A focus on film culture and the viewing experience

The Film Experience recognizes that film is so much more than a collection of shots on a screen. The book consistently explains the larger cultural contexts that contribute to the power of film in our lives — that undeniable "movie magic."

New coverage captures the latest technological and media innovations that are transforming our viewing experiences — from Internet streaming to the proliferation of Twitter marketing campaigns, like the one that generated Oscar buzz for *The Hurt Locker.*

New single history chapter and a streamlined theory chapter provide a rich, yet concise, look at how history and theory enhance the culture of film.

The tools that foster critical viewing and analysis

The Film Experience offers a vast array of learning tools, including compelling chapter-opening vignettes, helpful **Viewing Cues** in every chapter, in-depth **Film in Focus** essays, and the very best coverage of writing about film from Tim Corrigan, a recognized master teacher of the form.

Film in Focus essays ▶ provide close analyses of key films, demonstrating how certain techniques or concepts inform and enrich those films.

FILM IN FOCUS

From Angles to Animation in *Vertigo* (1958)

In Alfred Hitchcock's suspense film *Vertigo*, a wealthy businessman named Gavin Elster hires Scottie (played by James Stewart), a retired police detective who suffers from acrophobia (fear of heights), to watch his wife. Madeleine (Kim Novak), Elster claims, is troubled by her obsession with Carlotta, a woman from the past. After Scottie rescues Madeleine during an apparent suicide attempt, he falls in love with her, and when his acrophobia prevents him from stopping her as she races to leap from a mission tower, her death sends Scottie into a spiral of guilt. Later he believes he sees his lost love on the streets of San Francisco, and his pursuit of a look-alike woman, Judy (also played by Novak), entangles him in another twist to this psychological murder mystery in which the central crisis involves distinguishing reality from fictive images of it.

Vertigo takes advantage of almost every possibility in the film frame. Employing a particular brand of wide-screen projection called VistaVision, the aspect ratio of

3.55 *Vertigo* (1958). In this striking composition, Scottie's previously masked point of view becomes graphically juxtaposed with the mirror image of the woman he pursues.

angles as Scottie follows Madeleine through the streets, and the film's recurring motif about the terror of heights

THIRD EDITION

THE FILM EXPERIENCE
An Introduction

Timothy Corrigan
University of Pennsylvania

Patricia White
Swarthmore College

Bedford/St. Martin's
Boston • New York

For Bedford/St. Martin's

Publisher for Communication: Erika Gutierrez
Developmental Editors: Ada Fung Platt, Melissa Mashburn
Senior Production Editor: Harold Chester
Production Supervisor: Andrew Ensor
Senior Marketing Manager: Adrienne Petsick
Marketing Manager: Stacey Propps
Editorial Assistant: Emily Cavedon
Copy Editor: Denise Quirk
Indexer: Melanie Belkin
Photo Researcher: Julie Tesser
Permissions Manager: Kalina Ingham Hintz
Art Director: Lucy Krikorian
Text Design: Jerilyn Bockorick
Cover Design: Billy Boardman
Composition: Cenveo Publisher Services
Printing and Binding: RR Donnelley and Sons

President: Joan E. Feinberg
Editorial Director: Denise B. Wydra
Director of Development: Erica T. Appel
Director of Marketing: Karen R. Soeltz
Director of Production: Susan W. Brown
Associate Director, Editorial Production: Elise S. Kaiser
Managing Editor: Shuli Traub

Library of Congress Control Number: 2011933503

Manufactured in the United States of America.

6 5 4 3 2 1
f e d c b a

For information, write: Bedford/St. Martin's, 75 Arlington Street, Boston, MA 02116
(617-399-4000)

ISBN: 978-0-312-68170-8

Distributed outside North America by
PALGRAVE MACMILLAN
Houndmills, Basingstoke, Hampshire RG21 6XS
Companies and representatives throughout the world.

ISBN: 978-0-230-35909-3

A catalogue record for this book is available from the British Library.

This book is dedicated to Kathleen and Lawrence Corrigan and Marian and Carr Ferguson, and to Max Schneider-White.

Preface

"Experience is not what happens to you; it is what you do with what happens."

—Aldous Huxley

Virtually all of us have enjoyed the experience of watching movies, and we are well aware of the many pleasures they bring: becoming captivated by imaginary worlds brought to life, observing our favorite stars in familiar and unfamiliar roles, delving into different film genres, and witnessing the enthralling moments in film history projected onto the big screen. Yet these moments of enjoyment are usually scattered impressions that students rarely coordinate into a cohesive knowledge of film culture and film form—a knowledge that would inevitably add to their understanding, and appreciation, of the movies. Cultivating and encouraging that knowledge in a way that is accessible to beginning film students is the primary aim of this book.

The Film Experience: An Introduction offers students a serious, comprehensive introduction to the art, industry, culture, and—above all—the *experience* of movies, and it gives instructors the range and flexibility to adapt and use this book to complement a variety of approaches to film and media studies courses.

In publishing *The Film Experience*, our desire has always been to offer a new approach to film studies, one that simultaneously treats students as the avid movie fans they are while surpassing other texts in helping students understand the art form's full scope. As movie fans ourselves, we believe that one cannot grasp the *complete* film experience without an understanding of both the formal and the cultural aspects of cinema. Knowing how certain lighting angles create a specific mood as well as understanding how an actor's reputation affects the way his or her roles are perceived enrich our viewing experiences in equally important, albeit different, ways. *The Film Experience* ensures that students get the best of both worlds—strong formal coverage situated in the cultural contexts that inform the ways we watch movies. Lastly, the learning tools we have created help students make the transition from movie fan to critical viewer, allowing them to use the knowledge they acquire in this course to enrich their movie-watching experiences throughout their lives.

In short, with *The Film Experience*, our goal has been to offer a book that teaches students *how* to think about film and that helps them make the leap from movie buff to critical film viewer.

Given this goal, we are gratified that feedback from instructors and students over the years has affirmed for us that *The Film Experience*'s three-pronged approach to film—gaining formal knowledge, understanding cultural contexts, and engaging in critical analysis—works. In this new edition, we strive to make this proven approach even stronger and even more accessible to a wider range of instructors and students. Whether it's making the text even easier to read and learn from, adding new visual walkthroughs, or creating a brand-new suite of pedagogical videos, every improvement further reinforces one or more of the three major pillars of the book, making the third edition of *The Film Experience* the consummate introduction to film.

The Best Coverage of Film's Formal Elements

We believe that comprehensive knowledge of film practices and techniques allows students a deeper and more nuanced understanding of film meaning. Thus *The Film Experience* provides strong and clear explanations of the major concepts and practices in mise-en-scène, cinematography, editing, and sound, plus the best and most extensive coverage of the structure of narrative film, genre, documentaries, and experimental films. And going beyond mere descriptions of the nuts and bolts of film form, *The Film Experience* highlights how these formal elements can be analyzed and interpreted within the context of a film as a whole. From how jump cuts in *The Last Year at Marienbad* can leave viewers feeling disoriented, mirroring the characters' confusion between the past and the present, to how color is consciously used in *Pleasantville* to signify the characters' emotional awakening, we draw from a wide variety of movies to demonstrate for students how individual formal elements can contribute to a film's larger meaning.

   The Film Experience boasts the broadest range of film examples of any introductory text, because while we understand the importance of connecting with students through films they already know, we feel that it is also our profound responsibility to help students understand the rich variety of movies, as well as the diverse practices, audiences, and histories in the film landscape. Thus, we illustrate key concepts using classic and contemporary films from Hollywood (*Citizen Kane*, *Vertigo*, *Pulp Fiction*, *The Social Network*); experimental and independent films (*Sunless*, *Daughters of the Dust*, *Brand Upon the Brain!*, *Precious*); and international films (*Battleship Potemkin*, *Rashomon*, *Memories of Underdevelopment*, *The Apple*). (It is important to note that because films are not always released in the same year in which production is completed, the correct release year for certain films is debatable. Throughout this text, we have used the most widely agreed upon release dates for students' historical reference.)

Fully Encapsulates the Culture of Film

In addition to a strong foundation in film form, we believe that knowledge of the nature and extent of film culture and its impact on our viewing experiences is necessary for a truly holistic understanding of cinema. As such, one of the core pillars of *The Film Experience* story has always been its focus on the relationship among viewers, movies, and the industry. Throughout, the book explores how these connections are shaped by the social, cultural, and economic contexts of films through incisive discussions of such topics as the influence of the star system, the marketing strategies of indies versus blockbusters, and the multitude of reasons why we are drawn to some films over others. In particular, the Introduction, "Studying Film: Culture, Practice, Experience," explores the importance of the role of the viewer, recognizing that without avid movie fans there would be no film culture, and offers a powerful rationale for why we should study and think seriously about film. Chapter 1, "Encountering Film: From Preproduction to Exhibition," details how each step of the filmmaking process—from script to release—informs, and is informed by, the where, when, and why of our movie-watching experiences.

Learning Tools That Foster Critical Viewing and Analysis

The Film Experience transforms students from movie buffs to critical viewers by giving them the help they need to translate their movie experiences into theoretical knowledge and analytical insight. Our host of learning tools includes:

- **Compelling chapter-opening vignettes that immediately place students inside a film.** Each vignette draws from actual scenes in a real movie to connect what students know as movie fans to key ideas in the chapter's discussion. For example, Chapter 9 opens with a discussion of how the generic familiarity of the tongue-in-cheek horror conventions and formulas in *Shaun of the Dead* contributes to our enjoyment of the film.

- **Film in Focus essays in each chapter provide close analyses of specific films,** demonstrating how particular techniques or concepts inform and enrich those films. For example, a detailed deconstruction in Chapter 4 of the editing patterns in *Bonnie and Clyde* shows how they create specific emotional and visceral effects.

- **Marginal Viewing Cues adjacent to key discussions in the chapter highlight key concepts,** prompting students to consider these concepts while viewing films on their own or in class.

- **Concepts at Work give students opportunities to think more deeply about film concepts.** These include brief end-of-chapter summaries followed by activities that creatively extend the main ideas discussed in the chapter.

- **The best instruction on writing about film and the most student writing examples** of any introductory text. Praised by instructors and students as a key reason they love the book, Chapter 12, "Writing a Film Essay: Observations, Arguments, Research, and Analysis," is a step-by-step guide to writing papers about film—from taking notes, choosing a topic, and developing an argument to incorporating film images and completing a polished essay. It includes several sample student essays with helpful marginal annotations on such films as *Citizen Kane* and *Rashomon*.

New to This Edition

Thanks to the valuable feedback from our colleagues and from our own students, in this new edition we have taken the opportunity to make a strong book even better: *The Film Experience* is now even easier to read and navigate; it further cements its reputation of having the strongest art program of any introductory text with larger film frames plus brand-new visual walkthroughs of key film concepts; and it now boasts an exciting new media program, including a powerful pedagogical video resource. As ever, *The Film Experience* continues to be the best at representing today's film culture—with cutting-edge coverage of topics like 3-D technology, digital distribution, and social media marketing campaigns.

Briefer, Streamlined Text Makes *The Film Experience* Easier to Use

Now with a sharper focus on the most essential formal and cultural concepts of cinema, the third edition of *The Film Experience* is even easier for instructors to teach and even more accessible for students. In particular, the text clarifies for students the trickier aspects of film history and theory with these features:

- **A single, easy-to-teach "History and Historiography: Hollywood and Beyond" chapter** that provides students with a concise overview of film's historic movements and perspectives—from classical Hollywood cinema and Soviet silent cinema to French New Wave and Third Cinema—that influence how we watch and evaluate films.

■ A pared-down "Reading about Film: Critical Theories and Methods" chapter that clarifies the core schools and debates within film theory, giving students just what they need to begin to understand how theory informs the film experience, and encouraging them to seek out film theorists' writings on their own.

New Form in Action Visual Walkthroughs Bolster
The Film Experience's Strong Formal Coverage

Image-by-image analyses in each formal chapter (Chapters 1–9) give students a close look at how the formal concepts they read about translate onscreen. From Chapter 4's breakdown of how shots in the opening sequence of *Moulin Rouge!* are edited together to provide a whirling, frenzied rhythm to Chapter 9's detailed comparison of the formulas and conventions in *True Grit* (1969) and *True Grit* (2010) as a way to understand revisionist genres, each Form in Action essay brings key cinematic techniques alive and teaches students how to read and dissect a film formally.

The Strongest Art Program Available—Now More
Compelling and Better for Learning

With more than eight hundred images—the best and most extensive art program in any introductory film text—*The Film Experience* visually reinforces all the major techniques, concepts, and film traditions discussed in the text. This edition offers larger film frames and more detailed and incisive captions, providing students with the ability to see the detail in each image and giving them even better visual points of reference for analysis. The vast majority of the images are actual film frames from digital sources, rather than publicity or production stills. We have selected the best available source versions and preserved the aspect ratios of the original films whenever possible. (Because of differences in format, stills from older films will appear larger in this edition—making widescreen images smaller allows us to include more illustrations overall.)

Current Examples from a Broad Range of Films
Appeal to the Movie Buff in Every Student

Each generation of students that takes the introductory course (from eighteen-year-old first-year students to returning adults) is familiar with its own recent history of the movies; hence we have updated this edition with a number of new examples that reflect the diverse student body, from Hollywood blockbusters such as *Inception*, *Iron Man 2*, and *The Social Network* to independent fare like *The Kids Are All Right*, *The Hurt Locker*, and *Exit Through the Gift Shop*, as well as popular international films like *Persepolis*, *My Name Is Khan*, and *Ponyo*.

Cutting-Edge Coverage of the Film Industry,
Fandom, and Movie Watching

Today the movie experience means more than a ticket, a darkened theater, and a bucket of popcorn. This edition covers the latest technological and media innovations that are transforming our viewing experiences—from Internet streaming and watching movies on an iPad to the revolutionary 3-D technology developed for *Avatar* and the proliferation of Twitter viral marketing campaigns.

Brand-New Powerful Suite of Media Enhances Students' Learning Experience

For the first time, *The Film Experience* is accompanied by a full suite of media tools designed to make learning about film more dynamic and fun. Explore *VideoCentral: Film*, a collection of short videos that extend and bring to life the discussions in the text. *The Film Experience* is now also available as an e-book in a variety of digital formats for use on a computer, a tablet, or an e-reader.

Resources for Students

For more information on the student resources or to learn more about package options, please visit the online catalog at **bedfordstmartins.com/filmexperience/catalog**.

- New! *VideoCentral: Film* at bedfordstmartins.com/filmexperience. A collection of short videos, including unique annotated videos designed to give students a deeper look at important film concepts covered in the text, and a selection of early short films that introduce students to the rich early history of film. Each annotated video acts as an extension of the Film in Focus and Form in Action features—furthering the discussions in the book and bringing them to life. These videos are great as in-class lecture launchers or as motivators for students to explore key film concepts and film history further. *VideoCentral: Film* can be packaged for free with the print text.

- New! *The Film Experience e-Book*. *The Film Experience e-Book* is available in a variety of digital formats that can be used on computers, tablets like the iPad, or e-readers like the Nook. For more information, see **bedfordstmartins.com/ebooks**.

- **Book Companion Site** at bedfordstmartins.com/filmexperience. By James Fiumara of the University of Pennsylvania, this fully revised, free and open resource site includes chapter quizzes, short-answer questions, and chapter summaries that provide students with comprehensive practice and study of major film concepts discussed in the book. Students can also access links to other film resources, downloadable versions of additional Film in Focus features, the unabridged glossary, samples of film writing, and other support material.

Resources for Instructors

For more information or to order or download instructor resources, please visit the online catalog at **bedfordstmartins.com/filmexperience/catalog**.

- **Online Instructor's Resource Manual** by Amy Monaghan, Clemson University. The downloadable Instructor's Resource Manual recommends methods for teaching the course using the chapter-opening vignettes, the Viewing Cues, and the Film in Focus and Form in Action features. In addition, it offers such standard teaching aids as chapter overviews, questions to generate class discussion, ideas for encouraging critical and active viewing, sample test questions, and sample syllabi. Each chapter of the manual also features a complete, alphabetized list of films referenced in each chapter of the main text.

- *VideoCentral: Film* DVD. This instructor DVD for *VideoCentral: Film* gives you another convenient way to access our collection of early classic films and annotated videos of key film concepts. These videos are great as in-class lecture launchers or as motivators for students to explore key film concepts and film history further. The DVD is available upon adoption of *VideoCentral: Film*; please contact your local sales representative.

- **Content for Coursepacks.** Instructors can access content specifically designed for *The Film Experience* for coursepacks such as WebCT and Blackboard. Visit **bedfordstmartins.com/coursepacks** for more information.
- **The Bedford/St. Martin's Video Resource Library.** For qualified adopters, Bedford/St. Martin's is proud to offer in DVD format a variety of short and feature-length films discussed in *The Film Experience* for use in film courses, including films from the Criterion Collection. For more information, please contact your local sales representative.

Acknowledgments

A book of this scope has benefited from the help of many people. A host of reviewers, readers, and friends have contributed to this edition, and Timothy Corrigan is especially grateful to his students and his University of Pennsylvania colleagues Karen Beckman, Peter Decherney, Meta Mazaj, and Nicola Gentili for their hands-on and precise feedback on how to make the best book possible. Patricia White thanks her colleagues in Film and Media Studies at Swarthmore, Bob Rehak and Sunka Simon; the many colleagues and filmmakers who have offered feedback and suggestions for revision, especially Homay King, Helen Lee, and Jim Lyons (in memoriam); and her students and assistants, especially Mara Fortes, Robert Alford, Brandy Monk-Payton, Natan Vega Potler, and Willa Kramer.

Instructors throughout the country have reviewed the book and offered their advice, suggestions, and encouragement at various stages of the project's development. For the third edition, we would like to thank Kara Anderson, Brooklyn College; Craig Breit, Cerritos College; John Bruns, College of Charleston; Chris Cagle, Temple University; Donna Campbell, Washington State University; Jonathan Cavallero, The Pennsylvania State University; Shayna Connelly, DePaul University; Joe Falocco, Penn State Erie, The Behrend College; Neil Goldstein, Montgomery County Community College; Gregory Dennis Hagan, Madisonville Community College; Roger Hallas, Syracuse University; D. Scot Hinson, Wittenberg University; Michael Kaufmann, Indiana University–Purdue University Fort Wayne; Glen Man, University of Hawai'i at Mānoa; Sarah T. Markgraf, Bergen Community College; Tom Marksbury, University of Kentucky; Kelli Marshall, University of Toledo; Michelle McCrillis, Columbus State University; Michael Minassian, Broward College; Robert Morace, Daemen College; Scott Nygren, University of Florida; Deron Overpeck, Auburn University; Anna Siomopoulos, Bentley University; Lisa Stokes, Seminole State College; Richard Terrill, Minnesota State University, Mankato; and Robert Vettese, Southern Maine Community College.

For the second edition, we would like to thank Kellie Bean, Marshall University; Christine Becker, University of Notre Dame; David Berube, University of South Carolina; Yifen Beus, Brigham Young University Hawaii; Jennifer Bottinelli, Kutztown University; Donna Bowman, University of Central Arkansas; Barbara Brickman, University of West Georgia; Chris Cagle, Temple University; Shayna Connelly, Columbia College; Jill Craven, Millersville University; Eli Daughdrill, Santa Monica College; Clark Farmer, University of Colorado–Boulder; William Ferreira, Houston Community College Southwest; Anthony Fleury, Washington and Jefferson College; Rosalind Galt, University of Iowa; Neil Goldstein, Montgomery County Community College; Thomas Green, Cape Fear Community College; Ina Hark, University of South Carolina; Elizabeth Henry, Eastern Oregon University; Mary Hurley, St. Louis Community College; Christopher Jacobs, University of North Dakota; Brooke Jacobson, Portland State University; Kathleen Rowe Karlyn, University of Oregon; David Laderman, College of San Mateo; Peter Limbrick, University of California–Santa Cruz; William Long, Camden County College; Cynthia Lucia, Rider University; Glenn Man, University of Hawai'i at Mānoa; Jayne Marek, Franklin College; Kelli Marshall, University of Texas at Dallas; Adrienne

McLean, University of Texas at Dallas; Jeffrey Middents, American University; Stuart Noel, Georgia Perimeter College; Dann Pierce, University of Portland; Dana Renga, Colorado College; Susan Scheibler, Loyola Marymount University; Matthew Sewell, Minnesota State University, Mankato; Steven Shaviro, Wayne State University; Kathryn Shield, University of Texas at Arlington; Christopher Sieving, University of Notre Dame; Ed Sikov, Haverford College; Philip Sipiora, University of South Florida; Dina Smith, Drake University; Cristina Stasia, Syracuse University; Nickolas Tanis, New York University–Tisch School of the Arts; Kirsten Moana Thompson, Wayne State University; John Tibbetts, University of Kansas; Willie Tolliver, Agnes Scott College; Chuck Tryon, Fayetteville State University; Kenneth Von Gunden, Penn State Altoona; and Greg Wright, Kalamazoo College.

For the first edition, we are grateful to Nora M. Alter, University of Florida; Constantin Behler, University of Washington, Bothell; J. Dennis Bounds, Regent University (Virginia); Richard Breyer, Syracuse University; Jeremy Butler, University of Alabama; Jill Craven, Millersville University; Robert Dassanowsky, University of Colorado–Colorado Springs; Eric Faden, Bucknell University; Lucy Fischer, University of Pittsburgh; Stefan Fleischer; State University of New York, Buffalo; Brian M. Goss, University of Illinois at Urbana-Champaign; Mark Hall, California State University–Chico; Tom Isbell, University of Minnesota, Duluth; Christopher Jacobs, University of North Dakota; Jonathan Kahana, Bryn Mawr College; Joe Kickasola, Baylor University; Arthur Knight, College of William and Mary; Gina Marchetti, Ithaca College; Ivone Margulies, Hunter College, City University of New York; Joan McGettigan, Texas Christian University; Mark Meysenburg, Doane College (Nebraska); Charles Musser, Yale University; Mark Nornes, University of Michigan; Patrice Petro, University of Wisconsin–Milwaukee; Kimberly Radek, Illinois Valley Community College; Frank Scheide, University of Arkansas; Jeff Smith, Washington University (St. Louis); Vivian Sobchack, University of California, Los Angeles; Maureen Turim, University of Florida; Leslie Werden, University of North Dakota; Jennifer Wild, University of Iowa; Sharon Willis, University of Rochester; and Sarah Witte, Eastern Oregon University.

Special thanks go to the following individuals and organizations for their assistance and expertise in acquiring photo stills: Beth and Margaret at Narberth Video & Entertainment; and Rob Epstein and James Chan at Telling Pictures. James Fiumara provided assistance in many ways, most notably for his comprehensive revision of the chapter summaries and quizzes on the book companion Web site. Thanks also go to Amy Monaghan for her excellent work on the Instructor's Resource Manual.

At Bedford/St. Martin's, we thank Erika Gutierrez, publisher, for her belief in and support of this project from the outset. We are especially grateful to developmental editor Ada Fung for guiding us with patience and good humor throughout this project, for her precise work coordinating the art program and the media program, and for other tasks, big and small. Melissa Mashburn helped to launch this edition with energy, insight, and wit. We would also like to thank former editors Vik Mukhija and Lai Moy for their guidance during the project's earlier stages. We are indebted to photo researcher Julie Tesser for her extraordinary work acquiring every piece of art in this book and to Willa Kramer for all her work capturing the film grabs—the art program was a tremendous undertaking, and the results are beautiful. We thank Erica Appel, director of development; Simon Glick, executive editor; and Adrienne Petsick, senior marketing manager, for their support of this book. Thanks to Harold Chester, senior project editor; Andy Ensor, production supervisor; and Shuli Traub, managing editor, for their diligent work on the book's production. We also thank Lucy Krikorian, art director, for overseeing a beautiful design and Billy Boardman, designer, for a dynamic new cover. We are grateful to senior new media editors Tom Kane and Melanie MacFarlane for their guidance, expert advice, and help with *VideoCentral: Film*. Thanks also go to Sarah O'Connor, media producer, and Caitlin Quinn, new media editorial assistant, for helping to make the media for this book happen.

We are especially thankful to our families, Marcia Ferguson and Cecilia, Graham, and Anna Corrigan, and George and Donna White, Cynthia Schneider, and Max Schneider-White. Finally, we are grateful for the growth of our writing partnership and for the rich experiences this collaborative effort has brought us. We look forward to ongoing projects.

Timothy Corrigan
Patricia White

Brief Contents

Contents

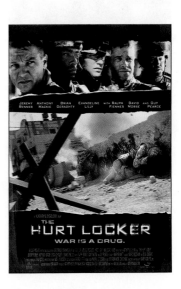

PART 2

FORMAL COMPOSITIONS:
film scenes, shots, cuts, and sounds   60

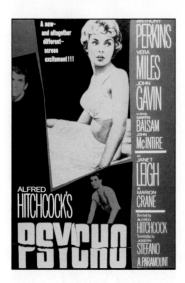

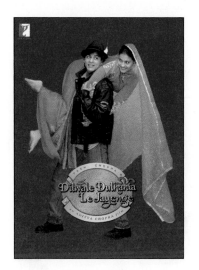

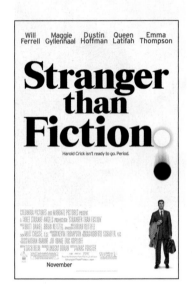

PART 4

CRITICAL PERSPECTIVES: history, methods, writing   352

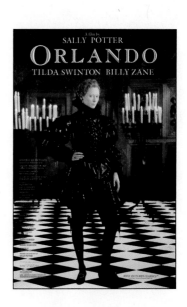

THE FILM EXPERIENCE

CULTURAL
CONTEXTS
making, watching,
and studying movies

In 2009, James Cameron's blockbuster *Avatar* created a sensation, not so much because of its well-worn story of an alien world threatened by exploitation and conquest but because of its dramatic use of 3-D and other new technology. Extensive newspaper, TV, and online coverage of its billion-dollar budget and spectacular 3-D images appeared well in advance of *Avatar's* release, and the film was widely distributed in a range of venues. By contrast, that same year Lee Daniels's *Precious, Based on the Novel* Push *by Sapphire*, with its tale of an illiterate African American teenager who finds a way to transform her life, reached audiences by means of a significantly different path. Modestly budgeted and independently produced, the film generated critical and word-of-mouth "buzz" and, most importantly, an American distributor, Lionsgate, at the Sundance Film Festival. In 2010, *Precious* garnered several Oscar nominations and two awards that confirmed its status as the most successful surprise of the year.

Social and institutional forces shaped these very different films in very different ways—from their production through their promotion, distribution, and exhibition. Part 1 of this book identifies institutional, cultural, and industrial contexts that shape the film experience, as well as shifts in these contexts over time, showing us how to connect our personal movie practices with larger critical perspectives on film. The Introduction discusses how and why we study film, while Chapter 1 introduces the movie production process as well as the mechanisms and strategies of film distribution, promotion, and exhibition. Understanding these different contexts will help us to develop a broad and analytical perspective on the film experience.

INTRODUCTION
Studying Film: Culture, Practice, Experience

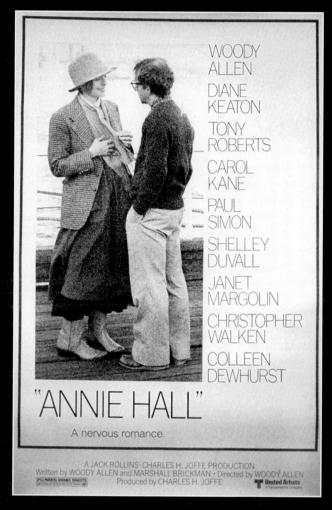

- Identifying the dimensions and importance of film culture
- Appreciating, interpreting, and analyzing film
- Understanding the changing film experience

CHAPTER 1
Encountering Film: From Preproduction to Exhibition

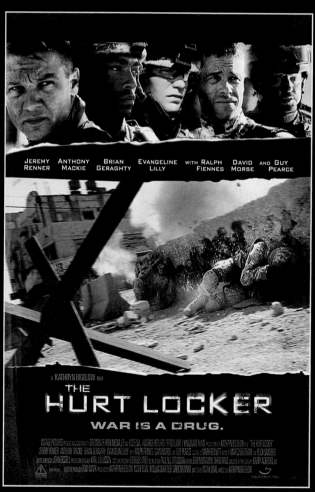

- Stages of narrative filmmaking
- Mechanisms of film distribution
- Practices of promotion and exhibition

WOODY
ALLEN

DIANE
KEATON

TONY
ROBERTS

CAROL
KANE

PAUL
SIMON

SHELLEY
DUVALL

JANET
MARGOLIN

CHRISTOPHER
WALKEN

COLLEEN
DEWHURST

"ANNIE HALL"

A nervous romance.

A JACK ROLLINS-CHARLES H. JOFFE PRODUCTION

Written by WOODY ALLEN and MARSHALL BRICKMAN · Directed by WOODY ALLEN

Produced by CHARLES H. JOFFE

PG PARENTAL GUIDANCE SUGGESTED

United Artists
A Transamerica Company

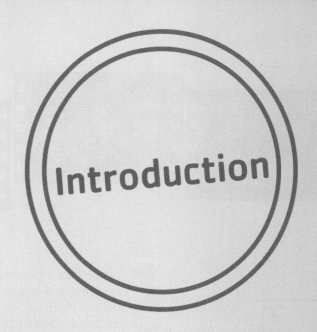

Introduction

Studying Film
Culture, Practice, Experience

In Woody Allen's 1977 film *Annie Hall*, Alvy Singer and Annie Hall stand in line to see the 1972 French documentary *The Sorrow and the Pity*. Next to them in line is a professor who pontificates about movies and about the work of media theorist and counterculture critic Marshall McLuhan, author of *Understanding Media* and *The Gutenberg Galaxy*. Alvy grows more and more irritated by the conversation, and finally interrupts the professor to tell him he knows nothing about McLuhan's work, as Annie looks on, embarrassed. When the professor objects, Alvy counters by bringing McLuhan himself out from a corner of the lobby to confirm that the professor is all wrong about McLuhan's writings. While this encounter among moviegoers comically exaggerates a secret wish about how to end an argument about the interpretation of movies, it also dramatizes, with typical Allen humor, the many dimensions of film culture—from scholarship to courtship—that drive our pleasure in thinking and talking, both casually and seriously, about film. For Alvy and many of us, going to the movies is a golden opportunity to converse, think, and disagree about film as a central part of our everyday lives.

For more than a century, the movies have been an integral part of our cultural experience, and as such, most of us already know a great deal about them. We know which best-selling novel will be adapted for the big screen and what new releases can be anticipated in the summer; we can identify a front-runner for a major award and which movie franchise will inspire a Halloween costume. Our encounters with and responses to motion pictures are a product of the diverse attitudes, backgrounds, and interests that we, the viewers and the fans, bring to the movies. These factors all contribute to the film culture that helps frame our overall film experience.

Film culture is the social and historical environment permeated with and defined by certain ideas, values, and expectations about movies. Film tastes, viewing habits, and viewing environments all inform film culture, and film culture transforms how we watch, understand, and enjoy movies in a variety of rapidly expanding ways. We can view a televised release of the epic *Lawrence of Arabia* (1962) on consecutive Sunday and Monday nights, join lines of viewers at an old movie palace for the latest installment of the *Twilight* franchise **[Figure I.1]**, enjoy the anime fantasy *Ghost Hound* (2007) instantly on the Netflix Web site, attend a documentary festival at a local museum, or watch the short silent films of Charlie Chaplin on an iPad. Our encounters with and responses to these films—how and why we select the ones we do, why we like or dislike them, and how we understand or are challenged by them—are all part of film culture and, by extension, film study.

I.1 ***Twilight* fans in line.** Experiencing the premiere of a movie becomes a singular social event with friends and other fans.

KEY OBJECTIVES

■ Define *film culture*, and discuss the various factors that create and distinguish it.

■ Appreciate the role and impact of film viewers, and note how our experience of movies and our taste for certain films have both personal and public dimensions.

■ Articulate the ways in which film culture and practice discussed in this textbook contribute to the film experience.

Why Film Studies Matters

As students, you bring to the classroom a lifetime of exposure to the movies. For example, your opinions about casting certain actors in the film *Precious* (2009) may reflect your understanding of how common movie character types appear and function; your mesmerized attraction to the special effects of *Inception* (2010) may pique your curiosity about new cinematic technology; your expectations of genre formulas, such as those found in the classic horror movie *The Shining* (1980), may provoke an outburst when a character heads down a darkened corridor. Film studies—the discipline—takes your common knowledge about and appreciation for film and helps you think about it more analytically and more precisely.

Film studies is a critical discipline that promotes serious reflection on the movies and the place of film in culture. It is part of a rich and complex history that overlaps with critical work in many other fields, such as literary studies, philosophy, sociology, and art history. From the beginning, the movies have elicited widespread attention from scientists, politicians, and writers of many sorts—all of them attempting to make sense of the film experience **[Figure 1.2]**. A film's efforts to describe the world, impose its artistic value, or shape society have long been the subject of both scholarly and popular debate. In the decades before the first public projection of films in 1895, scientists Étienne-Jules Marey and Eadweard Muybridge embarked on studies of human and animal motion that would lay the groundwork for the invention of cinema as we know it. In the early twentieth century, poet Vachel Lindsay and Harvard psychologist Hugo Münsterberg wrote essays and books on the power of movies to change social relationships and the way people perceive the world. By the 1930s, the Payne Fund Studies and later Margaret Farrand Thorp's *America at the Movies* (1939) offered sociological accounts of the impact of movies on young people and other social groups. Eventually courses about the art of the movies began to appear in universities, and elite cultural institutions such as the Museum of Modern Art in New York City began to take the new art form seriously.

After World War II, new kinds of filmmaking emerged in Europe along with passionate, well-informed criticism about the history and art of the movies, including Hollywood genre films and the accomplishments of certain directors **[Figure 1.3]**. Such criticism fueled film studies, which attained a firm foothold in North American universities by the 1970s. Today the study of film represents a wide spectrum of approaches and points of view, including

1.2 *Mon ciné.* Since the 1920s, *Mon ciné* and other movie magazines from around the world have promoted movies not just as entertainment, but also as objects of serious study with important sociological and aesthetic value.

I.3 *Cahiers du cinéma.* Appearing first in 1951, *Cahiers du cinéma* remains one of the most influential journals of film criticism and theory.

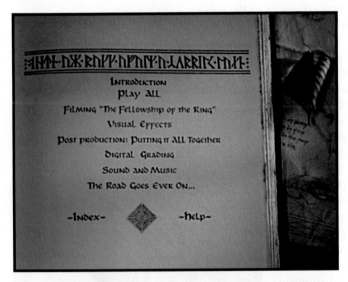

I.4 *Lord of the Rings* **DVD supplement index.** Expanded DVD formats and extras can now provide self-guided study tours of technical and even scholarly issues.

studies of different historical periods or national cinemas, accounts of economic and technological developments, studies of how race and gender are depicted in movies and affect audiences' responses to them, and explications of particular aesthetic or formal features of films ranging from experimental to documentary to narrative cinema.

One sign of today's rich film culture is the popular demand for DVD supplements—"extras" that have been called "film studies on a disk" **[Figure I.4]**. Many of us now rent or purchase DVDs and Blu-rays not just for the movies themselves but also for the extra features; these may include a film expert's commentary, a director's discussion of some of the technical decisions she made during filming, or historical background on the story behind the film. Some DVD editions address issues that are central to film studies, such as preservation of original promotional or textual materials. Trailers and posters that provide a glimpse of film culture at the time of the film's release, as well as scholarly commentary, are now available to the everyday film viewer. For example, in the *Treasures from American Film Archives* series, early films, hard-to-find gems, restored classics, and film experiments have been preserved and contextualized with scholars' voiceovers, making accessible to consumers works that were previously only available to experts. With research on movies facilitated by the Internet, the complexities and range of films and film cultures may now be more available to viewers than ever before.

The Film Experience provides a holistic perspective on the formal and cultural dynamics of watching and thinking about movies. It does not privilege any one mode of film study over another, but rather provides critical tools and perspectives that will allow individuals to approach film study according to their different needs, aims, and interests. Additionally, it provides the vocabulary needed to understand, analyze, and discuss film as industry, film as art, and film as practice. *The Film Experience* raises theoretical questions that stretch common reactions. These questions include psychological ones about perception, comprehension, and identification; philosophical ones about the nature of the image and the viewer's understanding of it; and social and historical ones about what meanings and messages are reinforced in and excluded by a culture's films. Far from destroying our pleasure in the movies, studying them increases the ways we can enjoy them thoughtfully.

Film Spectators and Film Cultures

Movies are always both a private and a public affair. Since the beginning of film history, the power of the movies has derived in part from viewers' personal and sometimes idiosyncratic responses to a particular film and in part from the social and cultural contexts that surround their experience of that film. Early viewers of the Lumière brothers' *Train Arriving at a Station* (1894) were rumored to have fled their seats to avoid the train's oncoming rush; new interpretations of such first-encounter stories suggest that viewers attended the screening precisely for a visceral entertainment not found in their normal social lives [Figure I.5]. In a more contemporary example, some individuals reacted on a personal level to *Avatar* (2009), breathlessly absorbed in a love story that harks back to *Romeo and Juliet* and overwhelmed by breathtaking visual movements that re-create the experience of amusement park rides. Other viewers dismissed the film because it offered what they saw as a simplistic political parable about corporate greed, terror, and exploitation far out of line with contemporary realities, disguising its bland characters and predictable story with jazzy special effects [Figure I.6].

I.5 **Poster for public screening of early films by the Lumière brothers.** The audience's reaction is as important an advertisement for the novelty as is the film onscreen, which represents the short comic sketch *L'Arroseur arrosé* (*The Waterer Watered*, 1895).

While certain approaches in film studies look first at a film's formal construction or at the historical background of its production, *The Film Experience* first emphasizes movie spectators and how they respond to films. Our different viewing experiences determine how we understand the movies, and, ultimately, how we think about a particular movie—why it excites or disappoints us. The significance of movies, in short, may lie not primarily in how they are made but rather in how we, as viewers, engage and respond to them. As movie spectators, we are not passive audiences who simply absorb what we see on the screen. We respond actively to films, often in terms of our different ages, backgrounds, educational levels, interests, and geographical locations. It is the richness and complexities of these factors that make film viewing and film study a profound cultural experience. In short, our engagement with a movie goes beyond determining whether we like or dislike it. As *active viewers*, we engage with a film in energetic and dynamic ways that *The Film Experience* aims to encourage and direct.

Our reactions are not only personal but also have important public and social dimensions. When *Precious* was released, for instance, many viewers were predisposed to appreciate it because of critics' reviews and word-of-mouth praise that followed the film's appearances at the Sundance and Cannes film festivals. As the film continued to play in wider release, its numerous Academy Award nominations and later wins for best supporting actress and best adapted screenplay also influenced audiences' curiosity about it and reactions to it. In a dramatic move, Oprah Winfrey, who came on board as one of the film's executive producers, energetically endorsed *Precious* on her

I.6 *Avatar* (2009). Many viewers responded favorably to Sigourney Weaver's strong female character in the film; others joined an Internet campaign against the film's depiction of smoking.

television show. All the while, buzz about the film spread via Twitter, Facebook, and other social media sites, as well as through the entertainment media and daily conversations. The film touched a cultural nerve in an American society still struggling in the twenty-first century with issues of racial inequality, the economic desperation of an urban underclass, sexual abuse, and body image. *Precious* arrived at the right time for many reasons, becoming an unexpected social barometer and provocation for audiences concerned about these issues. Discussions of the film's dramatic images and events thus connected emotional responses with wider social dynamics.

At the intersection of these personal and public experiences, each of us has developed different tastes—cultural, emotional, intellectual, and social preferences or interests—that influence our expectations and lead us to like or dislike particular movies. Some tastes vary little from person to person; most people prefer good characters to bad ones and justice served to justice foiled. Yet many tastes in movies are unique products of our experiential circumstances or experiential histories. *Experiential circumstances* are the material conditions that define our identity at a certain time and in a certain place, such as our age, gender, race, linguistic and socioeconomic background, and the part of the country or world in which we live. *Experiential histories*, such as our education, relationships, travels, and even the other films we have seen, are the personal and social encounters through which we have developed our identities over time. These histories help determine individual as well as cultural tastes. For example, American college students may be drawn to Wes Anderson's *Fantastic Mr. Fox* (2009) as fans of the director's debut film *Rushmore* (1998) or because they read Roald Dahl's books as children. A World War II veteran, because of his experiential history, might have a particular taste for WWII films **[Figure 1.7]**, ranging from such sentimental favorites as *Mrs. Miniver* (1942) to the harder-hitting dramas *The Longest Day* (1962), *Saving Private Ryan* (1998), and *Flags of Our Fathers* (2006). The big-screen **adaptation** of *Dreamgirls* (2006) might attract African American audiences familiar with the history of Motown music, Broadway fans familiar with the original musical, or fans eager to see pop star Beyoncé in a dramatic role **[Figure 1.8]**. An audience's taste in films can also be tied to historical events, drawing viewers to see films about contemporary experiences such as the Watergate scandal depicted in *Nixon* (1995) or the September 11 terrorist attacks on the United States dramatized in Oliver Stone's *World Trade Center* (2006).

Our experiential circumstances and histories may predispose us to certain

1.7 *Saving Private Ryan* (1998). The fiftieth anniversary of the end of World War II was widely commemorated in 1995. In 1998, Steven Spielberg's hard-hitting film was hailed by veterans as a realistic depiction of what American combat troops encountered during the invasion of Normandy.

1.8 *Dreamgirls* (2006). Musicals often draw their fan base from audiences familiar with the Broadway productions from which they are adapted or the pop singers featured in the cast.

tastes and responses, but these are activated when we actually watch a film by two psychological processes that come into play simultaneously: identification and cognition.

Identification, the complex process through which we empathize with or project onto a character, or participate in a place or an action, is commonly associated with our emotional responses. Both adolescent and adult viewers can respond empathetically to the portrayal of the social electricity and physical awkwardness of teenage sexuality in *American Graffiti* (1973), *The Breakfast Club* (1985), or *Superbad* (2007), though different generations might find the music of one movie or the fashions of another more resonant, and male viewers are likely to relate more easily—or uneasily—to the high school boys at the center of *Superbad* than are female viewers **[Figure I.9]**. Each of us may identify with different minor characters (such as the nerd Brian or the prom queen Claire in *The Breakfast Club*), but the success of a film often depends on eliciting audience identification with one or two of the main characters (such as Curt and Steve, the two boys who are about to leave for college in *American Graffiti*). Identification is sustained as the main characters face conflict and choices. Using another example, while watching the musical *An American in Paris* (1951) **[Figure I.10]**, one viewer may instantly relate to the carefree excitement of the opening scenes by identifying with the street life of the artistic Montmartre neighborhood where she had lived as a college student. Another viewer who has never been to Paris may participate vicariously because the film so effectively re-creates an atmosphere of romance with which he can identify. Sometimes our preference for a particular film genre aids—or detracts—from the process of identification. Viewers who favor the adrenaline rush of horror films may have less interest and enthusiasm when faced with the bright colors and romantic plotlines associated with American musicals of the 1940s and 1950s.

Cognition, the aspects of comprehension that make up our rational reactions and thought processes, also contributes to our pleasure in watching movies. At the most basic cognitive level, we process visual and auditory information indicating motion, temporality (the passing of time), and dimensionality as we watch movies. At another level, we bring assumptions about a given location or setting to most films, we expect events to change or progress in a certain way, and we measure characters against similar characters encountered elsewhere. Thus watching a movie is not only an emotional experience

I.9 *Superbad* (2007). Gender is an important, though not necessarily predictable, aspect of viewer identification.

▶ **VIEWING CUE**

What types of films do you identify with most closely? Are they from a particular country or era or particular genres? Do they feature certain stars or a particular approach to music or settings? ⏸

I.10 *An American in Paris* (1951). The setting of a film may be a source of identification.

I.11 **Gladiator** (2000). Watching this epic may combine historical knowledge, narrative recognition, and visceral response.

that involves identifying through processes of participation and empathy but also a cognitive process that involves the intellectual activities of comparison and comprehension. Engaged by our emotional identification with the terrors or triumphs of Russell Crowe's character in *Gladiator* (2000), for example, we also find ourselves engaged cognitively with other aspects of the film **[Figure I.11]**. We recognize and distinguish the Rome in the movie through particular visual **cues**—the Coliseum and other Roman monuments—known perhaps from studies in world history, pictures, or other movies. We expect we will know who will win the battles and fights because of what we've learned about such skirmishes, but that knowledge won't necessarily prepare us for the extreme and graphic violence depicted in the film. Because of other experiences, we arrive at the film with certain assumptions about Roman tyrants and heroes, and we appreciate and understand characters like the emperor Commodus or the gladiator Maximus as they successfully balance our expectations with surprises.

Even as we are drawn to and bond with places, actions, and characters in films, we must sometimes reconsider how those ways of identifying develop and change as part of our intellectual or cognitive development. Indeed, this process of cognitive realignment and reconsideration determines to a large degree our reaction to a movie. In *The Bridges of Madison County* (1995), for example, Clint Eastwood, best known for playing physically tough and intimidating characters, plays a reflective and sensitive lover, Robert Kincaid. Viewers familiar with Eastwood's other roles who expect to see the same type of character played out in *The Bridges of Madison County* must reconsider what had attracted them to that star, as well as assess how those expectations have been complicated and are now challenging their understanding of *The Bridges of Madison County*. Does this shift suggest that the film is about a human depth discovered within older masculinity or about the maturing of that masculinity through the encounter with an equally strong woman (Meryl Streep as Francesca Johnson)? Whether we are able to engage in that process and find the realignment convincing will lay the foundation for our response to the movie. Thus what we like or dislike at the movies often relates to the simultaneous and evolving processes of identification and cognition.

FORM IN ACTION

Identification, Cognition, and Film Variety

I.12a

The processes of cognition and identification that underlie how viewers interact with films contribute to the breadth of films produced and the different ways they are understood and enjoyed. Hollywood blockbusters like *Spider-Man 3* (2007) attract large audiences who expect to be entertained by special effects and comic-book spectacle without having to think too deeply about plot, character, or realism [**Figure I.12a**]. *Ponyo* (2008), a Japanese-made, Japanese-language animated fantasy about a surprising friendship, was released in the United States with well-known actors voicing the characters in English [**Figure I.12b**]. This family-friendly offering nevertheless captured plenty of anime enthusiasts as well as adults dazzled by its visual daring. The documentary *Client 9* (2010) is an engrossing dissection of former New York governor Eliot Spitzer's fall from power as well as an indictment of corporate greed. Its emphasis on contemporary American politics and its exploration of prostitution and corruption undoubtedly shaped its appeal while upping the ante on its perceived importance [**Figure I.12c**]. Independently produced films like *Juno* (2007), which deals in a humorous and sassy way with teen pregnancy, may appeal to a wealthier, more urban demographic comfortable with ironic, irreverent depictions of social problems [**Figure I.12d**].

I.12b

I.12c

I.12d

Studying *The 400 Blows* (1959)

I.13 François Truffaut. The director is closely identified with the French New Wave.

The 400 Blows (1959) is a realistic portrayal of a rebellious adolescent. It tells the tale of Antoine Doinel, whose search for identity on the streets of Paris is saturated with questions about sexuality, authority, family, economics, and education. One of the most important films in the birth of the French New Wave, François Truffaut's film relies extensively on location shooting across Paris to create a world that seems true to life as it is lived, not as it is portrayed in glossy, studio-produced films. Focusing this realism further, the **protagonist** of the film, Antoine Doinel, is played by

Jean-Pierre Léaud, a young teenager with no acting experience who brings an unrehearsed energy to the character of a young boy constantly confronting a seemingly endless variety of authority figures and institutions—schoolteachers, parents, police—bent on controlling him. The gritty street realism and the naive energy of the actors that underpin this production are the essence of what the film aims to communicate. Considering how viewers respond to this realism and Doinel—with sympathy, understanding, alienation, or confusion—is just one of the many paths into the experience of this landmark film.

The close relation between this character and the director provides the foundation for a sympathetic identification. Indeed, the film is semi-autobiographical. For many, this makes the film unusually personal and an obvious example of "auteurist" cinema, whereby a film expresses the director's individual vision **[Figure I.13]**. Like the protagonist of the film, Truffaut was himself both a bad boy and a writer, in both cases known for "raising hell"—which is an idiomatic translation of the film's French title, *Les quatre cents coups*. Truffaut's own youth, like that of Doinel, was that of a troubled truant and sometime thief ultimately redeemed by the cinema. Like Antoine, he was weaned on the cinema, and as a teenager he started his own cine-club, the Film Addicts Club. Shortly after this, he enlisted in the army, but after another of many "escapes" from various institutions, he was released because of an "unstable character." During this period, Truffaut found a surrogate father figure in the great film critic and scholar André Bazin, to whom *The 400 Blows* is dedicated in its credits and to whom Truffaut's parents even gave legal guardian rights. That Truffaut quickly became one of the most vociferous and polemical writers about film of the 1950s and was recognized as the primary scholar and archivist for the journal Bazin co-founded, *Cahiers du cinéma*, might extend this autobiographical or auteurist reading of the film to a larger cultural and historical understanding in which the film becomes a central document in the rapidly changing French cinema of the 1950s.

This autobiographical and historical dimension of the film also points to a way of reading and understanding *The 400 Blows* in terms of its distinctive stylistics. Such a formal approach triggers those cognitive dimensions of watching the film: its use of a discontinuous editing style and light-weight, handheld camera equipment produces a sense of freshness, energy, and immediacy. Numerous examples of Truffaut's experimentation with these kinds of innovations with cinematic language appear throughout the film, often as a way to reflexively call attention to a new kind of film-making and new ways of seeing. The sequence toward the conclusion of *The 400 Blows* when a female therapist interviews Antoine provides a good example: here the lack of a countershot of the therapist, the static position of the camera, and a stream of jump cuts through the entire sequence highlights Antoine's spontaneity and Léaud's extraordinary facial expressivity, as he is neither cowed nor contained by the interview's question-answer format.

Another example occurs in one of the central scenes in the entire film, which may be interpreted as a dense and explicit presentation of Truffaut's new film syntax embedded in a historical reflection about cinema's heritage and novelty. During the longer sequence when Antoine and René skip school and make a quick trip to the cinema, Antoine climbs aboard the spinning carnival ride called the "Rotor" **[Figure I.14]**. For film historians especially, the scene becomes an unmistakable metaphor for the cinema itself, as the ride resembles that nineteenth-century precursor of the cinema, the zoetrope, and contains a historical reference to the paternity of Alfred Hitchcock (specifically

the climactic carousel sequence in *Strangers on a Train* [1951]). More important, perhaps, Truffaut's cameo presence in this scene announces a new and more personal cinematic idiom. The rollicking celebration of movement is not just a vehicle for narrative but also the expression of energy and delight, both Antoine's and the filmmaker's. Antoine and René's wild ramble as they play hooky through the streets of Paris highlights the unpredictable realism of the film's aesthetic but simultaneously visually liberates the characters and the images from conventional laws of nature and cinematic realism.

Like those other stylistic innovations, the film's famous last shot—a track to a freeze frame of the young Antoine's face **[Figure I.15]**—can also be seen as a use of style to pose a cognitive dilemma, and to open up culturally embedded processes of interpretation. This unusually long track (lasting more than eighty seconds) of the fleeing Antoine usually unsettles first-time viewers, particularly since his goal or destination is unclear. This cognitive provocation continues when his face looks directly at the camera, perhaps as a question or perhaps as a confrontation. What is he thinking? What are we meant to understand happens next? The film leaves these questions unanswered, and we as viewers must reflect back on the boy's story and bring our individual experiential circumstances and histories to bear in our response.

I.14 *The 400 Blows* (1959). The carnival ride is a metaphor recalling the disorienting, exhilarating machinery of film.

I.15 *The 400 Blows* (1959). The film ends with a famous, ambiguous freeze frame in which Jean-Pierre Léaud as Antoine Doinel gazes directly at the camera.

The Film Experience

What a movie looks and sounds like is of course at the heart of any film experience, and much of *The Film Experience* is devoted to exploring in detail those many visual, audio, narrative, and formal features and forces that we see on the many screens around us. But it is viewers who ultimately process those images and sounds—in different and diverse ways that bring meaning to film culture and to their lives. The cinematic complexities of *Citizen Kane* (1941), for example, are technically the same for each person, but they provoke different responses in every viewer **[Figure I.16]**. Hardly a typical viewer, newspaper tycoon William Randolph Hearst reacted negatively to the film and claimed it to be an inflammatory portrait of himself, refusing to allow his papers to carry ads for it. In the 1950s, French writers and filmmakers hailed the film as evidence of the power of the filmmaker to create a personal vision of the world. In recent decades, the film's consistent ranking at the top of critics' polls has influenced increased viewing of *Citizen Kane*, thus illustrating how viewers respond to both the movie and its perceived place in film history. With any film, some viewers may find importance in the technological or economic features; others may highlight the aesthetic or formal innovations; and still others may emphasize a film's historical or social significance as its most meaningful quality. The same film, in fact, could lead different moviegoers to any one of these (or other) critical pathways, and it is less a question of which is the most important way to engage the film than one of which provides the most productive encounter for each individual viewer.

Viewers' experiences of the movies—their shared experiences of film culture as well as their individual interpretations guided by identification and cognition—are the starting point of *The Film Experience*. Part 1 examines how processes and patterns of production, distribution, and exhibition present a film in particular ways, creating social contexts in which audiences encounter the movies. Part 2 presents the four formal systems that structure films—mise-en-scène, cinematography, editing, and sound—showing how viewers derive meaning from familiar as well as innovative forms and patterns. Part 3 introduces and analyzes the primary modes through which viewers' encounters with the movies are shaped: narrative, nonfiction, and experimental organizations as well as genres. Part 4 offers critical perspectives on film, including an overview of film history, an account of major questions and positions in film theory, and a guide to writing a film essay.

The Film Experience encourages readers to choose and explore tactically different pathways into a film. This is not to say that studying film allows a movie to mean anything one wants; indeed, this book insists on a precise understanding of film forms, practices, and terminologies. Rather, having the tools and awareness to measure how and why a film engages us and provokes us in many different ways ultimately makes clear how rich and exciting films and film cultures are and, at the same time, how important and rewarding it is to think carefully, accurately, and rigorously about both.

Critical and scholarly interest in the movies is an outcome of—and an input into—the values and ideas that permeate our social and cultural lives. Not only are cultural values and ideas

I.16 *Citizen Kane* (1941). Even canonized films offer multiple entryways and the possibility of various responses for careful viewers.

reflected in the films and media that surround us, in other words, but values and ideas are *generated by* films as well. Both inside and outside the classroom, movies engage us, and we them. Public debates about violence in the movies, the crossover of movie stars into positions of political power, and the technological and economic shifts that have led to widespread participation in moving image production, as well as the vigorous marketing of new formats and playback devices, are only some of the constant reminders of how movies spread throughout the fabric of our everyday experiences. To think seriously about film and to study it carefully is therefore to take charge of one of the most influential forces in our lives. Expanding our knowledge of the cinema—from its formal grammar to its genres to its historical movements—connects our everyday knowledge to the wider sociocultural patterns and questions that shape our lives.

JEREMY RENNER   ANTHONY MACKIE   BRIAN GERAGHTY   EVANGELINE LILLY   WITH RALPH FIENNES   DAVID MORSE   AND GUY PEARCE

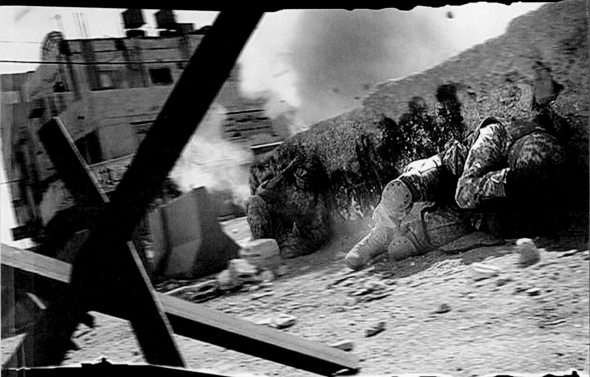

A KATHRYN BIGELOW FILM

THE HURT LOCKER

WAR IS A DRUG.

VOLTAGE PICTURES PRESENTS IN ASSOCIATION WITH GROSVENOR PARK MEDIA, LP & F.C.E.F.S.A. A VOLTAGE PICTURES / FIRST LIGHT / KINGSGATE FILMS PRODUCTION OF A KATHRYN BIGELOW FILM "THE HURT LOCKER" JEREMY RENNER   ANTHONY MACKIE   BRIAN GERAGHTY   EVANGELINE LILLY WITH RALPH FIENNES   DAVID MORSE AND GUY PEARCE CASTING BY MARK BENNETT MUSIC BY MARCO BELTRAMI AND BUCK SANDERS MUSIC SUPERVISOR JOHN BISSELL PRODUCTION DESIGNER KARL JÚLÍUSSON COSTUME DESIGNER GEORGE LITTLE SOUND DESIGN PAUL N.J. OTTOSSON EDITORS BOB MURAWSKI CHRIS INNIS DIRECTOR OF PHOTOGRAPHY BARRY ACKROYD, BSC EXECUTIVE PRODUCER TONY MARK PRODUCED BY KATHRYN BIGELOW MARK BOAL NICOLAS CHARTIER GREG SHAPIRO WRITTEN BY MARK BOAL DIRECTED BY KATHRYN BIGELOW

VOLTAGE PICTURES   GROSVENOR PARK

Encountering Film

From Preproduction to Exhibition

Long before James Cameron's *Avatar* (2009) arrived in theaters, viewers were primed by carefully vetted stories on the film's technological innovations and its imagined world—including the invented language spoken there. The hype surrounding *Avatar* was considered by many to be well earned. The film and the franchise facilitated a range of experiences: an immersive spectatorial environment, multiple viewings, companion games, successive releases of "special" DVD versions, fan-produced narratives, and even a museum exhibit. It quickly became the highest-grossing film of all time (though not if figures are adjusted for inflation). Even with a production budget of approximately $280 million (not including marketing costs or much of the costs of technological research and development), the film earned considerable profits.

Yet this epoch-defining production did not repeat Cameron's previous Oscar win. An outsized entertainment-oriented movie, it was passed over in favor of *The Hurt Locker* (2009), an independently produced film directed by Kathryn Bigelow about a U.S. military bomb squad in Iraq that had a more limited release. It may have been seen as more deserving of the award that year, amid the ongoing fighting in Iraq and Afghanistan, reminding us that criteria of artistic merit are influenced by social values. Bigelow's recognition as the first woman to receive the best director award lent another kind of historical significance to *The Hurt Locker*'s critical reception. As these two disparate films suggest, film production, distribution, and exhibition shape our encounters with movies, and these aspects of film are in turn shaped by how movies are received by audiences.

Whether we follow movie news or not, we know that a great deal has taken place before we as viewers experience a film. What steps are involved, and what challenges need to be overcome to ensure that a completed film finds an audience? The varied practices that go into moviemaking are not only artistic and commercial. They are also cultural and social, and they anticipate the moment of viewing at which meaning and value are generated. Understanding the process that takes a film from an idea to its final form not only deepens an appreciation for film form and the labor and craft of filmmakers but also reveals ways that social processes influence filmmaking itself. This chapter describes this process of production as well as the fate of a finished film through discussions of distribution, promotion, and exhibition. Such extra-filmic processes, which describe events that precede, surround, or follow the actual images we watch on the big screen, television monitor, or other device, are inseparable from the film experience. Where and when we see a movie shapes our response, enjoyment, and understanding as much as do the form and content of the film itself. The film experience encompasses rapidly expanding viewing technologies (from HDTV to movies viewed on computers, smartphones, and iPads), changing social environments (from IMAX to home theaters), and multiple cultural activities designed to promote interest in individual films (reading about films, directors, and stars, or consuming video games, special DVD editions, or social media connected to a film franchise). Waiting in line with friends for a midnight premiere and half-watching an edited in-flight movie are significantly different experiences that lead to different forms of appreciation and understanding. Overall, it is helpful to think of production and reception as a cycle rather than a one-way process: what goes into making and circulating a film anticipates the moment of viewing, and viewing tastes and habits influence film production and dissemination.

KEY OBJECTIVES

- Understand the ways the stages of filmmaking, from preproduction through production to postproduction, inform what we see on the screen.
- Describe how the mechanisms of film distribution determine what films we can see as well as when and how we can see them.
- Analyze how film promotion may predispose us to see certain films and to see them in certain ways.
- Evaluate the ways in which film exhibition both structures and is influenced by audience reception.
- Consider the ways in which media convergence and rapid technological advances are affecting virtually all aspects of the film experience from production to consumption.

Production: How Films Are Made

The aim at each step of filmmaking is to create an artistic and/or commercial product that will engage, please, or provoke viewers. In short, film **production** is a multi-layered activity in which industry, art, technology, and imagination intertwine. It describes the different stages—from the financing and scripting of a film to its final edit and, fittingly, the addition of production **credits** naming the companies and individuals involved—that contribute to the construction of a movie. Production may not seem like a central part of our film experiences as viewers, but the making of a film anticipates an audience of one sort or another and implies a certain kind of viewer. Does the film showcase the work of the director or the screenwriter, the cinematographer or the composer of the musical score? How does the answer to this question affect our perspective on the film? Understanding contemporary filmmaking in its many dimensions contributes to our appreciation of and ability to analyze films.

Preproduction

Although the term "production" is used to define the entire process of making a film, a great deal happens—and often a long time passes—before a film begins to be shot. **Preproduction** designates the phase when a project is in development and before the cameras roll. In narrative filmmaking, the efforts of the screenwriter, the producer, and sometimes the director, often in the context of a studio or an independent production company, combine at this stage to conceive and refine an idea for a film in order to realize it onscreen. Funds are raised, rights are secured, a crew is assembled, casting decisions are made, and key aspects of the film's design, including location scouting and the construction of sets and costumes, are developed during the preproduction phase. Documentary filmmakers might conduct archival or location research, investigate their subject, and interview subjects during this period.

Screenwriters

A **screenwriter,** or scriptwriter, is often the individual who generates the idea for a narrative film, either as an original concept or as an adaptation of a story, novel, or historical or current event. The screenwriter presents that early concept or material in a **treatment,** a short prose description of the action and major characters of the story. The treatment is then gradually expanded to a complete **screenplay** or **script,** including scene descriptions, dialogue, and other directions. This undergoes several versions, from the *temporary screenplay* submitted by the screenwriter to the *final shooting script* that details exact scenes and

1.1 *Adaptation* (2002). As its title indicates, screenwriting is the very topic of this inventive film, in which Charlie Kaufman, played by Nicolas Cage, is both a character and the credited writer.

camera setups. As these different scripts evolve, one writer may be responsible for every version, or different writers may be employed at each stage, resulting in minor and sometimes major changes along the way. Even with a finished and approved script, in the studio context an uncredited **script doctor** may be called in to do rewrites. From *Sunset Boulevard* (1950), about a struggling screenwriter trapped in the mansion of a fading silent-film star, to *Adaptation* (2002), about (fictional) screenwriter Charlie Kaufman's torturous attempt to adapt Susan Orlean's book *The Orchid Thief*, numerous films have found drama in the process of screenwriting itself **[Figure 1.1]**. One reason may be the dramatic shifts and instabilities in the process of moving from a concept to a completed screenplay to a produced film, a process that highlights the difficulties of trying to communicate an individual vision to an audience.

Producers and Studios

The key individuals in charge of movie production and finances are a film's producers. Although a director may also serve as a producer on his or her film, it is rare for a film not to have a producer at all. A **producer** oversees all of the different operations in putting a film together. At times, a producer may be fully involved with each step of film production from the selection and development of a script to the creation of an advertising campaign for the finished film; at other times, a producer may be an almost invisible partner who is responsible principally for the financing of a movie. Producers were extremely powerful in the heyday of the **studio system**, a term that describes the industrial practices of major studios in the 1920s through the 1940s. MGM was identified with the creative vision of the supervisor of production, Irving B. Thalberg, who as production head worked closely with studio mogul Louis B. Mayer from the mid-1920s until Thalberg's premature death in 1936. After leaving MGM to found his own studio, producer David O. Selznick controlled all stages of production, beginning with the identification of the primary material for the film. For instance, he acquired *Gone with the Wind* as a property even before the book was published. Selznick supervised every aspect of the 1939 film version of the best-seller, even changing directors during production—a process documented in his famous production memos.

With the rise of the independent film movement in the 1990s, independent producers have worked to facilitate the creative freedom of the writer and director, arranging the financing for the film as well as seeing the film through casting, hiring a crew, scheduling, shooting, **postproduction**, and distribution sales. For example, producer James Schamus first worked with Ang Lee on the independent film *Eat Drink Man Woman* (1994) and co-wrote the screenplays of *Sense and Sensibility* (1995), *Crouching Tiger, Hidden Dragon* (2000), and *Lust, Caution* (2007). As vice president of Focus Features (a specialty division of Universal), Schamus shepherded Lee's *Brokeback Mountain* (2005) through all stages of production **[Figure 1.2]**.

Regardless of the size or type of film being made, distinctions among the tasks and roles of types of producers exist. An **executive producer** may be connected to a film primarily in name, playing a role in financing or facilitating a film deal and having little creative or technical involvement. On a documentary, an executive producer might work with the television channel commissioning the program. A co-producer credit may designate an investor or an executive with a particular production company partnering in the movie, someone who had no role in its actual production. The **line producer** is in charge of the daily business of tracking costs and maintaining the production schedule of a film, while a **unit production manager** is responsible for reporting and managing the details of receipts and purchases.

The budget of a film, whether big or minuscule, is handled by the producers. In budgeting, **above-the-line expenses** are the initial costs of contracting the major personnel, such as directors and stars, as well as administrative and organizational expenses in setting up a film production. **Below-the-line expenses** are the technical and material costs—costumes, sets, transportation, and so on—involved in the actual making of a film. **Production values** demonstrate how the quality of the film's images and sounds reflects the extent of these two expenses; in both subtle and not-so-subtle ways, production values often shape viewers' expectations about a film. High production values suggest a more spectacular or more professionally made movie. Low production values do not necessarily mean a poorly made film. In both cases, we need to adjust our expectations to the style associated with the budgeting.

1.2 **James Schamus and Ang Lee.** Ang Lee's best director Oscar for *Brokeback Mountain* (2005) was the fruit of a long collaboration with producer James Schamus.

Financing Film Production

Of the many screenplays written and the many treatments sold, few in fact become movies, as movies require capital, and the film industry wants to generate money. Certainly some films are made primarily as personal or artistic expressions. For instance, Jonathan Caouette's *Tarnation* (2003) recounts the filmmaker's childhood and adolescence through a collage of snapshots, Super-8 footage, answering machine messages, video diaries, and home movies **[Figure 1.3]**. It does not use a conventional screenplay, and it was edited on a home computer with an alleged production budget of about $200. With John Cameron Mitchell and Gus Van Sant as executive producers, the film screened at the Sundance Film Festival. The publicity led to other festival invitations, a distribution deal—which enabled a limited theatrical release—and considerable critical attention. A mainstream action movie like Tony Scott's *Unstoppable* (2010), starring Denzel Washington, might cost over $100 million to produce and over $50 million to market—a significant investment that assumes a significant financial return. Developed alongside the conception of a film, therefore, is a plan to find a large enough audience to return that investment and, ideally, a profit.

Financing and managing production expenses is a critical ingredient in making a movie. Traditionally studios and producers have worked with banks or large financial institutions to acquire this financing,

1.3 *Tarnation* (2003). As Jonathan Caouette's debut film shows, even an ultra-low-budget independent production can be released theatrically if it lands an adequate distribution deal.

1.4 *The Kids Are All Right* (2010). A modestly budgeted independent production usually requires name stars to attract financing. Even with cast members committed, however, Lisa Cholodenko's comedic drama about lesbian parents took years to produce.

and the term "bankable" has emerged as a way of indicating that a film has the necessary ingredients—a famous star or well-known literary source—to make that investment worth the risk. Some films follow a less typical financing path, however. Kevin Smith made *Clerks* (1994) by charging expenses to various credit cards. The 1990s saw a rise in independent film as financing strategies changed. Instead of relying on a single source such as a bank or a studio, independent filmmaking is financed by organized groups of individual investors or pre-sales of distribution or broadcast rights in different markets. In the absence of studio backing, an independent film must appeal to potential investors with a known quantity, such as the director's reputation or the star's box-office clout. Although major star Julianne Moore was attached to Lisa Cholodenko's project *The Kids Are All Right* for five years, raising the film's $4 million budget was difficult **[Figure 1.4]**. Nonfiction films also require financing—documentaries may be sponsored by an organization, produced by a television channel, or funded by a combination of individual donors and public funds.

Casting Directors, Agents, and Super Agents

With the increasing costs of films and the necessity of attracting money with a bankable project, the roles of casting directors and agents have become more important. The practice of identifying the actors who would work best in particular scripted roles emerged during the advent of the star system around 1910. It was around this time when Florence Lawrence, the exceedingly popular star of Biograph Studio, known only as the "Biograph Girl," first demanded to be named and given a screen credit. **Casting directors** have since become bigger and more widely credited players in determining the look and scale of films. Representing actors, directors, writers, and other major individuals in a film production, **agents** negotiate with casting directors and producers and enlist different personnel for a movie. The significance and power of the agent extends back at least to the 1930s, when talent agent Lew Wasserman, working as a publicist for the Music Corporation of America (MCA), began to create independent, multiple-movie deals for Bette Davis, Errol Flynn, James Stewart, and many others. By the mid-1950s, Wasserman and others had established a **package-unit approach** to film production whereby the agent, producer, and casting director determine a script, stars, and other major personnel as a key first step in a major production, establishing the production model that would dominate after the demise of the traditional studio system. By the mid-1970s, so-called super agents would sometimes predetermine a package of stars and other personnel from which the film must be constructed. Michael Ovitz is perhaps the most famous of these; he co-founded the powerful Creative Artists Agency (CAA) in 1975, where he represented Tom Cruise and Barbra Streisand and packaged such blockbusters as *Jurassic Park*. Ovitz's story became exemplary of Hollywood hubris. After leaving CAA to seek power as a studio executive, he was fired from his position as president of the Walt Disney Company after only fourteen months.

Locations, Production Design, Sets, and Costumes

Documentary filmmaking is obviously very dependent on location—from the record of a strike in *Harlan County, U.S.A.* (1976) to nature documentaries like *Planet Earth* (2006)—but it also uses sets for interviews. In fiction films, the interaction between characters and the physical location of the action is often a central dimension of a film; hence choices about location and set design are critical.

Location scouting determines places that provide the most suitable environment for different movie scenes. Choosing a location is often determined by a series of pragmatic questions: Does the place fit the requirements of the script? How expensive would it be to film at this location? Many films rely on constructed sets that re-create a specific place, but the desire for movie realism often results in the use of actual locations to invigorate a scene. Few films more explicitly demonstrate the magic of movie set design than Laurence Olivier's *Henry V* (1944), where the drama shifts from the stage of Shakespeare's Globe Theatre to the comparatively realistic sets of ships leaving for war in France. In recent decades, the cinematic task of re-creating real-seeming environments has shifted to computer-graphics technicians. These technicians design the models to be digitally transferred onto film, becoming, in a sense, a new kind of location scout. Location scouting became commonplace in the early twentieth century. By 1915, **art directors,** those individuals responsible for supervising the conception and construction of movie sets in collaboration with **set designers,** became another integral and important part of filmmaking—although in those early years, they were "technical directors" doing "interior decoration." Today the term **production designer** is widely used for the person in charge of the film's overall look.

The role of **costume designers,** those who plan and prepare how actors will be dressed for parts, greatly increased as the movie business expanded in the 1930s. Costume designers such as Adrian **[Figure 1.5]** ensured the splendor, suitability, and sometimes the historical accuracy of movie characters' appearances, and their work was often as influential on clothing trends as was that of fashion designers. Indeed, for those films in which costumes and settings are central to the story—films set in fantasy worlds or historical eras, such as *Pan's Labyrinth* (2006), which uses both kinds of settings—one could argue that the achievement of the film becomes inseparable from the decisions about the art and costume design. In the end, successful films integrate all levels of the design, from the sets to the costumes, as in Jane Campion's period drama about John Keats and Fanny Brawne, *Bright Star* (2009), whose heroine's vivid clothing represents a passion and creativity to match the poet's **[Figure 1.6]**.

Production

Most mythologized of all phases of moviemaking is production itself—the weeks or months of actual shooting, on set or on location, known as a **film shoot.** Countless films, from *The Bad and the Beautiful* (1952), *Beware of a Holy Whore* (1971), and *Irma Vep* (1996) to *Sex Is Comedy* (2002), dramatize inspired or fraught interactions among cast, crew,

1.5 **Greta Garbo, George Cukor, and Adrian on the set of *Camille*** (1936). Costume designer Adrian contributed significantly to the sumptuous style of MGM films of the 1930s and 1940s.

1.6 *Bright Star* (2009). The heroine's fashions fit both the nineteenth-century setting of Jane Campion's film about Romantic poet John Keats and the film's theme of creativity.

and the person in charge of it all, the director **[Figure 1.7]**. The reality of production varies greatly with the scale of the film and its budget; but the director, who has often been involved in all of the creative phases of preproduction, must now work closely with the actors and production personnel—most notably, the camera units headed by the cinematographer—to realize a collaborative vision.

The Director

Although every film will afford a director a different degree of control, the **director** has been commonly regarded as the chief creative presence or the primary manager in film production, responsible for and overseeing virtually all the work of making a movie—from the directing of actors to the position of the camera and the selection of which images appear in the finished film. The earliest films of the twentieth century involved very few people in the process of shooting a film, with the assumption that the cameraman was the de facto director. By 1907, however, a division of labor separated production roles, placing the director in charge of all others on the film set.

Directors have different methods and degrees of involvement. Alfred Hitchcock claimed he never needed to see the action through the camera viewfinder since his script directions were so precise that there would be only one way to compose the shot; others are comfortable relinquishing important decisions to their assistant director (A.D.), cinematographer, or sound designer; still others, like Woody Allen and Barbra Streisand, assume multiple roles (from screenwriter to actor and editor) in addition to that of director **[Figures 1.8a and 1.8b]**. In Hollywood during the studio era, directors' visions were often subordinated to "house style" or a producer's vision; yet directors worked so consistently, and honed their craft with such skilled personnel, that critics have claimed to detect a given director's "signature" style across routine assignments, elevating directors like Howard Hawks and Nicholas Ray to the status of **auteurs** (directors considered "authors" of their films).

Today a company backing a film will choose or approve a director for projects that seem to fit with his or her skills and talents; for example, Chris Columbus's success with family films like *Home Alone* (1990) led to his early involvement with the *Harry Potter* franchise. Because of the control and assumed authority of the director, contemporary viewers often look for stylistic and thematic consistencies in films by the same director, and filmmakers like Quentin Tarantino have become celebrities. This follows a model prevalent in art cinema made outside Hollywood in which the vision of a director like Jean-Luc Godard or Tsai Ming-liang is supported by the producer and made manifest in virtually every aspect of the film.

1.7 *Irma Vep* (1996). Maggie Cheung stars in a film about making a film—starring Maggie Cheung.

1.8b   Yentl (1983). In Barbra Streisand's first film as a director, her protagonist dresses as a boy to study Torah.

1.8a   Barbra Streisand. Stardom as a singer and actress gave Streisand the opportunity to turn to directing.

The Cast, Cinematographer, and Other On-Set Personnel

The director works with the actors to bring out the desired performance, and of course these collaborations vary greatly. Mike Leigh is known for long improvisational rehearsal periods with his ensemble casts, from which his scripts and particular actors' roles emerge, giving films like *Another Year* (2010) a deeply affecting intimacy. David Fincher's exacting directorial style requires scores of **takes** (different versions of a shot), a grueling experience for *Zodiac* (2007) actors Jake Gyllenhaal and Robert Downey Jr. **Blocking**, or the planning of actors' movements on the set, may take precedence over the director's concern for the actors' emotional preparation. Because films are shot out of order and in a variety of shot scales, a film actor's performance must be delivered in bits and pieces. Some actors prepare a technical performance; others rely on the director's prompting or other, more spontaneous inspiration.

The **cinematographer**, also known as the director of photography or D.P., selects the cameras, film stock, lighting, and lenses to be used as well as the camera setup or position. In consultation with the director, the cinematographer determines how the action will be shot, the images composed, and, later, the kind of exposure needed to print the takes. The cinematographer oversees a **camera operator** and other camera and lighting crew. Many films owe more to the cinematographer than to almost any other individual in the production: the scintillating *Days of Heaven* (1978) profits as much from the eye of cinematographer Néstor Almendros as from the direction of Terrence Malick; and the consistently stunning work of cinematographer Michael Ballhaus, from R. W. Fassbinder's *The Marriage of Maria Braun* (1979) to Martin Scorsese's *The Departed* (2006), arguably displays the artistic singularity and vision that are usually assigned to film directors **[Figure 1.9]**.

Other personnel are also on the set, from the **production sound mixer** and other sound crew, including the boom operator; to the **grips** who install lighting and dollies; to the special effects coordinator, scenic, hair, and make-up artists; to the catering staff. A production coordinator helps this complex operation to run smoothly. During the shoot, the director reviews **dailies**, footage shot that day, and begins to make **selects**, takes that are suggested for the finished film. After principal photography is completed,

1.9   *The Departed* (2006). Cinematographer Michael Ballhaus suggests interpretations of the characters' motives through shot composition and lighting.

sets are broken down and the film *wraps,* or completes production. A film shoot is an intense, concentrated effort in which the contributions of visionary artists and professional crew mesh with schedule and budget constraints.

Postproduction

Some of the most important aspects of a finished film, including editing, sound, and visual effects, are achieved after **principal photography** is completed and production is over. How definitive or efficient the process is depends on many factors—a documentary may be constructed almost entirely during this phase, or a commercial feature film may have to be re-cut in response to test screenings or the wishes of a new executive who has assumed authority over the project.

Editing, Sound, and Special Effects

The director works closely with the editor and his or her staff to select, trim, and assemble shots into a finished film with a distinctive style and rhythm, a process that is now largely carried out with digitized footage and computer-based editing. **Editing** is anticipated in preproduction of fiction films with the preparation of a shooting script, and in production it is recognized in the variety and number of takes provided. Only a fraction of the footage that is shot makes it into the finished film, however, making editing crucial to its final form. In documentary production, editing may be the most important stage in shaping the film. When the editing is completed, the picture is said to be *locked.*

Postproduction also includes complex processes for editing sound and adding special effects. A sound editor oversees the work of creating audio patterns and relationships with the visual image. Less apparent than the editing of images, editing of sound can create noises that relate directly to the action of the image (such as matching the image of a dog barking), underpin those images and actions with music (such as the pounding beats that follow an army into battle), or insert sounds that counterpoint the images in ways that complicate their meanings (such as using a religious hymn to accompany the flight of a missile). In the **sound mix**, the score and all of the film's soundtracks are adjusted to their final levels and combined.

Special effects are techniques that enhance a film's realism or surpass assumptions about realism with spectacle. Whereas some special effects are prepared in preproduction (such as the building of elaborate models of futuristic cities), others can be generated in production with special camera filters or setups, or created on set, such as the use of pyrotechnics. But most special effects today are created in postproduction and are distinguished by the term **visual effects**. For most of film history, teams of technicians and artists worked in postproduction to create elaborate optical effects with expensive equipment. In the contemporary digital age, computer technicians have virtually boundless postproduction capabilities to enhance and transform an image. *Sky Captain and the World of Tomorrow* (2004), a film set in 1939 and giving that period's vision of the future, is the first film whose entire world (except the actors, whose performances were filmed using **green screen technology**) was generated in postproduction **[Figure 1.10]**. **Motion-capture technology** allows an

1.10 *Sky Captain and the World of Tomorrow* (2004). While the aesthetic of this film's visual effects was derived from the past, the technology used to achieve them was state of the art at the time of its release.

actor's physical movements to be transferred to figures created through **computer-generated imagery (CGI)**.

All of the personnel who work behind the scenes on these many levels of film-making are acknowledged when the **titles** and **credits** are added in the final stage of postproduction.

Distribution: What We Can See

The completed film reaches its audience through the process of **distribution**, in which films are provided to venues in which the public can see them. These include theaters and video stores, broadcast and cable television, Internet streaming and **video on demand (VOD)**, libraries and classrooms—even hotels and airlines. Despite these many outlets for distribution, many worthy films never find a distributor and are thus never seen. As avenues of distribution multiply, new questions about the role of film culture in our individual and collective experience arise. Our tastes, choices, and opportunities are shaped by aspects of the industry of which we may be unaware, and we, in turn, influence what we can see in the future.

From about 1895 to 1910, audiences flocked to see machines like the Vitascope (bought and marketed by Thomas Edison) project virtually any moving images, whether a couple kissing or a crowd walking across the Brooklyn Bridge. There they found and enjoyed a constant supply of short one-reel films, such as historical re-enactments found in movies like the gruesome *Execution of Czolgosz* (1901) and topical versions of fairy tales like *The "Teddy" Bears* (1907). Today we consume movies made available through different paths of distribution to theaters, television, and Internet sites. Our tastes for and knowledge of films are affected by these varying avenues of distribution. The discussion that follows, which emphasizes the U.S. feature-film distribution system since it often controls even foreign theaters, addresses how viewers and views of movies are prepared by the social and economic machinery of distribution.

Distributors

A **distributor** is a company or an agency that acquires the rights to a movie from the filmmakers or producers (sometimes by contributing to the costs of producing the film) and then makes that movie available to audiences by renting, selling, or licensing it to theaters or other exhibition outlets. The supply of films for distribution is, of course, dependent upon the films that are produced, but the inverse of that logic is central to the economics of mainstream movie culture: what is produced depends on what Hollywood and many other film cultures assume can be successfully distributed. Film history has accordingly been marked with regular battles and compromises between filmmakers and distributors about what audiences are willing to watch. United Artists was formed in 1919 by prominent Hollywood stars to distribute their independently produced films and became a major company. Decades later, in 1979, the independent distributor Miramax used aggressive promotional campaigns to make foreign-produced and independent movies viable in wide theatrical release, thus changing the distribution landscape.

The Feature Film

Consider the following examples of how the prospects for distributing and exhibiting a film can influence and even determine its content and form, including decisions about its length. From around 1911 to 1915, D. W. Griffith and other

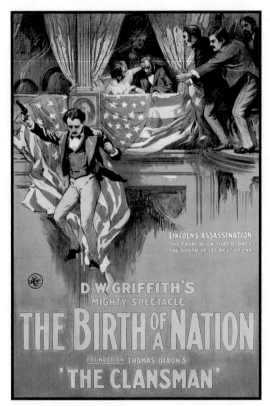

1.11   **Advertisement for *The Birth of a Nation***
(1915). The ambitious nature of D. W. Griffith's controversial epic was apparent in advertisements and its unprecedented three-hour running time.

filmmakers struggled to convince movie studios to allow them to expand the length of a movie from roughly 15 minutes to over 100 minutes. Although longer films imported from Europe achieved some success, most producers felt that it would be impossible to distribute longer movies because they believed audiences would not sit still for more than 20 minutes. Griffith persisted and continued to stretch the length of his films, insisting that new distribution and exhibition patterns would create and attract new audiences—those willing to accept more complex stories and to pay more for them. Griffith's three-hour epic, *The Birth of a Nation* (1915), was distributed as a major cultural event comparable to a legitimate theatrical or operatic experience and was an enormous commercial and financial success **[Figure 1.11]**. The film became a benchmark in overturning one distribution formula, which offered a continuous program of numerous short films, and establishing a new one, which concentrated on a single **feature film**, a longer movie that is the primary attraction for audiences. After 1915, most films would be distributed with 90- to 120-minute running times, rather than in their previous 10- to 20-minute lengths, though different combinations of accompanying shorts or double-bills were prevalent at different times.

Since 1915, this pattern for distribution has proved quite durable. In 1924, Erich von Stroheim handed his studio a nine-hour adaptation of Frank Norris's novel *McTeague*, retitled *Greed*. Appalled by the length, studio executives re-cut the film to about two hours, emaciating the story but allowing them to distribute it for a profit. In 1980, United Artists decided to reduce the length of Michael Cimino's massive epic *Heaven's Gate* (1980) from over four hours to 149 minutes in order to come closer to the standard film length **[Figure 1.12]**. After the catastrophic failure of its **first release** to movie theaters, and as a result of the flexible viewing conditions of home video, much of the original version was eventually restored. The recent trend toward longer running times, especially for "prestige" or "epic" films, acknowledges the flexible contexts in which films are now viewed.

Our experience of a movie—its length, its choice of stars (over unknowns, for example), its subject matter, and even its title—is partly determined by decisions made about distribution even before the film becomes available to viewers. Most movies are produced specifically to be distributed to certain kinds of audiences. Whether a movie is available everywhere for everyone at the same time, released during the holiday season, or available only in specialty video stores or on Internet sites, distribution patterns bring expectations that a particular film either fulfills or frustrates.

Release Strategies

As one of its primary functions, distribution determines how many copies of a film are available and the number of locations at which the movie can be seen. During the heyday of the Hollywood studio system, studios would either show their films in their own theater chains or sell them to theaters in

1.12   ***Heaven's Gate*** (1980). A disastrous theatrical release was later tempered when Michael Cimino's film was re-cut, re-released, and eventually restored for successful home video distribution.

packages, a practice known as **block booking**. An exhibitor would be required to show cheaper, less desirable films as a condition of booking the star-studded "A" pictures. This practice was one of the targets of antitrust legislation and was finally outlawed in the 1948 *U.S. v. Paramount* decision, which divorced the studios from their theater chains and required that films be individually sold. Typically, a distribution strategy starts with a **premiere**, a red carpet event attended by stars that attracts press attention. A film's initial opening in a limited number of first-run theaters as exclusive engagements would gradually be expanded, allowing for a series of premieres.

In 1975, Steven Spielberg's *Jaws* introduced the practice of **wide release**, opening in hundreds of theaters simultaneously. Since then, a film with a mass circulation of premieres, sometimes referred to as **saturation booking** or a saturated release, is screened in as many locations as possible in the United States—and increasingly abroad—as soon as possible. For a potential blockbuster such as *Iron Man 2* (2010), the distributors immediately release the movie in a maximum number of locations and theaters to attract large audiences before its novelty wears off **[Figure 1.13]**. In these cases, distribution usually promises audiences a film that appeals to most tastes (offering, perhaps, action sequences or breathtaking special effects rather than controversial topics) and is easy to understand.

Such a release may premiere on several thousand screens, whereas a **limited release** may initially be distributed only to major cities—Quentin Tarantino's *Reservoir Dogs* (1992) first appeared in only seventy-five theaters—and then expand its distribution, depending on the film's success. Audience expectations for films following a limited release pattern are generally less fixed than for wide releases: they will usually be recognized in terms of the previous work of the director or an actor but will offer a certain novelty or experimentation (such as a controversial subject or a strange plot twist) that will presumably be better appreciated the more the film is publicly debated and understood through the reviews and discussions that follow its initial release. The Weinstein Company's decision to limit the release of Todd Haynes's experimental biopic of Bob Dylan, *I'm Not There* (2007), to major cities was a bid to maximize critical attention to the film's daring and the intriguing promise of its star performances, which include Cate Blanchett playing the 1960s Dylan **[Figure 1.14]**.

As part of these more general practices, distribution strategies have developed over time to shape or respond to the interests and tastes of intended audiences. **Platforming** involves releasing a film in gradually widening markets and theaters so that it slowly builds its reputation and momentum through reviews and word of mouth. A movie can also be distributed for special **exclusive release**, premiering in only one or two locations. A dramatic example of this strategy was seen with the restored version of Abel

▶ **VIEWING CUE**

How might a distribution strategy determine a response to a film? Does knowing this strategy help you understand the film's aims better? ⏸

1.13   *Iron Man 2* (2010). As a major studio release and the sequel to the hugely successful adaptation of the Marvel comic, the film received a saturated release, opening on close to ten thousand screens in more than four thousand theaters.

1.14   *I'm Not There* (2007). Todd Haynes's experimental Bob Dylan biopic built up critical attention through a limited release pattern.

Gance's silent classic *Napoléon*, an epic tale of the life of the French emperor that periodically presents the action simultaneously on three screens. The original film premiered in April 1927 (although the film was not shown in its entirety until a month later to a private audience and was subsequently distributed in the United States as a single-screen presentation). In 1981, the exclusive release of the restored film featured distribution to one theater at a time, accompanied by a full orchestra. In this incarnation, *Napoléon* toured the country showing in only a very select group of cities and theaters so that seeing it became a privileged event. Although an exclusive release can be used in different ways, we generally approach these films expecting an unusual or singular experience created by epic subject matter (such as the history of a nation) or a remarkable technological or formal achievement (such as a three- or four-hour running time). The strategy for expanding a release depends upon box-office performance—if a film does well in its opening weekend, it will open in more cities on more screens. When the low-budget supernatural horror film *Paranormal Activity* (2007) was acquired and released by Paramount, audiences themselves became directly involved in determining where the film would open by voting on director Oren Peli's Web site.

Target Audiences

Since the latter part of the twentieth century, movies have also been distributed with an eye toward reaching specific target audiences—viewers who producers feel are most likely to want to see a particular film. Producers and distributors aimed *Shaft* (1971), an action film with a black hero, at African American audiences by distributing it primarily in large urban areas. Distributors positioned *Trainspotting* (1995), a hip tale of young heroin users in Edinburgh, to draw art-house and younger audiences in cities, some suburbs, and college and university towns. The *Nightmare on Elm Street* movies (1984–1989), a violent slasher series about the horrific Freddy Krueger, were aimed primarily at the male teenage audience who frequented cineplexes and, later, video stores. The initial success of *Transformers* (2007), one of many films based on cartoons (in this case, the cartoons were spawned by a line of toys by Hasbro), occasioned a later release of an extended IMAX version in which the special effects were even more dominant.

The various distribution strategies all imply important issues about how movies should be viewed and understood. First, by controlling the scope of distribution, these strategies determine the quality and importance of an audience's interactions with a film. As a saturated release, *Godzilla* (1998) aimed for the swift gratification of an exciting onetime event with a focus on special effects and shocks. Platformed gradually through expanding audiences, *Driving Miss Daisy* (1989) benefited from critical reflections on the relationship it depicts between an older white woman and her black chauffeur **[Figure 1.15]**. No distribution pattern produces a single set of expectations, nor does the distribution method determine the meaning of a film. Yet distribution methods can lead viewers, overtly or subtly, to look at a film in certain ways. We come to a saturated release perhaps prepared to focus on the performance of a star, on the relationship to a best-selling

1.15 *Driving Miss Daisy* (1989). Platforming this modestly budgeted film cultivated audiences and critical responses.

novel, or on the new use of computer technology. With a platformed release, ideas and opinions about the film are already in the air, and any controversy or innovation associated with it informs our initial viewing.

Second, in targeting audiences, distribution can identify primary, intended responses to the film as well as secondary, unexpected ones. *Scream* (1996) and *Scream 2* (1997) would probably offend or confuse adult audiences unfamiliar with teenage slasher films, but the targeted teenage audiences come prepared, knowing the formulas and clichés associated with this kind of movie, and are likely to see these films as spoofs and parodies **[Figure 1.16]**. The franchise also convinced distributors that girls were more likely to watch a more humorous version of the genre. Awareness of these strategies of targeting indicates how our identification with and comprehension of films are as much a product of our social and cultural location as they are a product of the film's subject matter and form.

1.16   *Scream* (1996). The franchise targeted the teenage audience for slasher films and expanded it through parody.

Ancillary Markets

Commercial cinema's reach has been expanding ever since studios began to take advantage of television's distribution potential in the mid-1950s. New technologies for watching movies continue to proliferate, and distribution has increasingly taken advantage of television, video, DVD, Blu-ray, and pay-per-view or other forms of video on demand (VOD). Today more of a film's revenue is generated by such **ancillary markets** than by its initial theatrical release.

Television Distribution

Historically the motion picture industry competed with broadcasting, which distributed entertainment directly to the home through radio and later television. As television became popular in postwar America, the studios realized that the new medium provided an unprecedented distribution outlet. While initial attempts to have viewers pay to see feature films on TV were abandoned in favor of licensing works to television networks and stations, this model returned with subscription cable in the 1980s. With the rise of cable television, studios were provided with even more lucrative opportunities to sell their vast library of films. Home video and the launch of dedicated movie channels like Turner Classic Movies (founded by Ted Turner to showcase his acquisition of MGM's collection) were a boon to cinema lovers as well.

With viewing options ranging from network to premium channels, and from On-Demand to subscription plans, more and more movies are presented through television distribution—the selection and programming, at carefully determined times, of films made both for theaters and exclusively for television. Historically there was a specific lag time between a theatrical release in a cinema and a cable or network release, but these relationships are changing. Some movies are distributed directly to video or cable, such as the two sequels to the film *From Dusk till Dawn* (1996). Whether a movie is released after its theatrical run or is made expressly for video and television, this type of distribution usually aims to reach the largest possible audience and thus to increase revenues. Part of the motive in these

1.17   *The Singing Detective* (1986). This eight-hour BBC production changed assumptions about the made-for-TV movie when it was broadcast in the United States.

cases may be to reach more people with a film's message, such as when *Schindler's List* (1993) was featured as a prime-time, commercial-free (though corporate-sponsored) television movie years after its original theatrical release. In an attempt to reach specialized audiences through subscription cable, distributors like IFC Films have made critically acclaimed foreign and U.S. independent films available on demand the same day they are released in art-house theaters in major cities, allowing television audiences in markets outside large cities access to such works as the Romanian *4 Months, 3 Weeks, 2 Days* (2007), winner of the Cannes Film Festival's top prize. Although the traditional wisdom is that such access will hurt the theatrical box office, the strategy allows such films to reach wider audiences, and positive word-of-mouth, for both the film and the distributor's "brand," might even enhance overall theatrical revenue.

Guaranteed television distribution can reduce the financial risk for producers and filmmakers and thus, in some situations, allow for more experimentation. This was certainly the case with the BBC's daring production of Dennis Potter and Jon Amiel's eight-hour *The Singing Detective* (1986), an extraordinary cinematic/televisual combination of musical and mystery genres that twists tales of World War II, childhood trauma, and the skin disease of a detective writer **[Figure 1.17]**. Over the period since, European television stations have become some of the only funders for artistic ("auteurist") filmmaking. Distribution rights sold to foreign television can help finance a film's production. In a fairly new trend, the flow between television and theatrical distribution is reversed. Premium (subscription) cable channels such as HBO increasingly produce their own films that include riskier documentary subjects. While these films are presented on their networks, a theatrical window for the film to receive reviews and become eligible for awards is sometimes allowed.

Television distribution has both positive and negative implications. In some cases, films on television must adjust their style and content to suit constraints of both time and space: scenes might be cut to fit a time slot, interrupted with commercial breaks, or, as with *Schindler's List*, the film may be shown on two different nights, thus potentially breaking the flow and impact of the movie. For many years, the size and ratio of the image was changed so that a widescreen film image would fit the shape of the television monitor, thus altering the picture to suit the format; now, widescreen ratios are sometimes the default, distorting films and programming originally produced in the standard, almost square, format. In other cases, television distribution may expand the ways movies can communicate with audiences and experiment with different visual forms. *The Singing Detective* uses the long length of a television series watched within the home as the means to explore and think about the passage of time, the difficulty of memory, and the many levels of reality and consciousness woven into our daily lives.

Video, DVD, and Internet Distribution

Each new format for the public or private consumption of media—VHS, laserdisc, DVD, Blu-ray—offers a new distribution challenge for media makers and a potential new revenue model for rights holders. Independent producers may find it difficult to transfer existing media to new formats or to make enough sales for a particular avenue of distribution to be viable. The home video era began with competition between Sony's Beta format and VHS. The VHS format won out, and with the widespread use of VCRs in the 1980s, studios quickly released films in the VHS home video format, first for rental and increasingly for sales. There have been similar dueling interests in recent years, like that between HD-DVD and Blu-ray.

One of the most significant challenges to distributors posed by new formats is **piracy**, the unauthorized duplication and circulation of copyrighted material. Despite anti-copying software, the circulation of pirated films is widespread and can bypass social and cultural controls as well as legal ones, bringing banned films to viewers in China, for example, or building subcultures and networks around otherwise hard-to-access films.

As with film distribution through cinema and television, distribution of consumer formats like video, DVD, and Blu-ray determines the availability of particular titles to audiences. A film may be made available for rental or purchase in stores, received by mail from companies like Netflix, or ordered from independent distributors such as Kino International. Before the closing of many video stores caused by the shift to subscriber and On-Demand services in the 2000s, the video store was a significant site of film culture. Since the selection in rental stores was based on a market perspective on local audiences as well as the tastes of individual proprietors, some films were distributed to certain cities or neighborhoods and excluded from other locations. While the dominant chains such as Blockbuster, which filed for bankruptcy in 2010, were likely to focus on high-concentration family-oriented shopping sites, offering numerous copies of current popular mainstream movies and excluding daring subject matter or older titles, local independent video stores specialized in art films, cult films, or movie classics such as those released on DVD by the Criterion Collection. Still other local stores might depend on X-rated films or video game rentals for their primary revenue. Sometimes distribution follows cultural as well as commercial logic. Bollywood films, available in video and even grocery stores in neighborhoods with large South Asian populations, provided a tie to cultural traditions and national stars and songs before access to such films became widespread.

For viewers, there were two clear consequences to these patterns of video distribution. First, video distribution can control and direct—perhaps more than does theatrical distribution—local responses, tastes, and expectations: as part of a community anchored by a particular video store, we see and learn to expect only certain kinds of movies when the store makes five or six copies of one blockbuster film available but only one or none of a less popular film. The second consequence highlights the sociological and cultural formations of film distribution. As a community outlet, video stores become part of the social fabric of a neighborhood. Viewers are consumers, and video stores can become forums in which the interests of a community of viewers—in children's film or art-house cinema, for instance—can determine which films are distributed. Michel Gondry's *Be Kind Rewind* (2008) shows an urban community coming together around the films made available at its locally owned video store after its employees begin to produce their own versions of rental titles to replace their demagnetized inventory **[Figure 1.18]**. Such ties are less likely to be forged around recent alternatives to dedicated stores, such as DVD kiosks in grocery stores.

The innovation in distribution of DVDs that is probably most responsible for the decline of the local video store is the rental-by-mail model launched by

1.18 *Be Kind Rewind* (2008). The employees at a neighborhood video store attract a loyal local audience with their do-it-yourself inventory, like this recreation of Stanley Kubrick's *2001: A Space Odyssey* (1968).

Netflix and followed by other companies. As part of a subscription system that offers viewers a steady stream of DVDs, Netflix members can select and return films as rapidly or as slowly as they wish. Because the DVDs arrive and are returned through the mail, this distribution arrangement emphasizes the rapidity of contemporary consumption of movies. And because preselected DVDs are sent automatically, it also reflects a kind of passivity and lack of social interaction in movie consumption.

But such models still involve a material object that is literally distributed to viewers. As high-speed Internet made downloading movies and live streaming a consumer option, many sites began to provide such opportunities, and distribution confronted yet another set of challenges. If a movie is purchased on demand, how many times can it be watched? On how many different devices? Unauthorized downloading and sharing became even more difficult for distributors to regulate; at the same time, new opportunities for viewing and for forming social relations around cinema were generated. Netflix updated its own model to allow subscribers to stream titles both to computers and to televisions linked through game consoles. Students were offered new forms of access to films and film history.

The success of streaming and downloading may indicate an audience's desire to see a growing variety of films, as Netflix, iTunes, and other sources expand their offerings of foreign, classic, and documentary films. With the ability to select from among a vast array of films, as well as to determine the time, place, duration, and even device upon which one views it, the viewer may feel that she has finally overcome the limits set by distribution, even though economic decisions still shape the circulation of film.

This emphatic attention to a new ease and freedom of film consumption raises different questions about changing viewing patterns and their implications, however. Do these new paradigms undermine the social and communal formations of the overall film experience, from browsing the video store to watching movies with an audience or a film class? Does an audience increasingly fragmented into individuals make shared movie culture a more remote possibility? Does increased ease of access to film traditions remote in time or location make for a richer film culture? Finally, how might these patterns influence and change the kinds of movies that are made?

Non-Theatrical Distribution

Many kinds of films are made without the intention of showing them for profit: artists' films, activist documentaries, alternative media, medical or industrial films. While many of these films are shown publicly, they are not shown in a traditional theatrical context, nor do they necessarily take advantage of commercial video or Internet distribution methods. These films require specialized distribution strategies. Some of these works serve a very specific training or promotional purpose and are distributed directly to their intended professional or target audience. Others may choose non-theatrical and educational distributors—from Smithsonian and PBS to Women Make Movies and Third World Newsreel—that bring alternative media to museums, community and cultural groups, libraries, schools, and universities. Some distributors specialize in foreign films or repertory films that are featured in cultural programming like festivals and film series before they are made available on DVD (if that ever occurs). In this way particular audiences can access experimental films, art cinema, shorts, and many forms of documentary that are not commercially viable in theatrical release or consumer video.

▶ VIEWING CUE

How might the distribution of a film that has been released in the last year have been timed to emphasize certain responses? Was it a seasonal release? ⏸

Distribution Timing

Distribution timing—when a movie is released for public viewing in certain locations or on certain platforms—is another prominent and changing feature of distribution (and, as we will see later in the chapter, of exhibition). Adding significantly to our experience of movies, timing can take advantage of the social atmosphere, cultural connotations, or critical scrutiny associated with particular seasons and calendar periods. The summer season and the December holidays are the most important in the United States because audiences usually have more free time to see thrill rides like *Speed* (1994) **[Figure 1.19]**. Offering a temporary escape from hot weather, a summer release like *Jurassic Park* (1993) offers roller-coaster thrills made literal in the Jurassic Park water ride at Universal Studios. Annual broadcasts of Christmas movies like *Miracle on 34th Street* (1947) promise a celebration of goodwill and community **[Figure 1.20]**.

1.19   *Speed* (1994). Action movies intended as summer amusements have become central to the release calendar.

The Memorial Day release of *Pearl Harbor* (2001) immediately attracts the sentiments and memories Americans have of World War II and other global conflicts. The film industry is calculating releases ever more carefully—for example, holding a promising film for a November release in order to vie for prestigious (and business-generating) awards nominations.

Mistiming a film's release can prove to be a major problem, as was the case with *A Little Princess* (1995), whose release unfortunately coincided with the more aggressively distributed *Pocahontas* (1995). Both films aimed for the same target audience of families with children, but *Pocahontas* was able to take advantage of Disney's large distribution system and was put in so many theaters that *A Little Princess* was virtually lost to audiences. As one would expect, avoiding unwanted competition with a film can be a key part of a distributor's timing **[Figure 1.21]**: distributors accelerated the timing of the opening of *The Matrix* (1999) precisely to avoid competition with *Star Wars: Episode I—The Phantom Menace* (1999).

▶ **VIEWING CUE**
Try to identify the target audience of one of the films you've discussed in class. How might this movie have gained different audiences through DVD distribution? ⏸

Multiple Releases

Of the several other variations on the tactics of timing, movies sometimes follow a *first release* or first run with a *second release* or second run; the first describes a movie's premiere engagement, while the second refers to the redistribution of that film months or years later. After its first release in 1982, for example, *Blade Runner* made a notable reappearance in 1992 as a longer director's cut **[Figure 1.22]**. While the first release had only modest success, the second (supported by a surprisingly large audience discovered in the home video market) appealed to viewers newly attuned to the visual and narrative complexity of the movie. Audiences wanted to see, think about, and see again oblique and obscure details in order to decide, for instance, whether Deckard, the protagonist, was a replicant or a human.

For *Blade Runner*'s twenty-fifth anniversary in 2007, a final cut was released theatrically, but it catered primarily to DVD customers. With multiple releases, financial reward is no doubt a primary goal, as the trend to reissue films in anticipation of or following major awards like the Oscars indicates. Steven Spielberg has followed this strategy on a grand scale, and the re-release of *Return of the Jedi* in 1997 testifies to the success of this formula. Distributed in 2,111 theaters, the film, now enhanced and titled *Star Wars: Episode IV–Return of the Jedi*, earned another $46 million in its reissue. Re-releases of either classic

1.20   *Miracle on 34th Street* (1947). Annual television broadcasts of classic Christmas movies compete with theatrical fare also timed to the season.

(a)

(b)

1.21   **(a) *The Matrix*** (1999) and **(b) *Star Wars: Episode I—The Phantom Menace*** (1999).
The summer 1999 release of *The Matrix* was moved up to avoid competition with the much-anticipated opening of
the first *Star Wars* prequel, *The Phantom Menace*.

or popular films such as animated Disney fare can also create new points of view, predisposing viewers to certain kinds of responses, such as appreciation for the techniques of animation before computers. They can initiate an emotional nostalgia for past experiences associated with an old film (ideally to be shared with new generations) or, in some instances, provoke curiosity about fresh material added to the re-release or about new information a viewer has acquired about a feature of the film such as its director or star.

1.22   ***Blade Runner*** (1982, 1994, 2007). While its initial opening was disappointing, Ridley Scott's dystopian "future noir" was an early success on home video. Theatrical releases of a director's cut for its tenth anniversary and a final cut for its twenty-fifth make the question of the film's definitive identity as interesting as the questions of human versus replicant identity posed by its plot.

With a film that may have been unavailable to viewers during its first release or that simply may not have been popular, a re-release can lend it new life and reclaim viewers through a process of rediscovery. When a small movie achieves unexpected popular or critical success or a major award, for example, it can then be redistributed with a much wider distribution circuit and to a more eager, sympathetic audience that is already prepared to like the movie. For example, the initial distribution of Werner Herzog's *The Mystery of Kaspar Hauser* (1975) in Germany proved unsuccessful; after it garnered film festival prizes and was acclaimed overseas, the film was successfully redistributed in Germany. A re-release may also occur in the attempt to offer the audience a higher-quality picture, or to clarify story lines by restoring cut scenes, as was done in 1989 with Columbia Pictures' re-release of the 1962 Oscar award–winning *Lawrence of Arabia*.

Similarly, television distribution can re-time the release of a movie to promote certain attitudes toward it. *It's a Wonderful Life* did not generate much of an audience when it was first released in 1946. Gradually (and especially after its copyright expired in 1975), network and cable television began to run the film regularly, and the film became a Christmas classic shown often and everywhere during that season **[Figure 1.23]**. In 1997, however,

1.23   ***It's a Wonderful Life*** (1946). A box-office disappointment when it was initially released, Frank Capra's film became a ubiquitous accompaniment to the holiday season on television. In recent years, NBC's broadcast restrictions attempted to restore the film's status as an annual family viewing event.

the television network NBC reclaimed the exclusive rights to the film in order to limit its television distribution to one showing each year and to try to make audiences see the movie as a special event.

Day-and-Date Release

The theatrical release **window** of a film—the period of time before its broadcast or cable premiere, or its distribution on video or DVD—has traditionally been about three to six months to guarantee box-office revenue. The period is becoming shorter and shorter. *Day-and-date release* refers to a simultaneous release strategy across multiple media. With *Bubble* (2006), an offbeat, low-budget murder mystery about a slacker working in a doll factory, director Steven Soderbergh and producers Mark Cuban and Todd Wagner effectively closed this window by releasing the film almost simultaneously to theaters (in limited release), stores, and cable television **[Figure 1.24]**. Director M. Night Shyamalan immediately denounced this strategy, claiming that it would dilute the fundamental experience of the movies as a singular, larger-than-life encounter with the fantasies of storytelling, an experience anticipated in the aesthetics of Shyamalan's own films, such as *The Sixth Sense* (1999) and *Lady in the Water* (2006) **[Figure 1.25]**. Since then, both mainstream and independent films have experimented with timing releases; in 2009 Warner Bros. released *Benjamin Button* on DVD/Blu-ray and made it available to iTunes and pay-per-view at the same time. Magnolia Pictures has even released its slate of independent films digitally on demand *before* their theatrical premieres. For a small film like *Night Catches Us* (2010), the word of mouth garnered by availability on demand can help extend the time it remains in theaters and the number of cities in which it opens theatrically **[Figure 1.26]**.

Whether or not this kind of distribution strategy actually announces a radical change in film distribution, it

text continued on page 42 ▶

1.24 *Bubble* (2006). Steven Soderbergh experimented with releasing simultaneously to theaters, cable, and DVD this modest digital film about a murder's impact on small-town workers at a doll factory.

1.25 *Lady in the Water* (2006). M. Night Shyamalan insists on the magic of encountering the movies on a big screen. Unfortunately, his fairy-tale film was a critical and box-office failure.

1.26 *Night Catches Us* (2010). Tanya Hamilton's film (starring Anthony Mackie and Kerry Washington) explores a racially divided Philadelphia neighborhood in the 1970s in the aftermath of the black power movement. Magnolia Films boosted awareness for this movie by offering it online prior to its theatrical release.

Distributing *Killer of Sheep* (1977)

Distribution is almost invisible to the public and hence much less glamorous than film production or exhibition, but it determines whether a film will ever reach an audience. Independent filmmakers often bring new perspectives to mainstream, formulaic filmmaking, but their visions need to be shared. African American filmmakers, who have historically been marginalized within the industrial system of production, often encounter additional challenges in getting their films distributed. The career of Charles Burnett, considered one of the most significant African American filmmakers despite his relatively small oeuvre, is marked by the vicissitudes of distribution. The successful limited release of his first feature, *Killer*

of Sheep (1977), in 2007, more than thirty years after it was made, not only illuminates black American filmmakers' historically unequal access to movie screens but also illustrates the multiple levels on which current distribution campaigns function. The way the film's distributor, Milestone Films, handled the film's theatrical, non-theatrical, and DVD release in order to maximize critical attention and gain significant revenue serves as a model for similar endeavors **[Figure 1.27]**.

Produced in the early 1970s as a master's thesis film, Burnett's *Killer of Sheep* emerged amid a flowering of African American filmmaking talent at the University of California, Los Angeles, film school. In place of the

1.27 *Killer of Sheep* (1977). Charles Burnett's legendary independent film about an African American family in Los Angeles's Watts neighborhood infuses its realism with poetic images, like the child wearing a mask. The film was finally distributed theatrically thirty years after it was made.

two-dimensional stereotypes of past classical Hollywood films, the almost-too-good-to-be-true characters played by Sidney Poitier in the 1960s, or the often cartoonish, street-smart characters of the so-called **blaxploitation** films that Burnett saw on urban screens at the time, he depicted his protagonist, Stan, as the father of a black family living in the impoverished Watts neighborhood in Los Angeles. A decent man whose slaughterhouse job and daily struggles have numbed and depressed him, Stan nevertheless gets by, and his bonds with his family and community, depicted in grainy, beautifully composed black-and-white images, are profoundly moving. In the film's final scene, Stan and his wife slow dance to a song by Dinah Washington, getting through another day.

Killer of Sheep was never distributed theatrically. Essential to the mood and meaning of the film is its soundtrack, composed of blues and R&B music by Paul Robeson, Dinah Washington, and Earth, Wind, and Fire. Without the resources to clear the music rights for public presentation, Burnett circulated his film over the years in occasional festivals and museum and educational settings. His artistic reputation became firmly established: in 1990, the film was among the first fifty titles named to the National Film Registry by the Library of Congress. But audiences never got to see the film. Only when Burnett was able to complete *To Sleep with Anger* in 1990 due to the participation of actor Danny Glover and Burnett's receipt of a prestigious MacArthur Fellowship, did one of his films receive theatrical distribution. But even *To Sleep with Anger*, a family drama that lacked violence and unambiguous resolutions, was overlooked amid the media's attention to more sensationalized depictions of ghetto culture set to hip-hop soundtracks, such as John Singleton's *Boyz n the Hood* (1991).

Eventually Burnett's critical reputation helped secure the restoration of *Killer of Sheep* by the UCLA Film & Television Archive just when its original 16mm elements were in danger of disintegrating beyond repair. The restoration, one of several planned for independent films of historical significance, was funded by Turner Classic Movies and filmmaker Steven Soderbergh, whose own debut feature, *sex, lies, and videotape* (1989), changed the landscape for the distribution of independent film. In March 2007, the specialty, or "boutique," distributor Milestone Films, whose founders (Dennis Doros and Amy Heller) have long been in the business of releasing important classic and contemporary films theatrically, opened *Killer of Sheep* in a restored 35mm print in New York. Excellent reviews that positioned the film in relation both to African American history and to filmmaking movements like **Italian neorealism**, and the grassroots support of the Harlem-based organization Imagenation, made the opening a record-breaking success, and the film soon opened in art cinemas around the country. The next phase was release on DVD to institutions such as universities that did not have the facilities to show *Killer of Sheep* on 35mm but wanted the rights to have a public screening. Finally, the film was released on DVD for the consumer market, packaged with another unreleased early feature by Burnett, *My Brother's Wedding*, along with a commentary track and other features. Thus an experienced "niche" distributor helped a thirty-year-old film win a place on critics' top-ten lists, a special prize from the New York Film Critics Circle, and a place in public memory.

does signal the kinds of experimentation that digital production and distribution can allow and the inevitable changes and adjustments that will occur in the future in response to shifting markets, tastes, and technologies. Across the exchange between Soderbergh and Shyamalan, it also suggests larger concerns about how these changes can affect our responses to films and the kinds of films that will be made.

The Repeat Viewer

Distributing a movie through one or more releases anticipates and capitalizes on an increasingly common variation in contemporary movie culture: the repeat viewer who returns to see the same movie more than once. *Love Story* (1970), a tale of tragically doomed young love, was among the first modern movies to draw viewers back to the theater for multiple viewings, but films like Rudolph Valentino's *The Sheik* (1921), *Gone with the Wind* (1939), *Toy Story* (1995), and *The Sixth Sense* (1999) have each exploited this viewing pattern **[Figure 1.28]**. Women returned with friends to share their adoration of Valentino; adults returned with children to *Toy Story*, more interested in the inside jokes than the story; and fans of *The Sixth Sense* returned to spot early clues that anticipate the surprise ending. Data taken from repeat viewings of *Titanic* (1997) revealed the extent of business brought to moviegoing by teenage girls—with repeat viewers like these, timing becomes more a function of the viewers' choices, not the distributor's. However, it also demonstrates the changing variety of experiences at the movies for the same individual: A different time and place, different companions, and more knowledge about a movie can alter or enrich expectations and assumptions, and determine how a viewer comes prepared to see a film.

Whether with an exclusive Christmas release or an experimental film, the distribution path implicitly identifies a certain kind of audience (in terms of age, gender, and other characteristics) watching the movie in a certain place (in a theater or at home) and a certain movie-goer (a midnight movie fan or the family that goes out during the holidays). Understanding a movie fully means considering carefully how it attempts to position us in a particular place and time.

> ▶ **VIEWING CUE**
>
> What recent film have you seen more than once? What elements or dimensions of this film suggest that the filmmakers would or would not have expected repeat viewings? ⏸

Distribution's influence on film culture can be significant. In post–World War II America, it was enterprising distributors, with access to theaters no longer monopolized by studio releases, who created a market for foreign films. Today studios easily "dump" a film directly into the video market because it does not think the film will be profitable; non-theatrical distributors circulate independent, experimental, educational, or special interest films to libraries, colleges, and media arts centers; and viewers access small DVD companies that distribute Iranian films by browsing the Internet. Access to movie culture determines viewers' experience of it, and distribution thus determines filmmakers' abilities to communicate with those audiences.

1.28 *The Sixth Sense* (1999). Repeat viewers may detect clues to this film's surprise ending in encounters like this one, in which a troubled boy's mother, played by Toni Collette, fails to meet the gaze of the main character, played by Bruce Willis.

Marketing and Promotion: What We Want to See

Why and how we are attracted to certain movies is directly shaped in the marketing and promotion that accompany distribution. A film might be advertised online as the work of a great director, for example, or it might be described as a steamy love story and illustrated by way of a sensational poster. A film trailer might emphasize the romantic story line in an otherwise cerebral spy film like *The Lives of Others* (2006). Although these preliminary encounters with a film might seem marginally relevant to how we experience the film, promotional strategies, like distribution strategies, prepare us in important ways for how we will see and understand a film.

▶ **VIEWING CUE**

Name a movie you believe has had a strong cultural and historical impact. Investigate what modes of promotion helped to highlight particular themes in and reactions to the film. ⏸

Generating Our Interest

Marketing and promotion aim to generate and direct interest in a movie. Film **marketing** involves identifying an audience in order to bring a product (the movie) to the attention of buyers (viewers) so that they will consume (watch) that product for financial return. Film **promotion** refers to the specific ways a movie can be made an object that an audience will want to see. No doubt the **star system** is the most pervasive and potent component of the marketing and promotion of movies around the world. One or more well-known actors (popular at a specific time and within a specific culture) act as the advertising vehicle for the movie, and, like other marketing and promotional practices, the star system aims to create, in advance, specific expectations that will draw an audience to a film. Quite often, these marketing and promotional expectations—that Tom Cruise stars or that Mexican filmmaker Alejandro González Iñárritu directs, for example—subsequently become the viewfinders through which an audience sees a movie.

The methods of marketing and promotion are many and creative. Viewers find themselves bombarded with everything from newspaper and billboard advertisements to previews shown before the main feature to tie-in games featured on the official movie Web site to trailers that appear when browsing the Internet **[Figure 1.29]**. Stars make public appearances on radio and television and are profiled in fan magazines; media critics attend early screenings and write reviews that are quoted in the ads for the film—all these actions contribute to movie promotion. In addition, while movies have long been promoted through prizes and gifts, modern distributors are especially adept at marketing films through **tie-ins**: ancillary products such as T-shirts, CD soundtracks, toys, and other gimmicks made available at stores and restaurants that advertise and promote a movie. *The Little Mermaid* (1989), for example, was anticipated with the replica toys of Ariel, and the song "Under the Sea" generated interest in the movie and vice versa.

Marketing campaigns for blockbuster films have become more and more extensive in recent years, with the promotion budget equaling and often even exceeding the film's production budget. A marketing blitz of note accompanied *Independence Day* (1996). Given its carefully timed release on July 3, 1996, following weeks of advertisements in newspapers and on television, it would be difficult to analyze first-run viewers' feelings about this film without taking into account the influence of these promotions. Defining the film as a science fiction thriller, the advertisements and reviews drew attention to its status as the film event of the summer, its suitability for children, and its technological wizardry. Promoted

1.29 Movie marquee. Promoting movies through prizes, giveaways, and product tie-ins dates back to the 1920s.

and released to coincide with the Fourth of July holiday, *Independence Day* ads emphasized its patriotic American themes **[Figure 1.30]**. In that light, many posters, advertisements, and publicity stills presented actor Will Smith together with Bill Pullman or Jeff Goldblum, not only to promote the film's stars but also to draw attention to the racial harmony achieved in the film and its appeal to both African American and white audiences. During the first month of its release, when U.S. scientists discovered a meteorite with fossils that suggested early life on Mars, promotion for the movie responded immediately with revised ads: "Last week, scientists found evidence of life on another planet. We're not going to say we told you so. . . ."

Typical Hollywood promotions and advertisements often emphasize the realism of movies, a strategy that promises audiences more accurate or more expansive reflections of the world and human experience. For *Dark Victory* (1939), a Bette Davis film about a socialite dying of a brain tumor, advertisements and press kits drew viewers' attention to the disturbing truth of a terminal illness, a reality that promotions claimed had never before been presented in movies. A related marketing strategy is to claim textual novelty in a film, drawing attention to new features such as technical innovations, a rising star, or the acclaimed book on which the film is based. With early sound films like *The Jazz Singer* (1927), *The Gold Diggers of Broadway* (1929), and *Innocents of Paris* (1929), marketing advertisements directed audiences toward the abundance and quality of the singing and talking that added a dramatic new dimension to cinematic realism **[Figure 1.31]**. Today promotions and advertisements frequently exploit new technologies. Promotions of *The Polar Express* (2004) flaunted its novel motion-capture technology, which used Tom Hanks's movements to animate several of the film's characters; *Avatar*'s marketing campaign emphasized its new 3-D technology. Marketers can also take advantage of current political events, as when Sam Mendes's *Jarhead* (2005) advertised its plot's timely encounter with debates and concerns around the ongoing war in Iraq **[Figure 1.32]**.

Stars are booked to appear on talk shows and in other venues in conjunction with a film's release, as official promotion tactics, but stars may also bring unofficial publicity to a film. Brad Pitt and Angelina Jolie boosted audiences for the film *Mr. and Mrs. Smith* (2005) when they became a couple during its filming. Conversely, unwelcome publicity can cause an actor's contract to be canceled or raise concerns about the impact on ticket sales **[Figure 1.33]**, as happened with Tom Cruise's often odd remarks and public appearances preceding the release of *Mission: Impossible III* (2006).

1.30 *Independence Day* (1996). The film's massive promotional campaign for its Fourth of July weekend opening drew on blatant and subtle forms of patriotism, such as the multicultural appeal of its cast.

1.31 *Innocents of Paris* (1929). The marquee promotes the novelty of sound and song and this early musical's singing star.

Older films in current release and independent, art, and foreign-language films have less access to the mechanisms of promotion than do current mainstream films, and social media have afforded new opportunities to spread the word to specialized audiences. In addition, audiences for these films are led to some extent by what we might call *cultural promotion*, academic or journalistic accounts that discuss and frequently value films as especially important in movie history or as aesthetic objects. A discussion of a movie in a film history book or even in a university film course could thus be seen as an act of marketing, which makes clear that promotion is not just about urging viewers to see a film but is also about urging them to see it with a particular point of view. Although these more measured kinds of promotion are usually underpinned by intellectual rather than financial motives, they also deserve our consideration and analysis.

How does a specific film history text, for instance, prepare you to see a film such as *Bonnie and Clyde* (1967)? Some books promote it as a modern gangster film. Others pitch it as an incisive reflection of the social history of the turbulent 1960s. Still other texts and essays may urge readers to see it because of its place in the oeuvre of a major U.S. director, Arthur Penn **[Figure 1.34]**. Independent movies promote the artistic power and individuality of the director; associate themselves with big-name film festivals in Venice, Toronto, and Cannes; or call attention, through advertising, to what distinguishes them from mainstream Hollywood films. For a foreign film, a committed publicist can be crucial to its attaining distribution by attracting critical mention. Documentaries can be promoted in relation to the

1.32 *Jarhead* (2005). Topical interest in the Iraq conflict and the best-selling memoir on which it was based fueled interest in this film about a Marine's baffling Gulf War experience.

1.33 **Tom Cruise.** The star's erratic behavior during daytime and late-night talk-show appearances to promote *Mission: Impossible III* (2006) contributed to Paramount's ending its contract with Cruise.

1.34 *Bonnie and Clyde* (1967). Critical accounts may position this film as an updated gangster film or as social commentary on the turbulent 1960s.

1.35 *The Kid* (1921). Chaplin, unlike in his well-known slapstick comedies, expresses a demeanor in the poster that suggests the serious themes of his first feature film.

topical subject matter or controversy. In short, we do not experience any film with innocent eyes; consciously or not, we come prepared to see it in a certain way.

Advertising

Advertising is a central form of promotion that uses television, billboards, film trailers or previews, print ads, banners on Web sites, and other forms of display to bring a film to the attention of a potential audience. Advertising can use the facts in and issues surrounding a movie in various ways. Advertising often emphasizes connections with and differences from related or similar films or highlights the presence of a particularly popular actor or director. The poster for Charles Chaplin's *The Kid* (1921), for example, proudly pronounces it "the great Film he has been working on for a whole year" [**Figure 1.35**]. For different markets, *G.I. Jane* (1997) was promoted as a star vehicle for Demi Moore or as the latest film from Ridley Scott, the director of *Alien* (1979), *Blade Runner* (1982), and *Thelma & Louise* (1991). It is conceivable that these two promotional tactics created different sets of expectations about the movie—one more attuned to tough female protagonists, the other to lavish sets and technological landscapes. As this example reveals, promotion tends not only to draw us to a movie but also to suggest what we will concentrate on as a way of understanding its achievement.

Trailers

One of the most carefully crafted forms of promotional advertising is the **trailer**, which previews carefully edited images and scenes from a film in theaters before the main feature film or on television or a Web site. In just a few minutes, these trailers provide a compact series of reasons why a viewer *should* see that movie. A trailer for Stanley Kubrick's *Eyes Wide Shut* (2000) is indicative: it moves quickly to large bold titles announcing separately the names of Tom Cruise, Nicole Kidman, and Kubrick, foregrounding the collaboration of a star marriage and a celebrated director of daring films. Then, against the refrain from Chris Isaak's soundtrack song "Baby Did a Bad Thing," a series of images condenses the progress of the film, including shots of Kidman undressing, Cruise as Dr. Harford sauntering with two beautiful women, a passionate kiss shared by the two stars, two ominous-looking

1.36 *Eyes Wide Shut* (2000). Advertisements and trailers for Stanley Kubrick's last film emphasized the film's director, its stars—Tom Cruise and Nicole Kidman, who were married at the time—and its sexual content.

men at the gate of an estate (where an orgy will take place), and Cruise being enticed by a prostitute. Besides the provocative match of two, then-married star sex symbols with a controversial director, the trailer underlines the dark erotic mysteries of the film within an opulently decadent setting. It introduces intensely sexual characters and the alternately seedy and glamorous atmosphere of the film in a manner meant to draw fans of Cruise, Kidman, Kubrick, and erotic intrigue [**Figure 1.36**].

That this promotion fails to communicate the stinging irony in the movie's eroticism may, interestingly, account for some of the disappointed reactions that followed its eager initial reception.

The availability of trailers on the Internet has increased the novel approaches to this format, and trailers are now rated and scrutinized like theatrical releases. Moreover, the trailer format lends itself to the increasingly

text continued on page 48 ▶

1.37a

1.37b

1.37c

1.37d

1.37e

1.37f

The Changing Art and Business of the Film Trailer

Initially shown trailing—after—the feature to give viewers accustomed to weekly movie attendance a taste of coming attractions, the film trailer later became a central form of movie marketing, positioned before the feature and subject to its own well-researched conventions and even to independent ratings. Through the 1950s, onscreen text was used to advertise a film's key features, including its stars, genre, plot mysteries, even the latest film technology, such as CinemaScope. Later, voiceover narration and scoring helped make a coherent message from a montage of images arranged in a three-act structure. In the era of the Internet, the movie trailer has become one of the most sought-out online experiences, a cultural touchstone that studios use to build expectations and engage viewers beyond a single ticket-buying experience.

The much-anticipated summer blockbuster *Inception* (2010) combines state-of-the-art special effects with director Christopher Nolan's trademark narrative complexity. *Inception*'s trailer for the Blu-ray and DVD release embeds some of the film's most spectacular visuals between shots of characters who look amazed and bewildered, much as the trailer's viewer is likely to be [**Figures 1.37a, 1.37b, and 1.37c**]. The main character, Dom Cobb, confides in a voiceover, "Something you should know about me: I specialize in a very specific type of security . . ." as images of a gun being loaded and a percussive soundtrack suggest fast-paced action. The line's direct address to "you" indicates that the viewer will soon be enlightened. ". . . Subconscious security," Cobb concludes, raising new questions and plot possibilities. Near the end of the trailer's two-minute condensation of the film's elaborate intrigue, two title cards, separated by shots of the film's improbable settings intercut with close-ups revealing the protagonist's emotional anguish, read: "Your mind—is the scene of the crime" [**Figures 1.37d, 1.37e, and 1.37f**]. From small scale to grand, from intimacy to action, the trailer, part of the film's $100 million advertising budget, succeeds in linking movie magic to the viewer's internal experience—as the tagline suggests.

Track the marketing techniques you encounter for a film in current release. Do the bus ads, trailers, banners, pop-up windows, and newspaper advertisements communicate a coherent message about this film? What is it? ⏸

prevalent practice of audience "remix," through which mainstream media content is re-edited by fans as tribute or satire. *Mary Poppins* remixed as a horror film trailer is a popular YouTube video, attesting to viewers' awareness of how promotional strategies direct our responses to and recognition of movie conventions.

Media Convergence

Movie advertising has always targeted consumers' changing habits and has adapted strategies for the era of **media convergence**, the coordinating and merging of media across a variety of platforms, such as print, television, and the Internet. A viewer might find and play an online game set in a film's fictional world on the film's Web site, read a print ad, and watch an online promotion with the films' stars, all before attending the movie in a theater. Indeed, the enormous sums spent on marketing a film's theatrical release are deemed worthwhile as they directly relate to the promotion of other media elements within the brand or franchise, such as video games, CDs, and later DVD releases. Viewers understand these tactics and may participate in this proliferation: a viewer who enjoys the film and its soundtrack might download a ringtone for her cell phone and place the title in her Netflix queue in anticipation of its release on DVD months later. But viewers may also decide to skip the theatrical release altogether and catch the film later on cable television or DVD.

The enormous popularity of social networking sites fosters the technique of **viral marketing**, which describes the process of advertising that relies on existing social networks such as word of mouth, Internet links, or sites like Facebook or Twitter to spread the word. Because viral marketing works through networks of shared interest, it is not as dependent upon market research and can be highly effective as well as an informative indicator of audience preferences. Yet it is also less easily controlled than deliberately placed ads based on target demographics. In many ways, viewers, due to media convergence, have even more of an impact on how films are understood and even produced today.

High Concept, A and B Pictures, and Other Marketing Labels

Trailers, posters, and newspaper advertisements carefully select not only their images but also their terminology in order to guide our perspective on a film even before we see it. Parodied brilliantly in Robert Altman's *The Player* (1992), the language of **high concept**, a short phrase that attempts to sell a movie through its main marketing features—stars, genre, or some other easily identifiable connection—is a feature of modern Hollywood [**Figure 1.38**]. In *The Player*, one film is memorably described as "kind of a psychic political thriller with a heart." Other high-concept movies might be advertised as "Stanley Kubrick's exploration of pornography" or "In *Lara Croft: Tomb Raider* (2001), superstar Angelina Jolie brings the CD-ROM game to life." The rhetoric of movie advertising frequently descends into such silly clichés as "two thumbs up" or "action-packed, fun-filled adventure," yet promotional and marketing language also uses succinct descriptive terms to position a movie for particular expectations and responses. As we have seen, the term "feature film" originated in 1912; by the 1930s it became a key promotional strategy to describe a movie of a certain length (over seventy minutes) that was positioned as the main attraction in an evening's movie program. The term is still used to describe a theatrically released film.

1.38 *The Player* (1992). Director Robert Altman and writer Michael Tolkin satirize the movie business; the screenwriter's "pitch" to a studio executive becomes a literal matter of life and death.

The Hollywood studios made a production distinction between a big-budget **A picture**, which promises high-quality stars and stories, and a **B picture**, a less expensive, more quickly made movie that plays on the bottom half of a double bill. (The term "B picture" later referred to a cheaply made **exploitation film**, made to "exploit" sensational or topical subject matter or genre conventions for profit.) Just as today the term **blockbuster** prepares us for action, stars, and special effects, and **art film** suggests a more visually subtle, perhaps slower-paced or more intellectually demanding movie, the terminology used to define and promote a movie can become a potent force in framing our expectations.

The Rating System

Rating systems, which provide viewers with guidelines for movies (usually based on violent or sexual content), are a similarly important form of advertising that can be used in marketing and promotion. Whether they are wanted or unwanted by viewers, ratings are fundamentally about trying to control the kind of audience that sees a film and, to a certain extent, about advertising the content of that film. In the United States, the current Motion Picture Association of America (MPAA) ratings system classifies movies as G (general audiences), PG (parental guidance suggested), PG-13 (parental guidance suggested and not recommended for audiences under thirteen years old), R (persons under age seventeen must be accompanied by an adult), and NC-17 (persons under age seventeen are not admitted). Films made outside the major studios are not required to obtain MPAA ratings, but exhibition and even advertising opportunities are closely tied to the system. Most countries, as well as some religious organizations, have their own systems for rating films. Great Britain, for instance, uses these categories: U (universal), A (parental discretion), AA (persons under age fourteen are not admitted), and X (persons under age eighteen are not admitted). Interestingly, the age limit for X-rated films varies from country to country, the lowest being age fifteen in Sweden.

A movie like *Free Willy* (1993), the tale of a child and a captured killer whale, depends on its G rating to draw large family audiences, whereas sexually explicit films like *Showgirls* (1995), rated NC-17, and Nagisa Oshima's *In the Realm of the Senses* (1976), not rated and confiscated when it first came to many countries, can use the notoriety of their ratings to attract curious adult viewers. An NC-17 rating can damage a film's box-office prospects, however, because many newspapers will not carry ads for such films. When promotion casually or aggressively uses ratings, our way of looking at and thinking about the movie already begins to anticipate the film. For example, with an R rating, we might anticipate a movie featuring a degree of sex and violence. A rating of G might promise happy endings and happy families. Such movies as *Men in Black* (1997) eagerly sought a PG-13 rating because it, ironically perhaps, attracts a younger audience of eight-, nine-, and ten-year-olds, who want movies with a touch of adult language and action **[Figure 1.39]**. *The King's Speech*'s (2010) R rating (for profanity used as speech therapy) was eventually amended to PG-13 after the film was cut to remove a few curse words.

1.39 *Men in Black* (1997). A PG-13 rating can suggest a certain edge to a film that makes it attractive to preteens.

Word of Mouth

Our experience at the movies is directed in advance of our viewing of the film in less evident and predictable ways as well. Word of mouth, the conversational exchange of opinions and information sometimes referred to as the "buzz" around

VIEWING CUE

How would you summarize the "buzz" that anticipated or surrounded a recent release? Can you analyze how it prepared viewers with certain expectations?

a movie, may seem a somewhat insignificant or at least hazy area of promotion, yet it is an important social arena in which our likes and dislikes are formed and given direction by the social groups we move in. The explosion of social networking sites, which allow us to list or indicate our "likes and dislikes" with a click, has expanded these groups exponentially. We know our friends like certain kinds of films, and we all tend to promote movies according to a culture of taste whereby we judge and approve of movies according to the values of our particular age group, cultural background, or other social determinant. When marketing experts direct a movie at a target audience, they intend to promote that film through word of mouth or "virally," knowing viewers communicate with one another and recommend films to people who share their values and tastes **[Figures 1.40a and 1.40b]**.

Examine, for instance, how a group of friends might anticipate *The Hunger Games* (2012) among themselves. Would they be excited about the casting of a rising star as the tough young heroine? The genre of science fiction films set in a dystopian future and the potential for interesting visual effects? The books by Suzanne Collins with which they are familiar? What would each of these word-of-mouth promotions indicate about the social or personal values of the person promoting the movie and the culture of taste influencing his or her views?

Fan Engagement

Fan magazines were an early extension of word of mouth as a form of movie promotion and have consistently shed light on the sociology of taste. Emerging in the 1910s and widely popular by the 1920s, such "fanzines" brought film culture home to audience members. Posing as objective accounts, many stories were actually produced by the studios' publicity departments. In recent years, fan magazines have evolved into Internet discussion groups, and promotional and user-generated Web sites and fan activity have become an even bigger force in film promotion and culture. Web sites, often set up by a film's distributor, have, in fact, become the most powerful contemporary form of the fanzine, allowing information about and enthusiasm for a movie to be efficiently exchanged and spread among potential viewers. In what is widely heralded as a breakthrough example of the Internet marketing trend, *The Blair Witch Project* (1999) Web site was established in advance of the film's release and used fake documents and clues to help generate word of mouth; the success of this strategy transformed this simple, low-budget horror film ($35,000) into a proportionally huge box-office hit ($15 million). Notoriously, the title *Snakes on a Plane* (2006) was so resonant with viewers in its very literalness that the Web activity around the film (even before its release) prompted changes to make the film more daring and campier **[Figure 1.41]**. The subsequent box-office disappointment may have been a measure of viewers' reaction to marketing manipulations.

VIEWING CUE

Consider a recent film release you've seen, and identify which promotional strategies were effective in getting you to attend. Was anything about the promotion misleading? Was there anything about the film you feel was ignored or underplayed in the promotion?

1.40a *Titanic* (1997). Word of mouth anticipating the release of James Cameron's film focused on special effects.

1.40b *Titanic* (1997). After the film's release, word of mouth fostered its success among young female fans of Leonardo DiCaprio and the romance plot.

To encourage and develop individual interest in films, these fanzines and Web sites gather together readers and viewers who wish to read or chat about their ongoing interest in movies like the *Star Trek* films (1979–1994) or cult favorites like *Casablanca* (1942) or share fan productions. Here tastes about which movies to like and dislike and about how to see them are supported and promoted on a concrete social and commercial level. Information is offered or exchanged about specific movies, arguments are waged, and fan fiction (**fanfic**) or user-generated videos are developed around the film. Magazines may provide information about the signature song of *Casablanca*, "As Time Goes By," and the actor who sings it, Dooley Wilson. Chat room participants may query each other about Mr. Spock's Vulcan history or fantasize about his personal life. Even before the release of *The Lord of the Rings: The Fellowship of the Ring* (2001), the filmmakers engaged fans of the Tolkien novels through e-mails and Web sites, trading information about the production for feedback on casting decisions and scene cuts. The Internet promotes word of mouth about a film by offering potential audiences the possibility of some participation in the making of the film, an approach that is increasingly common today.

As they proliferate, promotional avenues like these deserve attention and analysis in terms of how they add to or confuse our understanding of a film. Our different experiences of the movies take place within a complex cultural terrain where our personal interest in certain films intersects with specific historical and social forces to shape the meaning and value of those experiences. Here, too, the film experience extends well beyond the big screen.

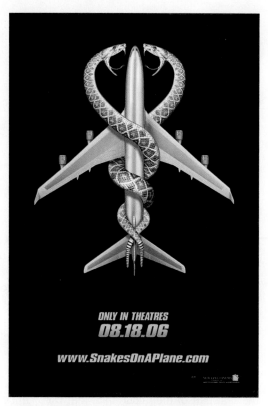

1.41 *Snakes on a Plane* (2006). Potential audiences had great fun with the film's advance publicity on the Web; the box-office performance did not live up to the hype.

Movie Exhibition: The Where, When, and How of Movie Experiences

Exhibition encompasses where and when we see films; it may involve promotional elements like movie posters and publicity events in a theater lobby or be related to distribution through the calendar of film releasing. But exhibition, closely tied to **reception**, the process through which individual viewers or groups make sense of a film, is at the heart of the film experience. **Exhibitors** own individual theaters or theater chains and make decisions about programming and local promotion; they are responsible for the actual experience of moviegoing, including the concessions that make a night out at the movies different from one spent watching films at home and that bring in an estimated 40 percent of theater owners' revenue. Like distribution and promotion, we may take exhibition for granted, forgetting that the many ways we watch movies contribute a great deal to our feelings about, and our interpretations of, film. We watch movies within a cultural range of exhibition venues: in theaters, at home on video monitors, or on a plane or train on portable devices. Not surprisingly, these contexts and technologies anticipate and condition our responses to movies.

The Changing Contexts and Practices of Film Exhibition

If production, distribution, and promotion already work to anticipate, shape, and direct our tastes, then exhibition contexts and practices can support or alter the intended aims and meanings of a movie. These contexts and practices include the

text continued on page 54 ▶

FILM IN FOCUS

Promoting *The Crying Game* (1992)

Neil Jordan's *The Crying Game* is an ingenious example of various promotional maneuvers that would characterize a new moment in making a modestly budgeted independent film into a **crossover** success in which it appeared on "ten best" lists and garnered high-profile award nominations. A hybrid of art film and thriller, its story about the sexual identity crisis of Fergus, a member of the Irish Republican Army (IRA), begins with the capture of Jody, a black British soldier. After witnessing Jody's violent, accidental death, Fergus flees to England, where he seeks out and falls in love with Dil, Jody's former lover. Complicating this plot, Fergus does not realize, during the first part of their courtship, that Dil's gender identity does not match her anatomy. Dil's transgender identity is revealed in a scene that surprises Fergus—and many audience members.

The film was first promoted on the basis of its artistic novelty and integrity, which was associated primarily with Jordan's cultural reputation as a serious director of such inventive British films as *Mona Lisa* (1986). That *The Crying Game* was only moderately successful when first released in England can be attributed, in part, to the social context of its release: renewed IRA activity in England at the time may have made it difficult for British audiences to look past the political subplot and concentrate on Jordan's artistry or on the intriguing relationship between Fergus and Dil **[Figure 1.42]**. The U.S. distributor, Miramax, also recognizing difficulties in distributing and promoting the film, was concerned about three traditional marketing taboos: race, political violence, and homosexuality. However, removed from the British–Irish political context, Miramax decided it could repackage the movie to promote it by drawing attention away from its political intrigue and focusing on the romantic and sexual "secret" of Dil's male anatomy **[Figure 1.43]**. This strategy both capitalized on the critical and modest box-office success of several concurrent independent films on lesbian/gay/bisexual/transgender topics dubbed "New Queer Cinema" and exploited the perception of breaking a taboo. The film broke box-office records in the United States for a British production. The promotional schemes in Britain and the United States resulted in significantly different ways of seeing and understanding the same movie.

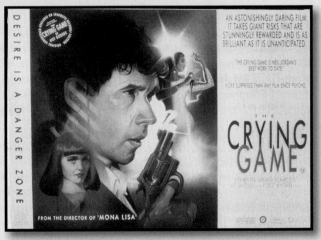

1.42 *The Crying Game* (1992). The British poster promotes the film's subject matter of political violence.

At the center of its promotional history, *The Crying Game* used two different advertising approaches, one for the British release and another for the U.S. release. The differences between these campaigns crystallize in the advertising posters used for the two promotions. In the British poster, a large profile of Stephen Rea as Fergus holding a smoking gun centers the image, surrounded by smaller images of Jaye Davidson as Dil and Miranda Richardson as the femme fatale, Jude. Numerous lines of print promote the film as "From the Director of *Mona Lisa*," "Neil Jordan's Best Work to Date," and as offering "More Surprises Than Any Film Since *Psycho*." The American poster features only the image of Miranda Richardson, with a smoking gun, set against a black backdrop. The print is equally spare: "Sex. Murder. Betrayal." and, under the film's title, "play it at your own risk." The British poster advertises the cinematic heritage of Jordan, while highlighting the masculine and political violence associated with Fergus's large image. The American poster conversely creates the dark atmosphere of sexual intrigue, notably offering audiences a participatory game rather than a serious political reality.

In the 1990s, after the film's box-office success in the United States, the Internet continued to promote the film's initial participatory lure. Dozens of Web sites about

52

The Crying Game appeared in numerous languages. Some sites, such as *The Crying Game* Fan Page, feature photos, Boy George's rendition of the title song, and links to movie reviews. Others are devoted to a single star, such as Forest Whitaker or Jaye Davidson.

Ratings and, especially, word of mouth created specific expectations and interests in *The Crying Game*. It received an R rating in the United States (no doubt for its frontal male nudity), where such a rating would more likely suggest sexual content rather than violence. But especially in the United States, word of mouth functioned as the most powerful strategy in the promotion of *The Crying Game*, in this way supplementing the poster. Viewers, including movie reviewers, were urged to keep the secret of Dil's anatomical gender as a way of baiting new audiences to see the film. A widely announced promotion—"Don't tell the secret!"—drew a continuous stream of audiences wanting to participate in this game of secrets. Word of mouth became part of a strategy to entice American audiences who, anticipating a sexual drama of surprises and reversals, would in most instances overlook the political tensions that complicated the film for British audiences.

1.43 *The Crying Game* (1992). The American poster promotes the film through an emphasis on sexual games, yet the central romance is not depicted.

physical environment in which we view a movie (spatial frameworks), when we watch a movie and the duration of the experience (temporal frameworks), and the technology through which we see the movie (technological frameworks).

Seeing the same movie at a cineplex or in a college classroom, watching it uninterrupted for two hours on a big screen or in thirty-minute segments over four days on a computer, can elicit very different kinds of film response. A viewer watching a film on an airplane monitor may be completely bored by it, but watching it later at home, he or she may find that film much more compelling, appreciating its visual surprises and interesting plot twists.

Movies have been distributed, exhibited, and seen in many different contexts historically. At the beginning of the twentieth century, movies rarely lasted more than 20 minutes and were often viewed in small, noisy **nickelodeons**, storefront theaters where short films were shown continuously to audiences passing in and out, or in carnival settings that assumed movies were a passing amusement comparable to other attractions. By the 1920s, as movies grew artistically, financially, and culturally, the exhibition of films moved to lavish **movie palaces** like Radio City Music Hall (which opened in 1932), with sumptuous seating for thousands amid the ornate architecture. By the 1950s, city centers gave way to suburban sprawl; as the theaters lost their crowds of patrons, drive-ins and widescreen and 3-D processes were introduced to distinguish the possibilities of film exhibition from its new rival, television at home. Soon television became a way to experience movies as special events in the flow of daily programming. In the 1980s, VCRs gave home audiences access to many movies and the ability to watch them when and how they wished, and the **multiplex** became increasingly important as a way of integrating a choice of moviegoing experiences with an outing to the mall. Today we commonly see movies at home on a DVD player or computer screen, where we can watch them in the standard 90- to 120-minute period, extend our viewing over many nights, or rewatch favorite or puzzling portions of films. Portable devices such as laptops, smartphones, and tablet computers give a new mobility to our viewing. As theaters continue to compete with home screens, film exhibitors have countered with so-called megaplexes—theaters with twenty or more screens, more than six thousand seats, and over a hundred showtimes per day. These new entertainment complexes may feature not just movies but also arcade games, restaurants, and coffee bars. Home exhibition has responded in turn with more elaborate digital picture and sound technologies and convergence between devices such as game consoles and television screens for streaming movies.

Technologies and Cultures of Exhibition

Changing viewing formats—how and where we watch a movie—contribute to the wider culture of exhibition space, the specific social activities that surround and define moviegoing. Theatrical exhibition highlights a social dimension of watching movies because it gathers and organizes individuals as a specific audience at a specific place and time. Further, our shared participation in that social environment directs our attention and shapes our responses.

A movie such as *Charlotte's Web* (2006) will be shown as a Saturday matinee in suburban theaters (as well as other places) to attract families with children to its famous children's tale of a spider who saves a pig **[Figure 1.44]**. The time and place of the showing obviously coordinate with a period when middle-class families can share recreation and amusement, making them more inclined to appreciate this light-hearted tale of family love and affection. Conversely, Peter Greenaway's *The Pillow Book* (1996), a complex film about a woman's passion for calligraphy, human flesh, poetry, and sex, would likely appear in a small urban theater frequented by individuals and young couples or groups of friends who also spend time in the theater's coffee bar **[Figure 1.45]**. This movie would probably appeal to an urban crowd with more experimental tastes, and to those who like to watch more intellectually stimulating and

VIEWING CUE

Imagine several different exhibition contexts—historical, cultural, technological—for the film you are studying. How would it fare in a nickelodeon, a movie palace, or on DVD?

VIEWING CUE

What do you imagine as the ideal "culture of exhibition" for the film you are studying? Would it appear in a particular type of theater, with a particular kind of projection? What types of audiences seem most apt? How would ads target those different groups?

conversation-provoking films. Reversing the exhibition contexts of these two films would indicate how those contexts could generate wildly different reactions.

The technological conditions of exhibition—that is, the industrial and mechanical vehicles through which movies are shown—shape the culture of exhibition space, whether public and theatrical or private and domestic. In a large theater, a movie can be shown on a 35mm or even 70mm projector that displays large and vibrantly detailed images. We might see another movie in a cineplex theater at a mall with a relatively small screen and a smorgasbord of other movies in the theaters surrounding it. We may watch a third movie on a DVD

1.44 *Charlotte's Web* (2006). G-rated family films are distributed widely to theater chains and exhibited in early time slots.

player that allows us to select just our favorite scenes. Today's movies exhibited on a computer screen can share the monitor with other kinds of activities. In the past, popular exhibition practices included inserting a short movie within a vaudeville performance or offering double features in drive-in theaters full of teenagers in cars.

Different technological features of exhibition are sometimes carefully calculated to add to both our enjoyment and our understanding of a movie. Cecil B. DeMille's epic film *The Ten Commandments* (1923) premiered in a movie palace, where the plush and grandiose surroundings, the biblical magnitude of the images, and the orchestral accompaniment supported the grand spiritual themes of the film. Thus the conditions for watching a film may parallel its ideas or formal practices. With the special projection techniques and 3-D glasses worn for *Creature from the Black Lagoon* (1954), the creature's appearance becomes even more startling. 3-D technology is in fact an excellent example of changing exhibition technologies and cultures; long regarded nostalgically as a gimmick of the 1950s, it made a comeback with Robert Zemeckis's *Beowulf* (2007) and was soon synonymous with state-of-the-art digital movie production and exhibition with the technology developed for *Avatar* **[Figure 1.46]**. Theater owners worldwide converted screens in order to show the film and to attract local audiences with the novelty of the spectacle.

1.45 *The Pillow Book* (1996). Art films, especially those that receive an NC-17 rating, are likely to be distributed primarily to specialty cinemas in urban locations.

1.46 **3-D exhibition.** Viewers enjoy a screening with special 3-D glasses in the 1950s, the first heyday of the technology. As a technological innovation, 3-D brings the focus to exhibition contexts and offers a chance for theater owners to increase revenue.

text continued on page 58 ▶

Exhibiting *Citizen Kane* (1941)

The tale of a man obsessed with power and possessions, *Citizen Kane* is often considered one of the greatest films ever made. It is usually hailed for Orson Welles's portrayal of Charles Foster Kane and Welles's direction of the puzzle-like story, and for the film's complex visual compositions. It is also a movie that ran into trouble even before its release because of its thinly disguised and critical portrayal of U.S. media mogul William Randolph Hearst [**Figure 1.47**]. Less often is *Citizen Kane* seen and understood according to its dramatic exhibition history, one that has colored or even decided the changing meanings of the film.

As the first film of a director already hailed as a "boy genius" for his work as a theater actor and director, *Citizen Kane* was scheduled to open with appropriate fanfare at the spectacular Radio City Music Hall in New York City, where RKO premiered its top films. Besides highlighting the glamorous and palatial architecture of this building, exhibiting the film in New York first would take advantage of the fact that Welles's career and reputation had been made there. The physical and social context for this opening exhibition would combine the epic grandeur of the Radio City building and a New York cultural space attuned to Welles's artistic experimentation. Already offended by rumors about the film, however, Hearst secretly moved to block the opening at Radio City Music Hall. After many difficulties and delays, the film's producer and distributor, RKO, eventually premiered the film simultaneously at an independent theater in Los Angeles and at a refurbished vaudeville house in New York City. The film's wider release was detrimentally affected by Hearst's attack on the film; Hearst newspapers were banned from running ads for it, directly affecting its box-office potential. When major theaters such as the Fox and Paramount chains were legally forced to exhibit the film, they sometimes booked *Citizen Kane* but did not actually screen it for fear of vindictive repercussions from Hearst. Where it was shown, the controversy overshadowed the film itself, making it appear for many audiences strange and unnecessarily confrontational, resulting in a box-office failure.

Changing sociological and geographical contexts for exhibition have continued to follow *Citizen Kane* as its reputation has grown through the years. After its

1.47 *Citizen Kane* (1941). William Randolph Hearst objected to the film's thinly veiled portrayal of his life and blocked it from opening at Radio City Music Hall. The film's wider release was negatively affected as well—major theater chains did not want to screen it for fear of incurring Hearst's wrath.

tumultuous first exhibition in the United States, the film was rediscovered in the 1950s by the art-house cinemas of France. There it was hailed as a brilliantly creative expression of film language. Today many individuals who see *Citizen Kane* watch it in a classroom—say, in a college course on American cinema. In the classroom, we look at movies as students or as scholars, and we are prepared to study them. In this context, viewers may feel urged to think more about the film as an art object than as entertainment or exposé. In the classroom, we may focus more on the serious aspects of the film (such as Kane's real and visual alienation from his best friends) than on the comic interludes (such as the vaudevillian dance number). This is not to say that someone watching *Citizen Kane* in an academic situation cannot see and think about it in other ways. It's clear, however, that exhibition contexts suggest certain social attitudes through which we watch a movie. The exhibition history of *Citizen Kane* likewise describes significant differences in how the film is experienced through different technologies. Its original 35mm exhibition showed off the imagistic details and stunning deep-focus cinematography that made the film famous. The visual magnitude of scenes such as

Susan Alexander's operatic premiere and Kane's safari picnic at Xanadu, or the spatial vibrancy and richness of Kane and Susan's conversation in one of Xanadu's vast halls, arguably require the size and texture of a large theatrical image. Since its first theatrical exhibition, the film has circulated to film societies and colleges on 16mm film and later appeared on the successive consumer technologies of video, laserdisc, DVD, and Blu-ray. The content of the film remains the same, but the different technologies have sometimes muted the visual power of its images and scenes because of lower quality or smaller image size. Digital formats enhance the image, perhaps redirecting our understanding to visual dynamics rather than the events of the story.

The shift in the exhibition context may also affect our level of concentration from focused to distracted attention. A viewing experience on television may be broken up because of commercials, and on a digital format we can affect the duration of the experience when we start and stop the movie ourselves. Whereas the large images in the theater may direct the viewer more easily to the play of light and dark as commentaries on the different characters, a DVD player might instead allow the viewer to replay dialogue in order to note levels of intonation or wordplay. Consumer editions of *Citizen Kane* give viewers the added opportunity to supplement the film with rare photos, documents on the advertising campaign, commentaries by filmmaker Peter Bogdanovich and critic Roger Ebert, and a documentary, *The Battle over Citizen Kane* (1996), that describes the history of its script and its exhibition difficulties. To whatever degree these supplemental materials come into play, it is clear that a DVD exhibition of *Citizen Kane* offers possibilities for significantly enriching an audience's experience of the film. Viewers taking advantage of these materials would conceivably watch *Citizen Kane* prepared and equipped with certain points of view: more attuned perhaps to Welles's creative innovation and influence on later filmmakers like Bogdanovich, or more interested in how the film re-creates the connections between Hearst and Kane detailed in the documentary supplement. That the DVD provides material on "alternative ad campaigns" for the original release of the film even allows viewers to investigate the way different promotional strategies can direct their attention to certain themes and scenes.

The fame of *Citizen Kane* among critics as the best film ever made (remaining at the top of the Sight and Sound poll taken each decade since 1962) and its frequent invocation as the effort of a "boy wonder" contribute to yet another exhibition context. Fans post excerpts on the Internet in video-sharing sites such as YouTube, and would-be filmmakers compare their efforts to Welles's or remix parts of his film, introducing new generations to the classic.

▶ **VIEWING CUE**

Consider how viewing the movie you most recently watched in class on a large screen versus a laptop would affect your response. ⏸

In contrast to viewing technologies that attempt to enhance the spectacular nature of the big-screen experience are those that try to maximize (sometimes by literally minimizing) the uniquely personal encounter with the film image, such as the individual screens of portable media players, iPads, and personal computers. In such cases, consumers have adapted quickly as distinct media (such as cinema, television, the Internet, and video games) and viewing platforms (such as television, computers, and cell phones) have become commercially, technologically, and culturally interdependent.

The Timing of Exhibition

Whereas distribution timing determines when a film is made available and in what format, the timing of exhibition is a more personal dimension of the movie experience. When and for how long we watch a film can shape the impact of and attitude toward a film as much as where we see the film and with whom. Although it is common to see movies in the early evening, before or after dinner, audiences watch movies of different kinds according to numerous rituals and in various time slots. Afternoon matinees, midnight movies, or in-flight movies on long plane rides give some indication of how the timing of a movie experience can vary and how that can influence other considerations about the movie. In each of these situations, our experience of the movies includes a commitment to spend time in a certain way. Instead of time spent reading, in conversation, sleeping, or working on a business project, we watch a movie. That time spent with a movie accordingly becomes an activity associated with relaxing, socializing, or even working in a different way.

Leisure Time

▶ **VIEWING CUE**

Think of a movie you've watched as a "leisure time" versus a "productive time" activity. How might the film be viewed differently in a classroom versus during a long airplane flight? How might your film choice be affected by the timing and context in which you view the movie? ⏸

Traditionally movie culture has emphasized film exhibition as *leisure time*, a time that is assumed to be less productive (at least compared to the time spent working a job) and that reinforces assumptions about movies as the kind of enjoyment associated with play and pleasure. To some extent, leisure time is a relatively recent historical development. Since the nineteenth century, when motion pictures first appeared, modern society has aimed to organize experience so that work and leisure could be separated and defined in relation to each other. We generally identify leisure time as an "escape," "the relaxation of our mind and body," or "the acting out of a different self." Since the early twentieth century, movie exhibition has been associated with leisure time in these ways. Seeing a comedy on a Friday night promises relaxation at the end of a busy week. Playing a concert film on a DVD player while eating dinner may relieve mental fatigue. Watching a romantic film on television late at night may offer the passion missing from one's real life.

Productive Time

Besides leisure time, however, we can and should consider film exhibition as *productive time*, meaning time used to gain information, material advantage, or knowledge. From the early years of the cinema, movies have been used to illustrate lectures or introduce audiences to Shakespearean performances. More strictly educational films, such as those shown in health classes or driver education programs, are less glamorous versions of this use of film. Although less widely acknowledged as part of film exhibition, productive time continues to shape certain kinds of film exhibition. For a movie reviewer or film producer, an early morning screening may be about "financial value" because this use of time to evaluate a movie will presumably result in certain economic rewards. For another person, a week of films at an art museum represents "intellectual value," as it helps explain ideas about a different society or historical period. For a young American, an evening watching *Schindler's List* can be about "human value" because that film aims to make viewers more knowledgeable about the Holocaust and more sensitive to the suffering of other human beings.

The timing of exhibitions may frame and emphasize the film experience according to certain values. The Cannes Film Festival introduces a wide range of films and functions both as a business venue for buying and selling film and as a glamorous showcase for stars and parties. The May timing of this festival and its French Riviera location ensure that the movie experience will be about pleasure and the business of leisure time. In contrast, the New York Film Festival, featuring some of the same films, has a more intellectual or academic aura. That it occurs in New York City during September and October, at the beginning of the academic year and

1.48 *Marie Antoinette* (2006). At the Cannes Film Festival, *Marie Antoinette* had a premiere as sumptuous as its mise-en-scène.

the calendars of arts organizations, associates this experience of the movies more with artistic value and productive time. The premiere of Sofia Coppola's *Marie Antoinette* (2006) at the Cannes festival exploited the high-profile glamour of that festival's party atmosphere and its French subject matter. That many French critics hostilely denounced the film indicates either a tactical error in the choice of an opening exhibition or the truism that all publicity is good publicity **[Figure 1.48]**.

Classroom, library, and museum exhibitions tend to emphasize understanding and learning as much as enjoyment. When students watch films in these kinds of situations, they are asked to attend to them somewhat differently from the way they may view films on a Friday night at the movies. They watch more carefully, perhaps; they may consider the films as part of historical or artistic traditions; they may take notes as a logical part of this kind of exhibition. These conditions of film exhibition do not necessarily change the essential meaning of a movie; but in directing how we look at a film, they can certainly shade and even alter how we understand it. Exhibition asks us to engage and think about the film not as an isolated object but as part of the expectations established by the conditions in which we watch it.

CONCEPTS AT WORK

Behind virtually every movie is a complex set of decisions, choices, and aims about how to make, distribute, market, and exhibit a film to reach audiences. In this chapter, we've highlighted some of the most important parts of that work as they anticipate and position viewers. We've seen how production methods, distribution strategies, marketing techniques, and exhibition places have responded to and created different kinds of movie experiences.

Activities

- Compare a story about a film in the arts section of your local paper with a discussion of the same film in the online version of the industry "trade" paper *Variety* or the independent film online source Indiewire.com. What does this tell you about the cultural priorities of the film industry today? How is film production valued and viewed in these different examples?
- Imagine that you and a group of investors plan to open a state-of-the-art movie theater in your hometown. Describe your plans for its design and its location. What kinds of films would you exhibit there? How would you use the timing of their distribution and exhibition to your advantage? How would these decisions reflect your intentions for the kinds of films you would show and the audience you'd hope to attract?

PART 2

FORMAL COMPOSITIONS

film scenes, shots, cuts, and sounds

To some extent, every movie mimics how we commonly use our senses to experience the real world. Film studies examines the ways that movies manage to activate our senses through the use of specific formal elements—the four categories of which are mise-en-scène, cinematography, editing, and sound. In *Broken Blossoms* (1919), D. W. Griffith uses composition to create the claustrophobic sensations of being physically trapped in a small room; in Rob Marshall's *Chicago* (2002), sets, cinematography, editing, and sound together communicate the robust energy and physical power of dance. By invigorating and manipulating the senses, film images and sounds create experiences viewers recognize and respond to—physically, emotionally, and intellectually.

The next four chapters identify the formal and technical powers associated with four different categories of film form. Chapter 2 on mise-en-scène explores the role of film settings and other onscreen elements. Chapter 3 examines cinematography, the art of how films are shot. Chapter 4 looks at film editing, while Chapter 5 focuses on film sound. Chapters begin with a short historical overview of the element and then detail the specific properties and strategies associated with each of these aspects of film form. Chapters conclude with our examination of some of the cultural values and traditions that help determine our reactions to, and interpretations of, scenes, shots, cuts, and sounds at the movies.

CHAPTER 2

Exploring a Material World: Mise-en-Scène

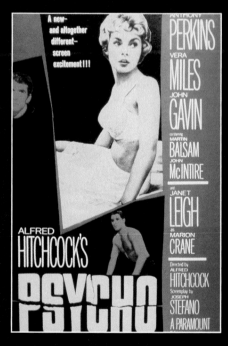

- Sets and settings
- Actors and performance styles
- Lighting
- Costumes and make-up

- Points of view of the camera
- Framing, depth of field, and movement
- Visual effects and digital technology

Relating Images: Editing

CHAPTER **4**
**Relating Images:
Editing**

- Construction of speech, music, and sound effects
- Meaning through sound
- Interactions between sound and image

- Organization through editing
- Construction of spatial and temporal relationships
- Continuity and disjuncture

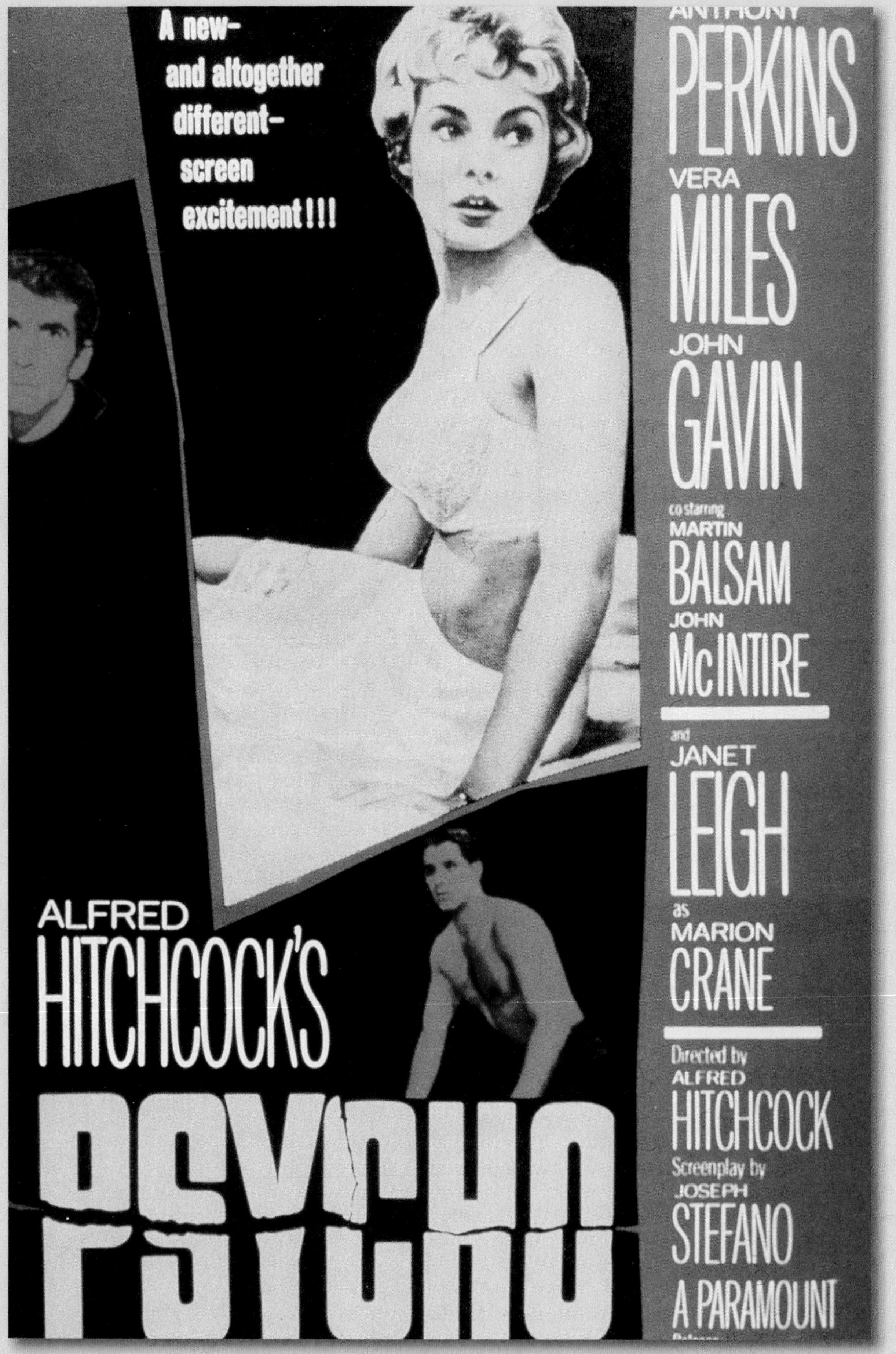
A new-
and altogether
different-
screen
excitement!!!
PERKINS
VERA
MILES
JOHN
GAVIN
co starring
MARTIN
BALSAM
JOHN
McINTIRE
and
JANET
LEIGH
as
MARION
CRANE
Directed by
ALFRED
HITCHCOCK
Screenplay by
JOSEPH
STEFANO
A PARAMOUNT
ALFRED
HITCHCOCK'S
PSYCHO

Exploring a Material World
Mise-en-Scène

In the trailer for his 1960 film *Psycho*, director Alfred Hitchcock takes the viewer on a tour of the film's now-legendary sets, treating them as actual locations. Walking through the ordinary-looking Bates Motel and the sinister old house behind it, Hitchcock blandly points out a steep staircase where a murder occurs, darkly hints at the significance of a picture on the wall, and finally reaches out to pull back the shower curtain. The viewer enjoys the trailer's manufactured suspense, which is more than likely enhanced by familiarity with the shocking events that occur in each of these sites, either because the viewer has already seen the film (this trailer postdates its release) or knows it by reputation. But outside the fictional world of the story, these settings don't quite carry the same charge of dread. Evoking the centrality of mise-en-scène to a film's mood, the trailer also shows how meticulously its effects are coordinated. But the full impact of these settings and props is not achieved until they are experienced in the course of watching *Psycho* itself.

A French term meaning literally "placement in a scene" or "onstage," **mise-en-scène** refers to those elements of a movie scene that are put in position before the filming actually begins and employed in certain ways once it does begin. Mise-en-scène (pronounced *meez-on-sen*) includes everything that is visible onscreen. Cinema orchestrates a rich and complex variety of formal and material elements inherited from theater, using principles of composition derived from painting and photography. The mise-en-scène contains the scenic elements of a movie, including actors, aspects of lighting, sets and settings, costumes, make-up, and other features of the image that exist independently of the camera and the processes of filming and editing.

Outside the movies, our surroundings function like mise-en-scène. The architecture of a town might be described as a public mise-en-scène. How a person arranges and decorates a room could be called a private mise-en-scène. Courtrooms construct a mise-en-scène that expresses institutional authority. The placement of the judge above the court, of the attorneys at the bar, and of the witnesses in a partially sequestered area expresses the distribution of power. The flood of light through the vast and darkened spaces of a cathedral creates an atmospheric mise-en-scène aimed to inspire contemplation and humility. The clothes, jewelry, and make-up a person chooses to wear are, in one sense, the functional costuming all individuals don as part of inhabiting a particular mise-en-scène: businessmen wear suits, clergy dress in black, and service people in fast-food restaurants wear uniforms with company logos. This chapter describes how mise-en-scène organizes and directs much of our film experience by putting us in certain places and by arranging the people and objects of those places in specific ways.

KEY OBJECTIVES

- Define "mise-en-scène" and understand how theatrical and other traditions affect the history of cinematic mise-en-scène.
- Delineate how sets and props relate to a film's story.
- Appreciate how actors and performance styles contribute to a mise-en-scène.
- Understand the ways costumes and make-up contribute to our perception of a character.
- Explain how lighting is used to evoke particular meanings and moods.
- Critically consider the ways mise-en-scène puts in play values associated with specific film traditions.

In many ways, we respond not only to physical settings and material surfaces and objects, but also to the sensations associated with them. Whether we actually touch the materials or simply imagine their texture and volume, this tactile experience of the world is a continual part of how we engage with and understand the people and places around us. This is also the case with the movies. Characters

attract or repulse us through the clothing and make-up they wear: in *Some Like It Hot* (1959), Marilyn Monroe's eroticism is inseparable from her slinky dresses; in *The Elephant Man* (1980), the drama hinges on Joseph Carey Merrick's deformed appearance (achieved through the magic of make-up) and the recognition that he is a sensitive human being inside a hideous shape **[Figure 2.1]**.

Actions set in open or closed spaces can generate feelings of portent or hopelessness: in *Lawrence of Arabia* (1962), the open desert shimmers with possibility and danger; in *127 Hours* (2010), a rock climber becomes trapped in a crevasse from which there seems to be no escape, and the viewer experiences his claustrophobia **[Figure 2.2]**. In *Vertigo* (1958), when the protagonist relives again and again the dizzying fear of heights that he first discovers when he watches a partner fall from a roof, viewers share his perspective. These tactile experiences can be culturally modified, influenced, or emphasized in very different ways by specific films. For instance, rarely has a taste for the texture and smell of food been re-created as intensely as it is in *Like Water for Chocolate* (1992) **[Figure 2.3]**.

Setting the artistic precedent for cinematic mise-en-scène is the theatrical stage, where our sensual and tactile engagement is based on the presence of real actors performing in real time on a physical stage. Film engages us in a different way. A film's material world may be actual objects and people set in authentic locations, like the stunning slopes of the Himalayas in *Seven Years in Tibet* (1997). Or it may include objects and settings constructed by set designers to appear realistic or fantastic, as in Tim Burton's *Alice in Wonderland* (2010) with its living cards and unusual creatures **[Figure 2.4]**. In all its variation, mise-en-scène—a film's places and spaces, people and objects, lights and shadows—is a key dimension of our movie experience.

2.1 *The Elephant Man* (1980). In many films, make-up accentuates features of the character; here it complicates that character and challenges the viewer to recognize the human being beneath his distorted features.

2.2 *127 Hours* (2010). The film's confined setting becomes a formal structure and a visceral experience, as the protagonist is trapped in a crevasse in the wilderness for the greater part of this film's running time.

2.3 *Like Water for Chocolate* (1992). Dark, luxuriant colors draw attention to the texture of the food being prepared in a *molcajete*, a Mexican mortar and pestle.

2.4 *Alice in Wonderland* (2010). Production designer Robert Stromberg worked with a team of art directors, costume designer Colleen Atwood, and an extensive make-up department to accomplish the Red Queen's distinctive look in this Disney remake.

A Short History of Mise-en-Scène

The first movies were literally "scenes." Sometimes they were quaint public or domestic scenes, such as pioneer filmmakers Auguste and Louis Lumière's films of a baby being fed or a pillow fight; often they were dramatic scenes re-created on a stage for a movie camera. The ancient sites and holy objects seen in *The Passion Play of Oberammergau* (1898) fascinated audiences with their realistic appearance. A mixture of slides and short films, *Old Mexico and Her Pageants* (1899) used scenes and costumes to enliven and illustrate a lecture. While early films usually presented what could be accomplished in a one-room studio or a confined outdoor setting, by 1907 mise-en-scène had become more elaborate. Movies like *The Automobile Thieves* (1906) and *On the Stage; or, Melodrama from the Bowery* (1907) began to coordinate two or three interior and exterior settings, using make-up and costumes to create different kinds of characters and exploiting the stage for visual tricks and gags. In D. W. Griffith's monumental *Intolerance* (1916), the sets that reconstructed ancient Babylon were, in many ways, the main attraction **[Figure 2.5]**. In the following section, we will sketch some of the historical paths associated with the development of cinematic mise-en-scène throughout more than a century of film history.

Theatrical Mise-en-Scène and the Prehistory of Cinema

The clearest heritage of cinematic mise-en-scène lies in the Western theatrical tradition that began with early Greek theater around 500 B.C.E. and evolved through the nineteenth century. The first stages served as places where a community's religious beliefs and truths could be acted out. Centuries later, European medieval theater celebrated

2.5 *Intolerance* (1916). The film's massive Babylonian set became a Los Angeles tourist attraction until it was dismantled in 1921.

Christian stories—of Adam and Eve or Christ's nativity—in mystery plays using a small cast with costumes, props, and scenery. During the Renaissance of the late sixteenth and early seventeenth centuries, the sets, costumes, and other elements of mise-en-scène that were used to stage, for example, the plays of William Shakespeare, reflected a secular world of politics and personal relationships through which individuals and communities fashioned their values and beliefs.

By the beginning of the nineteenth century, lighting and other technological developments rapidly altered the nature of mise-en-scène and began to anticipate the cinema. On the eighteenth-century English stage, actor and theater manager David Garrick is credited with unifying and professionalizing the theatrical experience and setting the stage apart from the audience with spectacular sets, costumes, and lighting, as well as encouraging new norms of audience behavior. In contrast to the drawing-room interiors that had prevailed before, stages and sets grew much larger; they could now support the massive panoramic scenery and machinery developed by innovators such as London artist P. J. de Loutherbourg, whose scenic illusions and breathtaking spectacles were designed to fascinate and stun audiences. In the nineteenth century, an emphasis on individual actors (such as Fanny and John Kemble and Ellen Terry in England) influenced the rising cult of the star, who became the center of the mise-en-scène. Non-Western theatrical traditions such as Sanskrit dramas in India and Japanese Kabuki featured recognizable characters in familiar plots.

1900–1912: Early Cinema's Theatrical Influences

The subjects of the first films were limited by their dependence on natural light. But by 1900, films revealed their theatrical influences. *The Downward Path* (1901), a melodrama familiar from the popular stage, used five tableaux—brief scenes presented by sets and actors as "pictures" of key dramatic moments—to convey the plight of a country girl who succumbs to the wickedness of the city. One of many early films that turned to famous playwrights for movie material was the 1904 release *Damnation of Faust*, which adapted Goethe's *Faust*. Further encouraging this theatrical direction in mise-en-scène was the implementation of mercury-vapor lamps and indoor lighting systems around 1906 that enabled studio shooting. By 1912, one of the most famous stage actors of all time, Sarah Bernhardt, was persuaded to participate in the new medium, starring in the films *Queen Elizabeth* (1912) and *La dame aux camélias* (1912). Besides legitimate theater, other aspects of nineteenth-century visual culture influenced the staging of early films. The famous "trick" films of Georges Méliès, with their painted sets and props, were adapted from magicians' stage shows. In the United States, Edwin S. Porter's *Uncle Tom's Cabin* (1903) imitated the staging of familiar scenes from the "Tom Shows," seemingly ubiquitous regional adaptations for the stage of Harriet Beecher Stowe's novel.

1915–1928: Silent Cinema and the Star System

The 1914 Italian epic *Cabiria*, which included a depiction of the eruption of Mount Etna, established the public's taste for movie spectaculars. Feature-length films soon became the norm, and elaborately constructed sets and actors in carefully designed costumes defined filmic mise-en-scène. By 1915, art directors or set designers (called "technical directors" doing "interior decoration" at the time) became an integral part of filmmaking. The rapid expansion of the movie industry in the 1920s was facilitated by the rise of studio systems in Hollywood, Europe, and Japan. Studios had their own buildings and lots on which to construct expansive sets and personnel under contract to design and construct them. Erich Kettelhut's famous, futuristic

2.6   *The Sheik* (1921).
The charismatic power of silent film star Rudolph Valentino is often linked to the romanticized Western notions of North Africa and the Middle East that were created through set and costume design.

set designs for Fritz Lang's film *Metropolis* (1927), constructed on the soundstage of the German Ufa studios, were influenced by the modernist architecture of the Manhattan skyline.

Beginning in the late 1910s, cinema developed and promoted its own stars, and the star system often identified an actor with a particular genre that had a distinctive mise-en-scène. Rudolph Valentino's films, for example, were set in a romanticized version of the Middle East **[Figure 2.6]**, and Douglas Fairbanks starred in swashbuckling adventure tales. Charlie Chaplin's "Little Tramp" was instantly recognizable by his costume. Costume also helped shape an individualized glamour for female stars; designers such as MGM's Adrian developed a very specific look for actresses Greta Garbo and Joan Crawford, whose films were showcases for clothing and décor that reflected the art deco style of the 1920s even when their settings were historical.

1930s–1960s: Studio-Era Production

The rapid introduction of sound at the end of the 1920s was facilitated by the stability of the studio system, in which a company controlling film production and distribution had sufficient capital to invest in production facilities and systems. **Soundstages**—large soundproofed buildings—were designed to house the construction and movement of elaborate sets, which were often complemented by an array of costumes, lighting, and props. Art directors were essential to a studio's signature style. During his long career at MGM, Cedric Gibbons was credited as art director on fifteen hundred films, including *Grand Hotel* (1932), *Gaslight* (1944), and *An American in Paris* (1951); he supervised a large number of personnel charged with developing each film's ideal mise-en-scène from the studio's resources. Producer David O. Selznick coined the title "production designer" for William Cameron Menzies's central role in creating the look of the epic *Gone with the Wind* (1939), from its dramatic historical sets, décor, and costumes to the color palette that would be highlighted by the film's Technicolor cinematography.

Studio backlots enabled the construction of entire worlds: the main street of a western town or New York City's Greenwich Village, for example. Other national cinemas invested considerable resources in central studios. Cinecittà (cinema-city) was established by Italian dictator Benito Mussolini in 1937, bombed during World War II, then subsequently rebuilt and used for Italian and international productions (including, in 2002, Martin Scorsese's *Gangs of New York*). The expense lavished on mise-en-scène during the heyday of the studio system shapes contemporary expectations of "movie magic."

1940–1970: New Cinematic Realism

Photographic realism and the use of exterior spaces and actual locations—identifiable neighborhoods and recognizable cultural sites—complement cinema's theatrical heritage. Although the Lumières' earliest films were of everyday scenes, and their operatives traveled all over the world to record movies, location shooting did not influence mainstream filmmaking until World War II. Ever since postwar Italian neorealist films were shot on city streets (as refugees were housed in the Cinecittà studios), fiction and documentary filmmaking have come to depend on location scouting for suitable

2.7a and 2.7b *Henry V* (1944). Produced in the midst of World War II, Laurence Olivier's film charts within its own frame an important shift from a theatrical mise-en-scène to a more realistic setting.

mise-en-scène. Few films more explicitly demonstrate the transformation within the history of mise-en-scène than Laurence Olivier's *Henry V* (1944), where the drama shifts from the stage of Shakespeare's Globe Theatre to the comparatively realistic setting of the French countryside **[Figures 2.7a and 2.7b]**. *Naked City* (1948) returned U.S. filmmaking to the grit of New York's crime-ridden streets. By the 1960s, cinematic realism in the United States was associated with youth rebellion. Italian filmmaker Michelangelo Antonioni used amateur actors and sensual desert locations in the counterculture classic *Zabriskie Point* (1970). Realistic mise-en-scène was central to many of the new cinema movements of the 1970s that critiqued established studio styles, including in the postrevolutionary cinema in Cuba and the emergence of feature-filmmaking in sub-Saharan Africa in such films as Ousmane Sembène's *Xala* (1975).

1975–Present: Mise-en-Scène and the Blockbuster

Since the mechanical shark (nicknamed "Bruce") created for Steven Spielberg's *Jaws* in 1975, the economics of internationally marketed blockbuster filmmaking have demanded an ever more spectacular emphasis on mise-en-scène, enhanced by photographic and computer-generated special effects. Spielberg's *Close Encounters of the Third Kind* (1977), for example, combined elaborate, built sets with special effects by Douglas Trumbull. Since the 1980s, the cinematic task of re-creating realistic environments and fantastical mise-en-scène alike has shifted to computerized models and computer-graphics technicians, who design the models to be digitally transferred onto film. *Pan's Labyrinth* (2006) portrays the internal world of its lonely child heroine in a rich mise-en-scène constructed from actual sets, costumes, prosthetics, and computer-generated imagery **[Figure 2.8]**. Realism remains a priority in some contemporary films, like *True Grit* (2010), however, while other films today benefit from the technical capacity of computers to re-create the exact details of historical eras, such as the nineteenth-century New York streets of Scorsese's *Age of Innocence* (1993). Many contemporary audiences look for and many contemporary movies provide an experience that is "more real than real," to adapt the motto of the Tyrell Corporation in *Blade Runner* (1982).

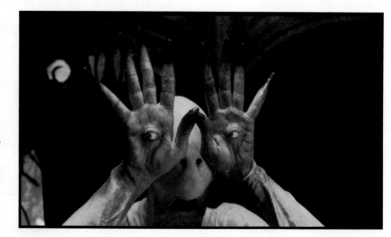

2.8 *Pan's Labyrinth* (2006). Computer-generated imagery often creates realistic nightmares.

The Elements of Mise-en-Scène

▶ **VIEWING CUE**

Describe, with as much detail as possible, one of the sets or settings in a movie you watch for class. Other than the actors, which features of the film seem most important? Explain why. ⏸

▶ **VIEWING CUE**

Examine the interaction of two important sets or settings in the film viewed for this unit. What is their relationship? Does that interaction suggest important themes in the film? ⏸

In this section, we will identify the elements of mise-en-scène and introduce some of the central terms and concepts underpinning the notion of mise-en-scène. These include settings and sets and how they contribute to scenic and atmospheric realism, as well as props, actors, costumes, and lighting, and the ways all of these important elements are coordinated through design and composition.

Settings and Sets

Settings and sets are the most fundamental features of mise-en-scène. The **setting** refers to a fictional or real place where the action and events of the film occur. The **set** is, strictly speaking, a constructed setting, often on a studio soundstage; but both the setting and the set can combine natural and constructed elements. For example, one setting in *Citizen Kane* (1941) consists of a fictional mansion located in Florida (based on the actual Hearst estate in San Simeon, California), which, in this case, is a set constructed on an RKO soundstage. **Set designers** supervise the construction of sets and the arrangement of props within settings to draw out important details or to create connections and contrasts across the different places in a film. In *The Hours* (2002), the lives of three different generations of women are reflected and connected by Virginia Woolf's novel *Mrs. Dalloway*, and similarities and differences are subtly drawn out by the careful coordination of color and design elements in scenes set in 1923, 1951, and 2001.

Historically and culturally, sets and settings have changed regularly. The first films were made either on stage sets or in outdoor settings, using the natural light from the sun. Films gradually began to integrate both constructed sets and natural settings into the mise-en-scène. Today's cinematic mise-en-scène continues to use constructed sets, such as the studio creation of the detective's residence for *Sherlock Holmes* (2009), as well as actual locations, such as the Philadelphia streets and neighborhoods of *The Sixth Sense* (1999) or the deserts and dusty streets of Jordan (standing in for Iraq) in *The Hurt Locker* (2009). Models and computer enhancements of mise-en-scène are used increasingly, notably in science fiction and fantasy films like *2012* (2009), which digitally depicts apocalyptic destruction **[Figure 2.9]**.

Scenic and Atmospheric Realism

Settings and sets contribute to a film's mise-en-scène by establishing scenic realism and atmosphere. One of the most common, complicated, and elusive yardsticks for the cinema, **realism** is the term most viewers use to describe the extent to which a movie creates a truthful picture of a society, person, or some other dimension of life. Realism can refer to psychological or emotional accuracy (in characters), recognizable or logical actions and developments (in a story), or convincing views and perspectives of those characters or events (in the composition of the image).

The most prominent vehicle for cinematic realism, however, is the scenic realism of the mise-en-scène, which

2.9   *2012* (2009). The computer-generated futuristic mise-en-scène depicts the destruction of Los Angeles.

enables us to recognize sets and settings as accurate evocations of actual places. A combination of selection and artifice, scenic realism is most commonly associated with the physical, cultural, and historical accuracy of the backgrounds, objects, and other figures in a film. Indeed, our measure of a film's realism is often more a product of the authenticity of this scenic realism than of the other features, such as the psychology or actions of characters. Movies like the animated *Beauty and the Beast* (1991) and the comic-book adaptation *Spider-Man 3* (2007) dramatize authentic human emotions (the blossoming of an unexpected love in the first, and the inner turmoil of a divided soul in the second), but these films would probably not be considered realistic because of the fantastic nature of their settings in magical castles and futuristic laboratories. Other movies, such as *Michael Collins* (1996), which depicts the Irish revolution at the turn of the twentieth century, establish a convincing realism through the physical, historical, and cultural verisimilitude of the sets and settings, regardless of how the characters or story may be exaggerated or romanticized **[Figure 2.10]**. Recognition of scenic realism frequently depends, of course, on the historical and cultural point of view of the audience. *The Blind Side* (2009), for example, set in an affluent American suburb, may seem realistic to many Americans but could appear to be a fantastic other world to farmers living in rural China.

In addition to scenic realism, the mise-en-scène of a film creates atmosphere and connotations, those feelings or meanings associated with particular sets or settings. The setting of a ship on the open seas might suggest danger and adventure; a kitchen set may connote comfortable, domestic feelings. Invariably these connotations are developed through the actions of the characters and developments of the larger story: the early kitchen set in *Mildred Pierce* (1945) creates an atmosphere of bright, slightly strained warmth; in *E.T.* (1982), a similar set describes the somewhat chaotic space of a modern, single-parent family; in *Marie Antoinette* (2006), the opulence of Versailles conveys the heroine's loneliness as well as her desires **[Figure 2.11]**.

2.10 *Michael Collins* (1996). The Irish countryside contributes to the convincing scenic realism in this twentieth-century epic.

▶ **VIEWING CUE**

While viewing your next assigned film, turn off the sound and analyze a single scene in the movie in terms of what is communicated through the elements of the mise-en-scène alone. ⏸

Props, Actors, Costumes, and Lights

As we have seen, unlike other dimensions of film form such as editing and sound, mise-en-scène was in place with the first films; hence the early decades of film history were explorations in how to use the materials of mise-en-scène. Here we will examine the multiple physical objects and figures that are the key ingredients in a cinematic mise-en-scène, moving from inanimate objects and human figures to the accentuation of those figures and objects with costumes and lighting.

2.11 *Marie Antoinette* (2006). Against a scenic background of extravagance, the character's discontent, desire, and duty come into sharp relief.

2.12 *Singin' in the Rain* (1952). An ordinary umbrella is transformed into a dancing prop, expressing how Gene Kelly's new love can transform a rainy world and all its problems into a stage for an exuberant song and dance.

Props

A **prop** (short for *property*) is an object that functions as a part of the set or as a tool used by the actors. *The Maltese Falcon* (1941) is named after its central prop, which its characters strive to possess or safeguard; *The Wizard of Oz* (1939) will be forever identified with the ruby slippers that Dorothy acquires upon accidentally killing the Wicked Witch of the East. Props acquire special significance when they are used to express characters' thoughts and feelings, their powers and abilities in the world, or the primary themes of the film. In *Singin' in the Rain* (1952), when Gene Kelly transforms an ordinary umbrella into a gleeful expression of his new love, an object that normally protects a person from rain is expressively used as an extension of a dance: the pouring rain makes little difference to a man in love **[Figure 2.12]**. In Alfred Hitchcock's *Suspicion* (1941), an ordinary glass of milk, brought to a woman who suspects her husband of murder, suddenly crystallizes the film's unsettling theme of malice hiding in the shape of innocence. In the same director's *Spellbound* (1945), parallel lines in the pattern of a bathrobe trigger a psychotic reaction in the protagonist, John Ballantyne, and in this film, too, a glass of milk suddenly appears ominous and threatening **[Figure 2.13]**. Even natural objects or creatures can become props that concentrate the meanings of a movie: in the 1997 Japanese film *The Eel*, the main character's bond with an eel becomes the vehicle for his poignant redemption from despair about human society.

Props appear in movies in two principal forms. *Instrumental props* are those objects displayed and used according to their common function. *Metaphorical props* are those same objects reinvented or employed for an unexpected, even magical, purpose—like Gene Kelly's umbrella—or invested with metaphorical meaning. The distinction is important because the type of prop can characterize the kind of world surrounding the characters and the ability of those characters to interact with that world. In *Babette's Feast* (1987), a movie that uses the joys and generosities of cooking to bridge cultural and other differences in a small Danish village, a knife functions as an instrumental prop for preparing a meal **[Figure 2.14a]**; in *Psycho* (1960), that same prop is transformed into a hideous murder weapon and a ferocious sexual metaphor **[Figure 2.14b]**. *The Red Shoes* (1948) might be considered a film about the shifting status of a prop, red dancing slippers: at first, these shoes appear as an instrumental prop serving Victoria's rise as a great ballerina, but by the conclusion of the film they have been transformed into a darkly metaphorical prop that magically dances the heroine to her death **[Figure 2.15]**.

2.13 *Spellbound* (1945). An ordinary but ominous glass of milk that may or may not have been poisoned.

2.14a *Babette's Feast* (1987). A knife is a simple instrumental prop.

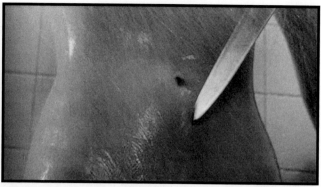

2.14b *Psycho* (1960). A knife can also be a murder weapon associated metaphorically with male sexuality.

In addition to their function within a film, props may acquire significance in two other prominent ways. *Cultural props*, such as a type of car or a piece of furniture, carry meanings associated with their place in a particular society. In *Herbie Fully Loaded* (2005), a sequel to the "flower-power" era's *The Love Bug* (1969), the heroine fixes up a tiny Volkswagen Beetle and the comedy revolves around associations with this inexpensive, "retro" car model and its remarkable magical powers; in *Easy Rider* (1969), the two protagonists ride low-slung motorcycles that clearly suggest a countercultural rebellion. *Contextualized props* acquire a meaning through their changing place in a narrative. *The Yellow Rolls-Royce* (1964) and *The Red Violin* (1998) focus on the changing meaning of the central prop: in the first film, three different romances are linked through their connection to a beautiful Rolls-Royce; the second film follows the path of a Nicolo Bussotti violin from seventeenth-century Italy to an eighteenth-century Austrian monastery, to nineteenth-century England, to the Chinese cultural revolution in the twentieth century, and finally to a contemporary shop in Montreal, Canada **[Figure 2.16]**. Some films play specifically with the meaning a contextual prop comes to acquire. In *Ronin* (1998), a mysterious briefcase unites a group of mercenaries in a plot about trust and betrayal, but its secret significance becomes ultimately insignificant. Alfred Hitchcock's famous "McGuffins"—props that appear to be important only at first, like the stolen money in *Psycho* (1960) and the uranium in *Notorious* (1946)—are props meant to move a plot forward but are of little importance to the primary drama of love, danger, and desire.

Staging: Performance and Blocking

At the center of the mise-en-scène is most often a flesh-and-blood **actor** who embodies and performs a film character through gestures and movements. A more intangible yet essential part of mise-en-scène, **performance** describes the actor's use of language,

► VIEWING CUE

Identify the single most important prop in the last film you watched for class. In what ways is it significant? Does the prop function as an instrumental prop, a metaphorical prop, or both? Explain.

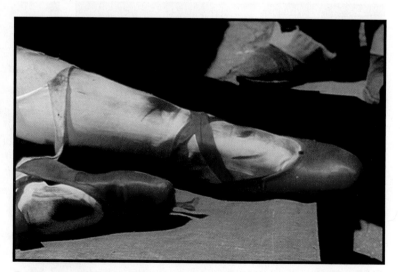

2.15 *The Red Shoes* (1948). Brilliantly red shoes become a prop that dominates and determines a tragic story of passion and obsession.

2.16 *The Red Violin* (1998). The changing significance of a violin dramatizes how contexts make meaning of objects.

physical expression, and gesture to bring a character to life and to communicate important dimensions of that character to the audience. Because characters help us see and understand the actions and world of a film, and because performance is an interpretation of that character by an actor, the success or failure of many films depends upon an actor's performance. In a film like *Kind Hearts and Coronets* (1949), in which Alec Guinness plays eight different roles, the shifting performances of the actor may be its greatest achievement.

In a performance, we can distinguish two primary elements: voice, which includes the natural sound of an actor's voice along with the various intonations or accents he or she may create for a particular role; and bodily movement, which includes physical gestures and, especially important to the movies, eye movements and eye contact. (As in many elements of mise-en-scène, these two features of performance also rely on other dimensions of film form such as sound and camera positions.) Woody Allen has made a career of developing characters through the performance of a strident, panicky voice and bodily and eye movements that dart in uncoordinated directions. At the heart of such movies as *The Blue Angel* (1930) and *Shanghai Express* (1932) is Marlene Dietrich's sultry voice, complemented by drooping eyes and languid body poses and gestures **[Figure 2.17]**.

Additionally, different acting styles define performances. With *stylized acting*, an actor employs emphatic and highly self-conscious gestures or speaks in pronounced tones with elevated diction; the actor seems fully aware that he or she is acting and addressing an audience. Much less evident today, these stylized performances can be seen in the work of Lillian Gish in *Broken Blossoms* (1919), in Joel Grey's role as the master of ceremonies in *Cabaret* (1972) **[Figure 2.18]**, and in the comic performances seen in virtually any Monty Python movie. More

2.17 *The Blue Angel* (1930). The body and eyes of Marlene Dietrich become the signature vehicles for her dramatic performances as an actor and character.

2.18 *Cabaret* (1972). Joel Grey is the master of ceremonies whose own stylized performance introduces a film replete with stylized performances on and off the stage.

influential since the 1940s, *naturalistic acting* requires an actor to fully and naturally embody the role that he or she is playing in order to communicate that character's essential self, famously demonstrated by Marlon Brando as Stanley in *A Streetcar Named Desire* (1951), a role in which the actor and character seem almost indistinguishable [**Figure 2.19**].

Types of Actors.
As part of the usual distribution of actors through mise-en-scène, **leading actors**—the two or three actors who appear most often in a film—play the central characters. Recognizable actors associated with particular character types or minor parts are sometimes referred to as **character actors**. They usually appear as secondary characters playing sinister or humorous roles, such as the bumbling cook in a western. **Supporting actors** play secondary characters in a film, serving as foils or companions to the central characters. Supporting actors and character actors often add to the complexity of a film's plotline or emotional impact. They may involve us more thoroughly in the action or serve to highlight a movie's themes. In the hands of a strong actor, such as James Earl Jones in a supporting role in *Field of Dreams* (1989) or Tatum O'Neal as a Bible salesman's precocious daughter in *Paper Moon* (1973), these supporting roles frequently balance our perspective on the main characters, perhaps requiring us to rethink and reassess the main character's decisions and motivations. In *Field of Dreams*, the writer that Jones plays, Terence Mann, fulfills his fantasy of entering the field and joining the baseball game, while lead actor Kevin Costner's character must remain behind [**Figure 2.20**]. Finally, realism and spectacle are enhanced by the role of **extras**, those relatively large groups of "background artists" who provide character and sometimes personality to large crowd scenes.

Actors are frequently cast for parts precisely because of their association with certain **character types** that they seem especially suited to portray due to their physical features, acting style, or previous roles. Tom Hanks portrays "everyman" characters, while Helen Mirren played both Queen Elizabeth I and Queen Elizabeth II in the same year. To appreciate and understand a character can consequently mean recognizing this intersection of a type and an actor's interpretation or transformation of it. Arnold Schwarzenegger's large and muscular physical stature, clipped voice, and stiff acting style suit well the characters he plays in *The Terminator* (1984) and *Total Recall* (1990); the comedy of *Kindergarten Cop* (1990) arises from his tough character's attempt to act "against type" in his undercover role of a kindergarten teacher.

2.19 *A Streetcar Named Desire* (1951). Ever since this landmark adaptation, it has become difficult to distinguish Marlon Brando's physical performance of Stanley from the essence of that fictional character.

> ▶ **VIEWING CUE**
>
> Consider the performance of a central character or actor in an assigned film. How would you describe his or her acting style in the film? Does that style seem compatible with the story? Why or why not? ⏸

2.20 *Field of Dreams* (1989). James Earl Jones as Terence Mann plays the supporting character with opportunities unavailable to the protagonist, acting as a parallel and counterpoint to the desires and choices of the leading actor, Kevin Costner.

2.21 *On Golden Pond* (1981). This film about a family cannot be fully appreciated without the resonance of its stars' careers: the longevity of Katharine Hepburn and Henry Fonda, and the fact that the couple's adult child is played by Fonda's daughter Jane, a star with a complex image of her own.

Stars. The leading actors in many films are, of course, movie stars—those individuals who, because of their cultural celebrity, bring a powerful aura to their performance, making them the focal points in the mise-en-scène. Unlike less famous actors, star performers center and often dominate the action and space of the mise-en-scène, bring the accumulated history and significance of their past performances to each new film appearance, and acquire a status that transforms their individual physical presence into more abstract or mythical qualities. For example, it is difficult to ignore the star power that Henry Fonda and Katharine Hepburn bring to their film *On Golden Pond* (1981) **[Figure 2.21]**. Stars thus combine the ordinary— they embody and play types audience members can identify with—and the extraordinary, bringing their distinct personality to their roles.

A star's performance focuses the action of the mise-en-scène and draws attention to important events and themes in the film. In *Casablanca* (1942), there are a multitude of individual dramas about different characters trying to escape Casablanca, but Humphrey Bogart's character Rick Blaine is, in an important sense, the only story: the other characters become important only as they become part of his life. In *The Bridges of Madison County* (1995), the story of a male photographer and a female immigrant who meet and fall in love in the isolated farmlands of Iowa, there are no characters other than those played by the stars Clint Eastwood and Meryl Streep for most of the film; this focus on their interactions intensifies the story. In a way, this film becomes the story of two stars creating an exclusive world bracketed off from other lives and characters. Johnny Depp's tongue-in-cheek performance as Jack Sparrow in *Pirates of the Caribbean: The Curse of the Black Pearl* (2003) contributed to the film's unexpected success and generated sequels highlighting the character's antics.

In fact, in all three of these films, much of the power of the characters is a consequence of the star status of the actors, recognized and understood in relation to their roles in other films—and in some cases, in relation to a life off the screen. Recognizing and identifying with Rick in *Casablanca* implies, especially for viewers in the 1940s, a recognition on some level that Rick is more than Rick, that this star-character in *Casablanca* is an extension of characters Bogart has portrayed in such films as *High Sierra* (1941) and *The Maltese Falcon* (1941). A similar measuring takes place as we watch Eastwood and Streep. Streep's performance in *The Bridges of Madison County* impresses viewers because the character she plays is so unlike the characters she plays in *Sophie's Choice* (1982) and *Out of Africa* (1985); part of our appreciation and understanding of her role is the skill and range she embodies as a star. Depp's pirate captain builds on the actor's association with eccentric characters and on cultural recognition of the rock star persona of Keith Richards of the Rolling Stones. We understand these characters as an extension of or departure from other characters associated with the star.

Blocking. The arrangement and movement of actors in relation to each other within the physical space of a mise-en-scène is called **blocking**. *Social blocking* describes the arrangement of characters to accentuate relations among them. In *Little Women* (1994), family and friends gather around the wounded father who has just returned from the Civil War, underscoring the importance of the familial bonds at the center of this society yet reminding us of his absence through the rest of the film [Figure 2.22]. *Graphic blocking* arranges characters or groups according to visual patterns to portray spatial harmony, tension, or some other visual atmosphere. Fritz Lang, for instance, is renowned for his blocking of crowd scenes: in *Metropolis* (1927), the oppression of individuality is embodied in the mechanical movements of rectangles of marching workers [Figure 2.23]; in *Fury* (1936), a mob lynching in a small town is staged as graphic-blocked patterns whose directional arrow suggests a kind of dark fate moving against the lone individual. Both forms of blocking can become especially dynamic and creative in dance or fight sequences. In *Kill Bill: Vol. 2* (2004), the choreographed movement of bodies visually describes social relations and tensions as well as freedom and control.

2.22 *Little Women* (1994). Blocking the family tightly around the father as a subtle expression of a symbolic social structure.

Costumes and Make-Up

Costumes are the clothing and related accessories worn by a character that define the character and contribute to the visual impression and design of the film overall. These can range from common fashions, like a dark suit or dress, to historical or more fantastic costumes. Cosmetics, or *make-up*, applied to the actor's face or body, highlight or even disguise or distort certain aspects of the face or body.

How actors are costumed and made up can play a central part in a film, describing tensions and changes in the character and the story. Sometimes a character becomes fully identified with one basic look or costume: through his many movie incarnations, James Bond has always appeared in a tuxedo at some point in the action. In three *Austin Powers*

2.23 *Metropolis* (1927). Masses of workers move in linear formation through a futuristic setting in which individuality itself is in doubt.

films (1997, 1999, 2002), much of the humor revolves around the often goofy fashions of the 1960s, which seem especially outrageous when transported to modern London. The dynamic of costuming also can be highlighted in a way that makes costuming the center of the movie. *Pygmalion* (1938) and its musical adaptation as *My Fair Lady* (1964) are essentially about a transformation of a girl from the street into an elegant socialite; along with language and diction, that transformation is indexed by the changes of costume and make-up from dirt and rags to diamonds and gowns [Figures 2.24a and 2.24b].

Costumes and make-up function in films in four different ways. First, when costumes and make-up support scenic realism, they reproduce, as accurately as possible, the clothing and facial features of people living in a specific time and place. Thus Napoleon's famous hat and jacket, pallid skin, and lock of hair across his brow are a standard costume and the basic make-up for the many films featuring this character, from Abel Gance's 1927 *Napoléon* to Sacha Guitry's 1955 *Napoleon*. Increasingly sophisticated **prosthetics**, artificial facial features or body parts, enhance realism in performance, as in Morgan Freeman's portrayal of Nelson Mandela in *Invictus* (2009).

▶ **VIEWING CUE**

Describe the ways costuming and make-up add scenic realism, highlight character, or mark the narrative development in the film viewed for class.

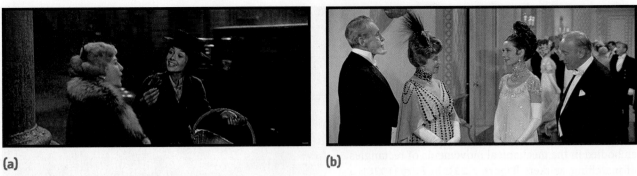

(a)   **(b)**

2.24a and 2.24b   *My Fair Lady* (1964). A flower girl transformed into a refined member of society through costume and set design by Cecil Beaton.

Second, when make-up and costumes function as character highlights, they draw out or point to important parts of a character's personality. Often these highlights are subtle, such as the ascot a pretentious visitor wears; sometimes they are pronounced, as when villains in silent films wear black hats and twirl their moustaches. In William Wyler's black-and-white film *Jezebel* (1939), Bette Davis's character shocks southern society when she appears in a red dress; her performance and the blocking of her entrance convey the tension created by the dress's scandalous color, even though the film is black and white. In Fellini's *Roma* (1972), an autobiographical panorama of the title city becomes a bombastic fashion show peopled by fantasy characters and memories of childhood **[Figure 2.25]**.

Third, when costumes and make-up act as narrative markers, their change or lack of change becomes a crucial way to understand and follow a character and the development of the story. Often a film, such as *Citizen Kane* (1941) or *The Age of Innocence* (1993), chronicles the story through the aging of the protagonist: gradually the hair is whitened and the face progressively lined. The use of more modern styles of clothing can also advance the story. In the adaptation *The Picture of Dorian Gray* (1945), the entire story concentrates on the lack of change in the facial appearance of the protagonist, who has sold his soul for eternal youth, and whose sequestered portrait shows the ravages of time **[Figure 2.26]**. In the *Lord of the Rings* trilogy (2001, 2002, 2003), the dark corruption of Gollum appears most powerfully in the changes in his physical appearance, measured in a dramatic flashback to his origins as the hobbit Smeagol at the beginning of *The Return of the King* (2003) **[Figures 2.27a and 2.27b]**.

Finally, make-up, prosthetics, and costuming can be used as a part of overall production design to signify genre, as they do in the fantasy world of the *Lord of the Rings* trilogy.

Costumes and make-up that appear as natural or realistic in films carry important cultural connotations as well. In *Rocky* (1976), the title character dresses to reflect his working-class background

2.25   **Fellini's** *Roma* (1972). Fellini's style is characterized by exaggerated and even grotesque costumes and make-up. Here costumes give shape to the excessive fantasies attached to a childhood memory.

in South Philadelphia, and his somewhat clownish hat in particular accentuates his bumbling but likeable personality. When Rocky boxes in the championship fight, however, he becomes a bare and powerful form whose simple trunks and cape contrast with the glitzy costume of his opponent. As the bout progresses, facial make-up exaggerates the gruesome violence of the fight, yet the character maintains an almost humble dignity and determination. After his valiant and heroic effort, his plain girlfriend in nerdy eyeglasses becomes more attractive through the power of make-up and costuming. In *The Devil Wears Prada* (2006), the maturation of the naive Andy Sachs (Anne Hathaway) becomes literally apparent in the changes in her outfits, which evolve from college frumpy to designer fashionable.

Lighting

One of the most subtle and important dimensions of mise-en-scène is **lighting**, which not only allows an audience to observe a film's action and understand the setting in which the action takes place but also draws attention to the props, costumes, and actors in the mise-en-scène. Our daily experiences outside the movies demonstrate how lighting can affect our perspective on a person or thing. Entering a dark, shadowed room may evoke feelings of fear, while the same room brightly lit may make us feel welcomed and comfortable. Lighting is a key element of cinematography, but since lighting choices relate

2.26 *The Picture of Dorian Gray* (1945). Facial make-up and costume help create an extremely composed and proper surface for a character with a dark secret in this production still.

profoundly to our experience of mise-en-scène, they are discussed here. *Mise-en-scène lighting* refers specifically to light sources located within the scene itself. This lighting may be used to shade and accentuate the figures, objects, and spaces of the mise-en-scène. As we will discuss in more detail in Chapter 3, the primary sources of film lighting are usually not visible onscreen, but they nevertheless affect mise-en-scène.

(a)

(b)

2.27a and 2.27b *The Lord of the Rings: Return of the King* (2003). Viewers waited until the trilogy's last installment for a glimpse of Smeagol, the hobbit whose greed will deform him into the shape of the creature Gollum.

text continued on page 82 ▶

From Props to Lighting in *Do the Right Thing* (1989)

In Spike Lee's *Do the Right Thing*, characters wander through the theatrical space of Bedford-Stuyvesant, a gentrifying African American neighborhood in Brooklyn. Here life becomes a complicated negotiation between private mise-en-scène (apartments, bedrooms, and businesses) and public mise-en-scène (city streets and sidewalks crowded with people). With Lee in the role of Mookie, who acts as a thread connecting the various characters, stores, and street corners, the film explores the different attitudes, personalities, and desires that clash within a single urban place by featuring a variety of stages—rooms, stores, and restaurants—with personal and racial associations. On the hot summer day of this setting, lighting creates an intense and tactile heat, and this sensation of heat makes the mise-en-scène vibrate with energy and frustration.

The central crisis of *Do the Right Thing* turns on the drama of instrumental props that become loaded with cultural meanings and metaphorical powers. Early in the film, Smiley holds up a photograph of Martin Luther King Jr. and Malcolm X as a call to fight against racism with both nonviolence and violence. Shortly thereafter, Da Mayor nearly instigates a fight because the Korean grocer has not stocked a can of his favorite beer, Miller High Life. It is the photographs of famous Italians in Sal's pizzeria—photos of Frank Sinatra, Joe DiMaggio, Liza Minnelli, Al Pacino, and others—however, that ignite the film **[Figure 2.28]**. When Buggin' Out complains that there should be photos of African Americans on that wall because Sal's clientele is all black, Sal angrily responds that he can decorate the walls of his pizzeria however he wishes. Later, when Radio Raheem refuses to turn down his boom box (an object that has become synonymous with who he is), he and Buggin' Out confront Sal with the cultural significance of the photo-props and the neighborhood residents' social rights within this mise-en-scène: why, they demand, are there no photographs of African Americans on the wall? Finally, at the climactic moment in the film, Mookie tosses a garbage can through the window of the pizzeria, sparking the store's destruction but saving the lives of Sal and his son.

2.28 *Do the Right Thing* (1989). The political flashpoint of props: nostalgic black-and-white photos of Italian Americans on the pizzeria wall.

Lee's performance as Mookie is certainly the central role, one that draws on his then-emerging status as a star actor and a star filmmaker. In fact, this double status as star and director indicates clearly that what happens in the mise-en-scène is about him. Physically unimposing, restrained, and cautious throughout the film, Lee's performance seems to shift and adjust depending on the character he is responding to. As the central performer in a neighborhood of performers, Lee's Mookie is a chameleon, surviving by continually changing his persona to fit the social scene he is in. By the end of the film, however, Mookie must decide which performance will be the real self he brings to the mise-en-scène—how, that is, he will "act" in a time of crisis by taking responsibility for the role he is acting.

Do the Right Thing features costumes that reflect the styles of dress in U.S. cities in the 1980s, and make-up that intends to suggest natural faces, thus adding to the scenic realism of the film. Yet their significance exceeds scenic realism because the costumes both highlight characters and mark the movie's narrative development. Da Mayor's dirty, rumpled suit contrasts sharply with the costumes that define the personalities of younger characters, such as Mookie's Brooklyn Dodgers shirt with

2.29 *Do the Right Thing* (1989). Mookie in his Brooklyn Dodgers shirt: a symbol of hometown and African American pride.

the name and number of the legendary baseball player Jackie Robinson on the back **[Figure 2.29]**, and Pino's white, sleeveless T-shirt with its white working-class connotations. Jade, Mookie's sister, stands out in her dramatic hats, skirts, earrings, and noticeably more elegant make-up and hairstyles, calling attention perhaps to the individuality and creativity that allow her, uniquely here, to casually cross racial lines.

Both social and graphic blockings become dramatic calculators in a film explicitly about the "block" and the arrangement of people in this neighborhood. Mother Sister sits in her window looking down at Da Mayor on the sidewalk, suggesting her dominance over and distance from the confusion in the street. In one scene, Pino, Vito, and Mookie stand tensely apart in a corner of the pizzeria as Mookie calls on Vito to denounce his brother's behavior and Pino counters with a call for family ties; their bodies are quietly hostile and territorial simply in their arrangement and in their movements around the counter that separates them. This orchestration of bodies climaxes in the final showdown at Sal's pizzeria. When Buggin' Out and Radio Raheem enter the pizzeria, the screaming begins with Sal behind the counter, while Mookie, Pino, Vito, and the group of kids shout from different places in the room. When the fight begins, the bodies collapse on each other and spill onto the street as a mass of undistinguishable faces. After the arrival of the police and the killing of Radio Raheem, the placement of his body creates a sharp line between Mookie and Sal and his sons on one side and the growing crowd of furious blacks and Latinos on the other. Within this blocking, Mookie suddenly moves from his side of the line to the other and then calmly retrieves the garbage can to throw through the window. The riot that follows is a direct consequence of Mookie's decisions about where to position himself and how to shatter the blocked mise-en-scène that divides Sal's space from the mob.

Do the Right Thing employs an array of lighting techniques that at first may seem naturalistic but through the course of the film become directional in particularly dramatic ways. From the beginning, the film juxtaposes the harsh, full glare of the streets with the soft morning light that highlights the interior spaces of DJ Mister Señor Love Daddy's radio station, where he announces a heat wave for the coming day, and the bedroom where Da Mayor awakens with Mother Sister. Here the lighting of the interior mise-en-scène emphasizes the rich and blending shades of the dark skin of the African American characters, while the bright, hard lighting of the exterior spaces draws out distinctions in the skin colors of blacks, whites, and Asians. This high-key lighting of exteriors, in turn, accentuates the colors of the objects and props in the mise-en-scène as a way of sharply isolating them in the scene: for example, the blues of the police uniforms and cars, the yellows of the fruits in the Korean market, and the reds of the steps and walls of the neighborhood **[Figure 2.30]**.

Other uses of lighting in the film are more specifically dramatic and complex. For example, the dramatic backlighting of Mookie as he climbs the stairs to deliver the pizza adds an almost religious and certainly heroic/romantic effect to the pizza delivery. When Pino confronts Vito in the storage room, the scene is highlighted by an overhead light that swings back and forth, creating a rocking and turbulent visual effect. In the final scene, Mookie walks home to his son on a street sharply divided between bright, glaring light on one side and dark shadows on the other.

More charged with the politics of mise-en-scène than many films, *Do the Right Thing* turns a relatively small city space into an electrified set where props, actors, costumes, and lighting create a remarkably dense, jagged, and mobile environment. Here the elements of mise-en-scène are always theatrically and politically in play, always about the spatial construction of culture in a specific time and place. To live here, people need to assume, as Mookie eventually does, the powers and responsibilities of knowing how and when to act.

2.30 *Do the Right Thing* (1989). The high-key lighting against a glaringly red wall adds to the intensity and theatricality of these otherwise casual commentators on the street.

The interaction of lighting, sets, and actors can create its own drama within a specific mise-en-scène. How a character moves through light or how the lighting on the character changes can signal important information about the character and story. In *Back to the Future* (1985), Marty McFly's face is suddenly illuminated from an unseen source, signaling a moment of revelation about the mysteries of time travel. More complexly in *Citizen Kane*, the regular movement of characters, particularly of Kane, from shadow to light and then back to shadow suggests Kane's moral instability.

The mise-en-scène can use both natural and directional lighting. **Natural lighting** usually assumes an incidental role in a scene; it derives from a natural source in a scene or setting, such as the illumination of the daylight sun or the lamps of a room. Spread across a set before more specific lighting emphases are added, **set lighting** distributes an evenly diffused illumination through a scene as a kind of lighting base. **Directional lighting** is more dramatically apparent; it may create the impression of a natural light source but actually directs light in ways that define and shape the object or person being illuminated. As illustrated in the shots presented here from *Sweet Smell of Success* (1957) **[Figures 2.31–2.39]**, the lighting used in the mise-en-scène has developed an even more specific technical grammar to designate its variety of strategies:

- **Three-point lighting** is a common lighting style that uses three sources: a key light to illuminate the object, backlighting to pick out the object from the background, and fill lighting that minimizes shadows **[Figure 2.31]**.
- **Key light** is the main source of lighting from a lamp; it may be balanced with little contrast (known as "high-key lighting") or the contrasts between light and dark may be stark (known as "low-key"). These terms indicate the ratio of key to fill lighting; high-key lighting is even (low ratio of key to fill) and used for melodramas and realist films; low-key lighting is (contrary to the colloquial use of "low-key") dramatic (high ratio of key to fill) and used in horror films and film noir **[Figures 2.32 and 2.33]**.
- **Fill lighting** can be used to balance the key lighting or to emphasize other spaces and objects in the scene **[Figures 2.34 and 2.35]**.
- **Highlighting** describes the use of the different lighting sources to emphasize certain characters or objects or to charge them with special significance **[Figure 2.36]**.
- **Backlighting** (sometimes called **edgelighting**) is a highlighting technique that illuminates the person or object from behind; it tends to silhouette the subject **[Figure 2.37]**.
- **Frontal lighting, sidelighting, underlighting,** and **top lighting** are used to illuminate the subject from different directions in order to draw out features or create specific atmospheres around the subject **[Figures 2.38 and 2.39]**.

The effects of lighting in the mise-en-scène range from a **hard** to a **soft lighting** surface that, in conjunction with the narrative and other features of the mise-en-scène, elicit certain responses. *Shading*, the use of shadows to shape or draw attention to certain features, can explain or comment on an object or a person in a way the narrative does not. Hard and soft lighting and shading can create a variety of complex effects through highlighting and the play of light and shadow that enlighten viewers in more than one sense of the word.

VIEWING CUE

Consider the role of lighting in a film you have recently watched. Is it low-key lighting or high-key lighting? Describe a scene in which lighting dramatically adds to the scene's emotional impact. Is there a scene where the lighting is less obtrusive but equally significant? If so, please describe it.

The Italian romance *Under the Tuscan Sun* (2003) depends on the soft natural light referred to in the title, and the shaded eyes of Jake in *Chinatown* (1974) indicate problems with his perspective well before the plot describes them. In a movie like *Barry Lyndon* (1975), the story is conspicuously inseparable from the lighting techniques that illuminate it: extraordinarily low and soft lighting, with

2.31

2.32

2.33

2.34

2.35

2.36

2.37

2.38

2.39

2.31–2.39 *Sweet Smell of Success* (1957).
In a classic film known for the dynamic lighting of celebrated cinematographer James Wong Howe, shades and contrasts become a drama in themselves: from the glare of a coffee shop and the shadows of a sexual encounter to the highlighting of power and the threatening underlighting of a policeman.

2.40 ***Barry Lyndon*** (1975). Low candle lighting and a murky color scheme add an eerie atmosphere and give the characters a ghostlike appearance.

sharp frontal light and little fill light on the faces, creates an artificial intensity in the expressions of the characters, whose social desperation hides their ethical emptiness **[Figure 2.40]**. One particular version of this play of light is referred to as **chiaroscuro lighting**, a pictorial arrangement of light and dark that can create the uneasy atmospheres found in German expressionist films such as Paul Wegener's 1920 tale of magic and supernatural creatures, *The Golem*. None of the elements of mise-en-scène—from props to acting to lighting—can be assigned standard meanings because they are always subject to how individual films use them. They have also carried different historical and cultural connotations at different times. While the shadowy lighting of German expressionist cinema, as in the 1924 horror film *Waxworks,* may be formally similar to that found in 1950s film noir, such as in *Kiss Me Deadly* (1955), the lighting has a very different significance, reflecting the distinctive perspective of each film and the cultural context that produced it. The metaphoric darkness that surrounds characters like Dracula and Jack the Ripper in the first film suggests a monstrous evil that may also be psychological; in the second, that shadowy atmosphere describes a corruption that is entirely human, a function of brutal greed and sexualized violence.

Space and Design

It is important to stress that elements of mise-en-scène that we have designated are used together to create the world of the film; mise-en-scène describes everything visible within the frame. Properties of cinematography that we will discuss in the next chapter (including framing, angle, and color) render the mise-en-scène in a particular way, but our visual impression starts with what is in front of the camera or later placed in the frame with special effects technology. The overall look of a film is coordinated by its design team, which uses space and composition to create a scene for the film's action. The set design of *2001: A Space Odyssey* (1968) is characterized by futuristic design elements arranged sparsely within the elongated widescreen frame. The crowded warrens of *Fantastic Mr. Fox* (2009) fill the frame but give the viewer little sense of depth, with stop-motion figures and props jumbled together. The sets William Wyler had built for *The Best Years of Our Lives* (1946) used realistic measurements; the ceilings visible in low-angle shots and the spaces between furniture give an impression of depth to the viewer. The frontal orientation of *Marie Antoinette* emphasizes the screens and drapes and wallpaper of Versailles, giving the film a compositional style reminiscent of decorative arts. The actors who move through these spaces, who are picked out by lighting, carefully made up, and clothed in costumes with specifically selected palettes, are integrated into the mise-en-scène, even as most designers would say their work is in the service of the story.

text continued on page 86 ▶

FORM IN ACTION

Mise-en-Scène in *Fantastic Mr. Fox* (2009)

2.41a

2.41b

2.41c

2.41d

Wes Anderson's *Fantastic Mr. Fox* (2009) uses stop-motion animation to bring a much-loved Roald Dahl children's book to life. The tale pits three ruthless farmers against Mr. Fox's thrill-seeking thievery, pulling an array of animals into the fray in the process. The film relies on an elaborately textured mise-en-scène to develop and enrich the story's largely underground action. A scene depicting the displaced animals' new home in Badger's Flint Mine opens with Mole playing the piano **[Figure 2.41a]** in a relaxed manner reminiscent of 1950s Hollywood. The space is large and tastefully lit by candles and a garland of what appears to be fruit and fake flowers entwined with twinkle lights. Even in this first image, however, the storage racks in the background indicate that the gracious living of Badger's home is being challenged by an influx of refugees and stolen supplies.

The camera tracks right to a kitchen area **[Figure 2.41b]**. Bright, cheery lighting highlights Rabbit chopping ingredients for a communal meal, and the cramped space and detailed abundance of food (like the roasting rack of stolen chickens) indicates both the large number and the camaraderie of the refugee animals. The camera moves right again to Mr. Fox and Badger, strolling past the opening to a bedroom where the feet of an exhausted animal can be seen lying on a top bunk **[Figure 2.41c]** and discussing the sustainability of the group's current living arrangement.

The scene ends at a punch bowl **[Figure 2.41d]**, beyond which the makeshift aspects of the living arrangements are evident: stolen cases of cider, bags of flour, and chicken carcasses are stored in the background. It is at this point in the shot that Ash, Mr. Fox's son, believing decisive action is needed to restore Mr. Fox's honor, asks his cousin Kristofferson to help him retrieve his father's tail from the ferocious Farmer Bean. Production design richly colors this tale in which animals dress and act more human than the humans hunting them.

The Significance of Mise-en-Scène

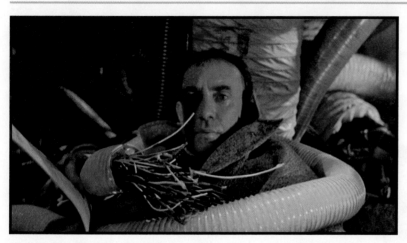

2.42   *Brazil* (1985). In this darkly comic film, a futuristic mise-en-scène of twisting and labyrinthine ductwork entangles the human actors in a disorienting present.

How does mise-en-scène "signify" in a film? Whether mise-en-scène presents authentic places or ingeniously fabricates new worlds, audiences look for and find particular meanings in sets, props, acting styles, blocking, lighting, and other elements of mise-en-scène. From the miniaturized reenactment of Admiral Dewey's naval victory in *The Battle of Manila Bay* (1898) and Georges Méliès's fantastic stage for *The Man with the Rubber Head* (1901) to the futuristic ductwork of *Brazil* (1985), located "somewhere on the Los Angeles–Belfast border" **[Figure 2.42]**, and the contemporary streets of Tehran in *The Circle* (2000), movie audiences have recognized the significance of and specific meanings created by a film through views of real lands and landscapes as well as through the sets, props, and costumes created with astonishing verve and style for fantasized worlds. In this final section, we explore how different approaches to and cultural contexts for mise-en-scène help us identify and assign meaning.

Defining Our Place in a Film's Material World

Whereas earlier we examined the historical foundations and formal strategies of mise-en-scène, here we will argue that those formal elements often impart emotional and intellectual values and meanings through a film. For most movie viewers, recognizing the places, objects, and arrangements of sets and settings has never been simply a formal exercise. The mise-en-scène has always been the site where viewers measure human, aesthetic, and social values; recognize significant cinematic traditions; and, in those interactions, identify and assign meaning to the changing places of films.

The most fundamental value of mise-en-scène is that it defines our location in the material world: the physical settings and objects that surround us indicate our place in the world. Some people crave large cities with bright lights and active crowds; others find it important that their town have a church as the visible center of the community. Much the same holds true for cinematic mise-en-scène, in which the place created by the elements of the mise-en-scène becomes the essential condition for the meaning of the characters' lives. As part of this larger cultural context, cinematic mise-en-scène helps to

- describe the physical conditions and limits of our natural, social, or imaginary worlds
- measure the ability of individuals and social groups to control and arrange their world in a meaningful way

On the one hand, mise-en-scène describes the limits of human experience by indicating the external boundaries and contexts in which film characters exist. On the other, how mise-en-scène is changed or manipulated in a film reflects the powers of film characters and groups. While the first set of values can be established without characters, the second requires the interaction of characters and mise-en-scène.

Mise-en-Scène as an External Condition

Mise-en-scène as an *external condition* indicates surfaces, objects, and exteriors that define the material possibilities in a place or space. The mise-en-scène may be a magical space full of active objects, or it may be a barren landscape with no borders. In *King Solomon's Mines* (1937) and *The African Queen* (1951), arid desert plains and dense jungle foliage threaten the colonial visitors, whereas films like *The Lady Vanishes* (1938) and *The American Friend* (1977), set in the interiors of trains and subways, feature long, narrow passageways, multiple windows, and strange, anonymous faces. An individual's

2.43 **Brokeback Mountain** (2005). In the expansive mountains and plains of the American West, two cowboys explore new sexual intimacies, as the film confounds expectations associated with setting.

movements are restricted as the world flies by outside. In each case, the mise-en-scène describes the material limits of a film's physical world; from those terms, the rest of the scene or even the entire film must develop.

Mise-en-Scène as a Measure of Character

Mise-en-scène as a *measure of character* dramatizes how an individual or a group establishes an identity through interaction with (or control of) the surrounding setting and sets. In *The Adventures of Robin Hood* (1938), the mise-en-scène of a forest becomes a sympathetic and intimate place where the outlaw-hero can achieve justice and find camaraderie; in *The Company of Wolves* (1984), a similar mise-en-scène becomes an environment fraught with psychological significance. In *Brokeback Mountain* (2005), the wide-open space of the mountain expands the horizons of the characters' sexual identities **[Figure 2.43]**. In the science fiction film *Donovan's Brain* (1953), the vision and the personality of a mad scientist are projected and reflected in a laboratory with twisted, mechanized gadgets and wires; essentially, his ability to create new life forms from that environment reflects both his genius and his insane ambitions. In both these interactions, the character and the elements of the mise-en-scène may determine more about each other's meaning than even the interactions between the characters do.

Keep in mind that our own cultural expectations about the material world determine how we understand the values of a film's mise-en-scène. To modern viewers, the mise-en-scène of *The Gold Rush* (1925) might appear crude and stagy; certainly the make-up and costumes might seem more like circus outfits than realistic clothing. For viewers in the 1920s, however, it was precisely the fantastical and theatrical quality of this mise-en-scène that made it so entertaining: for them, watching the Little Tramp perform his balletic magic in a strange location was more important than the realism of the mise-en-scène.

Interpretive Contexts for Mise-en-Scènes

Two prominent contexts for eliciting interpretations, or readings, of films include naturalistic mise-en-scène and theatrical mise-en-scène. A *naturalistic mise-en-scène* appears realistic and recognizable to viewers. A *theatrical mise-en-scène* denaturalizes the locations and other elements of the mise-en-scène so that its features appear unfamiliar, exaggerated, or artificial. Throughout their history, movies have tended to emphasize one or the other of these contexts, although many films have moved smoothly between the two. From *The Birth of a Nation* (1915) to *Amadeus* (1984), settings, costumes, and props have been selected or constructed to appear as authentic as possible in an effort to convince viewers that the filmmakers had a clear window on a true historical place: the first movie re-creates the historical sites and elements of the Civil War, whereas the second reconstructs the physical details of Wolfgang Amadeus Mozart's life in eighteenth-century Europe. In other films, from *The Cabinet of Dr. Caligari* (1920) to *Harry Potter and the Deathly Hallows: Part 1* (2010), those same elements of mise-en-scène have exaggerated or transformed reality as most people know it: *Caligari* uses sets painted with twisted buildings and nightmarish backgrounds, while magical animals and animated objects inhabit the fantastical settings of *Deathly Hallows*.

The Naturalistic Tradition

Naturalism is one of the most effective—and most misleading—ways to approach mise-en-scène. If mise-en-scène is about the arrangement of space and the objects in it, as we have suggested, then naturalism in the mise-en-scène means that how a place looks is the way it is supposed to look. We can, in fact, pinpoint several more precise characteristics of a naturalistic mise-en-scène:

- The world and its objects follow assumed laws of nature and society.
- The elements of the mise-en-scène have a consistently logical or homogeneous relation to each other.
- The mise-en-scène and the characters mutually define each other, although the mise-en-scène may be unresponsive to the needs and desires of the characters.

Naturalistic mise-en-scène is consistent with accepted scientific laws and cultural customs. Thus in a naturalistic setting, a person would be unable to hear whispers from far across a field, and a restaurant might have thirty tables and several waiters or waitresses. This kind of realistic mise-en-scène also creates logical or homogeneous connections among different sets, props, and characters. Costumes, props, and lighting are appropriate and logical extensions of the naturalistic setting, and sets relate to each other as part of a consistent geography. *The Battle of Algiers* (1966) uses location shooting in an attempt to re-create with documentary realism the revolution fought in the city's streets a decade earlier. In the submarine film *Das Boot* (1981), the individual sets are necessarily small, cramped rooms, and the characters wear the uniforms of World War II German sailors. Naturalism in the movies also means that the mise-en-scène and the characters mutually define or reflect each other. The gritty streets and dark rooms of a city reflect the bleak attitudes of thieves and femmes fatales in *The Killers* (1946); in *Up in the Air* (2009), the everyday world of airports, airlines, and hotel lobbies functions as a bleakly distorted home for a character unable to secure human companionship [**Figure 2.44**].

Two specific traditions have emerged from naturalistic mise-en-scène. A *historical mise-en-scène* re-creates a recognizable historical scene, highlighting those elements that call attention to a specific location and time in history: *All Quiet on the Western Front* (1930) can still stun audiences with its brutally accurate representation of trench warfare in World War I; *A Man for All Seasons* (1966) re-creates the sumptuous robes and august chambers of Parliament in the sixteenth-century England of martyr Thomas More.

2.44 *Up in the Air* (2009). Ordinary travel becomes a self-enclosed, naturalistic mise-en-scène from which the character cannot escape.

Calling attention to the ordinary rather than the historical, an *everyday mise-en-scène* constructs commonplace backdrops for the characters and the action. In *Louisiana Story* (1948), a swamp and its rich natural life are the always-visible arena for the daily routines of a young boy in the Louisiana bayous. In *Winter's Bone* (2010), the struggles of the heroine to protect her family home are set against the stark beauty and sparse settlement of the Ozarks. In the Brazilian film *Central Station* (1998), a railroad station in Rio de Janeiro and a poor rural area in the Brazilian countryside are the understated stages in a touching tale of a woman's friendship with a boy in search of his father.

The Theatrical Tradition

In contrast, theatrical mise-en-scène creates fantastical environments that display and even exult in their artificial and constructed nature. Films in this tradition define themselves in one or more of these terms:

- Elements of the mise-en-scène tend to violate or bend the laws of nature or society.
- Dramatic inconsistencies appear within one or between two or more settings.
- The mise-en-scène takes on an independent life that requires confrontations or creative negotiations between the props and sets and the characters.

Often violating the accepted laws of how the world functions, theatrical mise-en-scène can call attention to the arbitrary or constructed nature of that world. Horses change colors and witches melt in *The Wizard of Oz* (1939), and in movies from *Top Hat* (1935) to *Silk Stockings* (1957), Fred Astaire somehow finds a way to dance on walls and ceilings and transform spoons and brooms into magical partners. Dramatic inconsistencies within a film's mise-en-scène indicate the instability of those scenes, costumes, and props—and the world they define. The films of Monty Python offer innumerable examples. In *Monty Python's The Meaning of Life* (1983), a pirate ship sails through the streets of Manhattan and a darkly costumed grim reaper interrupts a classy dinner party to announce that all of the chatting friends have died of food poisoning. In a theatrical mise-en-scène, props, sets, and even bodies assume an independent (and sometimes contradictory) life that provokes regular confrontations or negotiations between the mise-en-scène and the characters **[Figure 2.45]**. Scorsese's *After Hours* (1985) describes the plight of Paul when he finds himself lost at night in the Soho neighborhood of New York City. Characters suddenly die, a woman surrounds herself with the objects and clothing of a 1960s lifestyle, and a vigilante group mistakes Paul for a robber; in this film, each apartment or street corner seems to be another individual's personal stage, and Paul becomes an unwilling participant in the play.

Two historical trends—expressive and constructive—are associated with theatrical mise-en-scène. In an *expressive mise-en-scène*, the settings, sets, props, and other dimensions of the mise-en-scène assert themselves independently of the characters and describe an emotional or spiritual life permeating the material world. Associated most commonly with the German expressionistic films of the 1920s, this tradition is also seen in surrealism, in horror films, and in the magic realism of Latin American cinema. Since Émile Cohl's

text continued on page 92 ▶

2.45 *Monty Python's The Meaning of Life* (1983). A dinner party is suddenly disturbed by the dramatic entry of Death in the midst of a theatrical mise-en-scène.

157010 157010 157010

Naturalistic Mise-en-Scène in *Bicycle Thieves* (1948)

The setting of Vittorio De Sica's *Bicycle Thieves* is post–World War II Rome, a mise-en-scène whose stark and impoverished conditions are the most formidable barrier against the central character's longing for a normal life. Antonio Ricci finds a job putting up movie posters, a humble but adequate way to support his wife and his son Bruno in an economically depressed city. When the bicycle he needs for work is stolen, he desperately searches the massive city on foot, hoping to discover the bike before Monday morning, when he must continue his work. The winding streets and cramped apartments of Rome appear as bare, crumbling, and scarred surfaces. They create a frustrating and impersonal urban maze through which Ricci walks asking questions without answers, examining bikes that are not his, and following leads into strange neighborhoods where he is observed with hostile suspicion. In what was once the center of the Roman Empire, masses of people wait for jobs, crowd onto buses, or sell their wares. The most basic materials of life take on disproportionate significance as props: the sheets on a bed, a plate of food, and an old bike are the center of existence. In the mise-en-scène, the generally bright lighting reveals mostly blank faces and walls of poverty.

Bicycle Thieves is among the most important films within the naturalistic tradition of mise-en-scène, associated specifically with the Italian neorealist movement of the late 1940s **[Figure 2.46]**. The laws of society and nature follow an almost mechanical logic that cares not at all for human hopes and dreams. Here, according to a truck driver, "Every Sunday, it rains." In a large city of empty piazzas and anonymous crowds, physical necessities reign: food is a constant concern; most people are strangers; a person needs a bicycle to get around

2.46 *Bicycle Thieves* (1948). Bare streets and a bicycle to steal become the heart of this mise-en-scène.

town; and rivers are more threatening than bucolic. Ricci and other characters become engulfed in the hostility and coldness of the pervasive mise-en-scène, and their encounters with Roman street life follow a path from hope to despair to resignation. In the beginning, objects and materials, such as Ricci's uniform and his bed linens, offer promise for his family's happiness in a barren and anonymous cityscape. However, the promise of these and other material objects turns quickly to ironic emptiness: the bicycle is stolen; the marketplace overwhelms him with separate bicycle parts that could never be identified; and settings (such as the church into which he pursues one of the thieves) offer no consolation or comfort. Finally, Ricci himself gets caught in this seemingly inescapable logic of survival when, unable to find his bike, he tries to steal another one. Only at the end of the day, when he discovers his son is not the drowned body pulled from the river, does he give up his search for the bicycle. Realizing that this setting and the objects in it will never provide him with meaning and value, he returns sadly home with the son he loves.

Bicycle Thieves's very purpose is to accentuate the common and everyday within a naturalistic tradition. Ricci and his neighbors dress like the struggling working-class population, and the natural lighting progresses from dawn to dusk across the various sets that mark Ricci's progression through the day. This film's everyday mise-en-scène is especially powerful because without any dramatic signals, it remains permeated by World War II. Even within the barest of everyday settings, objects, and clothing, *Bicycle Thieves* suggests the traces of history—such as Mussolini's sports stadium—that have created these impoverished conditions.

Along with these traces of history within its everyday mise-en-scène, we are reminded of a theatrical tradition that ironically counterpoints the film's realism. While performing his new duties in the first part of the film, Ricci puts up a glamorous poster of the movie star Rita Hayworth **[Figure 2.47]**. Later the sets and props change when Ricci wanders from a workers' political meeting to an adjacent theater where a play is being rehearsed. In these instances, a poster prop and a stage setting become reminders of a world that has little place in the daily hardships of this mise-en-scène—a world where, as one character puts it, "Movies bore me." For many modern tourists, Rome might be represented by that other tradition—as a city of magnificent fountains, glamorous people, and romantic restaurants. For Ricci and his son, however, that tradition is only a strange place and a fake set like the restaurant filled with rich patrons eating ravenously before returning to face the reality of the streets. For Europeans who lived through World War II (in Rome or other cities), the glaring honesty of the film's mise-en-scène in 1948 was, understandably, a powerful alternative to the glossy theatrical tradition of Hollywood sets and settings.

2.47 *Bicycle Thieves* (1948). Reminders of different values and traditions.

Fantasmagorie (1908) depicted an artist surrounded by sketches and drawings whose life and activity are independent of him, expressive mise-en-scène has enlivened the terrifying, comical, and romantic worlds of many films, including *The Birds* (1963), in which birds become demonic; *Barton Fink* (1991), in which wallpaper sweats; and *Lars and the Real Girl* (2007), in which a lonely and confused man falls in love with and introduces to friends and family the inflatable doll he purchases to be his companion.

In a *constructive mise-en-scène*, the world can be shaped and even altered through the work or desire of the characters. Films about putting together a play or even a movie are examples of this tradition as characters fabricate a new or alternative world through their power as actors or directors. In François Truffaut's *Day for Night* (1973), for example, multiple romances and crises become entwined with the project of making a movie about romance and crises, and the movie set becomes a parallel universe in which day can be changed to night and sad stories can be made happy. Other films, however, have employed constructive mise-en-scène to dramatize the wishes and dreams of their characters. In *Willy Wonka and the Chocolate Factory* (1971), the grim factory exterior hides a wonderland where, as one character sings, "you can even eat the dishes." In *The Dark Knight* (2008), spectacular costumes and electronic gadgets create a sinister version of a comic-book mise-en-scène in which good and bad characters battle each other for control, whereas the mise-en-scène of *Being John Malkovich* (1999) constantly defies the laws of spatial logic, as Craig the puppeteer and his co-worker Maxine struggle for the right to inhabit the body of the actor Malkovich.

We rarely experience the traditions of naturalistic and theatrical mise-en-scène in entirely isolated states. Naturalism and theatrics sometimes alternate within the same film, and following the play and exchange between the two can be one of the more exciting and productive ways to watch movies and to understand the complexities of mise-en-scène in a film—of how place and its physical contours condition and shape most experiences. In this context, Preston Sturges's *Sullivan's Travels* (1941) is a remarkable example of how the alternation between these two traditions can be the very heart of the movie **[Figure 2.48]**. In this film, Hollywood director John L. Sullivan, after a successful career making films with titles like *So Long, Sarong*, decides to explore the world of suffering and deprivation (as material for a serious realistic movie he intends to title *O Brother, Where Art Thou?*). He subsequently finds himself catapulted into a grimy world of railroad boxcars and prison chain gangs, where he discovers, ironically, the power of the movie fantasies he once created to delight and entertain others. The theatrical mise-en-scène of Hollywood, he learns, is as important to human life as the ordinary worlds people must inhabit.

VIEWING CUE

Describe why the mise-en-scène of the film you most recently watched fits best within a naturalistic or a theatrical tradition. Explain how this perspective helps you to experience the film. Illustrate your position using two or three scenes as examples.

Spectacularizing the Movies

Movie spectaculars are films in which the magnitude and intricacy of the mise-en-scène share equal emphasis with or even outshine the story, the actors, and other traditional focal points for a movie. Certainly many kinds of films have employed spectacular sets and settings as part of their narrative, but what distinguishes a movie spectacular is an equal or additional emphasis on the powers of the mise-en-scène to create the meaning of the film or even overwhelm the story. If low-budget independent films usually concentrate on the complexity of character, imagistic style, and narrative, movie spectaculars attend to the stunning effects of sets, lighting, props, costumes, and casts of thousands.

2.48 *Sullivan's Travels* (1941). The opposition between the "real" world and Hollywood fantasy may not be as absolute as its director-hero at first assumes.

The history of movie spectaculars extends back to the 1914 Italian film *Cabiria* [**Figure 2.49**], an epic about the Second Punic War, which became a clear inspiration for the making of D. W. Griffith's *Intolerance* (1916), with its four historical tales and sensational sets of ancient worlds. Since then, there have been many successful movie spectaculars and many colossal failures. Some of the most notable successes include *Napoléon* (1927), *The Ten Commandments* (1923, 1956), *Alexander Nevsky* (1938), *Gone with the Wind* (1939), *Lawrence of Arabia* (1962), *Gandhi* (1982), *Gladiator* (2000), and *Avatar* (2009).

Movie spectaculars fit squarely into two cultural traditions: that of the sublime and that of the epic. The *sublime* suggests the power of scenes and places to dizzy (or simply humble) the human mind before their breathtaking size, beauty, or magnificence. *Epics* tell heroic tales of nations or spiritual communities and the moments and events that defined them. More often than not, epics are about the importance of cul-

2.49   *Cabiria* (1914). In perhaps the first movie spectacular, the eruption of Mount Etna begins a cinematic tradition using mise-en-scène to show disaster.

tural place as a large national or spiritual mise-en-scène. Movie spectaculars often set epic stories about the birth or salvation of communities in a sublime mise-en-scène whose magnitude of place overwhelms and supersedes individual desires and differences. Through the last century, these sublime epics have tended to expand from visions of nationhood (*Gone with the Wind*) to spectacles of cities (the 2002 *Gangs of New York*), the stellar landscapes that surround our globe (*2001: A Space Odyssey*) and fantastical projections of an imagined world (*The Lord of the Rings*). In all their differences, however, movie spectaculars exploit one of the primary motivations of film viewing: the desire to be awed by worlds that exceed our day-to-day reality.

CONCEPTS AT WORK

Mise-en-scène describes the physical world of sets and settings, from props to actors and lighting. Yet as it is used in the service of the film as a whole, it can also be overlooked—think of the numerous times Universal has used the *Psycho* house in other movies and TV shows. It is the juxtaposition of its ordinary appearance with unthinkable horror that made the Bates Motel one of the screen's most memorable examples of mise-en-scène and emphasized the decisive role it played in the film's meaning. Viewers are sometimes even afraid to take showers after seeing *Psycho*! But, just as Hitchcock anticipated in the film's trailer, moviegoers actually enjoy being scared in this way. The motel remains one of the main attractions of the backlot tour at Universal Studios in Hollywood, which, when it began operating just four years after the release of Hitchcock's film, already included the *Psycho* house. These creepy three-fifths scale sets and facades remind viewers both of the movie's thrills and chills and of the artifice and manipulation that went into generating them.

Activity

Imagine a film, such as *The Wizard of Oz*, in which setting seems to determine plot ("follow the yellow brick road," for example), and transpose its characters to the world of another film: a mystery film or a social drama, for example. How would you design the new setting to conform to the new type of film? How would you rethink the plot based on a new setting?

Framing What We See
Cinematography

Based on a short story by Julio Cortázar, Michelangelo Antonioni's *Blow-Up* (1966) is a murder mystery in which the investigation of a possible death becomes an investigation of the meaning of images. A London photographer named Thomas wanders through a park taking photos, seeking a particularly lyrical image to conclude his latest collection. When he snaps a picture of two lovers, the woman involved insists that he give her the film. He refuses, however, to surrender it to her, and later, when he develops the photo, he notices something odd in the image. When he enlarges and refines it, blowing it up to reveal more and more detail, he discovers a dead body behind a bush in the image. As he unsuccessfully pursues this image and the mystery behind it through the course of the film, Thomas's faith in the reality of images and in reality itself gradually comes undone. By the end of the film, as he watches and then participates in an imaginary tennis match, Thomas has become a doubting Thomas who realizes that images of the world, like the world itself, do not simply show us a truth but rather require both analysis and imagination to see what they hold.

Visual stimuli determine a significant part of our experience of the world around us: we look left and right for cars before we cross a busy street, we watch sunsets in the distance, we focus on a face across the room. The visual dynamics through which we encounter our world vary. Sometimes we are caught up in the close-ups of a crowded sidewalk; sometimes we watch from a window high above the street. Vision allows us to distinguish colors and light, to evaluate the sizes of things near and far, to track moving objects, or to invent shapes out of formless clouds. Vision allows us to project ourselves into the world, to explore objects and places, and to transform them in our minds. In the cinema, we know the material world only as it is relayed to us through the filmed images (and recorded sounds) that we process in our minds. The filming of those images is called **cinematography**, which means motion-picture photography or, literally, "writing in movement."

This chapter describes the feature at the center of most individuals' experiences of movies: film images. Although film images may sometimes seem like transparencies or open windows on the world, they are purposefully constructed and filmed. Here we will detail the subtle and complex ways cinematography composes individual movie images in order to communicate feelings, ideas, and other meanings.

KEY OBJECTIVES

- Examine the development of the film image from a lengthy historical heritage of visual spectacles.
- Understand how the frame of an image positions our point of view according to different distances and angles.
- Explain how film shots use the depth of the image in various ways.
- Understand how film stock, color, lighting, and compositional features of the image can be employed in a movie.
- Describe the effects of different patterns of movement on the film image.
- Delineate the array of techniques used to create visual effects.
- Describe the significance of the film image in different cinematic traditions.

We go to the movies to enjoy stimulating sights, share other people's perspectives on the world, and explore that world through the details contained in a film image. In Ingmar Bergman's *Persona* (1966), a woman's tense and mysterious face suggests the complex depths of her personality. At the beginning of *Saving Private Ryan* (1998), we share the perspective of confused and wounded soldiers viscerally as bullets zip across the ocean surface during the D-Day invasion [Figure 3.1]. In *The Hurt Locker* (2009), brightly and starkly lit images capture not simply an arid desert landscape but also the brittle tension that seems to electrify the light [Figure 3.2].

Vision occurs when light rays reflected from an object strike the retina of the eye and stimulate our perception of that object's image in the mind. Photography, which means "light writing," mimics vision in the way it registers light patterns onto celluloid film. Yet whereas vision is continuous, photography is not; rather, it freezes a single moment in the form of an image. Movies connect a series of these single moments and project them above a particular rate of frames per second to create the illusion of movement. Recent studies of perception suggest that humans process the incremental differences among sequential still images just as we process actual motion—this effect is called short-range **apparent motion**, and it is now considered the psychological process that explains our perception of movement when watching films **[Figure 3.3]**. In brief, the brain is actively responding to the movie's visual stimuli exactly as it would in actual motion perception.

These technological and physiological mechanisms suggest that the power of the film image comes from its ability to re-create how we see the world through visual compositions that direct, expand, and even transform our natural vision. In the science fiction film *Blade Runner* (1982), Rick Deckard (Harrison Ford) uses a computer to explore unseen spaces in a photograph, using visual technology that surpasses the powers of human vision **[Figure 3.4]**. Deckard's technologically enhanced image reveals information that the traditional human perspective never could and serves as a metaphor for the power of film. Even conventional film images enhance and guide human perception. Whether in the slow-moving precision and clarity of the single forty-five-minute zoom image of Michael Snow's *Wavelength* (1967) or in the glowing and nostalgic textures of Federico Fellini's *Amarcord* (1974), through the film image we can see and understand the world with fresh eyes.

3.1 *Saving Private Ryan* (1998). The film uses visceral camera work to bring viewers close to the dying on D-Day.

3.2 *The Hurt Locker* (2009). In a very different war, very different images relay the tension that permeates its desert spaces.

3.3 **Optical illusion.** The difference between images on a strip of film is so slight that when they are projected at sufficient speed the viewer perceives continuous motion. Short-range apparent motion can be illustrated with optical illusions like this one.

3.4 *Blade Runner* (1982). The technology to explore unseen elements of a photograph imagined in Ridley Scott's science-fiction classic anticipated recent developments in computer imaging.

A Short History of the Cinematic Image

The human fascination with creating illusions is an ancient one; in the *Republic*, Plato wrote of humans trapped in a cave who mistake the shadows on the wall for the actual world. Leonardo da Vinci described how a light source entering a hole in a *camera obscura* (literally, "dark room") projected an upside-down image on the opposite wall, offering it as an analogy of human vision and anticipating the mechanism of the camera. One of the earliest technologies that used a light source to project images was the magic lantern. In the eighteenth century, showmen developed elaborate spectacles called *phantasmagoria*. The most famous of these were Étienne-Gaspard Robert's terrifying mobile projections of ghosts and skeletons on columns of smoke in an abandoned Paris crypt. These fanciful devices provided the basis for the technology that drives modern cinematography and the film image's power to control, explain, and entertain. In this section, we will examine the historical development of some of the key features in the production and projection of the film image.

3.5 **Zoetrope.** An early pre-cinema device that permitted individuals to view a series of images through a circular wheel, creating the illusion of movement.

1820s–1880s: The Invention of Photography and the Prehistory of Cinema

The components that would finally converge in cinema—photographic recording of reality and the animation of those images—were central to the visual culture of the nineteenth century. Combining amusement and science, the *phenakistiscope* (1832) and the *zoetrope* (1834), among other such pre-cinema contraptions, allowed a person to view a series of images through slits in a circular wheel, a view that creates the illusion of a moving image **[Figure 3.5]**. In 1839, Louis-Jacques-Mandé Daguerre produced the first still photograph (although Joseph Nicéphore Niépce laid the groundwork in 1826). Photography's mechanical ability to produce images of reality and make them readily available to the masses was among the most significant developments of nineteenth-century culture. Photography permeated everything from family albums to scientific study to private pornography collections. In the 1880s, both Étienne-Jules Marey in France and Englishman Eadweard Muybridge, working in the United States, conducted extensive studies of human and animal figures in motion using **chronophotography**, series of still images that recorded incremental movement and formed the basis of cinematography **[Figure 3.6]**. Muybridge's Zoopraxiscope, introduced in 1879, enabled moving images to be projected for the first time.

1890s–1920s: The Emergence and Refinement of Cinematography

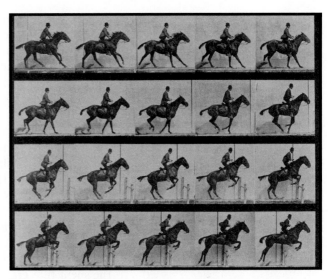

3.6   Eadweard Muybridge's motion studies. Experimenting with still photographs of motion, Muybridge laid the groundwork for cinematography.

Inventor W. L. K. Dickson invented the first motion picture camera, patented by his employer, Thomas Edison, as the Kinetoscopic camera in 1891. But the official birth date of the movies is widely accepted as 1895, when the brothers Auguste and Louis Lumière successfully joined two key elements: the ability to record a sequence of images on a flexible, transparent medium, and the capacity to project the sequence. The Lumières debuted their Cinématographe at the Grand Café in Paris on December 28, 1895, showing ten short films, including the famous scene of workers leaving the Lumière factory.

The very first movies consisted of a single moving image. The Lumières' early film *Niagara Falls* (1897) simply shows the famous falls and a group of bystanders, but its compositional balance of a powerful natural world and the people on its edge draws on a long history of painting that infuses the film with remarkable energy and beauty that the addition of motion renders almost sublime **[Figure 3.7]**. Referred to in one newspaper as "The Anatomy of a Kiss," the early Edison film *The Kiss* (1896) titillated viewers by giving them a playfully analytical snapshot of an intimate moment **[Figure 3.8]**.

3.7   *Niagara Falls* (1897). One of the Lumière brothers' nonfiction moving snapshots (or actualities) shows the wonder and balance of a single moving image.

3.8   *The Kiss* (1896). From the Edison company, one of the most famous early films regards an intimate moment.

In the early years of film history, technical innovations in the film medium and in camera and projection hardware were rapid and competitive. Eastman Kodak quickly established itself as the primary manufacturer of **film stock**, which consists of a flexible backing or base such as celluloid and a light-sensitive emulsion. The standard **nitrate** film base was highly flammable, and its pervasive use (it was not definitively replaced by **safety film** until 1952) is one reason why so much of the world's silent film heritage is lost. Early black-and-white film's emulsion was **orthochromatic**, sensitive only to blue and green light and processed using a red safety-light. Early in film history (by 1909), the width of the strip of film used for filming and exhibiting movies was standardized as 35mm. This **film gauge** is still dominant for theatrical exhibition worldwide, even as digital formats have begun to replace exhibition on film. Some common film gauges include 16mm, 35mm, and 70mm **[Figures 3.9a–3.9c]**. By the 1920s, the rate at which moving images were recorded (and later projected) increased from sixteen frames to twenty-four frames per second (fps), offering more clarity and definition to moving images.

The silent film era saw major innovations in lighting, mechanisms for moving the camera and varying the scale of shots, and the introduction of much more sensitive **panchromatic** stock, which responded to a full spectrum of colors and became the standard for black-and-white movies after 1926. Cinematographers like Billy Bitzer, working with D. W. Griffith in the United States, and Karl Freund, shooting such German expressionist classics as *Metropolis* (1927), brought cinematographic art to a pinnacle of visual creativity. These visual achievements were adversely affected by the introduction of sound in 1927, since bulky and sensitive sound recording equipment created restrictions on outdoor and mobile shooting.

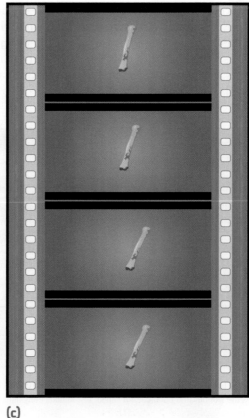

3.9   Common film gauges drawn to scale.
(a)   16mm film gauge.
The lightweight cameras and portable projectors used with this format have been effective for documentary, newsreel, and independent film as well as for prints of films shown in educational and home settings.

(b)   35mm film gauge.
The standard gauge for theatrically released films, introduced in 1892 by Edison.

(c)   70mm film gauge.
A wide, high-resolution gauge, in use since the early days of the film industry, but first used for feature films in the 1950s. A horizontal variant of 70mm is used for IMAX formats.

(a)   (b)   (c)

1930s–1940s: Developments in Color, Wide-Angle, and Small-Gauge Cinematography

Technical innovations increased even as the aesthetic potential of the medium was explored. By the 1930s, color processes, by which a single or a wide range of colors become part of the film image, had evolved from the individually hand-painted frames or tinted sequences of silent films to colored stocks and, finally, the rich **Technicolor** process that would dominate color film production until the 1950s. The Disney cartoon *Flowers and Trees* (1932) was the first to use Technicolor's three-strip process, which recorded different colors separately, using a dye transfer process to create a single image with a full spectrum of color. The process offered new realism but was often used to highlight artifice and spectacle, as in *The Wizard of Oz* (1939) **[Figures 3.10a–3.10c]**.

Meanwhile, the **camera lens**, the piece of curved glass that redirects light rays in order to focus and shape images, also changed significantly—in terms of lens speed, which determines how much light an aperture allows to be gathered (that is, the "f-stop"), and the introduction of new lenses—wide-angle, telephoto, and zoom. Each lens produces a different **focal length**—the distance from the center of the lens to the point where light rays meet in sharp focus—that alters the perspective relations of an image. Wide-angle lenses have a short focal length, telephoto lenses have a long one, and a zoom is a variable focus lens. The range of perspectives offered by these advancements allowed for better resolution, more **depth of field** (the portion of the image that is in focus), wider angles, and more frame movement.

3.10a–3.10c *The Wizard of Oz* (1939). Viewers sometimes find the opening, sepia-tinted scenes of *The Wizard of Oz* (1939) jarring **(a)**, having vivid memories of the film in Technicolor. When Dorothy first opens the door to Munchkinland, the drab tints of Kansas are left behind **(b)**. Technicolor's saturated primary colors are so important in the film **(c)**, the silver slippers of the book were changed to ruby slippers for the screen.

3.11 **The Heiress** (1949). Gregg Toland's cinematography made use of wide-angle lenses and faster film stocks to create images in which both foreground and background are in sharp focus.

During the 1920s, filmmakers used gauzy fabrics and, later, special lenses to develop a so-called soft style, through which the image could highlight the main action or character. From the mid-1930s through the 1940s, the development of the **wide-angle lens** (commonly considered a lens of less than 35mm in focal length) allowed cinematographers to explore a greater depth of field that could show different visual planes simultaneously. Cinematographer Gregg Toland is most closely associated with refinements in wide-angle cinematography, characterized by the dramatic use of deep-focus cinematography in his work on Orson Welles's *Citizen Kane* (1941) and William Wyler's *The Heiress* (1949) **[Figure 3.11]**.

Camera technology also developed, with the introduction of more lightweight **handheld cameras** (such as the Arriflex camera) that were widely used during World War II for newsreels and other purposes. Small-gauge production also expanded during this period, with the 8mm film developed in 1932 for the amateur filmmaker and the addition of sound and color to the 16mm format. In fact, 16mm's portability and affordability encouraged its use in educational films and other documentaries, as well as in low-budget independent and avant-garde productions.

▶ **VIEWING CUE**
Think about the cinematography of your class's most recent film screening in relation to the larger history of the image. Does the film include shots that seem like paintings, photographs, or other kinds of visual displays? How do these shots affect your understanding or interpretation of those images or the entire film? ⏸

1950s–1960s: Widescreen, 3-D, and New Color Processes

The early 1950s witnessed the arrival of several **widescreen processes**, which changed the size of the image—its *aspect ratio* (p. 106)—by dramatically widening it (in part, to distinguish the cinema from the new competition of television). One of the most popular of these processes in the 1950s, CinemaScope, used an **anamorphic lens**, which squeezed a wide-angle view onto a strip of 35mm film and then "unsqueezed" it during projection with another such lens. Other widescreen films, such as *Lawrence of Arabia* (1962), used a wider film gauge of 70mm **[Figure 3.12]**. This period, during which the popularity of television urged motion-picture producers to more spectacular displays, also saw a craze for 3-D movies such as *House of Wax* (1953). By now most movies were shot in color, facilitated by the introduction of Eastmancolor as an alternative to the proprietary Technicolor process. In the 1960s, Hollywood began to court the youth market, and cinematographers experimented more aggressively with ways to distort or call attention to the image through the use of **filters** (transparent sheets of glass or gels placed in front of the lens), **flares** (created by directing strong light at the lens), **telephoto lenses** (lenses with a focal length of at least 75mm and capable of magnifying and flattening distant objects and **zooming** by changing focal length), and fast motion, among other effects.

3.12 **Lawrence of Arabia** (1962). The film's 70mm widescreen format is suited to panoramic desert scenes and military maneuvers.

1970s–1980s: Cinematography and Exhibition in the Age of the Blockbuster

As we have seen, the history of film images is to a great extent that of film stock, cameras, and other recording and projection equipment. In the 1970s, the flexibility of **camera movement** was greatly enhanced with the introduction of the **Steadicam**, a camera stabilization device that allows the operator to follow action smoothly and rapidly, as evidenced in the uncanny camera movements in *The Shining* (1980). Visual effects technology also developed rapidly in the era of the blockbuster ushered in by *Jaws* (1975) and *Star Wars* (1977), movies in which expensive budgets meant shocking, stunning, or simply wondrous images **[Figure 3.13]**. The spectacular qualities of motion pictures are on display in modern IMAX and **Showscan** projection systems developed in the 1970s. IMAX systems store approximately three times as much information as a 70mm film image when projected horizontally rather than vertically. Showscan, developed by Douglas Trumbull and marketed in 1983, projects at sixty frames per second (rather than twenty-four frames) and creates remarkably dense and detailed images.

1990s and Beyond: The Digital Future

Television, documentary filmmakers, and artists in the 1970s first used **video** as an alternative medium to celluloid, and with the development of camcorders in the 1980s, it spread widely among consumers. Although the succession of broadcast and consumer video (including Portapak reel-to-reel, U-matic, Beta, and VHS) were analog formats (using a continuous signal to record on tape), they paved the way for the consumer embrace of digital technologies.

The broader shift to digital filmmaking is a critical transition in film history. Rather than using film or magnetic tape, digital images are generated by binary code and so allow for more flexibility, manipulation, and identical reproduction of the image (and, for some, more creativity and a higher-quality image). At first, the film industry developed digital technology for special effects and nonlinear editing before **digital cinematography** became a viable alternative to 35mm film. *Star Wars: Episode II—Attack of the Clones* (2002) was the first high-profile film to be shot in high-definition (HD) digital video.

Since the 1990s, digital technology, which does not use film stock and thus does not require processing in a laboratory, continues to transform cinematography in a number of ways from the amateur to the blockbuster level. Technically, the digital image offers advantages and disadvantages. Besides the economic advantage of lightweight and mobile cameras, the sharpness of the digital image suggests a kind of immediacy that distinguishes it from traditional celluloid images. The tale of a family gathering that is shattered through the horrifying revelation of a grown son, *The Celebration* (1998) uses the digital image to dramatize a stark reality with edgy directness. Director of such Hollywood films as *Leaving Las Vegas* (1995), Mike Figgis was also an early experimenter with digital recording equipment. In *Timecode* (2000), a frame

3.13 *Jaws* (1975). This Steven Spielberg film ushered in the blockbuster era with surprisingly modest special effects; a full glimpse of the mechanical shark, known on set as "Bruce," isn't obtained until 90 minutes into the film.

3.14   *Timecode* (2000). Real-time images made possible by digital cinematography are fractured in the gridlike presentation.

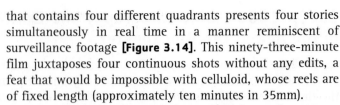

(a)   **(b)**

3.15   **(a) Russian icon painting from the sixteenth century and (b)** *Andrei Rublev* **(1969).** The composition and lighting of Tarkovsky's film about the great Russian icon painter evokes Rublev's medieval art.

(a)   **(b)**

3.16   **(a) Magic lantern slide** (1905) and **(b)** *Time Regained* **(2000).** Raoul Ruiz's adaptation of Marcel Proust's work evokes the past through lighting that recalls the rich color of magic lantern slides.

that contains four different quadrants presents four stories simultaneously in real time in a manner reminiscent of surveillance footage **[Figure 3.14]**. This ninety-three-minute film juxtaposes four continuous shots without any edits, a feat that would be impossible with celluloid, whose reels are of fixed length (approximately ten minutes in 35mm).

Digital moviemaking can be more intimate than 35mm cinematography, which involves large cameras and more crew members. Independent filmmakers quickly adapted to shooting on DV (digital video); for example, in Rebecca Miller's *Personal Velocity* (2002), cinematographer Ellen Kuras films three women's stories with emotional immediacy using mini-DV. Sophisticated camera systems made shooting on DV an option for large-budget films like David Fincher's *Zodiac* (2007). Steven Soderbergh has adopted the high-resolution Red One camera for his feature films since the two-part *Che* (2008), and technological innovation continues to drive both low- and high-end production. Well outside mainstream film culture, "machinima" has become one of the more interesting offshoots of digital cinema. With this practice, filmmakers (such as Hugh Hancock, the creator of *Ozymandias* [2000]) manipulate the digital graphics of popular computer video games in order to create original images and stories (*Ozymandias* is a free interpretation of the Percy Bysshe Shelley sonnet).

Digital image processing also has several disadvantages. While a cinematographer could predict how a particular film stock responds to light, shooting digitally depends more on familiarity with the camera's capabilities. Digital images are recorded and displayed in pixels (densely packed dots), rather than the crystal array or grain produced by the celluloid emulsion used for film. When converted to a digital file, a 35mm film frame contains about ten million pixels. A sophisticated digital camera, such as the Sony Panavision HD 24, records about two million pixels for each of the primary colors. This difference may not make one kind of image better than the other, but the digital image has less range and lacks the grains and tones found in the film emulsion. In addition, traditional film equipment outperforms digital equipment in difficult outdoor conditions.

Although the film image will continue to develop in new technological and aesthetic directions, traces of its past constantly resurface. Russian iconography permeates the images of Tarkovsky's *Andrei Rublev* (1969) **[Figures 3.15a and 3.15b]**. The Japanese tradition of *ukiyo-e* woodblock prints appears in the films of Kenji Mizoguchi, including *Utamaro and His Five Women* (1946). And in Raoul Ruiz's *Time Regained* (2000), rich color tones re-create the vibrancy of magic lanterns **[Figures 3.16a and 3.16b]**. In virtually every movie we see, our experience of its images is affected by the history of fine art, photography, and, of course, the movies.

The Elements of Cinematography

The basic unit of cinematography is the shot. The **shot** is the visual heart of the cinema: it is a continuous point of view (or continuously exposed piece of film); it may move forward or backward, up or down, but it does not change, break, or **cut** to another point of view or image. A film depicting a hotel room the morning after a wild party may shoot the scene, or employ cinematographic shots, in many different ways. One version might show the entire room with its broken window, a fallen chair, and a man slumped in the corner as a single shot that depicts the scene from a calm distance. Another version might show the same scene in a rapid succession of images made by multiple shots—the window, the chair, and the man—creating a visual disturbance missing in the first version. The core of most films, cinematography in general and the shot specifically offer a remarkable range of options for creating, representing, and understanding a cinematic point of view: from framing and depth through movement and color. For the astute viewer, recognizing and analyzing how these options are used in a film can be one of the most precise ways to experience and understand that film.

Points of View

In cinematographic terms, **point of view** refers to the position from which a person, an event, or an object is seen (or filmed). All shots have a point of view: a **subjective point of view** re-creates the perspective of a character through camera placement; an **objective point of view** represents the more impersonal perspective of the camera. A point of view may be discontinuous—for instance, in *No Country for Old Men* (2007) the perspective moves dramatically among a psychotic killer, Anton Chigurh; the man he pursues, Llewelyn Moss; and the sheriff attempting to capture Chigurh, Ed Tom Bell. During several tense moments towards the conclusion of the film, the perspective jumps from the position of the sheriff to that of the killer or, as the two men come closer to each other, shifts gradually across space between the sheriff and the hidden killer **[Figure 3.17]**. While the first is edited, cutting between two shots, the second is a single shot whose point of view is continuous. The specific object highlighted within a point of view is the shot's **focus**, the point in the image that is most clearly and precisely outlined and defined by the lens of the camera.

Four Attributes of the Shot

Every shot orchestrates four important attributes: framing, depth of field, color, and movement. The **framing** of a shot contains, limits, and directs the point of view within the borders of the rectangular frame. Usually framing is even, but sometimes it can appear unbalanced or askew, as in the **canted frame** that famously recurs in *The Third Man* (1949) **[Figure 3.18]**. Framing determines the image size by correlating with the camera's distance from its subject. In *Bend It Like Beckham* (2002), the framing at one point depicts only the face of the young female soccer player and, shortly

3.17 *No Country for Old Men* (2007). Different points of view alternate between a killer and the man who pursues him.

VIEWING CUE
Identify a subjective point-of-view shot from the movie you are watching for class. Describe what marks it as such.

3.18 *The Third Man* (1949). Suspicions about Orson Welles's character Harry Lime are reinforced by the canted framing.

thereafter, the entire field. Film images also create a depth of field, the range or distance before and behind the main focus and within which objects remain relatively sharp and clear: sometimes an image may create a short or shallow range and sometimes a long range or deep focus. From a viewing position in the bleachers behind the goalpost, for example, a film image may focus primarily on a penalty kick near midfield but create a depth of field that keeps the players before and behind that action—the kicker and the goalie—in focus.

Finally, a film image or shot may depict or incorporate movement. The subject of the shot may move, and the **mobile frame** of the image may follow an action, object, or individual, or it may move to show different actions, objects, or individuals. (Such movement requires the camera or lens to move during filming.) During the championship match in *Bend It Like Beckham*, the mobile frame of the shot shows the protagonist as she darts down the field on her way to scoring the winning goal, the movement of the shot capturing the strength and dexterity of her strides in a single motion **[Figure 3.19]**.

Framing

Although we may not attend to every individual image in a movie, its cinematography involves careful construction by filmmakers and rewards close observation by viewers. An early experiment with the power of framing, Abel Gance's *Napoléon* (1927) orchestrates multiple images to appear simultaneously on different projected screens in order to capture complex layers of Napoleon's life **[Figure 3.20]**; to shoot single scenes in *Dancer in the Dark* (2000), Lars von Trier used numerous digital cameras placed at different angles and distances in order to capture the exact images needed. Filmmakers have experimented with and refined ways to manipulate and use the film image and its properties for over one hundred years. The three dimensions of the film image—the height and width of the frame, and the apparent depth of the image—offer endless opportunities for representing the world and how we see it. Here we will examine and detail the formal possibilities inherent in every frame of a film, possibilities that, when recognized, enrich our experience of the movies.

3.19 *Bend It Like Beckham* (2002). A mobile camera increases the viewer's excitement during the winning goal.

3.20 *Napoléon* (1927). Abel Gance's historical tour-de-force juxtaposed images on multiple screens, creating visual connections between Napoleon and other dimensions of his complex life, such as his relationship with his wife Josephine.

Aspect Ratio. Like the frame of a painting, the basic shape of the film image on the screen determines the film composition. The **aspect ratio** describes the relation of width to height of the film frame as it appears on a movie screen or television monitor **[Figures 3.21a–3.21c]**. *Grand Illusion* (1937), *Citizen Kane* (1941), and other classic films employ the 1.33:1 image ratio standardized in 1932 by the American Academy of Motion Picture Arts and Sciences and used by most films until the 1950s. (Technically, this **academy ratio** is 1.375:1, which includes the portion of the filmstrip used for the optical soundtrack, which is not visible when projected.) These dimensions are closely approximated by the television screen and are rendered as 4:3 in DVD formats. This almost square image draws on associations between film frame and window or picture frame. **Widescreen ratios**, which have largely replaced academy ratio since the 1950s, range from 1.66:1 or 1.85:1 (the digital aspect ratio 16:9) to CinemaScope at 2.35:1.

Aspect ratios often shape our experience to align with the themes and actions of the film. For example, CinemaScope, which uses an anamorphic (or compressed) lens to achieve a widescreen ratio of 2.35:1, was first used for religious epics and musicals. In Nicholas Ray's 1955 drama of teenage frustration and fear, *Rebel Without a Cause*, the elongated horizontal CinemaScope frame depicts the loneliness and isolation of Jim Stark (played by James Dean) in a potentially violent showdown with a high school rival and bully **[Figure 3.21a]**. Outside the planetarium, Ray's cinematography conveys the city below as an unreachable place for these small-town youths who seem constantly overwhelmed by social and psychological spaces. While the more confined frame of *Citizen Kane* fits a film about a man driven to control the world, the widescreen space in *Rebel Without a Cause* suits the fitful search of restless teens, and both films use carefully composed frames that highlight screen dimensions. Although aspect ratio may not be such a crucial determinant in every movie, it does not escape the consideration of the filmmaker. For instance, Stanley Kubrick shot his war film *Full Metal Jacket* (1987) in academy ratio rather than widescreen, which had evolved into the standard ratio

(a)

(b)

(c)

3.21 **Common aspect ratios include CinemaScope (a), academy (b), and widescreen (c). (a)** *Rebel Without a Cause* (1955). Nicholas Ray uses the exaggerated width of the CinemaScope frame to show Jim Stark (James Dean) cornered despite the expanse of Los Angeles below. **(b)** *Full Metal Jacket* (1987). Stanley Kubrick's use of academy ratio emphasizes the role of television in transmitting the images of the Vietnam War to the American public. **(c)** *The Lord of the Rings: The Fellowship of the Ring* (2001). Epic films that use widescreen for elaborate visual compositions and effects are reduced in impact when seen in other formats.

by the time he shot the film **[Figure 3.21b]**. With this choice, Kubrick emphasizes a central theme: that the Vietnam War entered world consciousness through the boxlike screen of television.

The changes in film ratios over the years have presented interesting challenges when movies appear on television or are recorded to tape or disc. Most television broadcasts of movies now announce that they have been "formatted to fit your screen," and a DVD version of a film may be *letterboxed* by blocking off the top and bottom strips of the square frame to accommodate the widescreen image, or digitally

► **VIEWING CUE**

Identify the original aspect ratio of the film you are studying in class. How is it appropriate or inappropriate to this film's themes and aims? If the film is exhibited in a different ratio, explain how that process affects certain scenes. ⏸

altered and offered in several formats. In recent years, televisions themselves have taken on the horizontal proportions of widescreen cinema frames, even though much television programming does not utilize these dimensions. But before these innovations, and frequently even now, movies shown on television will have been altered through the **pan-and-scan process**. This process chops off outer portions of the image that are not central to the action or reconstitutes a single widescreen image into two consecutive television images. Reframing the image can alter our perception of the film and its story. In movies like *Rebel Without a Cause* and *The Lord of the Rings: The Fellowship of the Ring* (2001), to name just two, the surrounding space of the frame is an important part of the drama that helps us understand the characters and their actions **[Figure 3.21c]**. Even when these changes seem minor or barely noticeable, they can subtly influence our perceptions and responses to a film. In *Into the Wild* (2007), a widescreen image with an aspect ratio of 2.35:1 (rather than one formatted to fill the television frame) more appropriately displays the horizontal space that is so important to this road movie about the isolated wanderings of a young college graduate who hitchhikes to Alaska.

Masks. Besides the proportions determined by the aspect ratio, a film frame can be reshaped by various **masks**, attachments to the camera that cut off portions of the frame so that part of the image is black. Mostly associated with silent films—like D. W. Griffith's *Intolerance* (1916)—or modern movies recalling that earlier period, a masked frame may open only a corner of the frame, create a circular effect, or leave just a strip in the center of the frame visible **[Figure 3.22]**. An **iris shot** masks the frame so that only a small circular piece of the image is seen: in Harold Lloyd's *The Freshman* (1925), a shot of a timid collegian first appears in an **iris-in** (opening the circle to reveal more of the image) to show his seemingly safe location surrounded by a crowd of hostile football players. Conversely, a full image may be reduced, as an **iris-out** (closing the circle), to isolate and emphasize a specific object or action in that image: a shot of a courtroom, for example, might iris-out to reveal the nervous hands of the defendant's mother. In *The Night of the Hunter* (1955), an iris-out follows the demonic preacher as he walks toward the house of the children he threatens **[Figure 3.23]**.

Onscreen space refers to the space visible within the frame of the image, whereas **offscreen space** is the implied space or world that exists outside the film frame. Onscreen space is often carefully framed for compositional effect, with the position, scale, and balance of objects or lines within the frame directing our attention or determining our attitude toward what is being represented. Usually the action in offscreen space is less important than the action in the frame (as when a close-up focuses on an intimate

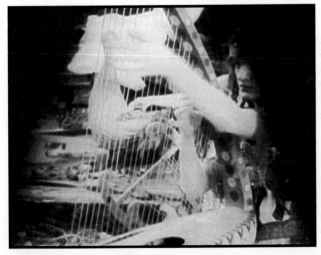

3.22 *Intolerance* (1916). A triangular mask isolates the triangular harp.

3.23 *The Night of the Hunter* (1955). An iris-out emphasizes the threat of a figure of evil.

3.24 *Alien* (1979). The horror genre makes significant use of offscreen space to generate suspense: what is Ripley (Sigourney Weaver) going to see?

3.25 *L'Argent* (1983). The agency of characters in Robert Bresson's films often seems to be limited by external forces signified by the emphasis on offscreen space.

conversation and excludes other people in the room). Offscreen space does, however, sometimes contain important information that will be revealed in a subsequent image (as when one of the individuals engaged in conversation looks beyond the edge of the frame—toward a glaring rival shown in the next shot). Offscreen spaces in horror films like *Alien* (1979) seethe with a menace that is all the more terrifying because it is not visible [**Figure 3.24**]. In Robert Bresson's films, offscreen space suggests a spiritual world that exerts pressure on but eludes the fragmented and limited perspectives of the characters within the frame [**Figure 3.25**].

Camera Distance. Another significant aspect of framing is the distance of the camera from its subject, which determines the **scale** of the shot, signals point of view, and contributes a great deal to how we understand or feel about what is being shown. **Close-ups** show details of a person or an object, such as the face or hands or a flowerpot on a windowsill, perhaps indicating nuances of the character's feelings or thoughts or suggesting the special significance of the object. An **extreme close-up** moves in even closer, singling out, for instance, the person's eyes or the petal of the flower. Carl Theodor Dreyer's *The Passion of Joan of Arc* (1928) and Ingmar Bergman's *Persona* (1966) are well-known examples of films that use close-ups and extreme close-ups to depict religious fervor and existential agony, respectively, through the heroines' facial expressions [**Figures 3.26 and 3.27**].

3.26 *The Passion of Joan of Arc* (1928). Carl Theodor Dreyer captures the intensity of religious faith through frequent close-ups of actress Renée Falconetti's portrayal of Joan of Arc.

3.27 *Persona* (1966). Existential questions are evoked by the use of close-ups and extreme close-ups in Ingmar Bergman's film.

3.28a   *Shane* (1953). Barely seen, Shane approaches through an extreme long shot.

3.28b   *Shane* (1953). The mysterious figure becomes more recognizable in a long shot.

▶ **VIEWING CUE**

Look for a pattern of framing distances in the next film you view for class. Do there seem to be a large number of long shots? Close-ups? Explain how this pattern reinforces themes of the film. ⏸

At the other end of the compositional spectrum, a **long shot** places considerable distance between the camera and the scene, object, or person filmed. A human figure remains recognizable but is defined by the large space and background that surrounds it. An **extreme long shot** creates an even greater distance between the camera and the person or object, so that the larger space of the image dwarfs small objects or human figures, such as with distant vistas of cities or landscapes. Most films feature a combination of these long shots, sometimes to show distant action or objects, sometimes to establish a context for events, and sometimes, as with the introduction and conclusion of *Shane* (1953), to emphasize the isolation and mystery of a character as he arrives in the distance **[Figures 3.28a and 3.28b]**.

Between close-ups and long shots, a **medium shot** describes a middle ground in which we see the human body from the waist or hips up, as in *The Maltese Falcon* (1941) **[Figure 3.29]**, while a **medium long shot** slightly increases the distance between the camera and the subject, showing a three-quarter-length view of a character (from approximately the knees up), a framing often used in westerns when a cowboy's weapon is an important element of the mise-en-scène **[Figure 3.30]**. A very

3.29   *The Maltese Falcon* (1941). A medium shot of Sam Spade (played by Humphrey Bogart).

3.30   *Red River* (1948). The medium long shot was often used in westerns to keep weapons in view. French critics dubbed it the *"plan américain"* or "American shot."

3.31 *Rebecca* (1940). The melodramatic tension of a medium close-up on the heroine Joan Fontaine's face.

3.32 *The Seven Samurai* (1954). An extreme long shot better shows off the open-air battles in this epic.

common framing, the **medium close-up** shows a character's head and shoulders and is frequently used in conversation scenes. Melodramatic or romantic films about personal relationships often feature a predominance of medium close-ups and medium shots to capture the facial expressions of the characters, such as in the story of a new bride's haunting by the memory of a former wife in *Rebecca* (1940) **[Figure 3.31]**. Open-air adventures, such as *The Seven Samurai* (1954), the tale of a sixteenth-century Japanese village that hires warriors for protection, tend to use more long shots and extreme long shots in order to depict the battle scenes **[Figure 3.32]**. As these descriptions imply, framing is defined relatively; there is no absolute cut-off point between a medium and a medium long shot, for example. As we have seen, the most common reference point for the scale of the image is the size of the human figure within the frame, a measure that is not a universal element of the cinematic image.

Although many shots are taken from approximately eye level, the camera *height* can also vary, as an element of a film's style, to present a particular compositional element or to evoke a character's perspective. Japanese director Yasujiro Ozu's signature camera level is low to the ground, an ideal position for filming Japanese interiors, where characters sit on the floor **[Figure 3.33]**. A camera might be placed higher to show larger-scale objects, such as tall buildings or landscapes. The opening shot of *Far from Heaven* (2002) takes a god's-eye view of its New England village setting, mimicking the opening of Douglas Sirk's *All That Heaven Allows* (1955) in its vision of 1950s small-town repression **[Figure 3.34]**.

Camera Angles. Film shots are positioned according to a multitude of angles, from straight on to above or below. These are often correlated with camera height, as demonstrated by the series of shots presented on the following page from Jane Campion's *The Piano* (1993), a powerful film about a mute Scottish woman who travels with her daughter

3.33 *Tokyo Story* (1953). A camera placed low to the ground presents characters sitting on tatami mats.

3.34   *Far from Heaven* (2002). The height of the opening shot establishes the setting and introduces a sense of distance.

to New Zealand to complete an arranged marriage. **High angles** present a point of view directed at a downward angle on individuals or a scene **[Figure 3.35a]**, while **low angles** view the subject from a position lower than it is **[Figure 3.35b]**. In either case, the exact angle of the shot can vary from very steep to slight. An **overhead shot** (sometimes called a **crane shot** because of the machinery on which the camera is mounted) depicts the action or subject from high above, sometimes looking directly down on it **[Figure 3.35c]**. In the Czech film *The Shop on Main Street* (1965), a clever opening crane shot looking down on the town reflects the point of view of a stork nesting on a chimney.

Shots change their angle depending on the physical or geographical position or point of view, so that a shot from a tall adult's perspective may be a high-angle shot, whereas a child's view may be seen through low angles. Such shots are often **point-of-view (POV) shots**, which are defined as shots that re-create the perspective of a character and may incorporate camera movement or optical effects as well as camera angle in order to do so.

Camera angles can sometimes indicate psychological, moral, or political meanings in a film, as when victims are seen from above and oppressors from below, but such interpretations must be made carefully in the context of the film's own patterns because formal features like these do not automatically assume particular meanings.

Shots can vary in terms of horizontal angles as well, with characters's faces more often shown in three-quarter view than in profile or frontally. Filming at a right angle to the scene characterizes the compositions of Ozu's films, producing a frontality that has had a strong influence on international art cinema directors from Chantal Akerman to Béla Tarr to Tsai Ming-liang.

3.35a   *The Piano* (1993). A high-angle long shot of the arrival on the beach.

3.35b   *The Piano* (1993). An extreme low-angle shot, slightly canted, shows the farmer/husband as he furiously descends toward his unfaithful wife.

3.35c   *The Piano* (1993). With this overhead shot, the film depicts a rare moment of contentment and harmony at the piano.

3.36 *The Best Years of Our Lives* (1946). The deep focus and balance indicate restored family harmony at a soldier's homecoming.

3.37 *The Best Years of Our Lives* (1946). The focused foreground of embracing lovers leaves the blurred background of the veteran's artificial arms barely visible.

Depth of Field

In addition to the various ways an image can be framed to create perspectives and meanings, shots can be focused to create different depths that subtly shape our understanding of the image. As noted in the history section, technological advances in camera lenses, most notably in the 1930s, played a central role in allowing filmmakers to experiment with this element in a variety of ways. One of the most dramatic products of these developments, **deep focus** means that multiple planes in the image are all in focus.

A film about three physically and psychologically brutalized veterans returning home from World War II, William Wyler's *The Best Years of Our Lives* (1946) provides superior examples of how deep focus can create relationships within a single image. In one image, the two grown children in the foreground frame the happy reunion of their parents in the background, all in harmonious balance and focus, with just a hint of the theme of isolation that will be developed after the homecoming **[Figure 3.36]**. In another image from the same film **[Figure 3.37]**, **shallow focus**, in which only a narrow range of the field is focused, is used. Here, too, the choice of a depth of field indicates what is significant in the image: the embracing lovers. With a **rack focus** (or **pulled focus**), the focus shifts rapidly from one object to another, such as refocusing from the face of a woman to the figure of a man approaching from behind her. During a dramatic scene in *L.A. Confidential* (1997), a young self-righteous police officer, Ed Exley, assures his captain he can force a criminal suspect to confess, and the shot rack focuses from the captain to Exley to catch the latter's determined expression as he turns toward the interrogation room **[Figure 3.38]**.

3.38 *L.A. Confidential* (1997). The shot refocuses to highlight the detective's expression against a blurry background.

3.39   *Nosferatu* (1922). Diffuse shadows and shades of gray create an atmosphere of dread.

3.40   *The Third Man* (1949). Sharply contrasting blacks and whites, with scintillating grays, intensify the drama of good and evil in Vienna.

Contrast and Color

Color profoundly affects our experience and understanding of a film shot; even black-and-white films use contrast and gradations to create atmosphere or emphasize certain motifs. In F. W. Murnau's *Nosferatu* (1922), black and white and tones of gray create an ominous world where evil lives, not in darkness but in shading **[Figure 3.39]**. In *The Third Man* (1949), black-and-white contrasts glisten on the slick surfaces of a morally slippery world **[Figure 3.40]**. No longer a necessity, the black-and-white format is used self-consciously in such modern films as *Raging Bull* (1980) and *Pleasantville* (1998) **[Figure 3.41]**. In *Raging Bull*, it suggests the violent extremities in the life of prizefighter Jake LaMotta as well as the style of films of the period and milieu in which it is set; in the second film, it parodies the superficial and simplistic lives of 1950s television, a world suddenly confused when emotional colors enter the characters' lives. Cinematographer Christopher Doyle, well known for his work with Hong Kong filmmaker Wong Kar-wai, shifts between black-and-white and color cinematography in less predictable ways, highlighting the surface of the image, the exposure, and the grain of the stock.

3.41   *Pleasantville* (1988). This film makes the shift from black-and-white to color cinematography a metaphor for the characters' emotional awakening.

Beginning with the colors of the mise-en-scène (natural colors, painted sets, locations, or actors' costumes), color describes the spectrum of color grades and hues used by a film, while **tone** refers to the shading, intensification, or saturation of those colors (such as metallic blues, soft greens, or deep reds) in order to sharpen, mute, or balance them for certain effects. Color film stocks allow a full range of colors to be recorded to film. Once colors are recorded on film stocks, that film can be manipulated to create **color balances** that range from realistic to more extreme or unrealistic palettes: these may appear as either *non-contrasting balances* (sometimes called a *monochromatic color scheme*), which can

text continued on page 116 ▶

3.42a

3.42b

3.42c

Color and Contrast in Film

The expressive use of color in film has evolved through artistic vision and technical innovation—from hand-tinting to Technicolor experiments to faster stocks and digital processing. Early silent films like *King Lear* (1910) created an impression of color film by hand-tinting each frame **[Figure 3.42a]**, but because of the time and labor involved this never became a widespread phenomenon. When Walt Disney released *Flowers and Trees* (1932), part of the *Silly Symphonies* series of short subjects, its full-color visuals, compliments of the new three-strip Technicolor process, were a sensation **[Figure 3.42b]**. The first Technicolor feature film soon followed: *Becky Sharp* (1935), an adaptation of William Thackeray's nineteenth-century novel, brings its historical tale to life with sumptuous colors in intimate scenes and dramatic contrasts in epic battles **[Figure 3.42c]**. DeLuxe color and CinemaScope were advertised along with the stars of *The Girl Can't Help It* (1956), a Jayne Mansfield rock-and-roll farce, to attract audiences to the movie spectacle **[Figure 3.42d]**. The advent of digital technology in the 1990s has made possible the saturated visuals of animated films like *Up* (2009) **[Figure 3.42e]**, as well as the subdued palette of the western exteriors of the Coen brothers' *True Grit* in 2010, which was shot on film and adjusted in postproduction **[Figure 3.42f]**.

3.42d

3.42e

3.42f

create a more realistic or flat background against which a single color becomes more meaningful, or *contrasting balances*, which can create dramatic oppositions and tensions through color.

In the first decades after the 1895 arrival of the cinema, before color film stock was available, some movies, like the 1910 version of Shakespeare's *King Lear,* used laboriously hand-tinted colored frames that appeared like moving paintings. In the 1930s, the introduction of Technicolor aided the construction of both more realistic and more fantastic worlds. The costume drama *Becky Sharp* (1935) was the first feature film to use the process, and Disney's popular *Snow White and the Seven Dwarfs* (1937) followed soon thereafter. But it wasn't until the 1950s, with the introduction of the less elaborate Eastmancolor stock, that the majority of films were produced in color. Former animator Frank Tashlin brought a comic-book look to such live-action films as *The Girl Can't Help It* (1956). Color is a key element in the composition of the image, with certain films being justly famous for the expressive use of color. For example, Néstor Almendros filmed Terrence Malick's *Days of Heaven* (1978) at the "magic hour" just before sunset to capture a particular quality of light for the historical setting in the Great Plains. Michael Mann's urban crime drama *Miami Vice* (2006) uses eerie blues.

Selection of film gauge and stock, which can vary in speed (a measure of a stock's sensitivity to light), manipulation of exposure, and choices in printing can all affect the color and tone of a particular film. Cinematographer Rodrigo Prieto used different stocks and cameras to achieve the looks of the three interconnected stories in *Babel* (2006). Lighting, a full discussion of which is included in Chapter 2 on mise-en-scène, is clearly crucial to a film's palette and color effects, and it comes under the direction of the cinematographer during the production process.

(a)

(b)

Movement

When the film frame begins to move, a film shot re-creates a quality of vision that has always been a part of the human experience but that could be adequately represented only with the advent of film technology. In our daily lives, we anticipate these movements of a shot: when, for instance, we focus on a friend at a table and then refocus beyond that friend and toward another at the door; when we stand still and turn our head from our left shoulder to our right; or when we watch from a moving car as buildings pass. Like these adjustments within our field of vision, the film image can move its frame and focus through changes in the view of the camera (such as pans or tracking shots) or through changes in the focus of the camera lens (such as zooms).

Reframing refers to the movement of the frame from one position to another within a single continuous shot. One extreme and memorable example of reframing is an early shot in *Citizen Kane* (1941). Here the camera pulls back from the boy in the yard to reframe the shot to include his mother observing him from inside the window; it then continues backward to reframe the mother as she walks past her husband and seats herself at a table next to the banker Thatcher, who will take charge of their son **[Figures 3.43a–3.43c]**. Often such reframings are much

(c)

3.43a–3.43c *Citizen Kane* (1941). Describing a dramatic turning point in Kane's story, a gradual camera movement reframes three planes of the image and four characters to condense a traumatic moment in Kane's lost childhood.

more subtle, such as when the camera moves slightly upward to keep centered in the frame a character who is rising from a chair.

Pan and Tilts.

In these mobile frames, the camera mount remains stationary. A **pan** moves the frame from side to side without changing the placement of the camera. In other words, the camera rotates on its vertical axis, as if a character were turning his or her head. For example, the long shot that scans the rooftops of San Francisco for a fugitive

3.44 *Death in Venice* (1970). A pan starts from the protagonist, crosses the beach, and scans the horizon, suggesting his state of mind as he calmly embraces suicide.

at the beginning of *Vertigo* (1958) is a pan (short for *panorama*), as are many similar establishing shots of a skyline. Or a pan may re-create a character's point of view. The opening sequence of *Rear Window* (1954) includes a pan around the courtyard of the protagonist's building—and we are surprised by the revelation that the man whose view we apparently share is in fact asleep. During the last scene of *Death in Venice* (1970), a slow pan leaves the main character, Gustav von Aschenbach, as he walks onto the beach, and then swings past a jetty to settle the shot on the turbulent ocean and the glowing horizon. The movement of this pan suggests the romantic yearning and searching that characterize the entire film and that now culminate in von Aschenbach's death **[Figure 3.44]**.

Less common, **tilts** move the frame up or down on a horizontal axis as the camera rotates on its mount, as when the frame swings upward to re-create the point of view of a man following a skyscraper from the street into the clouds. In Wim Wenders's *Paris, Texas* (1984), a story about a father and son searching for the boy's mother, repeated tilt shots become a rhetorical action, moving the frame up a flagpole with an American flag, along the sides of Houston skyscrapers, and into the sky to view a passing plane. In this case, vertical tilts seem to suggest an ambiguous hope to escape or find comfort from the long quest across Texas.

Tracking Shots.

A **tracking shot** changes the position of the point of view by moving the camera forward or backward or around the subject, usually on tracks that have been constructed in advance. Max Ophüls used fluid tracking shots extensively in his films—for example, following a waltzing couple in *The Earrings of Madame de . . .* (1953). In a **dolly shot**, the camera is moved on a wheeled dolly that follows a determined course. The term *traveling shot* is sometimes used interchangeably with both tracking and dolly shots. In the remarkable first shot of Jean-Luc Godard's *Contempt* (1963), a camera on tracks moves forward into the foreground of the image, following a woman reading. When the track reaches that foreground, the camera turns and aims its lens directly at us, the audience. When these two moving camera shots follow an individual, they are sometimes called **following shots**. In *The 400 Blows* (1959), a single following shot tracks the boy, Antoine Doinel, for eighty seconds as he runs from the reformatory school toward the edge of the sea.

Handheld and Steadicam Shots.

Even greater mobility is afforded when the camera is carried by the camera operator. Encouraged first by the introduction of lightweight 16mm cameras and later by the use of video formats, **handheld shots** are frequently used in news reporting and documentary cinematography or to

3.45   *The Blair Witch Project* (1999). Handheld video viscerally brings the viewer into the horror and confusion in this low-budget sensation.

create an unsteady frame that suggests the movements of an individual point of view. *The Blair Witch Project* (1999) uses handheld shots so that the audience participates in the characters' frightened flight through the haunted forest **[Figure 3.45]**. Thomas Vinterberg's *The Celebration* (1998) also employs handheld digital video techniques to express the tension, anger, and confusion at a family gathering. In both of these cases, the handheld point of view involves the audience more immediately and concretely in the action.

To achieve the stability of a tripod mount, the fluidity of a tracking shot, and the flexibility of a handheld camera, cinematographers may wear the camera on a special stabilizing mount often referred to by the trademarked name **Steadicam**. In *Goodfellas* (1990), a film about mobster Henry Hill, a famous Steadicam shot, lasting several minutes, twists and turns with Hill and his entourage through a back door, a kitchen, and into the main room of a nightclub, suggesting the bravura and power of a man who can go anywhere, who is both onstage and backstage **[Figure 3.46]**.

> ▶ **VIEWING CUE**
>
> Examine one or two shots from a film viewed for class in which camera movements (tracks, pans) or mobile framings (zooms) are important. Why is a moving frame of a single shot used here instead of a series of shots? ⏸

Zooms. Sometimes confused with a track-in or track-out, a zoom is technically not the result of a moving camera at all, but rather of adjustments to the camera lens during filming that magnify portions of the image. **Zoom lenses**, which employ a variable focal length of 75mm or higher, thus accomplish a different kind of compositional reframing and apparent movement. During a **zoom-in**, the camera remains stationary as the zoom lens changes focal length to narrow the field of view on a distant object, bringing it into clear view and reframing it in a medium shot or close-up. Less noticeable in films, a **zoom-out** reverses this action, so that objects that appear close initially are then distanced from the camera and reframed as small figures. One of the significant side effects of a zoom-in is that the image tends to flatten and lose its depth of field, whereas a track calls attention to the spatial depth that it moves through. Although camera movements (tracking or Steadicam shots) and changes in the lens's focal length (zooms) may look similar, there are differences in the image and in the historical development of these technologies and practices. Sometimes these techniques are used together. In two very different films, *An Occurrence at Owl Creek Bridge* (1962) and Ján Kádar's *Adrift* (1969), zoom-outs are combined with forward tracking shots, so that the respective

3.46   *Goodfellas* (1990). The long and winding trail of power behind the scenes is depicted in a three-minute Steadicam shot.

protagonists appear to be running forward but never making any progress.

Animation and Visual Effects

Our visual experience is not just naturalistic; it is also fantastical, composed of pictures from our dreams and imaginations. These kinds of images can be re-created in film through two important manipulations of the image, animation and visual (or special) effects, which can be used to make film seem even more realistic or completely unreal. Both practices have been employed since the earliest days of cinema, but, as described earlier (p. 103), the growing popularity of digital technologies since the 1990s has profoundly transformed both animation and visual effects.

3.47   *Alice* (1988). Jan Švankmajer's animated interpretation of Lewis Carroll's classic is considerably darker than the Disney version.

Animation traditionally refers to moving images drawn or painted on individual animation **cels**, which are then photographed onto single frames of film. In fact, animation includes several variations on that formula, as witnessed in films like *Chicken Run* (2000), the comic story of a chicken rebellion, and Czech filmmaker Jan Švankmajer's *Alice* (1988), which combines live action, puppets, and stop-motion animation to re-create the dizzying events of Lewis Carroll's story **[Figure 3.47]**. With both these films, **stop-motion photography** records, as separate frames in incrementally changed action, inanimate objects or actual human figures that are then synthesized on film to create the illusion of motion and action: **claymation** accomplishes this effect with clay figures (as in *Chicken Run*), while **pixilation** employs this technique (or instead simply cuts out images from a continuous piece of filmed action) to transform the movement of real human figures into rapid, jerky gestures.

If films from *Snow White and the Seven Dwarfs* (1937) to *Shrek* (2001) create graphic cartoon narratives through traditional frame-by-frame drawings, colorizing, and filming, today's animation is accomplished more and more through computer graphics. Since *Toy Story* (1995), produced by the pioneering Pixar studio, became the first feature-length film composed entirely of **computer-generated imagery (CGI)**, striking technological advances have contributed to the resurgence of animation as a genre **[Figure 3.48]**. The films of Japanese animator Hayao Miyazaki, such as *Spirited Away* (2001) and *Ponyo* (2008), were released successfully in the United States with English-language soundtracks. The renewed appreciation for the medium was reflected in the introduction in 2002 of a new Academy Award category: feature-length animated films. While Pixar and DreamWorks continue to produce CGI blockbusters for all ages, independent filmmakers have also engaged with animation. Richard Linklater's *Waking Life* (2001) and *A Scanner Darkly* (2006) recorded real figures and action on video as a basis for painting individual animation frames digitally in a technique

3.48   *Toy Story* (1995). Pixar's first feature and the first computer-animated feature film to be released. The exaggerated crayon colors leap from the more balanced, natural tones of the realistic background.

3.49 *A Scanner Darkly* (2006). For this Philip K. Dick adaptation, Richard Linklater had his actors filmed digitally and then animated using a rotoscope technique.

3.50 *Our Hitler* (1977). Puppets and process shots are a few of the special effects used in this film to unravel the illusion of a fascist dictator.

known as **rotoscoping** **[Figure 3.49]**. *Persepolis* (2007), an adaptation of Marjane Satrapi's graphic novels about growing up in Iran, was a successful art-house release, and *Waltz with Bashir* (2008), an Israeli film about the horrors of the 1982 Lebanon war, extended animation to documentary.

Visual effects, sometimes called **special effects**, is a term encompassing many practices, only some of which actually involve the camera or image processing (for example, many films employ pyrotechnics and other mechanical effects). Since early cinema, filmmakers have employed such basic manipulations as **slow motion** or **fast motion** to make the action move at unrealistic speeds (achieved by filming the action faster or slower than normal and then projecting it at normal speeds); **color filters** that change the tones of the recorded image with different tinted lenses; and **miniature** (or other) **models** used to create fantastic landscapes and machines of the kind seen in the *X-Men* series (2000–2009), which combines the use of models with CGI.

Another common visual effect that remakes more than one shot into a single image is a **process shot**, a term that describes many different ways that the image can be set up and manipulated during filming. A process shot might project a background for the action on a screen in order to add another layer to the reality of the image (such as a large dinosaur bearing down on a screen behind an unaware scientist who appears to be only inches away) or to intentionally undermine the realism of the image by suggesting two or more competing realities. Hans-Jürgen Syberberg's film *Our Hitler* (1977), for example, shows Hitler quietly eating dinner while, in the background, Jews arrive at concentration camps; at other times, the film reduces Hitler to a puppet onstage **[Figure 3.50]**. Finally, a **matte shot**, such as the ominous church tower in *Vertigo* (1958), joins two pieces of film, one with the central action or object and the other with the additional background, figures, or action (sometimes painted or digitally produced) that would be difficult to create physically for the shot.

Some visual effects use a combination of cinematography and computer techniques, such as the celebrated "bullet time" used to great effect in *The Matrix* (1999), in which images taken by a set of still cameras surrounding a subject are put together to create an effect of suspension or extreme slow motion. Similar effects are used in *Inception* (2010), in which recognizable images of cityscapes and mountain fortresses are remade as the fragile and malleable virtual shapes of a dreamscape [**Figure 3.51**]. Current blockbusters are driven more and more by these kinds of spectacular visual effects, additional sequences and explanations of which often fill their DVDs. The viewer experiences magical battles and chases in *Harry Potter and the Deathly Hallows: Part 1* (2010) through a combination of techniques, including **3-D modeling**. The fantasy world of Peter Jackson's *Lord of the Rings* trilogy (2001–2003) was created through a range of special effects [**Figure 3.52**]. Effects ranged from the use of simple forced perspective to put hobbit, elven, and human characters in the proper scale to the imaginative work of the New Zealand–based Weta Digital company that innovated **motion capture technology** to incorporate actor Andy Serkis's physical features into the computer-generated character Gollum.

3.51 *Inception* (2010). Images of real and virtual worlds merge in a drama that takes place in the layers of a dream.

3.52 *The Lord of the Rings: The Return of the King* (2003). The third film in the trilogy contained 1,448 visual effects shots, nearly three times as many as the first.

The Significance of the Film Image

From the chariot races in Enrico Guazzoni's *Quo Vadis?* (1913) to the dreamscapes of *Inception*, movie images have been valued for their beauty, realism, or ability to inspire wonder. Often these qualities are found in their production values because of the skill and money invested to generate such experiences. But film images carry other values in what they preserve and say about the world. French filmmaker Jean-Luc Godard's remark that film is truth at twenty-four frames a second is one way to describe the power and importance of the film image. Yet as Godard's many films themselves demonstrate, this "truth" is not just the truth of *presentation* but also the truth of *representation*. In short, film images are prized both for their accuracy in showing or presenting us with facts, as well as for how they interpret or represent those facts.

Image as Presentation or Representation

In earlier sections of this chapter, we investigated the cultural and formal structures of cinematography. In this section, we will examine how people intellectually and emotionally interact with film images. Having earlier addressed the historical background of the image and the compositional details we see, we turn to how we respond to film images according to the cultural and historical values and traditions that make images meaningful.

3.53   ***The Last Emperor*** (1987). The sumptuous cinematography gives access to the Forbidden City, illustrating the power of the cinema to "authenticate" through the image.

Images hold a remarkable power to capture a moment. Flipping through a photo album provides glimpses of past events. The morning newspaper collapses a day of war into a single poignant image. However, images can do far more than preserve the facts of a moment. They can also interpret those facts in ways that give them new meanings. A painting by Norman Rockwell evokes feelings of warmth and nostalgia, while the stained-glass windows lining a cathedral aim to draw our spiritual passions. Add motion, and the power of images to both show and interpret information magnifies exponentially. More often than not, a film image is designed to do both at once: to realistically and reliably show, or *present*, the visual truth of the subject matter, and to color that truth with shades of meaning; or to *represent* it in order to obtain an emotional or intellectual response.

The image as presentation reflects our belief that film communicates the details of the world realistically, even while showing us unrealistic situations. We prize the stunning images of the ancient Forbidden City in *The Last Emperor* (1987) as well as the dynamic close-ups of a boxing match in *The Fighter* (2011) for their veracity and authenticity in depicting realities or perspectives **[Figure 3.53]**. In pursuing this goal, cinematography may document either subjective images, which reflect the points of view of a person experiencing the events, or objective images, which assume a more general accuracy or truth. In *Little Big Man* (1970), images from the perspective of a 101-year-old pioneer raised by Native Americans succeed, for many, in both ways: they become remarkably convincing displays of known historical characters and events—such as General George Custer at the Battle of Little Bighorn—and they poignantly re-create the perspective of the pioneer as he lived through and now remembers those events.

The image also has an instrumental power to influence or even determine the meaning of the events or people it portrays by *re*-presenting reality through the interpretive power of cinematography. The image as representation is an exercise in the power of visual stimuli. The way in which we depict individuals or actions implies a kind of control over them, knowledge of them, or power to determine what they mean. When we frame a subject, we capture and contain that subject within a particular point of view that gives it definition beyond its literal meaning. This imagistic value to represent permeates the drama of *Vertigo*, in which Scottie tries so desperately to define Madeleine as an image, and the cinematography aids him by framing her as a painting. It can also be found at the heart of films as diverse as *Blonde Venus* (1932) and *Fight Club* (1999), which in different ways show the ability of the film image to capture and manipulate a person or reality in the service of a point of view. In *Blonde Venus*, as in many of the films directed by Josef von Sternberg starring Marlene Dietrich, the heroine is depicted as a self-consciously erotic figure, whether in an outrageous costume as a showgirl or as a housewife and mother at home; in *Fight Club*, the main character projects and represents himself, undetected for much of the film, as a violently sadomasochistic alter-ego image. In *Pan's Labyrinth* (2006), the viewer is invited into a young girl's fantasy world through artful cinematography, including special effects **[Figure 3.54]**.

Part of the art of film is that these two primary imagistic values are interconnected and can be mobilized in intricate and ambiguous ways in a movie (as indeed they are in all of these examples). When Harry Potter speaks in the language of snakes in *Harry Potter and the Chamber of Secrets* (2002), the cinematography highlights the fear and confusion among Harry's classmates. Is the image an objective presentation of the perspective of the Hogwarts students, or is it an interpretive representation on the part of the film itself, trying to make the viewer think Harry is deserving of fear? A perceptive viewer must consider the most

3.54 *Pan's Labyrinth* (2006). A lonely child's fantasy world is shared by the viewer.

appropriate meanings for the shot—whether it reflects the students' position or the film's position. Watching closely how images carry and mobilize values, we encounter the complexity of making meaning in a film and the importance of our own activity as viewers.

Image as Presence or Text

Traditional perspectives on the image in film reflect expectations about the imagistic values encountered in different movies, and these expectations, in turn, influence how we respond to certain kinds of shots and framings in other movies. For some kinds of movies, like documentaries and historical fiction films, we have learned to see the film frame as a window on the world, seeking accuracy. For others, such as avant-garde or art films, we learn to approach the images as puzzles, perhaps revealing secrets of life and society. Here we will designate two conventions in the history of the film image: the convention of image as presence, and the convention of image as text. In the first case, we identify with the image; in the second, we read it.

Image as Presence

The compositional practices of the film image that we call the conventions of *presence* imply the following:

- a close identification with the point of view of the image
- a response to the image that is primarily emotional
- an experience of the image as if it were a lived reality

Part of a varied history, images in this tradition fascinate us with a visual activity we participate in, overwhelm us with their beauty or horror, or comfort us with their familiarity. Although not entirely separable from the story and other elements of the film form, imagistic presence is what principally entertains us at the movies, what elicits our tears and shrieks. A shot of horses and riders dashing toward a finish line or of a woman embracing a dear friend communicates an immediacy or truth that engages us and leads us through subsequent images.

Two variations upon this convention are the phenomenological image and the psychological image. The *phenomenological image* refers to filmmaking styles that approximate and visually participate in the physical activity as we would experience it in

text continued on page 126 ▶

From Angles to Animation in *Vertigo* (1958)

In Alfred Hitchcock's suspense film *Vertigo*, a wealthy businessman named Gavin Elster hires Scottie (played by James Stewart), a retired police detective who suffers from acrophobia (fear of heights), to watch his wife. Madeleine (Kim Novak), Elster claims, is troubled by her obsession with Carlotta, a woman from the past. After Scottie rescues Madeleine during an apparent suicide attempt, he falls in love with her, and when his acrophobia prevents him from stopping her as she races to leap from a mission tower, her death sends Scottie into a spiral of guilt. Later he believes he sees his lost love on the streets of San Francisco, and his pursuit of a look-alike woman, Judy (also played by Novak), entangles him in another twist to this psychological murder mystery in which the central crisis involves distinguishing reality from fictive images of it.

Vertigo takes advantage of almost every possibility in the film frame. Employing a particular brand of widescreen projection called VistaVision, the aspect ratio of Hitchcock's film is one of its immediately recognizable and significant formal features: the especially open space that the widescreen frame creates becomes a fitting environment for Scottie and his anxious searches through the wide vistas of San Francisco. Although *Vertigo* does not employ masks in the artificially obvious way of older films, at times Hitchcock cleverly creates masking effects by using natural objects within the frame. For instance, the film uses doors or other parts of the mise-en-scène to create masking effects that isolate and dramatize Scottie's intense gazing at Madeleine [Figure 3.55].

Like many other Hitchcock films, *Vertigo* continually exploits the edges of the frame to tease and mislead us with what we (and Scottie) cannot see. In Scottie's pursuit of Madeleine, she frequently evades his point of view, disappearing like a ghost beyond the frame's borders. The mystery of Madeleine's fall to her death is especially shocking because it occurs offscreen, revealed only as her blurred body flashes by the tower window, which acts as a second frame limiting Scottie's perception of what has happened [Figure 3.56].

The angles of shots are crucial in *Vertigo*. The hilly San Francisco setting naturally accentuates high and low

3.55 *Vertigo* (1958). In this striking composition, Scottie's previously masked point of view becomes graphically juxtaposed with the mirror image of the woman he pursues.

angles as Scottie follows Madeleine through the streets, and the film's recurring motif about the terror of heights informs even the most commonplace scenes, as high angles and overhead shots ignite Scottie's panicked paranoia. Especially when these sharp angles reflect Scottie's point of view, they suggest complex psychological and moral concerns about power and control as well as about desire and guilt, perhaps dramatizing those moments when Scottie's desires leave him in positions where he is most out of control and threatened.

3.56 *Vertigo* (1958). The window frames Scottie's uncertain view of a falling body.

Certainly among the more striking dimensions of *Vertigo* is its moving frame. One casual scene demonstrates how common shot movements not only describe events in a complex way but also subtly invest those events with nuance and meaning. The scene takes place early in the film in Gavin's office as he works to enlist Scottie's help to follow his wife. The scene begins with Gavin sitting in his chair, but Scottie soon sits and Gavin stands and moves around the room: a pan of Gavin walking to a higher position in the room is followed by a low-angle shot of Gavin and a complementing high-angle shot of Scottie; a backward track then depicts the more aggressive Gavin as he moves to the front of the image toward the stationary Scottie **[Figure 3.57]**. As the moving frame continues to focus on Gavin trying to convince Scottie to help him track his wife, the framing and its movement indicate that this is not quite a conversation between equals: the moving frame makes clear that Gavin directs the image and controls the perspective.

A more clearly central series of camera movements takes place when Scottie finds Madeleine standing before a portrait of Carlotta in an art museum. Here the camera executes several complex moves that simulate Scottie's perspective: it simultaneously zooms in and tracks first on the swirl in Madeleine's hair and then reframes by tracking and zooming out on the same hair design in the painting of Carlotta **[Figure 3.58]**. Indeed, these reframings in the museum resemble the opening sequence in which Scottie hangs from the gutter and his frightened glances at the street below are depicted through a quick, distorting combination of zooming-in and tracking-out that describes his intense panic and spatial disorientation. Entirely through these camera movements, the film connects Scottie's original trauma and guilt with his mysterious attachment to Madeleine.

Although *Vertigo* seems to be a realistic thriller, it employs—dramatically and disconcertingly—both animation and special effects as a part of its story and description of Scottie's state of mind. An eerie matte shot re-creates a tower that is missing from the actual church at San Juan Bautista; its goal is perhaps largely to add a crucial ele-

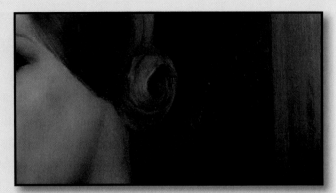

3.58 *Vertigo* (1958). Restless camera movement combining zooms and tracking shots traces Scottie's gaze at the portrait.

ment to the setting where Scottie's fear of heights will be exploited. Yet along with the nightmarish significance of that tower, in the final scene the matted image appears as an eerily glowing surface and color as the surreal tower looms over yet another dead body. More obvious examples of special effects include the rear projections and animation when Scottie begins to lose his grip on one reality and become engulfed in another. In one scene, Scottie and Judy's kiss spins free of the background of the room; earlier, during a nightmare triggered by his psychotic depression, an eruption of animation depicts the scattering of the mythical Carlotta's bouquet of flowers and a black abstract form of Scottie's body falling onto the roof of the church **[Figure 3.59]**.

Rather than mimicking or supplementing reality, these instances of animation and special effects in *Vertigo* point out how fragile the photographic realism of the film shot can be. *Vertigo* describes the obsessions of a man in love with the image of a woman (echoed from Carlotta to Madeleine to Judy). The film contains inordinately long periods without any dialogue, almost as a way to insist that Scottie's (and the film's) interest is primarily in images—in all their forms (from paintings to memories) and from many angles (high, low, moving, stationary, onscreen, and offscreen).

3.57 *Vertigo* (1958). A low-angle, backward tracking shot emphasizes the aggressive Gavin.

3.59 *Vertigo* (1958). The special effects of a nightmare: an abstracted black figure against the roof on which another body had fallen.

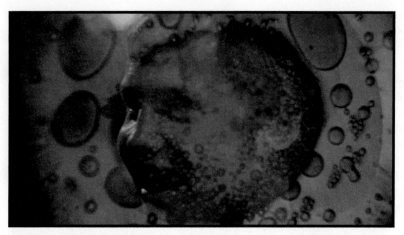

3.60 *Midnight Cowboy* (1969). Special effects and blurred, colored contrasts create a psychological representation of the cowboy's drug experience.

3.61 *3:10 to Yuma* (2007). Bodies in motion and pain are dynamically rendered through cinematography.

3.62 *Written on the Wind* (1956). Color, angles, composition, and deep focus contribute to the image's depiction of the character's emotional extremes in Douglas Sirk's melodrama of the unhappy rich.

the world—such as a shot that re-creates the dizzying perspectives from a mountaintop. As old as film history itself, this tradition appears in vastly different movies: from the remarkably visceral and physically chaotic battle scenes in Orson Welles's *Chimes at Midnight* (1966) to the painfully suspenseful *127 Hours* (2010), about a mountain climber trapped alone in the wilderness, phenomenological shots convey a sensual vitality in the image itself.

The *psychological image*, in contrast, creates images that reflect the state of mind of the viewer or a more general emotional atmosphere in a scene: in *10* (1979), a middle-aged man fantasizes the image of his dreams coming true as a beautiful woman running toward him in slow motion; in *Midnight Cowboy* (1969), disorienting, blurry images at a party re-create Joe's mental and perceptual experience after taking drugs **[Figure 3.60]**. Both traditions appear regularly in film history and in many different cultures, but certain film movements emphasize one over the other. Westerns—such as *3:10 to Yuma* (2007)—tend to rely on phenomenological images to imbue movement and conflict with energy **[Figure 3.61]**. Movies that concentrate on personal crises—such as the melodramatic *Written on the Wind* (1956), a tale of wealth and unhappiness in which high-strung emotions and mental stress are everywhere—often employ psychological images to reflect the states of mind of the characters **[Figure 3.62]**.

Image as Text

Textuality refers to a different kind of film image, one that demands

- an emotional distancing of the viewer from the image
- a reaction to the image that is primarily analytic
- an experience of the image as artifice or as constructed like a written statement or an aesthetic object to be interpreted

We stand back to look at textual images from an intellectual distance. They seem loaded with signs and symbols for us to decipher. They impress us more for *how* they show the world than for *what* they show. So-called difficult, abstract, or experimental films—from Germaine Dulac's surrealist film *The Seashell and the Clergyman* (1928) to *Pi* (1998)—enlist viewers most obviously within this tradition, but many films integrate images that test our abilities to read and decipher. A canted framing of an isolated house or a family reunion shot through a yellow filter may stand out in an otherwise realistic movie as a puzzle image that asks for more reflection: How do we read this image? Why is this unusual composition included? In *The Seashell and the Clergyman*, apparently about a priest in love with a beautiful woman, images resemble the cryptic language of a strange dream, requiring viewers to struggle to decipher them, perhaps as a way of understanding the film's complex drama of repression and desire [Figure 3.63].

3.63 *The Seashell and the Clergyman* (1928). Extreme angles, shadows, and highlighted patterns in the pavement suggest a complex dream image.

Two specific versions of the tradition of textuality can be referred to as the aesthetic image and the semiotic image. The *aesthetic image* asks to be contemplated and to be appreciated for its artistic re-creation of a world or a perspective through texture, line, color, and composition. While aesthetic images can be expected in art films like *The Seashell and the Clergyman*, they also surface in many other kinds of films: in the luxurious close-ups of Greta Garbo in *Queen Christina* (1933), in the elaborate patterns of the choreography of Busby Berkeley's musical *Dames* (1934), and in such films as *Run, Lola, Run* (1998) and *Requiem for a Dream* (2000). In *Run, Lola, Run*, for instance, a realistic shot of the mother watching a television tracks into the television itself, at which point it becomes an imaginatively animated tracking shot that follows the cartoon image of Lola as she dashes down the stairs [Figure 3.64]. The transformation signifies the malleable world of this movie.

The *semiotic image* presents images as signs (*seme* means "sign") to be interpreted like language or to be read like a poem. The puzzle-like paintings of René Magritte are a good example. Although such semiotic images are associated with experimental or new wave movies like Glauber Rocha's *Antonio das Mortes* (1969) and Jean-Luc Godard's *Numéro deux* (1975), they may also be found in historical avant-garde films like Sergei Eisenstein's *Battleship Potemkin* (1925) and Dziga Vertov's *Man with a Movie Camera* (1929) in which realistic and unrealistic images form strange compositions that demand a reflective reading. In R. W. Fassbinder's *In a Year of Thirteen Moons* (1978), a medium close-up shows the transsexual Elvira being violently forced to look at herself in a mirror. This painful

3.64 *Run, Lola, Run* (1998). The film image changes from live action to animation, inviting viewer participation in the film's aesthetic world.

text continued on page 130 ▶

Meaning through Images in *M* (1931)

Set in Germany around 1930, Fritz Lang's *M* constantly calls attention to its powers to present both objective and subjective experiences. *M* tells the gruesome tale of a child murderer, Franz Becker, whom both police and criminals pursue in an attempt to regain each group's stable, if corrupt, social situation. Throughout the film, objective images alternate with subjective ones: images seem at some points to describe the facts of a dark and anxious German society in 1930; at other points, they reproduce that world through the perspective of individual characters. Even in a fiction film such as this one, the images document a history of facial expressions, cultural products, and social activities, such as the uniforms of the German police and raucous criminal dens. At still other points in this film, the images present personal perspectives, such as the anxiety of a mother as she waits for her daughter, glances at the clock several times, and stares at an empty seat before a table setting **[Figure 3.65]**.

In *M*, the boundaries between these objective and subjective images regularly blur, and the film occasionally leaves unclear whether the images are a factual record of German street life or descriptions of anxious or even deranged minds. Early in the film, an extreme high-angle

3.65 *M* (1931). A seemingly benign shot of a child's place setting becomes ominous when it conveys the point of view of a mother whose daughter is missing.

shot presents an apparently objective view of children playing in a courtyard, but the angle of the shot also suggests the uneasy and oppressive feeling that suffuses the atmosphere. Soon afterward, a medium shot tracks laterally left to right as it follows the young girl, Elsie Beckmann, as she walks home bouncing a ball, straightforwardly depicting her carefree journey but also suggesting that someone might be following and watching her. Later a descriptive tracking shot of a man walking with a young girl is transformed into a scene of chaos, fear, and anger when the shot suddenly becomes identified with the subjective perspective of a crowd that sees the man as the murderer.

There are numerous examples in *M* of the power of the image to represent individuals by assigning them meanings and values, often in a self-conscious fashion that dramatically calls attention to this power. These representations are sometimes the common kind one finds in many films: a dark low-angle shot defines a criminal as dangerous, whereas a close-up of a mother emphasizes her internalized sorrow and pain. At other times, the structure of an image suggests more elaborate commentary: the detective Karl Lohmann is shot from an extreme low angle that not only describes him sitting in a chair but also depicts him as a grotesque, slovenly, and comical caricature. Sometimes other, darker judgments and meanings appear through the image. As part of a complex maneuver in that early tracking shot of Elsie, the image shifts subtly from being a description of her perspective to an ominously threatening point of view. When Elsie stops and bounces her ball off a poster warning of the murderer, the low camera angle assumes her point of view; but when, suddenly, the dark shadow of a man drifts across the poster and her perspective, the image acquires a darker and more threatening point of view that literally takes over Elsie's perspective with its own **[Figure 3.66]**. In a more diabolical way than in most films, vision is equated with control, and here the power of the unseen man's perspective over Elsie anticipates her murder. When, at the conclusion of the film, Becker stumbles into a vacant warehouse, he ironically finds himself the object of the same representational power in the image, the source of the perspective now being a

3.66 *M* (1931). A poster offering a reward for information on a child murderer becomes infused with horror when an anonymous shadow falls over it.

large crowd rather than a troubled individual. He suddenly finds himself literally captured by the gaze of a mob of street thieves and criminals prepared to judge him as the target of their eyes, just as he had done to Elsie.

M appears at the end of what is commonly called the "golden age" of German cinema, generally identified with two specific movie traditions: German expressionist films and German "street films." In street films, the movie image documents the tough and unglamorous social realities of criminals, prostitutes, or other desperate individuals. In German expressionism, film images often investigate emotional, psychological, and subconscious realities. *M* engages both these German film movements: while its documentary-like shots of criminals, tools, and weapons suggest the realism of street films, the expressionistic tradition allows Lang to use the textuality of the image to explore a different kind of presence, one associated with desires and fears.

A tradition of textual images that can be linked to German expressionism is both conveyed *in* the film, in which characters are often preoccupied with scrutinizing images for the mysteries they hold, and *by* it, as viewers detect the secrets within the film's own images. At one point, Becker examines his close-up reflection in a mirror, pulling his mouth down in a distorted frown, per-

haps as a bizarre attempt to see and comprehend the madman inside himself. At another, the police examine a note from Becker in close-up in order to analyze "the very particular shape of the letters," and several times they assemble images of fingerprints and maps to try to identify and locate the killer. In both cases, images become explicit instruments for investigating the crime and thus, the police hope, instruments with which to capture Becker. Finally, the plot turns dramatically when the criminals trailing Becker surreptitiously mark the back of his jacket with the letter *M*, thereby identifying this anonymous figure of a man on the street as the killer by making his image a legible text. Less directly, the film creates complex visual metaphors that ask viewers to decipher their significance: a balloon purchased by Becker for Elsie later appears in a medium shot tangled in telephone wires to suggest her death and perhaps the twisted person of Becker (whose body resembles the balloon figure) **[Figure 3.67]**.

The cinematography in *M* draws on both realist and expressionist traditions to create a mixture of documentary-style images and more symbolic representations that engage the viewer's powers of detection even as the crimes in the film are investigated. The exploration of the powers and limitations of the image in *M* link looking and seeing to matters of life and death.

3.67 *M* (1931). Reading a visual metaphor.

3.68 *In a Year of Thirteen Moons* (1978). The complexity and drama of the film image mirror the character's struggles.

image becomes inscribed with emotional and social divisions, hostilities, and imbalances **[Figure 3.68]**.

Recognizing the dominance of either the image as presence or the image as text within a single film or part of a film is one way to begin to appreciate and understand it. A romance like *Eat Pray Love* (2010) exudes the presence of location shooting in Italy, India, and Bali, and recognizing how it engages a larger tradition of presence, allows audiences to compare and contrast its exotic locales. A visually dense and complex film about an underground gang of Nazi "werewolves," Lars von Trier's *Zentropa* (1991) asks us to decipher images constructed with special effects and mixed media, but part of its success lies in how it engages the complexities of a tradition of textuality. Film compositions communicate information and tell tales, yet we experience and process—and enjoy—film images most fully by recognizing the values and traditions that underpin them and our expectations of them. The initial hostile reception of *Bonnie and Clyde* in 1967, for instance, turned to admiration several months later. One way of understanding the dynamics of this change is to note that viewers realized that the film's images belong not to a tradition of presence but to a tradition of textuality. At first, many viewers may have seen the film as glamorizing 1930s violence; only later did they recognize the distance of those images as an ironic commentary on 1960s violence. Film, like chance, favors the prepared mind.

CONCEPTS AT WORK

The experience and the art of the cinema are inseparable in cinematography—the moving image selected, framed, lit, tinted, and manipulated through effects. The emergence of cinema at the end of the nineteenth century joined a long-standing impulse to create moving images with the technological capacity to make such images and present them to audiences. Framing (variations in distances and angles), compositions that explore the depth of the images, and camera movements are some of the ways that cinematographers create and explore cinematic worlds. Technical developments in film stock, cameras and lenses, color processes, and eventually digital technologies allowed greater range in cinematic expression. Finally, moving images use all of the aspects specific to the language of film as well as the contexts and traditions in which the medium is embedded to generate meanings enriched by each viewer's experience.

Films tell their stories through moving images, adding dimension to a flat screen and allowing viewers to locate themselves in the narrative, follow its action, decode significance, and experience emotion. As we have detailed in this and the previous chapter, the properties of the film shot are determined by the infinite range of possibilities of mise-en-scène and cinematography and their interaction. In the next chapter, we learn how the juxtaposition of images enriches the experience and meanings of the film image.

Activity

Imagine filming a newsworthy event like a burning building for a fiction film. Imagine shooting this mise-en-scène through as many different cinematographic "lenses" as possible: both literal lenses such as wide-angle and zoom, and through variations in setups, lighting, framing, film stock, camera movement, and use of special effects. As you reflect on your particular cinematographic choices, note what specific film traditions (that is, image as presence, image as text) your "scenes" draw upon and why.

chapter

4

Relating Images
Editing

The longest-running movie in Hindi-language film history, the Shahrukh Khan–starring vehicle *Dilwale Dulhania Le Jayenge* (*The Big Hearted Will Take the Bride*, directed by Aditya Chopra, 1995) combines family comedy, romance, and musical numbers while exploring the changing relationships of Indians living outside India to the values and culture of the subcontinent. In spectacular production numbers, the central couple's predestined romance is emphasized by editing that defies barriers of space and time to unite them in song and dance. As the couple lip-sync to "Tujhe Dekha To" ("When I Saw You") in a flowering meadow, flashbacks to earlier moments depicted in the movie emphasize that the two were meant for each other. A shot of them fishing cuts to a shot of them dancing in formal wear, followed by a match cut—an edit that uses figure placement or gesture to match one shot to the next—in which the couple finishes the dance move but in different costumes. Such editing is typical of song-and-dance numbers in Hindi movies. But in *DDLJ*, as the film is almost universally known, such editing also implies the bridging of the distance between London, where the main characters live, and India, the home country of their families. The immediate connection forged by editing and music anticipates the one that fans develop for this film.

133

As we move through the world, we witness images that are juxtaposed and overlapped: in store windows, on highway billboards, on our desktops, or on television when we channel surf. As we recognize these different sights as part of a series of related images, we experience something like the logic of film **editing**, the process that links different images or *shots* (continuous images between cuts). Yet editing is a departure from the way we normally see the world. In our everyday experience, discrete images are unified by our singular position and consciousness. There are no such limits in editing. And unless we consciously or externally interrupt our vision (such as when we blink), we do not see the world as separate images linked in selected patterns. Editing may emulate ordinary ways of seeing or transcend them. The power and art of film editing lie in the ways in which the hundreds or thousands of discrete images that make up a film can be shaped to make sense or to have an emotional or a visceral impact.

KEY OBJECTIVES	

- Describe the evolution of the art and technologies of editing in their cultural and historical contexts.
- Understand that edited images are based on material cuts or breaks in the film.
- Examine the ways editing constructs different spatial and temporal relationships among images.
- Learn the ways editing establishes film continuity.
- Describe the particular graphic or rhythmic patterns emphasized by editing.
- Discuss the ways editing organizes images as meaningful scenes and sequences.
- Examine how editing strategies engage filmic traditions of continuity or disjuncture.

Many film theorists and professionals consider editing to be the most unique dimension of the film experience. This chapter will explore in depth how film connects separate images to create or reflect key patterns through which viewers see and think about the world.

A Short History of Film Editing

Long before the development of film technology, different images were linked to tell stories. Ancient Assyrian reliefs show the different phases of a lion hunt, while the 230-foot-long Bayeux tapestry chronicles the 1066 Norman Conquest of England in invaluable historical detail. In the twentieth and twenty-first centuries,

comic strips and manga have continued this tradition in graphic art: each panel presents a moment of action in the story **[Figures 4.1a–4.1c]**. Similarly, a story-board sketches out each shot of a film.

Indeed, a long history of cultural practices anticipates the structures of editing. Besides telling stories, juxtaposed images have been used symbolically, sensationally, and educationally. Religious triptychs convey spiritual ideas via three connected

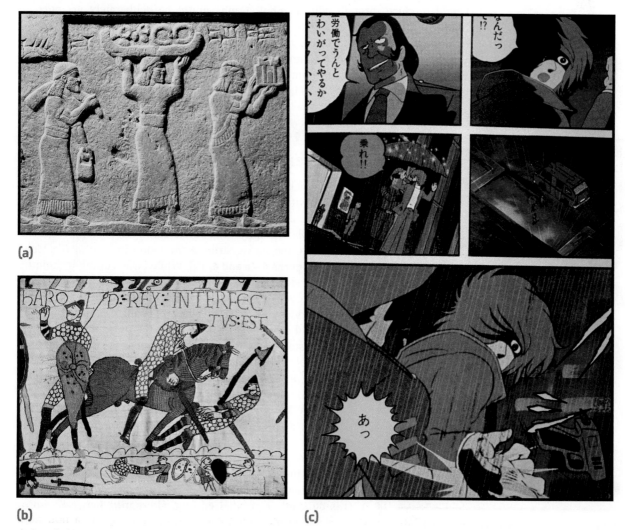

(a)

(b)

(c)

4.1a–4.1c **From ancient Assyrian reliefs (a) and the eleventh-century Bayeux tapestry (b) to comics (c),** cultures have told their stories in successions of images.

4.2 *Fencing Pose,* **Étienne-Jules Marey** (1890). Early photographic experiments in human and animal motion, known as chronophotography, anticipate the cinematic sequencing of images.

images. The **magic lantern**, developed in the seventeenth century, was used by showmen to create illusions of the supernatural. By the late nineteenth century, illustrated lectures using photographic slides were popular. Such practices have influenced film editing's evolution into its modern form.

One of the early mechanical and perceptual breakthroughs in the development of the cinema was Eadweard Muybridge's successful 1877 experiment to break down the movement of a galloping horse by taking a series of photographic images. Printed in sequence, the images suggested motion and the juxtapositions of editing. Such **chronophotography** was produced by Muybridge and by the French scientist Étienne-Jules Marey to study human and animal motion **[Figure 4.2]**.

Still photography found ways to achieve the effects of juxtaposition that film would produce through editing. Photographs might be deliberately arranged to highlight the relationship among the different images. Artists would often combine separate photographs to create particular motifs or visual patterns. In the photomontages of German artist Hannah Höch, produced in the 1920s, different images were juxtaposed into a new composition to suggest conceptual connections and to establish novel visual effects **[Figure 4.3]**.

4.3 *Astronomy and Movement Dada,* **Hannah Höch** (1922). Photomontages emulated the dynamism of contemporary cinema.

1895–1918: Early Cinema and the Emergence of Continuity Editing

Films quickly evolved from showing characters or objects moving within a single image to connecting different images. Magician and early filmmaker Georges Méliès used stop-motion photography and, later, editing to create delightful tricks, like the rocket striking the moon in *Trip to the Moon* (1902) **[Figures 4.4a and 4.4b]**. While basic editing techniques were introduced by other filmmakers, Edwin S. Porter, a prolific employee of Thomas Edison, synthesized these techniques in the service of storytelling in *Life of an American Fireman* (1903) and other early films. One of the most important films in the historical development of cinema, Porter's *The Great Train Robbery* (1903) tells its story in fourteen separate shots, including a famous final shot of a bandit shooting his gun directly into the camera **[Figure 4.5]**. By 1906, the period now known as "early cinema" gave way to cinema dominated by narrative, a transition facilitated by more codified practices of editing.

D. W. Griffith, who began making films in 1908, is a towering figure in the development of what is known as classical editing style. Griffith is closely associated with the use of **crosscutting**, or **parallel editing**, alternating between two or more strands of simultaneous action, a technique that he used in the rescue sequences that conclude dozens of his films. In *The Lonely Villa* (1909), shots of female family members

(a)

(b)

4.4a and 4.4b *Trip to the Moon* (1902). In a famous shock cut, Georges Méliès linked the launch of the rocket to its impact on the face of the moon in his ambitious science fiction film.

isolated in a house alternate with shots of villains trying to break in and with shots of the father rushing to rescue his family. The infamous climax of Griffith's *The Birth of a Nation* (1915) uses crosscutting to promote identification with the white characters the film construes to be "victims" of Reconstruction. Griffith cuts among a white family trapped in an isolated cottage and black soldiers trying to break in, a white woman threatened with rape by a mixed-race politician, and the Ku Klux Klan riding to the rescue of both [**Figures 4.6a–4.6c**]. The controversial merging of technique and ideology exemplified in Griffith's craft is a strong demonstration of the power of editing. After Griffith's *The Birth of a Nation*, feature filmmaking became the norm, and Hollywood's editing practices developed the classical style that remains the basis for many films today.

1919–1929: Soviet Montage

Within a decade after *The Birth of a Nation*, and in the wake of the 1917 Russian Revolution, Soviet filmmaker Sergei Eisenstein's first film, *Strike* (1924), developed the craft of editing in a different although equally dramatic fashion. Eisenstein's films and writings center on the concept of **montage** (the French word for editing), a style developed by the Soviets that emphasized the breaks and contrasts between images joined by a cut. To depict the mass shooting of workers in *Strike*, Eisenstein interspersed, or **intercut**, long shots of gunfire and of the fleeing and falling crowd with gruesome close-ups of a bull being butchered in a slaughterhouse [**Figures 4.7a and 4.7b**]. The effect of his montage is visceral and provocative.

Eisenstein and filmmakers Lev Kuleshov, Vsevolod Pudovkin, and Dziga Vertov advanced montage as the key component of modernist, politically engaged filmmaking in the Soviet Union of the 1920s. One of the most fascinating self-reflexive

4.5 *The Great Train Robbery* (1903). Edwin S. Porter is credited with advancing the narrative language of editing in this and other early films. The film's last cut is used to enhance the shock effect of the final image rather than to complete the narrative.

(a)

(b)

(c)

4.6a–4.6c *The Birth of a Nation* (1915). In this sequence of images, Griffith's white supremacist views are supported by the use of parallel editing, which encourages the viewer to root for the Ku Klux Klan to arrive in time.

sequences in film history is the editing sequence in Vertov's *Man with a Movie Camera* (1929), which features the film's own editor, Elizaveta Svilova, cutting film that the cameraman has been shown gathering. Images shown on the strips of film seem to freeze before our eyes, only to be reanimated to startling effect. Svilova was part of the "Kinoki" (cinema-eye) documentary filmmaking group, which included her husband, director Dziga Vertov, and the latter's brother (and the film's cameraman) Mikhail Kaufman. (A fascinating aspect of the social history of editing is its relative openness to the participation of women, even in Hollywood.) Other avant-garde movements in the 1920s and thereafter continued to explore the more abstract and dynamic properties of editing employed by the Soviets.

(a)

(b)

4.7a and 4.7b *Strike* (1924). The workers' massacre compared to the slaughter of a bull through montage.

1930–1959: The Studio Era

With the coming of sound and the full development of the Hollywood studio system, the storytelling style known as **continuity editing** was refined, while the new demand of simultaneously editing sound and image tracks was met. Indeed, the complexity of editing with a soundtrack initially resulted in fewer camera movements and fewer cuts, but by the early 1930s editors succeeded in establishing an integrated editing style that extended the continuity system, achieving an expansive sense of realism.

Beginning in the 1940s, cinematic realism became established as one of the primary aesthetic principles in film editing. The influence of Italian neorealism, which used fewer cuts to capture the integrity of stories of ordinary people and actual locations, was evident in other new wave cinemas and even in Hollywood. For example, Nicholas Ray's *In a Lonely Place* (1950) developed an editing style that emphasized imagistic depth and longer takes by cutting less frequently between images **[Figure 4.8]**. The continuity editing style would remain dominant until the decline at the end of the 1950s of the studio system, whose stable personnel, business models, and genre forms lent consistency to its products and techniques.

1960–1989: Modern Disjunctive Editing

Political and artistic changes during this period affected almost every dimension of film form, and editing was no exception. Both in the United States and abroad, alternative editing styles emerged and aimed to fracture classical editing's illusion of realism. Anticipated to some extent by the Soviet montage movement of the 1920s, these new styles reflected the temporal disjunctions, or disconnections, of the modern world. Editing visibly disrupted continuity by creating ruptures in the story, radically condensing or expanding time, or confusing the relationships among past, present, and future. The French New Wave of Jean-Luc Godard and Alain Resnais produced some of the first and most dramatic examples of disjunctive editing. Godard's *Breathless* (1960) used **jump cuts**, edits that intentionally create gaps in the action to defy the norms of continuity **[Figure 4.9]**. In the 1960s and 1970s, American filmmakers like Arthur Penn and Francis Ford Coppola incorporated such disjunctive styles within classical genres. In the 1980s, the fast-paced editing style used in commercials and music videos began to appear in mainstream films. Two popular and successful films, both made by former directors of television commercials, are indicative of this period: Adrian Lyne's *Flashdance* (1983), about a Pittsburgh woman who doubles as a welder

4.8   *In a Lonely Place* (1950). Postwar cinema tended to explore the depth of images, cutting less frequently between them to achieve a heightened realism.

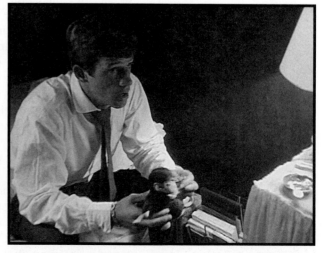

4.9   *Breathless* (1960). The fragmentations created by jump cuts become the visual vehicle for conveying the distractions and disjunctions in a petty criminal's life.

4.10 *Russian Ark* (2002). Wandering through the Hermitage Museum in St. Petersburg, and seeming to pass through historical eras, the digital camera is the vehicle for this film's meditation on art, politics, and Russian history as a single shot.

and exotic dancer, and Tony Scott's *Top Gun* (1986), about fighter pilots competing in flight school. Both combine an upbeat pop soundtrack with flashy, rapid editing to suggest the seductive energy of their protagonists' worlds.

1990s–Present: Editing in the Digital Age

One of the most significant changes to film editing is the emergence of nonlinear digital editing in the late twentieth century. Whereas for decades editors cut actual film footage by hand on a Moviola or flatbed editing table, editors today use computer-based nonlinear digital editing systems. In nonlinear editing, film footage is stored as digital information on high-capacity computer hard drives. Individual takes can be organized easily and accessed instantaneously, sound editing options can be simultaneously combined with picture editing, and such optical effects as dissolves and fades can be immediately visualized on the computer rather than added much later in the printing process. Because of the flexibility and efficiency of the new technology, the majority of feature films are now edited with nonlinear computer-based systems regardless of whether they are shot on 35mm film or digital video. Although one effect of the ease and affordability of digital editing seems to be the more rapid pace of films, digital filmmaking can also embrace the opposite aesthetic effect. On film, the length of a single take was limited by how much stock the camera could hold; on video, the duration of a shot is virtually limitless. Filmmaker Aleksandr Sokurov's *Russian Ark* (2002) is a virtuoso feature-length film with no cuts at all **[Figure 4.10]**.

The Elements of Editing

As we have established, film editing is the process through which different images or shots are linked. In terms of a movie's finished version, a shot is a continuous image, regardless of the camera movement or changes in focus it may record. Editing can produce meaning by combining shots in an infinite number of ways. One shot is selected and joined to other shots by the editor to guide viewers' perceptions. For example, the opening sequence of *Crooklyn* (1994) depicts the Brooklyn block where the film is set by editing together a high-angle moving crane shot that provides an overview of the neighborhood and its inhabitants and a variety of shots of people and their activities **[Figures 4.11a–4.11c]**.

If a shot presents mise-en-scène from a single perspective, film editing conveys multiple perspectives by linking shots in various relationships. Some of these relationships mimic the way an individual looks at the world (for example, a shot of someone looking off in the distance linked to an extreme long shot of an airplane in the sky), but often these relationships exceed everyday perception (for example, the shot of birds flying over Bodega Bay from above in *The Birds* [1963]). Edited images may leap from one location to another or one time to another and may show different perspectives on the same event. Editing is one of the most significant developments in the syntax of cinema because it allows for a departure from both the limited perspective and the continuous duration of a shot.

The Cut and Other Transitions

The earliest films consisted of a single shot, which could run only as long as the reel of film in the camera lasted. In his early trick films, pioneer Georges Méliès manipulated this limitation by stopping the camera, rearranging the mise-en-scène, and resuming filming to make objects and people seem to disappear. It was a short step to achieving such juxtapositions by physically cutting the film. In Méliès's 1903 film *Living Playing Cards*, a magician, played by Méliès himself, seems to make his props come alive [**Figures 4.12a and 4.12b**].

Even when they are intended to seem like magic, transitions between film shots, along with the technical labor of editing, are often obscured. Rarely can viewers describe or enumerate the edits that make a particular film sequence memorable. Learning to watch for this basic element of film language is a rewarding way to experience the art of film as a medium.

The foundation for film editing is the **cut**—that is, the break in the image that marks the physical connection between two shots from two different pieces of film. A single shot can depict a woman looking at a ship at sea by showing a close-up of her face and then panning to the right, following her glance to reveal the distant ship she is watching. A cut, on the other hand, renders this action in two shots, with the first showing the woman's face and the second showing the ship. While the facts of the situation remain the same, the single-shot pan and the cut joining two shots create different experiences of the scenario. The first might emphasize the distance that separates the woman from the object of her vision. The second might create a sense of immediacy and intimacy that transcends the distance. In a key scene from *The Best Years of Our Lives* (1946), we first see several characters occupying different spaces of the same shot [**Figure 4.13a**]. After the character on the right shifts his attention to the character in the background, we are presented with a cut isolating them [**Figures 4.13b and 4.13c**]. As these examples illustrate, the use of a cut usually follows a particular logic, in this case emphasizing the significance of the character's gaze. The less

(a)

(b)

(c)

4.11a–4.11c *Crooklyn* (1994). The credits sequence of Spike Lee's film juxtaposes a moving crane shot of a Brooklyn block with a series of short takes of daily activities to describe the neighborhood where the film is set.

(a)

(b)

4.12a and 4.12b   *Living Playing Cards* (1903). Pioneer George Méliès anticipated later editing techniques with magical transformations.

(a)

(b)

(c)

frequently used **shock cut** juxtaposes two images whose dramatic difference creates a jarring visual effect, such as the cut to a shot of a hand pierced by a nail in the opening montage of *Persona* (1966). Later in this chapter we will investigate additional ways that editing may create logical or shocking links among different images.

Edits can be embellished in ways that guide our experience and understanding of the transition. For example, **fade-outs** gradually darken and make one image disappear, while **fade-ins** do the opposite. Alfred Hitchcock fades to black to mark the passing of time throughout *Rear Window* (1954). A **dissolve** (sometimes called a *lap dissolve* because two images overlap in the printing process) briefly superimposes one shot

4.13a–4.13c   *The Best Years of Our Lives* (1946). Director William Wyler uses composition in depth and editing to bring out developing tensions in the friendship of three returning veterans. In the first shot, our attention is drawn to the figures in the foreground. When Al Stephenson turns to watch Fred make a difficult phone call in the background of the shot, the film cuts to a second shot that emphasizes the relationship between these two figures.

4.14   *The Scarlet Empress* (1934). Extended dissolves were a favorite device of director Josef von Sternberg. The layering of a conversation and the approach of a carriage appear almost as an abstract pattern.

4.15   *Broken Blossoms* (1919). The iris was often used in films by D. W. Griffith to highlight objects or faces. Here it focuses our attention and emphasizes the vulnerability of Lillian Gish's character.

over the next, which takes its place: one image fades out as another image fades in [**Figure 4.14**]. Usually these devices indicate a more definite spatial or temporal break than do straight cuts, and they often mark pauses between narrative sequences or larger segments of a film. A dissolve can take us from one part of town to another, while a fade-out, a more visible break, can indicate that the action is resuming the next day.

A number of other transitions between shots or scenes are most often found in older films, especially silent films. The **iris** masks the corners of the frame in a black, usually circular, form. An *iris-out* gradually obscures the image as if a camera shutter were closing; an *iris-in* gradually expands to reveal the entire image [**Figure 4.15**]. **Wipes** join two images by moving a vertical, horizontal, or sometimes diagonal line across one image to replace it with a second image that follows the line across the frame. Modern films, from *Star Wars* (1977) to the independent feature *Desert Hearts* (1985), have used wipes to reference an obsolete film style [**Figure 4.16**]. These transitional devices are traditionally known as **optical effects** because before digital editing they were created with a device called an **optical printer** that allowed for strips of film to be re-photographed and combined.

Although editing can generate an infinite number of combinations of images, as we will see, rules have developed within the Hollywood storytelling tradition to limit those possibilities. Other film traditions, most notably those of avant-garde and experimental cinema (see Chapter 8), can be characterized by their degree of interest in exploiting the range of editing possibilities as a primary formal property of film.

When watching movies, we manage to make sense of a series of discontinuous, linked images, understanding them according to conventional ways of interpreting space, time, story, and image patterns. We understand the action sequences

VIEWING CUE

Do a shot-by-shot breakdown of one scene from a film screened for class. What is the motivation behind each cut? What overall effect do these cuts have on the scene and the film?

4.16   *Desert Hearts* (1985). In a film set in the 1950s, a wipe creates a nostalgic reference to earlier editing techniques, but it may also suggest a certain kind of transience in the world of the characters.

▶ **VIEWING CUE**

Make a list of transitional devices besides cuts that are used in a film you've just watched for class. What spatial, temporal, or conceptual relationship is being set up between scenes joined by a fade, dissolve, iris, or wipe? ⏸

in *Fast & Furious* (2009) despite the improbable feats performed by the characters. Likewise, we make connections among the three separate narratives from three separate periods in *The Hours* (2002). As noted earlier, most of these patterns were established early in the course of film history; as we shall see in Chapter 6, editing patterns anticipate and form the foundation for numerous structural patterns in narrative organizations. The next three sections will explore the spatial and temporal relationships established by editing and will introduce the rules of the Hollywood continuity editing system, a dominant method of editing narrative films. Subsequent discussion will examine patterns of editing images based on graphic, movement, and rhythmic connections in order to show how different techniques provide very different experiences.

Continuity Style

In both narrative and non-narrative films, editing is a crucial strategy for ordering space and time. Two or more images can be linked to imply spatial and temporal relations to the viewer. **Verisimilitude** (literally, "the quality of having the appearance of truth") in fictional representations allows readers or viewers to accept as plausible a constructed world, its events, its characters, and their actions. In cinematic storytelling, clear, consistent spatial and temporal patterns greatly enhance verisimilitude, and, along with conventions of dialogue, mise-en-scène, cinematography, and sound, form part of Hollywood's **continuity style**. In the commercial U.S. film industry, spatial and temporal continuity are constructed through conventions of editing. Because its constructions of space and time are so codified and widely used, we will devote special consideration to continuity.

Continuity editing is a system that uses cuts and other transitions to establish verisimilitude and to tell stories efficiently, requiring minimal mental effort on the part of viewers. The basic principle of continuity editing is that each shot has a continuous relationship to the next shot. Two particular strategies constitute the heart of this style:

■ constructing an imaginary 180-degree space in which the action will develop
■ approximating the experience of real time by following human actions

Continuity editing has developed and deployed these patterns so consistently that it has become the dominant method of treating dramatic material, with its own set of rules that narrative filmmakers learn early. Minimizing the perception of breaks between shots, it is often called **invisible editing**.

Spatial patterns are frequently introduced through the use of an **establishing shot**, generally an initial long shot that establishes the setting and orients the viewer in space to a clear view of the action. A scene in a western, for example, might begin with an extreme long shot of wide-open space and then cut in to a shot that shows a stagecoach or saloon, followed by other, tighter shots introducing the characters and action.

The standard practice for filming a conversation presents a relatively close shot of both characters (also known as a **two-shot**) in a recognizable spatial orientation and context and then displays the character who is speaking in the next shot before cutting again to show the other character (often using an over-the-shoulder shot). The editing may proceed back and forth, with periodic returns to the initial view. Such **reestablishing shots** restore a seemingly "objective" view, making the action perfectly clear to the viewers. Early in Howard Hawks's *The Big Sleep* (1946), when detective Philip Marlowe (played by Humphrey Bogart) is hired by General Sternwood, the scene opens with an establishing shot, and their conversation follows this pattern **[Figures 4.17a–4.17h]**. Although many shots are edited together in the course of the conversation, the transitions remain largely invisible because the angle from which each character is filmed remains consistent and the dialogue continues over the cuts. Such editing practices are ubiquitous; we have learned to expect the coordination of conversations with medium close-ups of characters speaking and listening,

4.17a–4.17h *The Big Sleep* (1946). The simple interview, which provides a great deal of plot information, is broken down by many imperceptible cuts. After an initial establishing shot, alternating shots of the two characters in conversation cut in closer and closer and eventually focus our attention on the protagonist's face. Finally, the space is reestablished at the end of the interview.

4.18   *Fury* (1936). Lang dissolves from one shot of women chatting to another of chickens clucking to illustrate the concept of gossip in a rare example of a nondiegetic insert in a classical film.

just as we expect that these figures will be situated in a realistic space.

Another device that is used in continuity editing is the **insert**, a brief shot, often a close-up, such as a shot of a hand slipping something into a pocket or a smile another character does not see. The use of inserts helps overcome viewers' spatial separation from the action, pointing out details significant to the plot or underscoring verisimilitude—for example, showing us a ringing telephone. An insert that breaks continuity is referred to as a **nondiegetic insert**, such as the display of printed text in a Jean-Luc Godard film. More specifically, a nondiegetic insert introduces an object or a view from outside the film's world or makes a comparison that transcends the characters' perspectives, as in a famous nondiegetic insert of clucking chickens in Fritz Lang's *Fury* (1936) **[Figure 4.18]**.

Exceptions tend to prove the rules of continuity editing. In *Natural Born Killers* (1994), extraneous and disorienting cuts interrupt interactions among characters. The film's opening sequence dispenses with an establishing shot: a shot of a pot of coffee introduces the location and is followed by several exterior shots of the diner. The waitress's response to Mickey's order is repeated, and the second shot is in black and white **[Figures 4.19a and 4.19b]**. This disorienting introduction conveys a skewed perception of the diner's space, foreshadowing the eruption of violence later in the scene.

In continuity editing, after the establishing shot provides the initial view of a scene, subsequent shots typically follow the logic of spatial continuity. If a character appears at the left of the screen looking toward the right in the establishing shot, it is likely that he or she will be shown looking in the same direction in the medium shot that follows. Movements that carry across cuts will also adhere to a consistent screen direction. A character exiting the right of a frame will probably enter a new space from the left. Similarly, a chase sequence covering great distances is likely to provide spatial cues. The breakdown of a scene will proceed as if an imaginary line that the camera cannot cross traverses the action—a key characteristic of continuity editing.

(a)

(b)

4.19a and 4.19b   *Natural Born Killers* (1994). This scene uses overlapping editing, two shots in which the waitress repeats the same line. Violating continuity through this device and the use of different film stocks, the editing establishes a threatening mood.

Diagram A

Axis of
Action

Diagram B

Fig. 4.17f

Fig. 4.17d

Fig. 4.17b

Fig. 4.17g

Fig. 4.17e

Fig. 4.17c

4.20   **Diagram A** illustrates the 180-degree rule by showing the space of the conversation scene from *The Big Sleep* bisected by an imaginary line called the axis of action. All shots of the scene were taken from the white portion of the diagram. If the camera were to cross over to the shaded portion, the position of the characters onscreen would be reversed. **Diagram B** illustrates the editing of the conversation with references to Figures 4.17a–4.17h on page 145. Each character is depicted in tighter framings from a consistent camera angle.

180-Degree Rule

The **180-degree rule** is the primary rule of continuity editing and one that many films and television shows consider sacrosanct. The diagrams above **[Figure 4.20]** illustrate the 180-degree rule. In the scene from *The Big Sleep* discussed above, Marlowe and the general are consistently filmed as if the room is bisected by an imaginary line known as the **axis of action**. All of the shots illustrated by the still images from *The Big Sleep* in Figures 4.17a–4.17h were taken from one side of this axis. In general, any shot taken from the same side of the axis of action will ensure that the relative positions of people and other elements of mise-en-scène, as well as the directions of gazes and movements, will remain consistent. If the camera were to cross into the 180-degree field on the other side of the line (represented in Figure 4.20, Diagram A, by the shaded area), the characters' onscreen positions would be reversed. During the unfolding of a scene, however, a new axis of action may be established by figure or camera movement. Some directors do break the 180-degree rule and cross the line, either because they want to signify chaotic action or because conventional spatial continuity is not their primary aim.

30-Degree Rule

Although it is used less frequently, the **30-degree** rule illustrates the extent to which continuity editing attempts to preserve spatial unity. This rule specifies

(a)

(b)

4.21a and 4.21b *Rose Hobart* (1936). Joseph Cornell re-edited and re-scored the 1931 Hollywood action film *East of Borneo* to create this film (named after its star). The abrupt changes in mise-en-scène, mismatched eyelines, and other violations wreak havoc with continuity.

that one shot must be followed by another shot taken from a position greater than 30 degrees from that of the first. The rule aims to emphasize the motivation for the cut by giving a substantially different view of the action. A transition between two shots less than 30 degrees apart is perceived as unnecessary largely because the cut itself is likely to be visible. The editing is intentionally visible in Joseph Cornell's experimental film *Rose Hobart* (1936), a re-editing of the Hollywood film *East of Borneo* (1931); the original film's continuity editing principles are broken in Cornell's reassemblage, defying spatial and temporal logic **[Figures 4.21a and 4.21b]**.

Shot/Reverse Shot

One of the most common spatial practices within continuity editing, and a regular application of the 180-degree rule, is the **shot/reverse shot** (sometimes called *shot/countershot*) pattern. Often used during conversations, such as in the example from *The Big Sleep*, this pattern begins with a shot of one character taken from an angle at one end of the axis of action, continues with a shot of the second character from the "reverse" angle at the other end of the axis, and proceeds back and forth.

A scene from *Clueless* (1995) in which the protagonist, Cher, and her friends, Dionne and Tai, converse in a coffee-shop booth provides another example of a shot/reverse-shot sequence. The scene begins with a tracking establishing shot that depicts the overall environment and shows who is sitting where **[Figure 4.22a]**. Then the scene cuts back and forth across the booth, usually to depict the character who is speaking **[Figure 4.22b]**. Cher has the majority of the scene's shots, indicating that she is the focal point of our identification **[Figure 4.22c]**. Sometimes Dionne and Tai, sitting opposite, are depicted in a two-shot; occasionally these secondary characters receive individual shots **[Figure 4.22d]**.

Eyeline Match

Frequently the shots and reverse shots used in conversation scenes are taken over the shoulder of the participants, which helps remind viewers of their shared physical space. In general, continuity editing often implies spatial contiguity; in other words, it gives the impression that consecutively depicted spaces are adjacent ones. If a character looks offscreen toward the left, the next shot will likely show the

▶ **VIEWING CUE**
Does the film you watched most recently in class follow continuity patterns, such as the 180-degree rule? Can you identify other ways that spatial continuity is maintained?

4.22a–4.22d *Clueless* (1995). This scene follows the 180-degree rule and favors the film's heroine, Cher (played by Alicia Silverstone), as it alternates between characters.

character or object that the character is looking at in a screen position that matches the gaze. This is referred to as an **eyeline match [Figures 4.23a and 4.23b]**. Shot/reverse-shot sequences of characters in conversation often use eyeline matches. Eyelines give the illusion of continuous offscreen space into which characters could move beyond the left and right edges of the frame.

4.23a *The Silence of the Lambs* (1991). An eyeline match establishes the position of Clarice (played by Jodie Foster) in relation to Hannibal Lecter (Anthony Hopkins) in his cell.

4.23b *The Silence of the Lambs* (1991). The reverse shot.

Point-of-View Shots

Many of Alfred Hitchcock's most suspenseful scenes are edited to highlight the drama of looking. Often a character is shown looking, and the next shot shows the character's optical point of view, as if the camera (and hence the viewer) were seeing with the eyes of the character. Such point-of-view shots are often followed by a third shot in which the character is again shown looking, which reclaims the previous shot as his or her literal perspective. In a tense scene from *The Birds* (1963) in which the heroine, Melanie, sits on a bench outside a school as threatening crows gather on the playground behind her, Hitchcock uses both eyeline matches and point-of-view sequences. A bird flying high overhead catches her attention [**Figure 4.24a**]. When she turns her head to follow its flight, the shots are matched by her eyeline [**Figure 4.24b**]. Next comes a point-of-view sequence in which Melanie—and the viewer who shares her perspective—is horrified by the sinister sight of congregating birds [**Figures 4.24c and 4.24d**]. The editing of this scene serves both to construct a realistic space and to increase our identification with Melanie by focusing solely on the act of looking.

Elsewhere in the film, the point of view of Melanie's romantic interest, Mitch, is conveyed by partially masking the frame as if we were looking along with him through his binoculars. Similarly, when we share the point of view of a character waking from a knock on the head, we may see a blurry image. In contrast, over-the-shoulder shots used in a shot/reverse-shot sequence are not point-of-view shots because they do not show exactly what the characters see. However, if, as the conversation intensifies, the scene proceeds in tighter framings of characters' faces as if from the direct perspectives of the participants, then the film has introduced point-of-view shots.

4.24a   *The Birds* (1963). A low-angle shot of a flying bird . . .

4.24b   *The Birds* (1963) . . . is matched to Melanie's eyeline.

4.24c   *The Birds* (1963). Following its flight, Melanie registers shock at what she sees.

4.24d   *The Birds* (1963). A point-of-view shot of the gathering birds.

These components of the continuity system—shot/reverse-shot patterns, eyeline matches, and point-of-view shots—construct space in order to highlight human subjectivity. An emphasis on human perspective is also visible in the **reaction shot**, which depicts a character's response to something that viewers have just been shown **[Figure 4.25]**. The cut back to the character "claims" the view of the previous shot as subjective. Continuity editing constructs spatial relationships to create a plausible and human-centered world onscreen.

4.25 *The Way We Were* (1973). Barbra Streisand's face registers her character's emotion in this reaction shot, which records her response after seeing her former lover.

Although continuity editing strives for an overall effect of coherent space, films can reject continuity and use editing to construct less predictable spatial relations. For example, in Michelangelo Antonioni's film *L'Avventura* (1960), cuts join spaces that are not necessarily contiguous. The landscapes the characters move through express their psychological state of alienation, and a realistic use of space is rejected.

Editing and Temporality

Editing is one of the chief ways that temporality is manipulated in the time-based medium of cinema. A two-hour film may, for instance, condense centuries in a story. Through the power to manipulate **chronology**—the order according to which shots or scenes convey the temporal sequence of the story's events—editing organizes narrative time. Sequences of shots or scenes may describe the linear movement of time forward as one event follows another in temporal order. Often human activity directs the selection and ordering of events in this way.

Flashbacks and Flashforwards

Editing may also create nonlinear patterns in which events are juxtaposed out of their temporal order. Within the continuity system, such nonlinear constructions are introduced with strict cues about narrative motivation. A **flashback** follows one or more images of the present with one or more of the past; it may be introduced with a dissolve conveying the character's memory or with a voiceover in which the character narrates the past. In one sense, *Citizen Kane* (1941) uses a linear structure, organizing itself around a series of interviews and investigations conducted by a reporter looking for an angle on a great man's death. However, the story of Kane's life is provided in a series of lengthy flashbacks that make the film's chronology complex. Certain events are narrated more than once, a manipulation of **narrative frequency**. Like many film noirs in which the instability of appearances is important, *Sunset Boulevard* (1950) uses flashbacks motivated by voiceover narration. The film presents a particularly interesting case: continuity is maintained even though the protagonist-narrator is shown to be dead in the first sequence **[Figure 4.26]**.

4.26 *Sunset Boulevard* (1950). The entire story of *Sunset Boulevard* unfolds in flashback, introduced by the narrator's voiceover. The twist is that we discover in the first few moments of the film that the narrator is dead.

4.27 ***Don't Look Now*** (1973). Images of a small figure in red prove to be flashforwards to a horrifying encounter with the past.

(a)

(b)

4.28a and 4.28b ***The Limey*** (1999). Different shots of the protagonist (Terence Stamp) appear in the film without a clear sense of when they occurred.

The less common **flashforward** connects an image of the present with one or more future images. Flashforwards present a serious challenge to realistic motivation: how can the characters we are asked to identify with "see" the future? The technique is thus usually reserved for works that intentionally challenge our perceptions. In the countercultural film *Easy Rider* (1969), for instance, the protagonist has a brief flashforward vision of an aerial image of the accident that will be his demise at the end of the film. In Nicolas Roeg's *Don't Look Now* (1973), a couple is tormented by the recent death of their daughter, and haunting images of a small figure in a red rain slicker prove to be flashforwards to a revelatory encounter **[Figure 4.27]**. In *Memento* (2000), the chronology of scenes is completely reversed, but the maintenance of continuity within each scene allows us to follow the film.

Descriptive and Temporally Ambiguous Sequences

Certain edited sequences cannot be located precisely in time. The purpose of such a sequence is often descriptive, such as a series of shots identifying the setting of a film. In *An American in Paris* (1951), as one character describes the heroine to another, we see a series of shots depicting her different qualities (with different outfits to match). These little vignettes are descriptive; they do not follow a linear or other temporal sequence.

Art films often manipulate temporality through editing, defying realism in favor of psychological constructions of time. Writer Marguerite Duras and director Alain Resnais make time the subject of their film *Hiroshima Mon Amour* (1959), which constantly relates the present-day story, set in Japan, to a character's past. An image of her lover's hand sparks the female protagonist's memory of being a teenager in France during World War II, and the flashback begins with a matching image of another hand. But temporality is such an important dimension of film narration that even more traditional narratives explore the relationship between the order of events onscreen and those of the story. Steven Soderbergh's *The Limey* (1999) ingeniously inserts shots of the activities of the protagonist, played by Terence Stamp, into the narrative but out of sequence, keeping us guessing about temporal relations [Figures 4.28a and 4.28b].

Duration and Pace

Duration denotes the length of shots and can indicate the amount of time that passes in the story. Mike Figgis's *Timecode* (2001) is an experiment in filmic duration. In this film, the story time is identical to the screen time, whereas in most narrative films the story time is radically condensed and temporal relations are constructed through editing and complexly related to the film's story. Temporal continuity is maintained by cutting that constructs a sequence of cause-and-effect events.

Editing is one of the most useful techniques for manipulating narrative time. Although actions may seem to flow in a continuous fashion, editing allows for significant temporal abridgement, or **ellipsis**. Cutting strategies both within scenes and from scene to scene attempt to cover such ellipses. Grabbing a coat, exiting the front door, and turning the key in the ignition might serve to indicate a journey from one locale to the next. As we have seen, transitional devices such as dissolves and fades also manipulate the duration of narration. Without the acceptance of such conventions, time would be experienced in a disorienting fashion.

A specific continuity editing device used to condense time is the **cutaway**: the film interrupts an action to "cut away" to another image or action—for example, a man trapped inside a burning building—before returning to the first shot or scene at a point further along in time. We are so accustomed to such handling of the duration of depicted events that a scene in real time, such as the central character's taking a bath in *Jeanne Dielman, 83 quai du Commerce, 1080 Bruxelles* (1975), seems unnaturally long [Figure 4.29]. Less frequent than the condensation of time, the extension of time through **overlapping editing** occurs with the repetition of an action in several cuts. In *Battleship Potemkin* (1925), a sailor, frustrated with the conditions aboard ship, is shown repeatedly smashing a plate he is washing. The onscreen passage of time in this scene is longer than that of the action. Overlapping editing is a violation in a continuity system, and while it can be used for emphasis or for foreshadowing, it often appears strange or gimmicky.

The duration of individual shots helps determine the **pace** of a film's editing. What defines relative shot length and hence the experience of pacing can be personally subjective and culturally relative. The quick pacing characteristic of action sequences has become more prevalent in contemporary cinema. One obvious example of controlling pace is the use of **long takes**, or shots of relatively long duration; the image is sustained for what can seem an inordinate amount of time. In Claude Lanzmann's nearly ten-hour-long documentary about the Holocaust, *Shoah* (1985), the camera films an interview subject speaking and then holds on the subject while an onscreen translator conveys his or her words to Lanzmann, who is also present on camera. The long take, often filmed in deep focus with a wide-angle lens, became a significant aesthetic tool in William Wyler's *The Best Years of Our Lives* (1946). For film theorist André *text continued on page 155* ▶

4.29 *Jeanne Dielman, 83 quai du Commerce, 1080 Bruxelles* (1975). This long take records the protagonist's bath in real time; the film's pacing emulates the everyday routine of the housewife.

text continued on page 155 ▶

4.30a

4.30b

4.30c

4.30d

4.30e

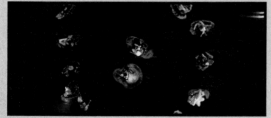

4.30f

Editing and Rhythm in *Moulin Rouge!* (2001)

Editing gives a film its rhythm, and musical sequences often emphasize this dimension of editing over its ability to convey spatio-temporal continuity. In the 1980s, music videos began to influence feature-film style, and in the 1990s the ease of digital editing facilitated a trend toward faster pacing. Today shot lengths average less than half those of studio-era Hollywood films. The frenetic editing of Baz Luhrmann's *Moulin Rouge!* (2001) contrasts markedly with the long takes used to highlight dance performances in *An American in Paris* (1951), which also featured a musical number inspired by Toulouse-Lautrec (he becomes a character in *Moulin Rouge!*).

Split-second shots of can-can dancers lip-synching the disco song "Lady Marmalade" **[Figure 4.30a]** bewilder viewers as much as they do the naive hero Christian on his first visit to the notorious nightclub, the Moulin Rouge **[Figure 4.30b]**. Incongruously, Nirvana's "Smells Like Teen Spirit" is introduced to the medley as the film cuts to the exterior of the club **[Figure 4.30c]** before a special effects shot rapidly returns us to a montage of a tumult of bodies **[Figure 4.30d]** dancing to the "Can Can Rap" of Zidler, the master of ceremonies. Cutting to the exterior again to highlight Zidler's direct solicitation of the audience **[Figure 4.30e]**, the film follows his superhuman dive back into the fray with jump cuts showing him commanding different stages. Abruptly, Zidler signals for silence, and after a brief pause, the music and dance (and editing) resume at an even more accelerated pace **[Figure 4.30f]**. The rhythmic nature of the nineteenth-century music hall dance form and a postmodern pastiche of musical styles are echoed in and whipped into a frenzy by editor Jill Bilcock's cutting of a three-minute musical sequence with close to two hundred individual shots.

Bazin, an advocate of Wyler's aesthetic and the use of the **sequence shot**, in which an entire scene plays out in one take, this type of filmmaking more closely approximates human perception and is thus more realistic than montage. Because of the preponderance of long takes, such films rely more heavily on mise-en-scène, including acting, and camera movement than on editing to focus viewers' attention. Yet the extended duration of shots fundamentally affects a film's rhythm and pace. Most films use shot duration to follow a rhythm that relates to the particular aims of the film. In *Flowers of Shanghai* (1998) by Taiwanese filmmaker Hou Hsiao-hsien, long takes evoke the city's past and vanished way of life. In contrast, the infamous shower murder sequence from *Psycho* (1960) uses seventy camera setups for forty-five seconds of footage, with the many cuts launching a parallel attack on viewers' senses.

As we have seen, continuity editing strives for a realistic space and time that approximate recognized perspectives, such as the crowded movement of a city street. Some narrative films aim to construct psychological space and time, creating such emotional and imaginative perspectives as the anxiety and suspense associated with horror films. In some films, the two may overlap: in *The Crowd* (1928), for example, images of New York City convey a specific setting as well as the hero's psychological impression of an overwhelming, disorienting sensory experience.

▶ **VIEWING CUE**

What is the temporal organization of the film you've just viewed for class? Does the film follow a strict chronology? How does the editing abridge or expand time? ❚❚

Graphic, Movement, and Rhythmic Editing

Earlier in this chapter, we introduced the term "montage" in relation to Soviet filmmaking of the 1920s. In the Hollywood tradition, montage is usually reserved to denote thematically linked sequences and sequences that show the passage of time by using quick sets of cuts or other devices, such as dissolves, wipes, and superimpositions. In studio-era Hollywood, Slavko Vorkapich specialized in creating such sequences, including the memorable earthquake in *San Francisco* (1936) **[Figures 4.31a–4.31c]**. In this specialized sense and in its use simply as a synonym for "editing" (Alfred Hitchcock, for example, often discussed it in this way), montage emphasizes the creative power of editing—especially the potential to build up a sequence and

(a)

(b)

(c)

4.31a–4.31c *San Francisco* (1936). Although continuity editing was the norm in studio-era Hollywood, montage sequences were created for special purposes such as this spectacular earthquake scene.

4.32　*Ivan the Terrible, Part Two* (1946). Strong graphic components of Sergei Eisenstein's image create forceful impressions in juxtaposition.

augment meaning, rather than simply to remove the extraneous, as the term "cutting" implies.

Editing may link images according to more abstract similarities and differences that make creative use of space and time. Here we distinguish among three such patterns in editing: *graphic editing, movement editing,* and *rhythmic editing.* Often these patterns work together to support or complicate the action being shown.

Graphic Editing

Linking or defining a series of shots in **graphic editing** are such formal patterns as shapes, masses, colors, lines, and lighting patterns within images. Graphic editing may be best envisioned in abstract forms: one pattern of images may develop according to diminishing sizes, beginning with large shapes and proceeding through increasingly smaller shapes; another pattern may alternate the graphics of lighting, switching between brightly lit shots and dark, shadowy shots; yet another pattern might make use of lines within the frame by assembling different shots whose horizontal and vertical lines create specific visual effects. Many experimental films highlight just this level of abstraction in the editing. A sequence of *Ballet mécanique* (see Chapter 9) cuts rapidly between circles and triangles. Among Stan Brakhage's hundreds of experimental films, *Dog Star Man* (1964) uses graphic editing and superimposition extensively. Frequently, narrative films employ graphic editing as well. Graphic elements of the mise-en-scène are incorporated in Sergei Eisenstein's editing design for *Ivan the Terrible, Part One* (1945) and *Ivan the Terrible, Part Two* (1946) **[Figure 4.32]**. Coherence in shape and scale often serves a specific narrative purpose, as in the continuity editing device called a **graphic match**, in which a dominant shape or line in one shot provides a visual transition to a similar shape or line in the next shot. One of the most famous examples of a graphic match is from Stanley Kubrick's *2001: A Space Odyssey* (1968) **[Figures 4.33a and 4.33b]**.

Movement Editing

To connect images through movement means that the direction and pace of actions, gestures, and other movements are linked with corresponding or contrasting movements in one or more other shots. Cutting on action, or editing during an onscreen movement, quickens a scene or film's pace. A common version of this pattern is the continuity editing device called a **match on action**, whereby the

▶ **VIEWING CUE**

What graphic patterns are constructed through the editing of the film you've just viewed? What effects do these patterns have on your viewing of the film? ‖

(a)

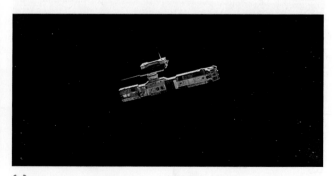

(b)

4.33a and 4.33b　*2001: A Space Odyssey* (1968). A famous graphic match from a prehistoric bone to a spaceship transcends millennia of history in one cut.

(a)   (b)

4.34a and 4.34b   *Meshes of the Afternoon* (1943). The power of cinema illustrated by matching the protagonist's steps across changing backgrounds.

direction of an action (such as the tossing of a stone in the air) is edited to a shot depicting the continuation of that action (such as the flight of that stone as it hits a window). Often a match on action obscures the cut itself, such as when the cut occurs just as a character opens a door; in the next shot, we see the next room as the character shuts the door from the other side.

In *Meshes of the Afternoon* (1943), Maya Deren depicts a continuous movement across diverse terrains by strictly matching the action of her character walking forward. The character's first stride is on the beach; her next strides are on dirt, among tall grasses, on concrete, and finally on carpet **[Figures 4.34a and 4.34b]**. This series of cuts works as an example of graphic matching as well, because the scale and distance are precisely matched in each shot. (Similarly, the example from *2001: A Space Odyssey*, cited in the preceding section, is also a match on action following the movement of the bone through the air.) Leni Riefenstahl's extraordinary editing of athletes in motion in her documentary *Olympia* (1938) has become a model for sports montages **[Figures 4.35a and 4.35b]**.

> ▶ **VIEWING CUE**
>
> Consider the last film you viewed in class. What is the relationship between figure and camera movement within specific shots and the film's cutting? ⏸

(a)   (b)

4.35a and 4.35b   *Olympia* (1938). The seemingly superhuman mobility of Olympic divers is enhanced by Leni Riefenstahl's editing.

(a)   **(b)**

4.36a and 4.36b   *Strangers on a Train* (1951). The movements of a carousel around, up and down, and finally out of control are intercut chaotically with the two characters' physical struggle in the climactic sequence of Alfred Hitchcock's *Strangers on a Train*.

Movement editing can, however, resist matching and instead create other patterns of movement in a series of images: rapid and slow movements, movements into various spaces of a shot, or different styles of movement can be edited together for visual effects. This is often the case in music videos. In pioneering experimental filmmaker Shirley Clarke's *Bridges-Go-Round* (1958), bridges—stationary structures—come alive and achieve a balletic movement through the editing. Chaotic movement editing appears in the climax of *Strangers on a Train* (1951) **[Figures 4.36a and 4.36b]**. Action sequences such as fights and chases also exploit the possibilities of movement editing, both relying on the spatial consistency of continuity editing to convey what's happening, and using variation to increase the surprise and excitement.

Rhythmic Editing

Finally, **rhythmic editing** describes the organization of the editing according to different paces or tempos determined by how quickly cuts are made. Like the tempos that describe the rhythmic organization of music, editing in this fashion may link a rapid succession of quick shots, a series of slowly paced long takes, or shots of varying length to modulate the time between cuts. Since rhythm is a fundamental property of editing, it is often combined with graphic, movement, or continuity aims. The early French avant-garde filmmaker Germaine Dulac defined film as "a visual symphony made of rhythmic images." Frequently, experimental films find their formal coherence in a rhythmic editing pattern, as in Hollis Frampton's *Zorns Lemma* (1970), which is structured around repeating and varying cycles of twenty-four one-second shots. However, narrative films also depend on editing rhythms to underpin the emotion and action of a scene, as depicted in the harrowing opening sequence of *Vertigo* (1958), for example **[Figures 4.37a and 4.37b]**. Directors in different genres and traditions work with their editors to achieve distinctive editing rhythms in their films.

Editing from Scene to Sequence

The coordination of temporal and spatial editing patterns beyond the relationship between two images results in a higher level of cinematic organization that

▶ **VIEWING CUE**

Time the shots of a specific sequence from any film you've viewed for class thus far. How does the rhythm of the editing in the sequence contribute to the film's mood or meaning? ⏸

(a)   (b)

4.37a and 4.37b   *Vertigo* (1958). This opening sequence uses almost no dialogue, relying on the rhythmic alternation of shots of Scottie looking down from the rooftop, where he hangs from his hands, and shots of the view below, occasioning the first use of the "vertigo shot"—a simultaneous zoom-in and track-out—to convey his distorted perspective.

is found in both narrative and non-narrative films. The shot is the single length of film, and combining it with another shot builds up edited units called either a scene or a sequence.

While these two terms for edited units are not always strictly distinguished, it may be helpful to conceive of them separately. Think of a **scene** as one or more shots that describe a continuous space, time, and action, such as the return of Ethan Edwards at the beginning of *The Searchers* (1956). Edwards's brother's family spies his arrival on the horizon and gathers on the porch to await his approach. He arrives, dismounts, and enters the homestead with them, at which point the scene ends. In contrast, a **sequence** is any number of shots that are unified as a coherent action (such as a walk to school) or as an identifiable motif (such as the expression of anger), regardless of changes in space and time. Later in *The Searchers*, one sequence covers several years' time as Ethan and Martin Pawley search for their abducted relative, Debbie, in a series of shots of them traversing different landscapes at different seasons.

One way to relate editing on a micro level to editing on a macro level is to attempt to divide a film into large narrative units, a process referred to as narrative **segmentation**. A classical film may have forty scenes and sequences but only ten large segments. Often locating editing transitions such as fades and dissolves will point to these divisions, which occur at significant changes in narrative space, time, characters, or action. Tracing the logic of a particular film's editing on this level also gives insight into how film narratives are organized. For example, the setting of a film's first scene may be identical to that of the last scene, or two segments showing the same characters may represent a significant change in their relationship. Sometimes the "seam" between segments will itself reveal something significant to viewers about the larger organization of the film.

In *Imitation of Life* (1959), director Douglas Sirk starkly contrasts a very upsetting scene in which Sarah Jane is beaten by her boyfriend after he discovers her mother is black with another scene in which her mother massages the feet of her white employer, Lora. Lora's exclamation—"That feels so good!"—acquires sickening irony in the juxtaposition. Here two scenes of black and white intimate relationships, one violent, one apparently benevolent, are deliberately contrasted. Once again, the connections among narrative units demonstrate how editing extends from the juxtaposition of shots to structure the film as a whole.

text continued on page 162 ▶

Patterns of Editing in
Bonnie and Clyde (1967)

Arthur Penn's *Bonnie and Clyde* represented a new kind of filmmaking in the late 1960s, in part because of its complex spatial and temporal patterns of editing. Based on the famous outlaws from the 1930s, the film describes the meeting of the title characters and their violent but clownish crime wave through the South. Clyde is able to enlist Bonnie in her first robbery because she is bored with her small-town life. As their escapades continue, they are naively surprised by their notoriety. Soon the gaiety of their adventures gives way to bloodier and darker encounters: Clyde's accomplice/brother is killed, and eventually the couple is betrayed and slaughtered.

Frequently, Dede Allen's editing of specific scenes emphasizes temporal and spatial realism. The scene depicting the outlaw couple's first small-town bank robbery begins with a long shot of a car outside the bank. The next shot, from inside the bank, shows the car parked outside the window. Spatially, this constructs the geography of the scene; temporally, it conveys the action

that takes place within these linked shots. The scene creates verisimilitude.

At other points in *Bonnie and Clyde*, the logic of the editing emphasizes psychological or emotional effects over realism. When Bonnie is introduced, for example, the first image we see of her is an extreme close-up of her lips; the camera pulls back as she turns right to look in a mirror. This is followed by a cut on action as she stands and looks back over her shoulder to the left in a medium shot and then by another cut on action as she drops to her bed, her face visible in a close-up through the bedframe, which she petulantly punches. Here Bonnie's restless movements are depicted by a series of jerky shots, and we sense her boredom and frustration through the editing **[Figures 4.38a and 4.38b]**. Next Bonnie goes to her window and, in a point-of-view construction, spots a strange man near her mother's car. She comes downstairs to find out what he is doing, and her conversation with Clyde is handled in a series

(a)

(b)

4.38a and 4.38b *Bonnie and Clyde* (1967). The lack of an establishing shot combines with the multiple framings to emphasize the claustrophobic mise-en-scène, taking us right into the character's psychologically rendered space.

(a)

(b)

(c)

4.39a–4.39c *Bonnie and Clyde* (1967). Clyde's famous death sequence uses slow-motion cinematography, cutting on movement, and overlapping editing.

of shot/reverse shots, starting with long shots as she comes outside and proceeding to closer pairs of shots. The two-shot of the characters together is delayed. The way this introduction is handled emphasizes the inevitability of their pairing.

The final scene of the sequence is the film's most famous and influential, and the strategies used serve as an instructive summary of the patterns and logic of editing. Accompanied by the staccato of machine-gun bullets, Bonnie's and Clyde's deaths are filmed in slow motion, their bodies reacting with almost balletic grace to the impact of the gunshots and to the rhythm of the film's shots, which are almost as numerous. In nearly thirty cuts in approximately forty seconds, the film alternates between the two victims' spasms and reestablishing shots of the death scene. Clyde's fall to the ground is split into three shots, overlapping the action [**Figures 4.39a–4.39c**]. The hail of bullets finally stops, and the film's final minute is comprised of a series of seven shots of the police and other onlookers gathering around, without a single reverse shot of what they are seeing. Like most films, *Bonnie and Clyde* matches the duration of scenes and editing rhythms to the actions and themes of the story, yet one of the more creative and troubling dimensions of the film is the striking combination of slow, romantic scenes and fast-paced action sequences, which culminate in this memorable finale.

For linking sex with violence, glamorizing its protagonists through beauty and fashion, and addressing itself to the anti-authoritarian feelings of young audiences, *Bonnie and Clyde* is among the most important U.S. films of the 1960s. Together with other countercultural milestones such as *The Graduate* (1967) and *Easy Rider* (1969), it heralded the end of studio-style production and the beginning of a new youth-oriented film market, one that revisited film genres of the past with a modern sensibility. However, as we have seen, it was not only the film's content that was innovative; *Bonnie and Clyde*'s editing and the climactic linkage of gunshots with camera shots also influenced viewers—ranging from French New Wave filmmakers to the American public.

The Significance of Film Editing

4.40 *The Cheat* (1912). Cecil B. DeMille's film made early use of the close-up to increase audience involvement.

4.41 *"I Want My MTV."* The energy and fragmentation of contemporary youth culture was evident in MTV's advertising in the 1980s—here using pop icon Cyndi Lauper—as well as the videos it broadcast.

The editing styles we have discussed so far are not simply neutral ways of telling stories or conveying information. The very word "continuity" represents a powerful and far-reaching value associated with spatial and temporal coherence and narrative clarity. Applied in different contexts—Hollywood, art cinema, or the avant-garde—each style conveys a different perspective on form and realism. Cutting to a close-up in a silent film such as *The Cheat* (1912) was an innovative way of smoothly taking the viewer inside the film's world **[Figure 4.40]**; it served the psychological realism of Hollywood story-telling. Early documentary films developed conventional editing patterns whose logic was made clear by a continuous voiceover narration. Experimental films like *The Flicker* (1965) employed various patterns of alternation or accumulation that generated aesthetic and structural values like those found in paintings or poetry.

In the 1960s, a "jumpy" kind of editing was introduced, one that simulated the freewheeling style of pop icons like the Beatles in Richard Lester's *A Hard Day's Night* (1964). Such modern editing often reinforced or promoted certain films' countercultural or even revolutionary themes. By the 1980s, the influence of the rapid and dynamic editing found in advertising was pervasive. MTV, the pioneering music television station, was launched in 1981, and fast-paced editing was evident in both its station identifications and the music videos it screened **[Figure 4.41]**. Directors like David Fincher, who got his start in music videos, introduced this style to feature films. In Fincher's *Fight Club* (1999), fragmentation of identity and the punishment of the body are conveyed in the cutting **[Figures 4.42a and 4.42b]**.

How Editing Makes Meaning

We have established how film editing assumes one or both of the following general aims:

(a)

(b)

4.42a and 4.42b *Fight Club* (1999). David Fincher's "jumpy" editing style allows the audience to truly feel the brutal self-inflicted punishment of the narrator (Edward Norton).

- to generate emotions and ideas through the construction of patterns of seeing
- to move beyond the confines of individual perception and its temporal and spatial limitations

In John Ford's *Stagecoach* (1939), for instance, we experience the approach of pursuing Indians and the subsequent battle and escape of the stagecoach's white passengers **[Figures 4.43a and 4.43b]**. Audience members almost involuntarily hope for the vanquishing of the pursuers, who are shown in long shots. We feel palpable relief, along with the surviving passengers, when their pursuers give up the chase. The editing, which breaks with the 180-degree rule, also constructs feelings of tension. Since we are not confined to the interior of the stagecoach, we see the initial threat and the close calls that the characters cannot see. Through logic and pacing, the editing does more than just link images in space and time; it also generates emotions and thoughts.

These potential effects of editing are well illustrated in the legendary (and no longer extant) editing experiments conducted by Soviet filmmaker Lev Kuleshov in the 1910s and 1920s. A shot of the Russian actor Ivan Mozzhukhin's face followed by a bowl of soup signified "hunger" to viewers, while the identical footage of the face linked to a child's coffin connoted "grief." In the absence of an establishing shot, viewers assumed these pairs of images to be linked in space and time—the so-called "Kuleshov effect." Editing a shot of a powerful leader with a shot of a peacock encouraged the audience to identify the leader with the concept of vanity, a more specifically conceptual association. Sergei Eisenstein referred to this intentional juxtaposition of two images in order to generate ideas as "intellectual montage." For example, in his own film *October* (1927), an intertitle with the slogan "In the Name of God" is followed by a series of iconic images from different religious traditions. This juxtaposition highlights the relativity of the concept of the divine by not associating the idea of "God" with any one religion, thereby pointing out the hypocrisy of the ruling class for invoking God's name in the film's plot.

A magisterial example of how editing overcomes the physical limitations of human perception can be found in *2001: A Space Odyssey*. No individual character's consciousness anchors the film's journey through space and time. Instead, our experience of the film is largely governed by the film's editing: long-shot images

▶ **VIEWING CUE**

In the film you've just viewed for class, what different emotional and intellectual responses are evoked by the editing choices? Be sure to jot down specific examples from the film to support your response. ⏸

(a)

(b)

4.43a and 4.43b   *Stagecoach* (1939). The editing of John Ford's classic *Stagecoach* uses humanizing close-ups of the passengers, medium long shots of the coach under siege, and long shots of the attackers to keep the viewers' sympathy with the stagecoach passengers.

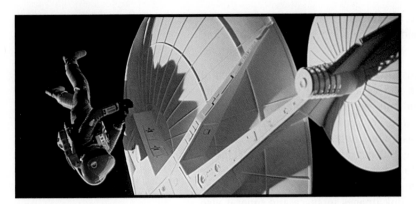

4.44 *2001: A Space Odyssey* (1969). From beginning to end, the editing of this film defies the limits of human perception.

that show crew members floating outside the spaceship, accompanied by Johann Strauss's *The Blue Danube* waltz, and a montage of psychedelic patterns that erases all temporal borders **[Figure 4.44]**. Our almost visceral response to these sequences is a result of the cinema's ability to defy our perceptual limits.

Of course, the two central aims of film editing often overlap. The abstract images in *2001: A Space Odyssey* make us think about the boundaries of humanity and the vastness of the universe—and, perhaps, about cinema as a manipulation of images in space and time. Many of Alfred Hitchcock's climactic sequences generate emotions of suspense—achieved in *Saboteur* (1942) by literally suspending the character from the Statue of Liberty **[Figures 4.45a and 4.45b]**. The scene also transcends the confines of perception by showing us details that would be impossible to see without the aid of the movie camera.

Our responses to such editing patterns are, of course, never guaranteed. We may feel emotionally manipulated by a cut to a close-up or cheated by a cutaway. Additionally, across historical periods and in different cultures, editing styles can seem vastly different, and audience expectations vary accordingly. Older transitional devices such as irises and wipes often generate laughter from audiences today. The slow, meditative editing of Iranian director Abbas Kiarostami's *Taste of Cherry* (1997) may appear boring to a viewer who has been raised on Hollywood action film sequences. However we respond, editing generates an experience unique to moving image media.

Continuity and Disjunctive Editing Styles

Since the beginning of the twentieth century, continuity editing has been paralleled and sometimes directly challenged by various alternative practices that we

(a)

(b)

4.45a and 4.45b *Saboteur* (1942). Suspense is made literal—and visceral—as a man's fate hangs by a thread.

refer to collectively as disjunctive editing. It is useful to distinguish these two styles to obtain more precise ways of discussing film form and to remark on philosophical differences in editing styles. However, in modern filmmaking it is quite possible to find these two editing methods converging in the editing style of a single film.

Continuity Editing

As noted earlier, continuity editing is not an inevitable or a "correct" style of cutting films. Rather, it creates shot patterns that shape space and time to approximate a closed and coherent fictional world, and it constructs a logic and rhythm that mimic human perception. In this section, we will focus on the Hollywood tradition of continuity editing and what critic André Bazin called "analytical editing," and we will also show how art cinema creates a different variant of continuity through editing.

Continuity editing proceeds as if organized around continuous human perception—even if there is no clearly identified person driving that perception, as in a series of establishing shots of decreasing distance. In the opening shots of *Rear Window* (1954), Hitchcock makes a kind of joke about how cinematic vision mimics human vision. An elaborate camera movement shows us the courtyard view from L. B. Jeffries's room while his protagonist sleeps. When Jeffries later wakes up and looks out the window, Hitchcock cuts from images of him to isolated views of the windows opposite, using editing to re-map the space with which we have already been made familiar in accordance with Jeffries's now-alert gaze **[Figures 4.46a and 4.46b]**.

Continuity style refers to an even broader array of technical choices that support Hollywood's principle of effacing technique to clarify the narrative and its human motivation. Lighting highlights the face. Mise-en-scène is scaled to the human figure and generally does not distract from the action. Plot is oriented to the perceptions and goals of a clearly drawn protagonist. The soundtrack also plays a major role, as we will see in Chapter 5. But it is editing that best exemplifies the principle of seamlessness in continuity style. Lighting must be consistent from shot to shot, and other aspects of mise-en-scène—such as costumes and make-up, props, and figure behavior—must be meticulously monitored from setup to setup by following the **continuity script**. The person in charge of continuity, for example,

(a)

(b)

4.46a and 4.46b *Rear Window* (1954). Editing together medium shots of Jeffries's gaze and long shots of the view across the courtyard, the film meticulously maintains spatial continuity.

(a)

(b)

4.47a and 4.47b *Plan 9 from Outer Space* (1959). The principles of continuity editing are illustrated by their failed execution in a film by notorious B-filmmaker Edward D. Wood Jr. When actor Bela Lugosi died before filming was complete on this low-budget sci-fi horror film, the director replaced him with another actor in a cape. Clearly props alone do not create continuity.

ensures that a cigarette almost burned down in one shot is not freshly lit in a later shot [**Figures 4.47a and 4.47b**].

In a Hollywood film, editing a scene in the service of narrative continuity and clarity is called **analytical editing**. In other words, the scene is analyzed or broken down by the camera to direct viewers' attention from the general perspective of an establishing shot to increasingly more specific views. Closer shots show character speech (shot/reverse-shot sequences) or denote the position of significant props or gestures (inserts, cutaways, reaction shots). Hitchcock's experiment with long takes in *Rope* (1948) illuminates the paradox that "continuity" traditionally depends on a large number of cuts. Containing just ten shots, the film is in many ways an "unnatural" viewing experience.

Spatially, the relationships set up in the Hollywood continuity tradition follow the logic of human interaction. Analytical editing cuts the world to the measure of the body, and camera distance is measured in anthropomorphic scale (a close-up is a shot in which the human face would be seen in its entirety). Point-of-view editing registers the impact of the world on humans, literally sandwiching a view between two shots of a person looking. The 180-degree rule outlines a field of interaction well illustrated by the shot/reverse-shot sequence, in which the camera takes turns "seeing" from different characters' perspectives.

Film theorists speculate that such spatial practices hide a source of potential anxiety for the viewer. If the conversation from *Clueless* illustrated earlier (Figures 4.22a–4.22d, p. 149) provided no shots of the protagonist Cher, we might be reminded of the fact that in order to film her friends, the camera occupies her seat. Our perception as viewers actually proceeds from what Dziga Vertov and his associates call the "camera eye," a fact we are encouraged to forget. In a subjective shot from a horror film that is not anchored by a reverse shot, we are forced to wonder whose point of view the camera is assuming. The mechanical eye becomes associated with that of a monster—perhaps the genre recognizes that being forced to share the point of view of an unknown entity (ultimately the camera itself) is anxiety-provoking.

▶ **VIEWING CUE**

In the film you just viewed, at what point is continuity editing used? How does this practice encourage you to identify with the characters or to believe in the story's world? ⏸

Editing in art cinema is often jarring for viewers who take Hollywood continuity for granted. Loosely defined, art cinema includes narrative feature films from outside Hollywood that are exhibited in specialty cinemas. Like Hollywood films, art films construct a fictional world, center on human perspective, and direct our view of unfolding events, but they construct space and time differently through editing. Although they provide a form of continuity between cuts, they are not governed by Hollywood continuity style.

Analytical editing, with its precise and often-redundant orientation to the spatial unfolding of a scene, is avoided in art films like Carl Theodor Dreyer's *The Passion of Joan of Arc* (1928), in which a series of close-ups against a white background conveys the psychological intensity of Joan testifying before the Inquisitors while never giving an overview of the space.

Dreyer's nearly exclusive use of close-ups of Joan and her interrogators elevates the spiritual subject matter rather than the worldly space of her surroundings that establishing shots and eyeline matches would provide [**Figures 4.48a–4.48c**].

Japanese director Yasujiro Ozu often uses graphic elements to provide continuity across cuts, and although in his *Early Summer* (1951) he conveys his characters' situations poignantly, he is more likely to set up his camera near the ground to show them sitting on the floor than he is to use their optical point of view. Cutting between handheld shots in films like *Faces* (1968) and *A Woman Under the Influence* (1974), U.S. independent pioneer John Cassavetes follows characters' conversations and reactions but disorients viewers' perception of the overall space in favor of immediacy of emotion. Art cinema, while often still tied to characters' perspective and location in space, nevertheless conveys a powerful alternative to Hollywood analytical editing.

Disjunctive Editing

While art cinema departs from the rules of continuity, **disjunctive editing** makes a definitive break from cutting based on how people perceive the world. Alternative editing practices based on oppositional relationships or other formal constructions can be traced back even to very

(a)

(b)

(c)

4.48a–4.48c   *The Passion of Joan of Arc* (1928). The juxtaposition of the inquisitors' faces with that of Renée Falconetti's as Joan ignores spatial continuity but is freighted with power and significance.

early developments in film syntax and are found in various countries and schools excited about the possibilities of film art. Disjunctive editing might be deemed *visible editing*. These practices confront viewers with juxtapositions and linkages that seem unnatural or unexpected with two main purposes:

- to call attention to the editing for aesthetic, conceptual, ideological, or psychological purposes
- to disorient, disturb, or viscerally affect viewers

When the viewer is asked, or even forced, to reflect on the meaning of a particular cut because it is so jarring, many filmmakers and theorists believe that he or she not only participates more fully in the film experience but may also develop a critical perspective on the film's subject matter or on the process of representation itself.

Disjunctive editing is not a single system with rules and manuals like Hollywood continuity editing, and it increasingly coexists with continuity editing. Disjunctive editing may be organized around any number of different aspects of editing, such as spatial tension, temporal experimentation, or rhythmic and graphic patterns. One primary principle behind the use of disjunctive editing is **distanciation**. In his plays and critical writings of the 1920s, German playwright Bertolt Brecht developed this concept to name a critical attitude adopted by the viewer when he or she is made aware of how the work of art is put together. A second approach, discussed earlier, is **montage**, primarily identified with Soviet filmmakers of the 1920s but subsequently incorporated to other editing practices.

Distanciation.
Brecht believed that a critical distance toward both the work of art and the social world on which it commented was achieved when the viewer had to think about a play's structure. This was accomplished through distanciation techniques, also known as *alienation effects*. A distanciation technique specific to film is the **jump cut**, a disjunctive cut that interrupts a particular action and, intentionally or unintentionally, creates discontinuities in the spatial or temporal development of shots. Used loosely, the term *jump cut* can identify several different disjunctive practices. Cutting a section out of the middle of a shot causes a jump ahead to a later point in the action. Sometimes the background of a shot may remain constant, while figures shift position inexplicably. Two shots from the same angle but from different distances will also create a jump when juxtaposed. Such jumps are considered grave errors in continuity editing. Films of the French New Wave, notably Jean-Luc Godard's *Breathless* (1960), reintroduced this disjunctive technique into the editing vocabulary, and contemporary films such as *Michael Clayton* (2007) have since appropriated this technique **[Figures 4.49a and 4.49b]**.

Jump cuts illustrate the two primary aims of disjunctive editing. In Wong Karwai's *Happy Together* (1997), they draw attention to the editing. Jumps in distance and time are combined with changes in film stock within a supposedly continuous

(a)

(b)

4.49a and 4.49b   *Michael Clayton* (2007). Hollywood films have increasingly appropriated jump cuts. Here, a corrupt attorney rehearses her boardroom speech.

(a)

(b)

4.50a and 4.50b *Happy Together* (1997). Here jump cuts draw attention to the restlessness and displacement of two men who have moved from Hong Kong to Buenos Aires.

scene **[Figures 4.50a and 4.50b]**. The viewer notices *how* the action is depicted, rather than simply taking in the action. The viewer may reflect on how the disjointed shots convey the characters' restless yet stagnant moods, recognize in them the film's theme of displacement, or appreciate the aesthetic effect for its own sake.

The jump cuts in Alain Resnais's *Last Year at Marienbad* (1961) are a central device through which the viewer is disoriented in space and especially in time. The major conceit of this classic art film is the characters' confusion between the present and the past (the previous year of the film's title); this diegetic confusion is inseparable from the viewer's disorientation through editing, because the viewer cannot tell whether shots of the two characters in the Marienbad resort depict the present or the past. Numerous images show the female protagonist striking poses around the hotel and gardens **[Figures 4.51a and 4.51b]**. The temporal relationship among such shots is unclear, as differences in costume and setting are countered by similarities in posture and styling. Finally, the strategy becomes a reflection on the process of viewing a film. How can we assume that the action we are viewing is happening now, when recording, editing, and projection/viewing are all distinct temporal operations?

The jump cut can also be used to explore the magical properties of the medium first explored by Georges Méliès. Maya Deren and Alexander Hammid's *Meshes of the Afternoon* (1943), for example, begins with a hand lowering a flower into the frame. In the film's second shot, the hand abruptly disappears. Later a hand reaches

(a)

(b)

4.51a and 4.51b *Last Year at Marienbad* (1961). Delphine Seyrig strikes poses against various backgrounds, challenging our perception of time and place. The technique was later adopted in music videos.

forward to remove a key from the table; then the key suddenly reappears in its original position. This action is repeated; we are invited to engage in existential reflection, enhanced by the fact that the disjunctive nature of these cuts is underscored by a distinctive, synchronized note on the soundtrack that Teiji Ito added to the film.

Jean-Luc Godard's films employ Brechtian distanciation devices in numerous ways beyond the jump cut. Many of his films are broken into numbered chapters, drawing the viewer out of the fictional world. He also uses frequent inserts; in *Two or Three Things I Know About Her* (1967), printed text and advertising images disrupt continuity.

Montage. The aim of grabbing viewers' attention through collision is at the center of Soviet theories of montage. Sergei Eisenstein's extensive writings, undertaken from the early 1920s to his death in 1945, have secured him a place as one of the foremost theorists of cinema. He first developed his concept of montage in conjunction with his work in theater before beginning his film experiments with *Strike* in 1924. Eisenstein advocated **dialectical montage**: two shots linked dialectically (that is, contrasted or opposed to one another) become synthesized into something greater, a visual concept. In *Battleship Potemkin* (1925), the shots of stone lions juxtaposed in sequence suggest that one stone lion is leaping to life **[Figures 4.52a–4.52c]**. According to Eisenstein, the concept of awakening, connected to revolutionary consciousness, is thus formed in viewers' minds even as they react viscerally to the lion's leap. Such an association of aesthetic fragmentation with a political program of analysis and action has persisted in many uses of disjunctive editing.

Whereas classical Hollywood films traditionally avoided a disjunctive style, alternative and experimental films have often employed it as the foundation of the film. The fragmentation of time and space (which is germane to editing) is an important aesthetic aim of artistic **modernism**. (Think, for instance, of cubism in painting, which aims to show different facets of an object through a distorted depiction of its shape, color, and composition, a very cinematic concept.) In the 1920s, for

(a)

(b)

(c)

4.52a–4.52c *Battleship Potemkin* (1925). Sergei Eisenstein rouses stone lions through montage.

example, experimental filmmakers in France organized their films' montage around the rhythms of poetry and music. In Germaine Dulac's surrealist film *The Seashell and the Clergyman* (1928), the central figure is as surprised as we are when his head suddenly appears on the seashell. During the same period, an international genre of "city symphony" films emerged. Walter Ruttmann's *Berlin: Symphony of a Great City* (1927) and Dziga Vertov's *Man with a Movie Camera* (1929) both create a conceptual whole through montage. In both films, the life of the metropolis is depicted through rhythmic patterns of images that emulate the condensed time and space of modernity. Vertov's film actually combines footage from different cities. In the documentary film style developed by British producer John Grierson in such films as *Drifters* (1929), images are cut together in a poetic montage.

Later avant-garde filmmakers also used montage. American filmmaker Kenneth Anger explores the ritual aspects of film in *Scorpio Rising* (1964), which edits the cult behavior of bikers to a rock-and-roll soundtrack. (In contrast, Andy Warhol's films are distinct for their lack of editing. *Empire* [1964], an eight-hour shot of the Empire State Building using a stationary camera, might be seen as a very prolonged homage to the first films of the Lumière brothers.) The very title of Trinh T. Minh-ha's *Reassemblage* (1982) references the process of editing **[Figure 4.53]**. In this short experimental documentary shot in Senegal, Trinh critiques ethnographic filmmaking's presumption that an image can tell the truth of another culture to an outsider. Her film makes use of disjunctive editing by repeating shots, using jump cuts, and refusing to synchronize the picture to a complex soundtrack. Films made from found footage, such as Bruce Conner's *A Movie* (1958), rely on montage to create humorous, sinister, or thought-provoking relationships among seemingly random images.

Video art has also made significant use of disjunctive editing through montage. With the use of effects, video editing can be layered as well as sequential, developing one of Eisenstein's principles: "each shot is a montage cell." In other words, relationships of contrast and opposition exist not only between shots, but within shots as well. Cecilia Barriga's low-budget video art piece *Meeting of Two Queens* (1991) is ingeniously constructed by re-cutting brief clips from the films of Greta Garbo and Marlene Dietrich. The montage creates comparisons between the glamorous movie star rivals, engineers their meeting, and suggests a romance between the two by making use of viewers' expectations of continuity editing and altering mise-en-scène through superimposition **[Figure 4.54]**. This "mash up" technique has become prevalent among amateur media makers on YouTube.

text continued on page 174 ▶

4.53 *Reassemblage* (1982). Trinh T. Minh-ha uses jump cuts and other devices to question the reliability of ethnographic images of African women.

4.54 *Meeting of Two Queens* (1991). Re-editing Hollywood films on video puts Greta Garbo and Marlene Dietrich, stars from rival studios, in the same film.

Montage in *Battleship Potemkin* (1925)

Soviet filmmaker Sergei Eisenstein's *Battleship Potemkin* is one of the most renowned examples of daring and innovative editing in film history. A 1925 silent classic based on a 1905 historical event, *Battleship Potemkin* describes the revolt of maltreated sailors aboard their ship, the sympathetic response of townspeople on shore, and the violent repression of those people by the czar's soldiers. Although the story itself is quite simple, Eisenstein uses complex montage to charge specific incidents with powerful energy and meaning, emphasizing the breaks and contrasts between images joined by a cut.

In a film with no single protagonist, numerous cuts join small groups to show the participation of the masses in anti-czarist sentiment, moving our perspective beyond the confines of individual perception and its temporal and spatial limitations. To give heightened drama or dynamic tension to an action, Eisenstein uses more shots than in a typical Hollywood film, sometimes overlapping the same action from one shot to the next in several points of view. When the ship's doctor is thrown overboard by sailors, the gesture is repeated from overhead and side angles, engaging viewers' emotions and leading them to a particular idea: the desperation of the sailors resulting in a mutinous act. After the doctor hits the water, Eisenstein employs an insert of the maggot-infested meat that the doctor had approved for the sailors' consumption. Appearing out of temporal sequence, this shot acts as narrative justification for the doctor's treatment.

The centerpiece of *Battleship Potemkin* is the famous Odessa steps sequence in which innocent citizens are shot and trampled by the czar's soldiers. The sequence is justly celebrated for its dynamic cutting, which makes dramatic use of movement and graphic patterns within shots to bring about Eisenstein's favored interaction between shots: collision. The sequence begins with the intertitle "Suddenly"; townspeople then begin to run from the imperial soldiers down the vast steps toward the camera. This action moves generally from left to right. Several figures are isolated in closer shots that are intercut throughout the sequence: a boy without legs propelling himself forward with his arms, a group of women, a mother running

with her child. When the orderly rows of troops are shown entering from top left, the shot provides a dramatic graphic contrast to the chaos of the mass of people. In the first major crosscutting episode within the sequence, the mother becomes separated from her son in the crowd. Shots of her turning back to retrieve him are vigorously contrasted with shots of him falling, with shots of the oncoming crowds, and with shots of the soldiers' inexorable progression behind them. Finally, the mother climbs high enough and enters a shot from the bottom left, which positions the soldiers across the top. The film cuts to peasants looking on, and in the next shot the mother is fired on and falls as the troops continue marching down. The use of movement in opposing directions is one of the key elements that organize this complicated editing sequence **[Figures 4.55a–4.55c]**.

As if this dramatic episode has not raised enough tension and pathos, after an intertitle announces the arrival of the Cossacks, Eisenstein embarks on one of the most famous editing sequences in film history. A young mother is shot and falls in several overlapping cuts. The baby carriage she had been clutching begins to roll down the stairs. Intercut with its descent (which is shown from changing screen directions) are repeated shots of onlookers who seem to be mimicking our own powerless, horrified gaze **[Figures 4.56a and 4.56b]**. No establishing shot puts these figures in spatial context. Just as the carriage reaches the bottom and begins to overturn, Eisenstein cuts to quick shots of a Cossack striking directly at us and then to the briefest of shots of the face of a woman wearing pince-nez. In a famous shock cut, her glasses are instantly shattered and bloodied **[Figure 4.57]**. The sequence fades out. As our vision is assaulted by the shock cut, the image of shattered glasses mirrors our own "injury," even as it stands in for an even more horrific, offscreen image of the baby's fate.

Battleship Potemkin made a similarly strong impact in the West when it was released in 1926. In the long term, Eisenstein's stylistic legacy has survived, even as the revolutionary purpose he associated with his aesthetic innovations has been questioned or abandoned.

His work has inspired more than one homage, including American director Brian De Palma's mimicking of the Odessa steps sequence in his gangster film, *The Untouchables* (1987). Some see a tour de force of suspenseful editing; others think the sequence is a distracting self-indulgence. Disjunctive editing like Eisenstein's helps open up multiple meanings, whereas the continuity tradition favors closure.

(a)

(b)

(c)

4.55a–4.55c *Battleship Potemkin* (1925). The conflict between the organized troops and the frightened masses is heightened by graphic collisions among shots showing different screen directions, different planes of action, patterns of light and shadow, and figure movement in the first part of the Odessa steps sequence.

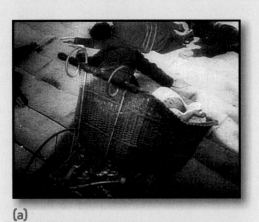

(a)

(b)

4.56a–4.56b *Battleship Potemkin* (1925). Repeated details of the baby carriage's descent convey a sense of helplessness in one of the most famous editing sequences in film history, which ends with a shock cut.

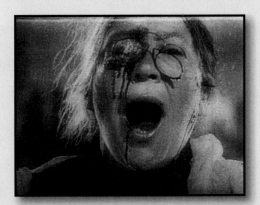

4.57 *Battleship Potemkin* (1925). Our vision is assaulted by this famous shock cut. The image of her shattered glasses mirrors our own "injury" even as it stands for the more horrific, offscreen image of the boy's fate.

Converging Editing Styles

Given the influence of other traditions and styles, editing in mainstream films arguably no longer strives for invisibility. Certainly it is no longer possible—if indeed it ever was—to assign specific responses, such as passive acceptance or political awareness, to specific editing techniques.

Digital technology has revolutionized the craft of editing, and stylistic changes such as faster pacing are becoming increasingly evident in movies. Lars von Trier's use of one hundred small digital video cameras to film *Dancer in the Dark* (2000) presented an editing challenge that an editor working with footage from a single film camera would never face. Von Trier's film breaks down actions much more minutely than standard analytical editing, and the arbitrariness of the cutting becomes apparent rather than remaining hidden **[Figures 4.58a and 4.58b]**. Fortunately, nonlinear digital editing allows the editor and director to sample many possibilities without affecting the original materials. As the two formal traditions of continuity and disjunctive editing converge, the values associated with each tradition become less distinct. For Eisenstein, calling attention to the editing was important because it could change the viewers' consciousness. For contemporary filmmakers, omitting establishing shots, breaking the 180-degree rule, and using rapid montage may serve the primary purpose of establishing a distinctive "look."

Editing is perhaps the most distinctive feature of film form. Editing leads viewers to experience images viscerally and emotionally, and it remains one of the most effective ways to create meanings from shots. These interpretations can vary from the almost automatic inferences about space, time, and narrative that we draw from the more familiar continuity editing patterns, to the intellectual puzzles posed by the unfamiliar spatial and temporal juxtapositions of disjunctive editing practices.

(a)

(b)

4.58a and 4.58b   *Dancer in the Dark* (2000). The use of many digital cameras makes it possible to intercut close shots from multiple perspectives.

CONCEPTS AT WORK

Editing has produced a vast array of strategies associated with different historical, cultural, and aesthetic perspectives. Against the background of a brief history highlighting changes in editing practices, we have detailed the many formal figures available in editing a film: from shot/reverse shot exchanges and continuity styles to graphic matches and disjunctive jump cuts. Finally, this chapter has emphasized how editing does not merely create formal patterns but associates these patterns with certain values, traditions, and meanings.

Activity

Imagine that you've been asked to remake a mainstream Hollywood movie as a provocative art film. To demonstrate how this would happen, "re-edit" one sequence of that film on paper, reimagining the continuity logic of the editing as a disjunctive style. How does this alter the meaning and the relationship between the viewer and the film?

THE PIANO

CIBY 2000 PRESENTS A JAN CHAPMAN PRODUCTION

HOLLY HUNTER   HARVEY KEITEL   SAM NEILL
A JANE CAMPION film

WITH ANNA PAQUIN KERRY WALKER GENEVIEVE LEMON – COSTUME DESIGNER JANET PATTERSON – SOUND DESIGNER LEE SMITH – MUSIC BY MICHAEL NYMAN – EDITOR VERONIKA JENET – PRODUCTION DESIGNER ANDREW McALPINE – DIRECTOR OF PHOTOGRAPHY STUART DRYBURGH – ASSOCIATE PRODUCER MARK TURNBULL – EXECUTIVE PRODUCER FOR CIBY 2000 ALAIN DEPARDIEU – PRODUCER JAN CHAPMAN – WRITTEN AND DIRECTED BY JANE CAMPION – DEVELOPED WITH ASSISTANCE OF THE AUSTRALIAN FILM COMMISSION AND NEW SOUTH WALES FILM AND TELEVISION OFFICE ⓒ 1992 JAN CHAPMAN PRODUCTIONS AND CIBY 2000

DOLBY STEREO

CiBy sales

Listening to the Cinema
Film Sound

Jane Campion's 1993 *The Piano* opens with its nineteenth-century heroine Ada McGrath's voiceover: "The voice you hear is not my speaking voice; it is my mind's voice." This is the first indication of the inventive uses to which the film will put sound—for Ada is mute, and we will not hear her "mind's voice" again until the film's final moments. She is about to emigrate from Scotland to New Zealand to marry a man whom she has never met, and the grand piano that she takes with her becomes her primary means of expression. And even when Ada is forced to leave the piano on the beach where she lands, as it is too large to transport, the film's soundtrack acts as a link between her and the piano. Later the piano becomes an instrument of exchange and erotic expression, when she must barter for its return from the man who buys it from her husband. *The Piano* recognizes from the start that film sound does not simply play a supporting role, nor is it restricted to human speech. Rather, film sound—as dialogue, music, or sound effects—can create a drama as complex as mise-en-scène, cinematography, or editing.

The cinema is an audiovisual medium, one among many that saturate our contemporary media experience. Many of the visual technologies we encounter in daily life are also sound technologies: you choose your smartphone's ringtone, battle villains to the soundtrack of your favorite video game, or notice that your television's volume soars when a commercial interrupts a program. These devices use sound to encourage and guide interaction, to complement visual information, and to give rhythm and dimension to the experience. The cinema works similarly, using complex combinations of voice, music, and sound effects. Too often given secondary status, sound engages viewers perceptually, provides key spatial and story information, and affords an aesthetic experience of its own. This chapter explores how speech, music, and sound effects are used in cinema and how they are perceived by a film's audience.

KEY OBJECTIVES	
	▪ Understand the importance of sound to the film experience.
	▪ Explore how the use and understanding of sound reflect different historical and cultural influences.
	▪ Discover how sounds convey meaning in relationship to images.
	▪ Learn how sounds are recorded, combined, and reproduced.
	▪ Understand the functions of the voice.
	▪ Describe the principles and practices that govern the use of music.
	▪ Understand the principles and practices that govern the use of sound effects.
	▪ Examine the cultural, historical, and aesthetic values that determine traditional relationships between sounds and images.

Sound is a sensual experience that in some cases makes an even deeper impression than a film's visuals. Viewers might cover their eyes during the infamous shower scene in *Psycho* (1960), but to lessen the scene's horror, they would have to escape from the shrieking violins that punctuate each thrust of the knife. To perceive an image, we must face forward with our eyes open, but sound can come from any direction. Listening to movies, just as much as watching them, defines the filmgoing experience, and with the advent of advanced technologies, sound has helped to make that experience even more immersive.

A Short History of Film Sound

Topsy-Turvy (1999) tells the story of the collaboration between Gilbert and Sullivan, the late-nineteenth-century British lyricist-composer duo, as they brainstorm, quarrel, and finally witness the first production of their operetta *The Mikado* [Figure 5.1]. The behind-the-scenes story culminates in a performance of

the operetta that brings together sound and image for the theater audience within the film and extends this experience to the film's viewers. As this film dramatizes, many of the traditions and technologies that became synthesized in the institution of the cinema combined sound, especially music, and visual spectacle in public performances.

Theatrical and Technological Prehistories of Film Sound

It is difficult to think of a theatrical tradition that does not have its own distinctive musical conventions. The practice of combining music with forms of visual spectacle in the Western tradition goes back at least as far as the use of choral odes in classical Greek theater. Perhaps most relevant to the use of sound in early cinema is the tradition of **melodrama**. Popularized in eighteenth-century France, melodrama, literally meaning "music drama," originally designated a theatrical genre that combined spoken text with music. In England, during a time when laws restricted "legitimate" theater to particular venues, melodrama permitted the mounting of popular theatrical spectacles. Stage melodrama became increasingly more spectacular throughout the nineteenth century and eventually came to dominate the American stage, where melodrama had an incalculable influence on cinematic conventions. Not only was the aural component of the form very important, but the up-and-down rhythms of melodrama's sensational plots also drew on the strongly felt but inexpressible emotions that music so powerfully conveys. All of these qualities were adopted by film melodramas like D. W. Griffith's *Way Down East* (1920), an adaptation of a nineteenth-century play.

Technological breakthroughs that led to such inventions as the phonograph were also important precursors of film sound. As far back as the end of the eighteenth century, inventors were engaged in the problems of sound reproduction. Thomas Edison's phonograph, introduced in 1877, had an irreversible impact on the public and on late-nineteenth-century science. Such inventions were often spoken about in terms of writing. "Phonography" means "sound writing," and Edison first thought of recorded sound as a way to record business letters.

5.1 *Topsy-Turvy* (1999). A film version of a filmic precedent: the making of the nineteenth-century operetta *The Mikado*.

5.2   Edison Studios' *Sound Experiment* (1895). A rare film fragment with synchronized sound from the dawn of cinema.

1895–1920s: The Sounds of Silent Cinema

Edison was also one of the primary figures in the invention of the motion-picture apparatus; the eventual coming together of film and sound haunted the medium from its inception. One of the first films made by Edison Studios in 1895 is a sound experiment in which Edison's chief inventor, W. L. K. Dickson, plays a violin into a megaphone as two other employees dance **[Figure 5.2]**. Sound cylinders provided a way of synchronizing image and sound very early in film history, and inventors continued to experiment with means of providing simultaneous picture and sound throughout the silent film era.

The term "silent drama" was sometimes used to distinguish film from stage drama that used spoken language. But, in fact, so-called silent cinema was often loud and noisy. Loudspeakers lured customers into film exhibitions that were accompanied by lecturers, pianos, organs, small ensembles, or, later, full orchestras **[Figure 5.3]**. In nickelodeons and other movie venues, audiences themselves customarily made noise, joining in sing-alongs between films **[Figures 5.4a and 5.4b]** and talking back to the screen. Often sound effects were supplied by someone standing behind the screen or by specially designed machines. Occasionally actors even provided dialogue to go along with the picture.

Music halls in Great Britain and vaudeville theaters in the United States lent early cinema popular talents, proven material, and formats such

5.3   Advertisement for Wurlitzer. The pianos, organs, and even orchestras of silent film were often as much of an attraction as the movie itself.

(a)   (b)

5.4a and 5.4b   Early nickelodeon slides. In early film programs, films were interspersed with sing-alongs, and slides like these provided the lyrics for an interactive experience.

as the revue, delivering audiences with specific expectations of sound and spectacle to the new medium. Because of the preexisting popularity of specific performers and styles in vaudeville, many ethnic voices were heard in cinema that might otherwise have been excluded from entertainment directed at mass audiences. For his sound film debut at MGM, director King Vidor chose to make *Hallelujah!* (1929), a musical with an all-black cast, capitalizing on the cultural association of African Americans with the expressive use of song **[Figure 5.5]**. Not only musical talent but also stage performers with training and experience were now in demand in Hollywood, and they soon displaced many of the silent screen's most beloved stars.

5.5   *Hallelujah!* (1929). With the coming of sound, musicals abounded, from backstage musicals to King Vidor's film, shot on location with an all-back cast.

1927–1930: Transition to Synchronized Sound

No event in the history of Hollywood film was as cataclysmic as the rapid incorporation of synchronized sound in the period 1927–1930. Many dynamics were at work in the introduction of sound, including the relationship of cinema to radio, theater, and vaudeville, the economic position of the industry as the United States headed into the Great Depression, and the popularity of certain film genres and stars. Yet exhibitors needed to be convinced to adopt the relatively untested new technology. The expense of converting a sufficient number of theaters to make the production of sound films feasible was considerable, and the studios had to be willing to make the investment.

From 1926 to 1927, two studios actively pursued competing sound technologies. Warner Bros. aggressively invested in sound and, in 1926, premiered its Vitaphone sound-on-disk system with a program of shorts, a recorded speech by Hollywood censor Will H. Hays, and the first feature film with a recorded score, *Don Juan*. Fox developed its Movietone sound system, which recorded sound optically on film, and in 1928 introduced its popular Movietone newsreels, which depicted everything from ordinary street scenes to exciting news (aviator Charles Lindbergh's takeoff for Paris was the first use of sound for a news item) and were soon playing in Fox's many theaters nationwide **[Figure 5.6]**. The new technology became impossible to ignore when it branched out from musical accompaniment and sound effects to include synchronous dialogue. Public response was enthusiastic.

5.6   Program for *Fox Movietone News*. Fox Studios developed a system to record sound optically on the film itself and then produced newsreels to show it off in its vast theater holdings. The newsreels ran from 1928 to 1963 in the United States.

5.7   *The Jazz Singer* (1927). Warner Bros.' Vitaphone sound-on-disk system became a sensation because of Al Jolson's singing and spontaneous dialogue.

5.8   *Dracula* (1931). Tod Browning's classic is one of a cycle of early sound-era horror films made by Universal.

5.9   *Dracula* (1931). The Spanish-language version was shot on the same sets as the English-language version, with different cast and costumes for the export market. This version was directed by George Melford.

The Jazz Singer, Warner Bros.' second feature film with recorded sound, released in October 1927, is credited with convincing exhibitors, critics, studios, and the public that there was no turning back. Starring vaudevillian Al Jolson, the country's most popular entertainer of the time, the film tells a story, similar to Jolson's own, of a singer who must turn his back on his Jewish roots and the legacy of his father, a cantor in a synagogue, in order to fulfill his show-business dreams. He introduces dialogue to the movies with a famous promise that came true soon thereafter: "You ain't heard nothing yet!" **[Figure 5.7]**. Talking pictures, or "talkies," were an instant phenomenon. In the wake of *The Jazz Singer*'s phenomenal success, the studios came together and signed with Western Electric (a subsidiary of AT&T) to adopt a sound-on-film system in place of the less flexible Vitaphone sound-on-disk process. The studios also invested in the conversion of their major theaters and in the acquisition of new chains to show sound films.

1930s–1940s: Challenges and Innovations in Cinema Sound

The transition to sound was not entirely smooth. The troubles with exhibition technology were more than matched by the difficulties posed by cumbersome sound recording technology. Despite such problems, the transition was extremely rapid: by 1930, silent films were no longer being produced by the major studios; only a few independent filmmakers, such as Charlie Chaplin, whose art grew from the silent medium, held out.

The ability of early films to cross national borders and be understood regardless of the local language, a much-celebrated property of the early medium, was also changed irrevocably by the addition of monolingual spoken dialogue. Film industries outside the United States acquired national specificity, and Hollywood set up European production facilities. Exports were affected by conversion-standard problems and patents disputes. For a time, films were made simultaneously in different languages. Marlene Dietrich became an international star in *The Blue Angel* (1930), produced in Germany in French, English, and German versions. Comparing variations not only in the language but also in the music and other sounds in these different versions is fascinating. The Spanish-language *Dracula* (1931), directed by George Melford, used the same sets and the translated script of Tod Browning's Hollywood classic but with a Spanish-speaking cast and more provocative women's costumes **[Figures 5.8 and 5.9]**. With adequate dubbing technology and other strategies, Hollywood's dominance of foreign markets was eventually reestablished, and foreign films, already dwindling on U.S. screens, became increasingly rare.

By this period, the Radio Corporation of America had entered the motion-picture production business, joining with the Keith-Orpheum chain of vaudeville theaters. The new studio, RKO, quickly became one of five studios known as the "majors" that would dominate sound-era cinema, and RKO's *King Kong* (1933) and *Citizen Kane* (1941) both contributed significantly to sound techniques.

1950s-Present: From Stereophonic to Digital Sound

The establishment of representational norms in sound recording and mixing practices proceeded rapidly after the introduction of sound. How movies sound—the crispness of voices, the lush quality of orchestral background music, the use of sound effects in conjunction with what is onscreen—supports ideas about the complementary relationship of sound and image, listening and viewing, and the value of realism. Further technological innovations in the 1950s (stereophonic sound), the 1970s (Dolby and surround sound), and the 1990s (digital sound) brought the aural experience of Hollywood cinema to the fore but did little to challenge these ideas. More than simple technological "improvements," these changes corresponded with historical shifts in film's social role, as television, home video, and computer games became competitive entertainments.

When **digital sound**, the most recent and radical change in sound reproduction, was introduced, the competitive formats recalled the period of sound's introduction in the late 1920s. Just as in the 1950s, when new film technologies such as CinemaScope and stereophonic sound were used to lure customers back to the theaters, today's digital sound systems attract audiences to theatrical exhibition. Audiophiles lead the companion trend toward home theaters with digital sound systems and speakers configured like those of movie theaters to emulate surround sound. Although cinema's mimetic capacity to reproduce images and sounds from the natural world is one of its strongest appeals, the perpetual quest for images and sounds that are bigger, better, and louder indicates that part of cinema's appeal is its ability to provide a heightened sensory experience that intensifies the ordinary.

The Elements of Film Sound

Despite our habitual references to motion *pictures* and to film *viewers*, sound is fully integrated into the film experience. In fact, one aspect of sound—human speech—is so central to narrative comprehension and viewer identification that we can often follow what happens even when the picture is out of sight. Sounds can interact with images in infinite ways, and strategies used to combine the two fundamentally affect our understanding of film. The song "We'll Meet Again"—a nostalgic 1940s song used to boost troop morale during World War II—that accompanies footage of H-bombs dropping in *Dr. Strangelove or: How I Learned to Stop Worrying and Love the Bomb* (1964) makes it impossible to read these images as noble or tragic; instead, a frame of dark satire determines our view of war **[Figure 5.10]**.

The relationship between the original sound and its reproduction differs from that between an object and its filmed image. Although a sound is altered when it is recorded, engineered, and reproduced, we feel that we are hearing a real sound in real time. With images, we readily recognize that we see only a two-dimensional copy of the original. Sound effects of footsteps to accompany an image of a character walking are not really necessary; such an image is easily interpreted. However, the sound of footsteps heightens the sense of immediacy and presence. In recent years, improvements in sound technology and developments in sound recording practices have

5.10 *Dr. Strangelove or: How I Learned to Stop Worrying and Love the Bomb* (1964). An image of aggression set to nostalgic 1940s music sets the film's dark satirical tone.

5.11   Playtime (1967). Jacques Tati's comic film emphasizes sound as much as image, often cueing the gag through sound effects.

▶ **VIEWING CUE**

Technologies of watching—and listening—to movies have changed rapidly in recent years. Characterize the audio experience of the last film you watched. How much of this experience was specific to the film's sound design and how much to the format, platform, or venue through which you watched the film?

resulted in ever greater "realism" and intensity, making contemporary films sound much richer than those of the past. Sound has also led the way toward digitization, with digital image manipulation and picture editing following in turn. In the next section, we will explore the relationship of sound and image and the often-unperceived meanings of sound, before considering more fully the technology and aesthetics of film sound.

Sound and Image

Any consideration of sound in film entails discussion of the relationship between sounds and images. Some filmmakers, such as the comic actor and writer-director Jacques Tati, have consistently given equal weight to the treatment and meaning of sound in their films. In *Playtime* (1967), as in Tati's other films, comic gags take place in long shots, and sounds cue us where to look **[Figure 5.11]**. In his unique films, filmmaker Jacques Demy pursues a vision of film's musicality. In *The Umbrellas of Cherbourg* (1964), all of the dialogue is sung to Michel Legrand's music, while the candy-colored sets and costumes are designed to harmonize with this heightening of experience **[Figure 5.12]**. Derek Jarman's *Blue* (1993), made after the filmmaker had lost his vision due to an AIDS-related illness, combines an image track consisting solely of a rich shade of blue with a soundtrack featuring a complex mix of music, effects, and voices reading diaries and dramatic passages. Gazing into a vast blue screen allows viewers to focus more carefully on the soundtrack's ideas and the emotions they evoke.

For many filmmakers, however, as for viewers, sound functions more as an afterthought that exists to enhance the impact of the image. Many possible reasons exist for this disparity. Film is generally considered to be a predominantly visual medium rather than an aural one, following a more pervasive hierarchy of vision over sound. The artistry of the image track is perceived to be greater, as the image is more clearly a conscious rendering of the object being photographed than the recording is of the original sound. The fact that sound came later in the historical development of cinema has also been offered as an explanation of its secondary status. Yet the importance and variety of aural experiences at the movies were great even before the introduction of synchronized soundtracks. Since the early years of sound cinema, certain directors and composers have struggled against a too-literal, and too-limited, use of sound in film, arguing that the infinite possibilities in image and sound combinations are germane to the medium and its historical development. French filmmaker René Clair feared that the introduction of sound would diminish the visual possibilities of the medium and reduce it to "canned theater." In his musical film *Le Million* (1931), he uses

5.12   The Umbrellas of Cherbourg (1964). The musicality of Jacques Demy's lovely tale of a small-town romance is represented in everything from the dialogue, all in song, to the brightly colored costumes and sets.

sound in a way that makes it integral to the film. Through scenes of characters and crowds singing songs essential to the plot, Clair demonstrates that sound's potential is more than additive; it transforms the film experience viscerally, aesthetically, and conceptually.

Synchronous and Asynchronous Sound

Because sound and image always create meaning in conjunction, film theorists attentive to sound have looked for ways to talk about the possibilities of the combination of sound and image. In his book *Theory of Film* (1960), Siegfried Kracauer emphasizes a distinction between **synchronous** and **asynchronous sound**. The former has a visible onscreen source, such as when dialogue appears to come directly from the speaker's moving lips, while the latter does not. (Some analysts prefer to call this distinction **onscreen** versus **offscreen sound**.) For instance, while most speech is synchronous, Ada's voiceover at the beginning of *The Piano* discussed in the chapter opener is asynchronous. A shot of an alarm clock accompanied by the sound of its ringing is synchronous. An asynchronous knock in a horror film might startle the characters with the threat of an offscreen presence.

Kracauer goes on to differentiate between **parallelism** in the use of sound, which occurs when the soundtrack and image "say the same thing," and **counterpoint** (or contrapuntal sound), which occurs when two different meanings are implied by these elements. In *Kill Bill: Vol. 2* (2004), as The Bride attempts to break out of a sealed coffin, the soundtrack by Ennio Morricone—music typically associated with spaghetti westerns—offers a counterpoint to this horrific situation **[Figure 5.13]**. Soon, the sound of the impact of her fist on the coffin lid, which parallels her methodical punching, combines with the music for heightened effect.

The two pairs of terms are distinct from each other. A shot of a teakettle accompanied by a high-pitched whistle is both synchronous and parallel. The teakettle accompanied by an alarm bell would be a synchronous yet contrapuntal use of sound. A voiceover of a nature documentary may explain the behavior of the animals in an asynchronous use of parallel sound. Idyllic images accompanied by a narration stressing the presence of toxins in the environment and an ominous electronic hum would be a contrapuntal use of asynchronous sound. A familiar example of how relationships between sound and image can achieve multiple meanings comes at the end of *The Wizard of Oz* (1939). The booming voice and sound effects synchronized with the terrifying image of the wizard are suddenly revealed to have been asynchronous sounds produced by an ordinary man behind the curtain. When we see him speaking into a microphone, the sound is in fact synchronous, and what was intended as a parallel is revealed to be a contrapuntal use of sound **[Figure 5.14]**.

5.13   *Kill Bill: Vol. 2* (2004). Spaghetti western music acts as a counterpoint to the horrific image of The Bride punching her way out of a sealed coffin.

▶ **VIEWING CUE**

Distinguish an example of synchronous sound (with an onscreen source) from an example of asynchronous sound (with an offscreen source) in the film you are studying. Are these sounds easy to distinguish? ⏸

5.14   *The Wizard of Oz* (1939). The source of the wizard's voice is revealed, interrupting the synchronous effect that frightened the travelers.

Parallelism—the mutual reinforcing or even the redundancy of sound and image—is the norm in Hollywood. For example, a shot of a busy street is accompanied by traffic noises, although viewers immediately understand the locale through the visuals. This parallelism is an aesthetic choice. In contrast, at the dawn of the sound era, Soviet theorists advocated a contrapuntal use of sound to maximize the effects of montage.

Diegetic and Nondiegetic Sound

One of the most frequently cited and instructive distinctions that is made in sound is between **diegetic sound**, which has its source in the narrative world of film, and **nondiegetic sound**, which does not belong to the characters' world. Materially, the source of film sound is the actual soundtrack that accompanies the image, but diegetic sound implies a visible onscreen source. **Diegesis** refers to the world of the film's story, including not only what is shown but also what is implied to have taken place. ("Diegesis" comes from the Greek word meaning "telling" and is distinguished from "mimesis," meaning "showing." The implication is that while mimetic representations imitate or mimic, diegetic ones use particular devices to tell about or imply events and settings.) One question offers a simple way to distinguish between diegetic and nondiegetic sound: can the characters in the film hear the sound? If not, the sound is likely to be nondiegetic. This distinction can apply to voices, music, and even sound effects. Conversations among onscreen characters, the voice of God in *The Ten Commandments* (1956), a voiceover that corresponds to a confession a character is making to the police, and the radio music that accompanies Mr. Blonde's sadistic assault of a police officer in *Reservoir Dogs* (1992) are all diegetic. Nondiegetic sounds do not follow rules of verisimilitude. For example, the voiceover narration that tells viewers about the characters in *The Magnificent Ambersons* (1942), background music that accompanies a love scene or journey, or sound effects such as a crash of cymbals when someone takes a comic fall are all nondiegetic. Audio practitioners refer to diegetic music, such as a shot of a band performing at a party or characters listening to music, as **source music** [Figures 5.15a and 5.15b].

The distinction between diegetic and nondiegetic sounds can sometimes be murky. Certain voiceovers, though not spoken aloud to other characters, can be construed as the thoughts of a character and thus as arising from the narrative world of the film. Film theorist Christian Metz has classified these as **semidiegetic sound**; they can also be referred to as **internal diegetic sound**.

▶ **VIEWING CUE**

Find an example of diegetic sound in the film you are studying, and one of nondiegetic sound. What would the movie be like without the nondiegetic sound? ⏸

(a)

(b)

5.15a and 5.15b   *Written on the Wind* (1956). Source music provides the dramatic soundtrack when Marylee's father has a heart attack as she dances in her room.

The uncertain status of the dead character's voiceover in *Sunset Boulevard* (1950) is an example of this. Diegetic music—such as characters singing "Happy Birthday"—is often picked up as a nondiegetic theme in the film's score. Such borderline and mixed cases, rather than frustrating our attempts to categorize, are illustrative of the fluidity and creative possibilities of the soundtrack as well as of the complex devices that shape our experience of a film's spatial and temporal continuity.

Sound Production

As early as the preproduction phase of a contemporary film, a **sound designer** may be involved to plan and direct the overall sound through to the final mix. During production, **sound recording** takes place simultaneously with the filming of a scene. When the slate is filmed at the beginning of each take, the **clapboard** is snapped; this recorded sound is used to synchronize sound recordings and camera images **[Figure 5.16]**. Microphones for recording synchronous sound (radio microphones) may be placed on the actors, suspended over the action outside of camera range on a device resembling a fishing pole called a **boom**, or placed in other locations on set. The placement of microphones is often dictated by the desire to emphasize clarity and intelligibility of dialogue, especially the speech of the stars, in the final version of a film. **Direct sound** is sound captured directly from its source, but some degree of **reflected sound**, captured as sounds bounce from the walls and sets, may be desired to give a sense of space. The **production mixer** (or sound recordist) combines these different sources during filming, adjusting their relative volume or balance. In the multitrack sound recording process introduced in Robert Altman's *Nashville* (1975), as many as twenty-four separate tracks of sound can be recorded on twelve tracks.

When a cut of the film is prepared, the crucial and increasingly complex phase of **postproduction sound** work begins. **Sound editing** interacts with the image track to create rhythmic relationships, establish connections between sound and onscreen sources, and smooth or mark transitions. When a sound carries over a visual transition in a film, it is termed a **sound bridge**. For example, music might continue over a scene change or montage sequence, or dialogue might begin before the speaking characters are seen by the audience. The director consults with the composer and the picture and sound editors to determine where music and effects will be added, a process called **spotting**. Sound effects may be gathered, produced by sound-effects editors on computers, retrieved from a sound library, or generated by **foley artists**. Named for the legendary sound man Jack Foley, these members of the sound crew watch the projected film and simultaneously generate live sound effects—footsteps, the rustle of leaves, a key turning in a lock—on what is called a foley stage. These effects are eventually mixed with the other tracks. The film's

5.16   On the set, *Wild at Heart* (1990). Clapboards are used to synchronize sound and image takes.

text continued on page 190 ▶

FILM IN FOCUS

Sound and Image in *Singin' in the Rain* (1952)

Hollywood has furnished its own myth about the introduction of synchronized sound in *Singin' in the Rain*. Directed by Stanley Donen and Gene Kelly, *Singin' in the Rain* demonstrates an escapist use of sound in film while also being *about* how sound in film achieves such effects. It addresses the relationship of sound to image, the history of film sound technologies, and the process of recording and reproducing sound.

Set in Hollywood at the end of the 1920s, *Singin' in the Rain* follows efforts at the fictional Monumental Pictures to make the studio's first successful sound film. Although the film's self-consciousness about the film-making process invites the audience into a behind-the-scenes perspective, the film itself continues to employ every available technique to achieve the illusionism of the Hollywood musical. One of the lessons of the film is that a "talking picture" isn't just "a silent picture with some talking added," as the studio producer assumes it to be. The film shows that adding sound to images enhances them with all the exuberance of song and dance, comedy, and romance. It also suggests that a great deal of labor and equipment are involved in creating such effects.

From the very beginning of *Singin' in the Rain*, the technology responsible for sound reproduction—technology that is usually hidden—is displayed. The film opens outside a Hollywood movie palace where crowds have gathered for the premiere of the new Lockwood and Lamont picture. Our first orientation is aural: "Ladies and gentlemen, I am speaking to you from. . . ." The asynchronous announcer's voice carries across the crowds and seems to address us directly. The second shot opens directly on a loudspeaker, underscoring the parallelism of image and soundtrack, and then begins to explore the crowd of listeners. When we first see the radio announcer, the source of the synchronous voice, the microphone is very prominent in the mise-en-scène **[Figure 5.17]**. Referring to the bygone days of radio and silent movies, the film celebrates its modern audience's opportunity to watch sound and image combined in a sophisticated MGM musical.

Singin' in the Rain immediately begins to exploit the resources and conventions of studio-era sound cinema.

When star Don Lockwood (Gene Kelly) tells the story of his past in a diegetic voiceover to the assembled crowds and the radio listeners at home, this is a contrapuntal use of sound because the series of flashback images belie his words. When his onscreen image gives way to his offscreen voice speaking of studying at a conservatory, we see him and his buddy, Cosmo Brown (Donald O'Connor), performing a vaudeville routine instead. This scene shows that images and voices can be out of sync, a theme that will become prominent in the film as a whole. It also shows the multiple ways the soundtrack can interact with the images. The comic vaudeville routine is, in turn, accompanied by lively music and humorous sound effects—the diegetic sound of the flashback world—encouraging our direct appreciation of the number. Next we hear the crowd's appreciative reactions to Lockwood's narration, a narration that we know to be phony. However, we do not experience these two different levels of sound—Don's self-serving narration and the debunking synchronized sound of the flashbacks—as confusing. It is clear that the film's unveiling of the mechanisms of sound technology will not limit its own reliance on the multiple illusions of sound–image relationships.

5.17 *Singin' in the Rain* (1952). A concern with sound recording technology is evident in the microphone's prominence in the first scene.

Later, when Don wants to express the depth of his feelings to Kathy Selden (Debbie Reynolds), he takes her to an empty soundstage. Ironically, his sincerity depends on the artifice of a sunset background, a wind machine, and a battery of mood lights, which together render the very picture of romance **[Figure 5.18]**. Yet the corresponding sound illusion is conjured without any visible sound recording or effects equipment, much less an onscreen orchestra. Indeed, each of Don's touches, such as switching on the wind machine, is synchronized with a nondiegetic musical flourish. It is possible to ask us to suspend our disbelief in this way because, in the film's world, music is everywhere.

The film pits the stilted, overblown style of silent costume drama against the rhythms of a vital, contemporary musical—a form so spontaneous that song even erupts backstage. In the "Make 'Em Laugh" sequence, Cosmo improvises a dance with props available on the set. When he begins to sing, an unseen orchestra starts up; when he takes a pratfall, cymbals crash in a parallel but asynchronous use of sound. The world in which illusions are made is itself illusory. In the course of the film, Don Lockwood will learn to incorporate his true self—the one who enjoys "singin' and dancin' in the rain"—into his onscreen persona. Lina Lamont (Jean Hagen), who represents image without the animating authenticity of sound (she's a beautiful woman with a comical accent, and ironically, her hilarious performance is one of the greatest aural pleasures of the film), will be replaced by Kathy, who dubs Lina's voice. Kathy is depicted as genuine because she can sing. Image and sound go together.

Nothing illustrates the film's paradoxical acknowledgment of the sound–image illusions constructed by Hollywood and its indulgence in them better than the contrast between the disastrous premiere of the non-singing *The Dueling Cavalier* and the film's final scene at the opening night of the musical *The Dancing Cavalier*, in which the truth of Lina's imposture comes out. In the former, a noisy audience laughs at and heckles the errors of poor synchronous sound recording: the actors' heartbeats and rustling costumes drown out their dialogue (for us, of course, the laughter and the heartbeats are both sound effects, the latter mixed at comically high levels). The film they have created fundamentally misunderstands the promise of "talking pictures." At the premiere of the musical *The Dancing Cavalier*, in contrast, the film finally makes the proper match, not only between sound and image (thus correcting the humorous synchronization problems of the first version) but also between Don and Kathy. After she's forced to dub Lina "live" at the premiere, and the hoax is exposed when the curtains are drawn for all the audience to see, the humiliated Kathy runs from the stage. Don gets her back by singing "You Are My Lucky Star" to her from the stage (thus demonstrating before the audience in the film that unlike Lina, he used his own singing voice during the film within a film). Cosmo conducts the conveniently present orchestra (the premiere is of a sound film that should not require accompaniment), and Kathy joins Don in a duet.

Lest we read the film as suggesting that the onscreen orchestra is more genuine than the romantic background music of the earlier scenes because it is synchronous, we must note that the film ends triumphantly with asynchronous music. A full, invisible chorus picks up "You Are My Lucky Star" as the camera takes us out into the open air, to pause on the billboard announcing the premiere of *Singin' in the Rain*, starring Lockwood and Selden (who, of course, are represented by images of the stars of the movie by the same name that we are watching, Gene Kelly and Debbie Reynolds) **[Figure 5.19]**. This patently fake chorus and the billboard advertising the film we are watching are the culmination of the film's effort to render Hollywood illusionism—so aptly represented by extravagant musicals such as *Singin' in the Rain*—natural. *Singin' in the Rain* dramatizes the arrival of sound in Hollywood as the inevitable and enjoyable combination of sound and image.

5.18 *Singin' in the Rain* (1952). The illusion of romance is visibly created on the soundstage, but the music the characters dance to has no apparent source.

5.19 *Singin' in the Rain* (1952). The film's final reflexive moment is accompanied by an invisible chorus on the soundtrack.

▶ **VIEWING CUE**

In the film you've just viewed, from what direction do particular sounds come? What are the most audible elements of the film's sound mix? Is the mix full, or are there relatively few sounds? ❚❚

composer begins composing the score, which is recorded to synchronize with the film's final cut **[Figure 5.20]**. The composer may actually conduct the musicians in time with the film. **Postsynchronous sound**, recorded after the fact and then synchronized with onscreen sources, is often preferred for the dialogue used in the final mix. Natural sound recorded during production may be indistinct due to noise, perspective, or other problems, and much of the actor's performance will depend on intelligibility of dialogue.

During **automated dialogue replacement (ADR)**, actors watch the film footage and re-record their lines to be dubbed into the soundtrack (a process also known as **looping** because actors watch a continuous loop of their scenes). Although dubbing can violate verisimilitude, in Italy and other countries it is used for all of a film's dialogue. Dubbing often replaces the original language of a film for exhibition in another country. Other common practices, such as assembling extras to approximate the sound of a crowd (known as **walla,** the word they were instructed to murmur) or recording **room tone** (the aural properties of a location when nothing is happening), may be used to cover any patch of pure silence in the finished film. Such practices show the extent to which the sound unit goes to reproduce "real-seeming" sound.

Sound mixing (or re-recording), an important stage in the postproduction of a film, can occur only after the image track, including the credits, is complete (that is, after the picture is "locked"). All three elements of the soundtrack—music, sound effects, and dialogue—that have been recorded on separate tracks will now be combined. As the tracks are mixed, they are cut and extended, adjusted and "sweetened" by the sound editor with the input of the director and perhaps the sound designer and picture editor. There are no objective standards for a sound mix. Besides making sure it is complete and clear, the director and technicians will have specific ideas for the film's sound in mind. The final mix might place extra emphasis on dialogue, modulate a mood through the volume of the music, or punch up sound effects during an action sequence. In a film like *Barton Fink* (1991), much of the sense of inhabiting a slightly unreal world is generated by a sound mix that incorporates sounds such as animal noises into the effects accompanying creaking doors **[Figure 5.21]**. At a film's final **mix**, a sound mixer produces a master track to match the final cut of the film. Optical tracks are "married" to the image track on the film print, whereas digital tracks may be printed on the film or recorded on separate disks.

Sound reproduction is the stage in the process when the film's audience (literally, those who listen) experiences the film's sound. During projection, optical soundtracks are illuminated and read by a solar cell that transfers the light to electrical energy, which is then amplified and transferred to the speaker system. Magnetic and digital soundtracks are also converted back to sound waves by the sound system during projection.

The reproduction of a sound is undoubtedly a copy. But it seems to have the same presence or effect on the ear as the original sound, even if its source, directionality, tonality, or depth has changed. We believe we are hearing the sound right here, right now, and indeed

5.20 **Production, *Far from Heaven*** (2002). Director Todd Haynes and composer Elmer Bernstein recording the film's score, which re-creates the sound of 1950s Hollywood movies.

we are, but we are hearing a recording of an airplane engine, not an actual airplane engine. Sound perspective enhances this impression of presence and can be manipulated with great nuance in digital sound mixing. The placement of speakers in the actual three-dimensional space of the theater may be used to suggest sounds emanating from the left or right of the depicted scene or from behind or in front of the audience.

Voice, Music, Sound Effects

Glengarry Glen Ross (1992), adapted by David Mamet from his own play, is dominated by the sound of actors' voices. *The Terminator* (1984) keys us to events in its futuristic world by noise, while the title of *The Sound of Music* (1965) announces

5.21   *Barton Fink* (1991). The subjective world of the main character, a playwright who has come to Hollywood to write for the movies, is rendered through the incorporation of unusual sounds in the mix.

what one can expect to hear on its soundtrack. Voice, music, and sound effects are the three elements of the film **soundtrack**, and they are often present simultaneously. In some sense a film's image track, composed of relatively discrete photographic images and text, is simpler and more unified. Nevertheless, although these three sound elements can all be present and combined in relation to any given image, conventions have evolved governing these relationships. Usually dialogue is audible over music, for example, and only in special cases does a piece of music dictate the images that accompany it. (Disney's *Fantasia* [1940] was an experiment in allowing the music to "go first.") Here we will examine each of the basic elements of the soundtrack and its potential to make meaning in combination with images and other sounds. We will uncover conventional usages of soundtracks and how they have both shaped the film experience and given direction to theorists' inquiries into the properties and potential of film sound.

Voice in Film

Human speech, primarily in the form of dialogue, is often central to understanding narrative film. Acoustic qualities of the voices of actors make a distinct contribution to a film: Jimmy Stewart's drawl is relaxed and reassuring; Robin Williams's cadences let us know we are watching something more antic and comic. But of course *what* actors say is crucial: speech establishes character motivation and goals and conveys plot information.

Making an intelligible record of an actor's speech quickly became the primary goal in early film sound recording processes, although this goal required some important concessions in the otherwise primary quest for realism. For example, think about how we hear film characters' speech. While the image track may cut from a long shot of a conversation to a medium shot of two characters to a series of close-up, shot/reverse-shot pairings, the soundtrack does not reproduce these distances accurately through changes in volume or the relationship between direct and reflected sound. Rather, actors are miked so that what they say is recorded directly and is clear, intelligible, and uniform in volume throughout the dialogue scene. **Sound perspective**, which refers to the apparent distance of a sound source, remains close.

5.22   ***Nashville*** (1975). Robert Altman's twelve-track recording process captures each character individually, and overlapping dialogue is used in the final mix.

Dialogue. A great deal of humor is derived from the depiction of early solutions to the miking of actors in *Singin' in the Rain*. First only every other word is caught as the actress Lina Lamont moves her head while speaking; then hiding the microphone in her bodice amplifies the sound of her heart, drowning out the words she speaks. Director Robert Altman's innovations in multi-track film sound recording in *Nashville*, mentioned earlier in this chapter, allowed each character to be miked and separately recorded. One stylistic feature of this technique is Altman's extensive use of **overlapping dialogue**, mixing characters' speech simultaneously, a technique Orson Welles had attempted with less sophisticated recording technology. In *Nashville*, characters constantly talk over each other **[Figure 5.22]**. This technique, which may make individual lines less distinct, is often used to approximate the everyday experience of hearing multiple, competing speakers and sounds at the same time. Dialogue is also given priority when it carries over visual shifts, such as shot/reverse-shot patterns of editing conversations. We watch one actor begin a line and then watch the listener as he or she continues. Sound preserves temporal continuity as the scene is broken down into individual shots. Speech occurs here and now, and thus it is a key support of verisimilitude. Sometimes the most outlandish plot premises and settings can be anchored by dialogue. Given the importance and authority we accord the spoken word, it is interesting that film sound often has second-class status in relation to the image.

5.23   ***M*** (1931). Use of offscreen sound and space implies the murderer's presence in Lang's masterpiece of early sound cinema.

Voice-Off. The **voice-off** technique refers to a voice that can be seen to originate from an onscreen speaker or from a speaker who can be inferred to be present in the scene but who is not currently visible. This technique is a good example of the greater spatial flexibility of sound over image. The opening shot of *Laura* (1944) follows a detective looking around a fancy apartment as a **narrator** introduces the film's events. Abruptly, the same voice addresses the detective from an adjacent room, telling him to be careful what he touches, a striking use of voice-off. Early in the film *M* (1931), the murderer's offscreen whistle is heard, followed by an onscreen shadow of a man, combining the expressive possibility of sound (just recently introduced when the film was made) with that of lighting and mise-en-scène **[Figure 5.23]**.

In an experimental film, voice-off may also serve to make the viewer/listener think about different levels of the film's fiction. How do we know that an offscreen voice shares the same space and time as the onscreen figures? The soundtrack of Chantal Akerman's *News from Home* (1976) consists of the director's voice reading letters in French from her mother back home in Belgium **[Figure 5.24]**. The images depict sparsely populated New York streets and lonely subway platforms and cars. The disjunction between voice and image reinforces the distance remarked upon in the correspondence. A more conventional example of voice-off appears in *Sin City* (2005), where the voice of "Yellow Bastard" precedes the revelation of his disfigured body and so creates a more disturbing effect when the two are connected.

While use of the voice-off in a classical film is a strong tool in the service of film realism, implying that the mise-en-scène extends beyond the borders of the frame, the illusion of realism can be challenged if the origins of the voice-off are not clear. The voice-off of HAL 9000, the computer in *2001: A Space Odyssey* (1968), is consistent with realism because the voice has a known source. However, the even level of volume makes it seem to pervade the spaceship even as it retains its intimate quality. In the film's uncanny combination of humanity and technology, it suggests how the voice-off can introduce distance into the customary match of sound and image.

Voiceover. A voice-off is distinguished from the familiar technique of **voiceover** by the simple fact that characters within the diegesis cannot hear the voiceover. The voiceover is an important structuring device in film: a text spoken by an offscreen narrator can act as the organizing principle behind virtually all of the film's images, such as in a documentary film, a commercial, or an experimental video or essay film. The unseen narrators of the classic documentaries *Night Mail* (1936) and *The Plow That Broke the Plains* (1936) offer a poem about the British postal service and an account of the U.S. government's agricultural programs, respectively, while the filmmaker's voiceover in Alex Gibney's *Taxi to the Dark Side* (2007) offers a somber description of contemporary torture in Afghanistan and Guantánamo Bay **[Figure 5.25]**. The voiceover device soon became the cornerstone of the documentary tradition, in which the voiceover "anchors" the potential ambiguity of the film's images. The sonic qualities of such voiceovers—usually male, resonant, and "unmarked" by class, regional, or foreign accent or other distinguishing features—are meant to connote trustworthiness (although today they can sound propagandistic). The traditional technique of directing our interpretation of images through a transcendent voiceover is sometimes referred to as the "voice of God." Confident male voices of this type can still be heard in nature shows, commercials, and trailers seen in movie theaters.

In the newsreel segment early in *Citizen Kane*, Orson Welles emulates, and gently mocks, this genre's characteristic sound, in particular the *March of Time* series shown in movie theaters from 1935 to 1951. The volume even increases notably at the start of the segment to emphasize the voiceover's booming authority. This sanctioned story of Kane's life remains impersonal, in contrast to the multiple on-camera narrators whose recollections organize the film's other segments. In the introduction to *History of the World: Part I* (1981), Mel Brooks casts Orson Welles himself as God the narrator, parodying precisely the theological transcendence with which voiceovers have been associated. More recently, *Stranger than Fiction* (2006) plays with many of the traditional

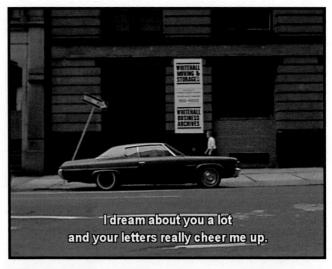

5.24   *News from Home* (1976). Letters from home are read over images of a lonely New York City.

▶ **VIEWING CUE**

Identify specific uses of voice in the film you will screen next in class. Is dialogue abundant? If voiceovers are used, what are their function and diegetic status?

5.25   *Taxi to the Dark Side* (2007). The somber and matter-of-fact voiceover in this documentary makes the realities it describes seem even more disturbing.

5.26 *Stranger than Fiction* (2006). Here voiceover ironically appears within the protagonist's world.

5.27 *Bridget Jones's Diary* (2001). The subjective voiceover of this film humorously articulates the desires and anxieties of the heroine.

assumptions when the main character, IRS agent Harold Crick, suddenly begins to hear a voiceover narration describing and directing his life and ultimately confronts the female author-narrator, Karen Eiffel, convincing her to alter her plans for his death **[Figure 5.26]**. What at first seems like a nondiegetic voiceover suddenly becomes discovered within the diegesis.

Voiceover narration has multiple functions in fiction films. *The Royal Tenenbaums* (2001) begins with a "once upon a time" voiceover as a way of introducing the world of the story. Voiceovers can also render characters' subjective states. Much of the humor of *Bridget Jones's Diary* (2001), for instance, comes from viewers' access to the heroine's internal (semidiegetic) comments on the situations she encounters **[Figure 5.27]**. But voiceover can also be an important structural device in narration, orienting viewers to the temporal organization of a story by setting up a flashback or providing a transition back to the film's present. For example, a voiceover narration in the present can accompany a scene from the past that uses both images and sounds from within the depicted world. Use of voiceovers to organize a film's temporality is prevalent in certain genres such as film noir, in which the voiceover imitates the hard-boiled, first-person investigative style of the literary works from which many of these stories are adapted. Sometimes, in keeping with the murky world of film noir or the limited perspective of the investigator, such voiceovers prove unreliable **[Figure 5.28]**.

Michael Curtiz's *Mildred Pierce* (1945) is a "woman's film"—featuring a female star whose character faces exaggerated versions of the problems many women encounter—but it is given a film noir framework, and the voiceover is an important element in this clash of styles. In the beginning, Mildred (played by Joan Crawford) confesses to a crime we eventually learn she did not commit. However, her voiceover's credibility is compromised by her gender as well as by genre conventions. Several flashbacks are introduced by scenes in which Mildred is interrogated by the police. "It seems as if I was born in a kitchen," she narrates **[Figure 5.29]**. These voiceovers are quickly abandoned as the flashback segments revert to and play out in synchronized sound. Eventually Mildred's version of events is discredited by the police, who use her words to convict her daughter; her voiceover ultimately confirms their point of view. In fact, critics note that in **women's pictures** such as *Mildred Pierce* and Alfred Hitchcock's *Rebecca* (1940), female voiceovers rarely carry through to closure, violating the symmetry we have come to expect from a classical Hollywood film.

5.28 *Laura* (1944). Shown writing in a tub, Waldo Lydecker (Clifton Webb) opens the film with a voiceover narration. His account of the heroine's death proves him unreliable when she is discovered to be alive.

Talking Heads.
Documentaries typically use sound to "explain" image. At one end of the spectrum is the authoritative, anonymous voiceover that sets up and interprets the film's images. At the other, **talking heads**—on-camera interviews, usually shot in medium close-up—tell the documentary's story through experts or ordinary people. This convention is widespread in the news media. In Lynne Fernie and Aerlyn Weissman's documentary about lesbian life in the 1940s to the 1960s, *Forbidden Love* (1992), there is no voiceover, printed text, or on-camera presence to lead the viewer through the material. The interviewed subjects are the authorities.

5.29 *Mildred Pierce* (1945). The voiceover of Mildred (played by Joan Crawford) increases our sympathy for her situation as a wife and mother in the flashbacks.

Synchronization.
Synchronization, the visible coordination of the voice with the body from which it is emanating, tends to be a valued practice in Hollywood films. It anchors sound that might otherwise seem to be autonomous or even call into question the seamless illusion of reality that Hollywood films strive for. Film theorist Kaja Silverman argues that synchronization is especially enforced for characters who are culturally more closely identified with the body, such as women and African Americans; these characters have not been allowed to achieve authoritative presence through speech alone. Thus Morgan Freeman's voiceover narration of *The Shawshank Redemption* (1994) is striking precisely because it validates the experience of an African American character. *Eve's Bayou* (1997) is narrated by a child, a device that infuses the film with wonder and a sense of having to decipher the narrative; the fact that Eve is female and African American makes the film's emphasis on untold stories even more urgent **[Figure 5.30]**.

Ever since "the talkies" were introduced, the human voice has organized systems of meaning in various types of film: narrative films are frequently driven by dialogue, documentaries by voiceover; and experimental films often turn voice into an aesthetic element. Some writers suggest that a theory of "voice" can open up cinema analysis to more meanings than a model devoted to the image alone. Although we have stressed how frequently film sound is subordinated to the image, the realm of the voice shows us how central sound is to cinema's intelligibility. In fact, the prevalence of the human voice is a measure of just how focused the universe of classical cinema is on depicting human experience.

Music in Film

Music is a crucial element in the film experience; among a range of other effects, it provides rhythm and deepens emotional response. Music has rarely been absent from film programs, and many of the venues for early film had been

5.30 *Eve's Bayou* (1997). A little girl's version of events gains credence through the voiceover device.

musical ones first. The piano, an important element of public and private amusements at the turn of the twentieth century, quickly became a cornerstone of film exhibition. Throughout the silent film period, scoring for films steadily developed from the distribution of collections of music cues that accompanists and ensembles could play to correspond with appropriate moments in films to full-length compositions for specific films. When D. W. Griffith's *The Birth of a Nation* premiered in 1915, a full orchestra, playing Joseph Carl Breil's score in which the Ku Klux Klan rallied to Wagner's "Ride of the Valkyries," was a major audience attraction. The architecture of the large movie palaces constructed during this period was acoustically geared to audiences familiar with listening to orchestral music in a concert setting. *The Jazz Singer* and other early sound films were conceived to show off the musical performances of their stars. As mentioned previously, speech made it to the screen as an afterthought—and thus the introduction of dialogue presented problems of scale and volume in the movie palaces.

Although the term "talkies" for the new sound films soon took over, movies of every genre—westerns, disaster films, science fiction films—relied on music from the beginning. Often this music contributes to categorizing such films *as* genre films. Vangelis's music for *Blade Runner* (1982), for example, distinctly marks it as a science fiction film. In contrast, Max Steiner's score for *Gone with the Wind* (1939) sets its nostalgic, romantic tone.

Narrative Music. When we think about the conventions of film sound, background music comes most immediately to mind. Music is the only element of cinematic discourse besides credits that is primarily nondiegetic. It can also move easily back and forth from the level of the story world to the nondiegetic level on which that world can be commented upon. In the back of our minds, we are aware that the practice of scoring films with music that has no source in the story violates verisimilitude, and yet we readily accept this convention. The celebrated gag in Mel Brooks's *Blazing Saddles* (1974), in which the musical soundtrack turns out to be coming from Count Basie's jazz orchestra playing in the middle of the desert, is entertaining because it shows the absurdity of the convention **[Figure 5.31]**. Occasionally we are jolted out of absorption in a film because the music is simply too overblown, its commentary on the action too obvious. Nevertheless, normally we value the musical score as a crucial element of our affective, or emotional, response to a film. The scoring for narrative films thus presents a notable paradox: much of what is valued in classical cinema—verisimilitude, cause-and-effect relationships—is completely ignored in even the most admired examples of film music.

The conventions of musical scoring, composition, orchestration, and mixing contribute to a particular kind of experience at the movies. Film music encourages us to be receptive to the information being conveyed by the visual as well as by the other acoustic dimensions of the film. It opens us to experience the movie as immediate and enveloping. It encourages us to let our barriers down. Many commentators speculate that these effects are psychologically related to the fact that the earliest human sensory experience is auditory. Because music is

5.31 *Blazing Saddles* (1974). Soundtrack music finds its onscreen source in Count Basie's orchestra playing in a desert in Mel Brooks's western spoof.

text continued on page 198 ▶

5.32a

5.32b

5.32c

5.32d

5.32e

5.32f

Music and Meaning in *I'm Not There* (2007)

Music often marks significance within a film narrative, so when film narratives explore the significance of music, the interdependence between these popular cultural forms is highlighted. In *I'm Not There* (2007), innovative filmmaker Todd Haynes uses six different characters to represent facets of Bob Dylan's persona; each inhabits a particular movie style, thus proliferating the possibilities of coordinating image, sound, and meaning.

The first "Dylan" is eleven-year-old drifter Woody Guthrie (Marcus Carl Franklin). He plays "Tombstone Blues" in a spontaneous, synchronous jam session with the man who takes him in (played by musician Richie Havens) **[Figure 5.32a]**. The next "Dylan" is folksinger Jack Rollins, whose story is framed as a documentary. Rollins is introduced through the rebel actor who plays him, Robbie Clark (Heath Ledger), in a scene that blends dialogue with the documentary's music track of "The Times They Are a-Changin'" **[Figure 5.32b]**. Next, we see the "actual" Rollins (Christian Bale) singing "The Lonesome Death of Hattie Carroll" **[Figure 5.32c]**, but the sincerity and immediacy of the performance is undercut by the documentary format, and by the fact that Rollins is preceded by his fictional double. Dylan's rock phase is dramatized through Jude Quinn (Cate Blanchett). As Jude and his band pull out electric guitars at a folk festival to play "Maggie's Farm" **[Figure 5.32d]**, the sound they emit is the parallel, though asynchronous, sound of a machine gun. But perhaps the most mysterious "Dylan" is Billy the Kid (Richard Gere), who encounters a diegetic band playing "Goin' to Acapulco" (sung by My Morning Jacket singer-songwriter Jim James) **[Figure 5.32e]** in the town of Riddle, surrounded by surreal figures drawn from Dylan's song lyrics. In a jarring transition from the Americana of this scene, we feel Dylan's alienation in swinging London as Michelle Williams's character taunts him while the Monkees' "(I'm Not Your) Steppin' Stone" spikes in volume in the background **[Figure 5.32f]**.

The distinction between diegetic and nondiegetic music is blurred throughout this complex film. The narrative significance of *I'm Not There* is as dependent upon the interpretations of the musical choices, and the level at which they are mixed on the soundtrack, as it is on the images that accompany and counterpoint the music.

197

nonrepresentational—it is not a copy of something specific in the world the way an image is—it can be more suggestive. Set apart from the diegesis and taking place right there in the theater, music eases our transition into the fictional world.

Because many of the practices of musical scoring were developed in tandem with the dominant form of narrative film, we will focus this discussion on narrative film music. In Hollywood and related mainstream film practices, the musical score has a direct connection to the story. However complex or lush the music may be, it serves a dramatic purpose. The term **underscoring**, also referred to as background music (in contrast to source music, which is diegetic), already emphasizes this status. Music quite literally underscores what is happening dramatically. A piece of music composed for a particular place in a film is referred to as a **cue**. When recording the score, the conductor watches the film for the cue to begin playing that particular piece of music. Often music reinforces story information through recognizable conventions. Action sequences in the *Indiana Jones* series are introduced by the inescapable "dum da-dum dum" as a parody of and a tribute to these recognizable themes. Through the use of motifs, themes assigned to particular figures, music also participates in characterization. We know when the main character has entered the scene not only visually but also aurally, because principal characters usually have a musical motif. The presence of "bad girl" Marylee Hadley in *Written on the Wind* (1956) is signaled by a distinctive sultry theme. Most notably, music is subordinate to that part of the narrative that competes in the realm of sound—the dialogue. A music cue will usually be audible during sequences in which there is no dialogue, often helping to smooth a spatial or temporal transition. When dialogue predominates, however, it will fade, the music volume will drop, or it will change to be less "competitive."

Composers for classical cinema, such as Erich Korngold, Dimitri Tiomkin, and Max Steiner, generated their own set of musical styles to suit the accepted function of film music, and many of these principles are still dominant in contemporary practice. In Steiner's more than three hundred scores, including those for *King Kong, Gone with the Wind, Now, Voyager* (1942), and *Mildred Pierce*, musical accompaniment was notable for being almost continuous. He composed using a **click track**—holes punched in the film to keep the beat of the action—and his style was highly illustrative, emphasizing what happens on the screen through music.

Much of Hollywood film music composition is derived from nineteenth-century, late-romantic orchestral music. Here the term "classical" is undoubtedly appropriate for studio-era Hollywood style, for popular music was rejected in favor of classical music. The work of such composers as Wagner and Strauss was rich in its ability to convey narrative information; reliant on compositional principles such as motifs assigned to different characters, settings, or actions; and lushly emotive, tonal, and euphonic. As such, it was perfectly suited to the musical experience that Hollywood was striving for with the integration of sound. This type of music was compatible with Hollywood storytelling not only because of its purely musical qualities but also because of the associations and values this music carried for audiences. These associations ranged from the high cultural status conferred on symphonic music of European origin (as opposed to the lower status of American jazz or pop) to the recognizable connotations of a particular instrumentation, such as somber horns for a funereal mood, violins for romance, and a harp for an ethereal or heavenly mood.

Classical film music developed practices of composition and mixing that supported the aim of storytelling and tended to efface its own presence. For example, Claudia Gorbman states in her book, *Unheard Melodies: Narrative Film Music* (1987), that the principle of inaudibility is analogous to the "invisible" editing style of the continuity system, meaning that conscious attention should not be paid to the score. Volume does not interfere with dialogue, the mood and rhythm of the music do not contradict those of the action, and compositions are matched to the

5.33 *Spellbound* (1945). Gregory Peck's character is stricken by an episode of vertigo, signaled by the theremin on the soundtrack.

5.34 *Secretariat* (2010). Composer Nick Glennie-Smith's score helps intensify the emotion and triumph the audience feels as Secretariat wins the Triple Crown.

narrative flow rather than allowed to follow their own progression. Ironically, screen music is at its best if we do not "hear" it.

Music is often used to carry a film's emotion. Dialogue and action fall short in their capacity to convey not only particular feelings but also the experience of feeling itself. Gorbman argues that there are three ways music's connotation of emotion is used. First, music conveys the irrational. In Hitchcock's *Spellbound* (1945), for example, the mental state of the hero is conveyed by the sound of the theremin, an unusual electronic instrument whose spooky sound is also used in science fiction films **[Figure 5.33]**. Second, music is associated with women, who are already culturally associated with emotion. Our pejorative idea of sappy music is derived from the sound of women's genres, where tears and musical notes fall with the same abundance. The music accompanying a brief scene in an empty bedroom in Gillian Armstrong's *Little Women* (1994) gives the viewer time to cry after Beth's death. Third, lush orchestration can ennoble specific events and make them feel timeless. In *Secretariat* (2010), the pre-race suspense and the triumph of winning the Triple Crown are made even grander by Nick Glennie-Smith's score **[Figure 5.34]**.

Narrative cueing is how music tells us what is happening in the plot. A return of the main theme signifies that *Gone with the Wind* is about to conclude; a western song over the credits of *Rancho Notorious* (1952) signifies the setting of a film of that genre. Narrative cueing is also connotative: violins on the soundtrack may indicate that the characters are falling in love; a few notes of "Deutschland über Alles" in the score of *Casablanca* (1942) signifies the looming Nazi threat. Music's role in relation to narrative may be to point something out or emphasize its significance. The most noticeable examples are called **stingers,** sounds that force us to notice the significance of something onscreen—like the one in *The Shining* (1980) that marks the moment when Wendy, the mother, looks at her bedroom door through her mirror and sees the word "murder" **[Figure 5.35]**. Overillustrating the action through the score, such as

5.35 *The Shining* (1980). When Wendy awakens and sees through the mirror what Danny has written on the door, a shocked look appears on her face. The audience is also forced to look and note the significance of what she sees—the word "murder"—because of the stinger on the soundtrack.

▶ **VIEWING CUE**

As you watch the film assigned for your next class, pay particular attention to its music. Is the film's score drawn from the classical tradition? Is popular music used? How do scoring choices contribute to the film's meaning? ⏸

accompanying a character walking on tip-toe with plucked strings, is referred to as **mickey-mousing**. (This term is a reference to the way cartoons often use the musical score to follow or mimic every action in synchronization, narrating through music rather than language.) Max Steiner is particularly noted for his habit of pointing out everything in his soundtracks in this manner.

We have already indicated the soundtrack's role in a film's continuity, another principle of film music that Gorbman notes. Discontinuities in visual information represented by cuts and scene changes are frequently bridged by the durational aspect of sound, and this function is most easily served by music. Various arrangements of the theme song of *High Noon* (1952) carry characters across space and help bridge transitions between scene changes. Although critics of studio-style film music complain that the composer's job involves nothing more than filling up any gaps in the film with the soundtrack, providing built-in unity through a structure of repetition and variation is a basic tenet of the classical film score.

Although musical scoring conventions have evolved and changed since the classical era of studio filmmaking, we can hear in the orchestral scores of John Williams, the most well-known composer of the past three decades, an homage to the romantic styles of the studio composers of earlier decades. Williams composes heroic, nostalgic scores that support and sometimes inflate the narrative's significance in films from *Star Wars* (1977) to *Harry Potter and the Prisoner of Azkaban* (2005). His five Academy Awards and more than forty nominations suggest that the film industry recognizes his style's consistency with that of classical Hollywood.

In Hollywood cinema of the studio era, nonclassical musical styles, such as jazz, popular, and dance music, might be used as source music and featured in musicals, but their incorporation into background music was gradual. One of the effects of the neglect of American musical idioms in favor of European influences was that African American artists and performers were rendered almost as inaudible as they were invisible in mainstream movies. African American performers were frequently featured in musicals, but they were there to provide entertainment and were rarely integrated into the narrative. Lena Horne's talent, for example, was shamefully underutilized because there were almost no leading roles for African American women in the 1940s and 1950s **[Figure 5.36]**. Film musicals (see Chapter 9), a dominant genre since the dawn of sound film, incorporated a range of American musical influences and performers.

As jazz music became more popular, jazz themes began to appear in urban-based film noirs of the 1940s. Henry Mancini's music for Orson Welles's *Touch of Evil* (1958) effectively connotes themes of crime, violence, and sexuality in the exaggerated border-town setting. Occasionally dissonance appeared in studio scores, but usually only when diegetically motivated—for example, to signify a psychological disturbance. In keeping with this connotation, the first atonal score was composed by Leonard Rosenman for *The Cobweb* (1955), a movie set in a home for the mentally ill. With other changes in the U.S. film industry in the postwar period, musical conventions shifted as well. Modernist and jazz-influenced scores, such as Leonard Bernstein's score for *On the Waterfront* (1954), became more common as different audiences were targeted through more individualized filmmaking practices. At the end of the studio era, the great tradition of the Hollywood musical also began to wane, but the persistence of the genre shows how central music is to the narrative film experience, even at the cost of verisimilitude.

5.36 **Lena Horne.** Most of the actress's appearances in mainstream films were restricted to cameo numbers because the industry was unwilling to allow an African American a leading role.

Prerecorded Music. Popular songs have long had a place in the movies, promoting audience participation and identification by appealing to tastes shared by generations or ethnic groups. Sheet music and recordings sales were profitable tie-ins even before sound cinema. In the 1980s, however, the practice of tying the emotional (and commercial) response of the audience to popular music on a film's soundtrack was so well established that the pop score began to rival originally composed music. *American Graffiti* (1973) helped inaugurate this trend with its soundtrack of nostalgic 1960s tunes, and *The Big Chill* (1983) captures the zeitgeist of its characters' and viewers' generation through popular music.

5.37 *Step Up 3D* (2010). The promotion of a film's soundtrack is crucial to the success of contemporary dance movies.

The centrality of prerecorded music is reflected in the increasing importance of the **music supervisor,** who selects and secures the rights for songs to be used in films. In youth-oriented, MTV-influenced films with pop music scores, such as *Step Up 3D* (2010), the promotion of the soundtrack is as important as that of the film **[Figure 5.37]**. In the 1990s, the proliferation of the pop soundtrack drew the film experience outside the theater to the record store, and music videos began to include scenes from upcoming films. Although theme songs have been composed for and promoted with films for decades, as in *Love Is a Many-Splendored Thing* (1955) to name one hit, the contemporary movie and recording industries have such close business relationships that even films without pop soundtracks often feature a tie-in song in their end-credits sequences. The extremely successful film careers of musicians like rapper-actor Will Smith demonstrate the increasing interdependency of these entertainment media.

Sound Effects in Film

Although the movies can represent the world in many ways, their capacity for successful mimesis, or imitation, has always fascinated audiences. Much of the mimetic impression in cinema comes from the use of sound effects, although, like other aspects of the soundtrack, viewers may not consciously notice these effects. Dialogue in film is deliberate; it tells a story and gives information. Background music is a clear enhancement, "unrealistic" if we pay attention to it. But sound effects appear unmanufactured, even accidental. This sense of the naturalness of effects is ironic because the sound texture of a film is so deliberately crafted and because in daily life we hardly notice such ubiquitous sounds as fluorescent lights humming, crickets chirping, and traffic going by—sounds that might be added to a film to achieve a "realistic" sound mix.

In most films, every noise that we hear is selected, and these effects generally conform to our expectations of movie sounds. Virtually nothing appears onscreen that does not make its corresponding noise: dogs bark, babies cry. A spaceship that blows up in outer space will usually produce a colossal bang even though in fact there is no sound in space. If a recording of a .38 revolver sounds like a cap gun on film, it will be dubbed with a louder bang. These expectations vary according to film genre. Traffic noise will be loud in an action film, in which we remain alive to the possibilities of the environment. In a romance, the sound of cars will likely fade away unless traffic is keeping the lovers apart. The extraordinary density of contemporary soundtracks does not necessarily mean that they are more "realistic" than the less dense soundtracks of classical Hollywood; they simply make more extensive use of the particular properties of sound to convey a visceral experience of the cinema. The change in the texture of contemporary soundtracks is based in new technological capabilities, but, as in other instances of "improved" technologies, this progress is not inevitable but rather a development that follows particular ideas and goals, although these are likely to remain unstated.

Sound effects are one of the most useful ways of giving an impression of depth to the two-dimensional image when they are reproduced in the three-dimensional space of the theater. Although the screen is itself only an illusory space of action, film presentation makes use of the directional properties of sound—a gunshot may come from the left-hand side of the screen, for example. In the mix, additional diegetic sounds such as thunderclaps can be added that were not present on set at all, adding significantly to a film's illusionism. Asynchronous sound effects, such as the hoot of an owl in a dark woods setting, both expand the sense of space and contribute to mood, often in very codified, even clichéd ways. Adding the clank of utensils and snatches of offscreen conversation to the soundtrack when two characters are shown at a table conjures a restaurant setting without having to shoot the scene in one.

The very manner in which noises are produced for a soundtrack illustrates their function in constructing, rather than reproducing, a particular experience. As we detailed earlier, incidental sounds—footsteps, the rustle of clothing, a punch in the stomach—are not even recorded at the same time as the film's dialogue. Rather, they are added later by the foley artist by walking on gravel, rubbing together different pieces of fabric, hitting a rolled-up telephone book, and so on. Our acceptance of these simulated synchronous sounds testifies to the strength of our impulse to perceive effects realistically. The process is a meticulous reconstruction of some but not all of the sounds that would have been present on set. The sounds selected are those that are deemed significant, if only because they establish a particular mood. Dramatic effects such as explosions are quite deliberately placed, and often enhanced, because of their narrative significance.

At the same time that they serve a mimetic function, sound effects have become part of how the cinema experience is distinguished from the ordinary. THX is a standards system devised by director George Lucas and named after his first feature film, *THX 1138* (1971), for evaluating and ensuring the quality of sound presentation. THX theaters promise to deliver an intense aural experience that is identical in each certified venue. Sound effects, like visual effects, draw in viewers. How crucial a film's sound is to the Hollywood illusion is marked in the relatively recent Academy Award category for sound-effects editing. Audiences are increasingly trusted to discern things aurally. In the films of master action film director John Woo, for example, each character may have a particular gunshot noise assigned to him or her so that the action can be followed throughout a protracted sequence without dialogue. The distinctive soundtrack of *Jaws* (1975) lent us not only what has now become the cliché of the shark's musical motif but also a rich new standard of sound-effects use. The film acknowledges a predecessor in the genre—and in the ingenious use of sound—when the death of the shark is accompanied by a sound effect of a prehistoric beast's death from *King Kong*. In these monster movies, sound effects take us beyond everyday events while also relying on their capacity to refer to familiar experiences.

As with music, the animated film illustrates the deliberately designed nature of film sound effects particularly well. In fact, most cartoon soundtracks are prepared in advance of the images, the reverse of live-action filmmaking [**Figures 5.38a and 5.38b**]. Cartoons thus demonstrate especially well the synchronization of sound effects to onscreen actions. Drawings do not "naturally" make sounds of their own; every sound in an animated film is conventionalized. In *Duck Amuck* (1953), for example, Daffy Duck is baffled by the cartoon he finds himself in and cannot follow

▶ **VIEWING CUE**

To what extent do sound effects add to a film's sense of realism? Locate an example in a film you recently watched that demonstrates how sound effects are primarily responsible for creating a particular impression of location, action, or mood. ⏸

▶ **VIEWING CUE**

Isolate a particular scene in a film you recently viewed for class and determine which sound seems especially responsible for conveying information to the spectator. How do voice, music, and sound effects work together? ⏸

(a)   (b)

5.38a and 5.38b   *Shrek* (2001). In most animated films, soundtracks and dialogue
are prepared in advance of the image track.

the logic of his mischievous animator. All sorts of mishaps befall him, and the abrupt termination of the soundtrack is one of the most disturbing of these mishaps. So unused are we to complete silence, that we are likely to look around us to see whether the theater's sound system really has gone out. Daffy holds up a sign demanding "Sound please!" and begins to play the guitar with which his animator has provided him. But the sound it "emits" is that of a machine gun, demonstrating with this synchronization error the arbitrary nature of the standard of matching image and sound. As Daffy's misadventures suggest, sound

5.39   *How to Train Your Dragon* (2010). Hiccup is able to interpret Toothless's feelings just from the dragon's purrs and growls. An angelic female choir accompanied by bells adds to the mystical atmosphere.

effects appeal to the audience subtly and viscerally. In *How to Train Your Dragon* (2010), the musical score certainly helps to set the mood, but the sound effects are even more crucial to the film—the sounds Toothless makes help Hiccup understand and communicate with him **[Figure 5.39]**.

The Significance of Film Sound

Sounds are grounded in viewers' everyday activities and contribute to movies' immediacy and sensory richness. Whether it is the pathos lent by Louis Gottschalk's score for D. W. Griffith's *Broken Blossoms* (1919), the stimulating interactions between the musical quotations of *2001: A Space Odyssey* and Alex North's original music for the film, the indelible aural record of Laurence Olivier's performance of *Hamlet* (1948), or the comical sounds of Jacques Tati's *Playtime*, film sound can intensify our viewing experience while conveying what seem like essential truths and meanings. Paradoxically, movie soundscapes often eschew realism and plausibility in order to heighten authenticity and emotion, like foregrounding actors' whispered conversation in a crowded room so we feel intimately connected to them.

The ways in which filmmakers choose to relate sound to image also has a distinctive effect on our viewing experience. Some filmmakers rely on sound continuity to support the narrative aim and smooth over gaps in a story. In contrast, others might remind viewers of sound's autonomy from the image through the use of sound montage—essentially employing sound to question, or act as a counterpoint to, the authority of the image.

Authenticity and Experience

▶ **VIEWING CUE**
How does the soundtrack of the next film you view "authenticate" the image? Would the absence of sound affect the film's authenticity? How? ❚❚

Film sound, because it surrounds and permeates the body of the viewer in a way that images alone cannot, contributes to the authenticity and emotion we experience while viewing a film. Sound in film can indicate a real, multidimensional world and give the viewer/listener the impression of being authentically present in space. Additionally, sound encourages the viewer to experience emotion, depending on the kind of sound, such as a particular piece of music.

The assumption that sound gives the viewer/listener the impression of being authentically present in space is supported by the preferences established in the standard techniques of sound recording, mixing, and reproduction. As previously mentioned, though the cinematic images and sounds that we see and hear were both captured at some other moment and are being reproduced for us, sounds feel immediate. Hearing the taps on Eleanor Powell's shoes in *Born to Dance* (1936) makes us witnesses to her virtuosity **[Figure 5.40]**. Foregrounding actors' voices through close miking and sound perspective and mixing that emphasizes dialogue also authenticate our perception. We are "in on" the characters' most intimate conversations. Sounds that are synchronized with the action by the depiction of their sources in the image, or even sounds that support the action while not being themselves "authentic"—for example, background music—all give us a central place in the fictional world that begins to seem present and real. The zither theme of *The Third Man* (1949) makes us feel disoriented in the streets of postwar Vienna, just as the film's characters are.

Sound encourages the viewer to experience emotion and to see the world in terms of particular emotions. When the lovers in *Now, Voyager* cannot really say what they mean to each other, the string section, performing Max Steiner's score, eloquently takes over. Sound reaches the viewer viscerally, seeming to involve the body directly. Excruciating suspense is generated in *Jurassic Park* when we hear the sound of the menacing tyrannosaurus rex **[Figure 5.41]**. Simply watching the dinosaur progress would be a less emotional experience.

5.40 *Born to Dance* (1936). Eleanor Powell's tap dancing is a perfect display of synchronized sound.

5.41 *Jurassic Park* (1993). On the digital soundtrack, the T-Rex's footsteps can be heard approaching the truck where the children are hiding, generating keen suspense.

The film environment attempts to duplicate our acoustic experience of the world, to orient us in this new space in a way that feels genuine and genuinely gets us to *feel*. This is not necessarily measured by strict realism. The sense of presence at the dance contest in *Saturday Night Fever* (1977) is better achieved through a sound mix that sacrifices background noise to focus on the Bee Gees' music.

Although film sound can have a great deal of complexity, and realism is thrown out the window every time background music appears, authenticity and emotion are often served by a subordination of the autonomy of sound to the cues given by the image. In contrast to this practice of sound–image continuity, however, a competing approach explores the concrete nature of sounds and their potential independence of images and of each other. This practice of sound montage, which characterizes the films of Jean-Luc Godard and others, does not serve the values of authenticity and emotion; rather, it makes us conscious of their violation by calling attention to the actual sound recording process or asking us to be aware of and reflect on emotional cues.

Sound Continuity and Sound Montage

Sound continuity describes the range of scoring, sound recording, mixing, and playback processes that strive for the unification of meaning and experience by subordinating sound to the aims of the narrative. *Sound montage* reminds us that just as a film is built up of bits and pieces of celluloid, a soundtrack is not a continuous gush of sound from the real world; rather, it is composed of separate elements whose relationship to each other can be creatively manipulated and reflected upon. The theme song from *Doctor Zhivago* (1965) is extremely lush and romantic, but it reinforces the big emotions of the film's characters at appropriate points in the plot and thus achieves continuity. In Andrei Tarkovsky's *Nostalghia* (1983), though the sound of an electric saw can be heard at different times and in different settings, the source is never revealed. This ambiguous sound functions as an element of montage. Most assumptions, shared by technicians and viewers, about what constitutes a "good" soundtrack emphasize a continuity approach. However, since the introduction of sound, many filmmakers have used it as a separate element for a montage effect. With the increasing sophistication of audio technology, it is possible that sound montage will find more practitioners.

Sound Continuity

Analyzing a film that adheres to sound continuity can be rewarding precisely because really hearing the soundtrack demands such attentiveness. As we have seen, matching up actors' voices with their moving lips and ensuring the words are intelligible were among the early goals of sound technology. Audiences were thrilled just to *see* the match. Despite our familiarity with film sound today, the degree of redundancy between image and sound in the continuity tradition still makes it difficult to analyze the soundtrack autonomously. From the priority granted to synchronization, we can define several compatible continuity practices:

- The relationship between image and sound and among separate sounds is motivated by dramatic action or information.
- With the exception of background music, the sources of sounds will be identifiable.
- The connotations of musical accompaniment will be consistent with the images (for example, a funeral march is unlikely to accompany a high-speed chase).
- The sound mix will emphasize what we should pay attention to.
- The sound mix will be smooth and will emphasize clarity.

Films that adhere to the principles of verisimilitude will use sound to amplify, as it were, what is taking place on the screen. Attention will be directed back to the

5.42 *Rocky Balboa* (2006). The *Rocky* film series's iconic theme song (Bill Conti's "Gonna Fly Now") ties together disparate images of Rocky doing pull-ups, jogging, and lifting weights.

characters, actions, and mise-en-scène by sound that supports it. In *The Big Sleep* (1946), a conversation in a car between the two protagonists, Marlowe and Vivian, begins with engine noise in the background. We see that there is a dog on the porch in the opening scene of *The Searchers* (1956), but when we hear it bark, the image comes alive. The relationship between image and sound and among separate sounds will also be motivated by dramatic action or information. In *The Big Sleep*, the engine noise will soon disappear so we can focus on the characters' avowal of love. The continuous use of music to cover a sequence of character activity draws our attention away from discontinuity in the image track. For example, continuous orchestral music links the "training montage" in *Rocky Balboa* (2006) **[Figure 5.42]**.

It may be easier to think of what sound continuity seeks to avoid than what it positively pursues. Sound should not intrude on the narrative. Unmotivated or unidentified sounds will not have a prominent place on the soundtrack. Nor will unidentified speakers be heard, unless in a conventional context such as a documentary, in which the voiceover explanation will demonstrate its own continuity with the content of the image. Characters' speech will not break with the diegesis to offer commentary or non sequiturs. Technology and techniques have developed in consort with these aims. Dolby noise-reduction technology improves frequency response and gives an almost unnatural clarity. Noise interferes with the sound signal and can call attention to the fact that the sound was recorded and, thus, to how the film was made. These are goals of continuity rather than of strict realism.

▶ **VIEWING CUE**

Identify two or three instances of sound continuity in a film you have watched for class. How do these instances support either the narrative action or the thoughts and feelings of a character? ‖

Sound Montage

Exploring the infinite possibilities of sound and image interactions, and interactions among sounds and images, is the province of montage. Often deriving its practices in direct opposition to the principles of sound continuity, sound montage calls attention to the distinct, autonomous elements that make up a film. Like the disjunctive image-editing practices discussed in Chapter 4, sound montage does not smooth over juxtapositions. In sound montage, sound may "come first," and the borders between the nondiegetic and the diegetic may be difficult to establish. In addition, the expectation that every element of the mise-en-scène will make a naturalistic noise is frustrated, and voices, whether diegetic or nondiegetic, do not always preserve the illusion of a closed world. The music might appear and disappear, giving it a more material presence, and sound effects can be "synchronized" to arbitrary sources.

When motivated relationships—for example, the image of a dog motivates the sound effect of barking—are given up, we see and hear something onscreen that is different from an attempted extension of our natural world. The intention may be to critique, as in a disturbing sequence in *Natural Born Killers* (1994) when Mallory's life at home with her abusive father is presented as if it were a situation comedy, complete with laugh track, applause, and perky theme music, directly commenting on how the media use sound to manipulate emotion. In a very different use of sound montage, the succession of still images that constitutes Chris Marker's *La Jetée* (1962) is anchored by a voiceover that tells of the time experiments in which the protagonist is participating, identifying the film as science fiction **[Figure 5.43]**. Prioritizing

5.43 *La Jetée* (1962). The fluidity of a voiceover accompanying a montage of still images creates a reflective distance between the two elements.

5.44 *Surname Viet Given Name Nam* (1989). The qualities of the film's voices—they are often accented and seem to belong to nonactors reciting—convey information that could not be gathered from images.

5.45 *Alexander Nevsky* (1938). The editing of Sergei Eisenstein's first sound film was planned with the score in mind.

sound makes us attend to the film's structure; the image track accompanies or provides counterpoint to what we hear.

The use of the voice can be opened up to include direct address to the viewer or the use of recitation or reading instead of naturalistic dialogue, as in Godard's *Weekend* (1967) or Isaac Julien's *Looking for Langston* (1989). The sensual quality of sounds can be explored as it might be in a musical composition, or poetic effects can be achieved by combining different sound "images." Voices are layered in Marguerite Duras's *India Song* (1975). A film can deliver ideas through multiple channels; the sound can contradict the image. Interview texts printed on the screen are read aloud with slight alterations by the voiceovers in Trinh T. Minh-ha's *Surname Viet Given Name Nam* (1989) **[Figure 5.44]**.

Overall, sound montage stresses the fact that images and sounds communicate on two different levels; rather than trying to make them equivalents, montage calls attention to what each contributes differently. Sergei Eisenstein, the primary theorist of montage, extended his ideas to sound even before the technology was perfected. In his first sound film, *Alexander Nevsky* (1938), he experimented with what he called "vertical montage," which emphasized both the simultaneity of and the difference between image and sound **[Figure 5.45]**. He also collaborated closely with composer Sergei Prokofiev to make a film in which every picture edit was influenced by the accompanying soundtrack. German filmmaker Ulrike Ottinger's *Madame X: An Absolute Ruler* (1977) makes ingenious use of postsynchronous sound. Her film's motley crew of female pirates do not speak; instead, their movements are "synchronized" with noises like animal growls or metallic clanking **[Figure 5.46]**.

Experimentation with sound montage began with the introduction of sound. Filmmakers such as Jean Vigo and René Clair in France and Rouben Mamoulian and King Vidor in the United States are identified with the early sound era because of the lyrical and creative ways sound and image are combined in their films. In films such as Mamoulian's

text continued on page 210 ▶

5.46 *Madame X: An Absolute Ruler* (1977). Sound montage without dialogue defines the characters' actions.

FILM IN FOCUS

1 5 7 0 1 0

1 5 7 0 1 0

The Ethics and Effects of Sound Technology in *The Conversation* (1974)

Directed by Francis Ford Coppola in collaboration with sound designer and editor Walter Murch, *The Conversation* is notable because its very topic is the exploitation of sound technology. While the film's own sound conforms to the principles identified with the continuity tradition, by virtue of its foregrounding of how sound is created and transmitted, it can also illustrate the aims of sound montage practice.

The film, set in San Francisco, follows the activities of a surveillance expert, Harry Caul (played by Gene Hackman), as he goes about what seems to be a routine job: eavesdropping on a pair of lovers in the park. Harry's expertise and interest in technology leave little space for human contact and complement his rather paranoid character. Interestingly, Harry's hobby is playing the saxophone. The warm sound of this instrument foreshadows his eventual awakening to the more human dimensions of the sounds he records for a living.

The first sequence of the film is a tour de force of sound and image counterpoint, which makes us partake in the activity of surveillance as we actively attempt to decode what is happening on the screen. Eavesdropping enhances the sound's quality of presence; we feel we are *right there* in the scene. Yet the activities of the on-camera sound recordists make us aware of those of the recordist, mixer, and director behind the scenes of the film we are watching.

The film opens with an aerial shot over San Francisco's Union Square; a slow zoom in is accompanied by jazz music, while sound perspective remains constant. As the music shifts from an instrumental theme to the banter of two singers, and as the hubbub of the busy square and then the applause become audible, we recognize that the music is diegetic, coming from the scene even though we cannot at first see the source. The music's festive and emotional connotations are immediately recognizable. Yet electronic interference comes in very early on; we begin to suspect that we are hearing the music through a device "within" the film as well as through the loudspeaker in the theater, and the emotional register turns slightly sinister.

In the next few shots, it remains difficult to tell who the object of the surveillance is and who the object of our attention should be, in part because the sound is not mixed to emphasize the action. Indeed, it is the gestures of a mime, taunting through his mimicry a figure whose crumpled raincoat suggests a desire for anonymity, that we must "listen" to in the first aerial shot if we want to pick out Harry in the crowd. The silent stalker is stalked. Finally, when Harry enters a van where his assistant is stationed, we learn that the target is a young couple, Ann and Mark, played by Cindy Williams and Frederic Forrest **[Figure 5.47]**.

5.47 *The Conversation* (1974). We eavesdrop on characters that the plot never brings us to know better.

The sound mix in the scene is quite complicated. The cut to the first shot taken at ground level corresponds to a notable shift in sound perspective with an increase in the diegetic music volume. Quickly a snatch of random conversation is heard, followed by a snippet of another—this time, the targeted couple—but the succession has already identified for us the arbitrariness of continuity sound mixing practices that isolate immediately what we should pay attention to. The closeness of our sound perspective is then given technical justification when we see both Harry and a man with a hearing aid in close proximity to the couple. We stay with Ann and Mark as they continue a conversation about a drunk passed out on the park bench; the volume of the conversation does not change as Harry climbs into the van. Here the continuity in sound perspective signals the importance of this apparently trivial conversation. And once again, what seemed like the film's sound—we hear the conversation—is revealed as sound produced within the story: what we hear is the recording of the conversation as we see the reel-to-reel tape recorder spinning **[Figure 5.48]**.

In the next scene, Harry plays a few lines of recorded conversation over and over again, discovering in the captured sounds clues to a suspicious event. Is the "guilty" party the couple, presumably engaged in an affair, or those who pay to have them watched? And what is the ethical role of the "invisible" bystander, the hired sound recordist, and by extension the film viewer? The opening scene of *The Conversation* functions like a puzzle as Harry and the viewer strive to find the truth behind the sounds captured in the square.

Toward the end of the scene, a new sound element is introduced. A nondiegetic moody piano theme begins as the couple parts; the music continues, with some street noise in the mix, as Harry starts home. The piano carries over the dissolve to the next scene and ends just as Harry turns the key in his door, when it is abruptly replaced by a shrill sound effect, his alarm being set off. Our newly honed attention to the concrete nature of each sound element encourages us to evaluate this nondiegetic musical theme. Associated almost exclusively with long shots of Harry making his way around town, the wandering theme played on a single instrument underscores his alienation, inviting us as viewers to feel the emotion Harry attempts to keep at bay. After Harry arrives home, we see him playing the sax. The sound of the saxophone is very solitary; it connects Harry to the piano theme we've just heard as well as to the musicians in the park. Interestingly, however, Harry plays his sax along with a record player, syncing up his own performance of the expressive qualities of music with prerecorded sound. This is emphasized by a shot of the record spinning. Such close-ups of sound technology are frequent in the film and remind us of the source of film voices, music, and effects. Often these cutaways are unmotivated by any character's specific attention to the sounds being emitted at that moment.

As the film progresses, Harry becomes increasingly suspicious of his employer's intentions, and he returns again and again to the evidence gathered in the first scene, in the form of the tape. The film's theme of paranoia finds a perfect echo in its setting in the world of sound technology, eavesdropping, and surveillance. Because of the claims to presence of sound, the incriminating audiotape, with the accidental music and noises it captures, appears "real" and convincing even in a film that is constantly showing off the paraphernalia of sound recording, mixing, and playback. By emphasizing that truth lies in the words spoken in that first conversation, the film upholds the privileged relationship between the voice and inner nature, while also facilitating Harry's (and the audience's) identification with other humans *through* technological mediation. Sound is used in service of narrative, but the narrative is about the uses of sound. Despite the period quaintness of the now-obsolete machines the film lingers on—reel-to-reel tape recorders and oversized headphones, the squeaky sound of rewinding, and the mechanical click of old-fashioned buttons—*The Conversation* remains an apt commentary on the values and practices of sound technology.

5.48 *The Conversation* (1974). Audio technology becomes a pervasive presence in the film.

Applause (1929), for instance, music and effects do not duplicate the image but create a more subjective and atmospheric setting. In the post–World War II art cinema, sound experimentation was renewed. French director Robert Bresson takes apart the usual fit between sound and image by a minimalist use of sound. In spare films such as *Pickpocket* (1959) and *L'Argent* (1983), which explore themes of predestination and isolation through scrutiny of details, Bresson achieves an uncanny presence of select sounds while refusing realistic indicators of space [**Figure 5.49**]. In "Notes on Sound," Bresson sums up his ideas: "what is for the eye must not duplicate what is for the ear." Without the use of room tone or other techniques to give spatial cues or to make sounds warmer, the minimalist sounds in his films become very concrete, a practice that has influenced many contemporary filmmakers in world cinema.

Other filmmakers layer sounds in ways that collide with images and other sounds. Dziga Vertov's early sound film *Enthusiasm* (1931) innovates the collection of documentary sounds, juxtaposing them as if in a collage. The sounds are not harmonized with each other or with the images but rather create disruptions or even shocks. A clock ticks over the image of a tolling bell, for example. The Soviet filmmaker was keenly interested in sound, and his work in radio and even his poetry showed a fascination with industrial noise. Jean-Luc Godard's many experiments with sound collage, which began early in his career, are indebted to Vertov's. Godard emphasizes music in the organization of many of his films; a favorite technique is to interrupt a music cue so that it literally cannot fade into the background. In *First Name: Carmen* (1983), we actually see a string quartet playing without knowing what its relationship to the story space might be. The abrupt cessation of a soundtrack element may be extended to voices and effects as well. In the café scene in *Band of Outsiders* (1964), one of the characters suggests that if the friends in the group have nothing to say to each other, they should remain silent. This diegetic silence is conveyed by the complete cessation of sound on the soundtrack, something that is rare indeed. By using nonauthoritative or noncontinuous voiceovers as well as frequent voice-offs, and by having on-camera characters address the camera, read, or make cryptic announcements, Godard challenges the natural role of the human voice in giving character and narrative information. Instead, language becomes malleable, an element in a collage of meaning.

Several examples from *Tout va bien* (*All's well*) (1972), made by Godard and Jean-Pierre Gorin, illustrate these strategies. The film opens with an unidentified male voice-off declaring his intention of making a film. A female voice responds that making films costs money. The image shows a hand writing checks for the production of the film *Tout va bien*. In another sequence, one of the film's protagonists speaks directly to the camera about his career as a political filmmaker turned director of commercials, and he is seated next to a camera as he does so. The speech makes us think about Godard's own position. Another memorable scene is set in a supermarket as it is taken over by anarchists. To add another element, the words of the journalist character played by Jane Fonda [**Figure 5.50**] are introduced by loudspeaker tones, such as those that would normally direct shoppers to a special bargain. This sound element confuses internal and external sound, layering sound in a collage effect.

5.49 *L'Argent* (1983). Robert Bresson's films carefully select sound to explore themes of isolation.

Over a more than forty-year career, Godard has earned a reputation as probably the most exemplary practitioner of sound montage.

But even in Hollywood films, sound montage can dominate. Although it is narratively motivated by the futuristic setting, the soundscape of Ridley Scott's *Blade Runner* resembles that of an experimental film. Sound is at least as responsible as the mise-en-scène and the story line for the theme of anxiety in a synthetic, syncretic world. Director David Lynch's sound designs are similarly integral to his disorienting onscreen worlds. In their richness, contemporary soundtracks draw more and more on montage traditions of layering sounds without necessarily encouraging reflection on the discrete functions of sound and image. The continuity tradition that subordinates sound to image and accords with screen realism is still dominant. One of the most interesting films to confront questions of sound practice in Hollywood film is *The Conversation* (1974). Although it does not depart from sound continuity in ways that an experimental film might do, the film asks viewers to consider the meanings and effects of sound as an autonomous element.

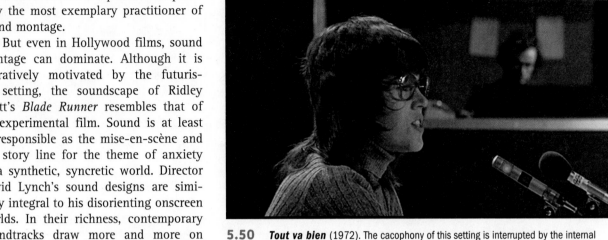

5.50 *Tout va bien* (1972). The cacophony of this setting is interrupted by the internal diegetic monologue of one the other main characters, a journalist played by Jane Fonda.

▶ **VIEWING CUE**

Is sound montage used to create meaning at certain points in the film? If so, how and to what effect? ⏸

CONCEPTS AT WORK

Films re-create sounds from the world around us and create new patterns of sound that construct or emphasize meanings and themes in the films. Listening carefully to films is a critical act that engages the films we watch in an audio dialogue that involves film history and culture, as well as specific formal elements and strategies. We listen—consciously or unconsciously—to a film with many layers of sound, from the dialogue to the background score. Depending on our familiarity with other films and film history, we note connections with and distinctions from other films, from offscreen sound to a rock music sound montage, that characterize the use of sound in a particular movie. While film sound may represent the least visible of the formal and technical elements of the movies, listening to movies can quite often provide the most insightful discoveries about a film's complex vision.

Activity

Select a scene or sequence from a film that uses orchestral music, mute the audio, and try accompanying the scene with other musical choices: jazz, part of a well-known score from a different film, a pop song. How do the changes redirect an understanding of the scene and its meaning?

PART 3

ORGANIZATIONAL STRUCTURES

from stories to genres

W e go to the movies not just to experience a film's elaborate scenes, brilliant images, dramatic cuts, and rich sounds. We also go for the gripping suspense of a murder mystery, the fascinating revelations of a documentary, the poetic voyage of a musical score set to abstract images and sounds, and the delight of seeing life as if it were a 1930s musical. We turn to films like *Syriana* (2005) for the twists and turns of a story about political and economic intrigue in the Middle East, to *Hoop Dreams* (1994) for the disturbing facts and human costs behind sports recruiting, to *Fantasia* (1940) for rhythms and sounds made into creative animated images, and to *Eternal Sunshine of the Spotless Mind* (2004) for its novel approach to romantic conventions and plots.

Besides the stylistic details found in the mise-en-scène, cinematography, editing, and sound, movie experiences are also encounters with larger organizational structures and attractions. Some of us may look first for a good story; others may prefer documentary or experimental films. Some days we may be in the mood for a melodrama; other days we may feel like watching a horror film. Part 3 explores the principal organizations of movies—narrative, documentary, and experimental films, and movie genres—each of which, as we will see, arouses certain expectations about the movie we are viewing. Each shapes the world for us into a distinctive kind of experience, offering a particular way of seeing, understanding, and enjoying it.

CHAPTER 6

Telling Stories: Narrative Films

■ Stories and plots

■ Characters

■ Narration and narrative point of view

■ Classical and alternative narrative traditions

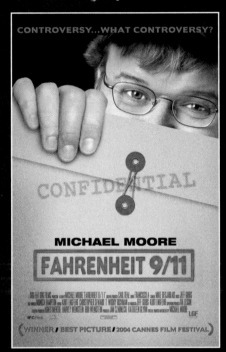

Will Ferrell Maggie Gyllenhaal Dustin Hoffman Queen Latifah Emma Thompson

Stranger than Fiction.

Harold Crick isn't ready to go. Period.

COLUMBIA PICTURES AND MANDATE PICTURES PRESENT
A THREE STRANGE ANGELS PRODUCTION "STRANGER THAN FICTION"
MUSIC BY BRITT DANIEL BRIAN REITZELL MUSIC SUPERVISION BY BRIAN REITZELL
EDITOR MATT CHESSÉ, A.C.E. PRODUCTION DESIGNER KEVIN THOMPSON DIRECTOR OF PHOTOGRAPHY ROBERTO SCHAEFER, ASC
EXECUTIVE PRODUCERS NATHAN KAHANE JOE DRAKE ERIC KOPELOFF
WRITTEN BY ZACH HELM PRODUCED BY LINDSAY DORAN DIRECTED BY MARC FORSTER

Read The Newmarket Press Shooting Script Book
StrangerThanFiction.com

November

6

Telling Stories
Narrative Films

In the surreal comedic drama *Stranger than Fiction* (2006), Will Ferrell plays IRS agent Harold Crick, who begins to hear the voice of a narrator telling the story of his rather boring and routine life with uncanny detail and accuracy. While we all may accept the notion that our lives often change and develop like stories, Crick suddenly faces the unusual crisis that his life seems to be someone else's story. In this bizarre twist on the role of narration in our lives, Crick recognizes the narrative voice in his head as that of a famous author, Karen Eiffel, whom he then seeks to meet. To his chagrin, he discovers that Eiffel has been researching how to bring closure to her story by killing off her central character, Crick, the typical ending for all her novels. Not surprisingly, Crick confronts his narrator with the hope of convincing her to change her standard formula. More self-consciously than most movies, *Stranger than Fiction* explores the complex and mutually formative relationships among life, narrative, and the movies. Along the way it raises fascinating issues about the relationship of life to narrative fiction and how the plots of those two realms interact.

Movies have thrived on **narrative**, the art and craft of constructing a story with a particular plot and point of view. Narrative film developed out of a long cultural, artistic, and literary tradition of storytelling, showing characters pursuing goals, confronting obstacles to those goals, and ultimately achieving some kind of closure. In general, narrative follows a three-part structure consisting of a beginning, a middle, and an ending; an opening state is disrupted in the middle of the narrative, and that disruption leads to a reestablishment of order in the ending. At its core, narrative maps the different ways we have learned to make sense of our place in history and the world, as well as how to communicate with others.

KEY OBJECTIVES	

- Explore the cultural ubiquity of storytelling in film.
- Discover the different historical practices that create the foundations for film narratives.
- Examine how film narratives construct plots that can arrange the events of a story in different ways.
- Learn the way film characters motivate actions in a story.
- Discuss the way plots create different temporal and spatial schemes.
- Examine the power of narration and narrative point of view and how they determine our understanding of a story.
- Describe the differences between classical and alternative narrative traditions.

Storytelling has always been a central part of societies and cultures. Stories spring from both personal and communal memories and reconstruct the events, actions, and emotions of the past through the eyes of the present. Stories entertain children before bed and sailors at sea, they communicate ideas about social behavior, they reconcile us to the changing of the seasons or the inevitability of death, and they strengthen both the memory and the imagination of a society. The many stories of the Bible, Hindu scriptures, Icelandic sagas, oral tales of indigenous cultures, and well-known stories of historical events (such as the Civil War) and people (such as Abraham Lincoln) are all driven by these aims. In a sense, stories are both the historical center of a culture and the bonds of a community. More often than not, history itself is recounted in narrative terms.

A Short History of Narrative Film

Over time, stories have appeared in a myriad of material forms and served innumerable purposes, many of which reappear in movie narratives. Some films, like *Little Big Man* (1970) and *Contempt* (1963), make explicit references to the narrative history that precedes them. *Little Big Man*, for instance,

depicts the heritage of Native Americans gathered around the fire listening to storytellers recounting the history of their people; *Contempt*, in contrast, struggles with the narrative forms found in Homer's *Odyssey* and those demanded by commercial filmmaking—between telling a tale as an epic poem and as a Hollywood blockbuster **[Figures 6.1a–6.1c]**. To appreciate the richness of film narrative, viewers must keep in mind the unique cultural history of narrative itself. For example, oral narratives, which are spoken or recited aloud, represent a tradition that extends from the campfire to today's stage performance artists. Written narratives, such as Charles Dickens's *Bleak House* (1853), appear in printed form, while graphic narratives develop through a series of images, such as the stories told through lithographs in the eighteenth century and through modern comic books like *Spider-Man* **[Figures 6.2a and 6.2b]**.

6.1b *Penelope with the Suitors* (Pinturicchio). Since the time of medieval and Renaissance paintings, the visual arts have incorporated stories and allegories, often orchestrating numerous character actions and events within a single frame, such as in this early-sixteenth-century scene from the *Odyssey*.

6.1a **Fifth-century Greek urn.** Ancient Greek epics, including the renowned *Odyssey*, were often depicted as visual narratives.

6.1c *Contempt* (1963). Jean-Luc Godard's film explicitly engages the history of narrative in his modern tale about the struggles to adapt Homer's *Odyssey* to the screen.

(a)

(b)

6.2a and 6.2b   *Spider-Man* (2002). The transformation of visual narrative from comic book page to big screen.

In these and other examples, the form and material through which a story is told affects aspects of the narrative, facilitating some characteristics of expression and prohibiting others. Oral narratives provide more direct and flexible contact with listeners, allowing a story to be tailored to an audience and to change from one telling to another. A visual narrative shows the appearance of characters more concretely than a literary one, while a literary narrative is able to present characters' thoughts more seamlessly than a visual narrative. A film narrative commonly draws from and combines these and other narrative traditions, and attending to how a particular film narrative might employ or emphasize the formulas or strategies of, say, oral narratives or operatic narratives illustrates the broad and complex history of storytelling embedded in cinematic form.

1900–1920s: Adaptations, Scriptwriters, and Screenplays

While the first movies were usually content to show simple moving images (such as a train arriving at a station), often these images referred to a story behind them. As film form developed, adaptations of well-known stories were a popular choice of filmmakers. Audiences' familiarity with the characters and plot helped them to follow emerging motion-picture narrative techniques. As early as 1896, the actor Joseph Jefferson represented Rip van Winkle in a brief short. By 1903, there appeared a variety of similar film tableaux (or images) that assumed audiences would know the larger story behind what was shown on the screen, including Shakespeare's *King John* (1899), *Cinderella* (1900), *Robinson Crusoe* (1902), and *Ali Baba and the Forty Thieves* (1905) **[Figure 6.3]**. *Uncle Tom's Cabin*, the most popular novel and stage play of the nineteenth century, was adapted for the screen numerous times in the silent film era, including by Edwin S. Porter **[Figure 6.4]**. Porter's films were among the first to use editing to tell stories, and by 1906 the movies were becoming a predominantly narrative medium.

These early historical bonds between movies and stories served the development of what we will call an *economics of leisure time*. In the first decades of the twentieth century, the budding movie industry recognized that stories take time to tell and that an audience's willingness to spend time watching stories makes money for the industry. In these early years, most individuals went to the movies to experience the novelty of "going to the movies," of spending an afternoon with friends or an hour away from work. By 1913, moviemakers recognized that by developing more complex stories they could attract larger audiences, keep them in their seats for longer periods, and charge more than a nickel for admission. Along with the growing cultural prestige of attending films that told serious stories, movies could now sell more time for more money through longer narratives. Quickly cinema established itself among the leading sources of cultural pleasures that included museums, art galleries, and traditional and vaudeville theaters. At the same time, cinema's own history came to be governed by the forms and aims of storytelling.

▶ **VIEWING CUE**

For the film you recently watched in class, describe as much of the story as you can. What are the main events, the implied events, and the significant and insignificant details of the film's story?

6.3 *Ali Baba and the Forty Thieves* (1905). An early tableau narrative that assumes the audience knows the larger story behind the image.

6.4 *Uncle Tom's Cabin* (1903). One of numerous silent film adaptations of the most popular nineteenth-century novel and stage play.

As narrative film developed, two important industrial events stand out: the introduction of screenplays, and the advancement of narrative dialogue through sound. Whereas many early silent movies were produced with little advance preparation, the growing number and increasing length of movies from 1907 onward required the use of **scriptwriters** (or **screenwriters**), who created film scenarios or scripts either by using original stories or by adapting short stories, novels, or other sources. As part of this historical shift, movies' narratives quickly became dependent on a **screenplay** (or film script), which standardized the elements and structures of movie narratives. A copyright lawsuit regarding an early movie version of *Ben-Hur* (1907) immediately underlined the importance of scriptwriters who could develop original narratives.

1927–1950: Sound Technology, Dialogue, and Classical Hollywood Narrative

While dialogue had an obviously limited function in silent movies (appearing only as **intertitles**, printed words inserted between the images), the introduction of sound technology and dialogue in the late 1920s proved to be one of the most significant advancements in the history of film narrative. While sound impacted the cinema in numerous ways, perhaps most important was that it enabled film narratives to create and develop more intricate characters whose dialogue and vocal intonations added new psychological and social dimensions to film. More intricate characters were used to propel more complex movie plots. In many ways a product of the new narrative possibilities offered by sound, screwball comedies such as *Bringing Up Baby* (1938) feature fast-talking women and men whose verbal dexterity is a measure of their independence and wit **[Figure 6.5]**. Other films of this period use sound

6.5 *Bringing Up Baby* (1938). The witty dialogue of the fast-talking, independent heroines of screwball comedies was made possible by the coming of sound to the movies. Such characters are epitomized by Susan Vance (played by Katharine Hepburn), whose "baby" in this film is in fact a pet leopard.

devices, such as a whistled tune in Alfred Hitchcock's *The Man Who Knew Too Much* (1934), to make oblique connections between characters and events and to build more subtle kinds of suspense within the narrative.

The continuing evolution of the relation between sound and narrative helped to solidify and fine-tune the fundamental shape of classical Hollywood narrative in the 1930s and 1940s. During this period, the structure of this increasingly dominant narrative form becomes firmly established according to three basic features: (1) the narratives focus on one or two central characters; (2) these characters move a linear plot forward; and (3) the action develops according to a realistic cause-and-effect logic. A trio of movies produced in 1939, often heralded as Hollywood's Golden Year—*Gone with the Wind*, *Stagecoach*, and *The Wizard of Oz*—illustrate sound-era movie narratives as modern-age myths and, despite their many differences, describe narrative variations on this classical Hollywood structure. During these years, the Hollywood studio system grew in size and power, and it provided a labor force, a central producer system, and a global financial reach that created an extraordinarily efficient industrial system for storytelling. This system became increasingly identified with lucrative narrative genres, such as musicals or westerns (see Chapter 9). Also during this period, the introduction and advancement of specific movie technologies—for example, deep-focus cinematography and Technicolor processes—offered ways to convey and complicate the narrative information provided by specific images. While the plot structure of the classical narrative remained fully intact, these technologies allowed movies to explore new variations on narrative in the atmosphere of a scene or in the dramatic tensions between characters.

With growing pressure from the Hays Office, the U.S. organization that determined the guidelines for what was considered morally acceptable to depict in films, and its strict Production Code, film narratives during the 1930s turned more conspicuously to literary classics for stories that could provide adult plots acceptable to censors. These classics included *Pride and Prejudice* (1938) and *Wuthering Heights* (1939). For an industry that needed more verbal narratives, Hollywood looked increasingly to New York and other places where literary figures like F. Scott Fitzgerald could be lured into writing new stories and scripts.

World War II (1939–1945) significantly jolted classical Hollywood narratives. The stark and often horrific events raised questions about whether the classic narrative formulas of linear plots, clear-headed characters, and neat and logical endings could adequately capture the period's far messier and more confusing realities. If the narrative of *The Wizard of Oz* (1939) followed the yellow brick road that led a character home, the war-scarred narrative of *The Best Years of Our Lives* (1946) poignantly questioned what path to follow, and even doubted whether one could ever go home again **[Figure 6.6]**.

1950–1980: Art Cinema

The global trauma of World War II not only challenged the formulaic Hollywood storytelling style of the time, but it also gave rise to an innovative art cinema that emerged in the 1950s and 1960s in Europe, Japan, India, and elsewhere. This new form of cinema questioned many of

6.6 *The Best Years of Our Lives* (1946). This postwar narrative questions the happy ending and closure that a return home usually signifies.

the cultural perspectives and values that existed before the war. Produced by such directors as Ingmar Bergman, Federico Fellini, and Agnès Varda, European art cinema experimented with new narrative structures that typically subverted or overturned classical narrative models by featuring characters without direction, seemingly illogical actions, and sometimes surreal events. In *Cleo from 5 to 7* (1962), for instance, Varda restricts the narrative to two hours in the day of a singer, capturing the real-time details of her life. Although the protagonist fears a cancer diagnosis, the narrative eschews melodrama for the joys of wandering through the everyday **[Figure 6.7]**. Influencing later new wave cinemas such as the New German cinema of the 1970s and the New Hollywood cinema of the 1970s

6.7 *Cleo from 5 to 7* (1962). Agnès Varda's narrative restricts itself to two hours of real time as it documents an afternoon in the life of a young woman in Paris.

and 1980s, these films intentionally subverted traditional narrative forms such as linear progression of the plot and the centrality of a specific protagonist. In addition, these narratives often turned away from the objective point of view of realist narratives to create more individual styles and tell stories that were more personal than public. These narrative turns toward personal or local subjects often resulted in self-reflexive styles that called attention to the very mechanisms of storytelling. François Truffaut's *The 400 Blows* (1959), a semiautobiographical tale of a boy growing up in Paris, is one of the best examples of these new narrative strategies (see Film in Focus, pp. 14–15).

1980s–Present: Narrative Reflexivity and Games

Contemporary movies represent a wide variety of narrative practices, but three can be identified as particularly significant and widespread in recent decades. In the practice of narrative reflexivity, filmmakers still tell stories but now call more attention to how they are telling those stories or how these stories are a product of certain narrative techniques and perspectives. *Adaptation* (2002) is thus a film about a screenwriter's struggles to adapt a *New Yorker* essay on orchids to the formulas of a Hollywood narrative. Replete with references to earlier films and narrative conventions, meanwhile, Quentin Tarantino's *Inglourious Basterds* (2009) is a self-conscious film fantasy about the destruction of the Nazi leadership (appropriately in a movie theater) **[Figure 6.8]**.

A second direction in movies of the last few decades is the appropriation of narratives directly from amusement park rides and a more general emulation of the physical and psychological thrills associated with them. *Pirates of the Caribbean: Dead Man's Chest* (2006) is an explicit example of this narrative practice (in this case, the film is based on a Disney World ride). *Harry Potter and the Order of the Phoenix* (2007), on the

6.8 *Inglourious Basterds* (2009). Contemporary narratives like this film are highly self-conscious and reflexive about the historical sources and materials that construct their stories.

6.9 *Mortal Kombat* (1995). The nonlinearity of plot allows for the convergence between game and film.

other hand, though based on J. K. Rowling's children's book, seems to aspire just as much to the model of a narrative ride, making its story perfectly suited for IMAX theaters.

As films move toward and into the digital age of the new millennium, a third tendency is to structure stories with the effects of video and digital gaming, making films, and their marketing campaigns, a kind of interactive game for audiences. While *Lara Croft: Tomb Raider* (2001) is one of the first narratives to be based on a video game, an increasing number of movies have either implicitly or explicitly constructed stories as an interactive exploration of spaces. *Mortal Kombat* (1995), for instance, is an example of a nonstory game (the objective of which was to become rulers of a specific space, the Earthrealm) being adapted into a nonstory film **[Figure 6.9]**. Film stories no longer depict a linear plot that an audience simply follows in every instance. Indeed, as film narrative evolves into the twenty-first century, the convergences and exchanges between games and films may represent one of cinema's most interesting new directions.

The Elements of Narrative Film

While narrative is universal, it is also infinitely variable. The origins of cinema storytelling in other narrative forms and texts, the evolution of narrative strategies across film history, and the distinct narrative traditions across cultures give a sense of this variety. However, we can identify the common elements of narrative and some of the characteristic ways the film medium deploys them.

Stories and Plots

As a starting point, let us identify the main features of any kind of narrative: story, character, plot, and narration. (Later in this chapter, we will explore and develop each of these four features in more detail.) A **story** is the subject matter or raw material of a narrative, with the actions and events (usually perceived in terms of a beginning, a middle, and an end) ordered chronologically and focused on one or more **characters,** those individuals who motivate the events and perform the actions of the story. Stories tend to be summarized easily, as in "the tale of a man's frontier life on the Nebraska prairie" or "the story of a woman confronting the violence of her past in Pakistan."

The **plot** orders the events and actions of the story according to particular temporal and spatial patterns, selecting some actions, individuals, and events and omitting others. The plot of one story may include the smallest details in the life of a character; another may highlight only major, cataclysmic events. One plot may present a story as progressing forward step by step from the beginning to the end; another may present the same story by moving backward in time. One plot may describe a story as the product of the desires and drives of a character, whereas another might suggest that events take place outside the control of that character.

Thus one plot of President John F. Kennedy's life could describe all the specifics of his childhood as well as the details of his adulthood; another plot might focus only on his combat experience during World War II, the major events of his presidency, and his shocking assassination in 1963. The first might begin with his birth, and the second with his death. Finally, how the plot is formulated can also differ significantly: one version of this story might depict Kennedy's life as the product of his energetic vision and personal ideals, whereas another version might present his triumphs and tragedies as the consequence of historical circumstances.

From early films like Edwin S. Porter's *Life of an American Fireman* (1903), regarded as one of the first significant narrative films, to recent movies like Christopher Nolan's *Memento* (2000), with its plot-in-reverse narrative, movies have relied on the viewer's involvement in the narrative tension between story and plot to create suspense, mystery, and interest. Even in the short and simple rescue narrative of Porter's film **[Figures 6.10a–6.10d]** some incidental details are omitted, such as the actual raising of the ladders. To add to the urgency and energy of the narrative, the rescue is actually repeated from two different camera setups. In *Memento*, the tension between plot and story is more obvious and dramatic: this unusual plot, about a

▶ **VIEWING CUE**

How do story and plot in a film differ? In what order does the plot in the film you've just viewed present the events of the story? ⏸

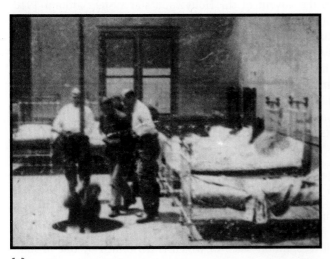
(a)

(b)

(c)

(d)

6.10a–6.10d *Life of an American Fireman* (1903). Told from two different perspectives, this story proceeds from a fire alarm sounded, to the racing of the firefighters through the streets, to the rescue.

6.11 *Memento* (2001). A crisis of memory becomes a crisis of plot in Christopher Nolan's innovative reverse narrative.

man without a short-term memory, begins with a murder and proceeds backward in time through a series of short episodes, as the film unveils fragments of information about who the man is and why he committed the murder **[Figure 6.11]**. In other films, we know the story (of President Kennedy's life, for instance) or the outcome of the story (that Kennedy was assassinated); in these cases, what interests us is discovering the particular ways the plot constructs that story.

Characters

The first characters portrayed in films were principally bodies on display or in motion: a famous actor posing, a person running, a figure performing a menial task. When movies began to tell stories, however, characters became the central vehicle for the actions; and with the advent of the Hollywood star system around 1910, distinctions among characters developed rapidly. From the 1896 *Lone Fisherman* to the 1920 *Pollyanna* (featuring Mary Pickford), film characters evolved from amusing moving bodies to figures with specific narrative functions, portrayed by adored actors whose popularity made them nearly mythic figures. With the introduction of sound films in 1927, characters and their relations began to be drawn according to traditions of literary realism and psychological complexity. Today the evolution of character presentation continues as characters now adapt the voices of real actors to animated figures and plots. Through all these historical incarnations, characters have remained one of the most immediate yet under-analyzed dimensions of the movies.

Character Functions

According to the discipline of **narratology**, the study of narrative structure, plots proceed through a fairly limited number of actions or functions—including prohibition, struggle, return, and recognition—each of which is performed by one or more characters. In the Russian folktales studied by narratologist Vladimir Propp, there are only a limited number of characters or *dramatis personae*, which include the villain, the hero, the donor (who prepares the hero), the helper (often an animal), and the princess or sought-for person. These character functions map surprisingly well onto the common narratives of popular cinema. Although we often think of film heroes and heroines as unique individuals, as the conventions of realist characterization and the casting of charismatic stars often encourage us to do, basic character types underlie these figures, and can even shape the personae of the stars who play them. In considering the function of character in the movies, it is useful to look at how we are encouraged to accept fictional entities as rounded individuals even while recognizing that familiar character types recur across different plots.

As indicated earlier, characters are either central or minor figures (usually, but not always, human beings) who anchor the events in a film. They are commonly identified and understood through aspects of their appearance, gestures and actions, dialogue, and the comments of other characters, as well as such incidental but important features as their names or clothes. Characters' thoughts, personalities, expressions, and interactions appear to focus the action of films and propel their narratives—although more interior qualities of film characters are less available to viewers than they are to readers of verbal narratives. Characters can be seen as motivating the actions of a film's story. Their stated or implied wishes and fears produce events that cause certain effects or other events to take place; thus the actions, behaviors, and desires of characters create the causal logic favored in **classical film narrative**, whereby one action or event leads to, or "causes," another action or event. In *The Wizard of Oz*, Dorothy's desire to "go home"—to find her way back to Kansas—leads her through various encounters and dangers that create friendships and fears; these events, in turn, lead to others, such as Dorothy's fight to retrieve the witch's broom. In the end, she returns home joyfully. The character of Dorothy is thus defined first by her emotional desire and will to go home and then by the persistence and resourcefulness that eventually allow her to achieve that goal **[Figure 6.12]**. A character's inferred emotional and intellectual make-up motivates specific actions that subsequently define that character.

Most film characters are a combination of both ordinary and extraordinary features. This blend of fantasy and realism has always been an important movie formula: it creates characters that are recognizable in terms of our experiences and exceptional in ways that make us interested in them. Often the differences and complexities of certain film characters can be attributed to this blending and balancing. For example, the title characters of *Million Dollar Baby* (2004), *Milk* (2008), and *The King's Speech* (2010)—a young working-class woman who becomes a prizefighter, the activist who fought for gay rights in San Francisco, and King George VI of Britain who overcame a speech impediment to rally his nation during World War II, respectively—all combine extraordinary and ordinary characteristics **[Figures 6.13a–6.13c]**. Even when film

6.12 *The Wizard of Oz* (1939). Narrative cause-and-effect logic finds Dorothy and her new companions on the yellow brick road toward the Emerald City.

(a)

(b)

(c)

6.13a–6.13c **(a)** *Million Dollar Baby* (2004), **(b)** *Milk* (2008), **(c)** *The King's Speech* (2010). These characters, whether based on historical figures or wholly invented, represent a balance of the ordinary and the extraordinary.

6.14 *Citizen Kane* (1941). Certainly one of the most complex characters in film history, Charles Foster Kane seems at first to resist simple models of character coherence and behavior.

▶ **VIEWING CUE**

Focus on a single character in the film you're currently studying. Is the character realistic or extraordinary? Explain how. Does the character's historical or cultural situation seem at odds with your own?

characters belong to fantasy genres, as with the tough but vulnerable heroine of *Alien* (1979), understanding them means appreciating how that balance between the ordinary and the extraordinary is achieved.

Character Coherence, Depth, and Grouping

No matter how the ordinary and the extraordinary, the unique and the typical, are blended in characters, narrative traditions tend to construct character behavior, emotions, and thoughts as consistent and coherent. **Character coherence** is the product of different psychological, historical, or other expectations that see people, and thus characters in fictional narratives, as fundamentally consistent and unique. We usually evaluate a character's coherence according to one or more of the following three assumptions or models:

■ *Values*. The character coheres in terms of one or more abstract values, such as when a character becomes defined through his or her overwhelming determination or treachery.
■ *Actions*. The character acts out a logical relation between his or her implied inner or mental life and visible actions, as when a sensitive character acts in a remarkably generous way.
■ *Behaviors*. The character reflects social and historical assumptions about normal or abnormal behavior, as when a fifteenth-century Chinese peasant woman acts submissively before a man with social power.

Within a realist tradition, the character Charles Foster Kane in *Citizen Kane* (1941) appears inexplicable in many ways: he madly seeks more and more art objects, rejects his friends, and changes from an idealistic and energetic young man into a bitter and reclusive old man **[Figure 6.14]**. A closer examination of his character, however, might suggest that he is unusually complicated but still coherent by virtue of his obsessive determination to control his world, his need for unconditional love, or the historical image of masculine wealth and power in U.S. society in the first part of the twentieth century.

Inconsistent, contradictory, or *divided characters s*ubvert one or more patterns of coherence. While inconsistent characters may sometimes be the result of poor characterization, a film may intentionally create an inconsistent or contradictory character as a way of challenging our sympathies and understanding. In films like *Desperately Seeking Susan* (1985)—about a bored suburban housewife, Roberta, switching identities with an offbeat and mysterious New Yorker—characters complicate or subvert the expectation of coherence by taking on contradictory personalities. *Mulholland Dr.* (2001) dramatizes this instability when its two characters become mirror images of each other. In its tale of an amnesiac woman and a young actress becoming entangled in a mysterious plot, fundamental notions about character coherence and stability are undermined **[Figure 6.15]**.

6.15 *Mulholland Dr.* (2001). The double characters of the amnesiac and the young actress complicate character coherence.

Film characterization inevitably reflects certain historical and cultural values. In Western cultures, movies promote the concept of "the singular character," distinguished by one or more features that isolate the character as a unique personality. For example, the unique character of Jason Bourne in the series of *Bourne* films (2004–2007) is a product of a complex mixture of traits—traits that reflect a modern notion of the advanced individual as one who is emotionally and intellectually complex and one-of-a-kind. The consequent **character depth** associated with the unique character becomes a way of referring to personal mysteries and intricacies that deepen and layer the dimensions of a complicated personality. The surface actions of Louise in *Thelma & Louise* (1991) clearly hide a deep trauma (a presumed sexual assault) that she tries unsuccessfully to repress. At other times, the uniqueness of a character may be a product of one or two attributes, such as exceptional bravery or massive wealth, that separate

6.16 *The Silence of the Lambs* (1991). Hannibal Lecter's dark depth of character is revealed.

him or her from all the other characters in the film. We should acknowledge that the value placed on singularity represents a social system that prizes individuality and psychological depth in ways that are open to question. After all, Hannibal Lecter in *The Silence of the Lambs* (1991) and its prequel and sequel is one of the most singular and exceptional characters in film history **[Figure 6.16]**; our troubling identification with him (at least in part) goes right to the social heart of our admiration for such uniqueness.

Character grouping refers to the social arrangements of characters in relation to each other. Traditional narratives usually feature one or two **protagonists,** characters we identify as the positive forces in a film, and one or two prominent **antagonists,** characters who oppose the protagonists as negative forces. As with the sympathetic relationship between a German officer and a French prisoner in *Grand Illusion* (1937), this oppositional grouping of characters can sometimes be complicated or blurred. In a film featuring an ensemble cast such as *Crash* (2004), the conflicting relationships and competing interests among a group of interrelated characters provide much of the film's drama. Surrounding, contrasting, and supporting the protagonists and antagonists, *minor* or *secondary characters* are usually associated with specific character groups. In *Do the Right Thing* (1989), Da Mayor wanders around the edges of the central action throughout most of the film. Although he barely impacts the events of the story, he becomes importantly associated with an older generation whose idealistic hopes have been dashed but whose fundamental compassion and wisdom stand out amidst racial anger and strife.

Social hierarchies of class, gender, race, age, and geography, among other determinants, also come into play in the arrangements of film characters. Traditionally movie narratives have focused on male protagonists and on heterosexual pairings in which males have claimed more power and activity than their female partners. Another traditional character hierarchy places children and elderly individuals in subordinate positions. Especially with older or mainstream films, characters from racial minorities have existed on the fringes of the action and occupy social ranks markedly below those of the protagonists: in *Gone with the Wind*, for example, character hierarchy subordinates African Americans to whites. When social groupings are more important than individual characters, the collective character of the individuals in the group is primarily defined in terms of the group's action and personality. Sergei Eisenstein's *Battleship Potemkin* (1925) explicitly fashions a drama of collective characters, crafting a political showdown among the czarist oppressors,

VIEWING CUE

Select a character in the film you're watching for class that you might define as singular. Does that singularity indicate something about the values of the film? Does the character seem coherent? How?

VIEWING CUE

What kinds of social hierarchies are suggested by the character groupings in the film you've just viewed?

6.17 *North Country* (2005). Dynamic and innovative characters, like the working-class female protagonist played by Charlize Theron, alter traditional character hierarchies of class and gender.

VIEWING CUE

Turn your attention to a film's most important minor characters. What do they represent?

the rebellious sailors, and the sympathetic populace in Odessa. Modern films, such as *North Country* (2005), may shuffle those hierarchies noticeably so that classes like blue-collar workers or groups like women and children assume new power and position, as in this story about a female mine worker's fight against institutionalized sexual harassment in the workplace **[Figure 6.17]**.

Character Types

Character types share distinguishing features with other, similar characters and are prominent within particular narrative traditions such as fairy tales, genre films, and comic books. A single trait or multiple traits may define character types. These may be physical, psychological, or social traits; tattoos and a shaved head identify a character as one type (a "skinhead" or punk, perhaps), while another character's use of big words and a nasal accent may represent another type (a New England socialite, perhaps).

We might recognize the singularity of Warren Beatty's performance as Clyde in *Bonnie and Clyde* (1967), yet as we watch more movies and compare different protagonists, we might come to recognize him also as a character type who—like James Cagney as gangster Tom Powers in *The Public Enemy* (1931) and Bruce Willis as John McClane in *Live Free or Die Hard* (2007)—can be described as a "tough yet sensitive outsider." Offering various emotional, intellectual, social, and psychological entrances into a movie, character types include such figures as "the innocent," such as Velvet Brown in *National Velvet* (1944); "the villain," such as Max Cady (played by Robert De Niro) in Martin Scorsese's remake of *Cape Fear* (1991); or the "heartless career woman," such as the imperious fashion editor played by Meryl Streep in *The Devil Wears Prada* (2006) **[Figure 6.18]**. These and other character types can often be subclassified in even more specific terms—such as "the damsel in distress" or "the psychotic killer." Usually character types convey clear psychological or social connotations and imply cultural values about gender, race, social class, or age that a film engages and manipulates. In *Life Is Beautiful* (1997), the father (played by director Roberto Benigni) jokes and pirouettes in the tradition of comic clowns from Charlie Chaplin and Buster Keaton to Jacques Tati and Bill Murray, outsiders whose physical games undermine the social and intellectual pretensions around them. In *Life Is Beautiful*, however, this comic type must live through the horrors of a Nazi concentration camp with his son, and in this context that type becomes transformed into a different figure, a heroic type who physically and spiritually saves his child **[Figure 6.19]**.

Film characters are also presented as *figurative types*, characters so exaggerated or reduced that they no longer seem at all realistic and instead seem more like abstractions or emblems, like the white witch in *The Chronicles of Narnia: The Lion, the Witch, and the Wardrobe* (2006). In some movies, the figurative character appears as an **archetype,** a reflection of a spiritual or abstract state or process,

6.18 *The Devil Wears Prada* (2006). The "heartless career woman" character type is depicted by Meryl Streep in her role as imperious fashion editor Miranda Priestly.

such as when a character represents evil or oppression. In *Battleship Potemkin*, a military commander unmistakably represents social oppression, while a baby in a carriage becomes the emblem of innocence oppressed. In different ways, figurative types present characters as intentionally flat, without the traditional depth and complexity of realistically drawn characters, and often for a specific purpose: for comic effect, as with the absentminded professor in *Back to the Future* (1985); for intellectual argument, as in *Battleship Potemkin*; or for the creation of an imaginative landscape, as in *The Wizard of* Oz and *Stardust* (2007).

6.19   *Life Is Beautiful* (1997). The "comic" character type, depicted by Roberto Benigni in his role as a prisoner in a Nazi concentration camp, is transformed into the "hero" type.

When a film reduces an otherwise realistic character to a set of static traits that identify him or her in terms of a social, physical, or cultural category—such as the "mammy" character in *Imitation of Life* (1934) **[Figure 6.20]** or the vicious and inhuman Vietnamese in *The Deer Hunter* (1978)—this figurative type becomes a **stereotype**. Although Louise Beavers's role and performance in *Imitation of Life* are substantive enough to complicate the way the role is written, the role is an example of how stereotypes can offend even when not overtly negative, because they tend to be applied to marginalized social groups who are not represented by a range of character types.

The relationship between film stars and character types has been a central part of film history and practice. For nearly one hundred years of film history, the construction of character in film has interacted with the personae of recognizable movie stars. Rudolph Valentino played exotic romantic heroes in *The Sheik* (1921) and *Son of the Sheik* (1926), and his offscreen image was similarly molded to make him appear more exotic, with his enthusiastic female fans differentiating little between character and star. In *Meet the Parents* (2000) and its sequels, Robert De Niro's character draws on familiar aspects of the actor's tough-guy persona—for example, his role as a young Vito Corleone in *The Godfather: Part II* (1974) or as Travis Bickle in *Taxi Driver* (1976)—to humorous effect. Our experience of stars, garnered through publicity and promotion, television appearances, and criticism, resembles the process by which characters are positioned in narratives. Elements of characterization through clothing or personal relationships, perceptions of coherence or development, all factor in to our interest in stars and, in turn, how aspects of stars' offscreen images affect their film portrayals. One way to contemplate the effects of star image on character types is to imagine a familiar film cast differently. Would *Cast Away*'s (2000) story of everyman encountering his environment be the same if, instead of Tom Hanks, Jack Nicholson or Beyoncé Knowles played the lead?

Character Development

Finally, film characters usually change over the course of a realist film and thus require us to evaluate and revise our understanding of them as they develop. In

6.20   *Imitation of Life* (1934). The "mammy" stereotype is identified by her social status and physical features.

6.21   *Juno* (2007). A sixteen-year-old's unexpected pregnancy and its social or moral implications are less the focus of the film than is her self-discovery.

a conventional story, characters are often understood or measured by the degree to which they change and learn from their experiences. Both the changes and a character's reaction to them determine much about the character and the narrative as a whole. We follow characters through this process of **character development,** the patterns through which characters move from one mental, physical, or social state to another in a particular film. In Hitchcock's *Rear Window* (1954), under the stress of a murder mystery, the beautiful Lisa changes from a seemingly passive socialite to an active detective. In *Garden State* (2004), an emotionally alienated twenty-something man undergoes a process of self-discovery as he reconnects with life through a chance encounter with a free-spirited young woman; in *Juno* (2007), the drama of a bright, sardonic sixteen-year-old's newly discovered pregnancy becomes ironically less about a social or moral crisis in the community and more poignantly and importantly about her own self-discovery of the meaning of love, family, and friendship **[Figure 6.21]**.

Character development follows four general schemes: external and internal changes, and progressive and regressive developments. *External change* is typically a physical alteration, as when we watch a character grow taller or gray with age. Commonly overlooked as merely a realistic description of a character's growth, exterior change can signal other key changes in the meaning of a character. Similar to the female protagonist in *Pygmalion* (1938) and *My Fair Lady* (1964), the main character in *The Devil Wears Prada*, Andy, is a rather naive recent college graduate who struggles with her first job at a fashion magazine. The course of Andy's personal and social growth and maturation becomes partly and problematically measured by her more and more fashionable outfits.

Internal change measures character changes from within, such as when a character slowly becomes bitter through the experience of numerous hardships or becomes less materially ambitious as he or she gains more of a spiritual sense of the world. In *Mildred Pierce* (1945), though there is minimal external change in the appearance of the main character besides her costumes, her consciousness about her identity dramatically changes—from a submissive housewife, to a bold businesswoman, and finally to a confused, if not contrite, socialite. Furthermore, as part of these external and internal developments, what we might call *progressive character development* occurs with an improvement or advancement in some quality of the character, whereas *regressive character development* indicates a loss of or return to some previous state or a deterioration from the present state. For most viewers of *The Devil Wears Prada*, Andy grows into a more complex and more admirable woman; Mildred Pierce's path resembles for many a return to her originally submissive role.

6.22   *The Tin Drum* (1979). Oskar's arrested character development is a symptom of the new Nazi society.

Using these schemes to understand character development can be a complex and sometimes even contradictory process. Some characters may seem to progress materially but regress spiritually, for instance. Other characters may not develop at all or may resist development throughout a film. Character development is frequently symptomatic of the larger society in which characters live. When the boy Oskar in Volker Schlöndorff's *The Tin Drum* (1979) suddenly refuses to grow at all, his distorted physical and mental development reflects the new Nazi society then developing in Germany **[Figure 6.22]**.

Diegetic and Nondiegetic Elements

Most narratives involve two kinds of materials: those related to the story, and those not related to the story. The entire world that a story describes or that the viewer infers is called its **diegesis,** which indicates the characters, places, and events shown in the story or implied by it. The diegesis of Steven Spielberg's *Amistad* (1997) includes characters and events explicitly revealed in the narrative, such as a rebellion on a slave ship in the first part of the nineteenth century and the subsequent defense trial featuring John Quincy Adams. However, the film's diegesis also includes viewers' knowledge of other unseen figures and events from American history, including a victorious war for independence and a near future that would erupt in the Civil War. The extent to which we find the film realistic or convincing, creative or manipulative, depends on our recognition of the richness and coherence of the diegetic world surrounding the story.

Some films intentionally leave the larger diegesis unclear or barely visible as a way of complicating viewers' understanding of the story. Andrucha Waddington's *House of Sand* (2005) tells the story of a woman taken to the remote and shifting dunes of Maranhão, in northeast Brazil, in 1910 **[Figure 6.23]**; there she remains isolated for fifty-nine years, barely catching glimpses of the major events of the twentieth century that exist outside her enclosed world. In this case, the very lack of a broader diegetic context serves to intensify the desperate loneliness of the woman but also to concentrate on her personal transformation.

The notion of diegesis is critical to our understanding of film narrative because it forces us to consider those elements of the story that the narration chooses to include or not include in the plot—and to consider *why* these elements are included or excluded. Despite the similarity of information in a plot and a story, plot selection and omission describes the exchange by which plot constructs and shapes a story from its diegesis. Consider a film about the social unrest and revolution in Russia at the beginning of the twentieth century: since the diegesis of that event includes a number of events and many characters, what should be selected and what should be omitted? Faced with this question for his film on the 1905 revolution, Sergei Eisenstein reduced the diegesis to a single uprising on a battleship near the Odessa steps and called the film *Battleship Potemkin.*

Information in the narrative that is **nondiegetic** includes material used to tell the story that does not relate to the diegesis and its world, such as background music and credits. These dimensions of a narrative indirectly add to a story and affect how viewers participate in or understand it. With silent films, nondiegetic information is sometimes part of the intertitles—those frames that usually print the dialogue of the characters but can occasionally comment on the action—as when D. W. Griffith inserts a line appropriated from Walt Whitman,

▶ **VIEWING CUE**

Describe the diegesis of the film you just watched in class. Which events are excluded or merely implied when that diegesis becomes presented as a narrative? ❚❚

6.23 *House of Sand* (2005). The omission of a broader diegetic context intensifies the narrative focus on the psychological and emotional plight of a single character.

6.24 *Jaws* (1975). In the opening sequence, Chrissie goes swimming during a late-night beach party. At first, all is tranquil, but the ominous thumping in the soundtrack foreshadows her violent death. This sound is used throughout the film to signal the presence of the shark.

VIEWING CUE

As you view the next film, identify the most important nondiegetic materials and analyze how they might emphasize certain key themes or ideas.

"Out of the cradle endlessly rocking," into his complex narrative *Intolerance* (1916). As discussed in Chapter 5, nondiegetic soundtracks are commonly musical scores or other arrangements of noise and sound whose source is not found in the story, as opposed to diegetic soundtracks whose source can be located in the story. Most moviegoers are familiar with the ominously thumping soundtrack of *Jaws* (1975) that announces the unseen presence of the great white shark: in this way, the story punctuates its development to quicken our attention and create suspenseful anticipation of the next event **[Figure 6.24]**.

Credits are another nondiegetic element of the narrative. Sometimes seen at the beginning and sometimes at the end of a movie, credits introduce the actors, producers, technicians, and other individuals who have worked on the film (with Hollywood movies today, the names of famous stars, the director, and the producers usually appear at the beginning, while the closing credits identify the secondary players and technicians). How this information is presented can often suggest ways of looking at the story and its themes as the story unfolds, or as we look back at it after it has ended. In *Se7en* (1995), for instance, the celebrated opening credits graphically anticipate a dark story about the efforts of two detectives to track down a diabolical serial killer. Filmed in a suitably grainy and fragmented style and set to the sounds of a pulsating industrial soundtrack, the opening credits depict the obsessive mind of a maniac as he crafts morbid scrapbooks, providing both atmosphere and expository narrative information **[Figure 6.25]**.

Narrative Patterns of Time

Narrative films have experimented with new ways of telling stories since around 1900, the beginning of movie history. One of the first such films, Edwin S. Porter's *The Great Train Robbery*, manipulated time and place by shifting from one action to another and coordinated different spaces by jumping between exterior and interior scenes. Since then, movie narratives have contracted and expanded times and places according to ever-varying patterns and well-established formulas, spanning centuries and traveling the world in Sally Potter's *Orlando* (1992) or confining the tale to two hours in one town in Agnès Varda's *Cleo from 5 to 7*. For over one hundred years and through different cultures around the world, intricate temporal organizations and spatial shapes have responded to changing cultural and historical pressures to develop and alter the art of storytelling on film.

Linear Chronology

A narrative can be organized according to a variety of temporal patterns. Individuals and societies create patterns of time as ways of measuring and valuing experience.

6.25 *Se7en* (1995). The presentation of the credits in a film can suggest ways for viewing its story and its unfolding themes.

text continued on page 234 ▶

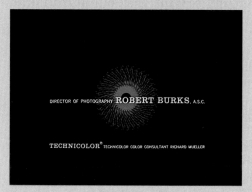

6.26a

6.26b

6.26c

6.26d

Nondiegetic Images and Narrative

Most moviegoers attend to the diegetic world of a film narrative: its characters, its story, and the world they inhabit. Punctuating, surrounding, and sometimes intruding on that diegetic world, however, are often important and illuminating nondiegetic actions and images.

Especially during the silent era, films relied heavily on nondiegetic intertitles to support the diegesis—by describing actions in the story, by providing the characters's dialogue, or by adding a perspective outside the narrative. This intertitle in D. W. Griffith's *Intolerance* (1916) offers a powerful poetic metaphor (from a Walt Whitman poem) about the course of human history **[Figure 6.26a]**. While intertitles are no longer commonly used, opening credit sequences are still a typical nondiegetic element in narrative films. As the first images audiences see, they frequently anticipate some of the main themes of a film without actually using images from the story itself. The opening credits of *Vertigo* (1958) begin with Saul Bass's powerful close-up of an eye containing a vertiginous spiral—an abstract pattern that resurfaces in various iterations throughout the credits and the diegesis **[Figure 6.26b]**, anticipating the complex themes of human vision trapped within the spirals of desire and fear in the film.

Closing credits offer other nondiegetic possibilities in a narrative film. In *Being There* (1979), the credits are run over outtakes from the film **[Figure 6.26c]**. By showing blundered takes, the film overtly calls attention to the fictional nature of the diegesis, and the realities of filmmaking outside that diegesis. Another way in which modern films challenge and break open the closed fictional world of narrative diegesis is by "breaking the fourth wall," or directly addressing an audience outside the walls of the diegesis. In *Ferris Bueller's Day Off* (1986), the always inventive and troublesome Ferris turns to the audience to detail his strategies for scamming parents **[Figure 6.26d]**.

6.27 *Little Miss Sunshine* (2006). En route to California from New Mexico in this linearly organized plot, the characters find themselves in hilarious predicaments.

Repeating holidays once a year, marking births and deaths with symbolic rituals, and rewarding work for time invested are some of the ways we organize and value time. Similarly, narrative films develop a variety of temporal patterns as a way of creating meaning and value in the stories and experiences they recount.

Most commonly, plots follow a **linear chronology** in which the selected events and actions proceed one after another through a forward movement in time. The logic and direction of a linear plot commonly follow a central character's motivation—that is, the ideas or emotions that make a character choose a course of action. In these cases, a character pursues an object, a belief, or a goal of some sort, and the events in the plot are constructed according to a logic that follows a cause-and-effect pattern centered on that character's motivation. The linear chronology of the plot will thus show how that character's motivating desire affects or creates new situations or actions: put simply, past actions generate present situations, and decisions made in the present create future events. The narrative of *Little Miss Sunshine* (2006) structures its linear action precisely in this way: a family of offbeat and dysfunctional characters travels from New Mexico to California to participate in a beauty pageant, and on their drive toward this single goal, over the course of several days, they must overcome numerous, sometimes hilarious, predicaments, obstacles, and personalities in order to complete their narrative journey and ultimately discover themselves anew **[Figure 6.27]**.

Linear narratives most commonly structure their stories in terms of beginnings, middles, and ends. As a product of this structure, the relationship between the narrative opening and closing is normally central to the temporal logic of a plot. How a movie begins and ends and the relationship between those two poles explain much about a film. Sometimes this relation can create a sense of closure or completion, as happens when a romance ends with a couple united or with a journey finally concluded. Other plots provide less certain relations between openings and closings. Michelangelo Antonioni's *Blow-Up* (1966) begins with a photographer at work developing pictures and concludes with his retrieving an imaginary tennis ball for an imaginary tennis match played by mimes. From the opening, the film's narrative follows the photographer's search for reality (in photos that suggest a possible murder); the conclusion offers only ambiguity, suggesting perhaps the impossibility of that search **[Figure 6.28]**.

Plot Chronologies

Despite the dominance of various versions of linear chronologies in movie narratives, most films deviate, to some extent, from straight linear chronologies to create different perspectives on events in order to lead viewers toward an understanding of what is or is not important in a story or to disrupt or challenge viewers' notions of the film as a realistic re-creation of events.

6.28 *Blow-Up* (1966). In Antonioni's art film, the photographer's search for reality leads only to ambiguous closure.

(a)

(b)

6.29a and 6.29b   *The Godfather: Part II* (1974). A retrospective plot of a father's formation of his Mafia family woven into a contemporary tale of the son's later destruction of it.

Plot order describes how events and actions are arranged in relation to each other to create a chronology of one sort or another. Either within a linear chronology or as a variation of it, actions may appear out of chronological order, as when a later event precedes an earlier one in the plot.

One of the most common nonlinear plot devices is the narrative *flashback*, whereby a story shifts dramatically to an earlier time in the story. When a flashback describes the perspective on the whole story, it creates a retrospective plot, which tells of past events from the perspective of the present or future. In *The Godfather: Part II*, the modern story of mobster Michael Corleone periodically alternates with the flashback story of his father, Vito, many decades earlier; this counterpointing of two different histories draws parallels and suggests differences between the father's formation of his Mafia family and the son's later destruction of that family in the name of the Mafia business [**Figures 6.29a and 6.29b**]. Conversely and less frequently, a film may employ a narrative *flashforward*, leaping ahead of the normal cause-and-effect order to a future incident. Thus a film narrative may show a man in an office and then flash forward to his plane leaving an airport before returning to the moment in the plot when he sits at his desk. In *They Shoot Horses, Don't They?* (1969), the plot flashes forward to a time when Robert, an unsuccessful Hollywood director during the Depression, is on trial; the unexplained scene creates a mysterious suspense that is not resolved until we later discover that he shoots Gloria, his partner in a marathon dance contest, at her request.

Other nonlinear chronological orders might interweave past, present, and future events in less predictable or logical patterns. In *Eternal Sunshine of the Spotless Mind*, the two main characters, Joel and Clementine, struggle to resurrect a romantic past that has been intentionally erased from their memories; the flashbacks here appear not as natural remembrances but as dramatic struggles to re-create a part of the personal narrative they have lost [**Figure 6.30**]. *Hiroshima Mon Amour* (1959) mixes documentary photos of the nuclear destruction of Hiroshima at the end of World War II, a modern story of a love affair between a French actress and a Japanese architect, and flashback images of the woman growing up

6.30   *Eternal Sunshine of the Spotless Mind* (2004). The film's chronology attempts to recover what has been lost from the couple's story.

6.31 *Hiroshima Mon Amour* (1959). The nonlinear mix of past and present engages us in the main character's attempt to reconstruct an identity across a historical trauma.

▶ **VIEWING CUE**

How is time shaped in the film narrative you just viewed? What especially important instances of frequency or duration can you point to in this narrative's time scheme? ⏸

in France during the previous war, when she had her first relationship with a German soldier **[Figure 6.31]**. Only gradually, and certainly not in chronological order, is the story of her past revealed. Conversations with her lover and images of Japan during World War II seem to provoke leaps in her memory; as the film narrative follows these flashbacks, we become involved in the difficulty of memory as it attempts to reconstruct an identity across a historical trauma. When a narrative violates linear chronology in these ways, the film may be demonstrating how subjective memories interact with the real world; at other times, as with *Hiroshima Mon Amour,* these violations may be ways of questioning the very notion of linear progress in life and civilization.

The Deadline Structure

One of the most common temporal schemes in narrative films, the **deadline structure** adds to the tension and excitement of a plot, accelerating the action toward a central event or action that must be accomplished by a certain moment, hour, day, or year. These narrative rhythms can create suspense and anticipation that define the entire narrative and the characters who motivate it. In *The Graduate* (1967), Benjamin must race to the church in time to declare his love for Elaine and stop her from marrying his rival. In the German film *Run, Lola, Run* (1998), Lola has twenty minutes to find 100,000 Deutsche marks to save her boyfriend. This tight deadline results in three different versions of the same race across town in which, like a game, Lola's rapid-fire choices result in three different conclusions **[Figure 6.32]**.

The deadline structure points to another common temporal pattern in film narrative: the doubled or parallel plot line. *Parallel plots* refer to the implied simultaneity of or connection between two different plotlines, usually with their intersection at one or more points. Quite frequently, a movie will alternate between actions or subplots that take place at roughly the same time and that may be bound together in some way, such as by the relationship of two or more characters. One standard formula in a parallel plot is to intertwine a private story with a public story. *Jerry Maguire* (1996) develops the story of Jerry's efforts to succeed as an agent in the cutthroat world of professional sports; concurrently it follows the ups and downs of his romance with Dorothy, a single mother, and his bond with her son, Ray. In some crime or caper films, such as *Ocean's Eleven* (2001), a murder or heist plot (in this case, involving a complicated casino robbery) parallels and entwines with an equally complicated love story (here, between Danny and Tess Ocean) **[Figure 6.33]**. In addition to recognizing parallel plots, we need to consider the relationship between them.

Narrative Duration and Frequency

Movie narratives also rely on various other temporal patterns, through which events in a story are constructed according to different time schemes. Not surprisingly, these narrative temporalities overlap with and rely on similar temporal patterns developed as editing strategies. Narrative duration refers to the length of time an

6.32 *Run, Lola, Run* (1998). In three different versions of the same race against time, Lola is forced to make different choices.

event or action is presented in a plot, whereas **narrative frequency** describes how often those plot elements are repeatedly shown. *Die Hard: With a Vengeance* (1995) features a now-standard digital countdown for a bomb that threatens to blow up New York City; the narrative suspense is, in large part, the amount of time the plot spends on this scene, dwelling on the bomb mechanism. Thus the thirty plot seconds devoted to this event in the film narrative take much longer than thirty real seconds, the temporal duration being not simply a real but also an extended

6.33   *Ocean's Eleven* (2001). The weaving together of the plot to rob a casino and a love story creates thematic and formal connections.

time. At the other end of the spectrum, a plot may include only a temporal flash of an action that really endures for a much longer period: in *Secretariat* (2010), a rapid montage of images condenses many months of victories during which the renowned racehorse of the title rises to fame. Instead of representing the many details that extend an actual duration of one or more events, the plot condenses these actions into a much shorter temporal sequence.

How often an event, a person, or an action is depicted by a plot—its narrative frequency—also determines the meaning or value of those events within a narrative. That is, when something is shown more than once, its value and meaning to the story increase. A movie may, for instance, return again and again to an exchange of glances between two specific characters, leaving no doubt that this relationship is central to the plot. In Eric Rohmer's *Claire's Knee* (1970), the witty plot returns again and again to the knee of the title. The frequency of this return suggests both the main character's obsession with this part of the young woman's body and, at the same time, how potentially comic that obsession can become through time **[Figures 6.34a–6.34c]**. In repetitions like this, it is important to recognize narrative frequency as a

(a)

(b)

(c)

6.34a–6.34c   *Claire's Knee* (1970). The frequency with which the knee is invoked becomes comical.

6.35 *My Dinner with Andre* (1981). The film takes place at a dinner table, a single space across which multiple narratives are spread.

6.36 *Roman Holiday* (1953). During an exploration of Rome, a sense of human history emerges.

6.37 *Walk the Line* (2005). When Johnny Cash bonds with the inmates, the ideological significance of Folsom Prison emerges.

way of drawing our attention to significant events, gestures, phrases, places, or actions.

Narrative Space

In Louis Malle's strange and unusual film *My Dinner with Andre* (1981), story after story is told, but the narrative takes place in a single visible space. The film occurs at a dinner table, where Andre Gregory and Wallace Shawn exchange anecdotes and memories, dreams, and secondhand stories **[Figure 6.35]**. That this film infuses a single mise-en-scène with such energy testifies to the imaginative power of stories to use and transform space. Thus along with narrative patterns of time, plot constructions also involve a variety of spatial schemes, spaces constructed through the course of the narrative as different mise-en-scènes (see Chapter 3). These narrative locations—indoors, outdoors, natural spaces, artificial spaces, outer space—define more than just the background for stories. Stories and their characters explore these spaces, contrast them, conquer them, inhabit them, leave them, build on them, and transform them. As a consequence, both the characters and the stories usually change and develop not only as part of the formal shape of these places but also as part of their cultural and social significance and connotations.

In conjunction with narrative action and characters, the cultural and social resonances of these spaces may be developed in four different ways: historically, ideologically, psychologically, and symbolically. Whether actual or constructed, the *historical location* abounds in film narratives as the recognized marker of a historical setting that can carry meanings and connotations important to the narrative. For example, in *Roman Holiday* (1953), a character visits the monuments of Rome, where she discovers a sense of human history and a romantic glory missing from her own life **[Figure 6.36]**. Films from *Ben-Hur* (1925) to *Gladiator* (2000) use the historical connotations of Rome to infuse the narrative with grandeur and wonder.

An *ideological location* in a narrative describes spaces and places inscribed with distinctive social values or ideologies. Sometimes these narrative spaces have unmistakable political or philosophical significance, such as the Folsom prison where Johnny Cash bonds with prisoners in *Walk the Line* (2005) **[Figure 6.37]** or the oppressive grandeur of the czar's palace in Eisenstein's *October* (1927). Less obviously, the politics of gender can underpin the locations of a film narrative in crucial ideological ways: in *9 to 5* (1980), the plot focuses on how three working women successfully transform the

6.38 *9 to 5* (1980). Three women transform the gendered politics of office space.

6.39 *Lost in Translation* (2003). The isolation of an American actor in Tokyo suggests a disaffected psychological space.

patriarchal office space of their jobs into a place where the needs of women are met **[Figure 6.38]**.

Psychological location in a film narrative suggests an important correlation between a character's state of mind and the place he or she inhabits at that moment in the story. In Sofia Coppola's *Lost in Translation* (2003), an American actor (played by Bill Murray) experiences confusion and communication difficulties while visiting contemporary Tokyo; these, along with his isolation in an expensive hotel, connect to deeper feelings of disaffection and disillusionment with his life back home **[Figure 6.39]**. Less common, *symbolic space* is a space transformed through spiritual or other abstract means related to the narrative. In different versions of the Robinson Crusoe story—from Luis Buñuel's *The Adventures of Robinson Crusoe* (1954) to *Robinson Crusoe on Mars* (1964) and *Cast Away* (2000)—the space of an island might become emblematic of the providential ways of life or of the absurdity of the human condition **[Figure 6.40]**.

Complex narratives often develop and transform the significance of one or more locations, making this transformation of specific places central to the meaning of the movie. In *Battleship Potemkin*, for example, the narrative infuses the Odessa steps with historical, psychological, ideological, and symbolic significance. In this case, the realistic mise-en-scène represents a famous location in the 1905 Russian Revolution, a psychological place of terror, an ideological location of oppression, and a symbol of the revolutionary uprising. In Jim Jarmusch's *Mystery Train* (1989), the narrative interweaves the stories of two Japanese tourists, an Italian woman on her way home to bury her husband, and three drifters who hold up a liquor store **[Figure 6.41]**. All happen to seek refuge in a sleazy

> **VIEWING CUE**
>
> Identify the three most significant narrative locations in the movie you've just viewed. How does the narrative construct different meanings for each location?

6.40 *Cast Away* (2000). The island as symbolic space becomes emblematic of the absurdity of the human condition.

6.41 *Mystery Train* (1989). Japanese tourists, ghosts of Elvis, and bungling drifters transform the space of a sleazy Memphis hotel into an offbeat carnival of loss and desire.

Memphis hotel. Although they never meet, the narrative location of the hotel becomes gradually infused with the meanings of their individual dramas: the hotel becomes simultaneously a place of historical nostalgia for 1950s America and of blues music for the Japanese couple; a comically ritualistic and spiritual location for the Italian woman, who takes leave of her husband's ashes after meeting Elvis Presley's ghost; and a weird debating hall where the drifters discuss contemporary social violence.

Narrative Perspectives

Plots are organized by the perspectives that inform them. Whether this perspective is explicit or implicit, we refer to this dimension of a narrative as its **narration**—the point of view that emotionally and intellectually shapes how plot materials appear and what is or is not revealed about them. Narration carries and creates attitudes, values, and aims that are central to understanding any movie.

Sometimes narration is associated primarily with the action of the camera and the selection of images, occasionally reinforced by verbal commentary on that action or other soundtrack cues. In other instances, as in *Memento*, narration becomes identified with the voiceover commentary of a single individual, usually (but not always) someone who is a character in the story; this perspective is called **first-person narration**, often recognized as one person's subjective point of view. In still other films, such as the epic *Curse of the Golden Flower* (2006), narration may assume a more objective and detached stance vis-à-vis the plot and characters, seeing events from outside the story; this is referred to as **third-person narration** (which we will later refine as "omniscient" or "restricted"). Even in cases of third-person narration, a presiding attitude or perspective defines the narration as it controls the plot. With third-person narrations like *Curse of the Golden Flower*, it still may be possible to describe a more specific kind of attitude or point of view. Far from being staid and detached, this film's narration is forceful and dynamic, igniting intimate and action sequences alike **[Figure 6.42]**.

Narrators and narrative frames are frequently used to signal the specific perspective of the narration. Both of these narrative elements describe formal tactics for drawing us into a story, and both direct the arrangement of the plot and create a specific position implying attitudes, standards, or powers. Additionally, they indicate certain cultural, social, or psychological perspectives on events of the story. The most common narrative perspectives are first-person narration, omniscient narration, and restricted narration.

VIEWING CUE

From what point of view is the narration of the film you are studying? If not controlled by an individual, how might the narration reveal certain attitudes about the story's logic?

6.42 *Curse of the Golden Flower* (2006). While third-person narration may maintain a level of objectivity, it can also create a dynamic relationship with the characters and action, infusing scenes with energy and wonder.

First-Person Narration and Narrative Frames

Some films use a narrator, a character or other person whose voice and perspective describe the action of a film from a point of view outside the story. This first-person narration is signaled by the pronoun "I" in written or spoken texts. Especially with first-person narrators, a standard device to mark the presence and perspective of that narrator is the voiceover commentary, a soundtrack commentary in which the narrator introduces the story and may occasionally make observations about it. First-person narration is an especially tricky notion for film narratives because this use of the voiceover to guide movie images can usually only approximate the full subjectivity of a first-person point of view. To attempt a literal first-person narration with film would require the film frame to become the narrator's eyes, re-creating only what the narrator sees. Narrated almost entirely through the first-person point of view of the detective Philip Marlowe, *Lady in the Lake* (1947) demonstrates how tiresome such a narration can become. The more common strategy is, accordingly, to signal a first-person narration through a voiceover narrator.

Appearing at the beginning and end of a narrative, a narrative frame is often a vehicle for introducing a first-person narration, but it serves many other narrative functions as well. A **narrative frame** describes a context or person positioned outside the story to bracket the film's narrative in a way that helps define its terms and meaning. Sometimes signaled by a voiceover, this frame may indicate the story's audience, the social context, or the period from which the story is understood. The frame may, for instance, indicate that the story is a tale told to children, that it is being told to a detective in a police station, or that it is the memory of a dying woman. In each case, the narrative frame indicates the crucial perspective and logic that define the narration.

In *Sunset Boulevard* (1950), the presence of the narrator is announced through the voiceover narration of the screenwriter-protagonist who introduces the setting and circumstances of the story. His voice and death become the narrative frame for the story. Through the course of the film, his voiceover disappears and reappears, but we are aware from the start that the story is a product of his perspective; how we understand the story is at least as dependent on this narrator and his attitudes as it is on the story's events. For this reason, viewers realize that although the story and plot seem focused on a delusional movie star whose glory has long since passed, the narrative (as opposed to the story) is perhaps even more about this writer's experience of her. That we learn from the start that this first-person narrator is dead becomes an unsettling irony.

Ang Lee's *The Ice Storm* (1997) also uses a narrative frame. The narrator in this case is a young man whose commuter train has stopped en route to his home because of a heavy ice storm **[Figure 6.43]**. The narrative begins as he waits in the night for the tracks to be cleared of ice and debris, and he reflects on his family; this isolated moment and compartment frame the flashback narration that follows. Although he, too, disappears as a narrator until we return to the train and his voice at the end of the movie, his salient position as a narrator makes clear that this tale of a pathetically dysfunctional family in the 1970s is, most importantly, about this young man at a turning point in his life. Indeed, both these examples suggest a question to ask about narrators: does it make a difference if the narrator is seen as part of the story?

Omniscient and Restricted Narrations

Most film narrators are not so visible, and the majority of film narratives employ some version of a third-person narration. The standard form of classical movie narration is **omniscient narration**, a version of third-person narration in which all elements of the plot are presented from many or all potential angles. An omniscient narrative perspective not only knows all; it also knows what's important and how to arrange it to reveal the truth about a life or a history. A limited third-person perspective, or **restricted narration**, organizes stories by focusing on one or two characters. Even though this narration also

text continued on page 244 ▶

6.43 *The Ice Storm* (1997). When a storm stops his train, a young man's thoughts on his past become the film's narrative frame.

Plot and Narration
in *Apocalypse Now* (1979)

Francis Ford Coppola directed *Apocalypse Now*, one of Hollywood's most ambitious film narratives, not long after his blockbuster successes *The Godfather* (1972) and *The Godfather: Part II* (1974) and his ingenious *The Conversation* (1974). Coppola and his first successful films were part of an American renaissance in moviemaking during the 1960s and 1970s, revealing the marked influence of the French New Wave filmmakers Jean-Luc Godard, François Truffaut, and others who brought decidedly experimental and ironic attitudes to film narrative. *Apocalypse Now* is also one of the first serious attempts by a U.S. director to confront the lingering anger and pain of the Vietnam War, a then-recent and traumatic memory that Americans struggled to make sense of.

The film's story is deceptively simple: during the Vietnam War, Captain Willard (played by Martin Sheen) and his crew journey into the jungle to find a maverick and rebellious U.S. army colonel named Kurtz (Marlon Brando). The story describes Willard's increasingly strange encounters in the war-torn jungles of Vietnam and Cambodia. Eventually he finds and confronts the bizarre rebel Kurtz at his riverside encampment in Cambodia.

As in other film narratives, *Apocalypse Now* constructs its story through a particular plot with a particular narrative point of view. The story of Willard and Kurtz could be plotted in a variety of other ways—by offering more information about the crew that accompanies Willard, for instance, or by showing events from an objective point of view rather than from one man's perceptions and thoughts. However, the film's plot concentrates less on the war or on how Kurtz became what he is (which is the main topic of the characters' conversations) than on Willard and his quest to find Kurtz. The plot begins with the desperate and shell-shocked Willard being given the assignment to seek out and kill Kurtz, to "terminate with extreme prejudice," and then follows Willard on his journey as he encounters a variety of strange and surreal

6.44 *Apocalypse Now* (1979). This scene depicts Willard's first-person narrative point of view.

people, sights, and activities **[Figure 6.44]**. In one sense, the plot's logic is linear and progressive: for Willard, each new encounter reveals more about the Vietnam War and about Kurtz. At the same time, the plot creates a regressive temporal pattern: Willard's journey up the river takes him farther and farther away from a civilized world and a rational truth, returning him to his most primitive instincts.

The mostly first-person voiceover narration of *Apocalypse Now* focuses primarily on what Willard sees around him and on his thoughts about those events. At times, the narration extends beyond Willard's perspective, showing actions from the perspective of other characters or from a more objective perspective, while still representing the other characters and events as part of Willard's confused impressions. Bound mostly to Willard's limited point of view, the narration colors events and other characters with a tone that appears alternately perplexed, weary, and fascinated. As a function of the film's narration, Americans, Vietnamese, and Cambodians appear increasingly bizarre, unpredictable, and even inhuman: rock music merges with the sounds of helicopters; soldiers surf during a violent attack on a village **[Figure 6.45a]**; tigers explode from the jungle; U.S. soldiers riot during a Playboy Bunny extravaganza in the depths of Vietnam **[Figure 6.45b]**.

In these and other ways, the narration, linked to Willard's control of the narrative point of view, communicates not just what happens but also the disturbing sense of a world gone awry. In *Apocalypse Now*, the traditional narrative pattern of personal progress and development is both acknowledged and severely challenged.

Indeed, as part of its exploration of the tragedies and horrors of the Vietnam War, *Apocalypse Now* continually raises questions about its own narrative debts and historical influences, thus suggesting a kind of narrative reflexivity. Characters tell each other stories about their lives, use the musical narrative of a Wagnerian opera as background for a vicious attack on a village, and (toward the end of the film) even act out a mythic narrative of ritual sacrifice as a bull and Kurtz are simultaneously slaughtered. The film makes no secret of its loose adaptation of Joseph Conrad's novella *Heart of Darkness* (1902), set in the nineteenth-century African Congo. Throughout the movie, passing references are made to various literary practices that question whether a traditional narrative can make sense of the brutality and emptiness of modern life, such as Joseph Campbell's well-known studies of narrative myths and T. S. Eliot's dark meditation in "The Hollow Men" (his 1925 poem that begins with a quote from Conrad's *Heart of Darkness*, "Mistah Kurtz—he dead"). Deep in Kurtz's dark jungle cavern, we catch glimpses of books on myth **[Figure 6.46]** and hear Kurtz reciting Eliot's poems, as if Coppola is acknowledging a narrative lineage that extends from Conrad's novella to *Apocalypse Now*, mapping the difficult relationship of narrative, modern history, and the darkness of the human heart. Almost a compendium of these narrative materials and traditions, *Apocalypse Now* seems to suggest that the history of war and colonization may well be bound up with a long history of attempts to control life and other people through the power of narrative.

(a)

(b)

6.45a and 6.45b   *Apocalypse Now* (1979). Here the traditional narrative pattern has been severely challenged.

6.46   *Apocalypse Now* (1979). The literary history of a cinematic narrative.

6.47 *The General* (1927). Restricted narration limits the plot to the experiences of the main character, Johnny Gray, as he rescues his locomotive and his girlfriend from the Northern army during the Civil War.

assumes objectivity and is able to present events and characters outside the range of those primary characters, it largely confines itself to the experiences and thoughts of the major characters.

The historical source of restricted narration is the novel and short story; its emphasis on one or two individuals reflects a relatively modern view of the world (since the eighteenth century) that is mostly concerned with the progress of individuals. Buster Keaton's *The General* (1927) **[Figure 6.47]** follows this pattern. Limiting the narration in this way allows the movie to attend to large historical events and actions (battles or family meetings, for instance) while also prioritizing the main character's—Johnny's—problems and desires. As a result, Johnny's ingenuity becomes apparent and seems much more honorable, and funny, than the grand epic of war that stays in the background of the narrative. With these and other restricted narrations, the logic and attitude of the narration determine why some characters receive more or less attention from the limited narrative point of view.

Reflexive, Unreliable, and Multiple Narrations

While omniscient narration and restricted narration are the most common kinds of classical narration, some films use variations on these models. **Reflexive narration** describes movies that call attention to the narrative point of view of the story in order to complicate or subvert their own narrative authority as a consistent perspective on the world. Robert Wiene's *The Cabinet of Dr. Caligari* (1920) is a well-known early example of reflexive narration that fractures the veracity and reliability of its narrative point of view when, at its conclusion, we discover that the narrator is a madman. Contemporary and experimental films commonly question the very process of narration at the same time that they construct the narrative. **Unreliable narration** (sometimes called *manipulative narration*) raises, at some point in the narrative, crucial questions about the very truth of the story being told: in *Fight Club* (1999), the bottom falls out of the narration when, toward the conclusion of the film, it becomes clear that the first-person narrator has been hallucinating the entire existence of a central character around whom the plot develops **[Figure 6.48]**.

6.48 *Fight Club* (1999). A dramatic example of a film whose narration suddenly appears to be the questionable fantasy of the film's narrator.

Multiple narrations are found in films that use several different narrative perspectives for a single story or for different stories in a movie that loosely fits these perspectives together. The 1916 movie *Intolerance* weaves four stories about prejudice and hate from different historical periods ("the modern story," "the Judean story," "the French story," and "the Babylonian story") and could be considered a precursor to the tradition of multiple narration. Woody Allen's comedy *Zelig* (1983) parodies the objectivity proposed by many narratives by presenting the life of Leonard Zelig in the 1920s through the onscreen narrations of numerous fictional and real persons (such as Saul Bellow and Susan Sontag). More recently, *Babel* (2006) weaves together different stories from around the world (those of a Moroccan family, tourists visiting Morocco, a Mexican nanny living in the United States, and a deaf and mute Japanese teenager) that are coincidentally linked by an accidental shooting of an American tourist. As these multiple narratives overlap and interact with each other, the film maps the struggle to find a common humanity and a common story in a complex global society **[Figure 6.49]**.

Compilation or anthology films—movies that feature the work of different filmmakers, such as *Germany in Autumn* (1978), *Two Evil Eyes* (1990), *Four Rooms*

6.49   *Babel* (2006). Overlapping multiple narratives in a film about the search for a common humanity.

(1995), and *Paris, Je T'Aime* (2006)—are more extreme versions of multiple narratives. This type of movie features a number of stories, each made by a different filmmaker. Although the stories may share a common theme or issue—a political crisis in Germany, adaptations of Edgar Allan Poe stories, or zany guests staying in a decaying hotel—they intentionally replace a singular narrative perspective with smaller narratives that establish their own distinctive perspectives.

▶ **VIEWING CUE**

What narrative perspective features most prominently in the film you've just viewed? If the narration is omniscient or restricted, how does it determine the meaning of the story? ⏸

The Significance of Film Narrative

In their reflections of time, change, and loss, film narratives engage viewers in ways that make time meaningful. From *The Birth of a Nation* (1915) and *The New World* (2005) (historical epics) to *The Hours* (2002) (a film about crises in the daily lives of three women), narrative movies have been prized as both public and private histories, as records of celebrated events, personal memories, and daily routines. Film, video, and computer narratives today saturate our lives with flashes of insight or events repeated again and again from different angles and at different speeds. As such, film narratives are significant for two reasons: they describe the different temporal experiences of individuals, and they reflect and reveal the shapes and patterns of larger social histories (of nations, communities, and cultures).

The significance of film narrative never functions independently of historical, cultural, and industrial issues. Many narratives in Western cultures are more inward, centering on individuals, their fates, and their self-knowledge. Individual heroes are frequently male, with female characters participating in their quest or growth primarily through marriage—a pervasive form of narrative resolution. Moreover, Western narrative models, such as the Judeo-Christian one that assumes a progressive movement from a fall to redemption, reflect a basic cultural belief in individual and social development. Of course, cultural alternatives to this popular logic of progression and forward movement do exist, and in some cultures individual characters may be less central to the story than the give-and-take movements of the community or the passing of the seasons. In *Xala* (1975) for instance, by Senegalese filmmaker Ousmane Sembène, the narration is influenced by oral tradition and the central character's plight is linked to a whole community. This tradition is associated with the griot, storytellers in some West African cultures who recount at public gatherings the many tales that bind the community together.

6.50   *Drumline* (2002). The narrative re-creates the familiar temporal experience of tense anticipation of a goal, climaxing in a final competition at the conclusion of the film.

Shaping Memory, Making History

Film narratives shape memory by describing individual temporal experiences. In other words, they commonly portray the changes in a day, a year, or the life of a character or community. These narratives are not necessarily actual real-time experiences, as is partly the case in the 95-minute *Russian Ark* (2002), which explores, without a cut, St. Petersburg's Hermitage museum. However, they do aim to approximate the patterns through which different individuals experience and shape time: time as endurance, time as growth, time as loss. In *Drumline* (2002), for instance, narrative time becomes about anticipation and action. In this film that concentrates on the rise of a talented but brash drummer in a college marching band, the tense excitement of the movie is summarized by the performances during a major marching band competition **[Figure 6.50]**. In the Dutch film *Antonia's Line* (1995), time becomes about women remembering and sharing experiences as their family expands in the years after World War II, and about the generational bonds of the love between mothers and daughters.

Through their reflections on and revelations of social history, film narratives make history. Narratives order the various dimensions of time—past, present, and future events—in ways that are similar to models of history used by nations or other communities. Consequently, narratives create public perceptions of and ways of understanding those histories. The extent to which narratives and public histories are bound together can be seen by noting how many historical events—such as the civil rights movement or the first landing on the moon—become the subject for narrative films. But narrative films can also reveal public history in smaller events, where personal crisis or success becomes representative of a larger national or world history. The tale of a heroic African American regiment, *Glory* (1989) **[Figure 6.51]**, tells a history of the Civil War left out of such other narratives as *The Birth of a Nation* (1915) and *Gone with the Wind*. While concentrating on the personal life of Mark Zuckerberg during his college years, *The Social Network* (2010) also reveals a key dimension of the larger cultural history of the digital revolution and specifically the social networking site Facebook **[Figure 6.52]**. In these cases, film narratives are about cultural origins, historical losses, and national myths.

Narrative Traditions

Based on how movies can both shape memory and make history, two prominent styles of film narrative have emerged. The classical film narrative usually presents a close relationship between individual lives and social history, whereas the alternative film narrative often dramatizes the disjunction

6.51   *Glory* (1989). A narrative of the heroic African American regiment that fought during the Civil War tells a different history of that war.

between how individuals live their lives according to personal temporal patterns and how those patterns conflict with those of the social history that intersects with their lives.

Classical Film Narrative

Three primary features characterize the classical film narrative:

- It centers on one or more central characters who propel the plot with a cause-and-effect logic (whereby an action generates a reaction).
- Its plots develop with linear chronologies directed at certain goals (even when flashbacks are integrated into that linearity).
- It employs an omniscient or a restricted narration that suggests some degree of realism.

6.52 *The Social Network* (2010). Here the personal history of the founder of Facebook reflects a much broader transformation in the social history of technology.

Classical narrative often appears as a three-part structure: (1) the presentation of a situation or a circumstance; (2) the disruption of that situation, often as a crisis or confrontation; and (3) the resolution of that disruption. Its narrative point of view is usually objective and realistic, including most information necessary to understand the characters and their world.

Since the 1910s, the U.S. **classical Hollywood narrative** has been the most visible and dominant form of classical narrative, but there have been many historical and cultural variations on this narrative model. Both the 1925 and 1959 films of *Ben-Hur* develop their plots around the heroic motivations of the title character and follow his struggles and triumphs as a former citizen who becomes a slave, rebel, and gladiator, fighting against the cruelties of the Roman Empire. Both movies spent inordinate amounts of money on large casts of characters and on details and locations that attempt to seem as realistic as possible. Yet even if both these Hollywood films can be classified as classical narratives, they can also be distinguished by their variations on this narrative formula. Besides some differences in the details of the story, the first version attends more to grand spectacles (such as sea battles) and places greater emphasis on the plight of the Jews as a social group; the second version concentrates significantly more on the individual drama of Charlton Heston as Ben-Hur, on his search to find his lost family, and on Christian salvation through personal faith [**Figure 6.53**].

Two important variations on the classical narrative tradition are the classical European narrative, films made in Europe since 1910 and flourishing in the 1930s and 1940s, and the **postclassical narrative**, a global body of films that began to appear in the decades after World War II and that strained but maintained the classical formula for coherent characters and plots. As discussed earlier, this latter tradition remains visible to the present day. Although it is difficult to offer broad or definitive models for

▶ **VIEWING CUE**

For the film you will watch next in class, what type of history is being depicted? What does the narrative say about the meaning of time and change in the lives of the characters? What events are presented as most important, and why? ⏸

6.53 *Ben-Hur* (1959). As the different versions of this film demonstrate, classical Hollywood narration can vary significantly through history—even when the story is fundamentally the same.

6.54   *The Rules of the Game* (1939). Do classical European narratives, such as this one by Jean Renoir, tend to accentuate social contexts more than classical Hollywood narratives?

these two narrative forms, the European model tends to situate the story in large and varied social contexts that dilute the singularity of a central protagonist and is usually less action-oriented than its U.S. counterpart. Thus in Jean Renoir's *The Rules of the Game* (1939), a diverse milieu of many classes and social types (from servants to aristocrats) interact on a large estate to create a narrative that seems less like a single plot than a collage of many stories about sexual escapades and bankrupt social mores. An exchange between two characters summarizes the range of this satiric narrative: one character exclaims, "Stop this farce!" and the other replies, "Which one?" **[Figure 6.54]**. Conversely, the postclassical model frequently undermines the power of a protagonist to control and drive the narrative forward in a clear direction. As a postclassical narrative, Martin Scorsese's *Taxi Driver* (1976) works with a plot much like that of *The Searchers*, but in Travis Bickle's strange quest to rescue a New York City prostitute from her pimp, he wanders with even less direction, identity, and control than his predecessor, Ethan. Bickle, a dark hero, becomes lost in his own fantasies (see pp. 372–73) **[Figure 6.55]**.

Alternative Film Narrative

Most visible in foreign and independent film cultures, these movies tell stories while also revealing information or perspectives traditionally excluded from classical narratives in order to unsettle audience expectations, provoke new thinking, or differentiate themselves from more common narrative structures. Generally, the **alternative film narrative** has the following characteristics:

- It deviates from or challenges the linearity of the classical narrative.
- It undermines the centrality of a main character.
- It questions the objective realism of classical narration.

   Both the predominance and motivational control of characters in moving a plot come into question with alternative films. Instead of the one or two central characters we see in classical narratives, alternative films may put a multitude of characters into play, with their stories perhaps not even being connected. In Jean-Luc Godard's *La Chinoise* (1967), the narrative shifts among three young people—a student, an economist, a philosopher—whose tales appear like a series

▶ **VIEWING CUE**

How would you describe the narrative tradition of the film you're now studying? What specific features of this film define it as part of one tradition or another? ⏸

6.55   *Taxi Driver* (1976). De Niro's character erupts into senseless violence and seems bent on his own destruction.

of debates about politics and revolution in the streets of Paris. A visually stunning film, Abbas Kiarostami's *Taste of Cherry* (1997) contains only the shadow of a story and plot: the middle-aged Mr. Badii wishes to commit suicide for no clear reason; after a series of random encounters and requests, his fate remains uncertain at the conclusion. Freed of the determining motivations of classical characters, the plots of alternative film narratives tend to break apart, omit links in a cause-and-effect logic, or proliferate plotlines well beyond the classical parallel plot. As an extreme example, David Lynch's *Lost Highway* (1997) seems to abandon

6.56   *Lost Highway* (1997). David Lynch's film is an example of an alternative narrative that upsets the audience's expectations about the characters' identities and linear stories.

its original story midway through the film when the protagonist inexplicably transforms into another character (played by another actor), leaving the audience unsure as to whether this change is actual, hallucinatory, or metaphorical **[Figure 6.56]**.

Many alternative film narratives question, in various ways, the classical narrative assumptions about an objective narrative point of view and about the power of a narrative to reflect universally true experiences. In *Rashomon* (1950), four people, including the ghost of a dead man, recount a tale of robbery, murder, and rape four different ways, as four different narratives **[Figure 6.57]**. Ultimately, the group that hears these tales (as the frame of the narrative) realizes that it is impossible to know the true story.

By employing one or more of their defining characteristics, alternative film narratives have also fostered more specific cultural variations and traditions, including non-Western narratives and new wave narratives. (With both these traditions, it should be noted, more state support and less commercial pressure have often abetted the experimentation with alternative narrative forms.) Alternative non-Western narratives, such as those found in the cinemas of Japan, Iran, and China, swerve from classical narrative by drawing on indigenous forms of storytelling with culturally distinctive themes, characters, plots, and narrative points of view. Indian filmmaker Satyajit Ray, for example, adapts a famous work of Bengali fiction for his 1955 *Pather Panchali* and its sequels, *Aparajito* (1956) and *The World of Apu* (1959), to render the story of a boy named Apu and his impoverished family. Although Ray was influenced by European filmmakers (he served as assistant to Jean Renoir on *The River* [1951], filmed in India), his work is suffused with the *text continued on page 252* ▶

6.57   *Rashomon* (1950). Four different narrative perspectives tell a grisly tale that brings into question the possibility of narrative objectivity.

Classical and Alternative Traditions in *Mildred Pierce* (1945) and *Daughters of the Dust* (1991)

Very much a part of the classical movie tradition, the narrative of Michael Curtiz's *Mildred Pierce* is an extended flashback covering many years—from Mildred's troubled marriage and divorce, her rise as a self-sufficient and enterprising businesswoman, and her disastrous affair with the playboy Monty. After the opening murder and the accusation of Mildred (its narrative frame), the narrative returns to her humble beginnings with two daughters and an irritating husband who soon divorces her. Left on her own, Mildred works determinedly to become a financial success and support her daughters. Despite her material triumphs, her youngest daughter, Kay, dies tragically, and her other daughter, Veda, rejects her and falls in love with Mildred's lover, Monty. The temporal and linear progressions in Mildred's material life are thus ironically offset in the narrative by her loss along the way of her emotional and spiritual life.

In *Mildred Pierce* we find all three cornerstones of classical film form. The title character, through her need and determination to survive and succeed, drives the main story. The narrative uses a flashback frame that, after the opening murder, proceeds linearly, from Mildred's life as an obsequious housewife to a wealthy and vivacious socialite to her final sad awareness of the catastrophe of life. Finally, the restricted narration follows her development as an objective record of those past events.

Set in the 1940s with little mention of World War II, *Mildred Pierce* is not a narrative located explicitly in public history, yet it is a historical tale that visibly embraces a crisis in the public narrative of America. While focused on Mildred's personal confusion, the film delineates a critical period in U.S. history. In the years after World War II, the U.S. nuclear family would come under intense pressure as independent women with more freedom and power faced changing social structures. *Mildred Pierce* describes this public history in terms of personal experience; but like other classical narratives, the events, people, and logic of Mildred's story reflect a national story in

which a new politics of gender must be admitted and then incorporated into a tradition centered on the patriarchal family. *Mildred Pierce* aims directly at the incorporation of the private life (of Mildred) into a patriarchal public history (of the law, the community, and the nation): Mildred presumably recognizes the error of her independence and ambition and, through the guidance of the police, is restored to her ex-husband, strikingly and perhaps ironically summarized in the final image of the film in which two laboring working women visually counterpoint the reunited couple **[Figure 6.58]**.

A very different kind of narrative, Julie Dash's *Daughters of the Dust* recounts a period of a few days in 1902 when members of an African American community prepare to move north from Ibo Landing, an island off the coast of South Carolina. The members of the Peazant family meld into a community whose place in time oscillates between their memories of their African heritage (as a kind of cyclical history) and their anticipation of a future

6.58 *Mildred Pierce* (1945). Mildred's story reflects a larger national story about gender and labor.

6.59 *Daughters of the Dust* (1991). The narrative drifts between past and present, merging history, memory, and mythology.

6.60 *Daughters of the Dust* (1991). Rather than focus on a single character, the narrative incorporates the perspectives of several Peazant family members.

on the U.S. mainland (where time progresses in a linear fashion) **[Figure 6.59]**. *Daughters of the Dust* avoids concentrating on the motivations of a single character. Instead, it drifts among the perspectives of many members of the Peazant family—Nana (the grandmother), Haagar, Viola, Yellow Mary, the troubled married couple Eula and Eli, and even their unborn child.

For many viewers, the difficulty of following this film is related to its nontraditional narrative, which does not move its characters forward in the usual sense but instead depicts individuals who live in a time that seems more about communal rhythms than personal progress, where the distinction between private and public life makes little sense **[Figure 6.60]**. The plot of *Daughters of the Dust* is structured as a denial of the dramatic turn of events that organizes the three-part movement of a classical plot. A fundamental question or problem appears quietly at the beginning of the film: will the Peazant family's move to the U.S. mainland remove them from their roots and African heritage? Yet the film is more about presentation and reflection than about any drama or crisis emerging from that question. Eventually that question may be answered when some of the characters move to the mainland, where they presumably will be recast in a narrative more like that of *Mildred Pierce*. But for now, in this narrative, they and the film embrace different temporal values.

In *Daughters of the Dust*, the shifting voices and perspectives of the narration have little

interest in a unified or objective perspective on events **[Figure 6.61]**. Besides voiceovers by Nana and Eula, the narrative point of view appears through Unborn Child, a mysterious figure who is usually invisible to the other characters and who narrates as the voice of the future. Interweaving different subjective voices and experiences, the film's narration disperses time into the communal space of its island world, an orchestration of nonlinear rhythms. Certainly a public history is being mapped in this alternative film, but it is one commonly ignored by most other American narratives and classical films. Especially with its explicit reflections on the slave trade that once passed through Ibo, *Daughters of the Dust* maps a part of African American history perhaps best told through the wandering narrative patterns inherited from the traditions and styles of African storytellers.

6.61 *Daughters of the Dust* (1991). As a story narrated in many voices, the film resists a unified perspective on events.

(a)

(b)

6.62   (a) *The River* (1951) and **(b) *Pather Panchali*** (1955). Jean Renoir's *The River* influenced Satyajit Ray's adaptation of *Pather Panchali,* but the films differ markedly.

6.63   *The Conformist* (1970). An alternative narrative set within a dreamy landscape where reality and nightmares overlap.

symbols and slow-paced plot of the original novel and of village life, as it rediscovers Indian history from inside India **[Figures 6.62a and 6.62b]**.

New wave narratives describe the proliferation of narrative forms that have appeared around the world since the 1950s; often experimental and disorienting, these narratives interrogate the political assumptions of classical narratives by overturning their formal assumptions. Italian New Wave director Bernardo Bertolucci's *The Conformist* (1970) is indicative: it creates a sensually vague and dreamy landscape where reality and nightmares overlap; through the mixed-up motivations of its central character, Marcello Clerici, the film explores the historical roots of Italian fascism, a viciously decadent world of sex and politics rarely depicted in the histories of classical narrative **[Figure 6.63]**.

Both these broad categories draw upon many narrative cultures that differ sharply from each other, and both suggest not so much a complete opposition to classical narrative as much as a dialogue with that tradition. In this context, Indian film narratives are very different from African film narratives, and the new waves of Greece and Spain represent divergent issues and narrative strategies. All, however, might be said to confront, in one way or another, the classical narrative paradigm.

CONCEPTS AT WORK

For most of us, narratives are the heart of our moviegoing experience as we seek out good films with interesting characters, plots, and narrative styles. All of these narrative elements and structures offer numerous possibilities for creating different kinds of stories, invariably related to the cultural and historical contexts that help shape them. Characters range across a myriad of roles and functions in films, from coherent characters to collective characters, who can develop in many different and meaningful ways. The narrative perspective of a film may provide an omniscient view of the world or one restricted to the point of view of a single character, while a film's narration may organize the diegetic materials of a film according to various plots and patterns of time and space. While many film narratives follow a classical pattern of linear development and parallel plots, many others deviate from those patterns and explore different ways of constructing a story and of infusing a film narrative with a larger significance. In all cases, film narratives allow us to explore and think about how time and history can be shaped as a meaningful experience.

Activity

Create a one-page treatment for your own film narrative, employing a classical narrative with parallel plots and five or six well-defined characters. As a commentary on your treatment, indicate the role of a particular narrative point of view in highlighting the themes of your narrative, as well as your goals in creating certain temporal and spatial schemes as part of your plot construction. Then create an "alternative narrative" of the same story, emphasizing the changes you would make in its major narrative features. How has this re-creation of the story through different structures changed the meaning of the story?

Representing the Real
Documentary Films

In 2001, at the site that is now known as Ground Zero, filmmakers Jules Naudet and Gédéon Naudet were working on a documentary about New York firefighters when Jules captured footage of an airliner striking the World Trade Center's North Tower. Thrown by chance into that monumental disaster, these directors found themselves making another documentary, now titled simply *9/11* (2002). Following the firefighters in the center of the chaos, the film depicted with immediacy and authenticity a catastrophe that would haunt America for years. In the following years, many other documentaries would attempt to make sense of that tragedy, the events that led up to it, and the politics that surrounded it; this variety of perspectives calls attention to the spectrum of possibilities within documentary filmmaking. For example, three years later Michael Moore released *Fahrenheit 9/11* (2004). In this case, however, the film arguably crossed the line between fact and fiction, as Moore himself became a larger-than-life character in the film, satirizing the Bush administration and investigating a wide range of political and economic forces that, for Moore, led to the 9/11 events. If we assume documentary cinema is fundamentally about representing reality, *9/11*, *Fahrenheit 9/11*, and the many other documentaries about that day remind us that documentary cinema can define and depict reality in very different ways and with very different goals.

For most of us, the film experience is primarily about the suspense of a thriller, the humor of a comedy, or the intense emotions of a romance. Yet that experience can also include the desire to be better informed about a person or an event, to engage with new and challenging ideas, or to learn more about what happens in other parts of the world. A movie that aims to inform viewers about truths or facts is commonly referred to as a **documentary** film, a term coined in 1926 by filmmaker John Grierson to describe a Robert Flaherty picture called *Moana* (1926) and its "visual account of events in the daily life of a Polynesian youth and his family." Broadly speaking, a documentary film is a visual and auditory representation of the presumed facts, real experiences, and actual events of the world. Documentary films usually employ and emphasize strategies and organizations that differ from those that define narrative cinema, such as plot and narration. Later Flaherty would team up with German filmmaker F. W. Murnau to integrate the documentary world of *Moana* into the narrative film *Tabu: A Story of the South Seas* (1931) **[Figure 7.1]**, and this hybrid film raises key questions: How are documentary films different from narrative ones? What attracts us to them? How do they organize their material? What makes them popular, useful, and uniquely illuminating?

7.1 *Tabu* (1931). Following the documentary breakthrough of Flaherty's earlier *Moana*, Robert Flaherty and F. W. Murnau's new project combines a tragic love story with documentary images of Polynesian life.

KEY OBJECTIVES

- Recognize that documentary films are best distinguished as cultural practices.
- Learn how documentary films employ nonfictional and non-narrative images and forms.
- Understand that documentary movies make and draw on specific historical heritages.
- Study the common formal strategies and organizations used in documentary films.
- Appreciate how documentary films have become associated with cultural values and traditions from which we develop filmic meaning.

If narrative films are prominently about memory and the shaping of time, then documentary movies are about insight and learning—expanding what we can know, feel, and see. Certainly narratives can enlarge and intensify the world for us in these ways as well, but without the primary task of telling a story,

documentary movies—whether they are news-reels, theatrical films, PBS broadcasts, or cable specials—can concentrate on leading our intellectual activities down new paths. Entertainment and artistry are of course not excluded from documentary films. A movie about the rise of skateboarding in Southern California, *Dogtown and Z-Boys* (2001) communicates, on the one hand, ideas and facts about the birth of a sport and the individuals who helped develop it; on the other hand, it creates a poetic collage of still photos, music, and talking heads, capturing the emotional energy and visual ballet in skateboarding that many of us may not have previously appreciated [Figure 7.2].

While narrative films are at the heart of commercial entertainment, documentary movies operate according to an *economics of information*. Many of the first films made in the 1890s and early 1900s, such as the traveling exhibitions and shows of Lyman H. Howe in America

7.2 *Dogtown and Z-Boys* (2001). Entertainment and artistry intermingle with the facts in this film on skateboarding.

and Walter Haggar in England, were part of lectures, scientific presentations, or visual illustrations of the art of motion. Churches, schools, and cultural institutions supported and financially subsidized these presentations, usually in the name of intellectual, spiritual, or cultural development. Since then, documentaries have remained, to some extent, tied to and often financially dependent on private and public sponsorship, such as museums, government agencies, local social activists, and cultural foundations—from projects of the Works Progress Administration (WPA) that funded U.S. documentaries in the 1930s to the grants of the National Endowment for the Humanities (NEH) that support some nonfiction films today. In addition, many documentaries are made for television, a phenomenon that has increased since the 1980s, when the deregulation of the broadcast industry encouraged the proliferation of such cable networks as Discovery Channel and History. For these channels, documentary programming has become a mainstay.

Although documentary films often claim and sometimes deserve the title "independent films," their survival has depended on a public culture that promotes learning as a crucial part of the film experience. Outside of or on the fringes of commercial cinema, this "other" culture of films has endured and often triumphed through every period of film history and in virtually every world culture. In the following sections, we will explore the many ways these films have expanded how we observe, listen, and think.

A Short History of Documentary Cinema

7.3   *President McKinley's Funeral Cortege at Buffalo, New York* (1901). Compelling images of events surrounding President William McKinley's assassination were recorded by motion-picture cameras. The Library of Congress has made these films available through the online American Memory Project.

▶ **VIEWING CUE**

What historical precedents (scientific treatises? essays? news reports?) might explain the strategies used in the film you've just viewed? ⏸

From ancient government records to family home movies, charts mapping new territories to school textbooks, we explain and learn about the world in ways that stories cannot fully explore. For example, the journals describing Marco Polo's travels through China or the early-nineteenth-century treatise by Sir Humphry Davy on the discovery of electricity have, in their own ways, recorded lost worlds, offered new ideas, or changed how we see society.

At the end of the nineteenth century, the search for empirical and spiritual truths produced new educational practices, technological tools, colonial expeditions, and secret societies—these were the vehicles to new experiences, pragmatic thought, and better worlds. In the midst of these trends, film was introduced in 1895 and used to illustrate lectures, offer cinematic portraits of famous people, and guide audiences through short movie travelogues. For many, film was not an art but a tool for investigating and explaining the physical and social worlds. The Edison Company stunned viewers in 1901 with a series of short films documenting the activities of President William McKinley on the day of his assassination, his funeral, and the transition of power to President Theodore Roosevelt **[Figure 7.3]**. Just as narrative films are rooted in cultural foundations and histories that preceded the cinema by centuries, so too are documentary films.

A Prehistory of Documentaries

For centuries, documentary cinema was anticipated by oral practices such as sermons, political speeches, and academic lectures; visual practices such as maps, photographs, and paintings; musical practices such as folk songs and symphonies; and written practices such as letters, diaries, poems, scientific treatises, and newspaper reports. The essay form, in particular, is considered to have had a great influence on documentary cinema, especially after 1945. Spearheaded by Michel de Montaigne, the essay form first appeared in the late sixteenth century and centered around personal and everyday subjects as a fragmented commentary on life and ideas.

Throughout the eighteenth and nineteenth centuries, journalism developed as a public forum for expressing ideas, announcing events, and recording daily happenings around town. Around 1800, Mary Wollstonecraft and Thomas Malthus wrote books, pamphlets, and lengthy essays describing the current state of society and insisting on practical ways that social science could improve people's lives. As the middle class moved to the center of Western societies in the nineteenth century, people demanded more information about the world.

Photography and photojournalism, evolving from new printing and lithographic technologies, became widespread and popular ways to record and comment on events. Unlike narrative practices, such as realistic novels or short stories, photojournalism presented virtually instantaneous and seemingly uncontestable records, factual representations of people and events frozen in time. One of the most dramatic combinations of social science and photography is Jacob Riis's *How the Other Half Lives* (1890) **[Figure 7.4]**,

7.4   *"Bandit's Roost," How the Other Half Lives* (1890). Jacob Riis documents the squalor and danger of tenement life in nineteenth-century New York.

which is part lecture, part photo essay; its pseudoscientific sermon exposes and condemns living conditions in New York City's tenement housing.

1895–1905: Early Actualities, Scenics, and Topicals

The very first movies appeared in 1895 and were frequently called **actualities**—that is, moving nonfiction snapshots of real people and events, with the most famous being Louis and Auguste Lumière's *Workers Leaving the Lumière Factory*. This film captivated audiences with its recording and presentation of a simple everyday activity without explanation or story line. **Scenics**, a variation of these early nonfiction films, offered exotic or remarkable images of nature or foreign lands. In Birt

7.5 *The Motion Picture Camera Goes to War* (1898). Many topicals produced between 1898 and 1901 depicted the ongoing Spanish-American War.

Acres's *Rough Sea at Dover* (1896), an immobile image shows waves crashing against a seawall, while other short scenics present views of Jerusalem or Niagara Falls. When these films captured or sometimes re-created historical or newsworthy events, they would be referred to as **topicals**, suggesting the kind of cultural, historical, or political relevance usually found in newspapers. Around 1898, for example, the ongoing Spanish-American War figured in a number of topicals, often with battle scenes depicting the sinking of the American ship *Maine*, which was re-created through miniatures. These factual and fabricated images of the war attracted large audiences **[Figure 7.5]**.

The 1920s: Robert Flaherty and the Soviet Documentaries

Footage of distant lands continued to interest moviemakers and audiences even after narrative film became the norm around 1910. American adventurers Martin and Osa Johnson documented their travels in Africa and the South Seas in such popular films as *Jungle Adventures* (1921) and *Simba* (1928) **[Figure 7.6]**. But it was Robert Flaherty, often referred to as "the father of documentary cinema," who significantly expanded the powers and popularity of nonfiction film in the 1920s, most famously with his early works *Nanook of the North* (1922) and *Moana*. Blending a romantic fascination with nature and an anthropological desire to document and record other civilizations, Flaherty identified new possibilities for funding these noncommercial films (largely through corporations) and, with the success of *Nanook*, identified new audiences interested in realistic films that were exciting even without stories and stars.

At the same time, a very different kind of documentary was taking shape in Soviet cinema. Filmmakers such as Dziga Vertov and Esfir Shub saw timely political potential in creating documentary films with strong ideological messages conveyed

7.6 *Simba* (1928). Early documentaries took the shape of explorations of new lands and cultures, frequently transforming those worlds into strange and exotic objects.

through the formal technique of montage. In *Fall of the Romanov Dynasty* (1927), Shub compiles and edits existing footage to show the historical conflicts between the aristocracy and the workers. In *Man with a Movie Camera* (1929), which would become one of the most renowned "city symphony" documentaries, Vertov re-creates and celebrates the energy of the everyday people and the activities of a modern city.

1930–1945: The Politics and Propaganda of Documentary

Perhaps more so than for other film practices, the introduction of **optical sound recording** in 1927 catapulted documentary films forward, as it made possible the addition of educational or social commentary to accompany images in newsreels, documentaries, and propaganda films. Public institutions such as the General Post Office in England, President Roosevelt's Resettlement Administration, and the National Film Board of Canada, as well as private groups such as New York City's Film and Photo League, unhesitatingly supported documentary practices in the 1930s and 1940s. These institutions prefigure the more contemporary supporters of documentary film, including the American Public Broadcasting Service (PBS), the British Broadcasting Corporation (BBC), and the German ZDF television station.

Indeed, documentary film history can never really be divorced from these critical sources of funding and distribution. Perhaps the most prominent figure to forge and develop a relationship between documentary filmmakers and those institutions that would eventually fund them was British filmmaker John Grierson. From the late 1920s through the 1940s, as the first head of the National Film Board of Canada, Grierson not only promoted documentaries that dealt with social issues but also established the institutional foundations that for years funded and distributed them. Government and institutional support for documentary cinema would proceed in a more troubling direction in the 1930s in the form of *propaganda films* **[Figures 7.7a and 7.7b]**—one of the famous examples being Leni Riefenstahl's *Triumph of the Will* (1935), commemorating the sixth Nazi rally in Nuremberg.

(a)   **(b)**

7.7   **(a)** *Triumph of the Will* (1935) and **(b)** *Japanese Relocation* (1943). Films like these represented the disturbing propagandistic power of documentaries controlled and supported by governments and other institutional agents.

1950s–1970s: New Technologies and the Arrival of Television

In the 1950s, changes in documentary practices followed the technological development of lightweight 16mm cameras (such as the Arriflex models), which allowed filmmakers a new kind of spontaneity and inventiveness when capturing reality. Most dramatic was the **cinéma vérité** movement that appeared in France at this time. Documentary filmmakers like Jean Rouch, with films like *Moi un noir* [*I, a Black* (1958)], could now participate more directly and provocatively in the reality they filmed. This new mobile and independent method of documentary filmmaking advanced again with the development of portable magnetic sync-sound recorders in the late 1950s (specifically the Nagra system in 1958), and then again in 1968 with the introduction of Portapak video equipment. Armed with a lightweight camera and the ability to record direct sound, filmmakers could now document actions and events that previously remained hidden or at a distance. Rouch's later film, *Chronicle of a Summer* (1961), has become a classic example of these new cinéma vérité possibilities, as it features random encounters with people on the streets of Paris, answering questions and giving their opinions on happiness, war, politics, love, and work.

Sometimes referred to as the golden age of television documentary, this period also brought a rapid expansion of documentaries aimed at a new television audience. Merging older documentary traditions with television news reportage, these programs were often noted for their tough honesty and social commitment (most famously identified with the work of television journalist Edward R. Murrow, whose battles with Senator Joseph McCarthy's indiscriminate attacks on individuals set a new benchmark for news reporting). Perhaps the best-known example of the convergence of new technology, a more mobile style, and television reportage is Robert Drew's *Primary*, the 1960 film about the Democratic primary in Wisconsin between John F. Kennedy and Hubert H. Humphrey **[Figure 7.8]**. This documentary was produced for the series "ABC Close-Up!" (1960–1961) by Drew Associates, the organization that would train many of the documentary filmmakers associated with **direct cinema**, the American documentary version of cinéma vérité that aims to capture unfolding events as unobtrusively as possible.

1980s–Present: Digital Cinema, Cable, and Reality TV

In the 1980s, the consumer video camera was taken up by artists and activists, such as the AIDS **activist video** collective Testing the Limits, as part of the democratization of documentary that would continue with the rapid shift to digital formats. With the introduction in the late 1980s of Avid's nonlinear digital editing process, documentary **shooting ratio** (the ratio of footage shot to footage used in the film), increased exponentially (since editing became so much easier and less expensive), and *personal documentaries* became a rapidly growing subgenre that would eventually achieve theatrical exposure in such films as Morgan Spurlock's quirky tale of his weight-gaining

7.8 *Primary* (1960). This documentary about John F. Kennedy's presidential campaign took advantage of the mobility and immediacy produced by new camera and sound equipment.

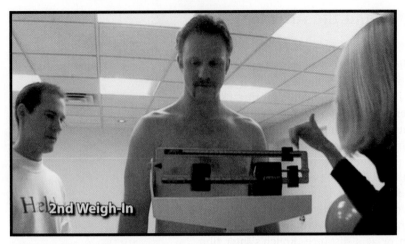

7.9 *Super Size Me* (2004). Morgan Spurlock at a checkup in this personal documentary on fast-food diets and their effects on American obesity.

7.10 *Planet Earth: Jungles* (2006). This bird of paradise from the jungles of New Guinea attempts to impress a potential mate with his elaborate dance. The high-definition documentary series was the most expensive nature documentary commissioned by the BBC.

quest, *Super Size Me* (2004) **[Figure 7.9]**. During this period, changes in the distribution and exhibition of documentaries significantly impacted the availability and popularity of these films.

In addition to increased festival and theatrical exposure and the expanding video rental market, cable and satellite television networks provide more and more opportunities for documentary projects. Under Sheila Nevins, premium cable channel HBO's documentary division has sponsored numerous powerful and acclaimed films, including *Born into Brothels* (2004) and *If God Is Willing and da Creek Don't Rise* (2010). *Planet Earth* (2006), the eleven-part nature series co-produced by the BBC and Discovery Channel, garnered awards, critical praise, and wide audiences on TV and DVD for its state-of-the-art, high-definition cinematography and conservation message **[Figure 7.10]**. While public television and cable networks provide more venues for independently produced documentaries that may otherwise have limited distribution, the relatively low production costs of nonfiction programming have also encouraged many channels to fill their schedules with reality television. From *Keeping Up with the Kardashians* and *Jersey Shore* to *American Idol* and *Top Chef*, these formats feature real people in situations that blur the lines between actual events, theatrical performances, and reenactments **[Figures 7.11a and 7.11b]**.

(a)   **(b)**

7.11 **(a)** *American Idol* (2002–) and **(b)** *Jersey Shore* (2009–). Just two examples of reality television shows that blur the boundaries between what is real and what is performed.

The Elements of Documentary Films

The documentary film, despite sharing elements of cinematic form with narrative and experimental films, organizes its material, constitutes its authority, and engages the audience in a distinct fashion. The following section outlines the modes of discourse, organizational patterns, and methods of presenting a point of view typical of the documentary film.

Nonfiction and Non-Narrative

Nonfiction and non-narrative, cornerstones of documentary films, are two key concepts that are often debated. Although documentary films and experimental films (see Chapter 8) can both be described as non-narrative, nonfiction has primarily been associated with documentary films. **Nonfiction films** present (presumed) factual descriptions of actual events, persons, or places, rather than their fictional or invented re-creation. Attempts to make a hard-and-fast distinction between "factual descriptions" and "fictional re-creations" have provoked heated debates throughout film history, since facts are arguably malleable. Nonetheless, a fundamental distinction can be made between, say, a PBS documentary about the life of Queen Elizabeth I of England and the feature film *Elizabeth: The Golden Age* (2007). The first film uses the accounts of scholars and historians, old paintings and artifacts, and the written accounts of her contemporaries to show the facts and complex issues in the life of one of the great women of history. The second film, a sequel to *Elizabeth* (1998), uses some of the same information but constructs it as an entertaining and easily comprehensible story.

However, it is also important to recognize that nonfiction can be used in a variety of creative ways. In *Enron: The Smartest Guys in the Room* (2005), Alex Gibney pursues a nonfictional, behind-the-scenes investigation of the cause behind the corporation's collapse through interviews with the actual participants in and victims of the event **[Figure 7.12]**. In contrast, in *Of Great Events and Ordinary People* (1979), Raoul Ruiz turns an assignment to conduct nonfictional interviews in a Paris neighborhood into a complex and humorous reflection on the impossibility of revealing any truth or honesty through the interview process.

Non-narrative films eschew or de-emphasize stories and narratives, instead employing other forms like lists, repetition, or contrasts as their organizational structure. For example, a non-narrative film might create a visual list (of objects found in an old house, for instance), repeat a single image as an organizing pattern (returning to an ancient carving on the front door of the house), or alternate between objects in a way that suggests different fundamental contrasts (contrasting the rooms, clothing, and tools used by the men and the women in the house).

A non-narrative movie may certainly embed stories within its organization, but those stories usually become secondary to the non-narrative pattern. In *Koyaanisqatsi* (1983), slow-motion and time-lapse photography capture the open vistas of an American landscape and their destruction against the drifting tones of Philip

7.12 *Enron: The Smartest Guys in the Room* (2005). Alex Gibney's film is a nonfiction investigation of the corruption that led to the collapse of a powerful American corporation.

7.13 *Koyaanisqatsi* (1983). A non-narrative catalog of images contrasting America's beauty and decay.

► **VIEWING CUE**

Is the film you have just seen in class best described as nonfiction or non-narrative? What elements helped you decide which categorization was more appropriate?

Glass's music: pristine fields and mountains, rusty towns, and garbage-strewn highways **[Figure 7.13]**. Through these images, one may detect traces of a story about the collapse of America in what the Hopi Indian title declares is "a life out of balance," but that simple and vague narrative is not nearly as powerful as the emotional force of the film's accumulating visual repetitions and contrasts. Diane Keaton's *Heaven* (1987) intersperses clips from old movies with angels and other images of heaven and presents a litany of faces and voices to answer such questions as "Does heaven exist?" and "Is there sex in heaven?" Although we may sense a religious mystery tale behind these questions and answers, this movie is better understood as a playful list of unpredictable reactions to the possibility of a life hereafter.

Nonfiction and non-narrative clearly suggest distinctive ways of seeing the world. Although they often overlap in documentary films, one form of presentation does not necessarily imply the other. A non-narrative film may be entirely or partly fictional; conversely, a nonfiction film can be constructed as a narrative. Complicating these distinctions is the fact that both kinds of practices can become less a function of the intentions of the film than of viewers' perception; what may seem nonfictional or non-narrative in one context may not seem so in another. For example, audiences in the 1920s mostly assumed that *Nanook of the North* (1922) was a nonfictional account of an Inuit tribesman and his family. Now, most viewers recognize that some of the central events and actions were fabricated for the documentary. Similarly, for some viewers, *The Cove* (2009) is a non-narrative exposé of the capture and slaughter of dolphins by a Japanese company, while for others it is a dramatic narrative about a group of activists on a rescue mission. Keeping in mind how the different meanings of nonfiction and non-narrative can historically and perceptually shift should, however, only make the categories more useful in judging the strategies of a particular documentary as part of changing cultural contexts and as a reflection of an audience's point of view.

Expositions: Organizations That Show or Describe

While narrative film relies on specific patterns to shape the material realities of life into imaginative histories, the documentary employs strategies and forms that resemble scientific and educational methods. For example, a narrative film of a young Thai girl longing to leave an isolated island might describe her adventurous escape to Bangkok. A documentary film, in contrast, might examine the details of her daily chores and intersperse those details with interviews in which she explains her frustrations and describes her hopes and wishes for another life. These different strategies alter our experience of the girl, thus making the character seem like two different people.

The formal expositional strategies used in documentary movies are known as *documentary organizations*. These organizations show or describe experiences in a way that differs from narrative films—that is, without the temporal logic of narrative and without the presiding focus on how a central character motivates and moves events forward. Traditional documentaries tend to observe the facts of life from a distance and organize their observations as objectively as possible to suggest some definition of the subject through the exposition itself.

text continued on page 266 ►

FILM IN FOCUS

Nonfiction and Non-Narrative in *Man of Aran* (1934)

Robert Flaherty's documentary film *Man of Aran* is an early, incisive example of how films employ, albeit in different ways, both nonfictional and non-narrative practices. *Man of Aran*, a documentary about a small community living on an island off the coast of western Ireland, does not identify the characters or explain their motivations; instead, it lists and describes the activities that make up their daily lives and records the hardships of living on a barren, isolated island. The members of this seemingly primitive community cart soil to grow potatoes on their rocky plots and struggle against the ferocious sea to fish and survive. In an important sense, the film is a historical and cultural record: it documents the routines of the residents' existence without the drama of a narrative beginning, climax, or conclusion. Adding to the distant atmosphere of a place that seems newly discovered by this film, the characters are not named, and the force of the sea constantly overwhelms their meager attempts to create order and meaning in their lives [**Figure 7.14**]. Well beyond learning about the customs of a distant way of life, audiences find in *Man of Aran* a dignity of living far removed from common experience and knowledge.

Stories and narratives are not the primary organizational feature in *Man of Aran*. Instead, the film mostly accumulates, repeats, and contrasts images. The brutal lifestyle on the island is presented by contrasting human activities with natural forces: images of people preparing meals, planting a garden, and repairing fishing nets alternate with images of crashing waves, barren rock coasts, and empty horizons.

Yet traces of fiction and narrative are still visible in the film, even if they are subsumed under alternative organizational patterns. Some situations are in fact fabricated, such as the episode in which the men are nearly lost at sea in the hunt for a basking shark (an activity that

was part of life two generations earlier but that, in 1934, no longer took place on the Aran Islands); the episode thus relies on the dramatic suspense that drives any good adventure story.

However innovative and distinctive this film is, it also reminds us of its cultural heritage. While explicitly working out of the tradition of an anthropological report, *Man of Aran* also adapts the tradition of the travel essay or travelogue, found in the works of writers from Henry James (1843–1916) to Bruce Chatwin (1940–1989). Whereas James describes the sights and sounds of his visits to Venice and Chatwin his encounters in Patagonia, Flaherty's film shows us a culture on the far reaches of the emerging modern civilizations of the twentieth century.

7.14 *Man of Aran* (1934). Inhabiting Irish islands unknown to many viewers, nameless individuals fight for survival against the barren and harsh world.

7.15 *Rain* (1929). The accumulation of images of different kinds of rain showers gradually creates a poetic documentary of various shapes and textures.

▶ **VIEWING CUE**

Examine carefully the organization of the film you've viewed most recently. Does it follow a clear formal strategy? Explain. ⏸

Here we will discuss three distinctive organizations of documentary films: the cumulative, the contrastive, and the developmental. These organizations may appear in different films or may be used in some combination in the same film. Then we will explore how the use of these organizational patterns is often governed by the perspective—or rhetorical position—from which a film's observations are made.

Cumulative Organizations

Cumulative organizations present a catalog of images or sounds throughout the course of the film. It may be a simple series with no recognizable logic connecting the images. Joris Ivens's *Rain* (1929) presents images from a rainstorm in Amsterdam, showing the rain falling in a multitude of different ways and from many different angles [**Figure 7.15**]. We do not sense that we are watching this downpour from beginning to end; rather, we see this rain as the accumulation of its seemingly infinite variety of shapes, movements, and textures. Another example of cumulative organization is *Thirty-Two Short Films About Glenn Gould* (1993). Although some viewers may expect a biography of the renowned pianist Gould, the film intentionally fragments his life into numerical episodes focused on his playing, on his acquaintances discussing him, and on reenactments of moments in his life [**Figure 7.16**].

Contrastive Organizations

A variation on cumulative organization, *contrastive organizations* present a series of contrasts or oppositions meant to indicate the different points of view on its subject. Thus a film may alternate between images of war and peace or between contrasting skylines of different cities. Sometimes these contrasts may be evaluative, distinguishing positive and negative events. At other times, contrastive exposition may suggest a more complicated relationship between objects or individuals. Among the most ambitious versions of this technique is a group of films by Michael Apted, beginning with his documentary *7 Up* (1963) and followed by successive films made every seven years; the films track the changing attitudes and social situations of a group of children as they grow into the adults of *42 Up* (1998) and *49 Up* (2005). With a new film appearing every seven years, these films contrast not only the differences among developing individuals in terms of class, gender, and family life but also the differences in their changing outlooks as they grow older.

7.16 *Thirty-Two Short Films About Glenn Gould* (1993). As an expositional organization, the film offers a glimpse into the life of the notoriously elusive genius through snippets of performance footage intermixed with reenactments of moments in his life.

Developmental Organizations

With *developmental organizations*, places, objects, individuals, or experiences are presented through a pattern that has a non-narrative logic or structure but still follows a logic of change or progression. For example, an individual may be presented as growing from small to large, as changing from a passive to an active personality, or as moving from the physical to the spiritual. With a script by W. H. Auden, *Night Mail* (1936) describes the journey of the mail train from London to Scotland, documenting and celebrating the many precisely coordinated tasks that make up this nightly civil service. With music from composer Benjamin Britten and poetry by Auden, the movement of this journey re-creates the rhythms of the train wheels as they accelerate, steady, and then slow in their developing path across England **[Figure 7.17]**. More recently, the 2007 *The King of Kong: A Fistful of Quarters* follows gamer Steve Wiebe in his attempt to break the record score of Donkey Kong champion Billy Mitchell. The film documents his progressive movement toward that goal and the showdown that threatens to derail it **[Figure 7.18]**.

Rhetorical Positions

Just as narrative cinema uses different types of narrators and narration to tell stories from a certain angle, documentary and experimental films employ their own *rhetorical positions*, or organizational points of view, that shape their formal practices according to certain perspectives and attitudes. Sometimes these films might assume the neutral stance of the uninvolved observer—referred to as the "voice of God" because of its assumed authority and objectivity. At other times, the point of view of the documentary assumes a more limited or even personal perspective. Whether clearly visible and heard, omniscient or personal, or merely implied by the film's organization, the rhetorical positions of documentary films generally articulate their attitudes and positions according to four principal frameworks:

- The first is associated with the effort to explore the world and its peoples.
- The second aims to interrogate or analyze an event or a problem.
- The third assumes the stance of a debater or polemicist who attempts to persuade the audience of a certain truth or point of view.
- The fourth foregrounds and reflects the presence and activity of the filmmaking process and/or the filmmaker.

Sometimes these frameworks will overlap in a single film. For example, the voice of Peter Davis's *Hearts and Minds* (1974) is both explorative and polemical as it tears apart, with

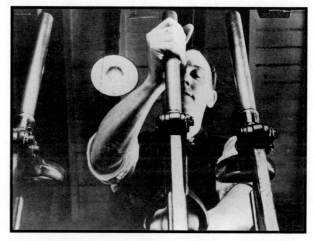

7.17 *Night Mail* (1936). Within the journey of mail from London to Scotland, a poetry of the everyday develops and progresses, as the film follows the tasks of sorting mail, picking up that mail by trains, and eventually delivering it at the end of the line.

7.18 *The King of Kong: A Fistful of Quarters* (2007). Gaming becomes a world of ever-rising scores, new records, and conquests, as we follow Steve Wiebe's journey from playing Donkey Kong in his garage to the Funspot Arcade in Laconia, New Hampshire, where he performs a live high score to prove his ability and legitimacy.

7.19 *Hearts and Minds* (1974). A documentary explores the realities of the Vietnam War, while trying to convince its audience of the misguided decisions that led to the disaster it became.

7.20 *Nanook of the North* (1922). Many documentaries mimic the anthropologist's project of exploring other cultures, in this case the rituals and daily routines of an Inuit family.

strategically placed interviews and newsreel footage, the myths supporting the Vietnam War **[Figure 7.19]**. *Winged Migration* (2001) uses both very little commentary and a "bird's-eye view" to present the flights of migratory birds around the world, while at the same time it subtly promotes the natural mysteries of those activities. *Capitalism: A Love Story* (2009), a film that centers on director Michael Moore's perspective on the recent financial crisis and the ensuing bailout, offers an often exaggerated performance as a clearly argumentative perspective meant to incite and arouse audiences and to sway opinion on the current economic situation in the United States.

Explorative Positions

Explorative positions announce or suggest that the film's driving perspective is a scientific search into particular social, psychological, or physical phenomena. Informed by this position, a documentary assumes the perspective of a traveler, an explorer, or an investigator who encounters new worlds, facts, or experiences and aims to present and describe these straightforwardly, often as a witness. Travel films have existed since the first days of cinema when filmmakers would offer short records of exotic locations such as Niagara Falls or the Great Wall of China. The first feature-length documentaries extended that explorative curiosity, positioning the travel film somewhere between the anthropologist's urge to show different civilizations and peoples, as in Flaherty's *Nanook of the North* **[Figure 7.20]**, and the tourist's pleasure of visiting novel sites and locations, as in Jean Vigo's tongue-in-cheek wanderings through a French resort town in *Apropos of Nice* (1930). More recently, Academy Award winner and box-office success *March of the Penguins* (2005) enhanced the traditional explorative position through the capabilities of new technologies to explore the migratory habits of Emperor penguins **[Figure 7.21]**.

7.21 *March of the Penguins* (2005). New technologies allow viewers to witness the delicate and unique exchange of the egg from mother to father.

(a)

(b)

7.22a and 7.22b   *Night and Fog* (1955). As images of liberated survivors of the Nazi concentration camps alternate with contemporary images of the same empty camps, the complex organizational refrain of the film becomes, "Who is responsible?"

Interrogative Positions

Interrogative or *analytical positions* rhetorically structure a movie in a way that identifies the subject as being under investigation—either through an implicit or explicit question-and-answer format or by other, more subtle, techniques. Commonly condensed in the interview format found in many documentary films, interrogative techniques can also employ a voiceover or an on-camera voice that asks questions of individuals or objects that may or may not respond to the questioning. Frank Capra's *Why We Fight* series (1943–1945) explicitly formulates itself as an inquisition into the motivations for the U.S. involvement in World War II, while in Trinh T. Minh-ha's *Surname Viet Given Name Nam* (1989) a question or problem may only be implied, and succeeding images may either resolve the problem or not. Harun Farocki's *The Interview* (1997) takes the logic of the interrogative position to a more reflexive level following unemployed individuals being trained to conduct themselves properly in a job interview. One of the most profound and subtlest examples of the interrogative or analytical form is Alain Resnais's *Night and Fog* (1955), which offers images without answers **[Figures 7.22a and 7.22b]**. In short, interrogative and analytical forms may lead to more knowledge, or may simply raise more questions than they answer.

Persuasive Positions

Use of interrogation and analysis in a documentary film are often (but not always) intended to convince or persuade a viewer about certain facts or truths. *Persuasive positions* articulate a perspective that expresses a personal or social position using emotions or beliefs and aim to persuade viewers to feel and see in a certain way. Some films do so through voices and interviews that attempt to convince viewers of a particular cause. In *An Inconvenient Truth* (2006), former vice president Al Gore positions himself like a professor before charts, graphs, and images in a sustained argument about the dangers of global warming **[Figure 7.23]**. Other

7.23   *An Inconvenient Truth* (2006). Graphs, charts, and expert opinion help to persuade an audience of the dangers of global warming.

7.24 *Titicut Follies* (1967). Much of the film's power resides in shocking images of the institutional abuses of the prisoners.

▶ **VIEWING CUE**

Describe the presiding voice or attitude of the film you just viewed. Is the dominant rhetorical position appropriate for the subject? Can you imagine another way of filming this subject? Explain. ⏸

movies may downplay the presence of the personal perspective and instead use images and sounds to influence viewers through argument or emotional appeal, as in propagandistic movies that urge certain political or social views. Leni Riefenstahl's infamous *Triumph of the Will* allows the grandiose composition of images to convince viewers of the glorious powers of the Nazi Party; meanwhile, Pare Lorentz's *The Plow That Broke the Plains* (1936) becomes an indictment of the lack of U.S. government planning that resulted in the environmental and social disaster in the West and Southwest known as the Dust Bowl. Persuasive forms can also rely solely on the power of documentary images themselves. Frederick Wiseman's *Titicut Follies* (1967), for example, exposes the treatment of and influences attitudes about the criminally insane without any overt argumentation **[Figure 7.24]**. With such movies, what we are being persuaded to do or think may not be immediately evident, yet it is usually obvious that we are engaged in a rhetorical argument that involves visual facts, intellectual statements, and sometimes emotional manipulation.

Reflexive and Performative Positions

Reflexive and *performative positions* call attention to the filmmaking process or perspective of the filmmaker in determining or shaping the documentary material being presented. Often this means calling attention to the making of the documentary or the process of watching a film itself. Certain films, like Laleen Jayamanne's *A Song of Ceylon* (1985), which references the classical documentary *Song of Ceylon* (1934) through its meditation on colonialism and gender in Sri Lanka, aim to remind viewers that documentary reality and history are always mediated by the film image, and that documentary films do not necessarily offer an easy access to truth. This focus can shift from the filmmaking process to the filmmaker, thus emphasizing the participation of that individual as a kind of performer of reality. In Ross McElwee's *Sherman's March* (1986), the filmmaker sets out on a journey to document the famous Civil War general's conquest of the South; along the way, however, this witty film becomes more about the filmmaker's own failed attempts to start or maintain a romantic relationship with the many women he meets. Werner Herzog's *Grizzly Man* (2005) alternates between the self-performative videos of Timothy Treadwell and Herzog's documentary of Treadwell's unusual life in an Alaskan bear colony—and his gruesome death. This back and forth makes the film a commentary on Treadwell, Herzog, and their different cinematic views of the world **[Figure 7.25]**.

7.25 *Grizzly Man* (2005). A documentary about another personal documentary, this film becomes a reflexive performance by filmmaker Werner Herzog about the relationship between images and nature.

The Significance of Documentary Films

Although moviegoers have always been attracted to a film's entertainment value, audiences have also appreciated the cultural and educational values of nonfiction movies produced as early as the 1890s. These films presented sporting events, political speeches, and dramatic presentations of Shakespeare. In 1896, for instance, the Lumière brothers took audiences on an educational railway trip with the "phantom ride" of *Leaving Jerusalem by Railway* **[Figure 7.26]**. According to these practices, then, the documentary could presumably offer unmediated truths or factual insights that were unavailable through strictly narrative experiences. Regardless of how this basic view of the documentary may have changed since then, presenting presumed social, historical, or cultural truths or facts remains the foundation on which documentary films were built.

Perhaps more than narrative cinema, documentary films expand and complicate how we understand the world, and the relationship between documentary films and the cultural and historical expectations of viewers plays a large part in how these movies are understood. Luis Buñuel's *Land Without Bread* (1933) might seem to be a kind of travelogue about a remote region of Spain—Las Hurdes—but its bitingly ironic soundtrack commentary, which flatly understates the brutal misery, poverty, and degradation in the region, makes the film a searing political commentary on the failure of the state and church to care adequately for the people who live there. So unmistakable was the message of this film, in fact, that the Spanish government repressed it. Without its cultural context, this film might seem odd or confusing to some viewers today, reminding us that in order to locate the significance of a film, we often must understand the historical, social, and cultural context in which it was made.

Throughout the history of documentaries, viewers have found these films most significant in their ability to reveal new or ignored realities not typically seen in narrative films, and to confront assumptions and alter opinions.

▶ **VIEWING CUE**

What makes a documentary film you have recently seen meaningful? How specifically does it achieve its aims and make its values apparent? ⏸

Revealing New or Ignored Realities

Because narrative movies dominate the cinematic scene, documentary films commonly have a differential value: successful documentary films offer different kinds of truth than narrative movies. Often this means revealing new or ignored realities by showing people, events, or levels of reality we have not seen before, because they have been excluded either from our social experience or from our experiences of narrative films. To achieve these kinds of fresh insight, documentaries often question the basic terms of narratives—such as the centrality of characters, the importance of a cause-and-effect chronology, or the necessity of a narrative point of view—or they draw on perspectives or techniques that would seem out of place in a narrative movie.

By showing us an object or a place from angles and points of view beyond the realistic range of human vision, such films place us closer to a newly discovered reality: we see the bottom of a deep ocean through the power of an underwater camera or the flight of migrating birds from their perspectives in the skies. Perhaps the object will be presented for

7.26 *Leaving Jerusalem by Railway* (1896). Early film allowed audiences to experience the pleasure and education of visiting new lands and vistas.

text continued on page 274 ▶

Organizational Strategies and Rhetorical Positions in *Sunless* (1982)

Chris Marker's *Sunless*, perhaps better known by its original French title, *Sans soleil*, is a global travelogue that moves through a dizzying catalog of different places and people, with commentary by a voice reading letters sent from an unnamed traveler to a friend in Europe. What makes this film such a beautiful and difficult movie is the precision and care with which different organizational strategies and rhetorical positions confront each other throughout the film, moving back and forth to parallel the correspondence between the traveler and his friend. At first glance, it appears that the film takes on a social science or ethnographic role, exploring the cultures of Japan and the African countries of Guinea-Bissau and the Cape Verde Islands. In looking closely at the organization of images, however, we see that the contrasts that these places dramatize are less about these cultures' surface differences than about their differing senses of time and the commentator's efforts to comprehend them. Thus the film also enacts a reflexive meditation on different conceptions of time and memory in the twentieth century.

In *Sunless*, conventional cumulative organizational forms seem to have a twist or a sense of irony running through them. At one point, we see a series of more than twenty faces of African women. Each face has its own expression and shape, and as the series accumulates one face after another, each seems to shine forth with more individual personality and intensity: one stares, another turns away; one smiles, another glares hostilely. While the series appears to offer a collective representation of African women, almost a sampling of types of faces, the specific expressions undermine any generalities that might otherwise describe the exposition [**Figures 7.27a and 7.27b**].

Just as it interrogates the scientific methods used to explore and colonize people of other cultures, *Sunless* also reflexively questions the methods used to romanticize those cultures by presenting images and simultaneously reflecting on them. Perhaps the most dramatic and important example occurs at the beginning and again toward the end of the film: at both points, the image of three children in Iceland appears, and the commentator, acting as the spokesperson for the unnamed letter writer, says about the effort to create a metaphor with this image, "He said that for him it was the image of happiness . . . and he has often tried to link it to other images but it had never worked." The image then goes black and is

(a)

(b)

7.27a and 7.27b   *Sunless* (1982). A sampling of facial types represents the accumulation of individual expressions.

replaced by three stationary U.S. fighter jets before the commentator continues, over another black image, with, "One day I'll have to put it at the beginning of a film with a long piece of black leader. If they don't see happiness in the picture, at least they'll see the black." With this admittedly complex association, the film seems to self-consciously struggle to create a meaning of happiness and innocence from one image and relate that to other experiences (in this case, perhaps the images of the entire film). But even in creating that meaning, the commentator seems to recognize that all film images disappear and fade to black as one image replaces the previous, sometimes fully alien, image.

One of the central themes of *Sunless* is the power and isolated integrity of "things"—or in the voiceover's quotation of an eleventh-century Japanese woman writer, "things that quicken the heart." The film follows a cumulative organization by presenting different examples of such "things"—Japanese pachinko games, dogs on the beach, the spiral image that recurs in many forms. These things and the images of them become documents of time and history: how people devote themselves to time or how time turns us constantly in its twists. The continual presentation of "things" through the film is always about why and how we make, need, and perform ourselves through things and their images—to help us anchor and explain living in a world so vexed by time and history.

Sunless thus makes continual references to the texture and structures of representation, film images, and other ways, such as rituals, that we try to organize our lives. At one point, the film's images move to abstract representation: one section shows a group of images filled with television sets whose multiple rectangular patterns fill the film frame [**Figure 7.28**]. In its most abstract moments, Marker's film shifts to computer designs, or what the voiceover refers to as images from "The Zone," where previously real images are now translated into quivering colors and lines. This shift suggests an almost utopian purity or intensification that the real world will never have.

In *Sunless*, the voiceover is that of a commentator rather than a narrator. This is an intricate example of how powerful and complex a non-narrative voice can be—whether it is actually heard or is simply implied by the perspective of the film. The unidentified voice of a woman reads letters sent by another fictionalized person, Sandor Krasna (named only in the closing credits), who may be a camera person, the filmmaker, or simply a traveler. This voice moves through multiple questions and the unresolved analysis of these questions in an almost scientific manner: What is the experience of happiness? What is memory? Is there a social politics to the experience of time? How can time be organized in life and on film? Meanwhile, the same voice grows poetically expressive and performative, providing a counterpoint to its more analytic questions with expressions of delight, meditative reflections, and occasional efforts at gentle persuasion. Sometimes the commentator verbalizes the emotionally drifting attitude of the film in its descriptions of its world: "poetry is born of insecurity . . . wandering Jews, quaking Japan . . . moving in a world of appearances, fragile, fleeting." At other times, the film silently illustrates that attitude: moving through still images of dead animals in the desert to frenetic and gay street festivals in Japan and Africa [**Figure 7.29**].

Sometimes frustrating and sometimes sublime, *Sunless* stands out as a remarkable orchestration of the many strategies and formal tools available to documentary filmmakers. If conventional documentaries reject the dominance of narrative organizations, Marker's movie challenges the idea that there are clear distinctions between these two practices. The result is a travelogue of a world that explodes into a collage of discrete particulars or "things," which fascinate us and elude our attempts to contain them.

7.28 *Sunless* (1982). Images of other images verge on abstraction.

7.29 *Sunless* (1982). The layered voice of the film's commentator ruminates across images about a "poetry born of insecurity."

7.30 *Grey Gardens* (1975). The relationship between two quirky and unusual women becomes a touching and entertaining documentary about individualism and humanity.

an inordinately long amount of time, showing minute changes rarely seen in our usual experiences: one movie condenses the gestation of a child in the womb, while another shows the dread and boredom experienced over one long night by a homeless person in Miami. David and Albert Maysles's *Grey Gardens* (1975) portrays the quirky extremes of a mother and daughter, relatives of Jacqueline Kennedy Onassis, living in a dilapidated mansion in East Hampton, Long Island. Slowly, by following their daily routines and dwelling on the incidentals in their lives, the film develops our capacity truly to see two individuals whose unique personalities and habits become less and less strange [Figure 7.30].

Confronting Assumptions, Altering Opinions

Documentary films may present a familiar or well-known subject and attempt to make us comprehend it in a new way. Some documentaries are openly polemical when presenting a subject: as an obvious example, documentaries about a political figure or a controversial event may confront viewers' assumptions or attempt to alter received opinions about the person or event. Other films may ask us to rethink a moment in history or our feelings about what once seemed like a simple exercise, as in *Wordplay* (2006), a documentary about crossword puzzles and how they inspire intellectual activity [Figure 7.31].

With any and all of the formal and organizational tools available to a documentary, these films attempt to persuade viewers of certain facts, attack other points of view, argue with other films, or motivate viewers to act on social problems or concerns. An especially explicit example, Michael Moore's *Sicko* (2007) very visibly and tendentiously argues that the health care system in the United States is antiquated and destructive, and that it needs to be changed. Released the same year, the documentary *Manufacturing Dissent: Uncovering Michael Moore* (2007) takes Moore and his many films to task for fudging or misrepresenting facts. Such polemic is central to this tradition of documentary cinema, which is always about which reality we wish to accept.

Serving as a Social, Cultural, and Personal Lens

From the two primary agendas discussed above come two traditions of documentary cinema: the social documentary and the ethnographic film. These two traditions encompass some of the main frameworks for understanding many documentary films throughout the twentieth century.

7.31 *Wordplay* (2006). This documentary presents viewers with new perspectives, such as that of Merl Reagle, longtime crossword constructor, on the seemingly ordinary subject of crossword puzzles.

The Social Documentary

Social documentaries examine and present both familiar and unfamiliar peoples and cultures as social activities. Using a variety of organizational practices, this tradition emphasizes one or both of the following goals: authenticity in representing how people live and interact, and discovery in representing unknown environments and cultures. Considered by some scholars and filmmakers as the father of documentary, John Grierson made his first film, *Drifters* (1929), about North Sea herring fishermen; another early British filmmaker, Humphrey Jennings, continued this tradition with *Listen to Britain* (1942), a twenty-minute panorama of British society at war–from soldiers in the fields to women in factories. Indeed, the social documentary tradition is long and varied, stretching from Pare Lorentz's *The River* (1937), made for the U.S. Department of Agriculture about the importance of the Mississippi River, to *Waste Land* (2010), about artist Vik Muniz's encounter with a community who live in and off the world's largest landfill on the outskirts of Rio de Janeiro. Two important spin-offs from the social documentary tradition are the political documentary and the historical documentary.

The Political Documentary. Partially as a result of the social crisis of the Great Depression in the United States and the more general economic crises that occurred in most other countries after World War I, *political documentaries* aimed to investigate and to celebrate the political activities of men and women as they appear within the struggles of small and large social spheres. Contrasting themselves with the lavish Hollywood films of the times, these documentary films sought a balance of aesthetic objectivity and political purpose. Preceded by the films of Dziga Vertov and the Soviet cinema of the 1920s (such as *Man with a Movie Camera*), political documentaries tend to take analytical or persuasive positions, hoping to provoke or move viewers with the will to reform social systems. Narrated by Ernest Hemingway, Joris Ivens's *The Spanish Earth* (1937) presents, for example, the heroic resistance of the "Loyalists" as they fight valiantly against the brutal forces of a fascist government **[Figure 7.32]**. While political documentaries such as these can sometimes be labeled *propaganda films* because of their visible efforts to support a particular social or political issue or group, they frequently use more complex arguments and more subtle tactics than bluntly manipulative documentaries.

Since World War II, political documentaries have grown more varied and occasionally more militant. In 1968, Argentine filmmakers Fernando Solanas and Octavio Getino produced *Hour of the Furnaces*, a three-hour-long examination of the colonial exploitation of Argentina's culture and resources that inspired heated political discussions and even demonstrations in the street. Emile de Antonio's *In the Year of the Pig* (1968) delivers a scathing attack on the Vietnam War. In recent decades, feminist documentaries, gay and lesbian documentaries, and documentaries about race have figured as prominent and important films in the traditions of political documentary as they explore political issues and identity politics that have traditionally not been addressed. The variety of these films indicates the power and purpose of this tradition. Focused on two sisters (who are later

7.32 *The Spanish Earth* (1937). A celebration of the heroic resistance of fighters in Spain against an emerging fascist political machine.

7.33 *Paris Is Burning* (1990). A sympathetic and witty portrayal of the subculture of drag balls in New York City.

7.34 *When the Levees Broke: A Requiem in Four Acts* (2006). Spike Lee's HBO documentary uses the medium as a powerful tool for political statements.

revealed to be actors) talking about their relationship with their mother, Michelle Citron's *Daughter Rite* (1979) expands as a much broader commentary on the development of female identity within the family. Robert Epstein and Richard Schmiechen's *The Times of Harvey Milk* (1984) describes the assassinations of the San Francisco mayor and of Milk, an activist who was the first gay supervisor elected in the city, and Jennie Livingston's *Paris Is Burning* (1990) explores the subculture of New York City drag balls, maintaining a serious, sympathetic, and witty tone throughout [**Figure 7.33**]. Spike Lee's HBO documentary *When the Levees Broke: A Requiem in Four Acts* (2006), about the government mishandling of the Hurricane Katrina disaster, is a worthy heir to a long tradition of documentaries that make the politics of race the centerpiece of the politics of the nation [**Figure 7.34**].

7.35 *Atomic Cafe* (1982). By employing archival footage and conventional documentary devices, this film satirizes the paranoia of 1950s culture.

The Historical Documentary. Another form related to social documentary is the *historical documentary*, a type of film that concentrates largely on recovering and representing events or figures in history. Depending on the topic, these films are often compilations of materials, relying on old film footage or other materials such as letters, testimonials by historians, or photographs. Whatever the materials and tactics, however, historical documentaries have moved in two broad directions. *Conventional documentary histories* assume the facts and realities of a past history can be more or less recovered and accurately represented. *Atomic Cafe* (1982), though a rather satirical documentary, uses media and government footage to describe the paranoia and hysteria of the nuclear arms race during the Cold War [**Figure 7.35**]. The films of Ken Burns, including the PBS series *The Civil War* (1990), *Baseball* (1996), and

The War (2007), use a range of materials, techniques, and voices to re-create the layered dynamics of major historical and cultural events.

Reflexive documentary histories, in contrast, adopt a dual point of view: alongside the work to describe an event (for instance, one associated with a historical trauma such as the Holocaust or the nuclear bombing of Hiroshima) is the awareness that film or other discourses and materials will never be able to fully retrieve the reality of that lost history. Despite their vastly different topics (the Nazi death camps and the racist murder of a Chinese automotive engineer), Claude Lanzmann's *Shoah* (1985) and Christine Choy and Renee Tajima's *Who Killed Vincent Chin?* (1988) engage specific historical and cultural atrocities and simultaneously reflect on the extreme difficulty, if not impossibility, of fully and accurately documenting the truth of those events and experiences **[Figure 7.36]**.

7.36   *Who Killed Vincent Chin?* (1988). This film documents a local hate crime that resonates in larger historical terms; at the same time, it reflects on the difficulty of communicating the full historical truth.

Ethnographic Cinema

Ethnographic documentaries, with roots in early cinema, are a second major tradition in documentary film. While social documentaries tend to emphasize the political and historical significance of certain events and figures, ethnographic films are typically about cultural revelations, aimed at presenting specific peoples, rituals, or communities that may have been marginalized by or invisible to the mainstream culture. Here we will highlight two practices within the ethnographic tradition: anthropological films and cinéma vérité.

▶ **VIEWING CUE**

Identify a documentary film you've seen that can be considered a social documentary. What type of social documentary is it? Explain. ⏸

Anthropological Films. *Anthropological films* explore different global cultures and peoples, both living and extinct. In the first part of the twentieth century, these films often sought out exotic and endangered communities to reveal them to viewers who had little or no experience of them. Such documentaries generally aim to reveal cultures and peoples authentically, without imposing the filmmaker's interpretations, but in fact they are often implicitly shaped by the perspectives of their makers. In the 1940s and 1950s, such works as Jean Rouch's *The Magicians of Wanzerbe* (1949) transformed film into an extension of anthropology, searching out the social rituals and cultural habits that distinguish the people of particular, often primitive, societies. Robert Gardner's *Dead Birds* (1965) examines the war rituals of the Dani tribe in New Guinea, maintaining a scientific distance that draws out what is most unique and different about the people **[Figure 7.37]**.

The scope and subject matter of ethnographic documentaries have expanded considerably over the years, sometimes finding lost

7.37   *Dead Birds* (1965). This remarkable ethnographic film provides audiences with a glimpse of life in the Dani tribe in New Guinea, focusing on Weyak, a farmer and warrior, and Pua, a young swineherd.

7.38 *Capturing the Friedmans* (2003). This domestic ethnography reveals the social intricacies and psychological complexities of a troubled middle-class family.

cultures in the West's own backyard. This contemporary revision of anthropological cinema investigates the rituals, values, and social patterns of families or subcultures, such as the skateboard clan of *Dogtown and Z-Boys* (2002), rather than directing its attention to cultures or communities that are "foreign" to its producers. Using found footage or archival prints of home movies made before 1950, Karen Shopsowitz's *My Father's Camera* (2001) argues that reality is sometimes best revealed by amateur filmmakers capturing everyday life though home movies and snapshots. *Capturing the Friedmans* (2003) also uses home videos and interviews to bring out the facts and contradictions in a Long Island family whose otherwise normal lifestyle is shattered when the father is accused of pedophilia **[Figure 7.38]**.

Cinéma Vérité and Direct Cinema. One of the most important and influential documentary schools related to ethnographic cinema is *cinéma vérité*, French for "cinema truth." Related to Dziga Vertov's *Kino-Pravda* ("cinema truth") of the 1920s, cinéma vérité insists on filming real objects, people, and events in a confrontational way, so that the reality of the subject continually acknowledges the reality of the camera recording it. This film movement arose in the late 1950s and 1960s in Canada and France before quickly spreading to film cultures in the United States and other parts of the world.

Aided by the development of lightweight cameras and portable sound equipment, filmmakers like Jean Rouch created in their images a jerky immediacy to suggest the filmmakers' participation and absorption in the events they were recording. Rouch's *Moi un noir*, filmed in Treichville, a neighborhood in Ivory Coast's capital city, portrays the everyday life of a group of young Africans accompanied by the voiceover narration of one who refers to himself as Edward G. Robinson (after the "tough guy" actor in American films of the 1930s). In this version of cinéma vérité, rules of continuity and character development are willfully ignored. Here reality is not just what objectively appears; reality is also the fictions and fantasies that these individuals create for and about themselves and the acknowledged involvement of the filmmaker as interlocutor. Moreover, unlike its American counterpart, French cinéma vérité draws particular attention to the subjective perspective of the camera's rhetorical position: in *Moi un noir*, the voiceover frequently makes ironic remarks about what is being shown.

The North American version of cinéma vérité, referred to as *direct cinema*, is more observational and less confrontational than the French practice. Its landmark film, *Primary*, follows Democratic candidates John F. Kennedy and Hubert H. Humphrey through the Wisconsin state presidential primary. D. A. Pennebaker and the Maysles brothers, who were all involved in the making of *Primary*, continued to work in this tradition, gravitating toward social topics in which the identity of the subjects is inseparable from their role as performers. Pennebaker made numerous cinéma vérité–like films such as *Don't Look Back* (1967) **[Figure 7.39]**, a portrait of the young Bob Dylan, and *The War Room*

(1993), about the 1992 political campaign of Bill Clinton. In addition to *Grey Gardens*, Albert and David Maysles made many films in direct cinema style, including *Salesman* (1968), about itinerant Bible salesmen, and *Gimme Shelter* (1970), a powerful and troubling record of the 1969 Rolling Stones tour across the United States. Albert Maysles continues to be active, serving as an adviser to new generations of documentarians.

Personal Documentaries, Reenactments, and Mockumentaries

In recent years especially, the line between the documentary traditions of social documentaries and ethnographic films has wavered and shifted, as the foundational structures of narrative, nonnarrative, nonfiction, and fiction have increasingly exchanged tactics and topics.

7.39 *Don't Look Back* (1967). Direct cinema contemplates the inside of the celebrity world of Bob Dylan.

Increasingly common in recent years, **personal** or **subjective documentaries** create films that look more like autobiographies or diaries. In *Lost, Lost, Lost* (1976), Jonas Mekas portrays his fears and hopes in a diary film about his growing up as an immigrant in New York; counterpointing home movies, journal entries, and a fragmented style that resembles a diary, the rhythmic interjections of the commentator-poet express feelings ranging from angst to delight. In *A Healthy Baby Girl* (1996), filmmaker Judith Helfland explores the causes of her cancer diagnosis in her mother's use during pregnancy of the drug DES (diethylstilbestrol), which was prescribed to prevent miscarriage. While the film exposes and indicts this breach of medical ethics and its impact on women's health, its primary focus is on the personal journey of the filmmaker and her family **[Figure 7.40]**.

Questions about the truth and honesty of documentaries have shadowed this practice since Flaherty's reconstruction of "typical" events for the camera in *Nanook of the North* and his other films in the 1920s. Recently more and more documentaries have seized on the question of the veracity of the camera in order to complicate or to spoof documentary practices. Increasingly visible and debated today, documentary **reenactments** use documentary techniques in order to present a reenactment or theatrical staging of presumably true or real events. An early example of this blurring of boundaries, *The Battle of Algiers* (1966) depicts the Algerian revolt against the French occupation (1954–1962) as a re-creation, a film about a real historical event that uses documentary techniques while developing the story with a script and actors. Indeed, an opening caption boasts that no documentary footage is used in the film. Errol Morris's *The Thin Blue Line* (1988) is a documentary about a man, Randall Adams, convicted of killing a Dallas police officer in 1976,

7.40 *A Healthy Baby Girl* (1996). Some documentaries, such as this one about the filmmaker and her mother, entwine a personal story with larger issues, here a breach of medical ethics.

7.41 *The Thin Blue Line* (1988). Reenacting a crime as a part of a documentary investigation, Errol Morris's film set the stage for more experimental documentary formats.

7.42 *This Is Spinal Tap* (1984). Mockumentaries like this cult film remind us that the authenticity of cinematic documentaries relies on the experiences and expectations of their audiences.

but it also becomes a mystery drama about discovering the real murderer. While it uses the many expository techniques of documentary film (such as close-ups of evidence and "talking-head" interviews), *The Thin Blue Line* alternates these with staged reenactments of the murder evening, invented dialogue, an eerie soundtrack, courtroom drawings, and even clips from old movies **[Figure 7.41]**. The debates and questions surrounding the practice of reenactment are explored in *Manufacturing Dissent*, Rick Caine and Debbie Melnyk's documentary on Michael Moore's use of reenactments in his films.

At the other end of the spectrum, **mockumentaries** take a much more humorous approach to the question of truth and fact by using a documentary style and structure to present and stage fictional (sometimes ludicrous) realities. The mockumentary is an extreme example of how documentaries can generate different experiences and responses depending on viewing context and one's knowledge of the traditions and aims of such films. For example, with the initial release of *This Is Spinal Tap* (1984), some viewers saw and understood it as a straightforward rock-music documentary (or "rockumentary"), while most recognized it as a spoof on that documentary tradition. The two responses dramatize how people's different ideas of, knowledge about, and associations with documentaries can elicit very different interpretations of the "reality" of the film **[Figure 7.42]**. The popular and controversial *Borat* (2006) integrates a similar mockumentary style by following a fictional Kazakh television talking head as he travels "the greatest country in the world" in search of celebrities, cowboys, and the "cultural learning" found on the streets of America. Actor Sacha Baron Cohen mixes his impersonation of the character Borat with interviews of people who accept his persona as genuine. As such, the film raises questions about the boundary between a parody of viewers' assumptions about the truth and a dangerous distortion of the integrity of documentary values **[Figure 7.43]**.

7.43 *Borat* (2006). Some of the most important assumptions about documentary integrity are violated in this film, perhaps as a way to satirize the pretensions of those assumptions.

7.44a

7.44b

7.44c

7.44d

The Contemporary Documentary: *Exit Through the Gift Shop* (2010)

Contemporary documentaries often appear especially conscious of the styles and forms that have preceded them; they experiment with old and new documentary tactics, such as emphasizing personal perspectives or exploring reenactments as a stylistic technique. Not surprisingly, mockumentaries, which self-consciously parody the common styles and strategies of traditional documentaries, have become increasingly popular.

Exit Through the Gift Shop (2010) may be one of the most puzzling and entertaining examples of the contemporary documentary, largely because it is unclear what is being documented, what is in fact authentic, and what or who it might be mocking. The film begins as the tale of Thierry Guetta, a Frenchman living in Los Angeles who decides to make a documentary about street artists, most notably the mysterious and famous Banksy. Gradually, however, Banksy assumes control of the film and, in a bizarre shift, the film becomes about Guetta's sudden rise as a celebrity street artist.

Much of the early part of the film depicts Guetta as a kind of cinéma vérité artist who captures the hidden world of street artists such as Space Invader and Shepard Fairey [Figure 7.44a]. However, when Guetta meets and joins forces with Banksy, the line between artistic value and self-parody begins to blur. After documenting Banksy's success at his farcically famous art exhibit in Los Angeles [Figure 7.44b], Guetta wonders: If Banksy can triumphantly mock the values and truth of public life [Figure 7.44c], then why can't I? With encouragement from Banksy, Guetta christens himself Mr. Brainwash and mounts his own extravagant opening of his newly discovered talents in Los Angeles [Figure 7.44d]. In the end, the mysterious and hooded Banksy [Figure 7.44e] can only wonder at (and regret) the monster he has created. If street art represents a way to intervene in day-to-day realities of the world, what does it mean when those interventions begin to look like a commercial scam? And if that art appears as a scam, does a documentary about it—by Banksy—also mock itself?

7.44e

7.45 *The Watermelon Woman* (1996). As a serious use of a mockumentary tradition, this film suggests a history that has not survived—or perhaps not yet arrived.

Closely related to the mockumentary but with more serious aims is the *fake documentary*, a tradition that extends from Buñuel's *Land Without Bread* through Orson Welles's *F for Fake* (1974), a movie that looks at real charlatans and forgers while itself questioning the possibilities of documentary truth. A more recent film, Cheryl Dunye's *The Watermelon Woman* (1996), is a fictional account of an African American lesbian documentary filmmaker researching a black actress from the 1930s. The archive of photos and film footage she assembles for the fake documentary within the film represents a lovingly fabricated work by the film's creative team—an imagining of a history that has not survived **[Figure 7.45]**.

As we have seen, documentary films create movie experiences markedly different from those of narrative cinema. While some of these experiences are non-narrative portraits that envision individuals in ways quite unlike the narrative histories of the same people, others are about the truth of events. Narrative movies encourage us to enjoy, imagine, and think about our temporal and historical relationships with the world and to consider when those plots and narratives seem adequate according to our experiences. Documentary movies remind us, however, that we have many other kinds of relationships with the world that involve us in many other insightful ways—through debate, through exploration, and through analysis.

> ▶ **VIEWING CUE**
>
> Consider a documentary you recently viewed. What were its aims and assumptions? How might seeing this documentary in a different historical or cultural context distort or change those aims and assumptions? ⏸

CONCEPTS AT WORK

Documentary cinema has a history as long and rich as that of narrative cinema, and while the two different organizations sometimes overlap and exchange tactics, documentary films emphasize less the entertainment found in a good story than the educational pleasure of new information or insight about events, people, and even ideas. These films have accordingly developed their own strategies and formal features: from expositional organizations that contrast, accumulate, or develop facts and figures to rhetorical positions that work to explore, analyze, persuade, or even "perform" the world. What we often value about these films is their ability to reveal that world to us in new ways and to provoke us to see it with fresh eyes, outcomes that have generated numerous and complex traditions from the many types of social documentaries to the many kinds of ethnographic films.

Activities

- Choose what you consider to be a very specific and very pressing contemporary social issue as the topic for a documentary you will make. Describe the presiding point of view that the film will use (its rhetorical position). Then sketch some of the central scenes or images you intend to use. How will these be organized? Describe in detail one important sequence in the film.
- Imagine that you've been contracted to make a mockumentary film about a particular documentary practice such as a travelogue. Highlight three central scenes that will demonstrate an awareness of the formal and thematic features of the films you're parodying.

OFFICIAL SELECTION
BERLIN
INTERNATIONAL FILM FESTIVAL
2007

OFFICIAL SELECTION
TORONTO
INTERNATIONAL FILM FESTIVAL
2006

OFFICIAL SELECTION
NEW YORK
FILM FESTIVAL
2006

"NUTTILY WONDERFUL!
One of the 10 BEST FILMS
of the year."
Manohla Dargis, NY TIMES

"UPROARIOUSLY FUNNY
and surprisingly touching.
A MAGICAL EXPERIENCE."
Michael Dwyer, IRISH TIMES

BRAND UPON THE BRAIN!

a film by
Guy Maddin

THE FILM COMPANY PRESENTS A GUY MADDIN FILM "BRAND UPON THE BRAIN!"
SULLIVAN BROWN GRETCHEN KRICH MAYA LAWSON
ERIK STEFFEN MAAHS KATHERINE E. SCHARHON
CASTING JOY FAIRFIELD COSTUME DESIGNER NINA MOSER PRODUCTION DESIGNER TANIA KUPCZAK
DIRECTOR OF PHOTOGRAPHY BENJAMIN KASULKE EDITED BY JOHN GURDEBEKE MUSIC BY JASON STACZEK
EXECUTIVE PRODUCERS JODY SHAPIRO AJ EPSTEIN PHILIP WOHLSTETTER PRODUCED BY AMY E. JACOBSON AND GREGG LACHOW
WRITTEN BY GUY MADDIN AND GEORGE TOLES DIRECTED BY GUY MADDIN
www.branduponthebrain.com

VITAGRAPH

Challenging Form
Experimental Film and New Media

The feverish imagery of Winnipeg-based auteur Guy Maddin's *Brand upon the Brain!* (2007) fuses memory, invention, and above all, film history in a strange tale of the hero Guy's return to the isolated lighthouse where his mother once ran a bizarre orphanage. Black-and-white cinematography reminiscent of German expressionist film and rapid montage set a spooky mood, silent film–style intertitles only hint at what we're seeing, and flashes of color footage disorient us. Twin teenage detectives, appalling science experiments, and expressionist paintings compound the mystery—and the fun—as Guy's past and present collide. At festivals and special exhibitions across North America, audiences could see *Brand upon the Brain!*, an ostensibly "silent" film, accompanied by live musicians, celebrity narrators (like rock star Lou Reed or Maddin's frequent collaborator actress Isabella Rossellini), and sound-effects artists. Turning experimental film into a theatrical event, Maddin invigorates its long tradition for contemporary viewers as he "brands" his vision upon the audience's perception.

W hile narrative films relate to the human desire for stories, and documentaries address the desire to see and understand society and history, other aspects of human experience—sensory states, intellectual puzzles, emotions, memories, and dreams—are invoked by the range of non-narrative, non-realist practices explored in experimental film, video, and other media. Experimental film is often likened to poetry, with narrative film likened to fiction. Not only does this analogy underscore the lyrical impulse that often drives experimental work, but it also captures something of its economic marginality. Experimental work is made by individuals rather than by large crews or studios, and its audiences are small ones, comprising those who seek out such films and are motivated to engage with experimental strategies.

8.1 **"Human Behavior"** (1993). Contemporary forms like the music video are indebted to experimental film traditions such as surrealism. This video by Michel Gondry combines pop culture and the avant-garde, as does singer Björk's music.

Experimentation with form and abstract imagery has occurred over the past century of film history. Adventurous filmmakers have used film to go outside the bounds of traditional narrative and documentary forms, combining images and sounds of the seemingly mundane, the unusual, and even the bizarre in order to address and challenge their audiences in fascinating ways. Cryptic imagery and music as structure were used in such experimental classics as the surrealist *The Seashell and the Clergyman* (1928). This impulse has carried over to other, more recent, forms; in Michel Gondry's music video for Björk's "Human Behavior" (1993), the singer inhabits a fairy-tale world in which animals and humans are no longer distinct and music allows us to transcend physical limits **[Figure 8.1]**. This chapter explores experimental audiovisual media from its origins to the present day, giving you the necessary tools to watch and discuss some of film history's most complex, challenging, and rewarding cinematic endeavors.

KEY OBJECTIVES

- Recognize experimental film and media as cultural practices.
- Explore how experimental works make and draw on aesthetic histories.
- Investigate how these works interrogate the formal properties of their media.
- Appreciate how experimental media can both challenge, and become part of, dominant film forms and institutions.
- Examine some of the common organizations, styles, and perspectives in experimental media.
- Learn how viewers can prepare themselves to watch and appreciate experimental works.
- Recognize that the challenges of experimental media contribute another dimension of significance to the film experience.

The word "cinema" is derived from the Greek word for movement, *kinema*. Arguably neither the storytelling ability of the medium nor its capacity to reveal the world is as basic to cinema as is the simple rendering of movement. So while narrative film defines the commercial industry and much of viewers' experience of the movies, and documentary builds on viewers' assumption of the camera's truth-telling function, experimental film focuses on the very properties that make film what it is—images in motion. Historically a variety of terms—notably **avant-garde cinema** (that is, advance guard or vanguard, derived from military terminology)—have been used to denote the works we discuss in this chapter. We have retained the more general term "experimental" precisely for its emphasis on the way filmmakers experiment with specific elements of film form for aesthetic expression or technical innovation.

Experimental films commonly reflect on the material specificity of the film medium and the conditions in which it is experienced by audiences—including such basic elements as film stock, sprocket holes, light, figure movement, editing patterns, and projection before an audience. Changes in technology bring changes in the form and object of these reflections. For example, filmmakers working in an amateur format like Super-8 may scratch directly on the film emulsion, as Su Friedrich does in *Gently Down the Stream* (1981), while a video artist might deliberately activate the vertical roll function to reflect on the medium of television, as Joan Jonas does in *Vertical Roll* (1972) **[Figure 8.2]**. The introduction of portable video equipment in the late 1960s and the shift to digital formats in the 1990s, as well as the convergence of computers and cameras at the end of the twentieth century, expanded the resources of artists working in what can be broadly termed moving-image media.

Although this chapter primarily discusses the larger body and longer history of experimental film, we will also attempt to show how its histories and preoccupations are related to those of video art and **new media**, a term used in both information science and communications as well as the arts to refer to an array of technologies, including the Internet, digital formats, video game consoles, smartphones, touchscreen devices, and the software applications and imaginative creations they support. Just as artists in the early twentieth century explored cinema's form and its place in modern life, many artists today use these technologies to reflect on life in the new millennium. The very fact that experimental films that were often difficult to see outside of urban arts or university contexts are now accessible through the Internet attests to a renewed energy in the realm of experimental moving-image media.

8.2 *Vertical Roll* (1972). Video artist Joan Jonas's piece reflects on the video medium, taking its name from a television malfunction.

A Short History of Experimental Film and Media Practices

The technology of experimental films and the vision they express have their roots in wider technological and social changes associated with **modernity**, a term that both names a broad period of history stretching from the end of the medieval era (with its primarily theological conception of the world) to the present, and identifies an attitude toward progress and science centered on the human capacity to shape history that is characteristic of our age **[Figure 8.3]**.

While modern society embraced progress and knowledge, some individuals rejected the scientific and utilitarian bias of the quest for facts. In "A Defence of Poetry" (1819), Romantic poet Percy Bysshe Shelley proclaimed that poets were the unacknowledged legislators of the world. Walter Pater, in *The Renaissance* (1873), argued for the power of art to reveal the importance of the human imagination and create experiences unavailable in commerce and science. Pre-Raphaelite paintings like those of Dante Gabriel Rossetti and the glimmering impressionist paintings of Claude Monet expressed aesthetic commitments to sensibility, creativity, and perception over factual observation **[Figure 8.4]**. Romantic aesthetic traditions influenced the emphasis on individual expressivity central to much experimental film practice **[Figure 8.5]**.

The early twentieth century, when motion picture technology was perfected, saw rapid industrial and cultural change that was mirrored and questioned in developments in the arts. Modernist forms of painting,

8.3   **Chicago World's Fair** (1893). Nineteenth-century modernity celebrated visuality and technology, anticipating cinema's ways of seeing.

8.4   **Claude Monet, *Water Lilies*** (c. 1916–1920). This panel from Monet's triptych anticipated experimental film in its energetic depiction of light.

8.5   ***The Garden of Earthly Delights*** (1981). The work of prolific experimental filmmaker Stan Brakhage is indebted to the nineteenth-century tradition of Romantic poetry and its conception of artistic insight. This two-minute film was made by pressing actual flowers and leaves between strips of film and optically printing the images.

music, design, and architecture captured new experiences of accelerated and disjunctive time, spatial juxtaposition, and fragmentation enabled by such technologies as the railroad, the telegraph, and electricity. Because cinema is literally made with machines, the medium was considered a central art of modernism, and experiments with space and time emerged early in the medium's history.

1910s–1920s: European Avant-Garde Movements

In the silent film era, experimental film practices and movements emerged in a number of countries and were often linked to other experimental art forms. In Germany, for instance, Dada artist Hans Richter began exploring abstract film along with Viking Eggeling **[Figure 8.6]**, and the expressionist painters in the group *Der Sturm* worked on the set designs of *The Cabinet of Dr.*

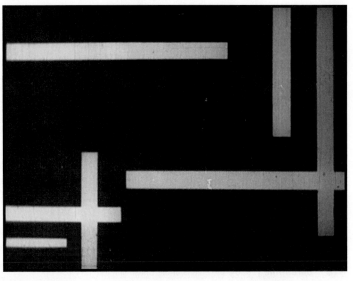

8.6 *Rhythmus 21* (1921). German artist Hans Richter claimed that this exploration of shapes in motion was the first abstract film.

Caligari (1920). In 1920s France, avant-garde filmmakers such as Jean Epstein and Germaine Dulac (see pp. 363–64) drew on impressionism and cubism in painting as well as new musical forms in their work. At the same time, film artists explored cinematography and editing to develop the cinema as a unique art form. In *Ballet mécanique* (1924), French cubist painter Fernand Léger collaborated with American director Dudley Murphy in a celebration of machine-age aesthetics originally intended as a visual accompaniment to American composer George Antheil's musical piece of the same name.

One of the most significant experimental film movements in history occurred in the Soviet Union after the Russian Revolution in 1917. Vladimir Lenin considered cinema the most important of the arts for the revolutionaries, and Soviet filmmakers were inspired by constructivism—dynamic, machine-age art that served a social purpose and influenced painting, theater, poetry, graphic design, and photomontage at the time. Though avant-garde cinema flourished in specific cities and countries, modernist filmmaking in the silent era was international in spirit, a characteristic that the introduction of sound (and hence language barriers) and the rise of fascism in Europe in the 1930s would inhibit. For example, the modern metropolis was paid tribute to in the transnational "city symphony" genre, three examples of which are Charles Sheeler and Paul Strand's tribute to New York City, *Manhatta* (1921) **[Figure 8.7]**, Walther Ruttmann's *Berlin: Symphony of a Great City* (1927), and Dziga Vertov's *Man with a Movie Camera* (1929). In Britain, such internationalism was advocated by Kenneth Macpherson, Bryher, and the American poet h.d. through their translation of writings by Soviet filmmaker Sergei Eisenstein in their journal *Close Up*, and in their strange and unique film, *Borderline* (1930). Featuring the politically outspoken African American actor Paul Robeson and his wife, Eslanda, *Borderline* evoked race and sexuality within the psychoanalytic

> ▶ **VIEWING CUE**
>
> What historical precedents in the arts might have shaped the strategies used in the film you just viewed? Does aligning the film with a historical precedent shed light on its aims? Explain. ⏸

8.7 *Manhatta* (1921). One of the first avant-garde films made in the United States, this tribute to the metropolis is echoed in European "city symphony" films.

8.8 **_Borderline_** (1930). The editors of the British film journal _Close Up_ put their modernist ideas into practice in this experimental narrative featuring the American actor Paul Robeson.

theories of the era, all while challenging conventional narrative filmmaking [**Figure 8.8**].

1930s–1940s: Sound and Vision

While many experimental filmmakers resisted synchronized sound and continued to produce silent films long after its introduction at the end of the 1920s, some were immediately attracted to the formal possibilities of the soundtrack. Vertov incorporated his interest in radio and industrial sounds in _Enthusiasm_ (1931). German animator Oskar Fischinger made abstract visual music in films such as _Allegretto_ (1936), produced after he emigrated to the United States [**Figure 8.9**]. American ethnomusicologist Harry Smith produced dozens of short films to be accompanied by musical performances, records, or radio; artist Joseph Cornell re-edited a Hollywood B-movie to make _Rose Hobart_ (1936) and played a samba record to accompany its projection. Playwright Jean Cocteau began making his influential poetic, surrealist films in 1930 with _The Blood of a Poet_, with music by Georges Auric [**Figure 8.10**].

Most historians consider _Meshes of the Afternoon_ (1943) by Russian-born Maya Deren and her Czech husband, Alexander Hammid, the beginning of the American avant-garde's historical prominence. Lightweight 16mm cameras, introduced as an amateur format and widely used during World War II for reportage, appealed to Deren and other midcentury artists seeking more personal film expression. The striking imagery and structure of Deren's films, and her tireless advocacy for experimental film as a writer and lecturer, shaped the conditions for, and aesthetics of, American "visionary film," the term coined by scholar P. Adams Sitney for this movement.

1950s–1960s: The Postwar Avant-Garde in America

Stan Brakhage, a protégé of Deren's, is the most influential of the next generation of American avant-garde filmmakers, with four hundred 16mm and 8mm films, mostly silent, produced in a career spanning almost half a century. While

8.9 **_Allegretto_** (1936). The films of animator Oskar Fischinger are designed as visual music.

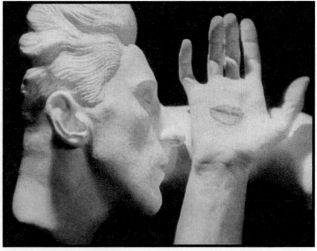

8.10 **_The Blood of a Poet_** (1930). Cocteau's first poetic experiment on film combines lyric imagery and music and remains one of the best-known avant-garde films.

8.11 *Window Water Baby Moving* (1959). The visceral impact of images of childbirth is tempered by silence and the lyrical play of light and water.

8.12 *Chelsea Girls* (1966). The singer and Warhol "superstar" Nico in Andy Warhol and Paul Morrissey's film. Composed of vignettes filmed in New York's Chelsea Hotel, the film was projected side by side on two screens.

most of his films arrange imagery in sensual, abstract patterns, they also rely on very personal subject matter, such as the intimate images of his wife giving birth in *Window Water Baby Moving* (1959) **[Figure 8.11]**. Working with the film stock itself—painting, scratching, and even taping moth wings to celluloid in *Mothlight* (1963)—Brakhage emphasized the materiality of film and the direct creative process of the filmmaker.

The American experimental film community established its own alternative exhibition circuit, including New York's Cinema 16 and the Anthology Film Archives (founded and overseen to this day by filmmaker Jonas Mekas) and distribution cooperatives such as The Film-Makers' Cooperative and Canyon Cinema. The exchanges fostered among artists and audiences profoundly influenced later generations of filmmakers working with film as personal expression.

The countercultural impulses of many U.S. filmmakers of the 1960s were reflected in their preferred term **underground film**. In New York, pop artist Andy Warhol definitively shaped the underground film movement. He explored the properties of cinema as a time-based medium in his eight-hour view of the Empire State Building, *Empire* (1964), the five-hour *Sleep* (1963), and other films. He also created his own version of the Hollywood studio system at the Factory, whose "superstars"—underground male and female devotees of glamour such as Viva, Mario Montez, and Holly Woodlawn—were featured in films he either directed or produced, including *Chelsea Girls* (1966) **[Figure 8.12]** and *Flesh* (1968), respectively. A legendary figure in this gay underground film scene, New York filmmaker Jack Smith incorporated his sublime and campy films and slides into erratically timed live performances in his downtown loft **[Figure 8.13]**. In one notorious incident, a screening of Smith's *Flaming Creatures* (1963) was shut down by the police for the film's provocative content—a rather listless pansexual "orgy."

8.13 *Flaming Creatures* (1963). Perhaps the most famous (and most notorious) of Jack Smith's works, this film, which featured several surreal and graphic sex scenes, was seized by the police during its premiere and banned for being "obscene." Despite the difficulty in viewing the film, it garnered a lot of attention from the public and the media.

text continued on page 294 ▶

Avant-Garde Visions in *Meshes of the Afternoon* (1943)

Maya Deren and Alexander Hammid's experimental film *Meshes of the Afternoon* forged a new American avant-garde cinema, drawing from Hammid's filmmaking experience in Europe and Deren's wide interests in poetry, dance and choreography, ritual, and psychoanalysis. Introspective and mysterious in its explorations of one woman's dream world, the film evokes symbolic associations and its sequences invite narrative speculations.

Meshes of the Afternoon opens with a brightly lit exterior shot of a flower in the street, then quickly lets us know it is about an interior reality of fantasies, fears, and unarticulated feelings when a hand reaches down and the flower disappears. A woman, played by Deren, enters a house with some difficulty and falls asleep in a chair. After images of her sleeping eyes alternate with a window to the outside world, we see symbolic objects—a key, a knife—begin to take on a life of their own. A figure cloaked in black turns, a mirror where its face should

be, suggesting both a double character and a figure of death **[Figure 8.14]**. A man enters the house: a phone is off the hook, a mirror breaks into shards on a bed. Are these images external or imagined? Is the broken mirror a symbol of violence or of insight? The woman sits down at a table, and is joined by two other figures of herself. Following the laws of the imagination rather than of reality, *Meshes of the Afternoon* is a visionary exploration of a woman's consciousness that deploys symbols of the unconscious, a puzzle that never comes completely together as a clear picture.

The challenge of the film lies in the fact that narrative is not its primary organizational feature. Instead, images accumulate, repeat, and contrast in associative chains that create internal patterns. The key to the door is dropped, it reappears in the woman's hand, then disappears **[Figure 8.15]**. The key suggests interpretation, but no interpretation is definitive. The knife is connected

8.14 *Meshes of the Afternoon* (1943). A cloaked figure seems to beckon, and then recedes around the corner; the figure's face is a mirror, adding to its ambiguity.

8.15 *Meshes of the Afternoon* (1943). The central image of the key suggests the viewer's search for the key that will unlock the film's meaning.

to the domestic when it is used to cut bread; it may perpetrate domestic violence when the woman appears to be dead on a bed, or it may be the instrument of self-inflicted violence when she approaches her double with it in hand.

The window, which represents the border between inside and outside, functions as a metaphor for the film frame [**Figure 8.16**]. As the woman who looks out of the window is played by Deren herself, *Meshes of the Afternoon* could be said to enact a woman's desires, fears, and struggle to escape domestic confinement. When the woman approaches her sleeping double with the dagger in her hand, each of the five different steps she takes is placed in a space that moves from outside to inside: a step by the ocean, another on the earth, the next on grass, the fourth on the pavement outside the house, and the last on the rug inside the room (see Figures 4.34a and 4.34b on p. 157). Interior and exterior are explored

psychologically—drawing on women's association with the home and on film genres such as gothic melodramas that render the domestic sphere threatening.

Meshes of the Afternoon infuses the emerging American avant-garde cinema with a deeply personal passion that Deren would bring to her future filmmaking, teaching, and writing. Like William Blake's illustrated poems about the dark side of the imagination or Odilon Redon's pictorial voyages into the subconscious, Deren's film aims to transform reality through the power of the imagination. As individually expressive as the film is, however, it also subtly shows a critical perspective on conventional film traditions. After the film's title appear the words "Hollywood 1943." Made within miles of the film studios often referred to as the "dream factory," *Meshes of the Afternoon* left the industrial tradition behind to pursue a dream of film as art.

8.16 *Meshes of the Afternoon* (1943). Deren looking out from the window has become an iconic image of this avant-garde film exploration of women's subjectivity.

The underground film movement frankly explored gender and sexual politics, but the increasing political radicalism of the period was more directly addressed at the border between documentary and experimental practice. African American actor, independent filmmaker, and documentarian William Greaves investigated the power relations on a film shoot in his feature-length *Symbio-psychotaxiplasm* (1968), made in Central Park **[Figure 8.17]**. Thirty-five years later, Greaves incorporated footage from the summer of 1968 with new scenes featuring the same actors in the sequel, *Symbiopsychotaxiplasm: Take 2 1/2* (2005), produced with the assistance of independent film stalwarts Steven Soderbergh and Steve Buscemi.

Experimental filmmaking also flourished outside of New York. San Francisco, the heart of the counterculture and gay and lesbian rights movements, hosted its own vibrant avant-garde film scene, exemplified in the work of poet and filmmaker James Broughton and the prolific lesbian experimental filmmaker Barbara Hammer, who began her career in the Bay Area with such short explorations of nature and the female body as *Multiple Orgasm* (1976). The influential *structural films* of Canadian filmmaker Michael Snow explore space, time, and the capacity of the camera to transcend human perception. In *La région centrale* (1971), a camera mounted on specially built apparatus pans, swoops, and swings to provide an unprecedented view of the mountainous Quebec region named in the film's title **[Figure 8.18]**. The avant-garde tradition is rich in Canada (whose arts funding has also fostered animation as an art form); some of its significant practitioners include Joyce Wieland (who was married to Snow), notable for films such as *Rat Life and Diet in North America* (1968), and, in the next generation, Bruce Elder, whose forty-two-hour cycle of films collectively titled *The Book of All the Dead* was completed in installments from 1975 to 1994.

1968 and After: Politics and Experimental Cinema

Outside North America, experimental film impulses have often been incorporated into narrative filmmaking and theatrical exhibition rather than confined exclusively to autonomous avant-garde circles. During the postwar period in Europe,

8.17 *Symbiopsychotaxiplasm* (1968). A hybrid of fiction and documentary, Bill Greaves's film about making a film in Central Park in 1968 is a fascinating record of the counterculture.

8.18 *La région centrale* (1971). Michael Snow's 16mm camera moves wildly on a special mount, rendering the landscape abstractly through mechanized vision.

Asia, and Latin America, innovative new wave cinemas challenged and energized commercial cinemas with their visions and techniques. Such experimentation was spurred by student unrest, Third World independence and decolonialization movements, and opposition to the American war in Vietnam. Radical content and formal rigor characterized the films of Jean-Luc Godard and Chris Marker in France, Alexander Kluge in Germany, and the French-born Jean-Marie Straub and Danièle Huillet. The massive traffic jam depicted in *Weekend* (1967) foregrounds Godard's revolutionary critique of consumerist culture through the consistent use of lateral tracking shots that are intended to hold viewers at arm's length **[Figure 8.19]**.

8.19   ***Weekend*** (1967). Godard's blistering critique of middle-class values is a famous example of the European avant-garde or counter cinema.

Kluge, a central figure in the New German cinema, addressed the Nazi legacy through experimental means in such films as *The Patriot* (1979), in which a history teacher literally digs for the past with a spade. Much of this work was informed by Marxist intellectual traditions. The critique of cinematic illusionism and narrative as ideologically complicit with capitalist culture was also central to a group of British filmmakers including Peter Wollen and Laura Mulvey, who were also noted film theorists. Peter Gidal, influenced by poststructuralism's interrogation of how representations convey meaning, made films that were anti-representational. He foregrounded the process of making films—the grain of the film stock, the repetition and duration of shots.

Cinema in the postrevolutionary and postcolonial periods of such countries as Algeria, Cuba, and Senegal was also very concerned with the politics of representation. However, limited means and populist intentions meant that experimental techniques were used in conjunction with realist filmmaking strategies. Under the political repression of a military dictatorship, Argentine filmmakers Fernando Solanas and Octavio Getino called for a *Third Cinema* for the Third World, one that rejected both commercial cinema and "auteur" or art cinema in order to engage directly with the people. Their epic documentary film *Hour of the Furnaces* (1968) covers the ongoing revolutionary struggles in Latin America and was intended to be debated with audiences. Cuban filmmaker Tomás Gutiérrez Alea's *Memories of Underdevelopment* (1968) uses experimental techniques such as the incorporation of documentary footage and self-reflexive voiceover in its narrative of a European-identified intellectual's sense of displacement in the aftermath of the Cuban revolution **[Figure 8.20]**. The first feature film made in sub-Saharan Africa, Ousmane Sembène's *Black Girl* (1966), about an African domestic worker's alienation

8.20   ***Memories of Underdevelopment*** (1968). Documentary footage interrupts the musings of an alienated intellectual in postrevolutionary Cuba in this commonly cited example of Third Cinema.

in France, makes an aesthetic virtue of economic necessity, notably in its use of postsynch sound. In *Perfumed Nightmare* (1978), Filipino filmmaker Kidlat Tahimik creates a witty parable of the clash between the "developed" world and the village of his birth by using a home movie aesthetic that incorporates cheap props and found footage.

Boundaries between experimental and documentary forms also began to blur during this period. In essay films by such filmmakers as Chris Marker in France, Harun Farocki and Alexander Kluge in Germany, and Jonas Mekas and Jill Godmilow in the United States, the "truth" of documentary is questioned. Self-reflexive techniques foreground experimental film's ability to see referential imagery in new ways. These richly interactive traditions are an important legacy for later video and digital-based media.

1980s–Present: New Technologies and New Media

While filmmakers continued to experiment using Super-8 and 16mm (and Super 16) formats, a radical shift to use and interrogate new technologies was driven by the introduction of consumer video formats. With the Sony Portapak in the late 1960s, electronic video technology became available to artists for the first time. Such pioneers as Nam June Paik brought television into confrontation with the art world in video works that were often also works of installation art **[Figure 8.21]**. Inexpensive consumer video formats of the 1980s spurred growth in both activist video and video art. Exemplary of both is Marlon Riggs's *Tongues Untied* (1989), a personal and poetic depiction of black gay men and HIV **[Figure 8.22]**. On the other end of the commercial spectrum, the launch of MTV in 1981 brought many previously experimental techniques—such as rapid montage, use of handheld cameras, breaking of continuity rules, and juxtaposition of different film stocks—into the mainstream, where they were quickly incorporated into commercials, television shows, and movies. Spike Jonze, for instance, developed the nonlinear narratives and inventive visuals

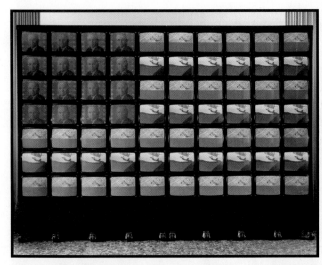

8.21 *Video Flag* (1985–1996). Nam June Paik's pioneering video art often incorporated multiple monitors.

8.22 *Tongues Untied* (1989). Marlon Riggs's *Tongues Untied* is one of the best known of the many experimental video works exploring issues of politics and identity that were facilitated by the availability of camcorders in the 1980s.

of his commercial and music video work in his feature film *Being John Malkovich* (1999).

The integration of computers and digital video in the 1990s blurred the lines between video and film-making. Commercial filmmakers used digital effects (for instance, the credit sequence of *Se7en* [1995] paid homage to Stan Brakhage), and video artists found new theatrical audiences for their work by transferring it to film. At the same time, new media artists drew on moving-image traditions in computer-based work. The development of the Internet revolutionized the potential for interactive art, allowing users to participate actively and determine their experience of the artwork. Lynn Hershman-Leeson's work as a video and performance artist in the

8.23 **"Country Weekend Pt. 1,"** *mini:mentals* (2006–). Denise Iris's Web series offers a weekly video on the beauties of everyday life, like this one in which a city girl lives a country life for a weekend.

1970s led to such pioneering interactive artworks as the networked installation *The Difference Engine #3* (1995–1998), which incorporates images of museum visitors and users logging on to the Internet to explore issues of identity and surveillance. The group Strange Company and other creators of **machinima** use video game engines to modify computer animation, creating new narratives from the game worlds. Web series, like Denise Iris's *mini:mentals* (2006–), have become a narrative format as well as a platform for artists to explore serial form **[Figure 8.23]**. Finally, widespread access to computer technology has blurred the boundaries between artists and viewers, democratizing experiments with media forms and technologies. For example, artist Natalie Bookchin knitted together hundreds of YouTube clips of solitary dancers into her video installation, *Mass Ornament* (2009).

The Elements of Experimental Media

A common understanding of the origins of cinema is that the Lumière brothers' short scenes of everyday life and scenic views represent the beginnings of the documentary tradition, and that Georges Méliès's trick films represent the beginnings of narrative film. But as film scholar Tom Gunning has pointed out, both types of film had a common objective—to solicit the viewer's desire simply to *see* something. Gunning suggests that early cinema's "look at me!" quality shapes such ongoing film traditions as special effects, musical numbers, comedy skits, and the formal techniques used by avant-garde cinema to demand that viewers see with fresh eyes. Gunning's framework also implies that documentary and narrative forms have connections to, even origins in, experimental practice. From Émile Cohl's *Automatic Moving Company* (1910), which used animation to show spoons and other household items magically packing themselves away, to Douglas Gordon's *24-Hour Psycho* (1993), which slows down Hitchcock's 1960 film to play around the clock in a museum installation, experimental media have intrigued, delighted, and sometimes alienated viewers by getting them to see things anew.

Formalisms: Narrative Experimentation and Abstraction

Film, and later video and multimedia, have been embraced as means of artistic expression distinct from, but drawing upon, other arts. Commonalities include the properties of camera lenses shared with photography, the unfolding in time shared with music, and the configuration of audience and spectacle shared with theater. And like avant-garde movements in these other arts, experimental films often explore formal questions specific to the medium. Indeed, a great many experimental films are **formalist**—concerned with problems of form over issues of content. Formal exploration of the qualities of light, the poetry of motion, and the juxtaposition of sound and image, as well as phenomenological inquiry into our ways of seeing, motivate many different experimental practices—from the camera-less film (made by exposing film stock) to video pastiche (made by re-editing television shows) to computer art (which depends on the user to determine the work's final form).

Within the wide range of experimental media, there are many different kinds of formalisms. William Wees refers to the avant-garde film tradition as "light moving in time," meaning that it foregrounds the three elements of light, motion, and time, which he argues are shared with human vision. Considered in these terms, Kenneth Anger's *Lucifer Rising* (completed in 1972 and released in 1981)—a richly imagistic film about esoteric ritual—is primarily about the principle of light (Lucifer is literally the light bearer) **[Figure 8.24]**. Chantal Akerman's films are formalist in a different way, through her consistent use of a stationary medium shot to frame images as flat planes. Frequently, as in her most widely praised film, *Jeanne Dielman, 23 Quai du Commerce, 1080 Bruxelles* (1975), her formal concerns are joined to narrative. A third example of formalist experimental film, Tony Conrad's *The Flicker* (1966) rigorously uses editing (black and white frames) to produce a phenomenological experience—the flicker effect to which the audience is subjected when the film is projected.

Many experimental films are *non-narrative* in that they lack well-defined characters or plots (see Chapter 6), and some are anti-narrative, explicitly refusing the seemingly passive relationship viewers have with storytelling film. But the unfolding of time itself introduces the basics of narrative—beginning, middle, and end—and so playing with narrative expectations is often central to experimental media. For some viewers, Alain Resnais's *Last Year at Marienbad* (1961) seems primarily a non-narrative study in the structural repetition and geometry of the rooms, hallways, and gardens of a baroque estate; for others, the film's formalism holds clues to an elusive plot about a man's efforts to seduce a woman **[Figure 8.25]**. Similarly, an interactive artwork can be thought of either in terms of game strategy or narrative archetypes. Often the relationship to cultural as well as particular narratives can be one of the most fruitful routes of interpretation for formalist films.

Formalism is central to one of the most fundamental impulses in experimental

8.24 *Lucifer Rising* (1981). Kenneth Anger's film about the occult uses esoteric imagery and a suggestive soundtrack, but it remains a formalist film exploring the principles of light.

8.25 *Last Year at Marienbad* (1961). Characters and mise-en-scène suggest a narrative, but formal patterns disrupt linear time and coherent space.

8.26 *Third Eye Butterfly* (1968). Patterns emerge from natural and spiritual imagery in Storm De Hirsch's abstract film.

film—abstraction. **Abstract films** are formal experiments that are also non-representational. They use color, shape, and line to create patterns and rhythms that are purely form-based or abstracted (that is, made more conceptual than concrete) from real actions and objects. Just as an abstract painting might foreground the texture of paint and the shape of the canvas, an abstract film might explore the specificities of film as a time-based medium by alternating forms rhythmically. Abstraction has been embraced by a range of movements, from the 1920s "absolute cinema" of Richter and Eggeling, to 1960s psychedelic films such as Storm De Hirsch's *Third Eye Butterfly* (1968) **[Figure 8.26]**, to current-day computer animation.

Experimental Organizations: Associative, Structural, and Participatory

While mainstream narrative films have predictable patterns of enigma and resolution, and documentaries follow one of a number of expository practices, experimental works organize experiences either in ways that defy realism and rational logic or in patterns that follow strict formal principles. Whether experimental forms are abstract or in some way representational, and whether or not they draw on narrative, we can think of their organizations in the following ways: associative, structural, or participatory.

Associative Organizations

Freud used free association with his patients to uncover the unconscious logics of their symptoms and dreams. *Associative organizations* create psychological or formal resonances, giving these films a dreamlike quality that engages viewers' emotions and curiosity. Later forms like the music video, whose narratives follow a dreamlike logic of imagistic or psychological association or violent juxtaposition, draw on similar traditions. Associative organizations can be abstract, such as in musicologist Harry Smith's films that relate shapes in succession or create resonances

text continued on page 302 ▶

> ▶ **VIEWING CUE**
> Consider how abstraction is achieved and used in a film screened for class. How do repetition and variation contribute to the film's shape? ⏸

> ▶ **VIEWING CUE**
> What is the formal organization of the next experimental film you see in class? Identify the most representative shot or sequence and discuss its meaning. ⏸

FILM IN FOCUS

Formal Play in *Ballet mécanique* (1924)

Painter Fernand Léger collaborated with filmmaker Dudley Murphy on *Ballet mécanique*, a film designed to accompany George Antheil's musical composition of the same title (which called for player pianos and airplane propellers among other instruments) yet released separately. Cubist painters broke from realism in order to present the process of perception in their work, transforming the flat canvas with angular shapes and lines. Léger's paintings borrowed from cubism and futurism's celebration of the machine age; his distinctive elongated shapes and thick black outlines suggest mechanical dynamism [**Figure 8.27**]. His film explores related principles, literally setting geometrical shapes in motion—quick cuts transform a circle to a triangle and back again. Léger was among the first of many modernist visual artists in the 1920s who saw cinema as a perfect medium to explore dynamism—one of the primary properties of the new art and the new age.

The circles and triangles are introduced in *Ballet mécanique* by abstracted photographic images: a straw hat filmed from above is echoed in the circle, the back-and-forth of a woman on a swing traces a triangular shape. Rather than referencing reality or building a story, these recognizable images become part of a rhythmic chain. Photographic images of moving parts are even less identifiable. Not only are they filmed in motion and moved onscreen and offscreen by the editing that associates one moving part with the next, but they are also refracted, mirrorlike, by optical printing techniques so that they are repeated in multiple sectors within the frame itself [**Figure 8.28**]. The title's suggestion of a mechanized dance is clearly figured in these groups of images.

The film's title also implies that cinema could be regarded as a mechanization of what we know to be a human activity—ballet. As in all visual arts, the human form onscreen has a special attraction to the viewer. It orients us, invites our identification and narrative expectations: who is the woman on the swing, and what does she want? Many modernist artists use the human figure in a notably different way, as an object rather than a subject, as an element like any other in the frame or as part of a machine. The swinging woman is the first image of the film, and we might think of the images that follow as her daydream, an interpretation supported by the final image of her smelling a flower. But we are also encouraged to abstract her image into one among many in a pattern of shapes and movements, as when the same footage of her swinging is shown upside down.

Indeed, one of the most notable ways that avant-garde art of the 1920s explored the connection between the human form and the machine was through fragmented images of modern women. In *Ballet mécanique,* a second

8.27 *Three Women (Le grand déjeuner)* (1921). Fernand Léger's paintings were inspired by mechanical forms, and their shapes—though not their colors—are carried over to his film.

8.28 *Ballet mécanique* (1924). Movement proliferates onscreen through refracted images of machine parts in motion.

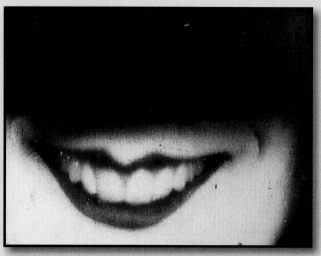

8.29 *Ballet mécanique* (1924). The fragmentation and abstraction of the female form is a common practice in modernist art.

female form appears first simply as a pair of lips sharply outlined in lipstick (cosmetics were widely popularized during this period) and isolated in the frame by a black mask over the rest of the face **[Figure 8.29]**. The lips smile and relax, intercut with the image of the straw hat. The same woman also becomes part of the patterns of the film—in a later shot her plucked eyebrows echo the curved shape of her eyes so that a quick cut of the eyes upside down goes by almost undetected. We do eventually see the woman's full head in profile, but the bobbed hair and stylized pose make her a sculptural image rather than a character to identify with. A later "dance" of alternating images of mannequin legs adorned with garters is at the same time a delightful visual joke and a disturbing evocation of dismemberment. The male form is treated differently in the film: a male head appears at the center of the refracted frame, perhaps signifying mind instead of body. Yet this image's closest visual rhyme is with a parrot framed in the same way, a surreal association that prevents us from reading him as a guiding consciousness behind the film's succession of images.

Approaching an abstract film, or any experimental media work, is made easier by close description of its formal elements, identification of its patterns, and synthesizing of its themes, as we have attempted here. An intriguing clue to the formal concerns of *Ballet mécanique* lies in the image that appears before the title: Hollywood silent film comedian Charlie Chaplin is rendered in a fragmented

form very reminiscent of Léger's paintings. The film, the credit says, is presented by "Charlot," the French name for Chaplin. At the end of the film, the image does a little animated dance of its own, a mechanized ballet **[Figure 8.30]**. An actor's iconic film image is thus first paid tribute to by a painter in a graphic form, and then enfolded into the last of the film's sequence of everyday objects set in motion, demonstrating the vibrant crossing back and forth between cinema and the other arts in this period of modernist experimentation.

8.30 *Ballet mécanique* (1924). Charlie Chaplin's iconic image animated by Fernand Léger.

8.31 *Film #7* (1951). Famous for his collections of American folk music, Harry Smith also made inventive animations in which found objects are organized in associative patterns.

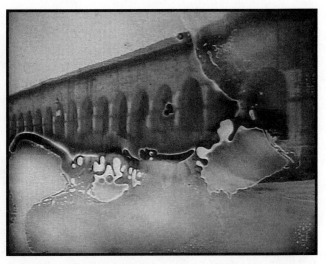

8.32 *Decasia* (2002). Patterns created by decaying nitrate film stock emerge on the surface of found footage, the layering suggesting impermanence and loss.

between objects and shapes or colors **[Figure 8.31]**, but they can also be representational, like in music videos.

Metaphoric associations link or associate different objects, images, events, or individuals in order to generate a new perception, emotion, or idea. In a film, this might be done by linking two different images, by indicating a connection between two objects or figures within a single frame, or by creating metaphors in the voiceover commentary as it responds to and anticipates images in the film. Juxtaposing images of workers being shot and a slaughtered bull, as Sergei Eisenstein does in *Strike* (1925), metaphorically evokes the brutal dehumanization of the workers. Derek Jarman's *Blue* (1993)—perhaps best described as an experimental autobiography—is a metaphoric meditation on the color blue and its chain of associations in the life of a man (the filmmaker) dying of AIDS. Accompanying one single blue image, a voice meditates: blue becomes associated with the "blue funk" created by a doctor's news, the "slow blue love on a delphinium day," and "the universal love in which all men bathe." Bill Morrison's *Decasia* (2002) edits together old films whose nitrate stock has deteriorated so that recognizable images and spaces blend into abstract splotches and blobs **[Figure 8.32]**. Metaphorical associations emerge in the dance of fleeting shapes, edited juxtapositions, and imagery called forth by Michael Gordon's symphonic soundtrack.

Unlike the concrete associations that bind metaphoric images, *symbolic associations* isolate discrete objects or singular images that can generate or be assigned abstract meanings—either those already given those objects or images by a culture, or ones created by the film itself. The symbolic significance may be spiritual (as with the Christian cross) or political (such as the flag of a particular country), or it may be tied to some other concept that has been culturally and historically grafted onto the meaning of a person, an event, or a thing. Building on his earlier work with

8.33 *The Hand* (1965). The hand symbolizes a figure of tyrannical power in this Eastern European puppet film.

puppet films, Czech filmmaker Jiří Trnka created his remarkable experimental film, *The Hand* (1965). A puppet struggles against the domination of a single, live-action hand that demands he make only other hands and not flowerpots [Figure 8.33]. The hand is a chillingly effective symbol of totalitarian regimes in Eastern Europe.

Structural Organizations

Films that employ *structural organizations* reject the illusionism of narrative film and challenge the audience's perceptions with a focus on the material of the film (its grain, sprockets, and journey through a projector past a beam of light). This organization, which follows a particular editing logic or other formal principle of construction, informs a wide variety of media artworks from the stationary camera films of Andy Warhol and the video works of artist Bruce Nauman, to digital artworks generated by algorithms.

Some filmmakers weave images, framings, camera movements, or other formal dimensions into patterns and structures that engage the viewer perceptually and often intellectually. Michael Snow's *Wavelength* (1967) is a forty-five-minute image that slowly moves across a room in an extended zoom-in and ends with a close-up of a picture of ocean waves [Figure 8.34]. Punctuated with vague references to a murder mystery, and accompanied by a high-pitched sound that explores another meaning of "wavelength," this movie is an almost pure investigation of the vibrant textures of space: as flat, as colored, as empty, and most of all, as geometrically tense.

Other films central to the structural film movement in the United States include Ernie Gehr's *Serene Velocity* (1970) and Hollis Frampton's *Zorns Lemma* (1970). *Serene Velocity* consists of images of the same hallway taken with structured variations in the camera's focal length, creating a hypnotic, rhythmic experience of lines and squares. In *Zorns Lemma*, a repeated sequence of one-second images of words on signs and storefronts arranged in alphabetical order creates a fascinating puzzle as they are replaced one by one with a set of consistent, though arbitrary, images [Figure 8.35]. The viewer learns to associate the images with their place in the cycle, in a sense relearning a picture alphabet. Such structural principles are fascinating intellectually, but Frampton's films, like the most effective structural films, also work on the viewer's senses.

8.34   Filmstrip showing frames of *Wavelength* (1967). An extended zoom-in for the duration of the film creates suspense through its formal structure.

8.35   *Zorns Lemma* (1970). Hollis Frampton's films are often organized around structural principles, as in this film's central sequence of images corresponding to cycles of the alphabet.

8.36   *Rapture* (1999). Shirin Neshat is one of many contemporary fine artists who use film and video in gallery contexts to generate meaning through audience interaction.

Participatory Experiences

A third approach to experimental film emphasizes *participatory experiences*—the centrality of the viewer and the time and place of exhibition to the cinematic phenomenon. Often the film is part of a live performance by the filmmaker. *Nervous System* (1994), a film performance by underground filmmaker Ken Jacobs, uses two projectors, a propeller, and filters through which audiences view the work. In 1970, Gene Youngblood coined the term **expanded cinema** for such work and predicted that video and computer technology would allow moving image media to extend consciousness. Nam June Paik delivered on this prediction in conceptual video art pieces like *Video Fish* (1975), which combined video monitors displaying images of fish and aquariums containing real fish.

Many filmmakers working in the art world design their works around the audience's experience. *Rapture* (1999), an installation by Iranian-born Shirin Neshat, projects 16mm film footage of men and women on opposite gallery walls to signify their separation in Iranian society under Islamic law, with the viewer both mediating and separating these worlds **[Figure 8.36]**. Multimedia artists may produce CD-ROMs for museum installations or home use that rely on users' selections, the sense of touch, and interface design as crucial artistic components. In an early Internet-based work, multimedia artist Shu Lea Cheang built several kinds of participatory experiences into the design of *Bowling Alley* (1995). A museum installation at the Walker Art Center in Minneapolis and an actual bowling alley were linked to a Web site that gathered contributions by collaborating artists. The actions of the bowlers and the online participants affected what museum visitors experienced. Artists now work with online interactive environments like *Second Life* and *World of Warcraft* as well as social media to create new user experiences. Fan art, video blogs, and the vast range of user-generated content on YouTube relate to these participatory traditions even when their content is not consciously artistic.

Styles and Perspectives: Surrealist, Lyrical, and Critical

Experimental organizations are often informed by specific styles and perspectives, including surrealism, lyricism, and critical positions, that stem from the intimate and personal impulse behind experimental filmmaking. More than any other kind of film, experimental films are driven by the efforts and point of view of individual filmmakers—they often shoot, edit, process, and even project their films themselves.

Surrealism

Surrealist styles use recognizable imagery in strange contexts—simultaneously defying the realist tendencies and narrative logic of mainstream film, and building on the medium's basis in photographic reproduction and the idea of unfolding images in time. **Surrealist cinema** was a driving force in Europe in the 1920s,

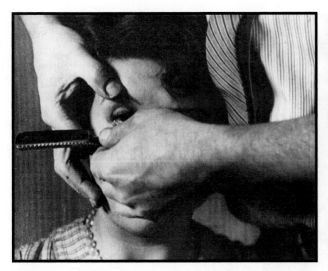

8.37   *Un chien andalou* (1928). The opening scene of a woman's eye being slit by a razor—arguably the most famous moment in experimental film history—exemplifies surrealism's use of shock.

8.38   *Destino* (1945, 2003). Dalí's unlikely collaboration with Disney remained unfinished until its release in 2003.

especially in France. Early works include René Clair's *Entr'acte* (1924) and Germaine Dulac's *The Seashell and the Clergyman* (1928), based on a script by Antonin Artaud, but certainly the most renowned surrealist film is Salvador Dalí and Luis Buñuel's *Un chien andalou* (1928). Beginning with a shocking assault on a woman's eye **[Figure 8.37]**, the film teases viewers with the possibility of a story about a woman and her relationship with one or more men, drifts among unexplained objects (like a recurring striped box), and never emerges from its dream state. Through the powers of film to manipulate time, space, and material objects, surrealist filmmakers confronted middle-class assumptions about normalcy and created a dream world driven by dark desires.

Since the 1920s, surrealism has had a great influence on animation, both directly, as in Dalí's collaboration with Disney, *Destino* (1945, 2003) **[Figure 8.38]**, and more indirectly, as in Czech animator Jan Svankmajer's *Alice* (1988) and Japanese master Hayao Miyazaki's *Spirited Away* (2001)—both of which create utterly unique, surreal worlds. Outside the realm of animation, the original worlds of Terry Gilliam's *Brazil* (1985) and Michel Gondry's *Eternal Sunshine of the Spotless Mind* (2004) are shaped by surrealist imagery and narrative logic.

Lyricism

Lyrical styles express emotions, beliefs, or some other personal position in film, much like the voice of a lyric poet does in literature. Lyrical films may emphasize a personal voice or vision through the singularity of the imagery or through such techniques as voiceovers or handheld camera movements. In his autobiographical film about his experience as an immigrant in New York, *Lost, Lost, Lost* (1976), Jonas Mekas portrays his fears and hopes. Home movies and journal entries are contrasted in a fragmented style that resembles a diary, while the rhythmic interjections of the commentator-poet express feelings ranging from angst to delight **[Figure 8.39]**.

8.39   *Lost, Lost, Lost* (1976). Jonas Mekas's diary-film uses a lyrical personal voice and is a key film in the important tradition of experimental documentary.

8.40 *Fireworks* (1947). Kenneth Anger's lyrical homoerotic reverie is one of the key early works of the American avant-garde.

▶ **VIEWING CUE**
Characterize the style of the film or media work you have viewed for class. What points to the artist's presence or position behind the work? ❚❚

Lyricism helped define postwar experimental cinema in the United States. Such work flourished in a climate of existential philosophy and with the help of lightweight 16mm cameras that the individual filmmaker could operate. As the movement's primary critic, P. Adams Sitney, argues, lyrical filmmaking carried forward traditions of inspiration and creativity based in Romanticism. These influences, together with an intimate community of viewers, helped create an unusually personal cinema that explored dreams, visions, and intricacies of human consciousness. Perhaps the most poetic and most prolific filmmaker of this movement, Stan Brakhage made films from the 1950s until his death in 2003. Themes of insight and blindness run through many of his films, which range in length from the nine-second-long *Eye Myth* (1967) to the five-hour-long *The Art of Vision* (1965). Kenneth Anger's lyricism fuses homoeroticism, ritual, popular culture, and esoterica, from his landmark *Fireworks* (1947) **[Figure 8.40]** made when he was seventeen, to *Invocation of My Demon Brother* (1969). Brakhage and Anger represent just two of the many avant-garde filmmakers whose visions are so distinctive that their work is instantly recognizable.

Video artists also draw on forms of lyricism. For example, Bill Viola uses extreme slow motion in his projection-based installation *Going Forth by Day* (2002) to envelop the viewer and to approach religious contemplation. Viewers experience an array of five 35-minute sequences that reflect upon the cycle of birth, death, and resurrection.

Critical Positions

Critical positions structure a film or media work through interrogation of its form, content, or communication with the viewer. In such works, experimental modes may overlap with documentary and narrative ones. In Jean-Luc Godard's *Two or Three Things I Know About Her* (1967), characters directly address the viewer, responding to questions such as "What is language?" whispered by the offscreen director. In Trinh T. Minh-ha's *Surname Viet Given Name Nam* (1989), Vietnamese women living in the United States act the roles of interviewees living in Vietnam, narrating their wartime experiences. The combination of this device, the filmmaker's voiceover text and other soundtrack elements, and unusual framings complicates the identities of these women and any effort to portray their experiences authentically or completely. As a result, the film raises more questions than it answers.

A film that employs critical techniques may present images so layered and complex that they are difficult to explain. Bruce Conner's experimental film *A Movie* (1958) contrasts wild races and chase scenes with images of refugees, an execution, and air crashes in an elusive questioning of what it means to watch a movie. Yvonne Rainer's *The Man Who Envied Women* (1985) uses a range of collage-like devices to make viewers think about what they are seeing, from using several actors in the same role to a camera tracking over a wall hung with a variety

text continued on page 308 ▶

8.41a

8.41b

8.41c

8.41d

8.41e

Lyrical Style in Bridges-Go-Round
(1958)

Pioneering American independent filmmaker Shirley Clarke (1919–1997) first trained as a dancer. But after studying with artist Hans Richter, who made some of the first abstract films in the early 1920s, she became drawn to avant-garde filmmaking. "You can make a dance film without dancers," Clarke believed. Using footage left over from another project, she did just that in *Bridges-Go-Round* (1958).

In four brief minutes, a series of tinted, superimposed, and rhythmically edited shots of New York bridges—taken from unusual angles with the lightweight 16mm camera favored by experimental filmmakers at the time—make these massive objects seem light as air and agile as gulls. At the start of the film, simple credits appear over rapidly moving shots of sparkling blue water. Next, the water is overlaid with structural elements of a bridge, animated by a series of pans, tracks, and tilts [**Figure 8.41a**]. Superimposition remains a common pattern across several sets of differently tinted shots. In one sequence, a city skyline seems to sail past its mirror image [**Figure 8.41b**]. This is followed by two horizontal images of the same bridge superimposed; as they move past each other we feel a sense of rapid transit. Later, the camera finally comes to rest—on a striking montage of identical, expressionistic images of a bridge shot from below, each image saturated in a different color [**Figure 8.41c**].

In the final sequence, a montage of brief shots converges in a rapid frontal flight over the bridge [**Figure 8.41d**], until in the last image the actual bridge has disappeared and we are left suspended in a gravity-defying shot that brings us back to the skyline and blue tint from the beginning of the film [**Figure 8.41e**]. Cinema itself becomes a kind of bridge leading to a new perception of the dynamism of the city. Finally, the lyrical style of Clarke's abstract editing is emphasized by the film's two very different commissioned soundtracks. The electronic score by Louis and Bebe Barron echoes industrial images with industrial noises; Teo Macero's arrangement uses voices and jazz instrumentation to uncanny effect. Clarke's collaborations with these composers, as much as the novel images and rhythms of this film, attest to her central role in the New York avant-garde.

8.42 *The Man Who Envied Women* (1985). Throughout the film, voiceovers analyze images pinned to a wall; the viewer of the film is similarly called upon to interrogate its images.

of clippings (of war photography, advertising, editorials) while an unidentified voiceover analyzes them **[Figure 8.42]**.

Many critical techniques are associated with political or theoretical positions that take apart the assumed natural relationship between a word or an image and the thing it represents. Critical filmmakers encourage audiences to take up similar critical positions by exposing them to formal experiments. Such aesthetic strategies are rooted in the social critiques of the late 1960s, and are sometimes referred to as *political modernism*. One of the most interesting and influential approaches to the image-oriented society of consumer capitalism was advanced by Guy Debord in a book and film called *The Society of the Spectacle* (1967 and 1973, respectively). Debord argued that images themselves—taken out of context through a process called *détournement*—were the only way to transform the image-oriented society. Feminist filmmakers like Yvonne Rainer, Laura Mulvey, and Peter Wollen used critical techniques to question the representation of women in film. In *Riddles of the Sphinx* (1977), for instance, Mulvey and Wollen took great care to avoid using camera work that would objectify the young mother featured in the film. In the 1980s, video artists extended this critical function toward mainstream media, and new media today often demand that viewers question *how* they are looking at something as well as *what* they are looking at.

The Significance of Experimental Media

Perhaps more than any other form of media, experimental film and video ask viewers to reflect actively on the viewing experience. Experimental media contemplates the way human senses and consciousness function. Some of these works, in setting out to explore the phenomenon of vision (or perhaps hearing and touch), are *about* perception and its relationship to consciousness; some can even be about the experience of boredom. Whether we are challenged to figure out the meaning of symbolism or to relate a film to an artist's wider body of work or to a social context, we are always required to participate in some way.

Just as the potential of the Internet and other new technologies generates excitement and even utopian claims today, so did the invention of cinema a little more than a century ago. French filmmaker Jean Epstein enthusiastically anticipated the way "slow motion and fast motion" could reveal secrets of the world; and Dziga Vertov celebrated the camera's capacity to see more, and differently, than the human eye in *Man with a Movie Camera* (1929). Decades later, television's ways of seeing became the object of similar reflection in video art. In *Technology/Transformation: Wonder Woman* (1978–1979), Dara Birnbaum scrutinized the TV heroine's gestures as she transforms into her superhero persona by slowing and repeating them in a ritualistic fashion **[Figure 8.43]**.

8.43 *Technology/Transformation: Wonder Woman* (1978–1979). Dara Birnbaum was one of the first artists to explore the video medium's relationship with television by appropriating pop culture imagery. *Courtesy of Electronic Arts Intermix.*

Challenging and Expanding Perception

As part of a thorough examination of the medium, experimental works make meaning through challenging and expanding how viewers see, feel, and hear. Such films, videos, and other artwork press us to open our senses and our minds in unaccustomed ways. For example, Hollis Frampton's *Lemon* (1969) presents only a single piece of fruit in changing light—for those seeing this film, a lemon will never look the same again. An experimental movie might use unusual filmic techniques or materials, such as abstract graphic designs and animation, as vehicles for seeing and thinking in fresh ways. It might present a rapid series of images that seem to skip about randomly—much like the experience of a dream. Shirley Clarke's *Bridges-Go-Round* uses unexpected camera angles and zooms to turn the massive structures of various bridges into an ethereal dance (see p. 307).

Each new medium brings new perceptual possibilities. Web 2.0—the current generation of the Internet as a site of user-generated content, social networks, and massively multiplayer online role-playing games—has given rise to new kinds of experiences. These experiences are based in representations of ourselves through avatars and connections with others whom we may never meet in the flesh. Works of art may explore these experiences by combining "old" and new media.

As with feature films or documentaries, the cultural and historical expectations of viewers play a large part in how experimental media are understood and what meanings are assigned to them. Education in ways of watching and artistic contexts plays a much greater part in the interpretation of experimental film, however, because of the difficulty and marginality of the medium or the technological platform.

Experimental Film Traditions

Old media were once new media. One paradox of the avant-garde is that it cannot remain a literal "advance guard" for very long. Innovations are absorbed into more dominant traditions, or artists' visions expand viewers' imaginations to encompass new forms. There are often historical precedents even for the most seemingly shocking, original, or technologically innovative works of art. Exploring these contexts not only is fascinating for its exposure of little-known traditions, but it also enriches our experience of current works that often make reference to previous traditions. In its early decades, cinema was heralded as the "seventh art," and its practitioners and theorists were proud of incorporating practices from all the others.

Experimental traditions also have direct ties to influences outside of film. Revolutions, resistance movements, and student unrest have influenced media politically. Despite celebrating their independence, often through the formation of journals, clubs, and societies that share their ideas, experimental filmmakers also rely on larger cultural institutions such as museums, government agencies, and private corporations (as in the case of new media) for sponsorship. And of course, audiences are essential to these traditions—not only for commercial viability but for the work of interpretation, advocacy, and aesthetic fulfillment. The ways in which experimental works interact and challenge their viewers can be categorized into two distinct traditions: expressive and confrontational.

VIEWING CUE

Consider your own interpretative process as you watch an experimental work. What specific images or sounds solicit your attention? What devices remind you of the elements of cinema? Are there any elements that bring to mind influences outside of film?

Expressive Traditions

Expressive traditions emphasize personal expression and communication with an audience and are tied to long-standing notions of artistic originality, authenticity, and interiority. Impressionist painters used new techniques to render color and light as they were perceived, not as academic painting traditions prescribed. Cubist painters attempted to integrate spatial perception and temporal duration into their canvasses. These ways of seeing had a significant influence on the emergence of film art. In Paris in the late 1910s, Louis Delluc founded journals and cine-clubs that defined the impressionist film movement. Germaine Dulac, Jean Epstein, and his sister Marie Epstein made films, wrote articles, and lectured about the new film art. While some argued that film should be composed like music, others embraced narrative components and photographic realism.

Expressive forms are generally rooted in lyrical and poetic traditions. From René Clair's *The Crazy Ray* (1925) to Jean Cocteau's *Orpheus* (1950), films that follow *poetic narratives* use stories as the skeletons on which to elaborate and explore novel cinematic techniques and special effects. Werner Herzog's *Heart of Glass* (1976) is based on a Bavarian legend about the death of a glassblower and the subsequent loss of a secret formula that supported the village industry; but with its characters wandering directionless and speaking in poetic non sequiturs, the heart of the film explores the hypnotic images floating through a world that has lost its sense of time. Stephen and Timothy Quay's *Street of Crocodiles* (1986), constructed through stop-motion photography and based on the memoirs of Polish author Bruno Schulz, is a dark tale of a porcelain doll trapped in a sinister, nightmarish environment of animate screws and threads. Here the remarkable life of thread and other objects—and not the thread of a story—shapes and organizes the film.

An expressive impulse is also at the heart of the American underground film. During the 1960s and 1970s, the American counterculture of "sex, drugs, and rock and roll" broke free of the perceived repressive social values, barriers, and gender roles of the 1950s. The San Francisco–based Kuchar brothers made campy films like *Hold Me While I'm Naked* (1966) **[Figure 8.44]**, while Marie Menken discovered a more personal expressive film language in such works as *Glimpse of the Garden* (1957). Subcultures—artistic and sexual—embraced filmmaking, and independent subcultures emerged around experimental filmmaking itself. A network of alternative cinemas and university screenings brought these works and their makers into contact with what became devoted audiences of filmmakers, critics, students, and other artists.

Expressive traditions also emerge from specific technologies and properties of the medium. For example, the small-gauge formats of 16mm and 8mm were developed in the 1920s and 1930s for the amateur film market and were taken up very early for artistic purposes. As video became more portable in the 1960s and was introduced to the consumer market, it too became a medium for artists. Artists exploited the intimacies of these media, such as the diary-like formula used by Jonas Mekas in the 1950s and adopted by video artists in the 1970s and digital filmmakers today. *Gina Kim's Video Diary* (2002) is a feature-length collection of video diaries made by a young Korean woman who immigrates to the United States. Exploring anorexia and family relationships with frank, startling imagery, the film captures experiences of transnational displacement that are common and yet completely personal.

8.44 *Hold Me While I'm Naked* (1966). This campy film by George Kuchar stars himself as the director of a film (within a film) who is frustrated by his failure to create the highly artistic film he envisions. The campiness and comic nature of the film are compounded by his pitiful getup.

New media present a range of expressive possibilities. YouTube is home to a plethora of user-generated content, and Vimeo plays host to many experimental filmmakers and new media artists. These moving-image artists use such sites to launch work that would otherwise have very limited chances of exposure. Although the vast majority of the work posted would not be associated with experimental film by their makers or viewers, the very technology that is being used and the expressive impulse fit very much into this tradition.

Confrontational Traditions

The shock of the modern—beautiful machines capable of brutal destruction; juxtapositions of commerce and art; time sped up and distances eliminated—was incorporated in the 1920s in a confrontational modernist impulse across the arts. Sometimes the urge was to shock the middle class—as in *Olympia* (1863), the frank painting by Édouard Manet whose subject was clearly a prostitute [Figure 8.45], or the eyeball slicing of *Un chien andalou* (see Figure 8.37, p. 305). Sometimes it was to document the democratization of art in a changing world, such as in Eugène Atget's photographs of Paris storefronts. As German cultural theorist Walter Benjamin argued in his famous 1936 essay, "The Work of Art in the Age of Its Technological Reproducibility," the very notion of artistic originality was challenged by the photograph and taken even further by film, which courted a mass, public audience. Because cinema was seen as the quintessentially modern medium, artists active in other media, like Dada artist Marcel Duchamp, experimented with the medium. Artists saw their role as vitally linked to the times, whether in embracing a machine aesthetic in their work, or in making films suitable to the proletarian revolution in the Soviet Union. Such an attitude goes against Romantic traditions of artistic expressivity and shapes the experimental film tradition of confrontation—of conventions, audiences, or expectations and associations in the context of a wider social, political, or aesthetic critique.

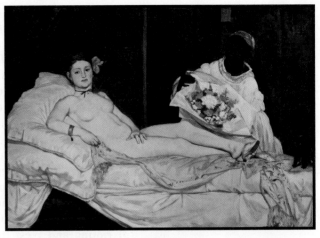

8.45 *Olympia* (1863). Édouard Manet's work was condemned at the time as vulgar and immoral, not because it depicted a nude woman but because the woman was clearly shown to be a prostitute.

The European avant-gardes of the 1920s were a conscious model for filmmakers like Jean-Luc Godard. His films in the 1960s were partly experimental, challenging commercial film conventions through unusual sound and image juxtapositions or by having actors go in and out of character. But as the critical and political environment of this period became more intense, the confrontational impulse of what became known as *counter cinema* went deeper. Godard started making consciously noncommercial films like *British Sounds* (1970) with collaborators under the name Dziga Vertov Group. In 1972, Godard and his partner, Jean-Pierre Gorin, made a film called *Letter to Jane* that scrutinizes a still photograph of liberal American actress Jane Fonda listening sympathetically on a visit to Vietnam. In voiceover, Godard and Gorin critique this image for its political naivete [Figure 8.46]. The radicalism of this period was hard to sustain, but the confrontational impulse informs all of Godard's work. For example, the intricate image and sound montages of the multipart

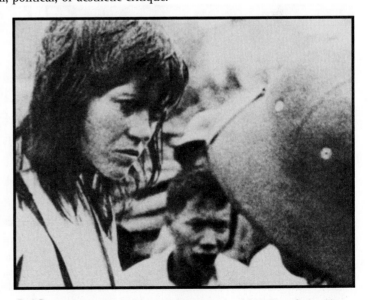

8.46 *Letter to Jane* (1972). Jean-Luc Godard and Jean-Pierre Gorin critique a photograph of American actress Jane Fonda for the liberal—rather than radical—politics it represents. While prescient in its scrutiny of celebrity culture, the film is also misogynist and even cruel in its confrontational style.

Histoire(s) du Cinéma (1988–1998) ask viewers to look at all the meanings that images accumulate over time.

In the 1980s, *activist video*—particularly that inspired by government indifference to the AIDS crisis—employed a confrontational style. While based in documentary in its presentation of information, it also used experimental techniques of editing, design elements drawn from advertising and propaganda, and self-conscious voiceover and personal reflection. Tom Kalin's *They Are Lost to Vision Altogether* (1989) combines elegiac imagery with footage of marches, portraying strategies of mourning and militancy employed by AIDS activists **[Figure 8.47]**. Also during this period, film and videomakers of color embraced experimental strategies in greater numbers than earlier, when documentary's directness was often preferred. In Britain, Sankofa's *Passion of Remembrance* (1986) combines political debate with newsreel footage and home movies, and the Black Audio Film Collective's *Handsworth Songs* (1986) juxtaposes footage of rioting and West Indian carnival traditions with a voiceover that analyzes colonial history and the reasons for current racial unrest. In *Night Cries: A Rural Tragedy* (1989), Australian Aboriginal artist Tracey Moffatt uses stylized sets and sounds and disjunctive editing to tell a story about the assimilation policies that forced Aboriginal children to be adopted by white families through the 1960s **[Figure 8.48]**. Experimental works that confront the audience's complacency or histories of injustice and misrepresentation may be hybrids of documentary and narrative work such as these. Sometimes voices and visions that have been marginalized find less-settled traditions like experimental film more fruitful areas to employ.

Confrontational tactics in new media are often about deflecting the messages of mainstream media. Groups like The Yes Men make fake Web sites offering corporate apologies for environmental degradation that mainstream news outlets sometimes pick up and report. With the increasing fragmentation of audiences by cable programming, blogs, and Internet video, confrontational media-making techniques are also multiplying.

▶ **VIEWING CUE**

Consider the film you've just viewed for class. Is it part of an expressive or a confrontational tradition? Explain. ⏸

8.47 *They Are Lost to Vision Altogether* (1989). Artist Tom Kalin conveyed competing impulses of mourning and militancy in response to the AIDS crisis in the elegiac imagery of this videotape.

8.48 *Night Cries: A Rural Tragedy* (1989). The fraught relationship between a grown Aboriginal daughter and the elderly white mother who adopted her as a child is conveyed without dialogue through the film's innovative sets, lush 35mm cinematography, and sound work.

CONCEPTS AT WORK

For the purposes of this chapter, we have distinguished experimental practices that are *alternative* to narrative cinema, to corporate- or state-sponsored documentary movements, or to the commercial interests of software developers or game manufacturers. It is thus crucial to understand the institutions and networks that support this alternative culture. In recent decades in the United States, media artists have been able to make their work through modest financial assistance of cultural foundations and government agencies such as the National Endowment for the Arts (NEA) and through teaching. Many experimental filmmakers influenced new generations through their positions teaching at places such as Cal Arts, the San Francisco Art Institute, the Art Institute of Chicago, the Rhode Island School of Design (RISD), Pratt Institute, and the School of Visual Arts. Museums like the Museum of Modern Art and the Whitney Museum of American Art have contributed to experimental film culture through their curatorial departments, collecting practices, and regular screening series. (Similar venues and networks exist in Britain, Canada, Germany, Japan, and elsewhere.) Other more traditional cultural institutions and funders, however, have resisted recognizing the medium, sometimes suspicious of its commercial relations. Interestingly, it has been somewhat easier for video art and new media to find a home in the gallery or museum than it was for film, because their installation components are more compatible with both traditional sculpture and the habits of museum goers.

Experimental movies remind us that we are involved with the world through fantasy, aesthetic experience, and analysis as well as through stories and informational modes. While experimental forms are in some ways the least accessible forms of film and media, they have fundamental bearing on how we see; this chapter has explored some implications of the fact that the word "experience" shares the same root as the word "experiment."

Activities

- Experimental media texts are difficult to access. Research the venues and other institutions that support this media and consider what kinds of audience expectations go into encounters with it.
- Explore film's connection with music, architecture, painting, and sculpture by tracing an element that occurs across each of these different media.

A Romantic Comedy.
With Zombies.
SHAUN OF THE DEAD
ROGUE PICTURES STUDIO CANAL
BIG TALK PRODUCTIONS "SHAUN OF THE DEAD" SIMON PEGG
KATE ASHFIELD LUCY DAVIS NICK FROST DYLAN MORAN BILL NIGHY PENELOPE WILTON
RONALDO VASCONCELLOS ANNIE HARDINGE MARCUS ROWLAND CHRIS DICKENS DAVID M. DUNLAP
NATASCHA WHARTON JAMES WILSON ALISON OWEN SIMON PEGG EDGAR WRIGHT NIRA PARK EDGAR WRIGHT
R RESTRICTED
For Zombie Violence/Gore And Language
STUDIO CANAL
ROGUE PICTURES
www.shaunofthedeadmovie.com
This September aim for the head.
"AN ABSOLUTE BLAST!"
-George Romero

chapter

9

Rituals, Conventions, Archetypes, and Formulas
Movie Genres

In *Shaun of the Dead* (2004), Shaun's life appears heading in all the wrong directions. He despises his job; his girlfriend constantly berates him about his slacker lifestyle; and his stepfather relentlessly complains about Shaun's treatment of his mother. To make matters worse, suddenly all the people around him seem to be turning into zombies. Quickly his dull and irritating life morphs into an apocalyptic horror film in which Shaun and his equally incompetent band of friends fight off and destroy the seemingly endless parade of slow-moving zombies, breaking apart gory bodies with cricket bats, shovels, pool cues, and any other objects on hand. The film is replete with tongue-in-cheek references to modern horror classics such as *Night of the Living Dead* (1968) and *28 Days Later* (2002) with their conventional pseudoscientific explanations about what started this gruesome epidemic of walking dead. But it also borders on parody, as early in the film it appears difficult to distinguish the behavior and gestures of presumably normal human beings from the slumping, mechanical movements of the zombies. Watching the film thus becomes a kind of generic game—we recognize and anticipate the formulas of horror films, and at the same time we watch the film reference slapstick and romantic comedy at various points. The pleasure of playing its game is at the heart of the intelligence and pleasure of watching many generic films.

A definition of **genre** can be derived from its root, meaning "kind." For film studies, it is a category or classification of a group of movies in which the individual films share similar subject matter and similar ways of organizing the subject through narrative and stylistic patterns. This chapter argues that film genres are not merely formulaic categories but practices connected to the human need for archetypes, rituals, and communication. The film industry has made this need part of an economic strategy in order to draw audiences back again and again to experience the genres they enjoy. Narrative, documentary, and experimental films have each created particular genres associated with their respective organizations, but in this chapter we will focus specifically on six narrative film genres: comedy, western, melodrama, musical, horror, and crime. For each genre, we will identify its primary formulas and conventions and consider how it reflects and regulates specific cultural and historical experiences.

KEY OBJECTIVES

- Understand why film genres attract audiences.
- Recognize that film genres spring from a long historical heritage, and that they can change over time.
- Learn the conventions and formulas of the six major genres—comedy, the western, melodrama, the musical, the horror film, the crime film—and their subgenres.
- Examine how genres function as cultural rituals that coordinate audience needs and desires.
- Explore how audiences' prescriptive and descriptive understanding of certain film types become ways of making meaning through genre.

Why do so many movies repeat formulas and conventions? How do those repetitions affect our responses to films? Indeed, we sometimes choose to see a movie because we identify it with a particular genre, and we return to genre films because we know and appreciate them. Movies rely on repetitions and rituals that allow audiences to share expectations and routines. Grounded in audience expectations about characters, narrative, and visual style, a film genre is a set of conventions and formulas repeated and developed through film history. To some degree, our understanding of a movie is a function of genre expectations. We enjoy science fiction films—from the 1927 *Metropolis* to the 1958 and 1986 versions of *The Fly*—because we recognize and appreciate some version of a "mad scientist" who works in a mysterious laboratory in which new technology leads to strange and dangerous discoveries. One viewer may rush out to see *The Fighter* (2010) for the very same reason that another viewer may resolutely choose not to see it: because it is a boxing movie whose formulas and images—a down-and-out working-class hero trying to redeem himself or herself, physically powerful and graphic fight scenes, overwhelming obstacles, and a usually triumphant ending—are part of a well-known genre designed to appeal to viewers' awareness of these conventions **[Figure 9.1]**. In an important sense, our different responses to particular genres define the film community to which we belong.

Genres also function as *cultural rituals*, the repetition of formulas that help coordinate our needs and desires. These rituals are both formal and ideological practices that can become a therapeutic means of responding to a situation that is too traumatic, confusing, or irrational to resolve in a simple or pragmatic way. Many religions celebrate a child's coming-of-age (around the age of thirteen) through ritualized ceremonies involving family and friends. Some communities acknowledge the transition from autumn to winter by acting out serious and playful rituals—such as those associated with Halloween—that testify to the coming months of darkness and death. As we will learn in this chapter, film genres carry their own specific cultural values.

9.1   **The Fighter** (2010). The genre formulas of the classic boxing film are recognizable but updated in this film.

A Short History of Film Genre

MGM's *Singin' in the Rain* (1952) reminds us more directly than most films that a film genre always carries the traces of an older and varied history. A musical comedy, it is as much about history as it is about music. It begins in 1928, with two silent film stars concluding one generic film, a historical romance in the model of a literary adaptation like *The Three Musketeers*, and follows them as they try, unsuccessfully, to adapt that genre to the new historical demands of "talking pictures" **[Figure 9.2]**. In the narrative confusion, failures, and frustrations that follow this clash of genre and history, they re-create their movie as a different film genre, the musical. The fact that the title song, as well as "You Are My Lucky Star" and several others, are drawn from early MGM musicals adds another historical dimension to the film. As the story unfolds, a romantic melodrama involving the two protagonists, Kathy and Don, sneaks into the musical, while the wacky antics of Don's sidekick, Cosmo, recall the slapstick comedies of the Keystone Kops, Charlie Chaplin, and Harold Lloyd. *Singin' in the Rain* itself later became many viewers'

9.2   **Singin' in the Rain** (1952). The film-within-the-film spoofs silent film genres.

9.3 *Shortly After Marriage* (1743). Prominent English genre painter William Hogarth painted satirical views of everyday life and contemporary mores.

9.4 *Human Nature* (1885). Nineteenth-century stage melodramas, like this one by Henry Pettitt and Augustus Harris, were forerunners of a central film genre.

reference point for the classical Hollywood musical; its awareness of genre history thus becomes incorporated in the history of film genres.

Historical Origins of Genres

Well before the advent of the movies, genres were used to classify works of literature, theater, music, painting, and other art forms. Tragedy was considered the most important genre in Aristotle's *Poetics* in 350 B.C.E., and more specific literary genres like poetic ballads, pastoral and epic poems, and dime novels were identified and refined in subsequent historical periods. Musical genres included classical sonatas and symphonies as well as popular love songs and children's lullabies. The seventeenth-century Dutch painter Pieter de Hooch created genre paintings that depicted scenes of domestic life and daily social encounters. In the eighteenth-century and early-nineteenth-century paintings of David Wilkie, William Hogarth, and others, genre came to suggest an image of a "slice of life," or scenes aimed at familiarity, recognition, and shared (if heightened) human emotions **[Figure 9.3]**. This combination of domestic realism and theatricality linked genres to the stage, particularly to the staging of melodramas, the most popular genre of the nineteenth century **[Figure 9.4]**. In these different forms, three functions for genre began to take shape:

- to provide models for producing other works
- to direct audience expectations
- to create categories for judging or evaluating a work

For painters in the eighteenth century, for example, historical paintings would need to follow certain generic rules about what objects to include in a painting about a naval victory; classical audiences would learn to expect all epic poems to begin with a generic invocation to the gods or a muse.

Early Film Genres

Early cinema immediately employed genres, building on the lessons of its predecessors in photography, literature, art, and music halls. Nineteenth-century portrait photography repeated standardized poses and backgrounds, and music halls developed formulas that would, for instance, predictably alternate a musical number with a comic skit, both of which would often feature recognizable conventions and rhythms. Although the first films of the 1890s searched out new subject matter, objects, and events, rough generic patterns quickly developed. Common formulas for short films included scenics such as *Panoramic View of*

Niagara Falls in Winter (1899), historical events as in *Carrie Nation Smashing a Saloon* (1901), and, less often acknowledged, semi-pornographic scenes in "blue movies," such as *From Show Girl to Burlesque Queen* (1903) **[Figure 9.5]**. As the film industry and its audiences expanded through the 1900s, other types of films filled the catalog of early genres: scenes from the theater, sporting events, and slapstick comedies. And as outdoor filming increased, westerns became common subjects.

1920s–1940s: Genre and the Studio System

Since the beginning of film history, the importance of genre and the popularity of specific genres have waxed and waned depending on the historical period and culture. Although films have used repeated subjects and formulas (such as Shakespearean plays and the chase, respectively) from their very beginnings, the rise of the studio system through the 1920s and 1930s provided extraordinarily fertile grounds for movie genres (see p. 20). In this context, the movie industry's model for genre parallels the industrial model for the Ford Motor Company. Fordism, the economic model that defined U.S. industry through much of the twentieth century, increased the amount and quality of output (of a kind of car) through the division of labor and the mass production of parts. As a result of that increased output, cost would decrease and, ideally, consumption of the product would increase. Tied to a studio system that adapted this industrial system of mass production, film genres enabled movie producers to reuse script formulas, actors, sets, and costumes to create, again and again, many different modified versions of a popular movie. In the same way that a consumer might buy a Ford automobile in a new color or different style every seven years, an audience might return every Memorial Day weekend to see the latest version of a swashbuckler adventure film franchise like *Pirates of the Caribbean: On Stranger Tides* (2011).

The most famous Hollywood studios differed in size, strategies, and styles—from the smaller United Artists to the massive MGM—but each used a production system based on the efficient recycling of formulas and conventions, stars, and sets. The system was headed by a mogul who assigned a producer, who in turn oversaw those many moveable parts that a studio had at its disposal. In this environment, individual studios refined their production line techniques, established their association with specific genres, and used and refined that expertise to develop those genres. Thus by the 1930s, Warner Bros. was identified with gangster films, Paramount with sophisticated comedies, MGM with musicals and melodramas, RKO with literary adaptations, Columbia Pictures with westerns, and Universal with horror films.

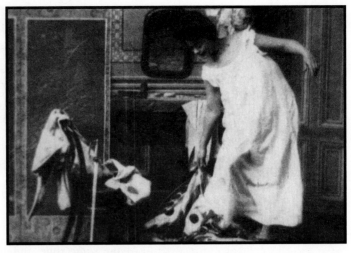

9.5 *From Show Girl to Burlesque Queen* (1903). Erotic "blue movies" emerged as an early film genre.

VIEWING CUE

Consider the historical precedents for the genre represented by the film screened in class. Do they come from literary or theatrical history? From a cultural or religious ritual?

1948–1970s: Postwar Film Genres

The *Paramount* decision of 1948, in which the Supreme Court ruled that the major studios violated antitrust laws by also owning movie theaters and therefore monopolizing the film business, undid the studio system and thus a cornerstone of movie genres. Without control of a distribution network of theaters to ensure the profitability of its production decisions, the studio system gradually

9.6   ***McCabe and Mrs. Miller*** (1971). Robert Altman and other New Hollywood filmmakers offered revisionist takes on Hollywood genres like the western.

began its decline, and with it waned the golden years of American film genres. Certainly genre movies continued to be made and enjoyed. Some, like film noir, appeared during this waning, and others, like blaxploitation, came about in the ensuing fragmentation: the former, with its shadowy characters and violent crimes, reflected the cultural stresses and instabilities that followed World War II, while the latter, featuring African American urban life and often machismo stereotypes, developed in the 1970s against the background of turbulent race relations.

At the same time, independent and less formulaic movies started to challenge the supremacy of genre films. Finally, the popularity of many genre films in the 1960s and 1970s depended upon a recycling of genres through other cultures and within American culture. These revisionist genre films, like Robert Altman's western *McCabe and Mrs. Miller* (1971) **[Figure 9.6]** and Wim Wenders's German film noir *The American Friend* (1977), often returned to the earlier conventions and icons but with an ironic and self-conscious perspective on those formulas and their relation to a changing world.

1970s–Present: New Hollywood, Sequels, and Global Genres

Jaws (1975) and *Star Wars* (1977) brought forth the era known as New Hollywood with film-school-educated directors drawing on established genres, special effects, and large advertising budgets to create blockbusters. Video and foreign sales helped such movies generate worldwide business, and the new corporate entities that owned the studios relied heavily on sequels and franchises, including those for blockbusters like *Star Wars*, to guarantee repeat successes. *The Godfather: Part II* (1974), for example, deepened the saga of the Corleone Mafia family and was hailed as a masterpiece, while contemporary sequels like *American Pie 2* (2001) and *Rush Hour 3* (2007) combine characters and plot elements with new situations to deliver familiar entertainment **[Figure 9.7]**. Franchises such as the live-action *Spider-Man* films (2002, 2004, 2007, 2012) spread genre elements into other platforms—for instance, video games.

Increasingly, the commercial movie business was not centered only on Hollywood. Hong Kong action films—for example, John Woo's *The Killer* (1989)—established a worldwide fan base by combining the successful national and regional genre of martial arts films with formulas of Hollywood action films, and they proved that films made outside Hollywood could be globally profitable. Bollywood films, characterized by their extravagant song-and-dance sequences and megastars, deepened their popularity beyond the Indian subcontinent and South Asian communities abroad by

9.7   ***Rush Hour 3*** (2007). Sequels and franchises cash in on the repetitive pleasures of genre formulas.

Rituals, Conventions, Archetypes, and Formulas: Movie Genres | CHAPTER 9 321

relying on the Internet and DVD distribution. *Devdas* (2002), a spectacular romance about two young soul mates separated when young and doomed to live lives of unfulfilled love, became widely distributed and popular, especially in England and the United States **[Figure 9.8]**.

As this section reveals, history renews some genres and demands the invention of new ones. Because genre is always a historical negotiation, an awareness of the vicissitudes of cultural history only makes movie genres more vital and meaningful.

9.8 *Devdas* (2002). Internationally successful, *Devdas* illustrates the successful globalization of national genres.

The Elements of Film Genre

Genres identify group, social, or community activity and seem opposed to the individual creativity we associate with many art forms, including the art film (see Chapter 8). A film may work creatively and individually within its genre, but the work must begin within the framework of acknowledged conventions and formulas that audiences expect. Our recognition of these formulas represents a bond between filmmakers and audiences, determining a large part of how we see and understand a film. Film genres thus describe a kind of social contract, one that allows us to see a film as part of both a historical evolution and a cultural community. For instance, the western, recognizable by scenes of open plains and lone cowboys, engages audiences' common knowledge of and interest in U.S. history and "how the West was won" in different ways and to different ends over time **[Figures 9.9a and 9.9b]**.

▶ **VIEWING CUE**

For a movie you have recently watched, identify the genre and describe three conventions typically associated with this genre.

(a)

(b)

9.9 **(a)** *My Darling Clementine* (1946) and **(b)** *Bad Girls* (1994). Genres represent a bond between filmmakers and audiences that must be renegotiated by each genre film. While one western may meet expectations about cowboys in gunfights, another may realign those expectations by making women gunfighters the center of the story.

9.10 *Hairspray* (2007). The set of *The Corny Collins Show,* around which much of the film revolves.

Conventions, Formulas, and Expectations

The most conspicuous dimensions of film genres are the conventions, formulas, and expectations through which we identify certain genres and distinguish them from others. *Generic conventions* are properties or features that identify a genre, such as character types, settings, props, or events that are repeated from film to film. In westerns, cowboys often travel alone; in crime films, a seductive woman often foils the hard-boiled detective. Generic conventions also include **iconography**, images or image patterns with specific connotations or meanings. Dark alleys and smoky bars are staple images in crime movies; the world of the theater and entertainment industry is frequently the setting for musicals, as in *Hairspray* (2007) **[Figure 9.10]**. These conventions and iconographies can sometimes acquire larger meanings and connotations that align them with other social and cultural *archetypes*—that is, spiritual, psychological, or cultural models expressing certain virtues, values, or timeless realities. For example, a flood is an archetype used in some disaster films to represent the end of a corrupt life and the beginning of a new spiritual life, such as in Peter Weir's *The Last Wave* (1977) with its ominous visions of a tidal wave that will destroy Australia, according to the Aborigines who predict it, as part of a spiritual process **[Figure 9.11]**.

When generic conventions are put in motion as part of a plot, they become *generic formulas*, the patterns for developing stories in a particular genre. Generic formulas suggest that individual conventions used in a particular film can be arranged in a standard way or in a variation on the standard. With horror films, such as Stanley Kubrick's *The Shining* (1980), we immediately recognize the beginning of one of these formulas: a couple and their child decide to live alone in a large, mysterious hotel isolated in the mountains of Colorado **[Figure 9.12]**. The rest of the formula proceeds as follows: strange and disturbing events indicate that the house/hotel is haunted (and in *The Shining* the haunting begins to take over and

9.11 *The Last Wave* (1977). Archetypal imagery, such as the tidal wave shown here, underpins generic conventions.

9.12 *The Shining* (1980). Jack Nicholson as a writer who suffers a mental breakdown within the walls of a deceptively peaceful Colorado hotel.

derange the husband/father); the haunting leads to frightening visions and begins to destroy the characters, who flee into the night.

In some cases, these generic formulas can also become associated with *myths*—spiritual and cultural stories that describe a defining action or event for a group of people or an entire community. All cultures have important myths that help secure a shared cultural identity. One may celebrate a national event associated with a particular holiday, such as the Fourth of July; another culture may see the birth and rise of a great hero from the past as the key to its cultural history. From *Patton* (1970) to *Malcolm X* (1992), historical epics often re-create an actual historical figure as a cultural myth in which the character's actions determine a national identity—in these cases, a U.S. army commander who turned the tide of World War II, and a black American Muslim minister who served as spokesperson of the Nation of Islam and is often considered the father of the Black Panther movement in the United States **[Figures 9.13a and 9.13b]**. The narrative formulas of science fiction films can also relate to broader myths, such as the Faustian myth of selling one's soul for knowledge and power or the story of Adam and Eve's eating from the tree of knowledge and their subsequent punishment. Science fiction films, such as Stanley Kubrick's *2001: A Space Odyssey* (1968), frequently recount explorations or inventions that violate the laws of nature or the spiritual world.

Triggered by a film's promotion or by the film itself, *generic expectations* describe a viewer's experience and knowledge while watching a film that help to anticipate the meaning of particular conventions or the direction of certain narrative formulas. Thus a narrative's beginning, characters, or setting can cue certain expectations about the genre that the film then satisfies or frustrates. The beginning of *Jaws*, in which an unidentified young woman swims alone at night in a dark and ominous ocean, leads viewers to anticipate shock and danger, participate in the unfolding of the genre, and respond to any surprises this particular film may offer. In the case of *Jaws*, the fact that much of the ensuing plot takes place on a sunny beach and open ocean, rather than in the darkened, confined houses of the usual horror film, is a clever variation that keeps the formula fresh and viewers' expectations attentive.

Indeed, generic expectations underscore the important role of viewers in determining a genre and how that role connects genres to a specific social, cultural, or national environment. Partly because of Hollywood's global reach and the extensive group of genre films it has produced, most audiences around the world will, for instance, quickly recognize the cues for a horror film or a western. Other non-Hollywood genres may not generate such clear expectations outside their native culture. Generic expectations triggered by a martial arts film are likely to be more sophisticated in China than in the United States. Likewise, the religious films, or *cine de*

▶ **VIEWING CUE**

Reflect on a film trailer you recently saw. Based on the generic expectations triggered by the trailer, what conventions or narrative formulas could you expect in the film itself? ⏸

9.13   **(a) *Patton*** (1970) and **(b) *Malcolm X*** (1992). Historical epics often use a heroic figure to build a national myth.

9.14 *Viridiana* (1961). Reactions to Luis Buñuel's film will vary according to the audience's familiarity with the genre of religious films it attacks.

sacerdotes, of the 1940s and 1950s were well known in Spain but their conventions and formulas may hardly be recognized by viewers from other cultures (even those international viewers familiar with Luis Buñuel's 1961 attack on this national genre, *Viridiana*) **[Figure 9.14]**.

Even within a culture the popularity of certain genres depends on shifting audience tastes and expectations over time. Movie producers make films based on beliefs about which films audiences are likely to identify with, enjoy, and therefore pay to go see. This economic formula thus reflects the historical periods and cultures in which genres take shape and the ability of these genres to assimilate historical and social conditions. For example, musicals proliferated in the 1930s because they offered audiences a clear escape from the anxieties of the Depression; film noir crime films flourished in the 1940s and early 1950s during and in the wake of the social upheaval of World War II; U.S. science fiction films had their heyday in the 1950s, when films like *The Day the Earth Stood Still* (1951) packaged and mythologized fears about political and other invasions as concrete aliens and monsters that could be confronted and understood **[Figure 9.15]**. Audience expectations signal the social vitality of a particular genre, but that vitality changes as genres move from culture to culture or between historical periods within a single culture. In this sense, genres can tell us a great deal about community or national identity.

Movie Genres: Six Paradigms

From their first days, movies were organized as genres according to subject matter: films about a famous person, panoramic views, and so on. As movies became more sophisticated, however, genres grew into more complex narrative organizations with recognizable formal conventions. By 1923, one poll of high school students identified their two favorite movies as Rex Ingram's epic war story *The Four Horsemen of the Apocalypse* (1921) and the exotic romance *The Sheik* (1921), both featuring Rudolph Valentino. Two or three times a week these young people would go to the movies, attracted to the clearly identified generic preferences for westerns, comedies, detective stories, romances, and melodramatic tragedies. As films developed and differentiated stylistic and formal conventions, these generic preferences would change and grow.

Assembling a list of movie genres can be more daunting and uncertain than it appears. Genres are a product of a perspective that groups individual movies together, sometimes in many different ways. For some scholars or viewers,

9.15 *The Day the Earth Stood Still* (1951). Science fiction films took over the Cold War era.

for instance, film noir is an important movie genre that surfaced in the 1940s, whereas for others, it is less a film genre than a style that appears in multiple genres of the period. Moreover, a particular genre designation may encompass too much or too little: comedies might appear too grand a category for some critics, and screwball comedies may seem too limited a group to be termed a genre. To better understand the multiple combinations and subdivisions of genres, two terms are helpful: **hybrid genres** are those created through the interaction of different genres to produce fusions, such as romantic comedies or musical horror films like *The Rocky Horror Picture Show* (1975) **[Figure 9.16]**. **Subgenres** are specific versions of a genre denoted by an adjective, for example, the *spaghetti western* (produced in Italy) or the *slapstick comedy*. The idea of genres as constellations suggests how genres, as distinctive patterns, can overlap and shift their shape depending on their relation to other genres or as extensions of a primary field. *Blazing Saddles* (1974), for example, belongs both to the subgenre of comedic western and to the hybrid genre of western comedy; seeing that film from one perspective or the other can make a difference in how we appreciate it **[Figure 9.17]**.

9.16   ***The Rocky Horror Picture Show*** (1975). A hybrid of horror film and musical comedy genres, this film also shares characteristics with other cult films.

While hybrid genres and subgenres show the complexity of genres as constellations, it is also helpful to demarcate major genres. Here we will focus on six important groupings of films that are generally talked about as genres: comedies, westerns, melodramas, musicals, horror films, and crime films. We'll aim to define each genre as it has appeared in different cultures and at different points in history, as well as how its social contract changes with different audiences. We will also highlight a selection of defining characteristics for each genre, including

▶ **VIEWING CUE**
Think back to a film you recently watched. Can you identify it as a particular hybrid and/or subgenre? ⏸

- the distinguishing features of the characters, narrative, and visual style
- the reflection of social rituals in the genre
- the production of certain historical hybrids or subgenres out of the generic paradigm

Although these generic blueprints will inevitably be reductive and the generic distinctions will overlap, mapping each of these paradigms can guide our explorations of specific films and how they engage their audiences.

Comedies

Film **comedies** have flourished since the invention of cinema in 1895, as comic actors took their talents to the screen where they could be appreciated even without synchronized sound. Rooted in the *commedia dell'arte*, Punch and Judy, and the

9.17   ***Blazing Saddles*** (1974). Comedic western or western comedy?

9.18 *Saturday Afternoon* (1926). Classic silent comedies, such as this Mack Sennett film, depend on physical gags.

vaudeville stage acts that would produce Buster Keaton and a host of other early comedians, film comedy is one of the first and most enduring of film genres. Its many variations can be condensed into these main traits:

- central characters who are often defined by distinctive physical features, such as body shape and size, costuming, or manner of speaking
- narratives that emphasize episodes or "gags" more than plot continuity or progression and that usually conclude happily
- theatrical acting styles in which characters physically and playfully interact with the mise-en-scène that surrounds them

From the 1920s comedies of producer Mack Sennett to the awkward and stumbling Woody Allen as Alvy Singer in *Annie Hall* (1977), comic figures stand out physically because of their body type, facial expressions, and characteristic gestures. Although comedies can develop intricate plots, their focus is usually on individual vignettes. In Sennett's *Saturday Afternoon* (1926), Harry Langdon balances between moving cars and hangs from telephone poles **[Figure 9.18]**. In *Annie Hall*, Alvy jumps around a kitchen chasing lobsters and later squirms at a family dinner table where he imagines himself perceived by others as a Hasidic Jew. In these episodic encounters, the comic world becomes a stage full of unpredictable gags and theatrical possibilities.

Comedies celebrate the harmony and resiliency of social life. Although many viewers associate comedies with laughs and humor, comedy is more fundamentally about social reconciliation and the triumph of the physical over the intellectual. In comic narratives, obstacles or antagonists—in homes, marriages, communities, and nations—are overcome or dismissed by the physical dexterity or verbal wit of a character, or perhaps by luck, good timing, or magic. In *Bringing Up Baby* (1938), Katharine Hepburn is a flighty socialite who moves and talks so fast that she bewilders the verbally and physically bumbling paleontologist Cary Grant, who will inevitably forsake his scientific priorities for the joys of an improbable romance with her. In *Groundhog Day* (1993), Bill Murray plays a weatherman with many social and professional flaws who falls into a magical world where he relives the day again and again, with the ability to correct his previous errors and romantic blunders. The unlikely hero of *Knocked Up* (2007) finds in his own childishness a resource for impending fatherhood **[Figure 9.19]**.

Perhaps the most obvious convention in comedies is the happy ending, in which couples or individuals are united in the form of a family unit or the promise of one to come. Very often, traditional comedies begin with some discord or disruption in social life or in the relationship between two people (lovers are separated or angry, for instance); after various trials or misunderstandings, harmony is restored and individuals are

9.19 *Knocked Up* (2007). In this film, slacker Ben, much like a child himself, attempts to prove his fatherhood potential.

united. In *The Proposal* (2009), for example, a demanding boss asks her assistant to marry her so she can avoid deportation back to Canada. Despite their mutual annoyance with the arrangement, they visit his family home in Alaska where they comically struggle to maintain the sham engagement, only to actually fall in love in the end [**Figure 9.20**].

9.20   *The Proposal* (2009). Comic resiliency ultimately brings a seemingly mismatched couple together.

Slapstick, Screwball, and Romantic Comedies. Historically, as the Hollywood film comedy responded to audience expectations in changing contexts, the genre itself endured numerous permutations and structural changes. Three salient subgenres emerged as a result: slapstick comedies, screwball comedies, and romantic comedies.

Slapstick comedies, marked by their physical humor and stunts, comprised some of the first narrative films. In the 1910s, the initial versions of this subgenre used printed intertitles rather than spoken dialogue and ran from a few minutes to about fifteen minutes in length. Early films like those of Mack Sennett's Keystone Kops revolved around physical stunts set within fairly restricted social spaces.

By the 1920s, comedy had integrated its gags and physical actions into feature-length films. This move allowed physical games to develop new twists and turns over the course of narrative time within a social arena. Even so, the singular slapstick instants are what stand out. For example, unforgettable is the moment in *The General* (1927) when Buster Keaton misfires the cannon vertically into the air and manages to avoid disaster when the cannonball fortuitously misses him and just happens to destroy an enemy bridge. Slapstick comedies reemerged in the 1980s with such films as *Porky's* (1982) and *Police Academy* (1984). The ingenuity of physical comedy gave way in these films targeted at young male audiences to scatological and sexual jokes. In *Monty Python's The Meaning of Life* (1983) [**Figure 9.21**] and *Monty Python and the Holy Grail* (1975), slapstick becomes an ingredient of nonstop social satire. Today the genre is popular again, featuring comic stars such as Mike Myers in *Austin Powers in Goldmember* (2002) and Zach Galifianakis in *The Hangover* (2009) [**Figure 9.22**].

In the 1930s and 1940s, **screwball comedies** transformed the humor of the physical into fast-talking verbal gymnastics, arguably displacing sexual energy with barbed verbal exchanges between men and women when the Production Code barred more direct expression.

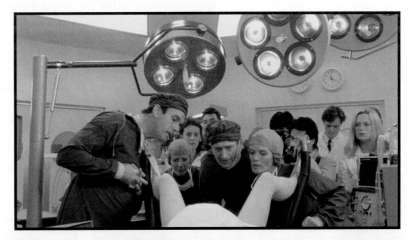

9.21   *Monty Python's The Meaning of Life* (1983). This birthing scene is an example of the slapstick that fills this social satire.

9.22   *The Hangover* (2009). Slapstick comedy has reinvented itself for new audiences, often through exaggerated physical humor involving sex and alcohol.

In effect, these films usually redirected the comic focus from the individual clown to the confused heterosexual couple. *It Happened One Night* (1934), *Bringing Up Baby*, *His Girl Friday* (1940), and *The Philadelphia Story* (1940) are among the best-known examples of screwball comedies; each features independent women who resist, mock, and challenge the crusty rules of their social worlds. When the right man arrives or returns, one who can match these women in charm and physical and verbal skills, confrontation leads to love. Focused on the nonstop chatter and quirkiness of its heroine, *All About Steve* (2009) revives some elements of this formula and its pleasures.

In **romantic comedies**, humor takes a second place to happiness. Popular since the 1930s and 1940s, romantic comedies like *Small Town Girl* (1936), *The Shop Around the Corner* (1940), and *Adam's Rib* (1949) concentrate on the emotional attraction of a couple in a consistently lighthearted manner. This subgenre draws attention to a peculiar or awkward social predicament (in *Adam's Rib*, for example, the husband and wife lawyers oppose each other in the courtroom) that romance will eventually overcome on the way to a happy ending. More recent examples of the "rom-com," as its recent exemplars have come to be known, include Nora Ephron's *You've Got Mail* (a 1998 remake of Ernst Lubitsch's *The Shop Around the Corner*), where the comic predicaments have contemporary twists—e-mail replaces the letters of the first version—but the formula and conventions remain fairly consistent. Stephen Frears's romantic comedy *My Beautiful Laundrette* (1985) suggests, however, the range of possibilities in the creative (and here political) reworking of any genre. In this case, the social complications include a wildly dysfunctional Pakistani family in London and the romance that blossoms between the entrepreneurial son and a white man who is his childhood friend and a former right-wing punk [**Figure 9.23**].

Westerns

Like film comedies, **westerns** are a staple of Hollywood, although their popularity has waxed and waned in different historical eras. This genre grew out of late-nineteenth-century stories, dime novels, and journalistic accounts of the wild American West [**Figure 9.24**]. The western began to take shape in the first years of the movie industry, as a kind of travelogue of a recent but now-lost historical period. From *The Great Train Robbery* (1903) to the HBO series *Deadwood* (2004–2006), the western has grown over one hundred years into a surprisingly complex

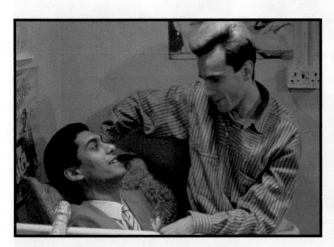

9.23 *My Beautiful Laundrette* (1985). Director Stephen Frears and writer Hanif Kureishi update romantic comedy to tell an interracial gay love story.

9.24 *Buffalo Bill's Wild West* (1899). At the end of the nineteenth century, William Cody's adventures as an army scout were reenacted in dime novels, stage melodramas, and his wildly popular show, establishing cowboy iconography for movie westerns to build upon.

genre while also retaining its fundamental elements:

- characters, almost always male, whose physical and mental toughness separate them from the crowds of modern civilization
- narratives that follow some version of a quest into the natural world
- a stylistic emphasis on open, natural spaces and settings, such as the western frontier regions of the United States

9.25 *Butch Cassidy and the Sundance Kid* (1969). Paul Newman and Robert Redford incarnate western heroes for the 1960s.

John Wayne as the Ringo Kid in *Stagecoach* (1939) has a physical energy and determination that is echoed by Paul Newman and Robert Redford as *Butch Cassidy and the Sundance Kid* (1969) **[Figure 9.25]**. Never at ease with the law or the restrictions of civilization, these men find themselves on vague searches for justice, peace, adventure, freedom, and perhaps a treasure that offers all these rewards. Quests through wide-open canyons and deserts seem at once to threaten, inspire, and humble these western heroes.

Through the trials of a lone protagonist, rugged individualism becomes the measure of any social relationship and of the values of most western communities. Even when they are part of a gang, as in *The Magnificent Seven* (1960), these individuals are usually loners or mavericks rather than representative leaders. More than in historical epics, violent confrontations are central to these narratives, and this violence is primarily measured by the ability and will of the individual rather than the mass, nation, or community, even when it is directed against Native Americans. In *High Plains Drifter* (1973), the moody Clint Eastwood must protect a frightened town from the vengeance of outlaws **[Figure 9.26]**. When a violent showdown concerns two groups—as in the gunfight at the OK Corral between the Earps and the Clantons in John Ford's *My Darling Clementine*—the battle is often about individual justice or revenge (of sons and brothers) or about who has the rightful claims to the frontier.

Epic, Existential, and Political Westerns.

Like most film genres, westerns have responded to changing audiences. During the early twentieth century, they were popular among the mass audiences of early cinema and associated with such popular forms as Wild West shows. With several significant exceptions, including *The Covered Wagon* (1923), westerns were not a particularly respected genre in the 1920s and early 1930s. Since then, however, three hybrids or subgenres have distinguished the western: the epic western, the existential western, and the political western.

Within the constellation of westerns, the **epic western** concentrates on action and movement, developing a heroic character whose quests and battles serve to define the nation and its origins. With its roots in literature and epic paintings, this genre appears early and often in film history, foregrounding the spectacle of open land and beautiful scenery. An early instance of the epic, *The Covered Wagon* follows a wagon train of settlers into the harsh but breathtaking frontier,

9.26 *High Plains Drifter* (1973). The western hero is often a loner for whom violence comes naturally.

9.27 *Dances with Wolves* (1990). Kevin Costner plays a sympathetic Civil War veteran who commiserates with Native Americans in this modern epic western.

where their fortitude and determination establish the expanding spirit of America. Years later, *Dances with Wolves* (1990) describes a more complex struggle for national identity as a traumatized Civil War veteran allies himself with Native Americans **[Figure 9.27]**.

In the 1950s, one of the most interesting decades for westerns, the **existential western** took shape. In this introspective version of the genre, the traditional western hero is troubled by his changing social status and his self-doubts, often as the frontier depicted in these films is more populated and civilized. *The Searchers* (1956), *The Furies* (1950), *Johnny Guitar* (1954), *Shane* (1953), and *The Left-Handed Gun* (1958) are existential westerns with protagonists who are troubled in their sense of purpose. The traditionally male domain of the West is now contested by women, evil is harder to locate and usually more insidious, and the encroachment of society complicates life and suggests the end of the cowboy lifestyle. Even during the 1990s, this subgenre endured, most notably with *Unforgiven* (1992): here the formerly unbendable Clint Eastwood is now financially strapped, somewhat hypocritical, and disturbingly aware that killing is an ugly business.

By the 1960s and 1970s, the **political western** had evolved out of the troubled territory of existential westerns: in this more contemporary and critical western, the ideology and politics that have always informed the genre are foregrounded; the heroism associated with individual independence and the use of violence naturalized in epic westerns become precisely what is questioned. In *The Man Who Shot Liberty Valance* (1962), the heroic myth of the American West is exposed as a lie. With only communities rather than frontiers to conquer in *The Wild Bunch* (1969), aging cowboys are less interested in justice and freedom than in indiscriminate and grotesque killing. More recently the western genre has remained visible in a variety of contemporary films, such as *There Will Be Blood* (2007) and *No Country for Old Men* (2007), where many of the conventional motifs and icons of violence and conquest reappear in more horrifying and exaggerated forms than ever before **[Figure 9.28]**.

Melodramas

Movie **melodramas** are one of the more difficult genres to define because melodramatic characters and actions can be part of many other kinds of movies. The word itself indicates a combination of the intensities of music (*melos*) and the interaction of human conflicts (*drama*). Indebted to a nineteenth-century theatrical heritage in which social and domestic oppression created heightened emotional dramas, film melodramas arrived virtually simultaneously with the first developments in film narrative. While the term "melodrama" was

9.28 *There Will Be Blood* (2007). Contemporary films incorporate traditional western conventions and formulas like frontiers and violent conquests—but often in more grotesque and unsettling ways, such as when Daniel Plainview beats Eli to death with a bowling pin at the end of this film.

used in different ways by early film critics, the contemporary definition developed by film scholars includes these fundamental formulas and conventions:

- characters defined by their situation or basic traits rather than their deeds, who struggle, often desperately, to express their feelings or emotions
- narratives that rely on coincidences and reversals and build toward emotional or physical climaxes
- a visual style that emphasizes emotion or elemental struggle, whether in interior scenes and close-ups or in action tableaux

From D. W. Griffith's *Way Down East* (1920) to Kimberly Peirce's *Boys Don't Cry* (1999), the central character is restrained, repressed, or victimized by more powerful forces of society. These forces may pit a dominating masculinity against a weaker femininity. In Griffith's film, a

9.29 *Way Down East* (1920). Claustrophobic interiors represent the melodramatic heroine's victimization.

city villain threatens an innocent virgin, and in *Boys Don't Cry*, Nebraska country boys assault and murder Brandon Teena when they discover that he was born female (and named Teena Brandon) and has been living as a male. In the first film, claustrophobic rooms dramatize this victimization **[Figure 9.29]**, until a climactic chase over a frozen river brings the conflict between good and evil outside for the world to witness. In the second, medium shots and close-ups of the protagonist emphasize the strains and contradictions of identity **[Figure 9.30]**. In each of these films, true to the conventions of melodrama, the story reaches a breaking point with the threat of death: one character almost drifts away on ice floes; the other is senselessly shot and killed.

As social rituals, melodramas parallel and contrast with westerns. Individualism and private life anchor this genre as well, but the drama is not about conquering a frontier and finding a home; rather, it is about the strain on and often failure of the individual to act or speak out within an already established home, family, or community. Melodramas thus develop a conflict between interior emotions and exterior restrictions, between yearning or loss and satisfaction or renewal. One or more women are typically at the center of melodrama, illustrating how historically women have been excluded from or limited in their access to public powers of expression. Mise-enscène and narrative space also play a major stylistic role in melodrama: for example, in Griffith's films, individuals, usually female, retreat into smaller and smaller private spaces while some obvious or implied hostile force, often male, threatens and drives them further into a desperate internal sanctuary. These rituals are often graphically acted out. In Elia Kazan's film version of

9.30 *Boys Don't Cry* (1999). Melodrama relies on close-ups to tell stories of contested identity—here the protagonist's expression of gender.

A Streetcar Named Desire (1951), Blanche and Stella, confined in a run-down, claustrophobic home in New Orleans, also confine and repress their memories of a lost family history; their desires to escape are channeled through their sexuality. For Stella, that means accepting her husband Stanley's violent control of her; for Blanche, it means becoming a victim of Stanley's power and, after he rapes her, retreating into madness.

Physical, Family, and Social Melodramas. Whereas early melodramas depicted female distress and entrapment in time and space, those formulas have grown subtler, or at least more realistic, over the years. Three subgenres of melodramas that usually overlap and rarely appear in complete isolation from one another can be distinguished: physical, family, and social melodramas.

Physical melodramas focus on the physical plight and material conditions that repress or control the protagonist's desires and emotions; these physical restrictions may be related to the places and people that surround that person or may simply be a product of the person's physical size or color. One of the first great film melodramas, D. W. Griffith's *Broken Blossoms* (1919) is also one of the most grisly: in an atmosphere of drugs, violence, and poverty, a brutal boxer, Battling Burrows, hounds and physically terrifies his illegitimate and frail daughter, Lucy. He eventually beats her to death (as she retreats into smaller and smaller rooms) and is himself killed by Lucy's one friend, a Chinese immigrant (identified in the subtitles only as the Yellow Man), who then commits suicide. Although most melodramas do not so definitively emphasize the physical plight of the heroine, viewers can still recognize this generic focus on bodily or material strain in such melodramas as *Dark Victory* (1939), about a woman with a terminal brain illness, and *Magnificent Obsession* (1954), about a blind woman whose vision is ultimately restored. Even a film like *Black Swan* (2010) might be best understood as a contemporary variation on a melodrama about sexual identity, bodily restraint, and the eruption of violence **[Figure 9.31]**.

Although physical arrangements play a part in them, **family** melodramas elaborate the confines and restrictions of the protagonist by investigating the psychological and gendered forces of the family. For many viewers, this is the quintessential form of melodrama, in which women and young people especially must struggle against patriarchal authority, economic dependency, and confining gender roles. In Douglas Sirk's *Written on the Wind* (1956), a Texas millionaire marries a beautiful but naive secretary and then tortures himself wondering whether the baby they are expecting is his or his best friend's (the man she should have married); the corruption and confusion of this household grow more intense and manic through the constant baiting and manipulations of a sister whose restlessness is expressed as sexual promiscuity. While the family melodrama came to prominence in the postwar period as gender and familial roles were being redefined, similar themes are found in soap operas and their nighttime serial counterparts such as *Dallas* (1978–1991) and *Desperate Housewives* (2004–2012). In *Ordinary People* (1980), an outwardly prosperous family is emotionally crippled by the loss of one son, the mother's withdrawal of affection from the other, and the father's powerlessness, while in Mira Nair's *The Namesake* (2006),

9.31 *Black Swan* (2010). While ostensibly about the world of ballet, this film is perhaps best understood as a melodrama about physical and sexual repression, as Nina battles pressures from her mother, her director, and herself to become the "perfect" Swan Queen.

family melodrama becomes a generational and transnational affair in which parents who emigrated from India and a son raised in New York struggle to find common ground [Figure 9.32].

Social melodramas extend the melodramatic crisis of the family to include larger historical, community, and economic issues. In these films, the losses, sufferings, and frustrations of the protagonist are visibly part of social or national politics. Earlier melodramas fit this subgenre—for example, John Stahl's *Imitation of Life* (1934), remade by Douglas Sirk in 1959, makes the family melodrama inseparable from larger issues of racism as a black

9.32 *The Namesake* (2006). Generations of an immigrant family struggle to find common ground in this transnational family melodrama.

daughter passes for white. Modern melodramas also commonly explore social and political dimensions of personal conflicts: in Lee Daniels's *Precious* (2009), the painful struggles of an overweight African American adolescent become inseparable from the social violence and poverty that surround her at home, in school, and on the streets of Harlem [Figure 9.33]. In *Brokeback Mountain* (2005), male lovers are kept apart by social conventions (and arguably generic ones as well, as cowboys are not usually shown falling in love with each other) [Figure 9.34].

Musicals

As we noted in Chapter 5, when synchronous sound came to the cinema in 1927, the film industry quickly embraced the new technology and moved to integrate music and song into the stories. Precedents for film **musicals** range from traditional opera to vaudeville and musical theater, in which songs either supported or punctuated the story. Since the first musicals, the following have been their most common components:

9.33 *Precious* (2009). In this successful indie film, melodrama underpins the social crises of an impoverished teen.

- characters who act out and express their emotions and thoughts through song and dance
- plots interrupted or moved forward by musical numbers
- spectacular sets and settings, such as Broadway theaters, fairs, and dramatic social or grand natural backgrounds, or animated environments

In *Gold Diggers of 1933* (1933) and *The Sound of Music* (1965), groups of characters escape the complexities of the situation

9.34 *Brokeback Mountain* (2005). The political melodrama of homosexual lovers kept apart by social and generic conventions.

9.35 *The Sound of Music* (1965). The Nazi threat cannot dampen the spirit expressed through song.

(Depression-era society and Austria threatened by Nazis, respectively) by breaking into song **[Figure 9.35]**. Whether on a Broadway stage or against the beauty of an Alpine setting, characters in musicals speak their hearts and minds most articulately through music and dance.

As social markers, musicals are the flip side of melodramas, highlighting the joy of expression rather than the pain of repression. With musicals, the tearful cries of melodrama give way to the beautiful articulations of music. Both focus on personal emotions, but in musicals, song and dance become the longed-for vehicles for the repressed and inexpressible emotions of the melodrama. In musicals, the present easily usurps the past. There are certainly romantic crises, social problems, and physical dangers in the narrative, but in most cases, these obstacles are secondary and any difficulties can be remedied or at least put into perspective by the immediacy of song, music, and dance. With more plot than most musicals, *West Side Story* (1961) features all the tragedy and violence found in Shakespeare's *Romeo and Juliet* (on which it is based) and a social commentary on Puerto Rican/white relationships in New York: gangs fight, lovers are separated, and horrible deaths happen. But even during the most troubling situations, song and dance transform battle cries into gaiety ("The Jet Song") **[Figure 9.36]**, patriotic idealism into comic satire ("America"), and even a tragic death into a peaceful vision ("Somewhere").

9.36 *West Side Story* (1961). Social antagonisms are expressed through song and dance.

Julie Taymor's *Across the Universe* (2007), similarly rich with plot and narrative, weaves together the stories of several characters living in New York City during the turbulent 1960s. Musical enactments of Beatles songs express the "free love" spirit and the darker, politically charged moments of the decade. "I Am the Walrus," parts of which were written by John Lennon while high on LSD, illustrates the drug-fueled art scene of the era, while "Let It Be" sums up the emotion and angst surrounding the tragic deaths of a brother and a boyfriend resulting from the 12th Street riot in Detroit and the Vietnam War. "All You Need Is Love" is of course the song that pleads for an end to the turbulence and the political and social strife that mark the period and the lives of the characters.

Theatrical, Integrated, and Animated Musicals. After the first feature-length musical, *The Jazz Singer* (1927), musicals adapted to reflect different cultural predicaments. Of the many types of musicals, we can identify three subgenres: theatrical, integrated, and animated musicals. Many examples of each subgenre are adaptations of Broadway musicals or other theatrical sources.

No doubt the best known, **theatrical musicals** situate the musical convention onstage or "backstage"; here it is unmistakable that the fantasy and art of the theater supersede the reality of the street. One of the finest early musicals, *42nd Street* (1933) is partly about the complicated love lives of its characters: a Broadway director who wants one last hit play; the starlet Dorothy Brock who juggles lovers offstage; and the chorus girl Peggy Sawyer who substitutes for the star and saves the show. What ultimately gathers all these hopes and conflicts is, of course, the musical show itself: through the remarkable choreography of Busby Berkeley and hit tunes like "Shuffle Off to Buffalo," jealousies and doubts turn into a spectacular celebration of life on Broadway **[Figure 9.37]**. Although theatrical musicals later waned in popularity, *All That Jazz* (1979) resurrected this subgenre as an exaggerated and even self-indulgent staging of the autobiography of choreographer Bob Fosse. In a recent resurgence, *Chicago* (2002) weaves the drama of abused and downtrodden women into an energetic musical in which the theatrics of song and dance burst open prison cells, and *Dreamgirls* (2006) dramatizes the story of Motown.

9.37 *42nd Street* (1933). The "Shuffle Off to Buffalo" number is presented as part of a Broadway show, which acts as the central mise-en-scène of the narrative.

When musicals began to integrate musical numbers into more common situations and realistic actions, they became **integrated musicals**. Here the idyllic and redemptive moments of song and dance are part of everyday lives. In *My Fair Lady* (1964), the grueling transformation of a street girl into a glamorous aristocrat is described by song; in the case of numbers like "The Rain in Spain," songs actually assist that transformation. *Dancer in the Dark* (2000) and *Pennies from Heaven* (1981) are more ironic versions of this subgenre. In both films, musical interludes allow the characters (a blind woman accused of murder and a sheet-music salesman during the Depression, respectively) to unexpectedly transcend the tragedies and traumas of life.

Beginning with *Snow White and the Seven Dwarfs* (1937) and increasing in popularity and frequency within the last decades, **animated musicals** use cartoon figures and stories to present songs and music. Moving in the opposite direction of integrated musicals, these films—from *Fantasia* (1940) and *Yellow Submarine* (1968) to the Disney features *The Little Mermaid* (1989) **[Figure 9.38]** and *Beauty and the Beast* (1991) and Sylvain Chomet's offbeat *The Triplets of Belleville* (2003) **[Figure 9.39]**—fully embrace the fantastic and utopian possibilities of music to make animals human, nature magical, or human life, as Mary Poppins says, "practically perfect in every way."

9.38 *The Little Mermaid* (1989). The resurgence of the animated musical highlights the utopian impulse of film genres, through which songs link the characters to fantasies and fantasy worlds.

9.39 *The Triplets of Belleville* (2003). An offbeat animated musical takes advantage of the magical and transformative powers of animation as they parallel the expressive power of song.

9.40 *The Golem* (1920). Horror takes monstrous physical form in this German expressionist film.

Horror Films

Horror has been a popular literary and artistic theme at least since Sophocles's account of Oedipus's terrifying realization of his fate, the horrifying suicide of his mother, and his ghastly self-blinding. The supernatural mysteries of Gothic novels such as *The Monk* (1796) were followed in the nineteenth century by tales of monsters and murder, such as *Frankenstein* (1818) and *Dracula* (1897). Occasionally overlapping with science fiction, **horror films** have crossed cultures and appeared in various forms throughout film history. The fundamental elements of horror films include

- characters with physical, psychological, and/or spiritual deformities
- narratives built on suspense, surprise, and shock
- visual compositions that move between the dread of not seeing and the horror of seeing

In Carl Boese and Paul Wegener's *The Golem* (1920) **[Figure 9.40]** and Ridley Scott's *Alien* (1979) **[Figure 9.41]**, monstrous characters terrify the humans around them with their grotesque shapes and actions, lurking on the fringes of the visible world. Each film is infused with a nervous tension at the mere prospect of seeing a horror that exists just out of sight, a suspense that explodes when the creatures suddenly appear.

9.41 *Alien* (1979). Suspense and terror build as the grotesque creature lurks on the fringes of the visible, until finally bursting into view.

Horror films are about fear—physical fear, psychological fear, sexual fear, even social fear. The social repercussions of dramatizing what we fear are often debated, but regardless of whether showing horror on film has any effect on society, the genre's widespread popularity suggests that it is a central cultural ritual. Like scary stories around a campfire, horror films dramatize our personal and social terrors in their different forms, in effect allowing us to admit them and attempt to deal with them in an imaginary way and as part of a communal experience. Horror films make terror visible and, potentially, manageable. An eerie tale about alien invaders taking over bodies in an American town, *Invasion of the Body Snatchers* (1956) acts out the prevalent fears in the 1950s about military and ideological invasion. The frightening story of a high school misfit with telekinetic powers, *Carrie* (1976) unveils all the anxiety and anger of female adolescence **[Figure 9.42]**.

9.42 *Carrie* (1976). The social and physical world of female adolescence erupts as a horror film about sexuality, violence, and revenge.

Supernatural, Psychological, and Physical Horrors. Within this genre, horror and fear have taken many shapes in many different cultures over the past century, addressing audiences in

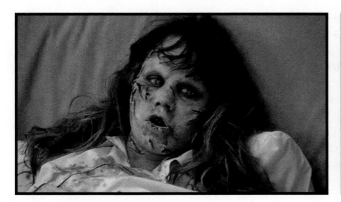

9.43 *The Exorcist* (1973). Satan possesses a young girl in this 1970s masterpiece of supernatural horror.

9.44 *The Host* (2006). A monstrously successful horror film, this Korean production pits a family against a frightening sea creature that suddenly emerges from the Han River in Seoul and terrorizes the entire community.

specific historical terms. Here we call attention to three subgenres characterized by dominant elements: supernatural, psychological, and physical horror (slasher) films.

In **supernatural horror films**, a spiritual evil erupts in the human realm, sometimes to avenge a moral wrong and sometimes for no explainable reason. This subgenre includes such movies as Henrik Galeen and Paul Wegener's *The Golem* (1915), an earlier film version of the myth of a clay monster brought to life to save the persecuted Jews; the Japanese film *Kaidan* (1964), which features four tales based on the writings of Lafcadio Hearn about samurai, monks, and spirits; and *The Sixth Sense* (1999), about a boy able to see the dead. In *The Exorcist* (1973), Satan possesses a young girl's body, deforming it into a twisted, obscenity-spewing nightmare **[Figure 9.43]**. *The Exorcist* is typical of supernatural horror in that how and why this evil has invaded the life of this modern and affluent family is never made entirely clear. Japanese horror films made in the aftermath of nuclear destruction featured ostensibly supernatural figures like Godzilla; the contemporary Korean horror film *The Host* (2006) taps into political relations with the United States as well as into environmental issues **[Figure 9.44]**.

Another variation on the threat to modern life, **psychological horror films** locate the dangers and distortions that threaten normal life in the minds of bizarre and deranged individuals. While German expressionist films like *The Cabinet of Dr. Caligari* (1920) dealt with psychological themes, the modern cycle of such films begins with *Psycho* (1960). *Whatever Happened to Baby Jane?* (1962), *Don't Look Now* (1973), *The Stepfather* (1987), *The Hand That Rocks the Cradle* (1992), and *Funny Games* (2007) **[Figure 9.45]** all participate in this subgenre. *The Silence of the Lambs* (1991) is characteristic: although it features scenes of nauseating physical violence, it is Hannibal Lecter's diabolically brilliant mind and his empathetic bond with the protagonist, Clarice Starling, that make this film so mentally, rather than physically, horrifying.

Films in which the psychology of a character takes second place to the depiction of graphic violence are examples of **physical horror films**, a subgenre with a long pedigree and a consistent place in

9.45 *Funny Games* (2007). When two seemingly normal young men arrive at the front door of a suburban home, an excruciating game of violence and terror begins.

every cycle of horror film. Again, *Psycho* is an originator, this time of the contemporary horror films known as **slasher films**. *The Texas Chain Saw Massacre* (1974) **[Figure 9.46]**, the story of a cannibalistic Texas family who attacks lost travelers; *Halloween* (1978), the first of a sequence of films about ghastly serial killings that spawned many imitators; and the grisly *Saw* (2004) belong to this subgenre. Cut and banned in many countries, Tod Browning's *Freaks* (1932) testifies to both the longevity and the more intelligent potential of physical horror. A morality tale of rejection and revenge, *Freaks* features performers from actual carnival sideshows who, despite their shocking appearance and the repulsive revenge they perpetrate, ultimately act in more generous and humane ways than the physically "normal" villains.

Crime Films

Like other genres, **crime films** represent a large category that describes a wide variety of films. From the mysteries of Edgar Allan Poe and the tales of Sherlock Holmes to the pulp fiction of the 1920s, such as Dashiell Hammett's *Red Harvest* (1929), and Walter Mosley's ongoing *Easy Rawlins* series, crime stories have been a staple of modern culture. When early movies searched for good plots, criminal dramas that contained physical action and relied on keen observation were recognized as a genre made for the cinema, where movement and vision are central. A crime film's chief characteristics include

- characters who live on the edge of a mysterious or violent society, either criminals or individuals dedicated to crime detection
- plots of crime, increasing mystery, and often ambiguous resolution
- urban, often dark and shadowy, settings

From *Underworld* (1927) to *The French Connection* (1971), the principal characters of crime movies are usually either criminals or individuals looking for criminals. In *Underworld*, gangster Bull Weed flees and then faces his relentless police pursuers in the mean streets of Chicago. In *The French Connection*, detective Popeye Doyle becomes entangled in New York's narcotics underworld. In the first film, the law triumphs but the tantalizing attraction of underworld life remains. In the second, legal victory is only partial and the glamour of the international drug market far outshines the tattered life of a New York cop **[Figure 9.47]**.

In crime films, deviance becomes a barometer of the state of society. If the outsider characters in horror films represent what we most physically and psychologically fear and repress, then the outsider characters in crime films describe what we socially reject as upholders of the status quo. As with horror films, the

9.46 *The Texas Chain Saw Massacre* (1974). This classic slasher film goes to extremes—cannibalism.

9.47 *The French Connection* (1971). Within the complex web of an international drug cartel, a determined New York detective relentlessly pursues its multiple and mysterious agents.

illegitimate groups and illegal behaviors of crime movies fascinate us as much as the savvy and determination of the detectives and other guardians of the law who track them. Perhaps the foundation for this fascination is that most people are capable of both social and antisocial inclinations at one time or another. Two of the most gripping and socially complex crime movies in film history, *The Godfather* (1972) and *The Godfather: Part II* (1974) offer a picture of twentieth-century America that culminates in the transformation of Michael Corleone from a respectable son and war hero into a ruthless mob boss willing and able to destroy any enemies or competitors **[Figure 9.48]**. The films reveal both sides of

9.48 *The Godfather: Part II* (1974). Michael Corleone balances a life of organized crime and power with familial dedication and loyalty.

the Mafia cult: its familial dedication and loyalty, and its vicious thirst for power at any cost. Echoing this duality, these films suggest that U.S. society has grown from a struggling immigrant community into a rich and intimidating nation.

Gangster and Hard-Boiled Detective Films.

The different incarnations of crime films, from the 1920s to the present, include three prominent and popular subgenres: the gangster film and the hard-boiled detective film, as well as the stylistically distinctive film noir.

Gangster films are typically (but not necessarily) set in the 1930s, when underworld criminal societies thrived in defiance of Prohibition. In these films, criminal activity characterizes a social world continually threatened by the most brutal instincts of its outcasts. *Scarface* (1932) depicts a vicious mob war in which rivals coolly manipulate and shoot each other **[Figure 9.49]**, while *The Public Enemy* (1931) follows Tom Powers's rise from a juvenile delinquent to a bootlegging killer who terrorizes Chicago. More recent versions of gangster films—*Scarface* (1983), *Goodfellas* (1990), *Road to Perdition* (2002), and *The Departed* (2006), for example—tend to escalate the violence and explore the peculiar personalities of the criminals or the strained rituals that define them as a subculture. The urban milieu of hip hop and so-called "gangsta" rap characterizes a cycle of African American crime films of the early 1990s, including *Boyz N the Hood* (1991), *New Jack City* (1991), and *Juice* (1992), in which the codes of loyalty and family are strained by the lure of fame, drugs, and cash. Japanese actor-director Takeshi Kitano has received wide acclaim for his reworking of the traditional Japanese

9.49 *Scarface* (1932). A classic gangster film from the genre's heyday in the 1930s.

9.50 *Exiled* (2006). Hong Kong gangster films such as this one are influencing recent Hollywood genre films.

gangster, or *yakuza*, film in *Hana-bi* (1997) and other films, while two Hong Kong films, Johnnie To's *Exiled* (2006) **[Figure 9.50]** and Andrew Lau and Alan Mak's *Infernal Affairs* (2002; remade in 2006 as Martin Scorsese's *The Departed*) demonstrate both the global reach of this genre and its ability to return from abroad to reshape Hollywood films.

On the other side of this generic coin, **hard-boiled detective films** focus on a protagonist who represents the law or a more ambiguous version of it, such as a private investigator. Usually these individuals must battle a criminal element (and sometimes the police) to solve a mystery or resolve a crime. In one of the most renowned films of this type, *The Maltese Falcon* (1941), detective Sam Spade pursues both a mysterious treasure (the falcon statue) and the murderers of his partner (killed for the statue). Suspected by the police, Spade embarks on a personal quest not so much for the treasure but, through his loyalty to his partner, for truth and integrity. Reinterpreted and reinvented in different cultures and with protagonists other than white males, this subgenre remains visible in such unusual movies as Jean-Luc Godard's meditation on crime detection, *Détective* (1985), and Lizzie Borden's feminist story of a sex crimes investigation in Georgia, *Love Crimes* (1992).

Film Noir. Although regularly discussed as a film style of shades and shadows, **film noir** can be considered a subgenre of crime films that emerged in the 1940s and one that distinctly elevates the legal, moral, and atmospheric ambiguity and confusion found in earlier examples of the genre. No longer simply about law versus crime or the ethical toughness of a detective, these films, such as the 1944 *Double Indemnity*, uncover a darkness and corruption in virtually all their characters that never seem fully resolved. Translated roughly as "black film," film noir suggests a visual style that emphasizes darkness and shadows that, in turn, reflect the shady moral universes common in these films. Protagonists waver between the law and lawlessness, and relationships commonly appear determined by violence and sexuality, characterized notably in the femmes fatales who surround the male protagonist. In recent decades, neo-noir films, such as the 1981 *Body Heat* and the 2005 *Sin City*, represent a more self-conscious awareness of the generic conventions of noir and often create characters and crimes far more confused and corrupt than their historical prototypes.

Orson Welles's *Touch of Evil* (1958) is one of the most powerful examples of film noir. Arriving in a Mexican town wild with drugs, prostitution, and murders, lawman Mike Vargas searches the dark alleys and filthy canals in pursuit of a murder mystery; he discovers that the heart of the corruption is Hank Quinlan, "a good detective but a lousy cop"

▶ **VIEWING CUE**

Identify the generic paradigm of the film you watch next in class. Which characteristics of this genre are most apparent? ⏸

9.51 *Touch of Evil* (1958). Orson Welles as Hank Quinlan, rotten with corruption in this classic example of film noir.

[Figure 9.51]. In David Lynch's neo-noir *Blue Velvet* (1986), the naive Jeffrey Beaumont takes on the role of detective to solve the mystery of a decaying ear found in a field. Soon he finds himself a participant in the kinky sexual world of Dorothy Vallens **[Figure 9.52]**. His girlfriend, Sandy, wonders whether he is "a detective or a pervert," and after his nightmarish wanderings through an underworld that he keeps returning to, Jeffrey can do no better than repeat that "it's a strange world, isn't it?"

9.52 *Blue Velvet* (1986). David Lynch makes the perversion at the heart of classic film noir explicit and surreal.

The Significance of Film Genre

Since the beginning of the twentieth century when chase films were an international fashion, the economics of the film industry were tied to the standardized formulas of film genre. Fashioned in accordance with the assembly-line productions of other industrialized businesses, these formulas, while meant to increase efficiency, also became the foundation for movie studios as they emerged through the 1920s. These studios would come to define themselves through the predictable scripts, sets, and actors of one or more genres. Gradually audiences learned what to expect from these genres and their associated studios. Although film genres have changed and spread considerably since the 1930s, they remain a critical measure of audience expectations as well as of the film's ability to satisfy or disappoint, and surprise or bore, the movie viewer.

Prescriptive and Descriptive Approaches

Broadly defined, film genres classify viewers' experience and understanding of a movie (as well as some directors' approaches to making a genre film). More specifically, a generic perspective on the movies can be prescriptive or descriptive. *Prescriptive approaches* assume that a model for a genre preexists any particular films in that genre; that a successful genre film deviates as little as possible from that model; and that a viewer can and should be objective in determining a genre. *Descriptive approaches*, on the other hand, assume that a genre changes over time by building on older films and developing in new ways; that viewers prize genres for different reasons; and that viewers' subjectivity can help determine a genre.

For example, a viewer approaching a genre prescriptively might stand back from, or outside of, the many specific musicals that have been made and identify, inductively and objectively, the main characteristics, rules, and conventions in order to determine "what the musical should be." With this model in mind, he or she can then evaluate any specific musical film in terms of whether it achieves or does not achieve that ideal. In this sense, Kenneth Branagh's *Love's Labour's Lost* (2000) may be seen as a terrific accomplishment, whereas *That's Entertainment* (1974) may be seen as a confused aberration of the prescribed terms of a musical.

A filmgoer looking at genre descriptively might survey the history of melodrama and deduce how its chief characteristics have altered through time. Admitting that such an exercise will necessarily depend on a person's particular perspective and knowledge (such as which films he or she has access to and the assumption that a particular genre exists), this viewer will value specific films

text continued on page 344 ▶

Generic *Chinatown* (1974)

Set in the 1930s Los Angeles of crime writers Dashiell Hammett and Raymond Chandler, Roman Polanski's *Chinatown* is a crime film that features elements of the gangster film, film noir, and especially the hard-boiled detective film. It opens in the offices of private investigator J. J. (Jake) Gittes, a location and a character that immediately recall such classics of the crime film genre as *The Maltese Falcon* and *The Big Sleep* (1946). The room is scattered with light and shade from partially closed venetian blinds, and the tough but cool Gittes (Jack Nicholson), wearing a white suit, controls the scene in every way **[Figure 9.53]** as he presents pictures of an unfaithful wife to the distraught husband who has hired him. A former police officer who worked the Chinatown district of Los Angeles, Gittes now operates between the legitimate law and the underworld, seeking out the seedy, dark side of human nature and exposing "other people's dirty laundry."

Familiar conventions and formulas are everywhere in this modern version of the crime film plot. Gittes takes what he believes is an everyday assignment to follow a husband, Los Angeles water commissioner Hollis Mulwray, who is suspected of having a sexual affair. Gittes becomes entangled, however, in events that are more complicated and devious than he can understand. The woman who hired him to spy on Mulwray turns out not to be his real wife, and the real Evelyn Mulwray becomes the foil that both attracts Gittes and makes it clear that, in this case, he is

no longer in control. Like other crime film detectives who survive with their independent moral vision, Gittes gradually and painfully uncovers the twisted and complicated truth that underlies this plot: that Noah Cross, Mulwray's former partner and Evelyn's father, has killed Mulwray as part of a vast scheme to exploit the water shortage in Los Angeles. Indeed, it slowly becomes clear that the cryptic title of the movie refers to a section of urban life—and by extension, to all of life in this film—where conventional law and order have little meaning, where, in Gittes's words, "you can't always tell what's going on." Shades and shadows, specialties of classic film noir, line the faces and spaces in this unclear world, and the addition of rich yellows, reds, and browns to the Los Angeles urbanscape creates a sickly, rather than sunny and natural, climate.

As in other crime films, the shadowy haze of corruption and violence appears also as a sexual darkness. However, unlike the aggressive sexuality of femme fatales in older crime films, the sexual danger and disorder in *Chinatown* is far more horrifying. Here Evelyn's sexuality poses little threat compared to the reality that Gittes discovers behind it: that she has been raped by her own father, Cross, and that her daughter, the mysterious "other woman" involved with Hollis Mulwray, is also her sister **[Figure 9.54]**. These facts are climactically revealed in the dark streets of Chinatown when Evelyn is killed trying to flee with her daughter/sister. The powerful and malevolent

9.53 *Chinatown* (1974). Jake Gittes, the classic bitter, smart, and handsome hard-boiled detective.

Cross walks away with his illegitimate daughter, the police stand idly by, and Gittes's only consolation is that "this is Chinatown." Although tentative and sometimes personal solutions to crime and corruption are a convention of crime films, the ambiguity is considerably darker and seamier in *Chinatown*.

Like the ending to *Chinatown*, many of the variations in these crime film formulas may be the product of changing times. With the Great Depression, Prohibition, and urban crowding and unrest, the crime film of the 1930s acted out social instabilities through the marginal success of a marginal detective, like Sam Spade and others. In the 1970s, after the government corruption of Watergate, the moral ambiguities of the Vietnam War, and the confused sexual legacy of the 1960s, the genre returned with a new relevancy. In *Chinatown*, hard-boiled detectives are less confident than before, femmes fatales are more neurotic, and corruption is more sickly and widespread.

9.54 *Chinatown* (1974). Not your typical femme fatale: Evelyn's dark backstory proves to be much more dangerous than her sexuality.

(a)

(c)

(b)

9.55a–9.55c **(a)** *All That Heaven Allows* (1955), **(b)** *Ali: Fear Eats the Soul* (1974), **(c)** *Far from Heaven* (2002). Melodrama's generic characteristics are both foregrounded and modified in loose remakes of Douglas Sirk's original by filmmakers Rainer Werner Fassbinder and Todd Haynes.

for how they develop, change, and innovate within a generic pattern. From this perspective, a film like Rainer Werner Fassbinder's *Ali: Fear Eats the Soul* (1974), about the social prejudices that hound the relationship between a young Arab migrant worker and an older German woman, may be a remarkable variation on the melodramatic formula, which in the different cultural context of the 1950s produced Douglas Sirk's *All That Heaven Allows* (1955), a version of the story in which a gardener and a wealthy socialite fall in love. With Fassbinder's "remake" in mind, Todd Haynes's *Far from Heaven* (2002) then reshapes and develops that same basic story and generic formula into a contemporary film in which the melodramatic crisis turns on a married man's discovery of his gay identity and his wife's potential interracial affair with their gardener **[Figures 9.55a–9.55c]**.

Both prescriptive and descriptive approaches can point viewers to particular readings of films. A studio, journalist, or filmmaker may, for instance, prescribe a particular genre as the framework for how a specific movie should be seen and evaluated. A studio may promote *In the Bedroom* (2001), a film about domestic violence and revenge, as a melodrama, whereas a journalist may urge audiences to see it as a murder mystery. Following one or the other of those prescribed genres will most likely result in different understandings of the film. Conversely, a movie historian may examine a number of similar films in order to describe the basic laws of a genre (say, science fiction), but if the body of films that generate his or her description is limited to Hollywood movies since 1950, that model will emphasize and overlook generic features that a wider survey (one including silent or Asian films, for example) might not. In both instances, the resulting model of a film genre reflects the prescriptive or descriptive approach used and generates meanings that limit, expand, or focus a viewer's understanding accordingly.

Classical and Revisionist Genres

The significance of a particular film's engagement with genre conventions and histories is also shaped by its situation within classical or revisionist traditions. *Classical genre traditions* are aligned with prescriptive approaches that place a film in relation to a paradigm that remains the same over time and that a genre film either successfully follows or not. Classical generic traditions establish relatively fixed sets of formulas and conventions, associated with certain films or with a specific place in history. Stemming from descriptive approaches, *revisionist genre traditions* see a film as a function of changing historical and cultural contexts that modify the conventions and formulas of that genre. A particular western, for example, will be understood differently from a classical perspective than from a revisionist one. Together these two traditions identify one of the central paradoxes of any genre: genres can appear to be at once timeless and time bound, to both create patterns that transcend history and to be extremely sensitive measures of history.

Classical genres can be viewed as both historical and structural paradigms. A *historical paradigm* presumes that a genre evolved to a point of perfection at some point in history and that one or more films at that point describe the generic ideal. For film critic André Bazin, John Ford's *Stagecoach* is the historical paradigm for the western that reached its pinnacle in the United States in 1939. For others, F. W. Murnau's *Nosferatu* (1922) is the historical paradigm for the horror film, achieving its essential qualities in the climate of 1920s Germany **[Figure 9.56]**. A *structural paradigm* relies less on historical precedent than on a formal or structural ideal that may or may not be actually seen, in a complete or pure form, in any specific film. For example, regardless of the many variations on science fiction films, a viewer familiar with the genre may develop a structural paradigm for the classic science fiction film. After viewing a wide spectrum of films—from *The Day the Earth Stood Still* (1951) to *The Man Who Fell to Earth* (1976)—a viewer may understand that the paradigm for the genre requires a visual and dramatic conflict between earth and outer space, the centrality of special effects, and a deadline plot structure. Some films will then fit this paradigm easily, whereas others, such as the frolicking *Repo Man* (1984; about teenage angst, the repossessing of cars, and a mad scientist), may seem less convincing participants in the genre.

In contrast, generic revisionism assumes that a genre is subject to historical and cultural flux, continually changing as part of a dialogue with films of the same genre. Films within a genre adapt their conventions and formulas to reflect different times and places. From this perspective, Fred Schepisi's *Barbarosa* (1982) is as much a western as *Stagecoach*, but it is adapted to a contemporary climate that sees outlaws and their myths in a more fantastic light. More modern films may demonstrate *generic reflexivity*—that is, they are unusually self-conscious about their generic identity and clearly and visibly comment on the generic paradigms. *Young Frankenstein* (1974) and *L.A. Confidential* (1997) surely fit this model, the first a goofy look at one of the most famous models for a horror film and the second a serious self-conscious reworking of the crime film. Less obviously perhaps, Werner Herzog's *Nosferatu the Vampyre* (1979) does not simply re-create the original *Nosferatu*, but also returns to many of its conventions and icons as a way of commenting on the continuing relevancy of the vampire myth and how it still reveals much about contemporary society **[Figure 9.57]**.

text continued on page 347 ▶

9.56   *Nosferatu* (1922). A historical paradigm for horror films.

▶ **VIEWING CUE**

Place a film you recently watched in a generic tradition and discuss whether, how, and why it exemplifies classical or revisionist characteristics. ⏸

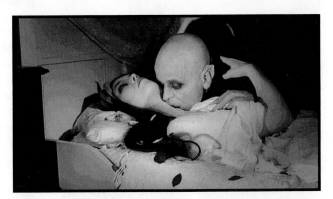

9.57   ***Nosferatu the Vampyre*** (1979). As an example of generic reflexivity, Herzog's film re-creates and manipulates the conventions and formulas of a horror film classic, specifically referencing images and themes from F. W. Murnau's 1922 *Nosferatu*.

9.58a

9.58b

9.58c

9.58d

9.58e

9.58f

Genre Revisionism: Comparing *True Grit* (1969) **and** *True Grit* (2010)

We can think of revisionist genres as a map of the history of film—they show how filmmakers regularly rethink and re-create generic formulas and conventions to reflect changing times and cultures. A comparison of the two versions of *True Grit* (1969, 2010) illustrates how a contemporary remake can be faithful to the original generic icons and formulas while revising and altering them to create a new film. That the Coen brothers's remake stays remarkably close to the original content and style only highlights those instances where it revises the western genre and Henry Hathaway's original film.

Central to *True Grit* is the tough and independent cowboy Rooster Cogburn (played by John Wayne in the 1969 version)—a true western icon [**Figure 9.58a**]. He is hired by the tough but refined fourteen-year-old Mattie to help track down her father's killer. But Jeff Bridges as the remade Rooster in the 2010 film is a more dissolute, lost, and troubled character—though equally iconic [**Figure 9.58b**]. Similarly, while both versions are set in the open plains of the U.S. frontier, the 1969 film often frames and focuses the sets and setting around concentrated actions, such as the gunfight around a cabin [**Figure 9.58c**], while the remake opens the spaces of the western in ways that seem to exaggerate the extreme isolation of the characters [**Figure 9.58d**]. Finally, in the climactic sequence in which Rooster races to find help for the dying Mattie, the 1969 film concentrates on the frantically clipped action in the bright light of day as Wayne drives a wagon pulled by horses [**Figure 9.58e**]. In contrast, the 2010 film presents a dramatic revision of this generic formula as it extends this long race through a surreal night, focusing on Mattie's features as she fights against time and death [**Figure 9.58f**]. The action of the western now becomes a strangely meditative space.

Local and Global Genres

Although major Hollywood genres may be the most recognizable, we also notice generic patterns in films connected to more specific times, places, events, and cultures—what we might call "local" genres. Modern American "teen films" such as *The Breakfast Club* (1985), *Heathers* (1988), *Clueless* (1995), *Bring It On* (2000), and *Easy A* (2010) **[Figure 9.59]** can be considered examples of a genre that relates in very particular ways to the characters, crises, and rituals of contemporary American youth.

9.59   *Easy A* (2010). This film about a teenage girl using rumors about her promiscuity to elevate her social standing is part of the cycle of teen films prevalent since the 1980s.

In a sense, all genres are local because they first take shape to reflect the interests and traditions of a particular community or nation. Westerns are essentially an American genre, although they have traveled successfully to Australia, Italy, Spain, and many other countries. Although horror is now a global genre, horror films may have their roots in the expressionistic cinema of Germany around 1920.

Of the many local genres that have appeared around the world, two clearly stress the connection between genre and a particular culture: the Japanese *jidai-geki* films and the Austrian and German *heimat* films. Popular since the 1920s, the Japanese *jidai-geki* films are period films or costume dramas set before 1868, when feudal Japan entered the modern Meiji period. Movies such as *Revere the Emperor* (1927) and *A Diary of Chuji's Travels* (1927) work as historical travelogues to resurrect the customs and glory of times long past. Like most nations' relationship to their preindustrial past, the Japanese view this period with curiosity, nostalgia, and pride, often seeing in these early films a kind of cultural purity that was lost in the twentieth century. Through the years, however, this genre, like all successful genres, has assimilated current affairs into its conventions and formulas: besides feudal courts and sword battles, *jidai-geki* films develop plots about class unrest and social rebellion. Akira Kurosawa's *Ran* (1985) is an interesting engagement with this essentially Japanese genre: a feudal Japanese costume drama replete with many of the *jidai-geki* conventions, it is a film adapted from Shakespeare's *King Lear* that, ultimately, describes the end of an ancient world **[Figure 9.60]**.

Set in idyllic countryside locales, Austrian and German *heimat* films depict a world of traditional folk values in which love and family triumph over virtually any social evil, and communities gather around maypoles and sing traditional German folk songs. Hailed by Austrian and German audiences

text continued on page 350 ▶

> **▶ VIEWING CUE**
>
> Consider whether and how the cultural or historical context seems to shade and shape the generic formulas used in a film you recently watched. ❚❚

9.60   *Ran* (1985). The classical Shakespearean story of King Lear retold in this essentially Japanese genre film.

The Significance of Genre History in *Vagabond* (1985)

For some, *Easy Rider* (1969) represents the historical center of the **road movie** genre **[Figure 9.61]**. A prescriptive definition of the road movie would doubtless place automobiles or motorcycles at the center of a narrative about wandering or driven men who are or eventually will become buddies. Structurally, the narrative develops along a linear path, as a quest that episodically unfolds and is punctuated by traveling shots of open roads and landscapes representing the stylistic heart of the genre. A descriptive definition would place at the center of this classically linear and episodic narrative an aimless odyssey toward freedom or an otherwise undefined place. If this structural paradigm can be found in *Easy Rider*, the genre has evolved and reappeared in numerous guises over the years.

The road movie genre has its origins in the 1930s, where the central motif of road travel occurs in such precursors as *Wild Boys of the Road* (1933), *You Only Live Once* (1937), and *The Grapes of Wrath* (1940), films that make traveling on the road the underpinning of the story. By the 1940s and 1950s, the more serious and existential dimensions of the road movie surface in *They Drive by Night* (1940), *Detour* (1945), and *The Wages of Fear* (1953), in which a lone male or male camaraderie (frequently inflected with anger and violence) moves to the center of the genre. During the 1950s in the United States, the social turbulence associated with the road movie began to spread (especially to adolescents who sought for ways to express their angst against their families). That the automobile became the country's social and industrial backbone only added to the pertinence of the central convention of this genre.

The 1960s and 1970s featured both classical road movies like Monte Hellman's *Two-Lane Blacktop* (1971) and, more often, revisionist versions such as *Weekend* (1967), *Duel* (1972), *Paper Moon* (1973), *Badlands* (1973), *Road Movie* (1974), and *The Car* (1977). If *Two-Lane Blacktop* is a straightforward account of two young men racing across America to a romantically apocalyptic end, the latter movies revised those central themes and icons to reflect the changing times and styles: irony and pathos now permeate the adventure, and junk and garbage strew the highways. In the 1980s and 1990s, both culturally displaced and formally reflexive versions of road movies appeared: *Mad Max* (1979), *Paris, Texas* (1984), and *Thelma & Louise* (1991). In *The Living End* (1992), which resurrects the genre with searing relevancy, the two HIV-positive road buddies have more on their minds than the direction of the road. More recently, the witty and self-conscious *O Brother, Where Art Thou?* (2000) returns the genre to its historical roots, reappropriating its title and certain scenes from

9.61   *Easy Rider* (1969). Two disaffected bikers go searching for the "real America" and ride, directionless, into violence, drugs, rock and roll, and eventually death.

9.62 *Vagabond* (1985). Unconventional in form and content, this movie opens up the road movie genre.

Vagabond, however, changes the terms of that search. Instead of following the protagonist's point of view as she searches the horizon or the rearview mirror for some insight into her present and past self, the film assumes the points of view of the eighteen people along the road, hoping their roadside perspectives will provide the key to this road warrior. Throughout, Mona remains an enigma, often refusing help and companionship, explaining herself only with quips like "being alone is good" and "I move" **[Figure 9.63]**. Her movement becomes a refusal to have an identity or a claim to a self, knowable either to herself or to others.

The key to the generic detours in this road movie is clearly that a woman has now taken the road

the 1941 comic road movie *Sullivan's Travels* as it remakes Homer's *Odyssey* into the frolicking road adventure of three escaped convicts.

As part of this historical development, French filmmaker Agnès Varda's feminist film, *Vagabond*, is one of the most radical contemporary revisions of the road movie. At first glance, this film about a hitchhiking vagrant only partly resembles a road movie, lacking that prominent icon of a car, motorcycle, or other motorized vehicle. Moreover, rather than moving forward down the road, this film moves backward, beginning with the corpse of the female protagonist, Mona, in a roadside ditch. In order to explain how her body ended up there, the narrative presents a series of flashbacks, tracing her wanderings as she hitchhikes through the French countryside **[Figure 9.62]**. It recounts forty-seven different episodes, eighteen of which describe individual meetings with Mona on the road. A migrant worker, a tree specialist named Landier and her assistant Jean-Pierre, a maidservant named Yolande, and Mona's temporary boyfriend David are some of the different people who befriend Mona and try to stop her wanderings or to just understand her.

An undefined search for identity propels the protagonists of most road movies and usually leads to some version of self-knowledge.

traditionally claimed by men. Road movies commonly focus on male anxiety and desire; *Vagabond*, like the later American film *Thelma & Louise* (1991), alters that central feature and, with this change, maps a new road and explores different questions about identity. Men may attack Mona or be put off by her, but on this road they will not contain or control her. As in the classic road movie, the narrative and the film image continually move and progress in *Vagabond*. Here, however, progression and movement are the means of staying alive to the potential inherent in one's self, rather than a way to search for some uncertain goal at the end of the road.

9.63 *Vagabond* (1985). Throughout the film, Mona is consistently impenetrable to those she meets on the road.

9.64 *Heimat* (1984). The traditional values of German home life are subjected to the conditions of postwar occupation.

throughout the first half of the twentieth century, this genre thrived in both countries with films ranging from *The Priest from Kirchfeld* (1914) and *Heimat* (1938) to *The Trapp Family* (1956). As German filmmakers became more self-conscious about their historical background and the connection between this political history and the movies, modern films resurrected the *heimat* genre, now reinterpreted as complicit in the social history of Germany. Peter Fleischmann's *Hunting Scenes from Bavaria* (1969), Volker Schlöndorff's *The Sudden Wealth of the Poor People of Kombach* (1971), Edgar Reitz's sixteen-hour *Heimat* (1984) **[Figure 9.64]**, and Stefan Ruzowitzky's *The Inheritors* (1998) are all explicit attacks on the mythology of this genre or reexaminations of its social meaning and power.

CONCEPTS AT WORK

The six genres examined in the central section of this chapter are broad, but hardly all-encompassing. Depending on the level of specificity used as criteria, one could expand this list of genres by a few entries, or by hundreds—as the mention of several among myriad local genres attests. Hybrid genres and subgenres extend the possibilities to the limits of generic frameworks, while many modern films try to bend the definition of one genre or another, or to defy definition altogether. Genres can blend into one another easily, as they should. Although classifying films by genre may seem like a way of restricting the entry of new ideas into the art form, forcing filmmakers to return to the same ideas time and again, nothing could be further from the truth. Identifying films by their genre simply helps to place them in their historical context by connecting them not just to other films, but to plays, books, and works of art that have come before. If a film is a dialogue between filmmaker and audience, then genre is an unspoken agreement on the language of that dialogue, one that is often made from a film's opening frames.

Activities

- As an example of the communicative power of genre conventions, examine a film trailer or teaser, preferably for a film you have not seen, and try to identify the film's genre as quickly as possible based on conventions and contextual clues. What visual and aural aspects indicate the film's genre? Trailers often attempt to establish a film as one genre to trick audiences into setting up particular expectations before suddenly introducing a generic shift. Does your initial assessment change by the end of the trailer/teaser?
- Choose a scene from a film that exemplifies that film's genre. For a horror film, this might be the moment when the killer finally steps out of the shadows. For a melodrama, this could be a scene of the heroine being physically or emotionally abused. Try to determine what subtle changes would need to occur to change this scene to one that would exemplify a different genre. Consider diegetic and nondiegetic sound, lighting, and mise-en-scène as you proceed.

PART 4

CRITICAL
PERSPECTIVES
history, methods, writing

Often our feelings and thoughts about a particular film linger well after we leave the theater, eject a DVD, or turn off our computer. We may puzzle over a film's meanings or over how it has managed to move us so deeply. We may then seek out reviews, essays, or books about the film, its director, or the country where it was made. As we become interested in film history, criticism, theory, and analysis through our reading, we can also be inspired to write about films.

In the next three chapters, we will explore and explain how knowledge of film history, film criticism and theory, and the act of writing about film deepen and enrich our experience of the movies. In Chapter 10, we survey film history and consider different models used to understand cinema's past. Determining a "correct" history of the cinema may be less important than recognizing the assumptions about film history that help shape our understanding and enjoyment. Chapter 11 introduces theories of film and examines different critical methods that have evolved over the years, while Chapter 12 maps the steps and procedures for turning our initial perceptions about a movie into a sophisticated essay. Through an understanding of film history and historiography, theoretical speculation, and critical analysis, our film experience grows and develops in as many directions as we are willing to take it.

WHAT IMPRISONS
DESIRES OF THE HEART?
JULIANNE
MOORE
DENNIS
QUAID
DENNIS
HAYSBERT
A FILM BY TODD HAYNES
FAR
FROM
HEAVEN
TF1 INTERNATIONAL PICTURES AND VULCAN PRODUCTIONS PRESENT IN ASSOCIATION WITH FOCUS FEATURES A KILLER FILMS/JOHN WELLS/SECTION EIGHT PRODUCTION
A FILM BY TODD HAYNES JULIANNE MOORE DENNIS QUAID DENNIS HAYSBERT "FAR FROM HEAVEN" PATRICIA CLARKSON CASTING BY LAURA ROSENTHAL
MUSIC BY ELMER BERNSTEIN ASSOCIATE PRODUCERS DIDIER SAPAUT JEAN CHARLES LÉVY COSTUME DESIGNER SANDY POWELL EDITED BY JAMES LYONS PRODUCTION DESIGNER MARK FRIEDBERG DIRECTOR OF PHOTOGRAPHY EDWARD LACHMAN, A.S.C.
CO-PRODUCERS BRADFORD SIMPSON DECLAN BALDWIN EXECUTIVE PRODUCERS JOHN WELLS ERIC ROBISON TRACY BRIMM JOHN SLOSS EXECUTIVE PRODUCERS STEVEN SODERBERGH GEORGE CLOONEY
VULCAN PRODUCTIONS
killer films
PRODUCED BY JODY PATTON PRODUCED BY CHRISTINE VACHON WRITTEN AND DIRECTED BY TODD HAYNES
SOUNDTRACK AVAILABLE ON VARÈSE SARABANDE CDs
TF1 INTERNATIONAL
www.farfromheavenmovie.com
ARTWORK: ©2002 FOCUS FEATURES, LLC. ALL RIGHTS RESERVED.

History and Historiography
Hollywood and Beyond

Three films retell a similar story at different points over nearly fifty years of film history: *All That Heaven Allows*, a Hollywood melodrama made in 1955 by German émigré director Douglas Sirk; *Ali: Fear Eats the Soul*, directed in 1974 by German filmmaker Rainer Werner Fassbinder; and *Far from Heaven*, made in 2002 by American independent Todd Haynes. The first, starring Rock Hudson and Jane Wyman in a romance between a middle-class widow and her gardener, is a glossy Technicolor tale of social prejudice in small-town U.S.A. The second, concentrating on the love affair between an older cleaning woman and a young Arab guest worker, is a grittier story about age, race, class, and immigration in modern Germany. The third juxtaposes a husband's desire for men with his wife's developing interracial intimacy with their African American gardener, critiquing the facade of a typical 1950s family. While these are very different films—one a product of the Hollywood studio system, the second a low-budget film by an acclaimed German filmmaker of the 1970s, and the third an independent art-house film—they are deeply connected as remakes of a love story as social critique. At the same time, they represent threads in the rich tapestry of the film past, approached as a series of partial histories and historical viewpoints.

n 1998, to commemorate the first one hundred years of cinema, the American Film Institute (AFI) released a highly publicized list of the "100 Greatest American Movies of All Time." This list generated instant credibility for, and renewed public interest in, its entries, none more so than Orson Welles's *Citizen Kane* (1941)—the film in the number-one spot. Many critics and viewers disagreed, however, with the list's claim to be "timeless," as it tended to reproduce current, dominant tastes. Only four silent movies made the list (*The Birth of a Nation* and three Charlie Chaplin films), for example, and works by African American and women filmmakers were all but absent. Further limiting this list, of course, was its sole focus on American films.

The debates surrounding the AFI list show that there is no single way to view the history of cinema. Like other histories, movie history can take many shapes and forms from "best of" lists to social and economic histories. In our discussion of film history, we aim not only to present key facts, names, and events, but also to indicate how our sense of history becomes richer and more insightful through an awareness of film **historiography**, the study of the methods and principles through which the past becomes organized according to certain perspectives and priorities.

KEY OBJECTIVES

- Learn the broad outlines and periods of film history.
- Understand film history as global, emphasizing the distinctive nature of different national cinemas as well as transnational influences.
- Examine film practices and filmmakers marginalized by traditional Hollywood-centered histories.
- Explore "lost" film history and the importance of film presentation.

Since the first days of moving pictures, movies have attempted to make history. The first movies, with their remarkable ability to present people and events as living images, began to record actual historical happenings and re-create historical moments. Since those early years, the cinema has become one of the most common ways people encounter the figures of the past. From the tale of the eighteenth-century Russian monarch Catherine the Great in *The Scarlet Empress* (1934) **[Figure 10.1]** to the story of John Reed and the Greenwich Village leftist movement in *Reds* (1981), movies have so powerfully and convincingly reconstructed the past that they have become the dominant framework through which many of us see and understand history.

Just as the movies construct visions of history for us, how we look at film history is the product of certain formulas and models. This chapter begins with one typical way of organizing film history: **periodization**. With this method, film history is divided into historical segments that help identify movies' shared thematic and stylistic concerns. For each of the following broad periods in our film

survey—early, between the wars, post–World War II, and contemporary—we will reference key social events that define film histories. We will highlight formal and stylistic features of each period, as well as a few representative films and filmmakers. While approaching film history according to its "masters and masterpieces" can downplay the many material forces that determine status and value, knowledge of such major figures and films is an essential orientation to film history.

While Hollywood has a dominant economic and stylistic position in world film history, any view of film history would be sorely incomplete if it were to ignore the rich traditions of filmmaking beyond Hollywood. This chapter will examine film cultures from around the world—some as old as Hollywood and some just beginning to emerge. In addition, we will consider lesser-known film cultures within the United States, exploring the extent to which women, African Americans, and lesbian, gay, transgender, and bisexual (LGBT) people have been marginalized in film history. Finally, we look at indigenous media and the issue of preserving our rich and diverse film history.

10.1 *The Scarlet Empress* (1934). History in the movies: Marlene Dietrich portrays a very glamorous Catherine the Great.

Early Cinema

The early cinema period, stretching from 1895 until roughly 1913, was characterized by rapid development and experimentation in filmmaking before Hollywood achieved dominance and settled into the more defined patterns of its classical period. In the United States, massive industrialization attracted large numbers of immigrants and rural Americans to urban centers, where the movie industry found many of its subjects and audiences. Traditional class, race, and gender lines began to shift, and the country experienced growth in economic prosperity. Industrialization also fostered the growth of leisure time and commercialized leisure activities. In the realm of this expanding free time, popular culture competed with the traditions of high culture as never before. Such patterns of modernization occurred all around the world, and the invention of cinema and its rapid integration into the life of the masses was an international phenomenon.

For many historians, the beginning of cinema history proper is the first screening of *Workers Leaving the Lumière Factory* on March 22, 1895, followed by the public screening of this and other Lumière films on December 18, 1895 (some historians would note that the German brothers Emil and Max Skladanowsky had projected

10.2   ***The Derby*** (1896). The finish of the annual horse race, captured by British filmmakers R. W. Paul and Birt Acres, stands at the beginning of cinema's evolution.

movies publicly in Berlin in November of the same year). Seeking the shock of the new, viewers in major cities all over the world flocked to see demonstrations of the new medium, like R. W. Paul's 1896 racing film *The Derby* **[Figure 10.2]**. Soon commercial and theatrical venues for showing movies to the general public arrived in the form of nickelodeon theaters, and in the United States, the major film companies standardized practices by forming the Motion Picture Patents Company (known as "the Trust").

Stylistically, early cinema was characterized by: (1) the shift from single to multiple shots, and (2) the beginnings of continuity editing and variations in camera distance in the early elaboration of narrative form. From simple scenes like *Fred Ott's Sneeze* (1896), movies quickly evolved to the dramatization of real or fictional events using multiple shots, logically connected in space and time. Released in 1903, Edwin S. Porter's *Uncle Tom's Cabin* presents fourteen shots introduced by intertitles to depict the highlights of the famous novel and play. By 1911, D. W. Griffith's *The Lonedale Operator*, a short film about burglars threatening a telegraph operator, used around one hundred shots to establish different spatial relations between an office interior and its exterior—to emphasize the action through variations in scale and to build narrative suspense through parallel editing.

As the movies experimented with undefined possibilities, the subject matter and themes reflected a multitude of topics and interests, and forms ranged from slapstick comedy to Victorian literary adaptations. The characters in these short films were originally anonymous actors and actresses, but the emergence of the star system enhanced the cultural power of film. By 1911, the "Biograph Girl" was identified as Florence Lawrence, and celebrities like Mary Pickford—"America's Sweetheart"—became the subject of fan magazines. In the 1910s, film industries thrived in many countries, and without language barriers, films produced in Italy, Denmark, and Japan circulated internationally. Eventually, American movie production advanced in length and complexity, and Hollywood extended its reach around the world, producing half the films made worldwide in 1914, on the cusp of World War I.

Cinema between the Wars

The devastating effects of World War I (1914–1918) in Europe and the emergence of the studio system and classical narrative style further consolidated Hollywood's dominance as an exporter of commercial films. However, before the introduction of sound at the end of the 1920s, artistic film movements flourished internationally outside the commercial model. And while Hollywood experienced a golden age during the 1930s, so did a number of other national cinemas, showcasing distinctive linguistic and cultural traditions.

Classical Hollywood Cinema

Classical Hollywood cinema can be divided into two periods: silent and sound films. The first encompasses Hollywood's classical silent period, from roughly 1917 to 1927, when the basic structures of classical narrative and the studio system were put into place. (The emergence of independents and longer films along with legal action against the Trust in the mid-1910s are often referred to as the *transitional period*.) Comedies, lavish spectacles, and thrilling melodramas attracted fifty million weekly moviegoers by 1920, and attendance soared during that decade.

Hollywood came of age during this time with three major historical developments: (1) the standardization of film production, (2) the establishment of the feature film, and (3) the cultural and economic expansion of movies throughout society. As the industry grew, standardized formulas for film production took root, creating efficient teams of scriptwriters, producers, directors, camera operators, actors, and editors. One product of this standardization process was the establishment of the feature-film model with a running time of approximately one hundred minutes for a narrative movie. Along with their technological and economic growth, movies found more sophisticated subject matter and more elegant theaters for distribution, reflecting their rising cultural status and their ability to attract audiences from all corners of society. Internationally, Hollywood continued to extend its reach: while World War I wreaked havoc on European economics, Hollywood increased its exports fivefold and its overseas income by 35 percent.

10.3 *Intolerance* (1916). D. W. Griffith intertwines stories set in four different historical periods in this landmark in the evolution of narrative film form.

The most pronounced and important aesthetic changes during this period included (1) the development of narrative realism, and (2) the integration of the viewer's perspective into the editing and narrative action.

Narrative realism came to the forefront of movie culture as the movies sought legitimization. From D. W. Griffith's *The Birth of a Nation* (1915) and *Intolerance* (1916) **[Figure 10.3]** through King Vidor's *The Big Parade* (1925), narrative films learned to explore simultaneous actions, complex spatial geographies, and the psychological interaction of characters through narrative. Adding to this new formal complexity, point-of-view shots, camera movement, and editing situated viewers *within* the narrative action rather than at the theatrical distance (that is, the view from a seat before a stage) found in early or preclassical films.

During this time, comedians and prominent silent film directors Charlie Chaplin and Buster Keaton drew audiences in with their slapstick vignettes and early narratives, defining the art of the comedy in 1920s Hollywood. Although Chaplin and Keaton each created distinct styles and stories, both replaced the clownish and chaotic gymnastics of early film comedies (such as Mack Sennett's Keystone comedies) with nuanced and acrobatic gestures that dramatized serious human and social themes. Chaplin's *The Kid* (1921), the first of his many feature-length films, is a tale about his Little Tramp character befriending an impoverished orphan boy. It displays Chaplin's ingenious ability to make his seemingly awkward body a vehicle for poetic improvisation motivated by the human need for companionship.

Providing a bombastic counterpoint to silent comedies and dramas, Cecil B. DeMille's *The Ten Commandments* (1923) is a lavish spectacle that marks another direction in silent film history **[Figure 10.4]**. Extremely expensive to produce at that time (costing $1.5 million) and technically advanced (using an early Technicolor process), this film about Moses's biblical journey stands at the crossroads of 1920s film culture, when

10.4 *The Ten Commandments* (1923). Cecil B. DeMille's first version of the biblical story was a silent movie spectacular.

the excesses of movies began to provoke social concern about their ethics. Perhaps the most interesting balancing act in *The Ten Commandments* is its portrayal of lurid sex and violence, scenes that are continually reframed by a clear and strong moral perspective. A similar contradiction characterized American attitudes toward the movies more generally; the early 1920s saw a series of shocking sex and drug scandals involving Hollywood stars, and calls for censorship became widespread.

The second part of the classical cinema period was brought about by the introduction of synchronized sound in 1927 and lasted until the end of World War II in 1945 (although aspects of classical style and the studio system continued long after). The Great Depression, triggered in part by the stock market collapse of 1929, defined the American cultural experience at the beginning of the 1930s. In the midst of economic unrest and other strains, fascist and Marxist ideologies began to make inroads in the United States, demanding major changes in the traditional way of life. Franklin D. Roosevelt's New Deal became the political antidote for much of the 1930s, pumping a determined spirit of optimism into society. The devastating conflict of World War II then defined the last four years of the classical period, in which the country fully asserted its global leadership and control.

The film industry followed these turbulent historical events with dramatic changes of its own. The "Big Five" studios (Fox, MGM, Paramount, Warner Bros., and RKO) along with the "Little Three" (Columbia, Universal, and United Artists) dominated the industry by controlling distributors and theater chains and exerting great industrial as well as cultural power. With social issues more hotly debated and the movies gaining more influence than ever, the messages of films came increasingly under scrutiny. Formed in 1922, the Motion Picture Producers and Distributors Association of America (MPDAA, now the MPAA) enlisted former Postmaster General William H. Hays to internally regulate movies' moral content in order to avert the threats of local censors through what became known as the "Hays Office." The Motion Picture Production Code, adopted in 1930, was at first widely ignored, but in 1934 the MPDAA set up the Production Code Administration, headed by Joseph I. Breen, to enforce it strictly. The code's conservative list of principles primarily governing the depiction of crime and sex kept censorship efforts within the industry.

At this time, Hollywood films followed these industry shifts with two important stylistic changes: (1) the elaboration of movie dialogue and the growth of characterization in films, and (2) the prominence of generic formulas in constructing film narratives.

The sensational arrival of sound technology opened a whole new dimension to film form that allowed movies to expand their dramatic capacity. Accomplished writers flocked to Hollywood, literary adaptations flourished, and outspoken characters became more verbally, psychologically, and socially complex. The rapid-fire witticisms of the Marx Brothers in *Duck Soup* (1933) **[Figure 10.5]** and the musically and verbally elaborate adaptation of Shakespeare's *A Midsummer Night's Dream* (1935) both reflected the new sound standards. Meanwhile, generic formulas, sometimes identified with a particular studio (for example, MGM's 1940s musicals), became the primary production and distribution standard. In fact, genres sometimes superseded the subject matter and actors in defining a film and expectations about it.

During Hollywood's golden age, an exceptional number and variety of studio classics emerged. Of the many celebrated films of the 1930s, Frank Capra's *It*

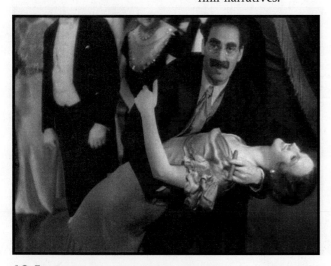

10.5 *Duck Soup* (1933). The introduction of sound brought dialogue and ushered in the comic talents of the Marx Brothers.

Happened One Night (1934) is perhaps one of the best representations of the energy that was making its way from the New York theatrical stage to the Hollywood screen after the arrival of synchronized dialogue. The film's social allegory about common people correcting the greed and egotism of the rich would continue to define Capra's vision throughout this decade and into the 1940s **[Figure 10.6]**.

Perhaps the most distinctive Hollywood genre, the western, first developed during the silent era and then became a staple of low-budget movie serial production in the 1930s. But in 1939, veteran director John Ford elevated the western with *Stagecoach*—a film widely considered one of the finest examples of classical Hollywood style. It depicted the tense journey of a mismatched group of passengers through the spectacular landscape of Monument Valley and established Ford's long-lasting partnership with John Wayne. *Stagecoach* joined *Gone with the Wind*, *The Wizard of Oz*, *Wuthering Heights*, and *Mr. Smith Goes to Washington* as a contender for the best picture Oscar, making 1939 a banner year for classical Hollywood.

10.6 *It Happened One Night* (1934). Frank Capra's delightful screwball comedy about a rebellious socialite (Claudette Colbert) who flees her wealthy father and takes up, reluctantly, with a reporter (Clark Gable) who hopes to use her scandalous behavior as a news scoop, is one of the quintessential 1930s Hollywood films.

German Expressionist Cinema

By the end of the 1930s, the aesthetic movements and national film industries that had developed in Europe during the silent and early sound eras were shaken by the threat of conflict. But the internationalism of the first decades of cinema meant that the aesthetic influences of these movements were still considerable and lasting. **German expressionist cinema** (1918–1929) veered away from the movies' realist drive, with aims to (1) concentrate on the dark fringes of human experience, and (2) represent irrational forces through lighting, set, and costume design.

Like the *film d'art* movement in France (1908–1912), German cinema first distinguished itself through imaginative interpretations of literature, such as theater director Max Reinhardt's adaptation of Hugo von Hofmannsthal's *The Strange Girl* (1913). After a national film industry was centralized toward the end of World War I, German films made under the postwar Weimar Republic began to compete successfully with Hollywood cinema. The most prominent achievements of the giant Universal Film AG, or UFA, studios exemplified the expressionist movement. Expressionism (in film, theater, painting, and the other arts) turned away from realist representation and toward the unconscious and irrational sides of human experience.

Weimar-era cinema differed from Hollywood models in that it successfully integrated an explicit commitment to artistic expression into a nationalized industry. The most famous achievement of the expressionist trend in film history is Robert Wiene's *The Cabinet of Dr. Caligari* (1920), a dreamlike story of a somnambulist who, in the service of a mad tyrant, stalks innocent victims **[Figure 10.7]**. Along with its story of obsessed and troubled individuals, the film's shadowy atmosphere and strangely distorted artificial sets became trademarks of German expressionist cinema. Two of the most important Weimar-era filmmakers are

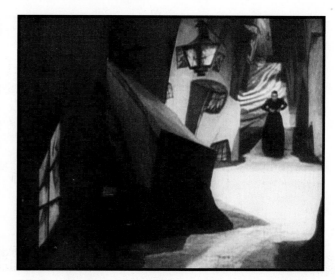

10.7 *The Cabinet of Dr. Caligari* (1920). Expressionist sets make this one of the most visually striking films in history.

10.8   *The Woman in the Window* (1944). Fritz Lang, the most prominent director in pre-Nazi Germany, later had a successful Hollywood career. This film—with its stylistic use of shadow and a protagonist whose obsession with a woman brings about his downfall—highlights the direct connection between American film noir and German expressionism.

Fritz Lang, director of *Dr. Mabuse: The Gambler* (1922), *Metropolis* (1926), and *M* (1931), and F. W. Murnau, director of *Nosferatu: A Symphony of Horror* (1922) and *The Last Laugh* (1924). In *Nosferatu*, Murnau re-creates the vampire legend within a naturalistic setting, one that lighting, camera angles, and other expressive techniques infuse with a supernatural anxiety. Other notable *street films*—so called for their exterior urban settings—are G. W. Pabst's *The Joyless Street* (1925) and Josef von Sternberg's *The Blue Angel* (1930). In both, the grim realities of the streets become excessive, morbid, and emotionally twisted. In the early sound film *The Blue Angel*, simultaneously filmed in German, French, and English, Marlene Dietrich plays her breakthrough role as a cabaret singer who seduces an aging professor. His decline into decadence under her erotic spell plays out the grim and seedy brilliance of German expressionism. During the rise of Nazism, much of the Weimar cinema's creative personnel emigrated to the United States, where they introduced expressionist formal elements and moral ambiguities to such Hollywood film noirs as Lang's *The Woman in the Window* (1944) [**Figure 10.8**].

Soviet Silent Films

Soviet silent films from 1917 to 1931 represent a break from the entertainment history of the movies. The Soviet cinema of this period developed out of the Russian Revolution of 1917, suggesting its distance from the assumptions and aims of the capitalist economics of Hollywood. This resulted in (1) an emphasis on documentary and historical subjects, and (2) a political concept of cinema centered on audience response.

Dziga Vertov, a seminal theoretician and practitioner in this movement, established a collective workshop—the Kinoki or "cinema-eyes"—to investigate how cinema communicates both directly and subliminally. He and his colleagues were deeply committed to presenting everyday truths rather than distracting fictions, yet they also recognized that cinema elicits different ideas and responses according to how images are structured and edited. Thus they developed a montage aesthetic suited to the modern world into which the Soviet people were being catapulted (see pp. 137–38). In the spirit of these theories, Vertov's creative documentary *Man with a Movie Camera* (1929) records not only the activity of the modern city but also how its energy is transformed by the camera recording it. Moving rapidly from one subject to another; using split screens, superimpositions, and variable film speeds; and continually placing the camera within the action, this movie does more than describe or narrate the city [**Figure 10.9**].

10.9   *Man with a Movie Camera* (1929). The image of the cameraman looms over the city, implying the central role of cinema in modern life.

Although Soviet cinema at this time produced many exceptional films, Sergei Eisenstein's *Battleship Potemkin* (1925) quickly became the most renowned outside the U.S.S.R. (see pp. 172–73). About an uprising of oppressed sailors that heralded the coming revolution, the film retains its place in film history because of its brilliant demonstration of how conflicting or unrelated images can be linked together, using what Eisenstein called *dialectical montage*, to generate an emotional, intellectual, and political understanding of events. The film's extraordinary international and critical success enabled Eisenstein to travel throughout Europe, and in 1930 he arrived in Hollywood with a contract from Paramount Studios (which was quickly terminated). Invited by painter Diego Rivera, he began shooting an ambitious project in Mexico. When his sponsors cut off his funds, Eisenstein returned to the Soviet Union, where, under Joseph Stalin, socialist realism had become the official program in filmmaking. Consequently, the careers of Eisenstein, Vertov, and the other major experimental filmmakers of the revolutionary period suffered.

French Impressionist Cinema and Poetic Realism

While Hollywood cinema was mostly preoccupied with the new possibilities of dialogue and the creation of generic formulas in the 1920s and 1930s, French directors conducted radical experiments with film form. As in contemporaneous visual arts like impressionist painting, **French impressionist cinema** destabilized familiar or objective ways of seeing and revitalized the dynamics of human perception.

Representative of the early impressionist films are Germaine Dulac's *The Seashell and the Clergyman* (1928), Jean Epstein's *The Fall of the House of Usher* (1928), Marcel L'Herbier's *L'Argent* (1928), and Abel Gance's three daring narrative films, *I Accuse* (1919), *The Wheel* (1923), and *Napoléon* (1927). Dulac's surrealist film illustrates the daring play between subject matter and form that these films deploy. Scripted by avant-garde writer Antonin Artaud, *The Seashell and the Clergyman* barely concentrates on its story (a priest pursues a beautiful woman). Instead, it focuses on the consciousness of the central character, who remembers, hallucinates, and fantasizes within a dream logic of split screens and other strange imagistic effects **[Figure 10.10]**.

Developing out of these avant-garde films in the 1930s are more narrative and commercial examples of poetic realism by René Clair, Jean Vigo, Marcel Carné, and Jean Renoir. These socially conscious directors integrated poetic innovations into traditional movie realism to unsettle perceptions.

Renoir's *The Rules of the Game* (1939) **[Figure 10.11]** is on one level a realistic account of social conflict and disintegration. A tale of aristocrats and their

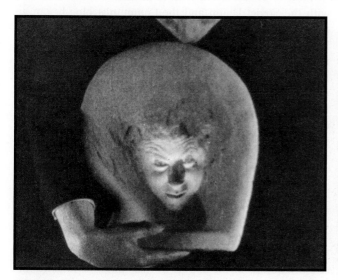

10.10 *The Seashell and the Clergyman* (1928). In a surreal image from the film collaboration between Germaine Dulac and Antonin Artaud, the main character sees his own head in the seashell.

10.11 *The Rules of the Game* (1939). Jean Renoir's masterwork of French cinema is known for its fluid style and critique of bourgeois society.

servants gathered for a holiday in the country, the film is a satirical and often biting critique of the hypocrisy and brutality of this microcosm of decadent society. The film's insight and wit come from lighting, long takes, and framing that draw out dark ironies not visible on the surface of the relationships. One of the film's most noted sequences features a hunting expedition in which the editing searingly equates the slaughter of birds and rabbits with the social behavior of the hunters toward each other.

Jean Vigo's *Zero for Conduct* (1933) takes up the themes of rebellion and social critique by depicting tyranny at a boys' boarding school. The spirit of rebellion in the boys is conveyed in a combination of realistic narrative and lyrical, sometimes fantastical, images. These images dramatize the wild and anarchistic vision of the young boys: at one point a pillow fight erupts in the dormitory, and the whirlwind of pillow feathers transforms the room into a paradise of disorder. The spirit of poeticism and critique that informed these directors' visions, while not impossible to convey in Hollywood films of the period, was discouraged by the industrial and commercial orientation of filmmaking in Hollywood.

Postwar Cinemas

The aftermath of World War II—from the inhuman nightmare of the Nazi concentration camps to the atomic bombing of Hiroshima and Nagasaki in 1945—overshadowed economic prosperity and surface optimism in the United States and reshaped geography and politics worldwide. This period, which extended roughly from 1946 to 1968, saw numerous global film movements, including the turbulent and transitional postwar Hollywood cinema, Italian neorealism, the French New Wave, the recognition of Japanese cinema in the West, and the emergence of Third Cinema. A new consciousness of film's role in national and cultural life, along with the great changes and challenges wrought by the war, such as decolonization, breathed vitality into cinemas globally.

Postwar Hollywood

In postwar America, unease permeated traditional institutions, especially the family and the sexual and social relationships associated with it. In addition, the Cold War with the Soviet Union and the Communist bloc began an extended period of tension and anxiety about national identity and security. In the 1950s and 1960s, the civil rights movement rigorously challenged social injustice. Amid the social and political turmoil of postwar America, the film industry was targeted for its capacity for ideological influence. The most prominent example of this was the congressional investigation of Communist infiltration of the motion-picture business in the late 1940s and 1950s, which was part of the postwar Red Scare associated with Senator Joseph McCarthy [Figure 10.12]. The film industry served as a high-profile target in the sensationalist hearings conducted by the House Un-American Activities Committee (HUAC).

Many Hollywood screenwriters, actors, and technicians embraced leftist politics during Franklin D. Roosevelt's administration in the 1930s. But the postwar mushrooming of anti-Soviet sentiment that stoked the Cold War cast suspicion on the left. In 1947, after a week of testimony about Communist influence in the industry from

10.12 Senator Joseph McCarthy. McCarthy's anti-Communist fervor planted the seeds for the blacklisting of numerous progressive film personnel, including directors, screenwriters, and actors.

"friendly" witnesses such as Walt Disney and Screen Actors Guild and later U.S. president Ronald Reagan, HUAC called "unfriendly" witnesses. Those who refused to answer the committee's question, "Are you now or have you ever been a member of the Communist Party?" were cited for contempt of Congress. These writers and directors, known as the "Hollywood Ten"—Alvah Bessie, Herbert Biberman, Lester Cole, Edward Dmytryk, Ring Lardner Jr., John Howard Lawson, Albert Maltz, Samuel Ornitz, Adrian Scott, and Dalton Trumbo—were eventually convicted and served short prison terms **[Figure 10.13]**.

Although HUAC's charges remained unconfirmed, its intimidation tactics were influential. Accusations of present or past Communist Party affiliation devastated Hollywood's creative pool and led to the blacklisting of more than three hundred screenwriters, directors, actors, and technical personnel, among them significant numbers of politically progressive Jews and African Americans. While some redress was achieved in 1960 when Dalton Trumbo, one of the Hollywood Ten, received screenwriting credit for *Exodus* and *Spartacus*, the careers of many others were irreversibly affected.

A number of other events had great impact on Hollywood during the postwar period. In the Supreme Court's 1948 *Paramount* decision, the studios were ordered to divest their theater chains and end their oligopolisitc control of the industry. This decline in studio power was accompanied by the arrival and rapid spread of television in the 1950s. Finally, in 1968, the Production Code era officially ended and the ratings system was introduced. Movies grew more daring and darker as they loosened or challenged the formulas of classical Hollywood and explored more controversial themes and issues. Competing with television, they also developed a more self-conscious and exaggerated sense of image composition and narrative structure.

Beginning with *The Best Years of Our Lives* (1946) and its layered tale of postwar trauma in small-town America, films delved into such subjects as family betrayal, alcoholism and drug abuse, sexuality, racial injustice, and psychological breakdowns. These topics introduced more unpredictable characters and narratives as well as sometimes subversive and violent visual styles, exemplified in Orson Welles's *Touch of Evil* (1958) and Alfred Hitchcock's shocking *Psycho* (1960). John Ford's westerns—from *My Darling Clementine* (1946) to *The Searchers* (1956)—can be seen as historical barometers of this transitional and turbulent period in Hollywood. *My Darling Clementine*, the prototypical western, is a meditation on the power of nature and communal individualism to overcome evil. *The Searchers*, however, is a morally ambivalent tale about where violence resides, featuring an older John Wayne as the racist cowboy Ethan Edwards **[Figure 10.14]**.

Michael Curtiz's *Mildred Pierce* (1945) and Howard Hawks's *The Big Sleep* (1946) both concentrate on the postwar period's social and personal instability, and explore the perceived threat of female sexuality. As if reflecting their troubled characters and actions in their form, these films' narratives

10.13   The Hollywood Ten. Refusing to answer HUAC's questions, these ten directors, screenwriters, and producers were jailed for contempt of Congress.

10.14   *The Searchers* (1956). John Ford's late western uses lead actor John Wayne, and the Monument Valley settings familiar from their long collaboration, to bring out dark themes of racist violence in the settling of the West. The film's structure and hero had a profound effect on the New Hollywood directors who would emerge in the 1970s.

10.15 *Mildred Pierce* (1945). This memorable look at gender roles in the 1940s is inflected with film noir style. Todd Haynes's 2011 HBO miniseries revisits the source novel by James M. Cain.

seem to lose their direction, and their visual styles are overwhelmed with gloom. Along with its superb performances—notably Joan Crawford's Oscar-winning portrayal of the title role—and compelling narration, *Mildred Pierce* stands out in its trenchant depiction of the cultural crisis that women faced in the 1940s **[Figure 10.15]** (see Film in Focus, pp. 250–51).

By the late 1950s and 1960s, younger audiences came to the forefront of movie culture: drive-ins and teenage audiences are one example; another is the college and urban audiences for art films and other alternative cinemas that proliferated after 1960. Nicholas Ray's *Rebel Without a Cause* (1955) gives a then-shocking depiction of a generational crisis in America in which teenagers drift aimlessly beyond parental guidance **[Figure 10.16]**. At the same time, with films like Ingmar Bergman's *The Seventh Seal* (1957) and Federico Fellini's *8½* (1963)—two very different meditations on existential questions—movies came to be considered complex artistic objects that justified aesthetic appreciation and academic study by college students.

Italian Neorealism

One of the most profound influences on the emerging international postwar art cinema was **Italian neorealism** (1942–1952), whose relatively short history belies its profound historical impact. At a critical juncture of world history, Italian cinema revitalized film culture by (1) depicting postwar social crises, and (2) using a stark, realistic style clearly different from the glossy entertainment formulas of Hollywood and other studio systems.

Earlier in the century, Italian film spectacles such as *Quo Vadis?* (1913) and *Cabiria* (1914) had created a taste for lavish epics (and influenced American cinema's transition to feature-length films). The films produced at the Cinecittà ("cinema city") studios under Benito Mussolini's Fascist regime (1922–1943) were glossy, decorative entertainments. During wartime in 1942, screenwriter Cesare Zavattini called for a new cinema that would forsake entertainment formulas and promote social realism instead. Luchino Visconti responded with *Ossessione* (1943), and Vittorio De Sica directed Zavattini's screenplays to produce such classics as *Bicycle Thieves* (1948). Perhaps the best example of the accomplishments and contradictions of this movement is Roberto Rossellini's *Rome, Open City* (1945), shot under adverse conditions at the end of the war **[Figure 10.17]**. Set during the Nazi occupation of Rome (1943–1944), the film intentionally approximates newsreel images to depict the strained and desperate street life of the war-torn city. The plot also employs the harsh reality of life in the city, as it tells of a community trying to protect a resistance fighter being hunted by the German SS and of the tragic deaths of those caught in between. One of its most shocking scenes shows the torture of one of these individuals. Despite the melodrama of its plot about lovers and families torn apart, the grim realism of *Rome, Open City* sounded a note that reverberated through postwar movie cultures, echoing in the later work of Italian director Pier Paolo Pasolini

10.16 *Rebel without a Cause* (1955). Teenage angst and juvenile delinquency are on display in Nicholas Ray's CinemaScope classic.

VIEWING CUE

How does the content of the film you just viewed identify it as part of a particular period? Which formal characteristics of this film seem common to this era?

and realist movements of the 1950s and 1960s, including the films of Senegalese director Ousmane Sembène (discussed later in this chapter). Subsequent Italian cinema—including the work of directors Michelangelo Antonioni, Vittorio and Paolo Taviani, Marco Bellocchio, Bernardo Bertolucci, and even Federico Fellini—follows from this neorealist history even when it introduces new forms and subjects.

French New Wave

A particularly rich period of cinema history occurs in the wake of Italian neorealism, from the 1950s through the 1970s, when numerous daring film movements, often designated as new waves, appeared in such countries as Brazil, Czechoslovakia, England, France, Germany, and Japan, among others. Despite their exceptional variety, these different new waves share two common postwar interests that counterpoint their often nationalistic flavor: (1) a break with past filmmaking institutions and genres, and (2) the use of film to express a personal vision.

The first and most influential new wave cinema, **French New Wave**, came to prominence in the late 1950s, with an exceptionally rich variety of films from such diverse filmmakers as Robert Bresson and Jacques Tati. This era brought three definitive films: Jean-Luc Godard's *Breathless* (1960), François Truffaut's *The 400 Blows* (1959), and Alain Resnais's *Hiroshima Mon Amour* (1959). Although the style and subject matter of these films are extremely different, they each demonstrate the struggle for personal expression and the formal investigation of film as a communication system.

The vitality of these films made a break with the past and an immediate impact on international audiences. Indeed, this vitality was often expressed in memorable stylistic innovations, such as the freeze frame on the boy protagonist's face that ends *The 400 Blows*, the jump cuts that register the restlessness of the antihero of *Breathless*, and the time-traveling editing of *Hiroshima Mon Amour*.

Much of the inspiration for the French New Wave filmmakers sprang from the work of film critic and theoretician André Bazin. In 1951, Bazin helped establish the journal *Cahiers du cinéma*, a forum from which emerged some of the most renowned directors of the movement, including Eric Rohmer and Claude Chabrol **[Figure 10.18]** as well as Truffaut and Godard. The revitalization of film language occurred in conjunction with the journal's policy of auteurism (*politique des auteurs)* or auteur theory, which emphasized the role of the director as an expressive author (see pp. 410–11). Writing and directing their own films, paying tribute to the important figures emerging in other national cinemas—like Michelangelo Antonioni, Ingmar Bergman, and Akira

10.17 *Rome, Open City* (1945). Roberto Rossellini's film exemplifies Italian neorealism in its use of war-ravaged locations, nonprofessional actors, and contemporary subject matter.

10.18 **Claude Chabrol** (1980). Chabrol was both a critic for *Cahiers du cinéma* and one of the directors associated with the rise of the French New Wave. His more than forty films were often influenced by Alfred Hitchcock, about whom he and Rohmer published a book in 1957.

10.19 *Tokyo Story* (1953). Carefully composed images suggest the rhythms of everyday life.

Kurosawa—and rediscovering the work of Hollywood directors, the young French filmmaker-critics helped shape the perspective and culture that elevated film to the art form it is considered to be today.

Japanese Cinema

Japan is one of the world's largest film-producing nations, with a long and varied tradition using distinct perceptual and generic forms and drawing on a range of cultural and artistic traditions. After World War II and the subsequent Allied occupation, Japanese films increasingly incorporated Hollywood forms and styles, yet generally they (1) place character rather than action at the center of a narrative, and (2) emphasize the contemplative aspect of images.

Kenji Mizoguchi, Yasujiro Ozu, Akira Kurosawa, and Nagisa Oshima are among the most celebrated names in Japanese cinema, with the long careers of the first two beginning in the silent period (which lasted into the 1930s in Japan). Ozu's midcareer masterpiece, *Tokyo Story* (1953) highlights his exquisite sense of the rhythms of everyday life, conveyed through carefully composed frames, long takes, and a low camera **[Figure 10.19]**. The energies of postwar cinema are especially evident in Kurosawa's *Rashomon* (1950), which uses multiple, contradictory narrations of the same event. The film won the top prize at the Venice Film Festival; and Mizoguchi's *Ugetsu* received the festival's Silver Lion soon after. Recognition at European film festivals established Japanese cinema's centrality to international postwar art cinema and helped Japanese auteurs achieve international notoriety. Even after the postwar era, Japanese filmmakers continued to make a mark on the international art cinema scene. Oshima's violent and erotic masterpiece, *In the Realm of the Senses* (1976) helped define Japan's new wave. Juzo Itami's *Tampopo* (1985) bridges the culturally specific and the culturally shared with its depiction of the pleasures of noodle eating.

Going beyond art cinema, many distinctly Japanese genres produced for national and Asian audiences eventually earned international followings. Indeed one of the most widespread influences on contemporary transnational cinema is *anime*, Japanese animation. The distinctive style and complex plots of such anime as *Ghost in the Shell* (1995) and *Ghost in the Shell 2: Innocence* (2004) have won worldwide audiences and influenced Hollywood productions **[Figure 10.20]**.

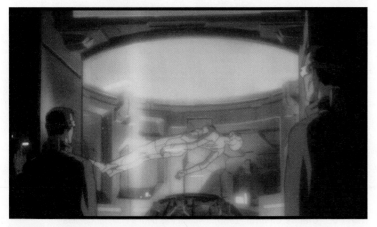

10.20 *Ghost in the Shell* (1995). The film's unique style and dramatic science fiction plot appealed to audiences all around the world and influenced *The Matrix* (1999).

Third Cinema

The growing influence of film festivals in the decades after World War II helped foster film art and commerce internationally. Inspired by the politicized atmosphere of Third World decolonization in the 1960s, Argentine filmmakers Fernando Solanas and Octavio Getino championed revolutionary films in opposition to Hollywood and to state-dominated film cultures elsewhere (which they dubbed "first cinema"), and in response to the elitist aesthetics of auteurist art cinema ("second cinema"). **Third Cinema**, a term coined in their 1969 manifesto

"Towards a Third Cinema," has been used to unite films from many countries under one political and formal rubric, including some made by Europeans, such as *The Battle of Algiers* (1966), directed by Italian Marxist Gillo Pontecorvo in cooperation with the victorious Algerian revolutionary government. In Latin America, Solanas and Getino's *The Hour of the Furnaces* (1968) incited political opposition and cultural renewal in Argentina, and *Black God, White Devil* (1964) by prominent Brazilian *cinema novo* director Glauber Rocha embraced cultural diversity and violence.

Third Cinema aimed to (1) reject technical perfection in opposition to commercial traditions, and (2) embrace film as the voice of the people. These goals often entailed combining modernist techniques drawn from Soviet montage and from filmmakers like Jean-Luc Godard— such as fragmented formal structures and analytical voiceovers—with populist documentary subject matter and traditions. The creation of the film institute ICAIC (Instituto Cubano del Arte e Industria Cinematográficos, or Cuban Institute of Cinematographic Art and Industry)

10.21   *Memories of Underdevelopment* (1968). The voiceover of Tomás Gutiérrez Alea's postrevolutionary Cuban film reflects on traditional culture, exemplifying Third Cinema.

in postrevolutionary Cuba provided the ideal testing ground for integrating film with an emerging nation's cultural identity. Tomás Gutiérrez Alea's *Memories of Underdevelopment* (1968) is one of the best-known examples of Third Cinema. Its story of a middle-class intellectual contemplating the changes in postrevolutionary society is innovatively filmed and politically engaged **[Figure 10.21]**.

The very term "Third Cinema" evokes its particular era in world politics—one that was dominated by First and Second World superpowers, preoccupied with the Cold War, and that witnessed the sometimes violent nation-building struggles of the Third World. The ways in which politics and culture intersect on global, regional, national, and local levels would continue to shift with the political changes beyond this era.

Contemporary Film Cultures

We designate the most recent period in film history, beginning around 1965 and continuing through the present, as contemporary cinema. In the United States, the social anger and confusion of the Vietnam War colored the early part of this era, and new pressures emerged when that war ended in 1975. Racial and gender politics, which had informed the strains and shifts of the 1950s, became a defining part of the landscape. These events and changes brought cultural issues like immigration, multiculturalism, and gender and sexual identity to the forefront of film culture.

The dissolution of the Soviet bloc in the 1990s redistributed global power. Postcolonial migrations continued to transform European societies and global cities, and international debt policies impacted developing nations. The rise of new nationalisms and fundamentalisms ignited violent conflicts and prolonged wars. Cinema and other kinds of cultural production became crucial to mediating individuals' experiences of these global events and transformations.

It would be impossible to be fully inclusive of contemporary global film culture in a few pages. New cinemas regularly leap to prominence on the global scene, and the economy of global film production and distribution reinforces the tendency toward international co-productions. We have selected a few examples that illuminate important histories and trends—contemporary Hollywood and

VIEWING CUE

Scan local film listings, noting how many different countries are represented. If the range is limited, why do you think this is so? If you have located foreign films, what kinds of venues or channels show them?

10.22 *The Godfather* (1972). Perhaps the key example of New Hollywood, Francis Ford Coppola's film was an economic and artistic success.

European, Indian, Chinese, African, and Iranian cinemas—with the recognition that there are a host of other national and regional cinemas, as well as directors, aesthetic movements, and institutions, that would reward attention.

Contemporary Hollywood

Since the 1960s, the commercial movie industry in the United States has been noticeably affected by four forces: the dominance of youth audiences, the increasing influence of European art films, globalization, and the rise of such economic and technological innovations as blockbusters, cable, and home video.

In the 1970s, Hollywood turned some of its power over to young filmmakers, who began to address the teenage audiences that made up larger and larger portions of the moviegoing public. *The Godfather* (1972) and *Taxi Driver* (1976) are part of a remarkable series of films from the so-called New Hollywood **[Figure 10.22]**. Influenced by European art cinemas, this movement took imaginative risks in form and subject matter. Hollywood's strategy for courting youth audiences changed significantly, however, when global conglomerate enterprises began to assimilate and shape Hollywood. Corporate Hollywood redirected youthful energy toward more commercial blockbusters and global markets. Finally, VCRs, cable television, and later technologies such as DVDs and Internet streaming disseminated movies in ways that offered viewers more variety and control.

Amid so many cataclysmic changes in film culture, two trends dominate the contemporary period: (1) the elevation of image spectacles and special effects, and (2) the fragmentation and reflexivity of narrative constructions.

On the one hand, contemporary movies frequently drift away from the traditional focus on narrative and instead emphasize sensational mise-en-scènes or dramatic manipulations of the film image. In this context, conventional realism gives way to intentionally artificial, spectacular, or even cartoonish representations of characters, places, and actions. Playful films like *Who Framed Roger Rabbit* (1988) **[Figure 10.23]** allow cartoon characters to interact with human ones, whereas a more serious drama like *The King of Comedy* (1983) shows an obsessive fan replacing the real world with strange fantasies. On the other hand, contemporary movies that do fully engage narrative traditions often intentionally fragment, reframe, or distort the narrative in ways that challenge its coherence. *Memento* (2000) reconstructs narrative through its continually changing retrospective perspectives, all subject to the narrator/protagonist's lack of short-term memory; the result is a series of overlapping episodes that eventually leads back to the murder that started the film. In *Babel* (2006), an international co-production directed by Mexican director Alejandro González Iñárritu, interlocking story lines unfold in multiple languages and on several continents. This new narrative complexity may relate to viewers' familiarity with game worlds and to their ability to watch and rewatch these complex works on DVD to piece together narrative strands.

One characteristic of the most recent chapter of Hollywood moviemaking, from about 1980 to the present, has been the idea of the auteur, most often the

10.23 *Who Framed Roger Rabbit* (1988). Cartoon characters interacting with actors exemplifies a contemporary interest in spectacle and a self-consciousness about film form.

director, as a brand. We can pinpoint three signature films of the 1980s and 1990s as evidence of this phenomenon: Ridley Scott's *Blade Runner* (1982), David Lynch's *Blue Velvet* (1986), and Quentin Tarantino's *Pulp Fiction* (1994). Each of these films is a dramatic visual and narrative experiment that investigates the confusion of human identity, violence, and ethics at the end of the twentieth century. In *Blade Runner,* Deckard (played by Harrison Ford) hunts down human replicants in a fascinatingly dark and visually complex dystopia where technology creates beings "more human than human." With *Blue Velvet,* Lynch fashions a nightmarish version of small-town America in which Jeffrey,

10.24   *Pulp Fiction* (1994). The running commentary of the hit men played by John Travolta and Samuel L. Jackson marks this as a Quentin Tarantino film.

the protagonist, discovers violence seething through his everyday community and his own naive soul. In *Pulp Fiction*, where violence is also a measure of human communication, the narrative follows the unpredictable actions and reflections of two hit men who philosophically meditate out loud about the Bible, loyalty, and McDonald's hamburgers **[Figure 10.24]**. These exceptional films demonstrate not only great imaginative quality but also professional skill and innovativeness. These filmmakers are in part able to produce such daring and disturbing projects and successfully distribute them within mainstream film culture because their own personae become part of what is marketed.

The prominence of the director in driving movie commerce is perhaps nowhere more evident than in the career of James Cameron. While the huge budgets, innovative technology, and massive promotional campaigns of *Titanic* (1997) and *Avatar* (2009) helped make them two of the highest-grossing films in both the United States and the worldwide box office, Cameron's reputation and "brand" were also key to their success.

In part because the big-budget Hollywood production model of the 1990s and 2000s is unattainable anywhere else, many national and regional cinemas have organized themselves around what makes them aesthetically distinctive, at the same time enacting funding, import/export, and distribution policies that can keep them competitive. One way that these cinemas have counteracted Hollywood's continuing commercial dominance is with an increasingly organized circuit of film festivals that foster contributions from many nations and the development of transnational and regional industrial alternatives.

Contemporary European Cinema

A number of youth-driven new wave movements emerged in both Eastern and Western Europe in the 1960s and 1970s (notably among them the Czech New Wave and New German cinema). Although the spirit of these movements, and the formal innovations of the films, challenged entrenched state- and commercially dominated national film industries, they were still largely identified with the concept of "the nation." European co-productions had emerged in the wake of World War II to increase available financing and to combat the perceived cultural and commercial threat of American imports. And since the fall of the Berlin Wall in 1989 and the founding of the European Union in 1993, trans- and supranational film production, distribution, and exhibition structures (such as the Eurimages Fund, created in 1989) are as prominent in the landscape of contemporary European cinema as are culturally and industrially distinct national cinemas. Here we chart a few of the key movements and trends in contemporary European cinema, from New German cinema to the pan-European productions of today.

text continued on page 374 ▶

Taxi Driver and New Hollywood (1976)

One reason Martin Scorsese's *Taxi Driver* remains such a powerful and rich film today is its keen self-consciousness about its place in film history and the complex historical references it puts into play. *Taxi Driver* is suffused with the historical events that colored and shaped U.S. society in the 1970s and shares many characteristics with other films of the era. At the same time, it echoes and recalls Hollywood's classical and postwar periods, suggesting that one of the defining features of contemporary film is its awareness of past cinematic traditions. For instance, Scorsese commissioned the film's haunting score from composer Bernard Herrmann, best known for his collaborations with Orson Welles on *Citizen Kane* and Alfred Hitchcock on *Vertigo*, *Psycho*, and other films. The darkness lurking in these films is fully embraced in *Taxi Driver* and resonates in Herrmann's music.

The story, written by filmmaker Paul Schrader, focuses on a New York cabdriver, Travis Bickle (played by Scorsese regular Robert De Niro), and his increasing alienation from the city in which he lives and works. As he cruises New York locked in the isolated compartment of his cab, his voiceover narration rambles and meditates on his entrapment in a world that has lost its innocence and seems to be progressing only toward its own destruction. Travis decries the filth and decadence of the city and considers violent and apocalyptic solutions like assassinating a politician. Attempting to break out of the bitter routines of his existence, he imagines himself the savior of Iris, a young prostitute, and attracts the ire of her pimp. The film ends with a ghastly bloodbath in which Travis murders the pimp, followed by the unsettling announcement that Travis has become a media hero.

The issues and atmosphere of 1970s U.S. society pervade *Taxi Driver*. Flagged by Travis's veteran's jacket and the traumatized personality associated with young soldiers returning from the Vietnam War, the specter of that war haunts the film. Travis's violent personality echoes a whole decade of U.S. violence: the assassinations of

John F. Kennedy and Martin Luther King Jr. and, as an explicit source for the film, Arthur Bremer's attempted assassination of Alabama governor George Wallace. The violence in *Taxi Driver* associates it with many other films made since the 1970s. These range from *A Clockwork Orange* (1971) to *Natural Born Killers* (1994), in which modern life and identity are tied to the psychological and social prevalence of violence, and graphic and often unmotivated violence becomes a desperate means of expression for lost souls. Five years after its release, *Taxi Driver* remained a barometer of modern America. When John Hinckley Jr. tried to assassinate President Ronald Reagan in 1981, he claimed to have been inspired by *Taxi Driver* and had hoped, in killing a president, to "effect a mystical union with Jodie Foster," the star who played Iris.

As a part of its consciousness about the burdens of the past, the film's plot explicitly recalls John Ford's *The Searchers* (1956) and implicitly recalls other classical westerns, such as Ford's *Stagecoach* (1939) (suggested by the Mohawk haircut Travis acquires midway through the film and the Native American look of the pimp Travis kills). Like Ford's Ethan Edwards (John Wayne) in *The Searchers*, Travis becomes alienated from most social interaction, yet he yearns, through his determination to "save" Iris, to restore some lost form of family and community. He wants to be a hero in an age when there is little possibility for heroic action. Yet the recollection of earlier periods of Hollywood history and the plots and characters they produced only highlights the historical differences of this film: Travis is a fully modern antihero, one with no frontier to explore and only imaginary heroics to motivate him. New York is not the Wild West, and Travis clearly lacks the proud, clear vision and the noble purpose of a western hero like the Ringo Kid in the classic *Stagecoach*. That a younger, more cynical audience was the primary target of and the vehicle for the success of *Taxi Driver* indicates that the changing social tastes and attitudes of audiences play a large part in determining the variations among films of different historical periods.

Stylistically, *Taxi Driver* consistently suggests a high degree of self-consciousness about its narrative organization and images. Scorsese employs two formal patterns typical of New Hollywood films: exaggerated or hyper-realistic cinematography and a self-conscious, often interiorized, narrative perspective. Both of these patterns suggest the influence of French New Wave directors on Scorsese and on other films of this period such as *Apocalypse Now* (1979). *Taxi Driver* paints New York City through hyper-realistic images that seem to be the product of either a strained mind or a strained society. Shots of New York at night gleam and swirl with flashing colors, creating a carnivalesque atmosphere of neon and glass. Frames (like those of the cab window and its rearview mirror) constantly call attention to a subjective, partial point of view **[Figure 10.25]**. This attention to the frames through which we see and understand the world then crystallizes in one of the most renowned shots of the movie. Midway through the film, Travis equips himself with various guns, and while he poses before a mirror, he repeatedly addresses himself with the famous line "You talkin' to me?" As he watches himself in the mirror, identity appears to split, one image of self violently confronting the other **[Figure 10.26]**. This line could be an epigraph for contemporary movies on divided identity.

Similarly, the first-person narration of *Taxi Driver* provides an almost psychotic staging of Travis's personal desires and anxieties. "One day, indistinguishable from the next, a long continuous chain," Travis rambles on through the private voiceover. This drifting interior narrative jumps from one psychological state and illogical action to another: Travis tries, for instance, to court a woman with a date at a pornographic movie, and later he plans to assassinate her employer, a politician running for office, for no apparent reason. When Travis initiates his final bloody attack on Iris's pimp, the narrative takes its most unpredictable turn: despite the bizarre motivation for this event (to rescue a young woman who does not wish to be rescued) and the shockingly graphic slaughter that leaves a trail of shredded bodies, Travis becomes a community hero, celebrated in newspapers for his rescue of Iris. At this moment of anticipated closure, narrative logic becomes strained to the point of fracturing. A "happy ending" to a narrative motivated and shaped by a narcissistic and unbalanced mind seems to subvert the possibility of a traditional narrative logic in *Taxi Driver*—and possibly even in this contemporary world.

Taxi Driver acts out the signs of its times, socially and artistically. However, this film demonstrates that recent cinema also bears the burden of its past. Being true to its present requires unusual awareness of the dramatic changes and fissures that distinguish the film from its historical heritage.

10.25 *Taxi Driver* (1976). The windshield functions as a frame for Travis Bickle's limited point of view.

10.26 *Taxi Driver* (1976). The famous scene in which the main character, Travis Bickle, confronts his mirror image demonstrates a divided and shifting identity.

10.27 *The Marriage of Maria Braun* (1979). Rainer Werner Fassbinder made forty feature films in a short career as one of the most celebrated representatives of New German cinema. This historical drama featuring frequent Fassbinder star Hannah Schygulla was one of his most commercially successful films.

New German cinema was launched in 1962, when a group of young filmmakers declared a new agenda for German film in a film festival document called the Oberhausen Manifesto. A unique mix of government subsidies, international critical acclaim, and domestic television and worldwide film festival exposure established New German cinema as an integral product of West Germany's national culture. This extraordinarily vital and stylistically diverse cinema can nevertheless be characterized by (1) a confrontation with Germany's Nazi and postwar past, approached directly or through an examination of the current political and cultural climate, and (2) an emphasis on the distinctive, often maverick, visions of individual directors.

Alexander Kluge, one of the political founders of New German cinema, uses modernist film practices to question the interpretation of history in *Yesterday Girl* (1966). Perhaps the movement's most celebrated and prolific director, Rainer Werner Fassbinder produced a trilogy of films about postwar Germany. The first, *The Marriage of Maria Braun* (1979), adapts the Hollywood melodrama to tell of a soldier's widow who builds a fortune in the aftermath of the war **[Figure 10.27]**. By 1984, Edgar Reitz's sixteen-hour television series *Heimat*, in part a response to the American television miniseries *Holocaust* (1978), demonstrated that the cultural silence about the Nazi era had definitively been broken.

On the international stage, however, the hallmark of New German cinema was less its depiction of historical, political, and social questions than the distinctive personae and filmic visions of its most celebrated participants. The visionary Wim Wenders, the driven Werner Herzog, and the enormously productive, despotic, and hard-living Fassbinder were easily packaged as auteurs with outsized personalities. Wim Wenders's films, including *Alice in the Cities* (1974) and *Wings of Desire* (1987), are philosophical reflections on the nature of the cinematic image and the encounter between Europe and the United States. Werner Herzog's *Aguirre: The Wrath of God* (1972) and *Fitzcarraldo* (1982) are bold depictions of extreme cultural encounters set in Latin American jungles. Several of the most successful directors began to work abroad, and with wider social shifts and changes in cultural policy in Germany, the heyday of New German cinema came to an end. In unified Germany, where many of these filmmakers continue to work, interesting new directions are indicated by Tom Tykwer's international hit, *Run, Lola, Run* (1998); Fatih Akin's films exploring Turkish-German culture, including *Edge of Heaven* (2007); and Florian Henckel von Donnersmarck's Academy Award–winning *The Lives of Others* (2006), set in the former East Germany.

As these examples of recent German filmmaking suggest, traditional understandings of the category of the national do not adequately encapsulate contemporary cinema. Take, for example, the success of recent Danish cinema. Subsidized by the government, sustained by the activities of the Danish Film Institute, and bolstered by the notoriety of the Dogme 95 film movement that called for a new realism facilitated by possibilities of digital filmmaking, Danish films have been embraced by Danish audiences, international festivals, and art-house audiences. The high profile of Danish film ranges from the controversial films of Lars von

Trier such as *Breaking the Waves* (1996) and *Antichrist* (2009) to Susanne Bier's socially conscious drama *In a Better World* (2010), which won the Academy Award for best foreign language film.

Both von Trier's films and Bier's *In a Better World* were produced by Zentropa (in which von Trier is a founding partner), an innovative company that fosters partnerships and co-productions across Europe. One such film is Andrea Arnold's remarkably assured debut feature *Red Road* (2006), in which the protagonist's job as a closed-circuit television worker in Glasgow brings her face to face with a trauma from her past. The low-budget collaboration between Zentropa and the Glasgow company Sigma Films won the Jury Prize in competition at the Cannes Film Festival, exemplifying how local and transnational film cultures are defining the current landscape.

Indian Cinema

Indian cinema is the world's most prolific, and it has thrived since the first Indian film premiered in 1913. The subcontinent's large population is served by films produced not only in Hindi in Mumbai (formerly Bombay) studios, but also in a number of other languages of India, including Bengali, Marathi, and Tamil. Audiences outside India—in South and Southeast Asia and the Middle East as well as Indian diasporan audiences in the West—contribute to the industry's success and influence.

The golden age of Indian cinema came after independence in 1948 with the ascendance of the Bombay-based industry with its stars, songs, and spectacular successes. During the same period, Parallel Cinema, an alternative to India's commercial cinema centered mainly in Calcutta and exemplified by the films of renowned director Satyajit Ray, achieved prominence. Ray's modest black-and-white film *Pather Panchali* (1955) has been heralded internationally as a masterpiece of realist style. This film, together with the two subsequent features in the "Apu trilogy" (named after their main character), is rooted in Bengali landscape and culture. Both traditions—popular blockbusters and realist, regional dramas—continue to thrive in contemporary Indian cinema.

In the 1970s, India overtook Hollywood as the world's largest film producer, driven largely by the hundreds of Hindi-language films produced annually in Mumbai. Often referred to as Bollywood films, they are a dominant cultural form notable for (1) rootedness in Hindu culture and mythology, and (2) elaborate song-and-dance numbers.

With an episodic narrative form based in theatrical traditions that accommodate musical numbers, many Hindi films highlight star performances: Nargis plays the title role of Mehboob Khan's *Mother India* (1957) **[Figure 10.28]**, and the phenomenally successful action star Amitabh Bachchan was featured in the most popular Bollywood film of all time, *Sholay* (1975). In the 1990s, Shahrukh Khan skyrocketed to popularity in such films as *Dilwale Dulhania Le Jayenge* (1995) and *Shanti Om* (2007), with a fan base numbering in the billions.

The cricket film *Lagaan: Once Upon a Time in India* (2001) capitalized on the international popularity of Indian cinema to bid for attention from more mainstream critics and audiences abroad, especially in North America and the United Kingdom. This strategy

▶ **VIEWING CUE**

Compare a Western and a non-Western film. What differences exist in the narrative or visual elements? ⏸

10.28 *Mother India* (1957). Nargis in the iconic role of a mother who withstands hardship and becomes an allegorical figure of an independent India.

10.29 *My Name Is Khan* (2010). This vehicle for power couple Shahrukh Khan and Kajol, the highest-grossing Bollywood film overseas to date, deals with anti-Muslim sentiment in the United States after 9/11. Ironically, during a promotional visit to the United States, Khan was detained by airport security—because of his name.

became more successful throughout the decade with *My Name Is Khan* becoming the highest-grossing Indian film internationally in 2010 **[Figure 10.29]**. The transnational dimension of Indian film can also be seen in movies directed by filmmakers of the Indian diaspora. For example, Gurinder Chadha's *Bride & Prejudice* (2004), an adaptation (with musical numbers) of Jane Austen's *Pride and Prejudice*, and Mira Nair's award-winning *Monsoon Wedding* (2001) borrow some of the visual and narrative tropes of Bollywood cinema. In 2008, when *Slumdog Millionaire*, British director Danny Boyle's film about a Mumbai street kid turned game-show contestant, won the Oscar for best picture, the international influence of Indian cinema could not be contested.

African Cinema

African cinema encompasses an entire continent and, hence, many languages, cultures, and nations, each with varying levels of economic development and infrastructure. An initial distinction can be made between North African and sub-Saharan African cinema. North African cinema has a long history, beginning with the Egyptian premiere of the Lumières's Cinématographe in 1896. After the introduction of sound, a commercial industry developed in Egypt that still dominates the movie screens of Arab countries. Youssef Chahine, working both in popular genres and on more political and personal projects (in which he sometimes appeared), was a cosmopolitan presence in Egyptian cinema from the 1950s to his death in 2008. His autobiographical trilogy, beginning with *Alexandria . . . Why?* (1979), is notable for its humor, frank approach to sexuality, and inventive structure. In recent Tunisian production, art films predominate, several of which are directed by and/or tell the stories of women. Moufida Tlatli's *The Silences of the Palace* (1994) opens in the postindependence period and follows a young woman singer as she remembers her girlhood as a palace servant. Many prominent filmmakers from Tunisia, Morocco, and Algeria have received training or financing from France, which allows for higher production values but also forces them to confront their countries' colonial past, at least in the filmmaking context.

Taking shape in the 1960s after decolonization, and often linked to the political and aesthetic precepts of Third Cinema, sub-Saharan African cinema encompasses the relatively well-financed francophone, or French-language, cinema of West Africa; films from a range of anglophone, or English-speaking, countries; and films in African languages such as Wolof and Swahili. Although it is difficult to generalize about this rapidly expanding film culture, some of its most influential features and shorts have been united by (1) a focus on social and political themes rather than commercial interests, and (2) an exploration of the conflicts between tradition and modernity.

At the forefront of this vital development is the most respected proponent of African cinema, Senegalese filmmaker Ousmane Sembène, who in 1966

10.30 *Black Girl* (1966). Simple long shots and a stark mise-en-scène depict the young woman's sense of entrapment and alienation.

directed sub-Saharan Africa's first feature film, *La noire de . . .* (*Black Girl*), with extremely limited technical and financial resources. The film, based on Sembène's own novel, follows a young woman who travels from Dakar, Senegal, to Monte Carlo to work with a white family as a nanny. She soon becomes disillusioned with her situation, trapped in the home, cooking and cleaning. Her French voiceover records her increasing despair. Simply composed long shots depict her as enclosed and restricted by her surroundings [Figure 10.30]. Although he made only eight features before his death in 2007, Sembène's films are remarkable for their moral vision, accessible storytelling, and range of characters. His protagonists represent aspects of traditional and modern African life without becoming two-dimensional symbols.

10.31 *Arugbá* (2010). The most recent film from veteran Nigerian filmmaker Tunde Kelani, which depicts the issues facing an accomplished young woman selected to participate in the annual community festival, was embraced by critics and audiences but economically undermined by video piracy.

Internationally known francophone filmmakers include Souleymane Cissé from Mali (*Yeelen*, 1987; *Finye*, 1982), Idrissa Ouedraogo from Burkina Faso (*Tilai*, 1990), and Abderrahmane Sissako from Mali (*Life on Earth*, 1998; *Bamako*, 2006). Sissako's films have been hailed as exquisite commentaries on the impact of globalization on Africa. Filmmakers are active all over the continent—in Ghana, Congo, Zimbabwe, and South Africa—and the shift to digital production has made a significant impact in these undercapitalized industries. The Nigerian film industry, known as Nollywood, has witnessed a stunning boom in the 1990s and 2000s driven by the hunger of audiences for African-produced images that are relevant to them and their lives. Producing popular genre films shot and distributed on video, such as Tunde Kelani's *Arugbá* (2010) [Figure 10.31], Nollywood overtook Hollywood in 2006 in terms of the number of films released annually.

Besides the limited financial and technical resources for film production, one of the biggest hurdles to the development of cinema in Africa is the lack of distribution and exhibition infrastructure that would enable African audiences to see African-made films in theaters. The Pan-African Film and Television Festival of Ouagadougou (FESPACO) in Burkina Faso is vital in this context. Filmmakers from all over the continent and the African diaspora meet at the festival, held every other year, to show and view others' work and to strategize about how to extend the cinema's popular influence.

Chinese Cinema

Chinese cinema poses its own challenge to models of national cinema because it includes films from the "three Chinas"—the People's Republic of China (or mainland China), Hong Kong, and Taiwan. Each of these areas developed under a different social and political regime, so the industries vary greatly in terms of commercial structure, the degree of government oversight, audience expectations, and even language. Yet they are all culturally united and increasingly economically interdependent. In mainland China after the 1949 Communist Revolution, cinema production was nearly halted and strictly limited to propaganda purposes. It was further disrupted during the Cultural Revolution in the 1960s, when leader Mao Zedong referred to American films as "sugar-coated bullets." It was not until the 1980s that a group of filmmakers emerged, the so-called Fifth Generation (referring to their class at the Beijing Film Academy), who were interested both in the formal potential of the medium and in critical social content. The enthusiastic reception given *Huang tu di* (*Yellow Earth*; 1985) at international film festivals made director Chen Kaige and cinematographer Zhang Yimou the most acclaimed filmmakers of this movement. The strong aesthetic vision of Fifth Generation films, stemming from the filmmakers' experiences growing up as marginalized artists during the Cultural Revolution, made a critical statement in its own right. However, this body of work, essentially art films, did not reach China's vast popular audiences.

With Zhang Yimou's directorial turn came a series of lush, sensuous films featuring Gong Li, an unknown actress who later became an international film star. Zhang's films *Ju dou* (1990) and *Raise the Red Lantern* (1991) **[Figure 10.32]** were the targets of censorship at home and the recipients of prizes and co-financing offers abroad. Later forays into *wuxia*, or martial arts films—*Hero* (2002) and *House of Flying Daggers* (2004)—and his direction of the Beijing Olympic ceremonies in 2008 established Zhang as a commercially successful, breathtaking visual stylist.

After the violent suppression of protests in Tiananmen Square in 1989, a new underground film movement emerged in the People's Republic of China. The so-called Sixth Generation explored urban life and controversial themes, such as gay sexuality in Zhang Yuan's *East Palace, West Palace* (1996), frequently making their films without official approval. One of the most internationally acclaimed filmmakers of this group, Jia Zhangke, was finally granted state approval to make his fourth feature, *The World* (2004), which depicts the uprooted lives of young employees at a Beijing theme park in heartbreaking, wry visual compositions **[Figure 10.33]**. Jia works modestly in both documentary and fiction, a versatility facilitated by his use of digital cinema. *Still Life* (2006), a drama set against the background of the Three Gorges Dam, won the Venice Film Festival's top prize.

After the phenomenal international success of low-budget Hong Kong kung-fu films in the 1970s, the Hong Kong New Wave led by producer-director Tsui Hark introduced sophisticated style, lucrative production methods, and a canny use of Western elements to the genre. Director John Woo became internationally known for his technical expertise and visceral editing of violent action films such as *The Killer* (1998). Along with legendary stunt star Jackie Chan, Woo brought the Hong Kong style to Hollywood in such films as *Face/Off* (1997). The stylish, even avant-garde work of Wong Kar-wai made an impact with its quirky stories of marginal figures moving through a postmodern, urban world, photographed and edited in an utterly distinctive style that finds beauty in the accidental and the momentary. *Happy Together* (1997) is the ironic title of a tale of two men drifting in and out of a relationship, set in a Buenos Aires that is not so different, in its urban anxiety, from the men's home of Hong Kong. Wong's *In the Mood for Love* (2000) is set

10.32 *Raise the Red Lantern* (1991). Gong Li became an international art-film star in the films of Fifth Generation Chinese director Zhang Yimou.

10.33 *The World* (2004). The Beijing theme park in which this film is set provides ironic visual commentary on the characters' limited options.

in the 1960s among cosmopolitan former residents of Shanghai who are trying to establish a pattern of life in Hong Kong **[Figure 10.34]**. Contemplative family sagas by acclaimed auteurs of the New Taiwan cinema, Hou Hsiao-hsien's *A City of Sadness* (1989) and Edward Yang's *Yi yi* (2000) reflect on the identity of contemporary Taiwan, positioned between mainland China, where much of its population comes from, and the West. In 2008, the box-office smash *Cape No. 7* by Wei Te-Sheng, featuring pop stars and a historical mystery, capped a recent trend of audiences supporting youth-oriented domestic films at the Taiwan box office.

10.34 *In the Mood for Love* (2000). In this film by Hong Kong auteur Wong Kar-wai, stylish characters make chance connections amid the urban alienation of Hong Kong.

Iranian Cinema

While many Chinese films have achieved strong commercial as well as critical success internationally, Iranian cinema is notable for its many festival prizes and critical acclaim abroad. The art films of this Islamic nation are characterized by (1) spare pictorial beauty, often of landscapes or scenes of everyday life on the margins, and (2) an elliptical storytelling mode that developed in part as a response to state regulation.

Following the 1978 Islamic Revolution in Iran, cinema was attacked as a corrupt Western influence and movie theaters were closed, but by the 1990s, both a popular cinema and a distinctive artistic film culture developed. The latter became a way to enhance Iran's international reputation, especially during the more moderate rule of Mohammad Khatami from 1997 to 2005. Films by such directors as Abbas Kiarostami and Mohsen Makhmalbaf became the most internationally admired and accessible expressions of contemporary Iranian culture as well as some of the most highly praised examples of global cinema. In Kiarostami's *Taste of Cherry* (1997), beautiful, barren landscapes are the settings for wandering characters' existential conversations. Jafar Panahi's popular *The White Balloon* (1995) depicts a little girl's search for a goldfish. Rural settings and child protagonists helped filmmakers avoid the censorship from religious leaders that contemporary social themes would attract. These strategies also evaded strictures forbidding adult male and female characters from touching—a compromise that at least avoided offering a distorted picture of domestic and romantic life.

More recently, however, filmmakers have used the international approval accorded Iranian films to tackle volatile social issues such as drugs and prostitution in portrayals of contemporary urban life. Panahi's *The Circle* (2000), banned in Iran, focuses on the plight of women, some of whom find prison a refuge; Makhmalbaf's *Kandahar* (2000) depicts the situation of neighboring Afghanistan just before that country became the focus of international attention and the target of a U.S.-led military campaign **[Figure 10.35]**. These depictions of controversial issues have tested the limits of the government's tolerance. In December 2010, Panahi was sentenced to a six-year jail term and banned from making films for twenty years by Mahmoud Ahmadinejad's regime.

One of the most interesting apparent contradictions in Iranian cinema is the prominence of women filmmakers. Strict religious decrees require female characters to keep their heads covered and forbid a range

VIEWING CUE

Compare at least two films from the same movement (such as New German cinema or Hong Kong New Wave). Do the characteristics discussed in this chapter apply?

10.35 *Kandahar* (2000). Makhmalbaf's film explores the volatile social issues in Afghanistan just prior to the U.S.-led military campaign there.

10.36 *Persepolis* (2007). Marjane Satrapi's autobiographical graphic novels satirize the Islamic Revolution, and their film adaptation, made with Vincent Paronnaud in France, was not looked upon favorably in the country of her birth. However, a number of women filmmakers working inside Iran also express a critical stance.

of onscreen behaviors, including singing. Nevertheless, behind the camera many Iranian women filmmakers—such as Tahmineh Milani, who was arrested for her film *The Hidden Half* (2001), and Samira Makhmalbaf (daughter of Mohsen Makhmalbaf), whose first feature film, *The Apple* (1998), was made when she was only eighteen—have achieved more than their contemporaries in many Western countries. Similar themes are more explicitly treated in the French animated film *Persepolis* (2007) by Vincent Paronnaud and Marjane Satrapi, based on the latter's graphic novel about her girlhood in Iran **[Figure 10.36]**.

In each of these examples of contemporary film cultures, we can see the role of cinema's powerful images and narratives in defining and challenging national and regional identities. A global perspective looks at cinema in the context of multiple and overlapping political and cultural histories.

The Lost and Found of Film History

Writing film history is not a straightforward enterprise; it involves interpretation and making choices about what to include. The process is made more difficult because important dimensions of the past remain hidden to the historian. For example, an estimated 80 percent of American films from the silent era are presumed to be lost. Moreover, standards of what's important are not timeless or universally shared. Debates about criteria of inclusion and exclusion are familiar in literary studies, where the accepted list of essential great works is called the **canon**. However, the concept of a film canon may give cultural weight to movies that audiences do not particularly enjoy, and it also inadvertently sets up some films and filmmakers as more authoritative than others.

Is it possible to write histories that remove the element of biased selection? One approach is to excavate the cinematic past for undervalued contributions and traditions and thereby to discover the unacknowledged antecedents of some of today's diverse film practices. Such a corrective history does not argue that rediscovered films should replace or even be put on a par with previously lauded masterpieces. Rather, it tries to (1) consider different questions about the past and its artifacts, and (2) uncover which version of the past has been accepted and supplement this version with missing perspectives.

In the shadow of canonized filmmakers and films, many others have been denied major status despite their significant historical contributions. Of these many omissions, we will focus on several histories that are key to a full understanding of U.S. cinema: women filmmakers, African American cinema, lesbian/gay/bisexual/transgender (LGBT) film culture, and indigenous media. Finally, we will provide an introduction to issues of film preservation through the concept of "orphan films." These are ephemeral or noncommercial films that, despite their lack of traditional cultural value, have survived or been rescued, yielding fascinating glimpses of the past.

Women Filmmakers

The American movie industry today remains male dominated, with women directing only 7 percent of the 250 top-grossing films in the United States in 2010. In independent, documentary, and experimental filmmaking, access for women is less prohibitive, but their participation is still unequal and these arenas are less visible.

However, in the early years of a wide-open industry, women entered film in great numbers as assistants,
writers, editors, and actresses as well as directors and
producers. Alice Guy Blaché, who made what some consider the first fiction film, *La fée aux choux* (*The Cabbage
Fairy*) in 1896 in France, set up her own U.S. company
and turned out hundreds of films from her New Jersey
studio **[Figure 10.37]**. Lois Weber, an actress turned
writer, director, and producer, was one of the most
important and highly paid American filmmakers in the
1910s—almost as well known as fellow directors Cecil
B. DeMille and D. W. Griffith. She directed scores of
movies, often on social issues. *Where Are My Children?*
(1916), for example, opposed abortion but advocated
birth control **[Figure 10.38]**. Nevertheless, both Alice
Guy Blaché and Lois Weber are excluded from most
mainstream histories of the cinema.

10.37   Alice Guy Blaché in 1915. The earliest and most prolific
woman director in history has barely been acknowledged in mainstream
film histories.

By the 1920s, as the movies became established in
Hollywood as big business, most women who were active
behind the scenes in the early U.S. industry began to
encounter difficulties. In the studios, only writers and editors continued to work in any
notable numbers. The most prominent and, for a considerable period, the only active
female director in sound-era Hollywood was Dorothy Arzner **[Figure 10.39]**. Her films
Christopher Strong (1933) and *Dance, Girl, Dance* (1940) feature strong heroines played
by top stars, and they portray significant bonds between women. The next woman
to achieve director credit in Hollywood, Ida Lupino, originally a well-known actress,
directed hard-hitting, low-budget independent films such as *Hard, Fast* and *Beautiful*
(1951), about a mother who pushes her daughter to succeed in a tennis career. Lupino
later had a successful directing career in television, which offered more opportunities
for women. Since their rediscovery by feminists in the 1970s, Arzner and Lupino have
been the focus of rewarding scholarship on what it meant to be a woman director in
the male-dominant power structure of the studio system.

Women in Independent Film

Because of their position outside the capital-intensive world of Hollywood mainstream filmmaking, the avant-garde, documentary, and independent movements

10.38   *Where Are My Children?* (1916). The film by Lois Weber
deals with the controversial social issues of birth control and abortion.

10.39   Dorothy Arzner. Arzner was the only woman to direct
Hollywood films in the 1930s, the heyday of the studio system.

have been more accessible to women filmmakers than feature filmmaking. Probably the best-known American avant-garde filmmaker is Maya Deren. A Russian immigrant, Deren began making her poetic, dance-inspired films in the early 1940s and paved the way for other female avant-garde filmmakers (see pp. 292–93). Shirley Clarke made both abstract films and the remarkable interview film *Portrait of Jason* (1967) and co-founded the influential Film-Makers' Cooperative of New York (see p. 307). Yoko Ono pursued filmmaking in addition to music and other areas of artistic expression, producing the humorous *Film No. 4 (Bottoms)* (1966) and the harrowing *Rape* (1969).

In the late 1960s and early 1970s, an explicitly feminist avant-garde movement emerged with such filmmakers as Carolee Schneemann, who filmed herself and her husband making love in *Fuses* (1967), and Yvonne Rainer, who incorporated her work as a dancer, as well as experiments with language and text, in the feature-length *Film about a Woman Who . . .* (1974). Barbara Hammer has used experimental film language to explore lesbian identity and eroticism, as well as other questions of representation, in more than eighty short films produced since the early 1970s. Lizzie Borden's *Born in Flames* (1983) imagined a postrevolutionary future in which women, still unequal citizens, organized to fight back **[Figure 10.40]**. Much of this work, as well as that of experimental feminist filmmakers outside the United States, including Belgium's Chantal Akerman, England's Sally Potter, and France's Marguerite Duras, was analyzed in and fostered by the galvanizing critical work by feminist film theorists such as Laura Mulvey in the 1970s and 1980s.

Feminism and other social justice issues are frequently highlighted in documentary and short film forms, where women have a strong foothold. Prominent among documentarians is Barbara Kopple, who has earned two Academy Awards for her documentaries on striking workers, *Harlan County, U.S.A.* (1976) and *American Dream* (1990). Christine Choy has produced many documentaries on social issues, including *Who Killed Vincent Chin?* (1988) made with Renee Tajima. African American filmmaker Ayoka Chenzira uses an animated format for *Hairpiece: A Film for Nappyheaded People* (1984). Julie Dash's influential short film *Illusions* (1982), the story of a black woman who "passes" as white in order to enter the motion-picture business during World War II, was a precursor to her breakthrough independent feature, *Daughters of the Dust* (1991). These and many other works by women filmmakers typically circulate outside theatrical exhibition structures, in places such as universities and media arts centers where they gain considerable influence on specialized audiences and scholars.

Independent features by women writers, directors, and producers are appearing in ever greater numbers. Allison Anders makes films based on her own experiences, such as *Gas Food Lodging* (1992), and on those of other girls and women, such as *Mi Vida Loca* (1993), about Chicana gang members. As an independent feature film producer, Christine Vachon has brought to the screen daring and acclaimed works by a number of women directors, including Rose Troche and Guinevere Turner's lesbian romance *Go Fish* (1994); Kimberly Peirce's debut drama based on the murder of transgender

10.40 *Born in Flames* (1983). A multiracial group of New York women rebel in the not-too-distant future in Lizzie Borden's collaboratively scripted feminist film.

Brandon Teena, *Boys Don't Cry* (1999); and Mary Harron's *The Notorious Bettie Page* (2005), a feminist take on the life of the 1950s pinup model. While there are still only a few independent women directors, such as Mira Nair (*The Namesake*, 2006) and Sofia Coppola (*Somewhere*, 2010), who have established the critical and commercial success needed to sustain high-profile careers, women like Nicole Holofcener (*Please Give*, 2010) and Debra Granik (*Winter's Bone*, 2010) **[Figure 10.41]** are garnering significant media and popular attention with their distinctive artistic visions. A number of women of color and lesbian directors are also making their mark in independent feature film-making, including Lisa Cholodenko (*Laurel Canyon*, 2002; *The Kids Are All Right*, 2010), Gina Prince-Bythewood (*Love & Basketball*, 2000; *The Secret Life of Bees*, 2008), Angela Robinson (*D.E.B.S.*, 2004; *Herbie Fully Loaded*, 2005), and Karyn Kusama (*Girlfight*, 2000; *Jennifer's Body*, 2009) **[Figure 10.42]**. Many of these directors work in television as they get their feature film projects off the ground—Harron, Troche, Cholodenko, Kusama, and Robinson have all worked on *The L Word* (2004–2009).

10.41 *Winter's Bone* (2010). Set in the Ozarks, Debra Granik's riveting film earned several Oscar nominations and launched Jennifer Lawrence's career.

Women in Contemporary Hollywood

Women entered contemporary Hollywood production slowly, with some of the first inroads to the prestigious position of director made by actresses who already had industry clout: Elaine May, Barbra Streisand, Penny Marshall, and Jodie Foster, for example. Women directors are rarely assigned to the highest-budget films, and therefore most are excluded from histories that focus on prestige films. Indeed, women have often more readily been hired as directors in such genres as youth

10.42 *Jennifer's Body* (2009). Screenwriter Diablo Cody teamed up with Karen Kusama to make this feminist horror film. Although it garnered pre-release buzz, it failed at the box office.

films and romantic and family comedies. Pioneering Hollywood women filmmakers who made interesting statements in these genres include Amy Heckerling with *Fast Times at Ridgemont High* (1982) and *Clueless* (1995), Penny Marshall with *A League of Their Own* (1992), and Penelope Spheeris with *The Decline of Western Civilization* (1981) and *Wayne's World* (1992). Susan Seidelman wrote and directed the New York–based comedy *Desperately Seeking Susan* (1985), giving Madonna her first film role.

On a larger scale, writer and director Nora Ephron mastered the romantic comedy formula in *Sleepless in Seattle* (1993) and continued to focus on women's themes in *Julie & Julia* (2009); Nancy Meyers (*It's Complicated*, 2009) was well established as a writer and producer before turning to directing films aimed comfortably at women consumers. A director with an art-school background who specializes in traditionally male genres, Kathryn Bigelow broke from this mold with films such as *Near Dark* (1987), a bizarre vampire film, and *Blue Steel* (1989). The war drama that won Bigelow an Oscar for best director (the first for a woman director) as well as a

▶ VIEWING CUE

Consider a recent film you watched that was directed by a woman. How would you characterize and distinguish the filmmaker's perspective behind the camera? **⏸**

10.43   Kathryn Bigelow. In 2010, Kathryn Bigelow was the first woman to be acknowledged by the Academy for best director— and only the fourth to be nominated in the history of the Oscars.

best picture award, *The Hurt Locker* (2008), is chock-full of adrenaline-pumping action sequences **[Figure 10.43]**

The rediscovery of women filmmakers in American film history and the advocacy for increased participation of women in all levels and forms of film production are crucial steps towards equity. However, the significance of women's role in film history goes beyond the recovery of forgotten names and films. It can be explored by asking such questions as these: What is the significance of a film's having been directed by a woman? Are women employed in other technical capacities? Whose story is told? Are women viewers specifically addressed by the film's characters, story, sounds, and images?

African American Cinema

Dominant Hollywood cinema has afforded only a limited range of representation for African, Asian, Latino, and Native Americans. When not absent from the screen altogether, these groups have traditionally been present in a small repertoire of stereotyped roles. The role of people of color behind the screen has historically been even more restricted.

Still, as a popular medium, film registers the diversity of U.S. culture even when it sometimes distorts it. Historian Michael Rogin has pointed to the prominence in American cinema of films that deal centrally with race, although in a biased way and often limited to the black-white dichotomy. In this perspective, *The Birth of a Nation* (1915), *The Jazz Singer* (1927), and *Gone with the Wind* (1939) show that the legacy of slavery and the symbolic meanings of blackness and whiteness are of crucial, though underacknowledged, importance to America's understanding of itself. Such mainstream representations have been challenged by the alternative perspectives put forward in films made by African Americans. To evaluate the movies' historical role in perpetuating and shifting racial inequities, we will look at how African Americans have been depicted in Hollywood movies before surveying the long history of cinema produced by African Americans.

Some of the earliest U.S. films featured racial themes, usually drawn from the egregious stereotypes circulating in minstrel shows and other forms of popular culture. Later, African American performers such as Lena Horne were highlighted in specialty numbers in Hollywood musicals but were denied starring roles except in films with all-black casts. Spike Lee's *Bamboozled* (2000) revisits this terrain: in order to expose his white boss's hypocritical appropriation of African American culture, a contemporary black television producer proposes a modern-day television minstrel show, replete with stock nineteenth-century stereotypes of subservient, caricatured African Americans **[Figure 10.44]**. The protagonist is stunned by the enormous success of the show, which even starts a fad for blackface. However, the film implies that the success of the show is in part due to the enormous

10.44   *Bamboozled* (2000). Spike Lee's aggressive and historically informed film confronts the legacy of racist stereotyping in American entertainment.

talent the performers channel into the songs and dances. Featuring the brilliant dancer Savion Glover, Lee's film acknowledges the genius of such historical performers as African American blackface artist Bert Williams and dancer Bill Robinson, the latter known for his pairings with Shirley Temple.

African American cinema provides an important case study because of its historical scope and contemporary breadth as well as its economic impact. In addition, African American identity bears a symbolic weight in a nation that is increasingly willing to acknowledge its historical conflicts in terms of black and white, though often still marginalizing the images and voices of other people of color.

Early Independent African American Cinema

Representing a distinguished and even heroic alternative to Hollywood history, early independent African American film culture developed in response to various phenomena—from the "race consciousness" of African American audiences cultivated by the burgeoning literature of the Harlem Renaissance and recordings by black musicians, to the realities of racism and segregation in the South. Opposition to the inflammatory depictions of blacks in *The Birth of a Nation* was a significant impetus for claiming film as a medium for self-representation. So-called **race movies** featured African American casts and were circulated to urban African American audiences in the North and shown in special segregated screenings in the South (including late-night screenings known as "midnight rambles") **[Figure 10.45]**. Some race movies were produced by white entrepreneurs, but several prominent production companies were owned by African Americans. As early as 1910, for example, Bill Foster founded the Foster Photoplay Company in Chicago, while in 1916, actor Noble Johnson formed the all-black Lincoln Motion Picture Company in Los Angeles with his brother and other partners.

The most important figure in early independent African American cinema is the novelist, writer, producer-director, and impresario Oscar Micheaux, who directed the first African American feature film **[Figure 10.46]**. Micheaux owned and operated his own production company from 1918 to 1948, producing nearly forty feature films on extremely limited budgets. He fashioned a distinctly non-Hollywood style whose "errors" have been interpreted as an alternative aesthetic. His most controversial film, *Within Our Gates* (1920), which realistically treated the spread of lynching, was threatened with censorship in Chicago, which had just seen a wave of race riots. Later, in *Body and Soul* (1925), Micheaux teamed up with actor, singer, and activist Paul Robeson in a powerful portrait of a corrupt preacher.

Another important writer-director-actor, Spencer Williams, contributed considerably to African American film history and aesthetics with his religious films. The pictorial beauty of his *The Blood of Jesus*

10.45 **Movie poster, *The Song of Freedom*** (1936). "Race movies" depicting African American lives and concerns targeted black audiences during the era of segregation.

10.46 **Oscar Micheaux.** One of film history's most resourceful figures, Micheaux wrote, produced, and directed feature films for African American exhibition networks from 1918 to the 1940s.

(1941) is echoed in scenes from Julie Dash's *Daughters of the Dust*. Although Williams contributed to sound-era cinema, and Micheaux continued to make films into the 1940s, the era of race movies peaked before the introduction of sound. By World War II, the participation of African Americans in the war effort led to increased expectations of equality in other sectors, including the Hollywood film industry. The studios themselves were eager to improve relations with audiences and journalists by updating the stereotyped images of the 1930s. Paradoxically, an agreement between the studios and the National Association for the Advancement of Colored People (NAACP) to enhance the portrayal of blacks contributed to the waning of the vibrant alternative culture of films about, for, and often by African Americans. Hollywood typically showcased black actors rather than creative personnel, though sometimes it made room for the voices of African American cultural producers, as with the major studio adaptation of Lorraine Hansberry's nuanced portrait of a black family, *A Raisin in the Sun* (1961). Actor Sidney Poitier, who appeared in the film, defined the era with his charismatic and dignified onscreen presence but was typically restricted to playing overly idealized characters.

From Blaxploitation to Contemporary African American Directors

After the studio system waned in the 1960s, new audiences for specialized films were sought by Hollywood, and the genre known as **blaxploitation** emerged. Although the term cynically suggests the economic exploitation of black film audiences (particularly an urban market likely to attend films about streetwise African American protagonists), the genre was also made possible in part by the black power movement. While many blaxploitation films were made by white producers, some African American filmmakers turned the genre to their own purposes with significant impact. The immensely successful *Shaft* (1971) was directed by noted photographer Gordon Parks. Melvin Van Peebles wrote, directed, scored, and starred in *Sweet Sweetback's Baadasssss Song* (1971), which incorporates revolutionary rhetoric in a kinetic tale of a black man pursued by racist cops **[Figure 10.47]**.

In the final two decades of the twentieth century, the commercial and artistic leader of the resurgence of African American cinema production was Spike Lee. With his debut feature *She's Gotta Have It* (1986), Lee helped revive independent cinema aesthetically and financially through a sophisticated use of cinematic language and engaging storytelling. Working through his production company, 40 Acres and a Mule, Lee addresses an important moment in African American history in the biopic *Malcolm X* (1992) **[Figure 10.48]** and explores personal issues in *Mo' Better Blues* (1990). He has also directed documentaries with HBO, such as *4 Little Girls* (1997), *When the Levees Broke* (2006), and the 2010 follow-up, *If God Is Willing and da Creek Don't Rise*. In addition, he produces the work of many other young filmmakers of color, including women like Darnell Martin (*I Like It Like That*, 1994).

Lee's success spurred an African American film boom in the early 1990s, centered on a wave of "hood" films about young men in urban settings. These included, for example, John Singleton's *Boyz N the Hood*

10.47   *Sweet Sweetback's Baadasssss Song* (1971). Melvin Van Peebles's militant blaxploitation hit.

(1991), Mario Van Peebles's *New Jack City* (1991), and the Hughes brothers' *Menace II Society* (1993). Offering a different perspective on African American life than that portrayed in urban films, Oprah Winfrey produced adaptations of acclaimed works by black women writers—*Beloved* (1998), based on Toni Morrison's 1987 novel of a former slave mother, and *Their Eyes Were Watching God* (2005), an adaptation of Zora Neale Hurston's 1937 classic.

The first decade of the 2000s saw the spectacular success with African American audiences of playwright-producer-actor-director Tyler Perry's comedies. *Diary of a Mad Black Woman* (2005) introduced his signature character, no-nonsense grandmother Madea (played by a cross-dressing Perry) to

10.48 *Malcolm X* (1992). Spike Lee argued that a big-budget biographical film about the slain leader should be directed by an African American.

the screen; more than a dozen films have followed, grossing half a billion dollars at the box office. When Lee Daniels's drama *Precious: Based on the Novel Push by Sapphire* (2009), an at once devastating and soaring story of an overweight young woman's life of physical, emotional, and sexual abuse, premiered at the Sundance Film Festival without a distributor, Perry and Winfrey came on board to help promote the film. Perry's and Winfrey's commercial clout helped bring the film to the attention of audiences and critics, making it an unexpected Oscar contender.

Films by and for other racial and ethnic groups have been made throughout U.S. film history and have increased in number as people of color obtain greater access to the means of film production. With the fostering of independent feature filmmaking in general and with more emphasis on the multicultural nature of U.S. society, Chinese American Wayne Wang launched his significant filmmaking career with *Chan Is Missing* (1982), and playwright and director Luis Valdez brought important stories from Chicano history to the screen with *Zoot Suit* (1981) and *La Bamba* (1987). It was not until 1998 that a feature film by and about Native Americans was produced: director Chris Eyre and writer Sherman Alexie's breakthrough film, *Smoke Signals,* provided a gently funny picture of the contradictions of contemporary Native American life.

In addition to these feature films, many experimental, documentary, and community-based works are produced by artists of color. Each year film festivals dedicated to Asian-Pacific American and Latin American cinema showcase hundreds of short films, videos, and documentaries, as well as feature-length films from Asian and Latin American countries. All of these traditions expand the concept of American cinema beyond the genres, personalities, and stories that Hollywood has promoted.

Lesbian/Gay/Bisexual/Transgender (LGBT) Film History

The history of lesbian, gay, bisexual, and transgender (LGBT) people in film provokes reflection on the relationship between representation and sexuality in general. Looking at LGBT film history tells us not only about changing representations of same-sex desire but also about continuity and discontinuity in definitions of sexual identity and community and about the social regulation of sexuality and its representations. This history has become more accessible since the 1990s, when mainstream images of lesbians and gay men became much more common and less stigmatized, provoking interest in the images of the past.

text continued on page 390 ▶

Lost and Found History:
Within Our Gates (1920)

Oscar Micheaux's *Within Our Gates* is a crucial film in the counterhistory of American cinema because of its content, its circumstances of production and reception, and its fate **[Figure 10.49]**. Produced independently in 1919 and released in 1920, it is the earliest surviving feature film by an African American filmmaker. Despite its historical significance, however, the film was lost for decades. Greeted with controversy upon its initial release, it came back into circulation in the 1990s after the Library of Congress identified a print titled *La Negra* in a film archive in Spain as Micheaux's lost film and then restored it. The film's recovery was part of the efforts of film historians and black cultural critics to reinvestigate the vibrant world of early twentieth-century race movies and the remarkable role Micheaux played in this culture. The film's long absence from the historical record deprived generations of viewers and cultural producers of a picture of African American life and politics in the North and South during that era, and of any concept of the audience that Micheaux addressed.

Within Our Gates is important to an alternative film history because it offers a corrective view of a devastating historical phenomenon, the lynching of African Americans, which had reached epidemic proportions in the first decades of the twentieth century. When the film was returned to circulation in the 1990s, viewers immediately saw it as a countervision to D. W. Griffith's *The Birth of a Nation,* which boldly uses cinematic techniques like parallel editing to tell the inflammatory story of a black man pursuing a white virgin, who commits suicide rather than succumb to rape. The Klan is formed to avenge her death, and the would-be rapist is captured and punished in what the film depicts as justified vigilante justice. Micheaux offers an equally visceral story that counters the myth of lynching as a reaction to black male violence by presenting a testament to white racist mob violence against African Americans. In his film, after an African American tenant farmer, Jasper Landry, is unjustly accused of shooting the wealthy landowner Girdlestone (the guilty party is actually an angry white tenant), a lynching party attacks Landry's family. *Within Our Gates* poignantly depicts the lynching of the mother and father and the last-minute escape of their small son as a

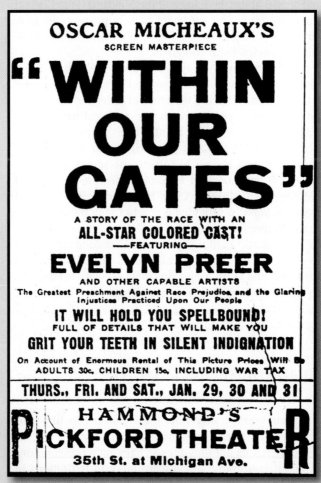

10.49 **Poster for *Within Our Gates*** (1920). Oscar Micheaux's rediscovered film about the lives and philanthropic work of middle-class African Americans includes dramatic scenes of lynching.

public spectacle attended by the townspeople, including women and children, a historically accurate depiction of lynching. This powerful sequence stands as perhaps the strongest cinematic rebuttal to *The Birth of a Nation*'s racist distortion of history. It uses the power of the visual to make history, just as Griffith's film does. Finally, as a director, Micheaux offers an important contrast to Griffith. Whereas Griffith has been consistently heralded as a father of American cinema, Micheaux's diverse talents, his unique approach to film language, his business savvy, and his modernity have waited decades for full recognition.

The structure of Micheaux's film also rewards historical inquiry because it requires viewers to think about how certain modes of storytelling become naturalized. Although *Within Our Gates*'s treatment of lynching is its most noted feature, this controversial material, which threatened to prevent the film's exhibition in Chicago where racial tensions had recently erupted in rioting, is buried in an extensive flashback. The flashback fills in the past of Sylvia Landry, described by a title card as someone "who could think of nothing but the eternal struggle of her race and how she could uplift it." The language of racial uplift directly addresses the racially conscious, middle-class black audiences for Micheaux's film. Sylvia's quest to raise funds for a black school in the South, her romance with the politically active Dr. Vivian [Figure 10.50], and several side plots featuring less noble characters, make the lynching story at the film's

heart feel even closer to the historical record. The story serves a didactic purpose in the film: the demonstration of the racial injustice that propels Sylvia's struggle. But the film does not spare melodramatic detail. We learn that Sylvia, the Landrys' adopted daughter, escapes the lynch mob only to be threatened with rape by landowner Girdlestone's brother [Figure 10.51]. The attack is diverted when the would-be rapist notices a scar that reveals she is actually his daughter. The film's inclusion of white male violence against black women is another rebuttal of the distortions in *The Birth of a Nation*. The unlikeliness of the rescue scenario can be understood as the use of melodramatic coincidence to right wrongs that cannot easily receive redress in other ways. In other words, Micheaux uses the form of the movies to imagine social reality differently.

Micheaux's films were made with extreme ingenuity on low budgets. When Micheaux's affecting melodrama of African American hardship and determination disappeared from film history, a great deal was lost. The film's subject matter was not undertaken in mainstream cinema. The perspective of African American filmmakers was absent in Hollywood, and black audiences were not addressed by Hollywood films. The title *Within Our Gates* speaks to the film's own status—a powerful presence within American film history too long unacknowledged.

10.50 *Within Our Gates* (1920). In the framing story of Oscar Micheaux's film, Dr. Vivian hears the story of Sylvia Landry's past.

10.51 *Within Our Gates* (1920). In the flashback, a last-minute coincidence saves the heroine from being attacked by a white man who is later revealed to be her biological father.

10.52 *The Children's Hour* (1961). Lillian Hellman's 1936 play was finally faithfully adapted to the screen after the Production Code was relaxed in the 1960s, but by then its depiction of the main character's suicide was dated and damaging.

Homosexuality and Gender Deviance Onscreen

In 1934, the U.S. motion-picture industry began to strictly enforce self-imposed restrictions on film content. The document known as the Production Code stated that "homosexuality and any inference to it are prohibited." Lillian Hellman's play *The Children's Hour* dealt with the consequences of a malicious child's lies about the lesbian relationship between the two headmistresses of her school. The play was a hit on Broadway in 1934, but the 1936 movie version, *These Three*, implied that the child's gossip was about one teacher's heterosexual affair with the other's fiancé, a change that was transparent to the many members of the audience who were familiar with the play or the publicity surrounding it. Strictures on the theme of homosexuality finally relaxed in the 1960s, in part due to a Supreme Court decision declaring that the movies were entitled to the constitutional protections of freedom of speech. One of the first films to capitalize on this shift was William Wyler's remake of *The Children's Hour* (1961) **[Figure 10.52]**. However, nearly a quarter of a century after the original, and with the feminist and gay rights movements just around the corner, the film's depiction of one teacher's suicide (when the child's accusations provoke her recognition of her own desire for her friend) had a negative impact. The trend of dead or murderous gay characters continued in mainstream treatments for a considerable period, including the notorious examples *Cruising* (1980) and *Basic Instinct* (1992). The vocal protests surrounding both films' perpetuation of stereotypes were probably more instrumental in achieving lesbian and gay visibility than were the films themselves.

During the 1980s, mainstream heterosexual stars began to appear in films offering more complex images of gay men and sometimes lesbians, such as William Hurt's award-winning performance in *Kiss of the Spider Woman* (1985). While openly gay comic and character actors like Harvey Fierstein and Nathan Lane benefited from increased LGBT visibility in the 1990s, it remains difficult for openly gay actors to obtain leading roles. Two later films that featured gay and lesbian characters and appealed to a wide cross-section of audiences, Ang Lee's cowboy love story *Brokeback Mountain* (2005) **[Figure 10.53]** and lesbian director Lisa Cholodenko's comedy *The Kids Are All Right*, had popular heterosexual stars in the main roles. In fact, *The Kids Are All Right* would not have been viable without its stellar cast of Annette Bening and Julianne Moore.

LGBT Filmmaking

Much like the absence of LGBT representation onscreen, the contributions of LGBT filmmakers are often erased or overlooked. It is important to recognize that, like any cultural identity, the sexual orientation of a filmmaker does not necessarily have any specific impact on his or her work. However, knowing whether a filmmaker identified himself or herself as lesbian, gay, bisexual, or transgendered, or whether there is significant biographical evidence of same-sex erotic attachments,

10.53 *Brokeback Mountain* (2005). An appealing cast and new take on the traditional western made a gay male love story a mainstream success.

can make a difference in two contexts: (1) when sexual identity arguably affects the filmmaker's subject matter or aesthetic approach, and (2) when withholding information about a filmmaker's sexual identity erases a specific historical legacy.

Filmmakers might choose to be explicit about their sexual identity and affiliation with the LGBT community or movement in order to target a specific audience or LGBT cause, or because they consider sexuality an integral part of their experience and vision as artists. The first LGBT activist movie, *Anders als die Andern* (*Different from the Others*), was produced in Germany in 1919 in the socially tolerant period between the two world wars. Dramatizing the risk of blackmail to a prominent citizen because of his sexual preference, the film advocates the decriminalization of male homosexuality (no statute specifically prohibited lesbianism) and features a lecture by German sexologist Magnus Hirschfeld. Another famous Weimar-era film, *Mädchen in Uniform* (1931), was written by lesbian author Christa Winsloe and based on her own play **[Figure 10.54]**. Featuring an all-women cast and directed by a woman, Leontine Sagan, the film depicts a young woman's boarding-school crush on a sympathetic teacher. It achieved international success despite its censorship, including in the United States.

Withholding information about a filmmaker's sexual identity can sometimes erase a significant historical legacy. George Cukor, the MGM studio director whose classic films include *The Women* (1939) and *A Star Is Born* (1954), was often called a "women's director" because of the excellent performances given by such female stars as Greta Garbo, Judy Garland, Katharine Hepburn, and Judy Holliday under his direction. The term was also intended as a euphemism, often pejorative, for gay, and Cukor was even replaced as director of *Gone with the Wind* at the behest of its macho star Clark Gable. But this characterization of Cukor can also be the basis of a more nuanced reading of his work. Another important example of how a historiography sensitive to gay presence can illuminate the cinema's past can be found in the underground films of the 1960s. Chroniclers of the films of Jack Smith, Andy Warhol, and Kenneth Anger sought to have them taken seriously as art, describing their outrageous transvestite actors and transgressive sexual content but failing to mention that the directors themselves were gay. Correcting this omission enriches both social history and film interpretation.

The 1970s saw the rise of the gay rights movement, which was documented in Rob Epstein's *Word Is Out* (1977). He later went on to make the award-winning *The Times of Harvey Milk* (1984) and, with Jeffrey Friedman, a series of acclaimed documentaries on LGBT issues, including *The Celluloid Closet* (1995), based on Vito Russo's book about the depiction of lesbians and gay men in film. Their most recent film, *Howl* (2010), features James Franco as beat poet Allen Ginsberg. Epstein and Friedman's first fiction feature, it draws on elements of documentary and animation **[Figure 10.55]**.

During the 1980s, there was an explosion of activist video advocating for money for AIDS research and combating the stigma associated with the epidemic. At the same time,

10.54 *Mädchen in Uniform* (1931). This Weimar-era film about a student's crush on her teacher features an all-female cast and was written and directed by women.

> **VIEWING CUE**
> What models or types of sexuality appear in one of the films you've recently seen? How does its historical moment shape these models?

10.55 *Howl* (2010). James Franco as Allen Ginsberg in Rob Epstein and Jeffrey Friedman's imaginative film about Ginsberg's famous poem.

10.56   *Paris Is Burning* (1990). This documentary about New York City drag balls won critical acclaim, but it was shut out of the Oscars, possibly due to what was deemed its unconventional subject matter.

British director Derek Jarman produced a significant oeuvre, including such lyrical and subversive interpretations of historical and literary subjects as *Caravaggio* (1986) and *Edward II* (1991). Probably the most internationally celebrated gay filmmaker, Jarman became one of many talented artists lost to AIDS.

By the early 1990s, gay-themed works had prepared critics and audiences for a crop of commercially successful, aesthetically innovative films by an impressive group of young LGBT filmmakers. This trend, dubbed New Queer Cinema, arose from a cultural moment when the LGBT community had become more militant in response to the AIDS crisis, embracing the formerly pejorative term "queer" for its connotations of going against the norm; the best of these films were "queer" in relation to cinematic as well as gender and sexual norms. Key New Queer Cinema works include Jennie Livingston's documentary *Paris Is Burning* (1990) [Figure 10.56] and fiction films such as Todd Haynes's *Poison* (1991) and *Safe* (1995), Gregg Araki's *The Living End* (1992), and Rose Troche and Guinevere Turner's *Go Fish*. The industry took notice, and big-budget dramas like *Philadelphia* (1993) and comedies like *In and Out* (1997) addressed gay issues more openly than ever before. Preceding and accompanying these feature films' recognition is the burgeoning of independent LGBT documentaries produced for non-theatrical exhibition, notable examples of which include Pratibha Parmar's *Khush* (1991), about South Asian lesbians and gays, and Marlon Riggs's acclaimed video *Tongues Untied* (1989), about African American gay men.

With the proliferation of LGBT images in mainstream television and films, some commentators felt that the political edge of New Queer Cinema had been blunted. What had before been an activist audience was now courted as a lucrative market segment. The success of a film like *Milk* (2008), the story of the murder of openly gay San Francisco City Supervisor Harvey Milk in 1978—a watershed moment in the gay rights movement—testifies to the significantly changed terrain for films by and about, and also for, the LGBT community. Directed by Gus Van Sant, one of the most significant figures in catalyzing New Queer Cinema, the film brings the story of the LGBT community to the forefront of American history.

Indigenous Media

Thus far we have offered corrective histories of American cinema that to a certain degree emphasize the politics of identity and the image. The history of indigenous media is perhaps even more concerned with self-representation, but it also challenges the purposes of the film medium as primarily about entertainment or communication. The history of depicting native cultures is one of asserting power through the control of the image.

One of the earliest uses of film was to record the ways of life of other cultures for exhibition to audiences in the West. In the first decades of film history, little distinction was made between science and sensation: Ernest B. Schoedsack and Merian C. Cooper, the team that made *Grass* (1925), a record of an Iranian migration, went on to make *King Kong* (1933), whose premise, it is sometimes forgotten, is a movie-making expedition to Sumatra. But with the increased specialization of anthropology, a distinct practice of *ethnographic documentary*—the use of film to document cultures for others to study—emerged as an indispensable tool.

Film can record rituals in a way that written ethnographies cannot. Filming interviews minimizes the mediation of an interpreter by capturing the subject's own words and gestures through the lens. However, the camera can never grant complete access to a cultural context. In a culture that does not use cameras, the equipment can hardly be invisible or neutral. But because it can capture conversations and gestures, sounds and settings, time and space, film can give a strong impression of documenting a culture despite such mediations.

Nowhere do claims of film as an impartial record become more loaded than in the filming of indigenous people by Western observers, and not until recently have indigenous groups been able to appropriate video and film technology to tell their own stories. Deploying a technology like the movies in such a cultural encounter means claiming the power to represent others and their history. The camera conveys a profound feeling of presence that puts the viewer in the place of the observer or "expert."

10.57   *Nanook of the North* (1922). Robert Flaherty re-created traditional activities for the camera, but his images are nevertheless striking records of the Inuit.

Widely considered the first feature-length documentary film and certainly one of the most influential movies ever made, Robert Flaherty's *Nanook of the North* (1922) is a record of the lives and customs of the Inuit people of the Canadian Arctic. The isolation of the people in a harsh environment, and the duration of Flaherty's stay among them, required that the film be produced in close collaboration with its subjects. In the film, Nanook (played by the uncredited Allakariallak), his family, and others engage in traditional behavior, including an exciting seal hunt and the construction of an igloo. Although some of these activities were performed and modified for the purposes of the film, they were "real" records of Inuit people carrying out Inuit hunting and building techniques **[Figure 10.57]**. Part of *Nanook of the North*'s impact at the time lay in the use of a still relatively new technology to deliver an image of a technology-free universe, so that the viewer marveled at both.

Flaherty's claims that he presented an accurate representation of Inuit life are compromised by the reenactments and by his having paid his subjects. The film is also often *primitivist*, reinforcing stereotypes of non-Western people as simple, childlike, and outside the process of history. For example, Nanook is shown trying to eat a gramophone record, yet he and other native collaborators were familiar with modern technology and worked as Flaherty's (uncredited) crew, operating the film cameras and developing the footage. The complex legacy of this film is explored in the video *Nanook Revisited* (1988), which returns to the village where Flaherty's classic was made to take on the myths and realities surrounding his great film among the people whose ancestors participated in its making. *Nanook Revisited* gives a glimpse of another side to the story of the conjunction of "camera" and "primitive," one that characterizes the end of the twentieth century.

The introduction of video technology to indigenous people, such as the Kayapo and Waipai Indians in the Amazon Basin of Brazil, has resulted in considerable output that has several empowering uses **[Figure 10.58]**. These include the preservation of traditional culture for future generations; video activism for land rights and

10.58   *The Spirit of TV* (1990). Amazon Indians, such as the Waipai, have used video to record their culture and assert their rights.

10.59 *Atanarjuat* (2001). Shot on digital video in the Canadian Arctic, this epic is the first feature made in the Inuktitut language by Inuit filmmakers.

▶ **VIEWING CUE**

Think about a film you recently watched that depicts another culture. What questions do you have about what you are seeing? How would you put the film in context to answer those questions? ⏸

the environment; and a new form of visual expression in a culture that has always relied on pictorial communication. While the Kayapo are entering a new historical moment by employing this technology, the video work's primary purpose is to preserve the past.

The indigenous people of Canada also left behind their legacy as objects of ethnographic film and campaigned for self-representation. Organized activism resulted in the licensing of the Inuit Broadcasting Network in 1982, featuring programming by, for, and about native Canadians. In 1999, the Canadian government ordered cable companies to carry the Aboriginal Peoples Television Network, bringing this culture and its video productions to the whole country. A new phase of indigenous media making was marked by the historic release of *Atanarjuat* (*The Fast Runner*; 2001). Shot in digital video, this extraordinary film, directed by Inuit filmmaker Zacharias Kunuk, appropriately enough deploys the genre of epic to explore a people's past [**Figure 10.59**]. But it portrays a cultural legend, not a factual past. Although at first it resembles an ethnographic film, *Atanarjuat* is set a millennium ago. By setting its depiction of the traditional way of life in the mythic past, the film represents an Inuit claim to self-representation on several levels. The film's use of amateur actors lends an "authenticity" to the scripted scenes, and its script represents the longest text ever written in the Inuit language. Its images also implicitly acknowledge and respond to the beauty as well as the ideological dimensions of a film like *Nanook of the North*. Two subsequent films made in 2006 and 2009 complete the *Fast Runner* trilogy.

Excavating Film History

As we consider the different ways that film history can be regarded, it is important to remember that the very idea of reflecting on our film heritage is a relatively recent one. Precisely because film and photography capture the fleeting moment, they have been regarded as ephemeral and of little long-term value. Film is also materially ephemeral—because the earliest nitrate-based film stock was extremely flammable, negatives and prints of countless titles have been lost or simply destroyed. Film prints that were once in circulation have been altered by censors, damaged in transit and projection, and improperly stored. Approximately 80 percent of our silent film heritage has been lost. The later format of video, which deteriorates over time, has suffered a similar fate, with television stations routinely recording over the only records they have of earlier programs. Even some films that were celebrated and successful in their day no longer exist and so cannot be consulted by contemporary historians or shared with new audiences.

The historical record looks as it does because of lucky accidents—informed and not-so-informed decisions about what to keep and what to throw away—and rare acts of foresight. The Library of Congress requested copies of all film materials submitted for copyright consideration and thus has records of the very first movies. The Museum of Modern Art, under the leadership of its first curator of film, Iris Barry, made the decision to treat film as a modern art and collected prints and stills beginning in 1935. Most Hollywood films that survive today were stored in vaults by the film studios that produced them; later owners of these companies discovered a new source of revenue in the preservation and re-release of old movies on television, video, or DVD.

10.60 *What You Should Know About Biological Warfare* (1952). The U.S. government instructs citizens in Cold War protocol.

10.61 Fox Movietone News Story 4-171: *World's Youngest Acrobat* (1929). Newsreels, like this one from Fox Movietone, captured the small moments in the daily lives of American people as well as major events.

Orphan Films

Orphan films are films that have been abandoned by their owners or copyright holders, or have otherwise been neglected. This is a catchall category devised by those interested in film preservation, including everything from amateur films, training films, and documentaries to censored materials, commercials, and newsreels. When we consider the reach of this term, we get a glimpse of how daunting, and costly, the task of saving all the orphans might be. These films have no commercial interests to pay the costs of their preservation, so often these works enter the public domain. At times, however, the word "orphan" is used to emphasize films that have been neglected by canonical film histories and need to be recovered materially as well as critically. Dorothy Arzner's *Working Girls* (1931), for example, was an orphan until its restoration through the UCLA Film and Television Archive; and almost all surviving race movies can be considered orphans.

Today, it is up to those who discover orphan films to evaluate what they have to tell us about the past: they function like time capsules of cinematic history and of history in general. For example, a 1952 informational film about biological warfare conveys the anxieties of the government and citizens of the United States during the Cold War **[Figure 10.60]**. Newsreels offer glimpses of past events just as the people of that era saw them—fleeting moments in history that only film can record **[Figure 10.61]**. Looking carefully at the variety of forms, styles, and uses of orphan films helps us understand how central—and how taken for granted—film was to the twentieth century. Although orphans are a worldwide phenomenon, rescuing such films is a particular challenge in the United States because of the volume and commercial concentration of film.

VIEWING CUE
View an "ephemeral film" on the Internet Archive at www.archive.org/details/ephemera. What does it tell us about history?

Film Preservation and Archives

Some orphans have special needs that raise interesting questions about the goals of preservation. Do we want to keep all of these films? With the vast storage capacities computers have for digital media, it may not seem like we have to make such choices. Indeed, given today's technology, it can seem absurd that so many orphan films are inaccessible. But it is also important to preserve the materials in their

10.62 *The Night of the Hunter* (1955). This dark fable was restored with the support of Martin Scorsese and the Film Foundation.

original format. Numerous reasons exist for saving as much as possible:

- Historians can have access to a wide range of images from particular times, places, and institutions.
- Filmmakers can ensure that their work survives and even attracts new viewers.
- Other filmmakers may use orphan films as sources for their work, such as compilation films or documentaries.
- Audiences can have new educational, eye-opening, and outrageous film experiences.

The importance of archives and preservation is especially vital to silent film history. Kevin Brownlow and David Gill's 1981 restoration of Abel Gance's *Napoléon* (1927) is a complex and particularly sensational example of restoration. Frustrated with the tattered versions of this silent French classic in circulation, Brownlow pursued the confused history of the film, searching out different versions from private and public archives and eventually patching together an accurate reproduction of the film. In 1990, Martin Scorsese established the Film Foundation with a group of fellow filmmakers to support restoration efforts for American films. Hundreds of projects have been completed, including a restoration of *The Night of the Hunter* (1955)—a dark, offbeat tale of a religious con man pursuing his two stepchildren and a hidden stash of money **[Figure 10.62]**. The World Cinema Foundation expanded this effort, releasing its first restored film, the documentary *Trances* (1981) by Moroccan filmmaker Ahmed El Mannouni in 2007.

Undoubtedly, we have made a good deal of progress in considering films not only as documents of history but also as having a history in their own right, one that is worth preserving. Film archives, which are key to the efforts of film preservation, became central institutions beginning in the 1930s. Among the most prominent are at the Cinémathèque Française, identified with longtime archivist Henri Langlois and New York's Museum of Modern Art. As early as 1898, Polish scholar Boleslaw Matuszewski argued the need for film archives, and today more than 120 archives dedicated to the preservation and proper exhibition of films and their study constitute the International Federation of Film Archives (FIAF), itself founded in 1938. Several DVD initiatives such as Kino International's five-disc collection *The Movies Begin: A Treasury of Early Cinema* and the Natural Film Preservation Foundation's ongoing series, *Treasures from American Film Archives*, have resulted in the distribution of rare movies that viewers previously had not been able to see. Different versions of older films—such as Fritz Lang's *Metropolis* (1927) or Orson Welles's *Touch of Evil* (1958)—pieced together from materials found in archives and collections, are generating debates about which is the authoritative version. A film's history includes not only the definitive version reconstructed by archivists but also the vicissitudes of its exhibition and audience reception over time.

CONCEPTS AT WORK

Historical knowledge helps our thinking about any subject, and movies are no exception. When watching films made in another era, we must consider them, to some degree, as documents whose style and subject matter need a historical context to be appreciated. For example, contemporary viewers of James Whale's *Frankenstein* (1931) might find its story simplistic, the acting clumsy, and its audiovisual style primitive. With a historical perspective on the period, however, we have provided viewers with an understanding of the film as a product of particular historical constraints and possibilities.

In addition, by looking, however cursorily, at global histories, we have attempted to move beyond a single progression to multiple sites on the map and beyond stylistic periods to a more dynamic sense of the interaction of national history and film. Finally, by introducing films and filmmakers that have been hidden from film history, we hope to have prompted new explorations of the past.

Activities

- Elaborate the connections between a film and its historical period in political, technological, industrial, economic, and cultural terms.
- Compare and contrast two films from different traditions that "remake" similar material. For example, the Hollywood *Carmen Jones* (1954) and *U-Carmen eKhayelitsha* (2005) from South Africa, Akira Kurosawa's *Throne of Blood* (1957) and Roman Polanski's *Macbeth* (1971), or *Sita Sings the Blues* (2008) and *Ramayana: The Epic* (2010). How do different cinematic histories influence these films?
- Research a "lost and found" tradition in American cinema that is not covered here. Examples include Latino film, Asian American film, documentary, and exploitation films. In what ways does this particular tradition challenge mainstream film history?

"ONE OF THE MOST HOTLY DEBATED AND HANDS-DOWN EXCITING SELECTIONS AT THIS YEAR'S CANNES FILM FESTIVAL COMES FROM ONE OF THE MEDIUM'S RELATIVELY UNSUNG MASTERS, THE AUSTRIAN FILMMAKER MICHAEL HANEKE. DANIEL AUTEUIL AND JULIETTE BINOCHE, BOTH SUPERB..."
-Manohla Dargis, THE NEW YORK TIMES

"MAINTAINS SUCH A TIGHT REIN ON OUR EMOTIONS THAT WE SIT SPELLBOUND."
-Ken Tucker, NEW YORK MAGAZINE

DANIEL AUTEUIL   JULIETTE BINOCHE

CACHÉ

(H I D D E N)

FESTIVAL DE CANNES
BEST DIRECTOR
MICHAEL HANEKE

CLOSING NIGHT SELECTION
NEW YORK FILM FESTIVAL
2005

7 EUROPEAN FILM AWARD
NOMINATIONS
INCLUDING
BEST PICTURE
BEST DIRECTOR
BEST SCREENPLAY

A FILM BY
MICHAEL HANEKE

A SONY PICTURES CLASSICS RELEASE ··········· LES FILMS DU LOSANGE WEGA FILM BAVARIA FILM BIM DISTRIBUZIONE ···········
ARTE FRANCE CINEMA FRANCE 3 CINEMA ORF FILM/FERNSEH ABKOMMEN ARTE/WOR ··········· STUDIOCANAL CANAL+ CENTRE NATIONAL DE LA CINEMATOGRAPHIE ÖSTERREICHISCHES FILMINSTITUT
FILMFONDS WIEN FILMSTIFTUNG NRW ··········· MEDIA ··········· DANIEL AUTEUIL JULIETTE BINOCHE ··········· MICHAEL HANEKE "CACHE (HIDDEN)" MAURICE BENICHOU ANNIE GIRARDOT BERNARD LE COQ
DANIEL DUVAL NATHALIE RICHARD DENIS PODALYDES ··········· AISSA MAIGA ··········· CHRISTIAN BERGER ··········· MICHAEL HUDECEK NADINE MUSE ··········· EMMANUEL DE CHAUVIGNY CHRISTOPH KANTER
··········· LISY CHRISTL ··········· MICHAEL KATZ MARGARET MENEGOZ ··········· MICHAEL WEBER VALERIO DE PARIS ··········· MARGARET MENEGOZ VEIT HEIDUSCHKA ··········· MICHAEL HANEKE
WWW.SONYCLASSICS.COM   WWW.CACHEMOVIE.COM

Reading about Film
Critical Theories and Methods

The opening shot of Michael Haneke's *Caché* (*Hidden*; 2006) depicts a closed doorway on a quiet street. This commonplace image appears to conceal nothing of significance; yet slowly the disturbing realization dawns on the viewer that this is surveillance footage of the entrance to the main characters' home. At least three distinct points of view are thus implied by the shot: that of the person who has taped the footage; that of the couple to whom the video has been sent; and that of the viewer, who is thus uncomfortably split between characters who solicit empathy and an anonymous other who scrutinizes those characters' lives. As the plot unfolds and Georges, the husband, begins to investigate why the tapes are being sent, those initial visual perspectives become imbued with social perspectives shaped by divisions of history and power. In the film's final long take, the viewer may or may not find a clue about what is "hidden" in the film's mysteries and moral quandaries; however, the stakes of reading that image have been raised by what has come before. Such complex ways of seeing lie under the surface of all films. Film theorists from the early days of the medium to the present explore both the aesthetics of sound and image and the visceral, ethical, and historically situated encounters between viewers and images that *Caché* depicts.

Audiovisual technologies are now more prevalent and more integrated with our experience than ever before. When television was introduced in the mid-twentieth century, and later when home video and computer games became popular, predictions abounded that moviegoing would be eclipsed by the new leisure forms. However, these pronouncements on the death of cinema were premature. What is it about the film experience that resonates so meaningfully with modern life? This question, which emerged with the first projected moving images, continues to drive our thinking about mediated experiences today. Such reflection on the nature and uses of the medium is the province of film theory. The books and essays that constitute this field undertake a sustained interrogation of propositions about the nature of the medium, the features of individual films or categories of films, and the interaction between viewers and films. In this chapter, we will make explicit the issues that inform the theoretical study of film by framing these issues in terms of specific histories and positions of film theory.

KEY OBJECTIVES

- Explore the concept of cinematic specificity and the method of formal analysis.
- Recognize the interdisciplinary nature of film and media studies.
- Understand the major positions in classical film theory, from Soviet montage theory to formalism and realism.
- Learn about the key schools of thought within contemporary film theory, including semiotics, structuralism, and ideological critique; poststructuralism and psychoanalysis; feminist theory; cultural studies; philosophical approaches; and postmodernism and new media.

Precisely because cinema is so accessible and familiar, the very idea of theorizing it makes some viewers skeptical. Yet the knowledge that comes with avid moviegoing can itself be the foundation of a theoretical position. Every time we go to the movies, we evaluate elements about the film beforehand: when we choose drama or comedy, we invoke genre; if we buy a ticket for the new Spielberg film, we draw on auteur theory; and if we elect, while acknowledging the dismissive quality of the term, a "chick flick," we invoke some understanding of reception theory, which focuses on how different kinds of audiences regard different kinds of films. When we speak of the fictional world of *The Godfather* (1972) **[Figure 11.1]** as if it were real, we invoke the concept of verisimilitude, or "having the quality of truth." Even when we select a seat at the movie theater, implicit in our choice is an ideal vantage point from which the film illusion will be most complete.

As these examples suggest, every theoretical approach to cinema foregrounds some elements and relegates others to the background. Besides looking at different aspects of the experience, film theories vary in their level of analysis, selecting

different features to address. Some theories regard the cinema as a mass phenomenon that needs to be approached on the basic level of the significance and organization of the institution of cinema, from the industry to the broad-based reception of films, while others are concerned with formal principles alone. It may be helpful to think of each theory we will introduce as part of the tool kit of the cultural critic. This metaphor implies that different theories are needed to address different questions; it also reminds us that theoretical inquiry is not only about taking something apart, but also about building models and connections. An overview such as this one cannot fully survey this diverse field. We encourage you to read these thinkers' own words; only then will the stakes of the debates be driven home.

11.1 *The Godfather* (1972). Audiences' evaluation of the verisimilitude of the world of the Corleone crime family deploys a theoretical concept in an experiential way.

Film Theory: Cinematic Specificity and Interdisciplinarity

Before we present an overview of the history and debates of film theory, let us draw out two issues that are at the heart of the discipline and yet seemingly at odds with each other: the specificity of the cinematic medium and the interdisciplinary nature of its study. By specificity, we mean that which makes the medium of film distinct as an aesthetic form or mode of communication. This has been one of the reigning concepts of film theory, and it has received renewed attention since the advent of the digital era. Yet we also acknowledge that film, characterized early on as "the seventh art," represents a combination of other art forms as well as commercial, artistic, and social interests, and thus we must also consider film from an interdisciplinary perspective. Moreover, the lenses through which we understand film are drawn from history and sociology; art history and philosophy; literature and economics—adding to the interdisciplinary nature of film study. The excitement of studying film theory lies in the challenge of illuminating these two seemingly contradictory dimensions of cinema. Sustained critical interrogations—such as the writings by filmmakers, philosophers, and academics examined here—help us see the specificities of cinema as an aesthetic form and social institution, as well as its commonalities with other arts and cultural experiences.

Theories of an artistic medium often begin by trying to define their object. "What is cinema?" asks French film theorist André Bazin in his classic book of the same title. In philosophy, this is called the question of ontology or being. Sometimes theorists approach film ontologically in an attempt to define the medium in relation to other artistic media. How does cinema differ from painting, for example? Both use pictorial imagery. But film differs from painting and drawing because it is composed of photographic images captured with a camera (even if the images are of drawings, as with traditional animation). Film differs from photography in that its images are displayed to give the illusion of motion. As a storytelling medium, cinema borrows from the novel; yet the way it associates images with emotions resembles poetry. Like music, film is a time-based performance. Each of these comparisons can and has been extended considerably and productively. Theorists hope that from ever more precise statements of its properties, they will arrive at the genuine specific definition of cinema.

One advantage of honing a definition of cinema to its specifics is that theorists who accept that definition can then share terms of analysis and point to concrete elements as the basis for interpretations. Although some theorists might postulate that cinema is defined by some ineffable essence, most would characterize it by its form, or the configuration of its specific parts. **Formalism** is a method of analysis that considers a film's form, or its structure, to be primary. The theoretical position behind formalism is that meaning is to be found in the work itself. Like the formalist art historian, the film analyst examines how elements such as light, color, and composition are used in a particular film. Likewise, elements unique to cinema, such as camera movement and distance, shot duration and rhythm, will provide further insights into the film's effectiveness.

Formalist approaches to specific film texts are often called *close readings*. As the term implies, this technique is derived from literary studies. Close readers analyze texts by isolating, naming, and considering the effects of individual elements and their interrelationships. One method of close reading is to look at a segment of film shot by shot. This technique of *textual analysis* is exemplified in the work of French film theorist Raymond Bellour. Bellour's detailed studies of films by Alfred Hitchcock, Howard Hawks, and others are accompanied by charts listing all the shots in the sequence to be analyzed as well as such variables as camera distance or movement. From such a chart, the analyst notes and interprets the interrelations among different formal elements and their patterns of development. For example, how do variations in camera distance correlate with camera movements in a given sequence? What effect do these variations have?

Analysts such as Bellour refer to elements such as shot duration, camera movement, and lighting as **codes**. A code is essentially a rule, and it structures a particular act of communication, a message. The code must be shared by the sender and the receiver for the message to be understood. For example, viewers understand that the shadows in a shot from *The Big Heat* (1953) signify a threat because they recognize the code of film noir lighting. The textual analyst draws conclusions from the interactions of various codes over a series of shots. For instance, dark shadows and threatening music reinforce each other to connote danger. Some codes used in cinema, such as lighting and dialogue, are shared with theater. Other codes, such as framing, camera movement, and shot duration, are specific to film. Textual analyses are an especially effective way to train oneself to look—and listen—to the movies more closely.

Questions of cinema's specificity and its interdisciplinary nature are especially pertinent today as recent technological developments—from videotape playback and virtual reality to computer-generated imagery (CGI), digital cinematography, and digital projection—raise profound ontological questions about cinema. The image is no longer a product of the physical contact between light and its referent, the actual object that is then captured on film stock; instead, the properties of the image are digitally coded and thus mutable. A computer-generated image does not have a real-world referent; the image *is* the thing **[Figure 11.2]**. Interestingly, film theory's long history of thinking about specificity puts it in an excellent position to make sense of what the unique properties of this new, digital medium might be. We have used the concept of interdisciplinarity to refer both to how film draws on a variety of other art forms and to how a range of academic disciplines offer invaluable perspectives on the significance and social role of cinema. Now cognitive science, computer science, and game theory play a key role in the study of contemporary film and media studies, making this inquiry an interdisciplinary one as well.

11.2   ***Final Fantasy: The Spirits Within*** (2001). The nature of the film image—its ontological status—is challenged by computer-generated imagery (CGI) in this first film to feature human "actors" produced entirely through this technology.

There are no clear boundaries—either chronological or intellectual—to the field of film theory. However, a historical overview of film theory allows us to contextualize important thinkers and to understand how key principles and terms have been defined and debated over time. Film theory, and the emerging theories that address new and related audiovisual media, will undoubtedly take on new questions in the future. Yet these concerns will be shaped by an intellectual history of considerable longevity and complexity.

VIEWING CUE

Compare a scene from a film you have viewed either in class or on your own with a passage from the book from which it was adapted. What elements are specific to the film?

Early and Classical Film Theory

In this section, we begin with the earliest reflections on film that occurred not long after the first public exhibitions by Thomas Edison and the Lumière brothers. We then consider the body of work designated as **classical film theory**, which emerged with the maturity of the medium in the 1920s and finds a convenient endpoint with the publication of Siegfried Kracauer's major work *Theory of Film* in 1960.

Early Film Theory

"Last night I was in the Kingdom of Shadows. If you only knew how strange it is to be there," wrote the Russian novelist Maxim Gorky after attending a film screening in 1896. When movies were new, observers searched for metaphors to describe the experience of seeing them. Struck by movies' magical properties, viewers attempted to pinpoint what was distinctive about the medium. Some early critics considered moviegoing a social phenomenon, a new form of urban entertainment characteristic of the dawning twentieth century. Others viewed the cinema in aesthetic terms, heralding it as the "seventh art."

While today film theory is considered part of an academic discipline, earlier writers on the topic came from many contexts and traditions, making any overview of the history of film theory a disjunctive one. A few early theorists wrote books, yet equally important theoretical contributions have been made in journals, essays, and other forms. Early writers on film might have been critics of other art forms or scholars in other disciplines. Or they might have been filmmakers who shared their ideas and excitement about the developing medium with each other in specialized publications. Some of the questions film theorists have examined since the inception of film theory include:

- Is cinema an art form? How does it relate to photography, painting, theater, music, and other art forms?
- Does film resemble language or have a language of its own?
- Is film's primary responsibility to tell a story?
- Is film by nature a "realist" medium?
- What is the place of film in the modern world that fostered its development?

Two noteworthy books on movies appeared in the United States as early as the 1910s. Poet Vachel Lindsay's *The Art of the Moving Picture* (1915) responded enthusiastically to the novelty and the democratizing potential of the medium. "I am the one poet who has a right to claim for his muses Blanche Sweet, Mary Pickford, and Mae Marsh," he gushed, invoking the popular movie stars of the day. In his idiosyncratic but suggestive book, Lindsay likened film language to hieroglyphics. This metaphor of picture-writing indicated cinema's promise of universality, which excited many early observers.

A more systematic elaboration of ideas about cinema was contributed by Harvard psychologist Hugo Münsterberg in *The Photoplay: A Psychological Study* (1916). For Münsterberg, viewing films was linked to the subjective process of thinking. The properties of cinema that distinguished it from the physical reality to which its images referred were what made it of interest aesthetically and psychologically. Unlike watching a play, watching movies requires specific mental activities to make sense of cues of movement and depth. "The photoplay tells us the human story by overcoming the forms of the outer world, namely, space, time, and causality, and by adjusting the events to the forms of the inner world, namely, attention, memory, imagination, and emotion," wrote Münsterberg. His ideas thus emphasized the viewer's interaction with the medium. Decades later, theories of spectatorship would do the same. While Lindsay's work praised specific films, Münsterberg referred to the idea of photoplay in general. In a sense, their works mark the division between criticism, which reflects on a given aesthetic object, and theory, which is broader and sometimes more abstract.

Outside the United States, much early writing about cinema came from filmmakers themselves. Although movies immediately became commercialized, they emerged, and flourished, in the context of modernist experimentation in the arts—music, writing, theater, painting, architecture, and photography. Because film was based on new technology, many considered it an exemplary art for the machine age. Film influenced new approaches to established media, such as cubism in painting and the "automatic writing" of the surrealists. In turn, filmmakers adopted avant-garde practices, and painters like Hans Richter took up filmmaking, exploring graphic and rhythmic possibilities **[Figure 11.3]**. Modernist intellectuals debated cinema's aesthetic status and its relationship to the other arts.

In the 1910s and 1920s in France, the first avant-garde film movement, impressionism, was fostered by groups known as ciné-clubs and by journals dedicated to the new medium. In *Cinéma*, Louis Delluc coined the term *photogénie* to refer to a particular quality that distinguishes the filmed object from its everyday reality. Jean Epstein elaborated on this elusive concept in such poetic writings as "Bonjour Cinéma" and in his film adaptation of Edgar Allan Poe's story, *The Fall of the House of Usher* (1928) **[Figure 11.4]**. Germaine Dulac compared film to music in her extensive writings and lectures. Film theory and practice began to flourish during this time and would continue to develop in tandem in the period between the world wars.

11.3 *Rhythmus 21* (1921). Frames of prominent German artist Hans Richter's early abstract film.

Soviet Montage Theory

After the 1917 Russian Revolution, a group of artist-intellectuals in the Soviet Union set about defining an artistic practice that could participate in revolutionary change. Like the avant-garde graphic and set designers, painters, and composers who were their comrades, they were eager to incorporate the materials of industrial modernity in their art. The cinema, with its technological base and its populist reach, provided a perfect medium. Lev Kuleshov's teaching at the state film school put the theory of montage at the center of Soviet filmmaking, and these ideas went well beyond the world of film theory to influence filmmaking worldwide.

As we noted in Chapter 4, Vsevolod Pudovkin and Sergei Eisenstein, Kuleshov's students, elaborated the theory of montage in their own writings and films (pp. 137-38). In his *Mother* (1926) **[Figure 11.5]** and other films, Pudovkin used montage as a way of breaking down a scene to direct the spectator's look and understanding. Eisenstein's theory of montage, in contrast, emphasized the effects of collision between shots. He correlated the exponential increase of meaning to be gained by the juxtaposition of shots to the dialectic, a philosophical concept that Karl Marx had adopted and incorporated in his theory of historical materialism. Simply defined, a dialectic consists of a thesis that is countered by an antithesis, or opposing element, which results in a synthesis of both that is more forceful and truthful than either element on its own. Eisenstein's extensive body of writing, amply illustrated with examples from his celebrated films, spans several decades and constitutes the most significant contribution to film theory by a filmmaker.

Filmmaker Dziga Vertov also contributed to film theory in the form of manifestos signed by the Kinoki, or "cinema-eye" group **[Figure 11.6]**, that emphasized the new way of seeing made possible by the movie camera's ability to overcome the limitations of the human eye. Resisting systemization in his poetic, avant-garde writings, Vertov rejected the fiction film in favor of "life caught unaware" and experimented with the possibilities of sound. Eisenstein denounced Vertov's trick shots as "formalist jackstraws"; Vertov scorned Eisenstein's "filmed theater." The polemics and practices of these two great filmmakers were later championed by the 1960s generation of critic-filmmakers in France.

Film was seen as a vital force within the revolutionary culture of the early Soviet Union, one that could bring the masses, many of them illiterate, into modernity. The intensity of discussion about the properties and potential of the medium contributed as much to the cinema's importance as did the films themselves; at this time and place, theory was an indispensable part of film culture. Above all, the concept of montage survived as one of the central theoretical and

11.4 *The Fall of the House of Usher* (1928). Jean Epstein's interest in the poetic quality of an object when filmed shares affinities with the writing of Edgar Allan Poe, whose short story he adapted in this impressionist film.

11.5 *Mother* (1926). Like other Soviet filmmakers, Vsevolod Pudovkin emphasized the power of montage. But while Eisenstein favored dissonant effects, Pudovkin pioneered the orchestration of emotion through cutting, as in this powerful adaptation of Maxim Gorky's novel.

11.6 **Poster for Vertov's *Man with a Movie Camera* (1929).** This dynamic poster by Soviet designers the Stenberg brothers shows the close relationship between the graphic arts and cinema of the period.

11.7 *Arrival of a Train at La Ciotat* (1896). Whether a truthful account or a myth, audiences were said to be so frightened by the image of a life-sized train coming directly at them that they screamed and ran from their seats.

practical concerns of cinema. It is as significant to film analysts as it has been to filmmakers from Alfred Hitchcock to Soviet editor Slavko Vorkapich, who lent his name to the "montage sequences" he supervised for classical Hollywood films.

Classical Film Theories: Formalism and Realism

While integral to the historical context in which they emerged, Sergei Eisenstein's formalist writings were also taken up by thinkers and academics outside the Soviet Union, including Béla Balázs, Rudolf Arnheim, André Bazin, and Siegfried Kracauer, whose body of works spanned the shift from silent to sound filmmaking and into the post-World War II period. The momentous technical development of synchronized sound was accompanied by ontological speculation: does sound allow film to fulfill a mission to reproduce the world as it is, or does sound hinder cinema's visual expression?

One of the organizing debates of classical film theory centers around the appeal to **realism** made first by photography and then by film. Realism, generally speaking, relates to mimesis, or imitation of reality, in the arts. The mimetic quality has been valued in the Western artistic tradition since ancient Greece. However, the term "realism" itself only came into use in the nineteenth century to designate a style—developed in the most important genre of the era, the novel—that embraced subject matter drawn from the experience of everyday life. Realist style was highly descriptive, a function that the photographic nature of cinema fulfills. For theorists such as Bazin and Kracauer, film's referential quality—that is, its ability to refer to the world through images that resemble and record the presence of objects and sources of sounds—sets it apart as a realist medium. In contrast, theorists such as Arnheim and Balázs emphasize film form as fundamental; for them, realism is only a style that uses this form in a particular way.

Viewers and commentators addressed the question of cinematic realism from the beginning, and digital media theorists pose it anew today. Stories of the presentation of the Lumière brothers' first films at the Grand Café in Paris invariably tell how audiences shrank from the arriving train or feared they would be splashed by the waves of the sea [**Figure 11.7**]. Whether or not these stories are true, they characterize cinema as lacking the aesthetic distance of the other arts. For many, film seems too "natural" to be a vehicle for making meaning or an object to which traditional aesthetic criteria apply. Others, including the French and Soviet modernists, were concerned primarily with cinema's status as an art, distancing themselves from the impression it gives of reproducing the world, perhaps because the artist's role is downplayed by such a notion.

Formalism: Béla Balázs and Rudolf Arnheim

Like Sergei Eisenstein, Béla Balázs and Rudolf Arnheim championed formalist theories of film. They were especially interested in how film became an art form precisely by transcending its referential quality.

Béla Balázs, a Hungarian screenwriter and film critic, published his first book on film in 1924, making him one of the earliest important film theorists. Later, his writings were published in the influential volume *Theory of the Film* (1952). Balázs was passionate about the new ways of observing the world that cinema made possible, and he argued that film was a new "form-language" that broke with the language of theater. In particular, Balázs wrote eloquently on the power of the close-up, an element of film art impossible to approximate on stage: "by means of the close-up the camera in the days of the silent film revealed also the hidden main-springs of a life which we had thought we already knew so well" **[Figure 11.8]**. Balázs also explored

11.8   **Asta Nielsen as *Hamlet*** (1921). Theorist Béla Balázs believed the close-up could reveal the soul onscreen and wrote eloquently about Danish silent film star Asta Nielsen's face in close-up.

the crucial phenomenon of identification in cinema as an aspect of film language, describing how in watching a movie, "we look up to Juliet's balcony with Romeo's eyes and look down on Romeo with Juliet's." Thus for Balázs, film was able to reveal aspects of reality that could not otherwise be seen. More important, he championed the pursuit of film theory itself, arguing that the new form-language required systematic elaboration.

German art historian Rudolf Arnheim argued even more strongly for a formalist position in his 1933 study *Film*, which was later revised for English publication as *Film as Art* (1957). For Arnheim, the quest for film realism was misguided, a betrayal of the unique aesthetic properties of the medium that allowed it to transcend the imitation of nature. He set out to "refute the assertion that film is nothing but the feeble mechanical reproduction of real life." For example, in his view the two-dimensionality of the screen image was not a limitation but an aesthetic parameter to be exploited by filmmakers and emphasized by theorists. Lighting effects and various other artistic manipulations were what allowed film to go beyond mere duplication. Arnheim's position recalls Hugo Münsterberg's arguments about the distinctive properties and processes of film. Indeed, both theorists were interested in the psychology of perception and did not value the perception of resemblance above other responses.

> ▶ **VIEWING CUE**
>
> From the last film you viewed for class, explore a shot or scene in terms of (1) Béla Balázs's arguments about the close-up or (2) Rudolf Arnheim's arguments about the two-dimensional screen. ❚❚

Realism: André Bazin and Siegfried Kracauer

While theorists in the 1920s and 1930s tended to align themselves with formalist positions, in the post–World War II period, a reconsideration of realism was prompted by political events as well as by technical innovations and new filmmaking movements. One of the most prominent film critics and theorists of the 1950s and 1960s, André Bazin, saw film as quintessentially realist, a medium "in which the image is evaluated not according to what it adds to reality but what it reveals of it." Bazin responded directly to the formalists who preceded him, and he serves as an important predecessor of contemporary film studies in turn (Bazin's influence through *Cahiers du cinéma* is discussed later in this chapter).

In his essay "The Evolution of the Language of Cinema," Bazin expressed the view that cinema's ability to capture a space and event in real time is its essence. Montage interfered with this vocation, he argued, by altering spatial and temporal relationships. He advocated instead for the use of composition in depth, made

11.9 *Footlight Parade* (1933). In his writings of the 1920s and early 1930s, Siegfried Kracauer cited the almost abstract patterns of chorus girls in performance as examples of what he called "mass ornament." He later advocated filmic realism.

possible by deep-focus cinematography, which kept all planes of the image in view, making cutting between shots taken from different distances less necessary. For Bazin, a filmmaker like Jean Renoir, who staged scenes in depth using long takes, conveyed "respect for the continuity of dramatic space and, of course, of its duration." Bazin saw the image not only as a reference to reality but also as a record of it—and ultimately as a means of transcending time.

Another formidable thinker on film, Siegfried Kracauer, is, like Bazin, best known for his strong advocacy of realism, though Kracauer's position evolved over time. In the 1920s, he began writing newspaper essays in Weimar Germany amid modernist experimentation with film form. In "The Mass Ornament," Kracauer explored the aesthetics of mass culture and the new rhythms of life it inspired [**Figure 11.9**]. And though he published his well-known *From Caligari to Hitler: A Psychological History of the German Film* in 1947, it was not until 1960 that he elaborated his views on film's capacity for realism in his major work, *Theory of Film: The Redemption of Physical Reality*. Kracauer argued that the cinematic medium "is uniquely equipped to record and reveal physical reality." It was not just that film provided a window on the phenomenal world. More important, for Kracauer film was able to preserve what would otherwise meet with destruction: the momentary, the everyday, the random.

▶ **VIEWING CUE**

From a realist position, analyze a recent film you viewed. Can you identify a scene that corresponds with André Bazin's ideas about the long take or Siegfried Kracauer's ideas about photography's power to capture the everyday?

Modernity and Cinema: Walter Benjamin

Walter Benjamin, Siegfried Kracauer's Weimar-era contemporary, was particularly interested in how cinema participated in the transformation of perception in the modern world. Benjamin wrote about cinema as well as photography in his famous, and complex, essay, "The Work of Art in the Age of Its Technological Reproducibility." For Benjamin, the comparison of photography and film with painting did not hinge on their relative artistic value or even their technique. Rather, they differed because these new art forms did not produce unique objects with the "aura" of an original artwork. Instead, film captured, in multiple widely circulating copies, the sense of accelerated time and effortlessly traversed space typical of contemporary urban life. Benjamin regarded the distracted state of the film viewer as characteristic of the historical moment. Written in 1935 as the Nazis rose to power, Benjamin's essay closed with an epilogue critiquing fascism's manipulation of the masses through traditional aesthetics. Benjamin did not survive the war, and his writings on cinema remained too sparse to put him at the center of classical debates in film theory. However, his influence on contemporary theorists, particularly his description of the transformation of the senses by twentieth-century modernity, has been great.

Postwar Film Culture and Criticism

As mentioned earlier, theorists' interest in cinematic realism was shaped by the devastating events of World War II and its aftermath. Kracauer's experience as a German Jewish refugee influenced his views on cinema as a kind of historical evidence. Bazin, an activist Catholic and member of the French Resistance, invested film with similar redemptive properties. For example, Bazin valued the postwar Italian neorealist movement, exemplified in films like *Germany Year Zero* (1948) with its location shooting and amateur actors [**Figure 11.10**], because it demonstrated what Bazin called "faith in reality."

In the period of recovery from the trauma and destruction of the war, a vigorous international film culture of art cinema, film festivals, and journals emerged. In fact, it can be argued that film theory could not have taken hold had it not been for the flurry of filmmaking and lively debates of this period.

Film Journals

Postwar film culture was fostered in an international array of film journals. One of the most famous journals, *Cahiers du cinéma*, was founded by Bazin in 1951. For many film buffs, the distinctive yellow cover of *Cahiers du cinéma* in the 1950s is as iconic an image of film history as that of Fay Wray in King Kong's hairy palm [Figure 11.11]. Under Bazin's mentorship, the magazine published the criticism of the young cineastes—François Truffaut, Jean-Luc Godard [Figure 11.12], Eric Rohmer,

11.10 *Germany Year Zero* (1948). For André Bazin, Roberto Rossellini's film, set on location in postwar Berlin, puts its "faith in reality."

11.11 *Cahiers du cinéma.* The journal, with its iconic yellow cover, introduced auteur theory in the 1950s.

11.12 *Jean-Luc Godard.* From his feature debut *Breathless* (1960) to the honorary Academy Award for lifetime achievement that he refused in 2010, Godard is an *auteur* whose persona is as distinctive as the innovative sounds and images of his many films.

FILM CULTURE

JANUARY, 1955   Volume I   No. 1

ERICH VON STROHEIM / Queen Kelly; Walking Down Broadway
ORSON WELLES / For a Universal Cinema
HANS RICHTER / Film as an Original Art Form
EDOUARD L. DE LAUROT / Towards a Theory of Dynamic Realism
HERMAN G. WEINBERG / The New Films
GEORGE N. FENIN / Motion Pictures and the Public
WILLIAM K. EVERSON / A Family Tree of Monsters
    also articles by GORDON HENDRICKS, FRANCIS BOLEN, ROGER TILTON,
    JOSE CLEMENTE, RICHARD KRAFT, and others

11.13   *Film Culture*. The first issue of the influential U.S. film magazine started by Adolfas and Jonas Mekas.

▶ **VIEWING CUE**

Look at several issues of one of the journals mentioned in this section. Characterize the publication's perspective on film culture, giving concrete examples. ⏸

Jacques Rivette, and Claude Chabrol—who would shape the French New Wave (see Chapter 10, pp. 367–68). These writers were getting much of their film education at the Cinémathèque Française, where Henri Langlois screened an eclectic menu of world film—including the hundreds of American studio films that had not been released in France during the Vichy period. Their writings, and the films that the *Cahiers* critics went on to make, energized world film culture and made possible the emergence of the discipline of film studies in universities.

Rival journals in France, *Positif* and *Cinéthique*, also flourished, and the polemics among them catalyzed film enthusiasts. English-language publications like *Movie* in England and the English-language *Cahiers du cinéma* edited by Andrew Sarris disseminated French criticism and ideas, like auteur theory. In the United States, *Film Culture* was at the heart of the avant-garde New American cinema movement in the 1950s and 1960s **[Figure 11.13]**, and the University of California's *Film Quarterly*, published under that title since 1958, introduced many key ideas of film theory.

After the cultural upheaval provoked by general strikes in France in May 1968, *Cahiers du cinéma* became more political and more theoretical. In its pages, films from *Hiroshima Mon Amour* (1959) to *Young Mr. Lincoln* (1939) were analyzed in depth, drawing on the Marxist theory of Louis Althusser. These articles became the basis for academic film studies and the contemporary film theory discussed in the next section. In the 1970s, writers for the British journal *Screen* introduced the Marxist, semiotic, and psychoanalytic language and ideas that would permeate Anglo-American cinema studies for more than a decade. Film publishing was not limited to periodicals. Monographs and series on individual directors, specific decades of film production, national cinemas, and genres proliferated. Many of these "little books"—low-cost, portable texts—combined the popular and the scholarly and encouraged the development of academic publishing in the field.

Auteur Theory

The ideas that emerged from this intense cultivation of film culture informed both criticism and theory. **Auteur theory**, which asserts that a film bears the creative imprint of one individual (typically the director), emerged in the 1950s when specific directors were vocally championed by the French critics. The retention of the French term "auteur" in English marks this origin. *Cahiers du cinéma* promoted what its writers called "*la politique des auteurs*," a "policy" or doctrine of singling out for praise certain filmmakers, such as Orson Welles, Fritz Lang, Samuel Fuller, and Robert Bresson, whose distinct styles made their films immediately identifiable. European art cinema was in its ascendance, with such figures as Ingmar Bergman and Michelangelo Antonioni fitting the definition of an auteur as an autonomous writer-director. Yet *Cahiers du cinéma*'s concept of authorship was also applied to a group of filmmakers for whom the idea of such conscious and consistent creative artistry seemed less appropriate: directors working in the heyday of the Hollywood studio system.

Despite studio constraints on artistic autonomy and the primacy of market considerations, critics argued that Hollywood auteurs such as Raoul Walsh and Howard Hawks left their signature on their films in the form of characteristic motifs or striking compositions. Debates arose over whether a particular director should be classified a true auteur or a mere **metteur en scène** (French for "director," derived from theatrical usage), a label that conveyed technical competence without a strong individual vision. In America, *la politique des auteurs* was popularized by Andrew Sarris in *Film Culture* and the *Village Voice*. In his 1968 collection *The American Cinema: Directors and Directions, 1929–1968*, Sarris lists his "pantheon," including Hawks, Chaplin, Welles, and John Ford. At the same time, he deflates the reputations of such Academy Award winners as William Wyler. In Sarris's hierarchy of Hollywood talent, the judgment of the critic prevails in assigning relative status to a wide array of directors based on their personal signature. Like that of the French critics, Sarris's work depends on a deep **cinephilia,** or love of cinema, and an almost exhaustive knowledge of the films—major and minor—released throughout the previous several decades. Sarris's rendering of *la politique des auteurs* as auteur theory is somewhat misleading; it is less a fully worked-out theory than a critical method, and the political connotation is lost in translation.

However, the auteurist approach tends to minimize the fact that cinema is a collaborative, commercial, and highly technologically mediated form. Making a film is not as personal as authoring a poem, and because so many individuals usually contribute to a film, it can be hard to assign credit to a single authorial vision, especially in studio-produced work. Critic Pauline Kael counters Sarris's position in one famous instance, asserting that writer Herman Mankiewicz rather than Orson Welles should be credited for coming up with *Citizen Kane*'s original structure and that cinematographer Gregg Toland's work is what distinguishes the film's look. In commercial cinema, a producer, studio, or franchise may be more important than a director. Today, a credit such as "a Tom Cruise film" or even "an Oliver Stone film" may be more a matter of contractual obligations and financial arrangements than of authorship **[Figure 11.14]**.

Another challenge to auteur theory is that it extended the cultural prestige of the literary author to filmmakers at the same time that literary critics were calling the traditional notion of authorial genius into question. In a 1968 essay, French literary critic Roland Barthes declared "the death of the author," arguing that the artist's conscious intention and biography should be set aside in favor of an analysis of the formal qualities of the work itself. These new perspectives on authorship had their roots in **structuralism,** an approach to linguistics and anthropology that, when extended to literary and filmic narratives, looks for common structures rather than originality. In the case of films, these common structures might be plots or characters that recur across works. In his influential 1969 book, *Signs and Meaning in the Cinema*, Peter Wollen advocates a structural approach to authorship, placing the film author's name in quotation marks to designate a critical construct rather than a biographical individual. For example, John Ford's films return again and again to the opposition between garden and wilderness. One can see this common "Ford" structure developed differently from *My Darling Clementine* (1946) to *The Man Who Shot Liberty Valance* (1962). Through his approach, Wollen attempts to reconcile the contradiction between the heralding of artistry that always informs criticism and the skepticism toward individual creative intention that is characteristic of structuralist theory.

11.14 ***Wall Street: Money Never Sleeps*** (2010). Though promoted as "an Oliver Stone film" in some advertisements, this sequel relies on the established *Wall Street* franchise and Michael Douglas's reprisal of the infamous Gordon Gekko as much as the name of the director to attract audiences.

Genre Theory

As we note in Chapter 9, the theory of genre, which categorizes the different structures, motifs, and effects of a particular form of art, dates back to Aristotle's *Poetics*. In film, genre criticism, like auteur theory, was invigorated by the film culture of post–World War II France when American films that had not been released during that country's occupation by Germany were finally exhibited all at once, making commonalities easy to identify. Like auteur criticism, genre criticism also depends on cinephilia—making generalizations based on only a few films would be imprudent. Sometimes genre criticism is considered at odds with auteurism: geniuses could not make run-of-the-mill films—or if they did, it was an exception in their oeuvre. But auteurist approaches essentially developed in tandem with genre perspectives—it can be argued that the mark of the auteur on a genre is what distinguishes his or her work. This is certainly the case with John Ford and the western. Critics might consider how an artist's preoccupations and style intersected with the formulas and conventions of a genre.

11.15 *His Girl Friday* (1940). Howard Hawks made classics in disparate genres, including westerns, musicals, adventure films, and comedies such as this one.

Auteur criticism might also praise the handling of different genres by a particularly gifted auteur. Critic Robin Wood looks at the elaboration of Hawksian themes in both Howard Hawks's male adventure films and his screwball comedies and finds them to be related to the same concerns **[Figure 11.15]**. Similarly, a contemporary auteur such as Quentin Tarantino is known for his self-conscious use of martial arts, blaxploitation, and crime film genres; and Ridley Scott made an utterly original film in *Blade Runner* while respecting science fiction conventions **[Figure 11.16]**. The positive critical view toward popular cinema, especially Hollywood movies, that auteurism began to bring about in the 1950s was carried on through genre criticism more directly—and without auteur theory's dependence on the literary analogy.

11.16 *Blade Runner* (1982). The convergence of auteurist and genre criticism is apparent in assessments of Ridley Scott's science fiction film.

Westerns are popular examples for genre theory. When we go to see a western, we know what we are getting: horses, open horizons, good guys in white, bad guys in black. Or do we? Critics have documented how genres evolve and cultural myths shift. For example, later existential westerns featured more complicated moral scenarios, differing greatly from the easy identification of good guys and bad guys in earlier westerns. In *The Searchers* (1956), John Wayne's character's racism is evident, and in *Unforgiven* (1992) violence seems pointless **[Figure 11.17]**. We see westerns featuring independent women in *The Quick and the Dead* (1995) and African American cowboys in *Posse* (1993), redefining our notions of history and heroism. That an epic western can be transposed to an outer-space setting in *Star Wars* (1977) suggests ways in which the geography of the western United States that the

11.17 *Unforgiven* (1992). Clint Eastwood's existential western revived the genre in the 1990s.

genre usually features may itself be an imaginary space. Different genres work out different cultural questions or problems; hence their emergence and decline in particular periods. Critic Thomas Schatz, in his 1981 book *Hollywood Genres*, for example, sees musicals as celebrating cultural integration, often symbolized by the couple coming together, whereas westerns require the establishment of a home, one that the wandering hero cannot himself enjoy.

Critical Questions in Contemporary Film Theory

By the 1970s, film studies had become an established discipline, with strong footholds in English and art history programs as well as in its own academic departments, societies, and journals. During this time, the vocabulary of film theory became very specialized. Theorists became interested in a more systematic approach to cinema than was offered by the often subjective and impressionistic legacy of film criticism. More recently, online journals, blogs, and streaming sites have helped democratize film theory, reflecting a greater engagement between the public and the scholarly, and reconnecting with the discipline's origins in a wider film culture.

The following necessarily partial overview of **contemporary film theory** is organized according to major critical schools within the discipline. There are important interrelationships among these schools, and often one set of questions grows out of another. For example, feminism overlaps with psychoanalytic theory on the one hand, and with cultural studies on the other. However, establishing the evolution and broad outlines for each area of contemporary film theory is useful, and it can inspire new questions for further study.

Semiotics, Structuralism, and Ideological Critique

The academic discipline of film studies has been heavily influenced by European thought, especially by several currents converging in postwar France, including semiotics, structuralism, and the ideological critique that grew out of Marxism. At first glance, these ideas may seem to have little to do with film, but in fact such iconoclastic systems of thought are well suited to questioning a medium of comparable freshness and vitality, like cinema.

Semiotics

In order to introduce **semiotics** (also called semiology) and structuralism, we must understand that a language model, one that compares a given object or system to the structure of language, is central to 1970s film theory. This might at first seem curious: after all, films consist predominantly of pictures. How can a model that compares a given object or system to the structure of language be crucial to understanding film and film theory?

The influence of linguistics was pervasive in French thought of the 1960s, and it can be traced back to the work of Ferdinand de Saussure in the early part of the century. Saussure used linguistics as the most exemplary case of a new science of signs he called semiology, which could include pictures, gestures, and a wide range of other systems of communication or perception. A **sign**, for Saussure, is composed of a *signifier*, the spoken or written word, picture, or gesture, and a *signified*, the mental concept it evokes. Together, the signifier "c-a-t" and the signified mental image of a domesticated feline form a sign, and the two parts cannot be imagined without each other. In a particular instance, the sign "cat" might refer to a specific tabby, which would be its *referent*.

text continued on page 416 ▶

FILM IN FOCUS

Genre and Authorship in *Touch of Evil* (1958)

Touch of Evil is a police thriller based on the novel *Badge of Evil* by Whit Masterson, who specialized in the genre. Set in an unnamed, unsavory town on the U.S.-Mexico border, the film follows the power struggle between the Mexican official Vargas (Charlton Heston), recently married to an American woman named Susan (Janet Leigh), and the corrupt American detective Quinlan (Orson Welles). In the very first shot—a remarkable mobile crane shot—a wealthy American and his girlfriend are killed, and the film leads us from the crime investigation into an investigation by Vargas of Quinlan's long history of witness intimidation and evidence tampering. Meanwhile, Susan is assaulted and then framed for drug use and homicide by the Grandi family, the border town's small-time criminal mob. It turns out that Quinlan is behind the attack on Susan; and in the end he is shot and killed by his formerly loyal sidekick, and Vargas and Susan are happily reunited.

Elements of story, setting, and character quickly establish *Touch of Evil* as a crime thriller that can be rewardingly discussed in comparison to other films of the genre and period shot in a similar film noir style. Generic characteristics include "criminal" locations such as nightclubs and bars, cheap motels, and deserted streets and alleyways. Most of the important scenes take place at night. The characters include a range of recurrent generic figures: a taciturn streetwise hero, Vargas; and a physically and morally monstrous villain, Quinlan. The two principal female characters suggest, even as they complicate, the common division between good girl and bad in the film noir. Susan is an all-American blonde bride, and Tanya, a woman from Quinlan's past, is a dark-haired, ethnically indeterminate fortune-teller who runs a suspect establishment on the Mexican side of the border. Stylistically, *Touch of Evil* displays and exaggerates the conventions associated with film noir. It is shot in black and white, and the extremely effective low-key lighting produces sharp contrasts that emphasize the sinister quality of people and places and the mysteriousness of unfolding events. Unbalanced composition, wide-angle lenses,

and figures lit from below produce distortions in everyday perceptions that frighten or unsettle **[Figure 11.18]**. The film's score by Henry Mancini reflects the incorporation of jazz in film noir's urban night world.

By the time *Touch of Evil* was made at the end of the 1950s, the film noir cycle had nearly run its course. *Touch of Evil* supports Thomas Schatz's contention that the end of a genre's life span is characterized by "self-conscious formalism"; the film's style is so baroque that it overtakes the story. Consider, for example, the grotesque low-angle shot, taken from Susan's point of view, of Grandi after he has been strangled **[Figure 11.19]**. The film's cynicism takes the pessimistic values of film noir to the extreme. In the exaggerated rottenness of Quinlan, the law itself is shown to be corrupt. And although Vargas and his wife may seem to get their happy ending, they are pictured in a convertible at the end of the film, a sinister echo of the couple who had been blown up by a car bomb in the first shot.

In fact, the strangeness of *Touch of Evil* made it difficult to market. At the other end of the spectrum from the one-of-a-kind superproductions that were beginning to be produced in Hollywood, *Touch of Evil* was intended as the kind of low-budget film that uses genre to let audiences know what to expect. Welles seems to have violated

11.18 *Touch of Evil* (1958). Low-key lighting and unbalanced composition characterize the film noir mise-en-scène.

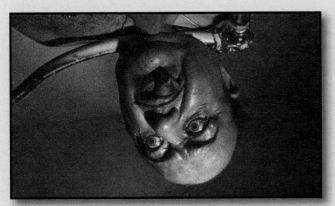

11.19 *Touch of Evil* (1958). The drugged Susan wakes up to this shocking point-of-view shot. Wide-angle lenses increase distortion in the images.

11.20 *Touch of Evil* (1958). The virtuosity of the moving crane shot that opens this film shows off Welles's authorial presence in this otherwise standard Hollywood fare. The sequence shot also establishes the film's genre, as we know a ticking bomb is hidden in the trunk of the car.

such expectations; the industry publication *Variety* called it a "confusing, somewhat 'artsy' film" with "so-so prospects." Interestingly, however, it is precisely as a genre film that *Touch of Evil* supports an assessment of Orson Welles's greatness as an auteur, for he certainly made the most of his "routine" assignment. In sharp contrast to his unprecedented (and short-lived) autonomy when he first arrived in Hollywood to make *Citizen Kane* in 1941, *Touch of Evil* was not designed as "an Orson Welles film." It was offered to Welles to direct at the behest of the film's star, Charlton Heston.

Welles's almost accidental participation mitigates against assigning too much original intention to him as an author. Universal agreed to allow him to adapt the screenplay and to direct because they thought he would make an interesting Quinlan. But Welles's appearance in the film enforces his authorship, drawing our attention to his character and away from his foil, the ostensible "good guy" protagonist, Vargas. Welles's flamboyant presence and his willingness to play a remarkably unappealing character reference his performances in films he directed, most notably *Citizen Kane*, whose hero is also larger than life—and flawed.

Auteurism, of course, goes beyond the visual presence or "signature" of the author. It is a way of connecting stylistic and thematic similarities across an individual's films. Welles had been known for stylistic excess since making brilliant innovations in camera, sound, lighting, acting, and composition in *Citizen Kane*. Many of these techniques are used in *Touch of Evil*. The use of deep-focus cinematography, so characteristic of *Citizen Kane* and *The Magnificent Ambersons* (1942), results in menacing and distorted images as the edges of the frames

stretch. Wide-angle lenses include more in the frame, allowing a shot to run longer without cutting, for naturalistic or virtuosic effects. An example of the latter is *Touch of Evil*'s famous opening shot, which lasts approximately 2.5 minutes; it covers a great deal of territory and ultimately explosive action [**Figure 11.20**]. French critics were particularly admiring of this "sequence shot," so named because a whole sequence unfolds in one continuous camera take; after they saw the film, these critics helped canonize Welles as Hollywood's greatest auteur. Truffaut wrote, "You could remove Orson Welles's name from the credits and it wouldn't make any difference, because from the first shot, beginning with the credits themselves, it's obvious that Citizen Kane is behind the camera."

Because of Welles's fame, today it is almost impossible to consider the film outside of an auteurist framework. Although *Touch of Evil* is revived in series surveying film noirs, its reputation as a classic is owed to its being a sleazy police film directed by a genius. The 2000 release of the restored "director's cut" of *Touch of Evil* demonstrates the importance of the auteurist perspective on the film. This version is not a recovered copy of the film Welles originally submitted. Rather, the restoration team construed his intentions by referring to an extensive memo that Welles wrote upon viewing Universal's cut of the original release. The story of the artist's vision being sacrificed to the studio's wishes helps construct Welles's authorial persona as a misunderstood artist. Readings of *Touch of Evil* based on genre or authorship reveal different patterns of meaning and ultimately demonstrate how film theory goes beyond abstraction, using concrete evidence to test the usefulness of propositions about how films work.

11.21 *The Treachery of Images* (1928-1929). René Magritte's painting contrasts verbal and visual signs. Neither the picture nor the word is an actual pipe.

For late-nineteenth-century American philosopher C. S. Peirce, who coined the term "semiotics," there are three varieties of signs. A word is a *symbolic sign*. Photography and film, in contrast, are *iconic signs*, meaning they resemble their referents. Finally, since photographic images are a product of a process in which light, when reflected from an object, produces an image that is fixed by the chemical emulsion on film, these images are also *indexical signs*, Peirce's third type of sign. In other words, a direct causal relationship exists between the sign and the object depicted—a relationship that can be likened to pointing or indicating, implied by the word "index." A footprint indicates that a person has walked in a particular path; a weathervane points in the direction the wind blows. Like photographs, both are indexical signs.

Therefore, pictures, especially photographs and film or video images, have a stronger identification with their referents than do words, whose connection to what they designate is purely arbitrary. In René Magritte's painting *The Treachery of Images*, the words "*Ceci n'est pas une pipe*" ("This is not a pipe") seem absurd because we take them to refer to what is unmistakably a picture of a pipe [**Figure 11.21**]. But a picture of a pipe is not a pipe. There is no essential nature of an object that is captured in a sign, of whatever kind. Semiotics is anti-essentialist, stressing the human invention and social convention aspects of language rather than its essential qualities. The scientific methodology devised by linguistics to describe these conventions has been useful to theorists attempting to approach cinema systematically, rather than relying on subjective evaluations such as beauty and truth.

The comparison of film and language is by no means new. Classical film theorists—from Vachel Lindsay to Sergei Eisenstein and Béla Balázs—have used linguistic metaphors of hieroglyphics, rhetoric, and grammar in their writings, and filmmakers like D. W. Griffith sought a visual Esperanto, or common language. But contemporary theorists, most notably Christian Metz in his book *Film Language: A Semiotics of Cinema* (1990), use the analogy even more systematically. Eisenstein had concluded that a shot was more like a sentence than it was like a word, in that a shot could be subdivided again and again and its components would still "make sense." On the one hand, Metz posited that since shots can be combined in an infinite number of ways, no film grammar exists. But on the other hand, he recognized that in narrative filmmaking there are many similarities among types and sequences of narrative units. Metz gives names to the limited number of units in use, such as "scene," "sequence," and "alternating **syntagma**" (a crosscutting sequence), to build something like a narrative grammar of film.

Structuralism

The legacy of linguistics has also been felt in theories of film narrative. French anthropologist Claude Lévi-Strauss titled his important 1957 work *Structural Anthropology*, building on Saussure's structural linguistics. Lévi-Strauss studied thousands of myths and discovered that they share basic structures that profoundly shape cultural life. Russian folklorist Vladimir Propp noticed a similar unity in his study of folktales. There are a limited number of what he called character functions (eight) and plot elements (thirty-one), and certain kinds of plot events always occur in the same order. From hundreds of tales he discerned basic plots; interestingly, these are echoed in many other narrative forms. **Narratology**, the study of narrative forms, is a branch of structuralism that encompasses stories of all kinds, including films. Are there a limited number of basic plots available to filmmakers? Are genres like myths? Because movies are so formulaic and so strikingly similar to myths and folktales even when not explicitly based on them, narratological studies had fruitful results. The characters in the *Star Wars* series, for example, closely match the heroes, antiheroes, magical help-ers, princesses, and witches of the folktales Propp studied **[Figure 11.22]**.

The linguists known as the Russian formalists, contemporaries of Sergei Eisen-stein and Vladimir Propp, have contributed the important distinction between *syuzhet* (plot) and *fabula* (story) to the study of narrative. *Syuzhet* refers to the way events are arranged in the actual tale or film, and *fabula* refers to the chronologically ordered

11.22 ***Star Wars: Episode IV—A New Hope*** (1977). George Lucas acknowledged the influence of mythologist Joseph Campbell (though not that of French structuralists) in the plot of the first *Star Wars* movie. Narratologists would recognize the *dramatis personae* of the hero, the helper, and the princess in the film's main characters.

sequence of events as we rationally reconstruct it. For example, a detective story's *syuzhet* follows the detective's progress through the investigation. Its *fabula* com-mences with the circumstances leading up to the committing of the crime.

Structuralist theorists reduce narrative to its most basic form: a beginning situation is disrupted, a hero takes action as a result, and a new equilibrium is reached at the end. The novel, the distinctive middle-class cultural form of the nineteenth century, gave that hero psychological depth and a realistic field of action. The novel's basic narrative form is adopted by motion pictures, yet film theory and certain film practices have challenged the idea of classical narrative form as "the norm." According to its critics, classical narrative form affirms values of middle-class culture, such as the agency of the individual, the transparency of realism, and the inevitability of the status quo, through processes of identification, verisimilitude, catharsis, and closure. **Modernism** favors a more fragmented human subjectivity, a foregrounding of style, and an open-ended narrative. *Postmodern-ism* mixes and matches different kinds of narratives and formal approaches. The disjunctive incidents of surrealist films, abstract films by avant-garde filmmakers such as Maya Deren and Michael Snow, and murky postmodern tales such as *Blade Runner* and *Fight Club* (1999) intentionally reject classical narrative characteristics adopted from the realist novel.

▶ **VIEWING CUE**

Compare *The Wizard of Oz* (1939) to a fairy tale. Do they share a similar narrative structure? ⏸

Ideological Critique

In many of the preceding examples, the rejection of narrative is based on an ideo-logical argument against the naturalization of conventions and the mystification of how things work. This ideological critique is derived from Marxist theory. Marxism is most immediately understood as a political and economic discourse, one that looks at history and society in terms of unequal class relations. Marxist approaches to film and mass culture exerted a profound influence on shaping film theory long before the 1970s. As we have seen, the work of Sergei Eisenstein, Dziga Vertov, Vsevolod Pudovkin, and other practitioner-theorists in the Soviet Union was made possible by a Marxist state. Walter Benjamin also drew on Marxism when he welcomed the democratization of culture made possible by "the age of technological reproducibility." At the same time, the Frankfurt School, a group of thinkers based in Frankfurt, Germany, with which Benjamin was associated, critiqued film and other forms of mass culture for reinforcing the capitalist social structure. Theodor Adorno and Max Horkheimer's essay "The Culture Industry," written in the United States in 1944 but not widely read until its republication in 1969, greatly influenced postwar academic and popular perceptions that mass culture duped its viewers, churning out movies in the same manner as it did new cars or brands of toothpaste, with only superficial differences among the products. Approaches to mass communication in the United States in the 1960s and 1970s tended to follow the thesis of "The Culture Industry."

At the same time, however, a different strain of Marxist thinking became prominent in French film theory, which was catalyzed by the radical social disruptions, political protests, and intellectual currents of the late 1960s. One of the most important theorists to influence contemporary film studies, French Marxist Louis Althusser approaches the traditional Marxist question of the nature of **ideology**—a systematic set of beliefs that is not necessarily conscious—with a new understanding of the structures of representation in order to explain how people come to accept ideas and conditions contrary to their interests. Althusser defines ideology as "the imaginary representation of the real relations in which we live." According to him, real relations, such as paid work that contributes to the profits of others, disempower working people in the interests of the ruling class, and our imaginary representations (that this is the way it is supposed to be, according to narratives such as the evening news and fashion magazines) make this powerlessness seem inevitable and tolerable.

For the critics at *Cahiers du cinéma*, film is an important test of Althusser's theories about ideology. Jean-Luc Comolli and Jean Narboni open their 1969 editorial "Cinema/Ideology/Criticism" by acknowledging that their own work as critics is "situated fairly and squarely inside the economic system of capitalist publishing." They then look at varieties of film practice and classify films in seven categories (a–g) according to their relationship with the "dominant ideology." Comolli and Narboni reject category "a" films, those they perceive as most politically and formally consistent with the dominant ideology. They most highly value category "b" films, those that break with this ideology, not only on the level of content (for example, films that portrayed decolonization and the conflict over U.S. involvement in Vietnam), but also on the level of form (for example, experimental films that disturb easy viewing processes).

But Comolli and Narboni's editorial set an even more lasting agenda for film theory. In their alphabetical list of categories of films to study, they use category "e" to designate films that seem to uphold the status quo but register, in their formal excesses or internal contradictions, the stresses and strains of trying to make the dominant ideology work, thus exposing it to close viewers as a representation rather than as an unchangeable reality. Soon, other critics followed Comolli and Narboni's lead in reading films in this way. For example, studio-era auteur Douglas Sirk's 1950s melodramas, including *All That Heaven Allows* (1955), were considered too color-coordinated, his characters too hysterical, and their environments too crammed with artificial commodities to be taken at face value [**Figure 11.23**]. These glossy surfaces were seen to be cracking under the brittle hypocrisies characterizing prosperous, Eisenhower-era America, including anti-Communist hysteria, repression of

▶ **VIEWING CUE**

Does the film you are watching put forth a clear ideological position? Are there ways to see conflicting positions in it? ⏸

11.23   *All That Heaven Allows* (1955). Critics regarded Douglas Sirk's melodramas as "progressive texts" whose formal excesses and improbable situations showed the cracks in Eisenhower-era America's facade of prosperity and social consensus.

civil rights movements, and enforcement of gender roles and sexual codes that had been challenged during the war. Sirk's films are what these critics called "progressive texts"; the uneasy feeling they leave us with is itself a critique of dominant ideology. This subtle, and sometimes wishful, approach is known as "symptomatic reading," a fruitful legacy of Althusser's ideological critique in contemporary film theory.

Poststructuralism: Psychoanalysis, Apparatus Theory, and Spectatorship

As the term implies, poststructuralism is the intellectual development that derived from structuralism and in some sense supplanted it. **Poststructuralism** questions the rational methodology and fixed definitions that structuralists bring to their various objects of study and includes many areas of thought, from psychoanalysis to postcolonial and feminist theory. Poststructuralism is a position of critique, asking us to reconsider the truths and hierarchies we take for granted. For example, our implicit standard that a satisfying film ties up all its loose ends is a structuralist position that posits closure as a basic narrative element. Poststructuralism counters that closure is a relative quality and stresses the open-endedness of stories: what if we daydream about the characters we have been introduced to or pick up on the relationship between a film and topical events?

Structuralism attempted to be systematic with empirical observation by looking for transhistorical patterns into which specific data would fit. Poststructuralism, in turn, questions structuralism's assumption of objectivity and the disregard for cultural and historical context. Hence it is a great deal messier as an intellectual movement. A shorthand definition might be: structuralism + subjectivity = poststructuralism. Most of contemporary film theory is poststructuralist in orientation; key movements that investigate and elaborate on the intersection of subjectivity with film structures include psychoanalysis, apparatus theory, and spectatorship.

Psychoanalysis

Louis Althusser's elaboration of how an individual comes to believe in ideology as "imaginary representation" draws on **psychoanalysis** and in particular the French psychoanalyst Jacques Lacan's definition of the *imaginary.* In his teachings from the 1950s through his death in 1981, Lacan spoke of three domains of psychic experience: the *imaginary,* the *symbolic,* and the *real.* The Lacanian imaginary realm deals in images, the symbolic realm is the domain of language, and the real is the domain of trauma that cannot be directly represented. The human subject relates to pictures (the imaginary) in a particularly powerful way, rooted in one of the earliest images to leave an impression on us, our own reflection in the mirror. In the *mirror stage,* the infant comes to recognize himself or herself as a human individual. But this recognition is also a "misrecognition," as the image is really an illusion. Lacanian film theorists like Jean-Louis Baudry and Christian Metz liken this early sense of self, which is both powerful and illusory, to the experience of viewing a film and "believing" in its world. We are immobile and surrounded in darkness when we watch, and a grandiose image appears lit up on the wall. Moreover, films are peopled with stars and characters with physical powers superior to ours and with whom we identify **[Figure 11.24]**. While the symbolic and the real also come into play in our encounters with movies, it is the imaginary that accounts for their power.

11.24   *Casino Royale* (2006). Daniel Craig's character James Bond represents an idealized object of identification, an aspect of spectatorship highlighted in psychoanalytic film theory.

Apparatus Theory

In Plato's ancient parable of the cave, people chained underground watching shadows on the wall could not know that what they saw was not real. Film theorist Jean-Louis Baudry saw the cinema as an ideological mechanism based in a physical set of technologies, with the power to convince us that an illusion is real. He used Althusser's term "apparatus" to argue that the arrangement of equipment, such as the hidden projector and the illuminated screen, influences our unconscious receptivity to the image and to ideology—as if we too were trapped in Plato's cave.

Apparatus theory explores the values built into film technology through the particular context of its historical development. The camera's monocular (single-eyed) perspective incorporates the values of human-scaled Renaissance art, which posits that a viewer stands at the point where perspective lines converge. The film viewer is in the same position as the camera that filmed the image and can thus imagine himself or herself as the originator or possessor of the illusion on the screen. Apparatus theory asserts that this position is not neutral but embodies Western cultural values like anthropocentrism (human-centeredness), individualism, possessiveness, and placing the visual over other senses. A culture that did not put the possessive individual at the center of representation—a culture that equally valued animals and people, for example, or senses other than sight in the arts—might never have developed the technology of photography.

Poststructuralism argues that an individual who stands in front of a Renaissance painting or watches a classical Hollywood movie is "subjected" to the apparatus's positioning and understands his or her "subjectivity" or sense of self in predetermined conditions. Theorists argue that subjects are constituted through language or through other acts of signification (meaning-making), such as film. For example, the word "I" has no definite meaning until it is used by someone in a conversation, and its meaning shifts as each speaker in the conversation uses "I" to refer to himself or herself. As viewers cannot "talk back" when they watch a movie (as they can with video games, Web sites, and interactive films), they can be said to be constituted as the object of the film's address: they are meant to laugh, cry, or put clues together as the film unfolds.

Spectatorship

How subjects interact with films and with the cinematic apparatus is addressed through the theory of **spectatorship.** Spectatorship has been a concern in film theory since Münsterberg, who used psychology to explain the mind's role in making sense of movies. In the poststructuralist theory of the 1970s, however, spectatorship stood at the convergence of theories of language and subjectivity, psychoanalysis, and ideological critique.

Christian Metz was one of the most prolific and influential contemporary promoters of spectatorship theory. He refers to linguistic and psychoanalytic terminology in the title of his influential book *The Imaginary Signifier* (1977), which argues that film's strong perceptual presence—giant images projected in a dark room, immersive sound—makes it an almost hallucinatory experience. Going to the movies gratifies our voyeurism (looking without being seen ourselves) and plays to our unconscious self-image of potency. It is as if what's on the screen is made possible by our presence. The work of Metz and other French theorists appeared in translation in the English journal *Screen* in the early 1970s, and the psychoanalytic theory of spectatorship is sometimes known as *screen theory* (or *gaze theory*).

Theories of Gender and Sexuality

The poststructuralist concern with spectatorship, subjectivity, desire, and identification remains abstract if spectatorship is generalized and the specific nature of subjectivity is left unquestioned. Theories of gender and sexuality, which have been

VIEWING CUE

Consider your experience as a spectator of the film screened most recently for class. Did you relate to the point of view of a particular character or was your perspective more omnipotent? Were you aware of the apparatus (the camera, the projection)?

integral to film theory's exploration of how subjectivity is engaged by and constructed in cinema, help make these concerns concrete.

Feminist Film Theory

As feminism began to have wide social and intellectual currency during the 1970s, commentators pointed out that the female image is treated differently from the male image in film. In advertising, pornography, and painting, the objectification of the female image seems to solicit a possessive, implicitly male gaze [**Figure 11.25**]. In film, feminist critics note, the spectator is envisioned in a similarly gendered way. "Is the gaze male?" asks E. Ann Kaplan in an essay of the same title, noting that vision is often associated with ownership and power—typically seen as male—in our culture.

British theorist and filmmaker Laura Mulvey's "Visual Pleasure and Narrative Cinema," published in *Screen* in 1975, is one of the most important essays in contemporary film theory. Arguing that psychoanalysis offers a compelling account of how the difference between the sexes is culturally determined, Mulvey observes that the glamorous and desirable female image in film is also a potentially threatening vision of difference, or otherness, for male viewers. Hollywood films repeat a pattern of visual mastery of the woman as "Other" by attributing the onscreen gaze to a male character who can cover for the camera's voyeurism—its capacity for looking without being seen—and stand in for the male viewer. Film narratives also tend to domesticate or otherwise tame the woman, Mulvey shows, offering analyses of Alfred Hitchcock's *Vertigo* (1958) and *Rear Window* (1954), whose stories are driven by voyeurism and female makeovers. Essentially, Mulvey argues that the standard dichotomy in Hollywood film is: "woman as image/man as bearer of the look."

In her own films, Mulvey champions "a political use of psychoanalysis" and a style of filmmaking that would "free the look of the camera into its materiality in time and space" so that it cannot be ignored through assimilation to the viewer's or characters' perspective. In their film *Riddles of the Sphinx* (1977), Mulvey and Peter Wollen use 360-degree pans, with the camera positioned at about waist level, to emulate the circularity of a young mother's rhythms of work and to avoid objectifying her body in a centered, still image [**Figure 11.26**]. The film deliberately sets out to destroy conventional visual pleasure and narrative satisfaction. Like many theorists of this period, Mulvey and Wollen believed in making spectators think about what they were seeing.

Building on Mulvey's provocative argument, other feminist critics raise the question of female spectatorship. If narrative cinema so successfully positions the viewer to take up a male gaze, why are women historically often the most enthusiastic film viewers? One way to approach this question is to consider films produced with a female audience in mind. During Hollywood's heyday, women's pictures featured female stars who had a strong appeal to women, such as

11.25 *And God Created Woman* (1956). Brigitte Bardot's character exemplifies what Laura Mulvey calls woman's "to-be-looked-at-ness."

11.26 *Riddles of the Sphinx* (1977). Laura Mulvey puts her own theories about images of women into practice in a film made with Peter Wollen.

11.27 *Volver* (2006). Pedro Almodóvar revisits the Hollywood genre of the maternal melodrama in this family story, empowering his female characters.

Bette Davis and Joan Crawford. At first glance, women's pleasure in these films seems self-defeating: what these heroines seem to do best is suffer. However, feminists argue that a film like *Now, Voyager* (1942) enables female spectators to explore their own dissatisfaction with their lives by fantasizing a more fulfilling version of that existence. The movie shows Davis as a dowdy spinster taking control of her life—through psychoanalytic treatment, romance, and new clothes! Today's commercial films aimed at women are not that different from those of the 1940s. Many feminist critics argue that women's pleasure in these complicated, mixed-message movies should be taken seriously. Because film is a mass medium, it will never radically challenge existing power relations, but if it speaks to women's dilemmas, it is doing more than much official culture does. Sometimes filmmakers succeed in evoking these emotions and mass cultural traditions in more reflexive and satisfying ways, such as in Pedro Almodóvar's revisiting of maternal melodramas in *All About My Mother* (1999) and *Volver* (2006) **[Figure 11.27]**.

Overall, feminism has had more of an impact on the relatively young discipline of film theory than on many more established ones. Arguably, gender in film cannot be ignored. As Mulvey's work suggests, cinema—certainly entertainment film but also the avant-garde—depends on the stylized images of women for its appeal. Moreover, the cinema, because it is part of the fabric of daily life, necessarily comments on the everyday, private sphere of gender relations. Feminism's significant inroads in film theory have laid the groundwork for related, though not always parallel, critiques of cinema's deployment of sexuality, race, and national identity.

► VIEWING CUE

Describe the interrelated issues of gender representation and gendered spectatorship in a film you viewed recently.

Lesbian, Gay, Bisexual, and Transgender (LGBT) Film Studies

Feminist and psychoanalytic theory stress that unconscious processes of desire and identification are at play when we go to the movies. Like cinema itself, however, psychoanalysis historically concentrates on heterosexual scenarios (such as the Oedipus complex) and pathologizes gays and lesbians (as cases of "arrested development," for example). LGBT film theory critiques and supplements feminist and psychoanalytic approaches, allowing for more flexible ways of seeing and experiencing visual pleasure than are accounted for by the binary opposites of male versus female, seeing versus seen, and being versus desiring that are the basis of Mulvey's influential model of spectatorship.

LGBT film theorists posit that the gender of a member of the audience need not correspond with that of the character he or she finds most absorbing or most alluring. Marlene Dietrich, whom Mulvey often cites as an example of a "fetish" or mask for male desire, cross-dressed for songs in many films and even kissed a woman on the lips in her first American movie, *Morocco* (1930) **[Figure 11.28]**.

11.28 *Morocco* (1930). LGBT theorists interpret Marlene Dietrich—here kissing a woman—in a different way than feminist theorist Laura Mulvey does in her influential essay, "Visual Pleasure and Narrative Cinema."

Dietrich's gender bending is more than theoretical. Her onscreen style borrows directly from the fashions of the lesbian and gay subculture of Weimar-era Germany, where her career began. Dietrich thus appealed on many different levels to lesbian and gay viewers, as well as to heterosexual women and men. In fact, this multiplicity could be seen more generally as a key to cinema's mass appeal.

Although movies tend to conform to the dominant values of a society—in this case, to heterosexuality as the norm—they also make unconscious appeals to our fantasies, which may not be as conformist; anyone may identify with or desire a character of either gender in a particular movie. Moreover, films leave room for viewers' own interpretations and appropriations, such as when fan writers continue the adventures of particular mainstream characters or celebrities and share them on the Internet. Spectators positioned at the margins, such as gay men and lesbians, often "read against the grain" for cues of performance or mise-en-scène that suggest a different story than the one onscreen, one with more relevance to their lives. An interest in stars may extend beyond any particular film they are cast in and ignore those films' required romantic outcomes. For example, Dietrich's and Jodie Foster's strong images have historically appealed to LGBT viewers. Lesbian and gay portrayals in and responses to the cinema constitute one of many areas that have demanded fresh concepts in film theory.

Cultural Studies

Cultural studies scrutinizes aspects of cinema embedded in the everyday lives of individuals or groups at particular historical junctures and in particular social contexts; it does not analyze individual texts or theorize about spectatorship in the abstract. A useful way of understanding the fresh approach that cultural studies takes toward cinema lies in a shift in the very definition of "culture." Instead of defining culture as great works produced by transcendent artists and appreciated by knowledgeable patrons, cultural studies uses an anthropological definition: culture as a way of life, including social structures and habits. In other words, it is how movies are encountered, understood, and "used" in daily experience that interests cultural studies scholars. Critics at the influential Birmingham Centre for Contemporary Cultural Studies in England were among the first to use the term, in studies of youth culture and of television audiences in the 1970s. The way social background and education influence taste; legal decisions on monopoly practices or censorship in film; how films were exhibited in the first decade of cinema; the reception of particular films by particular groups at particular times; and the activities of movie fans are all topics that have been pursued under the rubric of cultural studies. We will look at a few key approaches within cultural studies: reception theory, star studies, and race and representation.

Reception Theory

Reception theory focuses on how a film is received by audiences, rather than on who made a film or on its formal features or thematic content. As suggested throughout this book, audiences are at the center of the film experience. Composed of actual individuals whose habits and preferences may be researched through surveys and testimonies, audiences provide a concrete basis for theorizing. Collecting information about audience composition or preferences is not itself film theory—the film industry is as interested in audience demographics as is the sociologist, and the studios themselves have initiated some of the best viewer surveys. Cultural studies goes further, theorizing that a work's meaning is only achieved in its reception. This implies a theory of audiences as active rather than passive. An obvious example is participatory viewing practices, including the costumes and call-and-response of fans in *The Rocky Horror Picture Show* (1975)

11.29 *The Rocky Horror Picture Show* (1975). Participatory audiences and repeat viewers are studied by reception theory.

viewings **[Figure 11.29]**. Reception theory also recognizes that films from the past may be received by today's audiences in entirely new ways, like rooting for the Native Americans rather than the cowboys or enjoying a supporting character's subversive wit rather than investing in the romance of a pair of bland leads.

Beyond the idiosyncrasies of personal history and circumstances, aspects of our *cultural identity*—for instance, age, ethnicity, and educational background—can predispose us toward particular kinds of reception. The homoerotic subtext of *Rebel Without a Cause* is likely to be more salient to an audience knowledgeable about the gay subcultural following of actors James Dean and Sal Mineo **[Figure 11.30]**. Such an audience is referred to as an *interpretive community* because its members share particular knowledge, or *cultural competence*, through which a film is experienced and interpreted, and their responses are known as *situated responses*. The panoply of West African–derived hairstyles in *Daughters of the Dust* (1991) is more likely to be enjoyed and recognized by black women than by other audience members; indeed, filmmaker Julie Dash intended this special gratification as part of the movie's address, its vision of its ideal audience. Theorists see these multiple ways of interacting with a text as confirmation that individuals actively make meaning even in response to otherwise homogenous mass media.

The methodologies associated with reception theory include comparing and contrasting the protocols of reviews drawn from different periodicals, countries, or decades; conducting detailed interviews with viewers; tracking commodity tie-ins, the goods that are marketed with the "brand name" of a particular film or characters; and studying fan activity on the Web. Given the multitude of possible approaches, it's no surprise that reception studies has a wide scope.

Reception studies differs from theories of spectatorship in that it deals with actual audiences rather than a hypothetical subject constructed by the text. While spectatorship is concerned with the unconscious patterns evoked by a particular text or by the process of film viewing in the abstract, reception studies addresses both actual responses to movies and the behavior of groups. British cultural studies scholar Stuart Hall has argued that groups respond to mass culture from their different positions of social empowerment. They may react from the position the text slots them into—the *dominant reading*; offer a *negotiated reading* that accommodates different realities; or reject the framework in which a dominant message is conveyed through an *oppositional reading*. Reception studies thus suggests that social identity considerably complicates the picture of subjectivity offered in poststructuralist film theory.

VIEWING CUE

Conduct a reception study of the film you just viewed by surveying your classmates about which characters and situations they responded to most favorably. Compare and contrast their opinions with those of film reviewers.

Star Studies

An important component of reception is our response to *stars*, performers who become recognizable through their films

11.30 *Rebel Without a Cause* (1955). Subcultural knowledge about actor Sal Mineo's gay identity reinforces the film's homoerotic subtext about Plato's feelings for Jim Stark, played by James Dean.

or who bring celebrity to their roles. In addition to analyzing how a star's image is composed from various elements—film appearances, promotion, publicity, and critical commentary—theorists are interested in how audience reception helps define a star's cultural meaning (see pp. 75–76). Although one of the most pervasive aspects of cinema, stars may seem one of the least likely topics to be considered in a theoretical approach—after all, stars are the province of entertainment and newsmagazines, tabloid journalism, and online chats. But these familiar and ephemeral sources such as fan magazines have an important place in cultural studies, as do the responses of fans themselves. One understands a film in relationship to what one knows of its stars outside the world of the film's fiction. From Judy Garland to Lindsay Lohan, stars with troubled offscreen lives are perceived differently in wholesome onscreen roles [**Figures 11.31a and 11.31b**].

(a)

Beyond the range of roles that a star becomes familiar for playing, other discourses about stars—including promotion (studio-arranged exposure such as Web sites and television appearances), publicity (romances, scandals, and political involvement), and commentary (critical evaluations and awards)—help construct their images. Star images become "texts" to be read in their own right. Sean Penn's promise as a teen star was associated with his acting rather than his looks. His volatile marriage to Madonna and his arrest for assaulting a photographer; his major film roles (a condemned man in *Dead Man Walking*, 1995, his Oscar-winning role in *Milk*, 2008, and the cryptic protagonist of *Tree of Life*, 2011); his work as an independent director (*Into the Wild*, 2007); and his outspoken politics and humanitarian work around Hurricane Katrina and the 2010 Haitian earthquake construct him as an individualist, even an "outlaw," a persona that carries connotations of "authenticity" [**Figure 11.32**]. Even when a particular star is billed as "just an ordinary guy," like Tom Hanks, or "the girl next door," like 1950s star Doris Day, this image is carefully orchestrated. Hence the fascination of so many paperback star biographies that purport to look behind the facade.

We will never have access to the star as a real person. Instead, we experience his or her constructed image in relation to cultural codes (including age, race, class, gender, religion, fashion, and more) and according to filmic codes (genre, acting, and even lighting). For example, the silent film star Lillian Gish was sometimes lit from above as she stood on a white sheet. The reflected light enhanced her pallor and the radiance of her blonde hair, connoting a virginal whiteness that was an important component of her star image in her films with D. W. Griffith. Stars are often considered the embodiment of types. For example, John Wayne connotes rugged individualism; Meg Ryan, perky romanticism; Morgan Freeman, quiet dignity; Robin Williams, manic mayhem. Different film roles, such as Robin Williams's creepy stalker in *One Hour Photo* (2002), add new inflections to these personas.

(b)

11.31a and 11.31b **Lindsay Lohan's wholesome character in *Mean Girls*** (2004) contrasts with contemporary viewers' knowledge of her troubled offscreen life.

11.32 Sean Penn. Penn's maverick star image is composed of the ensemble of his film roles over time, critical assessments, and publicity; cultural studies of stars analyzes the cultural significance and function of celebrities.

VIEWING CUE

Research the star of the film you are about to watch for class. What does your previous knowledge of this star bring to your viewing? Is the role at odds with his or her established image?

We also construct our own identities and communities through stars whom we will never know, and this is not necessarily a negative aspect of the phenomenon. Young girls who patterned themselves after plucky singing star Deanna Durbin in the 1940s, Madonna in the 1980s, or Miley Cyrus in the early 2000s incorporated the quality of independence these stars embodied, and identified themselves in solidarity, rather than in competition, with other girls who shared their appreciation. According to critic Richard Dyer, a basic conflict between the ordinary and the extraordinary is at the root of the star phenomenon. Stars are not better people than the rest of us, which facilitates our identification with them. And yet they are a breed apart.

Star discourse is a particularly revealing and useful critical approach to cinema because it is based in our everyday experience as fans. We have many immediate and unexamined responses to stars, from crushes to antipathies. But we also appreciate stars in nuanced ways that yield considerable critical understanding. Cultural studies of stars often begins with viewer testimonials, taking them not at face value but using them as a starting point for a more sociological analysis. What ethnic groups are represented in a nation's most popular stars? Do popular female stars transgress the boundaries of what is considered proper female behavior? Are people of color limited to supporting roles? Stars are powerful forces for understanding what is important to a culture at any given moment.

Race and Representation

The concept of race—for race is not an objective fact but a socially constructed category based on historical experiences and valuations of perceived difference—intersects with the film experience on many different levels, including questions of spectatorship and reception. The psychoanalytic models that have proven valuable for understanding gender in film may be inadequate when it comes to explanations of race. However, cultural studies models are flexible and can address such topics as stereotypes and how they are received by diverse audiences, and how discourses of imperialism, colonialism, and nationalism are embedded in film stories, genres, and star images. It is helpful to distinguish in this area two senses of the term "representation": (1) the *aesthetic* sense, whereby we may speak of representations of African Americans in the films of Spike Lee versus those of *Gone with the Wind*, for example, and (2) the *political* sense of standing for a group of people, as an elected representative does. Both senses are at play in the cinematic representation of race. Finally, theories of exile and homeland, cultural hybridity and diaspora, and the global and the intercultural have added to the store of explanatory frames we have for looking at race and representation in cinema.

Identification across race is a fraught and often obligatory process for nonwhite viewers because of the historical lack of racial diversity onscreen. Cinematic history reinforces the assumption of a white, Western, "unmarked" spectator-subject. In classical Hollywood films, nonwhite characters are relegated to the periphery of the action as villainous or comic or sometimes noble, but always secondary, characters. Colonialism, the assumed primacy of Western values, peoples, and power over people from other parts of the globe, pervades such genres as the western and the adventure film. In the musical *The King and I* (1956), one white Englishwoman proves to be a match for the Siamese king and his entire court [**Figure 11.33**]. In *Unthinking Eurocentrism* (1994), theorists Robert Stam and Ella Shohat show how a Western gaze and voice are reproduced in such popular films as the *Indiana Jones* series, in which ancient cultures provide colorful backgrounds for the exploits of a Western hero. They also discuss how non-dominant cultures are marginalized by casting, when white actors play other races [**Figure 11.34**], and even by sound, when everyone speaks English in films set in another country or when jazz scores are used in films in which all the characters are white. But Stam and Shohat's examples show that American cinema often reflects a multicultural society in other ways. The importance of the western as a genre, or of the plantation as a motif, gives evidence of a cultural preoccupation with racial difference and conflicts. Although stereotyped in such film representations, people of color stand at the center of the nation's definition of itself. Recent Hollywood films, from dramas like *Crash* (2004) to animated films like *Rio* (2011), often incorporate multiculturalism as part of the very definition of America.

11.33   *The King and I* (1956). Colonialism becomes a charming musical romance told from a white Englishwoman's perspective.

11.34   *West Side Story* (1961). The film's Puerto Rican heroine is played by white actress Natalie Wood.

The increasing success of filmmakers of color in the United States has paralleled theoretical explorations of alternative aesthetics. The trickster figure of West African tradition, which appears in *To Sleep with Anger* (1990) by Charles Burnett and in *Zajota and the Boogie Spirit* (1989) by Ayoka Chenzira, is an expression of the identification of these African American filmmakers with the diaspora, a scattered community of people who share an original homeland. Finally, aesthetic expressions of politics are a major concern in postcolonial cinemas that have emerged around the world. Third Cinema, discussed in Chapter 10, is one such example. These works often use narrative forms more in keeping with specific cultural traditions or political ideas than the linear cause-and-effect structures of Hollywood films. Humberto Solás's *Lucía* (1968), for instance, uses a three-part structure to link the fates of three Cuban women in different historical moments [**Figure 11.35**].

By arguing that there is room for agency and divergence in our reception experiences, and in increasing the kinds of films and related

11.35   *Lucía* (1968). Humberto Solás's film uses formal innovation to reflect on Cuban history through the stories of three women.

cinematic phenomena that are deemed worthy of theoretical attention, critics associated with cultural studies take apart the unity and inevitability that characterized poststructuralist film theory in the 1970s. With roots in sociology, cultural studies also takes a broader approach to contemporary media than film studies based in the humanities often do. This wider scope has opened up space to address the distinctiveness of television and new media, as well as the many social and economic transactions that surround cinema today, from the viewing of works on cable, DVD, or the Internet to the incorporation of movie franchises into our daily lives.

Film and Philosophy

While cultural studies critics reject the overt formalism as well as the abstractions of 1970s film theory, film philosophers critique the same dominant school for its lack of empirical support and theoretical rigor.

To some extent, all film theory is related to philosophy and characterized by a search for underlying principles and a logical argument. However, some film theorists identify more strongly than others with philosophical methods. In *Mystifying Movies: Fads and Fallacies in Contemporary Film Theory* (1991), Noël Carroll carefully and gleefully debunks the analogy of film to dreams; other scholars point out the flawed reasoning in using linguistic models to describe sounds and images. David Bordwell, one of the most prolific and well-respected film scholars, advocates a cognitivist approach to the medium. *Cognitivist film theory* understands our response to film in terms of rational evaluation of visual and narrative cues. Based in psychological research, it advocates verifiable scientific approaches. Rejecting analysis that invokes unconscious fantasy or employs idiosyncratic interpretation, cognitivism claims that we respond to the visual stimuli of the moving image with the same perceptual processes we use to respond to visual stimuli in the world—adjusting film images for lack of depth, perceiving the identity of objects that are moving and changing in time. Not simply a backlash against the obscure terminology and French-influenced syntax of poststructuralist theory, cognitive film theory argues for a less metaphorical, more scientific, and historically verifiable definition and practice of film studies.

Phenomenology, which stresses that any act of perception involves a mutuality of viewer and viewed, has also had a profound effect on film theory. Jacques Lacan and Christian Metz derived their emphasis on the gaze from phenomenologists, but the psychoanalytic concept of the unconscious diverged from the more embodied consciousness that phenomenology described. Vivian Sobchack uses the phenomenology of perception to account for the film experience as a reciprocal relationship between viewer and screen, also distinguishing between the different phenomenologies of film and television viewing.

French philosopher Gilles Deleuze has made a distinctive contribution to recent film theory, building on the semiotics of C. S. Peirce and the work of philosopher Henri Bergson. More than the writings of almost any other film theorist, Deleuze's work must be studied on its own terms because he develops ideas through specific interrelated terminology. But the investment is rewarding. In his two books on cinema, Deleuze distinguishes between two types of cinema that correspond roughly to two historical periods. The "movement image," prevalent in the cinema of the early twentieth century, reflects what might be called a cause-and-effect view of the world. The physical comedy of Buster Keaton and the collision at the heart of Sergei Eisenstein's montage represent action and a linear or dialectical forward movement that provoke a response in the viewer. In contrast, the "time image" is displayed in films by such masters as the neorealist

Roberto Rossellini and the more meta-phorical Michelangelo Antonioni, both working in the wake of the disillusion-ment and uncertainty of postwar Italy. In such movies, images and sounds do not give clear signals of spatial connec-tion or logical sequence; instead, they represent the open-endedness of time and the potentiality of thought [Figure 11.36]. Deleuze's philosophy of film goes beyond the specific films and di-rectors he uses as examples to suggest new ways of imagining the relationship between images and the world: *referen-tiality*, the idea that filmic images refer to actual objects, events, or phenomena, is no longer a basic tenet of film theory. For Deleuze, the film image is not a representation of the world; it is an experience of movement or time itself. For other thinkers, referentiality is no longer a tenet of film theory because neither film nor the world is what it used to be.

11.36   *L'Avventura* (1960). According to philosopher Gilles Deleuze, this classic art film presents "a direct image of time," in part through its unpredictable editing patterns.

Postmodernism and New Media

Obviously, film is no longer the only medium that organizes our audiovisual experience. At least since the 1940s, when television was rapidly adopted into U.S. homes, other moving-image media have challenged cinema's dominance, and many predict that digital media will soon replace film stock. However, such developments also suggest that this book's title is more apt than ever before: film has so thoroughly transformed our overall experience that it has prepared us for the integration of digital media and other image technologies in our lives. Rather than defining film more narrowly in the digital era, we can think of it more broadly.

This predominance of visual media is characteristic of the culture of postmod-ernism. As we have mentioned, the term "modernism" refers both to a group of artistic movements (from atonal music to cubist painting to montage filmmaking) and to the period in which those movements emerged and to which they responded (generally, the first half of the twentieth century). **Postmodernism** also has two primary definitions:

1. In architecture, art, music, and film, postmodernism incorporates many other styles through fragments or references in a practice known as *pastiche.*
2. Historically, postmodernism is the cultural period in which political, cultural, and economic shifts challenged the tenets of modernism, including its belief in the possibility of critiquing the world through art, the division of high and low culture, and the genius and independent identity of the artist.

The most important thinkers on postmodernism have addressed both aspects of this definition. Fredric Jameson defines postmodernism historically as "the cultural logic of late capitalism," referring to the period in postwar economic history when advertising and consumerism, multinational conglomerates, and globalization of financing and services took over from industrial production and circulation of goods. Stylistically, postmodern cinema represents history as nostalgia, as if the past were nothing more than a movie style.

text continued on page 432 ▶

Clueless about Contemporary Film Theory? (1995)

Theory will be present in all the sites that a culture uses for debate and conversation, including popular films. Although the title of the 1995 film *Clueless* would seem to disclaim any form of knowledge whatsoever, many theoretical issues are raised by the film. *Clueless* helps "clue us in" to the concerns of postmodern cinema and is of particular interest to feminist and cultural studies critics.

Clueless takes place in Los Angeles, a city whose freeways, location, cultural diversity, entertainment industry, commercial and artistic gems of pastiche architecture, and rampant consumerism have made it exemplary for theorists of postmodernism. The film's main character, played by Alicia Silverstone, is a high school student, and thus marginal in terms of social power. But as a blonde, white, rich girl, she represents the relative power of consumerism. A "remake" or update of Jane Austen's novel *Emma*, the film could be considered a nostalgic but inauthentic citation of the culture of another era. The main character's name, Cher, is another citation, this time of the "inauthentic" culture of the recent past (pop star Cher is known for her costumes and physical transformations). The multiculturalism of postmodern Los Angeles is signaled by Cher's group of school friends. Yet this is a tongue-in-cheek depiction because Cher's African American best friend, Dionne, is as fabulously wealthy as she is: the girls are worlds apart in socioeconomic terms from Cher's Latina housekeeper, for example.

The film opens with a montage of fresh-faced teenagers, and with postmodern irony Cher's voiceover compares what we have just seen to an acne-product commercial. The definition of identity as a matter of surface appearance is underscored in the next set of images: Cher "tries on" different outfits using a computer program containing simulations of the ample contents of her closet [**Figure 11.37**]. While Cher does undergo a transformation in character during the course of the film, she nevertheless understands social problems in commodity-culture terms: she donates her skis to the homeless. And it is while window-shopping that Cher finally realizes what she truly wants. Bits of the film replay in her mind, a thorough confusion of "real" and cinematic perception that perfectly illustrates what Anne Friedberg calls postmodernism's "mobilized virtual gaze."

Admittedly, the description thus far makes the film seem as if it is concerned only with the trivial. But feminist theorists point out that women's consignment to the domestic sphere with its "trivial" concerns of shopping and romance has a direct effect on the public sphere, which was as true in Jane Austen's day as it is in our own. Cher's ostensibly minor concerns have important

11.37 *Clueless* (1995). Postmodern style and attitude characterize a film that found a welcome reception among young audiences, especially young women.

consequences in her world, and by portraying her subjectivity through her voiceover and her optical point of view, the film gives her perspective validity. *Clueless* was directed by a woman, Amy Heckerling, who has specialized in youth genre films that pay special attention to young women's perspectives; Austen, too, was consigned to a circumscribed genre within which she made enduring works of art.

Viewers might find *Clueless*'s romantic ending predictable, even disappointing, in that it undermines what has so far been the film's most important relationship—the one between Cher and Dionne and the other girls—by conflating plot closure with heterosexual coupling. But in fact, the film winks at the happily-ever-after convention, ending with a wedding and suggesting for a moment that it is Cher's. "As if!" her voiceover exclaims: two schoolteachers she helped fix up are getting married. She escapes the strictures of the plot with postmodern irony.

One of the most remarkable aspects of *Clueless* is its reception. It successfully addressed a teenage interpretive community, both in and outside the United States, which quickly adopted the film's styles in fashion and slang. Young women's "use" of the film was generally positive. *Clueless* validated and enabled (coded) communication among young girls, who, far from being treated yet again as know-nothings, were now the only ones fully "clued in." Their multiple viewings made for an open-ended text; *Clueless* sums up the complexity of postmodern simulation in a succinct "as if!"

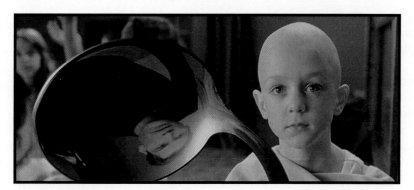

11.38   *The Matrix* (1999). "What is the matrix?" the film's ad campaign asked. Postmodern theorist Jean Baudrillard is quoted in the film.

For Jean Baudrillard, the triumph of the image in our cultural age is so complete that we live in a *simulacrum*, a copy without an original, of which Disneyland is one of his most illuminating examples. In *The Matrix* (1999) and its sequels, the characters' belief that they live in the "real world" is mistaken: the city, food, intimate relationships, and physical struggles are all computer-generated **[Figure 11.38]**. This lack of referentiality is frightening in that it represents the absence of any overarching certainty to ground postmodern fragmentation. But on the hopeful side, the "real" is now open to change. When *The Matrix* shows a (fake) book written by Baudrillard, the film is both making an in-joke and illustrating postmodernism's feeling that there is nothing new in the world.

It is no accident that the postmodern world is most vividly presented in a movie because movies themselves are simulations. Film theorist Anne Friedberg notes that the way we consume film images can be generalized to a society characterized by image consumption and mobility. The variety of "looks" one finds by window-shopping or identifying with other characters at the movies has a positive side. The postmodern breakdown of singular identity has as its corollary a recognition of identities formerly relegated to the margins. Postmodernism also recognizes the reality of today's increasing globalization. New technologies make the flow of images even easier—from Hollywood to the rest of the world, from formerly peripheral cinemas to U.S. audiences, and between local cultures.

Our survey of the history of contemporary film theory evokes the auspicious institutional climate of the academic discipline of film studies in Anglo-American universities, which has consolidated and developed ideas from France and elsewhere since the late 1960s. This story of the origins of contemporary film theory can be told fairly smoothly, and that should make us suspicious. Fields of knowledge advance by active questioning and dissent. As we have noted, cultural studies and cognitivism have challenged the orthodoxies that began to emerge in film theory by the 1970s, and their pluralism and skepticism add a welcome perspective on ideas that might otherwise become rote and ossified, simply "applied" to new cases.

The challenges posed by the digital image to film since the 1990s go beyond technological and economic ones: they are also intellectual. As we discuss earlier in the chapter, the photographic basis of the medium, long considered key to cinematic specificity, is no longer what defines cinema. While in some ways new technology can be seen as merely enhancing the film experience as we have known it (for example, the return of 3-D technologies), in other ways it alters both the medium and our experience of it (for example, the puzzles, interactivity, and convergence culture of video games). Scholars continue to draw on the legacies of previous inquiries in film theory in order to identify the salient questions our contemporary audiovisual experience raises and to develop tools with which to address those questions.

CONCEPTS AT WORK

This chapter has aimed to demystify the field of film theory, which is not to imply that readers will not have to struggle with theory or do some work to understand film on a more abstract plane. Because film theory is a notoriously difficult discourse, any summary gives it much more continuity than it actually warrants. In reading and picking apart theorists' work, it is important to recall that referring to "theory" in the abstract is misleading. The term is a useful, shorthand way to refer to a body of knowledge and a set of questions. We study this corpus to gain historical perspective, to acquire tools for decoding our experiences of particular films, and above all to comprehend the hold that movies have on our imaginations and desires.

Activities

- Do a shot-by-shot analysis of the opening sequence of a film. What codes—of lighting, camera movement, framing, or figure movement—are used to create meaning?
- Compare reviews of a film from a number of different sources (and periods if relevant). Pay particular attention to the time and place each review appeared. What does the range of reviews tell you about the film's reception context(s)?

A film by
SALLY POTTER

ORLANDO

TILDA SWINTON   BILLY ZANE

ADVENTURE PICTURES

PRESENTS A CO-PRODUCTION WITH

LENFILM MIKADO FILM RIO
SIGMA FILMPRODUCTIONS

WITH THE PARTICIPATION OF
BRITISH SCREEN

DEVELOPED WITH THE SUPPORT OF THE
EUROPEAN SCRIPT FUND

A FILM BY
SALLY POTTER

BASED ON THE BOOK BY
VIRGINIA WOOLF

ORLANDO

TILDA SWINTON
BILLY ZANE
LOTHAIRE BLUTEAU
JOHN WOOD
CHARLOTTE VALANDREY
HEATHCOTE WILLIAMS
QUENTIN CRISP

COSTUME DESIGN
SANDY POWELL

PRODUCTION DESIGN
BEN VAN OS JAN ROELFS

MUSIC COMPOSED BY
DAVID MOTION
AND SALLY POTTER

MUSIC SUPERVISOR
BOB LAST

EDITOR
HERVE SCHNEID

DIRECTOR OF PHOTOGRAPHY
ALEXEI RODIONOV

PRODUCED BY
CHRISTOPHER SHEPPARD

WRITTEN AND DIRECTED BY
SALLY POTTER

Read the HARCOURT
BRACE book

DOLBY STEREO

PG-13 PARENTS STRONGLY CAUTIONED
Some Material May Be Inappropriate for Children Under 13

SONY PICTURES CLASSICS™
©1993 Sony Pictures Entertainment, Inc.

Writing a Film Essay
Observations, Arguments, Research, and Analysis

Based on British novelist and critic Virginia Woolf's celebrated novel, Sally Potter's *Orlando* (1992) is a film about reading, writing, and imaginative self-expression. Leaping through time from the seventeenth to the twentieth century, Orlando encounters poets and writers such as Jonathan Swift and Alexander Pope and changes historical—and even gender—identities as if walking through different film sets of history. Throughout, the poet-writer Orlando reflects on experience, relationships, and cultures in an effort to find and define a personal voice that is expressive, creative, and critical. At one end of history, he struggles to compose poetry in Elizabethan England; at the other end, her new daughter playfully captures her with a video camera. Whatever the means and wherever the place, Orlando recognizes that forms of writing as self-expression can transform one's experiences and enrich life. In a sense, Orlando's journey through history mirrors that of all good writers.

W riters can be found everywhere in films and film history. In modern movies alone, famous and not-so-famous writers populate and drive many kinds of stories about many kinds of experience. *Mishima* (1985) describes the intense blend of radically conservative politics and restless creativity in the life of Japanese author Yukio Mishima. In *Central Station* (1998), a middle-aged woman, Dora, sets up a stand in the middle of a crowded railroad station where illiterate people go to have her write letters to their friends and loved ones. And in Cameron Crowe's semiautobiographical *Almost Famous* (2000), a young music reviewer, William Miller, encounters rock journalist Lester Bangs [Figure 12.1], who gives Miller the advice that motivates his life: "Write honestly and mercilessly." As with other arts and cultural activities, movies inspire a common and fundamental human need to explain one's feelings about and responses to a significant experience. In this chapter, we will see how writing about film develops from these needs and inspirations, and we will show how it can become a rich extension of our fundamental film experiences.

KEY OBJECTIVES

■ Understand the difference between reviews and critical essays.
■ Learn how to take notes on films and how to organize those notes.
■ Choose a topic and develop it into a thesis and argument for a paper.
■ Conduct research and integrate sources.
■ Acquire the skills to turn your work into a polished essay.

12.1 *Almost Famous* (2000). Lester Bangs's advice to a young music reviewer is "Write honestly and mercilessly."

Writing about film has been a significant part of film culture since the beginning of movies. Almost simultaneously with the arrival of the cinema, writers debated the function and value of this new art form. In the first few decades of film history, film critics such as Vachel Lindsay (in his 1915 book *The Art of the Moving Picture*) and Dorothy Richardson (in the 1920s art magazine *Close Up*) wrote passionately about movies. Since then, movie reviews, scholarly essays, and philosophical books—by writers including James Agee, Pauline Kael, Trinh T. Minh-ha, and Umberto Eco—have debated the achievements of individual films and the cultural importance of movies in general.

Writing an Analytical Film Essay

Writing extends the complex relationship we have with films by challenging us to articulate our feelings and ideas and to communicate our responses convincingly. In 1915, early reviewers and critics often focused on the dangerous or uplifting effects that movies might have on women or children. In the 1960s, film was frequently discussed in terms of its political impact or social meaning. Today's writers focus on a range of topics—from characters, stars, and stories to new film technologies or historical questions, such as how 1930s censorship influenced film content or how 1950s teenage audiences encouraged the making of certain kinds of films.

Personal Opinion and Objectivity

Writing about a film usually involves a play between subject matter and meaning. The subject matter of a film is the material that directly or indirectly comprises the film, whereas the meaning is the interpretation a writer discovers within that material. In *Crouching Tiger, Hidden Dragon* (2000), for instance, the subject matter includes the five main characters and their adventures in feudal China. The warrior Li Mu Bai returns to a town where he encounters his soul mate, Yu Shu Lien, the vengeful Jade Fox and her ferocious but naive companion Jen Yu, and Jen Yu's lover, the desert fighter Lo. The interaction of these characters describes a journey through China that ends in love and death. The subject matter's meaning, however, is more complicated than any simple description; the meaning depends on the film's style and organization, the historical and cultural significance of those techniques, as well as the experience and thinking of the viewer responding to it. Other films certainly use the subject matter of martial arts combat or the trials of love and honor in ancient China, but *Crouching Tiger,*

Hidden Dragon creates and elicits more specific meanings for those who have seen it. For some writers, this martial arts tale of love and honor weaves subtle and often complex points about women and their desires and about the importance of love over mastery **[Figure 12.2]**. For other writers, the film transforms its Asian subject matter into a Western take on self-knowledge and sacrifice.

The meanings a writer finds in a film are not simply personal and arbitrary. No film can mean whatever one chooses to make it mean, and useful and insightful

12.2 *Crouching Tiger, Hidden Dragon* (2000). Discovering the more complex meaning behind a deceptively simple subject matter.

12.3 *Crouching Tiger, Hidden Dragon* (2000). Is the interpretation of this final leap as suicide or liberation a matter of opinion?

writing always balances opinion and **critical objectivity**. *Opinion* or *subjectivity* indicates personal responses and evaluations. Critical objectivity, however, refers to a more detached response, one that offers judgments based on facts and evidence with which others would, or could, agree. Good writing about film is a balance of both: your personal views and opinions are where insights and evaluations usually begin, but for your essay to make sense to others, you must convince your readers that your insights identify a larger, more objective truth.

An essay that hides behind personal opinion—constantly stating "I feel" or "In my opinion"—will seem too personal to have any value for others. Writing about *Crouching Tiger, Hidden Dragon*, a writer may attempt to hide behind a lack of certainty about the meaning: "In my opinion, Jen's final leap off the mountainside is very ambiguous. I think her decision was probably a suicide, but it seemed to me to be a strangely beautiful act" **[Figure 12.3]**. Conversely, flat descriptive statements fail to interest readers in an essay's argument and often miss the subtleties of a film: "Jen's leap off the mountain is a suicide. It is not a liberating act." Balancing opinion and critical objectivity, as in the following passage, results in writing that engages and convinces the reader that your insights could be useful revelations for most viewers of the film:

VIEWING CUE

Examine a short critical essay about a film you have seen in class. What subjective or objective claims does the writer make about the film? What evidence from the film does he or she provide? Be specific.

> The conclusion of *Crouching Tiger, Hidden Dragon* is both shocking and uplifting, a combination that disturbs and confuses me, as it probably does most viewers. This confusion about Jen's motives is, however, part of the strange and mysterious beauty of the film because it asks us to recognize a central theme: the possibility that love and passion can transcend any physical limitations when we have faith in that love.

Identifying Your Readers

Knowing or anticipating your readers is central to writing about film and indeed to all writing, often guiding a writer in balancing opinion and objectivity. If we think of writing about film as an extension of conversations or arguments we have with friends about a film, we realize that the terms and tone of these discussions change with different people. A conversation between two knowledgeable fans of war films would likely presume that they have both seen many of the same films and know a great deal about special effects. Their discussion might thus get quickly to the finer points about how successful the portrayal of a famous battle between the Japanese and the Americans during World War II was in *Letters from Iwo Jima* (2006), told from the perspective of Japanese soldiers **[Figure 12.4]**. In talking about *Of Gods and Men* (2010) with an American film buff, an Algerian

12.4 *Letters from Iwo Jima* (2006). Director Clint Eastwood portrays one of World War II's fiercest battles from the perspective of the Japanese.

student might have to provide some cultural and historical background about the religious beliefs of Islam, the rise of various sects, and the Trappist monks who live in northern Africa.

Possessing an awareness of your readers is like knowing the person you are talking with: it helps determine the amount of basic information you need to provide, the level of complexity of the discussion, and the kind of language you should use. The following four questions are useful guidelines in gearing your essay to certain readers: (1) how familiar are your readers with the film being discussed? (2) what is your readers' level of interest in the film? (3) what do your readers know about the film's historical and cultural contexts? and (4) how familiar are your readers with the terminology of film criticism and theory?

For most critical essays, anticipating your readers' knowledge of the film means assuming they have seen the film at least once and thus do not require an extensive plot summary. Such readers are not primarily concerned with whether a movie is good or bad or with other general observations. Rather, they want to be enlightened about a specific dimension of the film (such as the opening shot) or about a complicated or puzzling issue in the film (for instance, how the different cityscapes in *The Bourne Ultimatum* [2007] carry specific thematic points important to the action of the film) **[Figures 12.5a and 12.5b]**. An effective writer works to convince readers that their interests can be deepened and enriched by following the writer's argument about a film.

Knowledge of a film's historical and critical contexts refers to how much your readers know about the place and time of the film's appearance. If the film was made in the United States in the 1920s, would information about that period help your readers better understand the film? Finally, determining your readers' level of familiarity with the terminology of film criticism and theory allows you to choose language that can efficiently and clearly communicate your argument. Can you assume that a term like *continuity editing* will be easily understood, or do you need to define it? In making these decisions, keep in mind that overly simplistic language or dense jargon can equally undermine your analysis.

In most college-level film courses, your audience will be not only your professor but also your peers: intelligent individuals who have seen the film and who share information and knowledge about film criticism, but who are not necessarily experts. For this audience, you can concentrate on a particular theme or sequence that may have been overlooked by a critical viewer. Note that your writing style and choice of words should be more rigorous and academic than in the typical movie review.

Elements of the Analytical Film Essay

Two common forms of film writing are film reviews and analytical essays. Aimed at a general audience that has not seen the film, a **film review** tends to be a short essay that describes the plot of a movie,

▶ **VIEWING CUE**

As you prepare to write an analytical essay about a film you have seen in class, consider your readers. What defines them? What are their interests? What do they need or want to know about the film? ⏸

(a)

(b)

12.5a and 12.5b *The Bourne Ultimatum* (2007). The various cityscapes through which Jason Bourne travels might be the basis of an argument about the film.

12.6   *O Brother, Where Art Thou?* (2000). Three escaped convicts: the focus for a precise analysis.

provides useful background information (about the actors and the director, for example), and pronounces a clear evaluation of the film to guide its readers. In contrast, the **analytical essay**, distinguished by its intended audience and the level of its critical language, is the most common kind of writing done by film students and scholars. It typically focuses on a particular feature or theme of a film, provides an interpretation of that material, and then gives a careful analysis to prove or demonstrate that interpretation. Unlike the writer of a movie review for a magazine, the writer of an analytical essay presumes that readers know the film and do not require an extensive plot summary or background information. Although a clear and engaging style is the goal of any kind of writing about film, the writer of an analytical essay often chooses words and terms that can effectively communicate complex ideas.

Consider this passage from a hypothetical essay about *O Brother, Where Art Thou?* (2001), written for a college film course **[Figure 12.6]**. Whereas a newspaper review might summarize the plot, offer some background information, and employ more casual language, note how this analytical essay concentrates on a specific and perhaps less obvious argument:

> Joel and Ethan Coen's *O Brother, Where Art Thou?* (2000) is much more than a musical comedy loosely structured around *The Odyssey*. Woven through the distinctive soundtrack, the plot set in Depression-era America, and the comic exaggerations of its characters, is a sharp ideological critique of race and class in modern America. Regularly mistaken to be African Americans, the three escaped convicts, Everett, Pete, and Delmar, learn quickly that their lower-class white status binds them most importantly to the fate of the black men and women they encounter, and from this predicament the film explores the economic and political power structures that then and now make poverty color-blind. Two sequences in particular dramatize this less noticed but more provocative dimension of the film: the arrival of the prisoners at a church to see a movie (a direct reference to Preston Sturges's film *Sullivan's Travels*, in which the Coens found the title for their movie) and the Ku Klux Klan rally where the fugitives rescue their black comrade Tommy.

Here the essay's focus is relatively refined and sophisticated. It assumes its readers have seen and know the film, and it concentrates not on general information, but on a specific thesis about race and class **[Figure 12.7]**. Along with its choice of a polemical thesis (an analysis directed at two particular sequences that viewers may not have carefully considered), this critical essay employs terms suited to academic writing, such as "ideological critique."

12.7   *O Brother, Where Art Thou?* (2000). An analytical paper on race and class in this comic film can be shaped around two specific sequences, the first about the arrival of the prisoners in a black church and the second about their witnessing a Ku Klux Klan rally.

Preparing to Write about a Film

Despite some common ground, an effective film essay does differ from a casual conversation or a debate about a movie. Few writers can dash off a perceptive commentary on a film with little preparation or revision. Instead, most writers gain considerably from anticipating what they will write about and later reviewing carefully what they have written. Few could watch *The Sorrow and the Pity* (1972), a powerful documentary about fascism in France during World War II, and then immediately type a brilliant paper on Marcel Ophüls's use of documentary strategies to expose certain myths about French history or the French Resistance. Like all good writers, you must follow certain steps in preparing to write an essay.

Asking Questions

First, try to identify your own interests *before* you view the film. Ask yourself, How does the film relate to my own background and experiences? What have I heard about the film? Am I drawn to technology or to questions about gender? To a particular filmmaker or period in movie history? To a certain national cinema? In what direction of inquiry does my interest point? In Howard Hawks's 1938 *Bringing Up Baby*, Katharine Hepburn plays an audacious heiress, Susan, whose pet leopard Baby becomes the foil in her zany relationship with a bumbling pale-ontologist, David, played by Cary Grant [**Figure 12.8**]. Perhaps you've seen other films by Hawks, like *His Girl Friday* (1940), or other films with Hepburn, like *The Philadelphia Story* (1940). Might you consider comparing the two Hawks films or Hepburn's two different roles?

 This sort of preparation is not meant to preclude your being drawn to new ideas and in unexpected directions when you view the film. Surprising discoveries are certainly one of the bonuses of approaching films with an open mind. While watching *In the Bedroom* (2001), one viewer might become puzzled by how the film seems to suddenly change direction: after depicting the excruciating pain of two parents who have lost a son, the movie then becomes a revenge tale in which the father seeks out and murders his son's killer. For the viewer, what seems at first a slow meditation on inexpressible grief becomes a tense thriller. How do the two parts work together? Does loss always require retribution? Does violence always beget violence? By asking these kinds of questions, you can intellectually interact with a film, sharpening your responses and shaping the direction of your essay.

Taking Notes

Note taking, an essential part of writing about film, stimulates critical thinking and generates precise and productive observations. Whereas most students find it natural to take notes on a biology experiment or on their reading of a Shakespearean play, annotating a film is both awkward and unnatural; it is difficult to write while watching a movie in a darkened room, and most films ask that we constantly attend to them so that we do not miss information that passes quickly. Note taking is, however, absolutely necessary to writing about film because a good analytical essay must include concrete evidence to support its

▶ **VIEWING CUE**

Before viewing your next film, jot down three or four questions you want to direct at the film. During the film, write down three or four more about specific shots or scenes. Later, attempt to answer all of your questions as precisely as possible. ❙❙

12.8 ***Bringing Up Baby*** (1938). Katharine Hepburn's role as an audacious heiress involved with a blundering paleontologist could start a writer's critical thinking about the film.

text continued on page 445 ▶

Analysis, Audience, and
Citizen Kane (1941)

For more than seventy years, viewers have responded to Orson Welles's *Citizen Kane* with a seemingly endless variety of opinions. Some find it fascinating; others feel it is boring or confusing. The character of Susan Alexander attracts some viewers; the final sequence in which the camera surveys a large room full of Kane's many acquisitions intrigues others. Any of these opinions about, or reactions to, *Citizen Kane* could be developed into a provocative essay about the film, but only if those ideas can be substantiated or proven useful, true, and important—that is, only if they can be shown to have objective accuracy. One such viewer decides to write a review of *Citizen Kane* for his college newspaper in anticipation of the film's upcoming appearance at the college art house. Despite the celebrity of the film, the writer presumes that many of his potential readers have not yet seen it and need both information and balanced opinions. He proceeds with a clear sense of what his readers already know, don't know, and need to know about the film.

Background information on the director and film help provide context for readers.

Citizen Kane is one of those movies that everyone talks about but few have ever seen. When it first appeared in 1941, the film was surrounded by enormous hype about the debut of the "boy genius" Orson Welles and his ballyhooed transition from the New York stage to the Hollywood screen. Before the film even appeared, rumors also connected *Citizen Kane* to the life of William Randolph Hearst, the U.S. newspaper mogul, and this too made the movie something of a fascinating scandal. In the seven decades since its release, *Citizen Kane* has appeared at the top of almost every list of the "greatest movies ever made," and it appears in practically every film course in the world.

Be prepared for a bit of a disappointment. The story is simple enough: played wonderfully by Welles himself, Charles Foster Kane grows, with the help of a windfall fortune, from a boy torn from his childhood home in Colorado into a lonely man obsessed with power and possessions. For me, the story is melodramatic and overblown, and Kane never becomes a very likeable character. What redeems *Citizen Kane*, however, is the construction of the story: different parts of Kane's story are told through the eyes of his friends and acquaintances, and these shifting perspectives create a kind of visual puzzle that the movie never really solves, enlivening an otherwise dull tale.

Reviews should still have a point of view. Here, although finding the film "a bit of a disappointment," the writer argues that the film is redeemed through the dramatic construction of its story.

This black-and-white film is a continuous series of stunning (and famous) shots, such as the opening sequence of dark shots that takes viewers past a No Trespassing sign to Kane's deathbed. In our age of digital technology and new-wave television commercials, these images will probably seem less surprising and innovative than they did when the movie first appeared. Yet

Citizen Kane remains a film to see—if only to judge for yourself whether it is among the "greatest movies ever made."

The same writer later chooses to compose the following critical essay about *Citizen Kane* for a film history course. In this case, his readers are his professor and the other students in the class, readers who are familiar with the film and have even read other material about *Citizen Kane*. Note this student's inclusion of images from the film. These images do not serve merely as a visual embellishment for the paper but as concrete and precise evidence in support of his argument.

In the many critical essays on *Citizen Kane*, three different perspectives on its meaning dominate: analyses that focus on the mythic character of Kane, discussions of the kaleidoscopic narrative structure that shapes the story, and detailed interpretations of the stylistic compositions (such as the use of deep-focus and dramatic editing techniques). Engaging all three analytical perspectives, I will examine a single, early scene in *Citizen Kane* that demonstrates the legendary visual power of the film. In this scene, *Citizen Kane* crystallizes a family drama of loss and division that is inseparable from a life lived in dense and complex spaces and perceived from many points of view.

> Even a short critical essay benefits from demonstrating some familiarity with other writings about film.

In this tale of Charles Foster Kane's rise to a position as one of the richest and most powerful men in America, the scene in question sets the stage for the entire film. It succinctly describes the sudden wealth of Kane's mother, who receives an unexpected windfall from a deed to a gold mine (mistakenly presumed useless), and her subsequent decision to send Charles to be educated on the East Coast. The scene's setting is the rustic family cabin in Colorado, with glimpses of the snowy yard outside where the child, Charlie Kane, plays.

> The writer concentrates on one or two scenes that can be analyzed in detail.

In this scene, one shot begins by showing Charlie making snowballs in the field; then it moves back to show his mother in the foreground watching from inside and, through an open window, the boy building a snowman in the background **[Figure CK.1]**. Here the window frame within the film frame calls attention to how a point of view can control perspective, specifically the point of view on the child Kane. As the shot pulls back further, the frame expands to include the central conversation about the boy and the money, while the original subject of the shot, Charlie, becomes a much smaller, background figure in the action and the frame.

The shot pulls back even further, following the mother's movement away from the window, and the frame creates visible tensions and conflicts among the individuals. Mrs. Kane's stern face and upper body dominate the center of the image, flanked by the banker Thatcher, while Charlie's father drifts along the edges of the frame, complaining, "You seem to forget I'm the boy's father." Moments later, Thatcher and Mrs. Kane sit at a table in the foreground of the image and prepare to sign papers authorizing the child's departure, while the father protests in vain in the middle ground and Charlie remains barely visible in the far background, playing outside in

CK.1   *Citizen Kane* (1941). Framing emphasizes the point of view.

CK.2 *Citizen Kane* (1941). This famous shot uses reframing, along with deep focus, to convey the drama of Charles Foster Kane's boyhood.

CK.3 *Citizen Kane* (1941). Kane's obsession with the power of images could be his semiconscious way of replacing the image of his lost childhood.

The writer's careful analysis of the details show how they lead to a complex and subtle interpretation that viewers may have missed.

the snow **[Figure CK.2]**. The rectangular shape of the frame crowds these characters within a tight visual space, even including the ceiling on the top of the frame as a way of further drawing in the space. Positioned between the adults but in the far background is the diminutive shape of Charlie, the subject of their quarrel over plans to remove him from the home. Visually it is fairly clear how power and control are being distributed through this frame: the mother and Thatcher visually overwhelm the father, and the tiny figure of Charlie is the impotent object of exchange.

In *Citizen Kane*, Charles Foster Kane grows up to become obsessed with the power of images, such as paintings, newspaper pictures, and images of himself **[Figure CK.3]**. This obsession perhaps acts out his semiconscious struggle to replace the image of his lost childhood and family. Throughout the remainder of his life, Kane struggles to create, own, and control the people and things around him by imposing his perspective on them—just as the perspective of others controlled him early in his life. The film is also a narrative constructed around the multiple points of view of Kane's friends, wife, and associates, all of whom dramatize how points of view can attempt to frame a man's life as a way of understanding or interpreting that life. The irony and tragedy of Charlie Kane's life is that no one, not even Kane himself, is able to reconstruct the complete picture and harmony that were lost in that early childhood scene.

The writer expands his interpretation to show how it resonates through the entire film.

argument—and precise notes provide that support. The three general rules for anno-tating a film are (1) take notes on the unusual—events or formal elements that stand out in the film; (2) take notes on events or techniques that recur with regularity; and (3) take notes on oppositions that appear in the film.

For instance, most viewers of *Bringing Up Baby* would agree that the sequence involving David and Susan at the local jail, with Hepburn pretending to be a hard-ened gangster's moll, stands out as one of the funniest and most unusual moments in the film. Equally important, however, are those actions or images whose repetitions suggest a recurring theme or pattern, such as David's repeatedly losing his clothes or glasses. Oppositions can be equally illuminating, such as the contrast between the rival women: the goofy Susan and David's staid fiancée, his scientific assistant.

Each writer develops his or her own shorthand for taking notes on films. The trick is to jot down information about the story or characters that seems significant while also recording visual, audio, or other formal details. Some common abbrevia-tions for visual compositions include the following:

es: establishing shot   **la:** low angle   **mls:** medium long shot
ha: high angle   **trs:** tracking shot   **nds:** nondiegetic sound
ct: cut   **ls:** long shot   **vo:** voiceover
cu: close-up   **ds:** diegetic sound
mcu: medium close-up   **ps:** pan shot

More specific camera movements and directions can often be re-created with arrows and lines that graph the actions or directions. The following drawings sug-gest the movements of the camera:

low camera angle ↗   high camera angle ↙   tracking shot ∿

For example, part of the jailhouse sequence in *Bringing Up Baby* **[Figures 12.9 and 12.10]** might be annotated as follows to indicate cuts, camera movements, or angles.

— mcu of constable and Susan through bars
— ct mcu David

Later, these notes would be filled in, perhaps by again reviewing the sequence for more details—for example, pieces of the hilarious monologue of "Swinging

▶ VIEWING CUE

Which events, sounds, or shots in the film you just viewed stand out as unusual? As most important? As examples of a pattern of repetition? Describe clearly and concretely one or two events, sounds, or shots from the film. ⏸

12.9 *Bringing Up Baby* (1938). "Swinging Door Susie" engages the sheriff . . .

12.10 *Bringing Up Baby* (1938). . . . and baffles her cellmate, David.

Door Susie." Drawings of shots can supplement such details. Critical comments or observations might also be added—for instance, about how the organization of the shot composition and editing provides the contrast between the officious and tongue-tied sheriff and the zany and loquacious Susan.

Selecting a Topic

After taking and reviewing your notes on the film, you need to choose the topic for the paper. Because there are so many dimensions of a film to write about—character, story, music, editing—selecting a manageable topic can prove daunting. Even a lengthy essay will suffer if it attempts to address too many issues. Narrowing your topic will allow you to investigate the issues fully and carefully, resulting in better writing. In a five- or six-page essay, a topic such as "fast-talking comedy in *Bringing Up Baby*" would probably need to rely on generalities and large claims, whereas "gender, order, and disorder in the jailhouse" would be a more focused and manageable topic.

Formal Topics

Although good critical analysis usually considers different features of a film, we can distinguish two sets of topics for writing about film: formal and contextual. Formal topics, which concentrate on forms and ideas within a film, include character analysis, narrative analysis, and stylistic analysis. As a formal topic, **character analysis** focuses its argument on a single character or on the interactions between two or more characters, while **narrative analysis** deals with a topic that relates to the story and its construction. **Stylistic analysis** concentrates on a variety of topics that involve the formal arrangements of image and sound, such as shot composition, editing, and the use of sound.

Although writing a character analysis may appear easier to do than other kinds of analyses, a good essay about a character requires subtlety and eloquence. Rather than write about a central character, like Susan in *Bringing Up Baby* or the tormented musician Johnny Cash in *Walk the Line* (2005) **[Figure 12.11]**, an essay might concentrate on a minor character, such as Susan's aristocratic aunt or Cash's wife Alicia. Similarly, a narrative analysis should usually be refined so that the paper addresses, for instance, the relationship between the beginning and end of a film or the way a voiceover comments on and directs the story. A paper that deals with a stylistic topic will be more controllable and incisive if, for instance, it isolates a particular group of shots or identifies a single sound motif that recurs in the film. One student may find a topic for a paper by examining the role of the various narrators in Terrence Malick's *The Thin Red Line* (1998). Another student may choose to look more carefully at repeated editing patterns in *Battleship Potemkin* (1925) or at the use of framing in Yasujiro Ozu's *Tokyo Story* (1953). Any one of these topics will grow more interesting and insightful if you continue to ask questions during the writing process: How is the character David in *Bringing Up Baby* shaped by costuming or shot composition? How do the various narrators in *The Thin Red Line* reflect different attitudes about war?

12.11 *Walk the Line* (2005). Character analysis of a primary role, the tormented musician Johnny Cash, played by Joaquin Phoenix, risks the obvious.

Contextual Topics

Contextual topics, which relate a film to other films or to surrounding issues, include comparative analysis and historical or cultural analysis. A **comparative analysis** evaluates features or elements of two or more different films or perhaps a film and its literary source. A comparative analysis might thus contrast Susan in *Bringing Up Baby* with one or more heroines in more recent films, such as Julia Child in *Julie & Julia* (2009). **[Figure 12.12]**. A comparative analysis always calls for some common ground in order to link what you are comparing and contrasting. Conversely, **cultural analysis** investigates topics that relate a film to its place in history, society,

12.12 *Julie & Julia* (2009). The endearing and sassy Julia Child, as played by Meryl Streep, becomes a rich subject of a comparative analysis.

or culture. Such a topic might examine historical contexts or debates that surround the film and help explain it—for example, the social status of women or the importance of class in 1938 America. With historical or cultural analysis, the pertinence of the topic to understanding the film is crucial (in our example, the role of women is obviously important; the historical status of leopards probably is not).

Once a topic has been selected (the more specific, the better), the writer should view the film again. This second viewing allows the writer to refine and build on those initial notes, now that he or she has a topic in mind. The writer who comes to *Bringing Up Baby* with a vague interest in how it portrays the battle of the sexes might, after seeing the film again, find that he or she wishes to refocus the topic on how the leopard becomes a metaphor for that battle.

Elements of a Film Essay

With notes in hand and a topic clearly in mind, writing a film essay becomes a less daunting task. The next step, composing a first draft, will be less cumbersome because the writer has prepared for the task. Ideally, the writer should view the film once again while working through the following stages of the writing process, in order to sharpen the analysis and confirm details from the film. When a topic leads to a clearly defined thesis, focus, and argument, this additional viewing of the film inevitably reveals other useful details and leads to new or better formulated ideas and interpretations.

Interpretation, Argument, and Evidence

Whether your topic is a formal analysis of a sequence or a comparison of the narrative point of view of a novel and its filmic adaptation, it needs to be honed and shaped into a precise interpretation and argument. Your interpretation is your explanation of what the film or a part of it means. In addition, a good essay must construct a logical argument by presenting **evidence** from the film—concrete details that convince readers of your point of view—and then analyzing that evidence. Although different audiences may interpret all or part of a movie somewhat differently, a valid and interesting argument distinguishes itself by how well the analysis of evidence supports the interpretation. Without good evidence, precise analysis, and logical argument, an essay will appear to be simply one viewer's impression or opinion.

▶ VIEWING CUE

Sketch an argument for your essay. What is the logic of its development? What conclusions do you foresee making? ⏸

▶ **VIEWING CUE**
Write a precise thesis statement.
Is your thesis specific enough,
or does it need refinement? Is it
sufficiently interesting to encourage
readers to continue reading your
essay? ⏸

Thesis Statement

Perhaps the most important element in a good analytical essay is the **thesis statement**, a short statement (often a single sentence) that succinctly describes the interpretation and argument and anticipates each stage of the argument. The remainder of the essay should prove that thesis with evidence. As a significantly refined version of the topic, the thesis statement identifies clearly the writer's critical perspective on the film; it should indicate what is at stake in the argument and perhaps how that argument is important to understanding the film. A strong thesis anticipates each stage of the argument that will follow in the paper. Usually this statement, which appears in the first paragraph of the essay, undergoes various revisions during the writing process. Having a *working thesis*, a rough version of a thesis, in mind as you begin your first draft, however, will help anchor your argument. In its final form, a precise and assertive thesis statement is likely to engage readers' interest in the essay.

As with most films, Steven Soderbergh's *Traffic* (2000) and Stephen Frears's *My Beautiful Laundrette* (1985) both offer a wide variety of topics that could be developed into specific arguments and thesis statements. For *Traffic*, a film about the drug trade that flows from Mexico into various U.S. communities, one student writer considers analyzing either the cinéma vérité camera movements used in the Mexican settings or the transformation of the central character, a U.S. drug czar who sees his daughter destroyed by heroin **[Figure 12.13]**. For *My Beautiful Laundrette*, a contemporary romance between a young Pakistani man and a male friend involved with right-wing British gangs, the writer weighs the advantages of two possible topics: the developing sexual relationship of the two main characters or the mise-en-scène of the laundrette where the climactic scenes take place **[Figure 12.14]**. After reflecting on these topics and seeing the films again, the student opts for the second film and develops a thesis statement that demonstrates a clear and specific direction: "*My Beautiful Laundrette* looks at contemporary British politics from numerous angles: family politics, sexual politics, racial politics, and economic politics. In the end, these various motifs coalesce and climax in a single space that is both practical and fantastic, the mise-en-scène of the laundrette." As clear and intelligent as it is, this proposed thesis statement will no doubt be revised for the final draft of the paper, as the writing will certainly generate new insights and possibly new issues.

12.13 *Traffic* (2000). A character destroyed by drug abuse presents an abundance of issues for analytical writing.

12.14 *My Beautiful Laundrette* (1985). The climactic mise-en-scène of the laundrette.

Outline and Topic Sentences

Although some writers prefer other methods of organization, preparing an outline results in a valuable blueprint of an essay, allowing the writer to see and examine the different parts and overall development of the argument as it proceeds out of a strong thesis. An outline can consist of a simple list of ideas to address or shots and scenes to highlight—such as "weak father figures," "house squatting as metaphor for identity," and "description of the laundrette"—or a more complete (and more useful) list that includes subheadings and perhaps full sentences, which can be used as topic sentences in the essay.

Here is an excerpt from the detailed outline prepared by the student working on the essay about *My Beautiful Laundrette*.

VIEWING CUE

Formulate a specific interpretation for the film you are writing about. Why is that interpretation important? What new light does it shed on the film for your readers?

The Politics of Laundry in *My Beautiful Laundrette*

Working Thesis: *My Beautiful Laundrette* looks at contemporary British politics from numerous angles: family politics, sexual politics, racial politics, and economic politics. In the end these various motifs coalesce and climax in a single space that is both practical and fantastic, the mise-en-scène of the laundrette.

- I. Family politics: the most immediate and complicated type
  - A. Fathers and authority
  - B. Family traditions and repression
- II. Sexual politics: underpins family situations in way that exposes hypocrisy
  - A. Heterosexual politics: Nasser, his wife, and his mistress Rachel
  - B. Feminist politics: Tania, Nasser's daughter
  - C. Gay politics: Johnny and Omar
- III. Racial politics: nearly lost in this drama is the way they permeate all other relationships
  - A. Johnny, race, and right-wing politics (National Front)
  - B. Papa, race, and left-wing politics
- IV. Economic politics: where the other confrontations are—presumably and ironically—resolved
  - A. Papa as businessman
  - B. Salim as drug dealer
  - C. Johnny and Omar as laundry entrepreneurs
- V. Political motifs coalesce and climax in a single space that is both practical and fantastic: the mise-en-scène of the laundrette
  - A. Detailed description of mise-en-scène of laundrette
  - B. Pragmatic meets fantasy
  - C. Analysis of climactic gathering

As this example illustrates, a detailed outline allows the writer to review the structure of the essay and note any problems with the scope or logic of the argument or with the transitions from one section to another. At this stage the topic should be focused on a specific thesis whose parts develop as logical steps in the body of the paper.

Whether or not you work from an outline, a clear organization and structure—most notably, coherent paragraphs introduced and linked by topic sentences—are paramount for an effective essay. Well-developed paragraphs, which tend to consist of several sentences, demand coherence and evidence. Critical to a good paragraph is the **topic sentence**, usually the first sentence, which announces the central idea to which all other sentences within the paragraph are related. The remainder of the paragraph develops the idea stated in the topic sentence and provides evidence from the film as support.

VIEWING CUE

Create a detailed outline of your essay. Does your outline include subsections that can later be developed with details and evidence from the film?

In this excerpt from the essay on *My Beautiful Laundrette*, note how the strong and lucid topic sentence opening the paragraph is then supported by evidence:

In *My Beautiful Laundrette,* the drama of the characters is invariably about space, territory, and most important, home. In the first sequence, Salim and a henchman evict Johnny and another squatter from an abandoned tenement, and for the rest of the film the metaphor of squatting describes the characters' unstable and temporary relations to the places in which they live and with which they interact. Although most of the characters are driven by the idea that, as one character puts it, "people should make up their minds where they want to live," places and homes are never more than shifting locations, foreign territory where one lives uncomfortably. In this sense, "home" is at best a dream and usually just a temporary convenience. Nasser's daughter Tania wants to be anywhere but with her family, and she is willing to have either Johnny or Omar as a lover, depending on who will take her away from her home. In the end, Nasser watches from a window as a medium shot shows Tania being visually swept off the platform by a series of trains that rush off the screen, on her way to another home that she will define for herself.

Revision, Manuscript Format, and Proofreading

A completed first draft of an essay is not a completed essay. The final stage in writing about film requires at least one revision of the paper, with special attention to manuscript format and proofreading. Last-minute corrections should be kept to a minimum and should be clear and simple.

A good revision begins by reading the essay with fresh eyes, achieved best by allowing time away from the first draft—at least a few hours and at best a few days—before returning to work on the revision. A revision should examine, clarify, and rewrite word choices, sentence structures, paragraphs, the logic and organization, and the coherency of the ideas; it should improve the presentation and the efficiency of the argument and analysis. In addition, carefully check the manuscript format, including margins, title position, footnotes, and other mechanics. Typically, the format for a film essay should follow these guidelines, which are based on recommendations by the Modern Language Association.

▶ **VIEWING CUE**
In your draft, look for consistent errors and troublespots that you need to pay special attention to during revision. ⏸

- Put your name in the top left-hand corner of the first page, along with your instructor's name, the course title and number, and the date of submission. Your title should be centered on the next line.
- The entire essay, including quotations, should be double-spaced.
- Quotations running more than four lines should be indented ten spaces at the left margin and reproduced without quotation marks.
- Leave one-inch margins at the top, bottom, and sides of each page. Indent paragraphs five character spaces or one-half inch.
- Put your last name and the number of each page (including the first) in the upper right-hand corner.
- Be certain quotations and documentation are in the proper format.

Note: For more information, see the *MLA Handbook for Writers of Research Papers,* 7th ed. (2009).

Once your final revision is completed, proofreading—checking the revision for grammatical and structural errors, typos, or omissions that can be easily corrected—is essential. With any kind of writing, the presentation helps determine how your reader views your work, and an accurate, professional look will promote an accurate, professional reading of it. Typographical mistakes and other small goofs do not ruin a good essay, but they do undermine it by creating an impression of carelessness.

While not all writers about film precisely follow the guidelines for outlining, formulating a thesis statement, revising, proofreading, and so on, experienced writers almost always do so, even if unconsciously or in abbreviated ways. Keeping a checklist of these mechanics in mind can alleviate much of the anxiety about writing, providing a working framework that leads to stronger and more interesting essays.

Using Film Images in Your Paper

With computer and Internet technologies, writers can now easily capture film images from a DVD or streaming video and incorporate them in a critical essay to illustrate a part of an argument and analysis. Being able to "quote" from a film to support an interpretation or insight can be quite important since such images can provide the evidence that underpins a strong argument.

Many instructors prefer that students avoid using images because often these images function simply as ornaments and distractions from the real work of the writing. Therefore, if film images are used in an essay, they should be used judiciously to support a key point in the argument. As with the example from the paper on *Citizen Kane* (pp. 442–44), use a specific image or series of images that illustrates important visual information (about image composition or editing, for example) that your text discusses. If useful, provide a short caption that encapsulates what you wish your reader to see in the images.

> ▶ **VIEWING CUE**
>
> Locate areas in your essay where an image might improve your argument. Are there technical aspects, such as the use of lighting or types of camera movements, that could be further explained with an illustration? ⏸

Writer's Checklist

As you grow more confident as a writer, you will be able to write about films in a fluid motion: watching the film, taking some notes, sketching an outline, and writing the first draft and final essay. Even the most competent writers, however, pause to reflect on their work by consulting a checklist like this one.

1. Review your notes, filling in details where you can. Ideally, view the film one more time.
2. Try to summarize the most important themes or motifs in the film.
3. Formulate a working thesis and an argument for the essay.
4. Outline the argument. If possible, use full sentences for headings because they can then become your topic sentences.
5. Develop the central idea of each paragraph using details from the film that support that paragraph's topic sentence.
6. Rewrite your thesis statement to reflect any changes or refinements in your thinking that occurred while you were writing your first draft.
7. If you are writing a research essay, be sure to use the correct documentation format for in-text citations and the Works Cited list (see pp. 459–61 and 466).
8. Revise your essay, checking for such problems as vague or illogical organization, and proofread for surface errors in spelling and grammar.
9. Select a title that reflects the main argument of your paper.
10. Print out the essay and correct any remaining typographical errors.

> ▶ **VIEWING CUE**
>
> After writing your first draft, revise your thesis statement to reflect changes in your thinking. Be sure to sharpen your thesis statement to better describe your argument. ⏸

Researching the Movies

12.15 *Orpheus* (1950). Researching this film may also mean researching the poetry of the surrealist movement.

While in some critical film essays writers aim simply to convey a personal response to a film based on critical distance and careful reflection, in other essays they might want or need to use research in order to sharpen and develop their interpretation of a film. Research enables writers to identify significant issues surrounding a film and to contribute their opinions and ideas to the ongoing critical dialogue about it. A student intending to write about Jean Cocteau's *Orpheus* (1950), for example, may be intrigued by the film but uncertain about his or her specific argument. With some reading and research about Cocteau, his relation to the surrealist movement, and his work as a poet and painter, the student discovers a more specific argument about the complicated role of poetry in the film and the relevance of the Orpheus myth to Cocteau's vision of the modern artist **[Figure 12.15]**.

Distinguishing Research Materials

Whether limited or extensive, research helps determine why your essay is important and what critical questions are at stake in writing it. Research is also a dialogue with other opinions and writings—they help distinguish or support your ideas about a film or group of films. Various kinds of materials qualify as research sources for a film essay, including primary, secondary, and Internet resources.

Primary Research

Primary research sources—such as 16mm films, videotapes, DVDs, and film scripts—have a direct relationship with the original film. Some of these materials are readily available in libraries, including the many classic scripts now published as books; others, such as 16mm films, can be far more difficult to locate, except in film archives. A student planning to write a research essay on Don Siegel's *Invasion of the Body Snatchers* (1956) might first view a 16mm or DVD projection of that film, and then access other primary sources, such as a script, as follow-ups to the first screening **[Figure 12.16]**. With primary sources, however, keep in mind that they may approximate, but not duplicate exactly, the look of a film when seen in a theater. Videotapes and DVDs may format images differently from the format used in theatrical screenings, while scripts may represent a simple blueprint from which the actual film dialogue deviates.

12.16 *Invasion of the Body Snatchers* (1956). Watching a film closely and following its script allow you to analyze it with precision and depth.

Secondary Research

Secondary research sources—including books, critical articles, Web sites, supplementary DVD materials, and newspaper

text continued on page 457 ▶

Interpretation, Argument, and Evidence in *Rashomon* (1950)

After reviewing his notes on Akira Kurosawa's *Rashomon*, a student writer considers some possible topics. He begins by thinking about the film's unusual narrative structure: Three men, including a priest, seek shelter from a rainstorm under an ancient city gate. They hear the tale of a murder and rape through four different points of view—those of a bandit, the woman, the ghost of the dead man, and a woodcutter. The narrative tension in the film, the writer realizes, develops around the discrepancies in these competing points of view; the result is a dark ambiguity about the truth of this violent and tragic event. After seeing the film again and trying to refine his thinking about it, the writer develops the following thesis, a clear interpretation of the film.

> In Akira Kurosawa's *Rashomon*, four different perspectives present four different versions of the truth about a violent attack. At the conclusion of the film, after we have seen and heard these various perspectives and have been presented with the evidence, the opening confusion of the three men is even more pervasive, setting the stage for the only possible response to a world defined by egotism and uncertainty: compassion.

The student's next step is to sketch an outline, one in which he uses topic sentences to mark the development of the argument and the places where key evidence will appear.

Rashomon: Beyond Understanding and Evidence

Thesis statement: *Rashomon* is a drama of evidence and interpretation.
  I. Central to this film is the drama of interpretation and evidence.
      A. Four accounts of same horrifying event
      B. The opening focus on evidence
  II. Although more evidence appears through the perspective of the different witnesses, that evidence does not always agree and seems to befuddle a clear interpretation.
      A. Overlaps and inconsistencies in describing the facts
      B. The dagger as key piece of evidence
  III. The heart of the fragmented narratives of *Rashomon* is the egotism that fashions the various perspectives.
      A. The bandit's violent sexual desire and the crime
      B. His story of conquest and surrender

IV. Both the wife's and the husband's perspectives are likewise mostly about themselves.

    A. The wife's tale of a helpless woman

    B. The husband's tale of honor and self-sacrifice

V. The woodcutter's narrative is more problematic, but equally locked into its own needs for self-justification and protection.

    A. His revised vision: a base and cowardly world

    B. His acknowledging stealing the evidence of the dagger

VI. Each of these perspectives is distorted by the ethical failures of the individuals telling them, indicating the horrifying indeterminacy of a world determined by isolated egos, as well as the corruption of these perspectives by human egotism.

    A. Natural disaster and moral depravity

    B. Editing and shot compositions add to confusion, disorientation, and failure to see facts and events clearly.

VII. Although the humane conclusion of the film seems unexpected (and somewhat sentimental), its unexpectedness is what makes the film so engaged with modern times.

After writing his first draft, the writer sets the paper aside for three days before undertaking a careful revision. He proofreads a printed version of the essay and then submits his final copy, which follows.

Fred Stillman   Stillman 1

Professor White

Film 101

10 Oct. 2011

Beyond Understanding and Evidence:

The Surprise of Compassion in *Rashomon*

A brief summary of the films is followed by a concise thesis that maps out the main points of the paper's argument.

The setting that opens and closes Akira Kurosawa's *Rashomon* is the collapsed Rashomon gate in the ancient city of Kyoto. Amidst a torrential rainstorm, a woodcutter, a commoner, and a priest huddle together, and the first recounts a horrifying tale of rape, murder, and possibly suicide told through four different perspectives that structure the narrative of the film. Seen through the eyes of a criminal, the female victim, the dead husband, and a woodcutter, each of these perspectives offers a contrasting version of events and the truth of what happened, and each introduces pieces of evidence to support that particular version. Despite having heard these witnesses, however, the priest can only murmur, "I don't understand." At the film's conclusion, moreover, the uncertainty of the men is more pervasive than ever, setting the stage for the only possible response to a world defined by egotism and uncertainty: compassion.

The initial topic sentence introduces the first part of the argument.

Rashomon is a drama of evidence and interpretation. As the priest and woodcutter explain to the commoner, the original staging of the different testimonies was a police court trying to gather evidence about a horrible crime in which a noblewoman and her husband were attacked in the wilderness—she was raped and he was killed. Appropriately, the first point of view presented is that of the woodcutter, who follows a trail of evidence through the woods—a woman's hat, a man's hat, a belt, and an amulet case—to the sudden discovery of the dead body of the samurai nobleman, his stiffened arms and hands stretched grotesquely toward the horrified woodcutter in a low-angle shot **[Figure R.1]**. Shortly thereafter, a man describes how he captured the bandit Tajomaru, emphasizing the discovered evidence of the samurai's horse as well as "seventeen arrows" and a "Korean sword" found on the criminal. Yet this seemingly incontestable claim and evidence become subject to doubt when the bandit suddenly denounces and denies the man's interpretation of certain details.

Although more evidence is given through the perspective of the other witnesses, that evidence does not always agree, and it seems to befuddle a clear interpretation. Most important, the significance of a pearl-handled dagger, the

R.1   *Rashomon* (1950). The mystery of a horrifying death.

weapon that supposedly killed the husband, changes dramatically in the different narratives, acting as an evidential marker to distinguish the interpretations of events.

Focused on the shifting place of the dagger, the center of the fragmented narratives of *Rashomon* becomes the egotism that informs each perspective. Or more exactly, each version becomes more about the personal desire and greed of the person explaining what happened than about the factual events and evidence. What initiates the horrendous crime is the violent sexual desire of the bandit, who happens to witness—in a sharp-shot/reverse-shot exchange beginning with his awakening eyes—the exposed face and feet of the wife. After that, his entire account emphasizes greed and desire: he deceives and entraps the nobleman by suggesting he will sell him riches from an old tomb, and his leering gaze at the young woman turns quickly to a brutal sexual attack. Not surprisingly, in the bandit's version, his desires and demands fulfill the woman, and she becomes the mirror image of his greed and lust when she ecstatically surrenders to his assault. At this moment, the critical object, the dagger, drops passively from her hand, according to the bandit, who claims to then kill the husband "honestly."

Both the wife's and the husband's perspectives are likewise mostly about themselves. From the beginning, she appears discreet and demure, partly hidden by veils and white makeup and barely moving as she rides her horse through the forest. In her account, she becomes a "poor helpless woman" whose husband turns viciously on her after the assault. Unable to bear his hateful stare, she claims to have fainted—only to later discover her dagger in her husband's chest. The husband's narrative, in contrast, paints a picture of his suffering devotion and lost honor, weeping from the grave as he recounts killing himself with the controversial dagger. Light and shadow fill the images of this account, suggesting an ambiguity and lack of certainty even in this testimony by a dead man.

Finally, the woodcutter's narrative is more problematic, but equally locked into its own needs for self-justification and protection. After introducing the story at the beginning of the film, he returns to offer a final version that reveals deceptions and lies in his first account. Now he admits to having witnessed the entire scene. His subsequent description of the part-clownish, part-terrified fighting

Excellent visual detail indicates that the writer's interpretation is grounded in film form and not just content.

R.2 *Rashomon* (1950). Trying to make meaning in a chaotic world.

of the two men shows a world that is fundamentally base and cowardly, a reflection of his own base and cowardly position in failing to intervene or fully disclose the truth of what he saw. Most disturbing perhaps, he tacitly acknowledges stealing the crucial piece of evidence, the dagger, in order to sell it for personal gain.

That each of these perspectives is distorted by different degrees of ethical failure on the part of the individual indicates the source of the horrifying indeterminacy and chaos of this world **[Figure R.2]**. This is a world described by the priest in the opening as full of "war, earthquake, wind, fire, famine, plague . . . each year full of disaster . . . hundreds of men dying like animals." Stylistically, the stunning editing and shot compositions of *Rashomon* dramatize this world of confusion and disorientation, in which seeing and understanding seem to constantly combat each other. Witnesses are introduced with a wipe that crosses the screen in one direction or the other, almost violently wiping out the perspective of the preceding account. Within the different accounts, rapid tracks and flash pans re-create the desperately unsettled struggle to discover facts through perspectives that dart across surfaces blocked by branches and leaves.

Within all this moral darkness and despair, however, the conclusion of *Rashomon* suggests a possible way out of the terror and blindness that results from so much visual and narrative ambiguity. In this final sequence, the threesome who tell and hear that tale of violence discover an abandoned baby in the ruins of the gate. The commoner urges them to steal the baby's blankets and clothing because "you can't live unless you're what you call selfish." At this point, a dramatic turn occurs: in a head-to-head confrontation in the rain, the commoner accuses the woodcutter of hiding his theft of that crucial piece of evidence, the dagger. In dazed silence, the priest and the woodcutter stand against a wall. As the rain stops, the commoner suddenly insists on taking the child home with him to his already crowded family. Despite his shame about his selfishness and despite the missing evidence of the stolen dagger, a glimmer of human value returns to the world. Compassion overcomes the evidence of mistakes, and as they all depart, the sun gleams through the clouds and the saved child becomes the emblem of a new future. During this sequence, the priest shouts the fundamental truth so often lost in this violent courtroom: "If men don't trust each other, then the world becomes a hell."

The conclusion recalls the main points of the argument and expands it to claim a broader meaning for the film.

Although this conclusion seems unexpected (and somewhat sentimental), its unexpectedness is what makes the film so engaged with modern times. Danish philosopher and theologian Søren Kierkegaard uses the term "leap of faith" to describe the only possibility for a spiritual faith in modern times. What his term implies is that both spiritual and human faith—the grounds for ethical behavior— often occur *despite* the evidence before our eyes and *despite* the failure of human reason to understand it. As in *Rashomon*, truth and morality may need to leap over the confusion of facts and logic in order simply to do what is right.

reviews—contain ideas or information from outside sources such as film critics or scholars. The student researching *Invasion of the Body Snatchers* might include film reviews published at the time of release, scholarly essays on Siegel's work, and perhaps a book on 1950s American cinema. Even in our electronic age, libraries and their databases remain the most reliable places to find solid secondary materials. Check such databases as the Humanities Index, Lexis-Nexis, and Comindex for essays and books on your subject, and don't underestimate the more conventional approach of exploring the library's shelves. Annual bibliographic indexes and their electronic versions identify journal articles and books that may support and broaden your thinking, including especially *The Readers' Guide to Periodical Literature*, the *MLA International Bibliography*, and the *Film Literature Index*. Once you have a topic and a working thesis, you can search for sources relevant to your topic and argument. After checking general categories like "film," "cinema," and "movies," a more precise topic, such as "contemporary Australian cinema" or "sound technology and the movies," will lead you more quickly to pertinent research materials.

In addition to databases and bibliographic indexes, specialized encyclopedias, which identify important topics and figures in film studies, are useful resources for initiating research on a film. Examples include Ephraim Katz's *The Film Encyclopedia*, Pam Cook's *The Cinema Book*, Leonard Maltin's *The Whole Film Sourcebook*, Ginette Vincendeau's *Encyclopedia of European Cinema*, David Thomson's *The New Biographical Dictionary of Film*, Leslie Halliwell and John Walker's *Halliwell's Filmgoer's and Video Viewer's Companion*, and Amy Unterburger's *The St. James Women Filmmaker's Encyclopedia*. Film guides such as these provide factual information about and short introductions to a subject. The entries typically do not offer the sort of detailed analysis or arguments required for a good research paper, but they can suggest pertinent information and issues that can lead you to more research and a refined argument.

Internet Sources

The Internet offers useful discussion groups, access to various library and media catalogs, and numerous other information sites. However, with so many Web sites available, the writer must be careful to consult the three kinds of reputable Internet sources for film studies:

- sites and databases that provide basic facts about a film and the individuals involved with that film, including biographical facts about the director, the running time of a film, and the like.
- sites that offer reviews or essays from academic film journals, such as *Film Comment*, *Jump Cut*, and *Sight and Sound*.
- film-specific sites that provide information ranging from production facts to gossip as well as reviews and interviews. Almost every major film now has its own Web site, as do the studios and distributors.

While the Internet is an important source of information of all kinds, film researchers and writers must be cautious about the quality of the material found there. For one thing, it can be difficult to determine the authenticity of some Internet-based information. Unlike material published in academic journals or books, Internet essays and articles may not have been through a review process to determine their value. Virtually anyone can post on a Web site any opinion or "facts," often without substantial evidence. When using the Internet for research, therefore, writers need to differentiate substantial and useful material from chat and frivolous commentary. Especially with Internet sources, there are three important rules to follow.

- Determine the quality of the Internet source. Does it provide reliable information and a carefully evaluated argument supported by research? Is the source a refereed publication (one whose material is evaluated by experts) or a reputable

▶ **VIEWING CUE**

Locate at least five secondary research sources for your essay topic. What are the most recent books on the film or topic? Find at least two relevant scholarly articles on this topic. ⏸

▶ **VIEWING CUE**

Search the Internet for information about your film and topic, and locate at least one useful source. What distinguishes this source from other online information about your topic? ⏸

institution? Is its information supported by references to other research? What are the credentials of the authors?

■ Define your search as precisely as possible. Instead of just the title of a film, focus your search on, for example, "lighting in *Double Indemnity*" or "politics and Iranian cinema." Pursue your topic through the advanced search option.

■ Explore links to other sites. Does your research link you to sites on other films by the same director or to such related issues as the film genre or the country in which the film was made?

Here is a short list of Web sites useful for film research:

■ *American Film Institute* (www.afi.com): recent industry news, events, educational seminars, and reviews.
■ *Berkeley Film Studies Resources* (www.lib.berkeley.edu/MRC/filmstudies): a growing collection of online bibliographies and sources for film and media studies.
■ *Cinema Sites* (www.cinema-sites.com): a comprehensive listing of links to hundreds of sites.
■ *The Criterion Collection* (www.criterion.com): DVD distributor of well-known masterpieces of international art cinema, Hollywood classics, and often overlooked gems from film history.
■ *EarlyCinema.com* (www.earlycinema.com/resources/index.html): a solid introduction to the filmmakers, technologies, and social environments for early cinema, including suggestions for further research.
■ *Film Literature Index* (webapp1.dlib.indiana.edu/fli/index.jsp): an index, with more than two thousand subject heads, of the publications in 150 film and media journals.
■ *Film-Philosophy* (www.film-philosophy.com/): an international journal that features a wide range of book reviews, theoretical essays, and sophisticated analyses of individual films.
■ *FilmSound.org* (www.filmsound.org): covers all topics related to film sound—including definitions of terms, links to scholarly articles, and interviews with sound designers—and is useful for students and practitioners.
■ *Internet Movie Database* (www.imdb.com): plot summaries, links to reviews, and background information on individual films.
■ *Kino International: The Best in World Cinema* (www.kino.com): DVD distributor of many of the most important films from throughout film history and around the world.
■ *Library of Congress Motion Picture & Television Reading Room* (www.loc.gov/rr/mopic/): the library's catalog, the national Film Registry preservation list, and the American Memory Collection of online early films.
■ *Offscreen* (www.offscreen.com): an extremely well-organized online film journal that covers genres, directors, and individual films, along with reviews of festivals and other journals.
■ *Oxford Bibliographies Online* (www.oxfordbibliographiesonline.com): annotated and regularly updated bibliographies on a wide variety of topics in film and media studies.
■ *Rovi* (www.allrovi.com/movies): film and video reviews and production credits, cross-referenced by actor, director, and genre.
■ *Society for Cinema and Media Studies* (www.cmstudies.org/): academic society dedicated to the scholarly study of film, television, and new media.
■ *UbuWeb* (www.ubu.com/): allows users to download rare and remarkable documents from literary, film, video, and music history, such as a Dadaist magazine from 1917 or a documentary on Andy Warhol.
■ *Vectors*: *Journal of Culture and Technology in a Dynamic Vernacular* (www.vectorsjournal.org): a cutting-edge journal that combines scholarship and analysis with new design and delivery technologies.

■ *Yale University Library Film Studies Research Guide* (http://guides.library.yale .edu/film/): an introductory guide to conducting library and Internet research in film studies.

Using and Documenting Sources

Writers gather research material in a variety of ways: some record paragraphs and phrases on handwritten note cards, while others prefer to type that material directly into their computers, allowing them to sort, move, and insert text easily. In either case, the bibliographic information for quotations should be double-checked for accuracy. It should include all of the publication data required for the Works Cited list (and sometimes the Works Consulted section) of your research paper. Just as sloppy technical errors—such as a boom microphone appearing in a frame—can undermine a film's look and effect, inaccurate or careless source documentation can make a research paper look amateurish.

Integrating research material into the text of your paper requires both logic and rhetoric. Sometimes research can be used to describe how your argument differs from prevailing positions on a film or an issue. In this case, the writer frequently identifies one or more opposing positions as a way of highlighting how the essay will distinguish itself: "While Annette Michelson has claimed that Kuleshov's films are best understood as part of a debate with Eisenstein, this paper argues that the French films of Jean Epstein are equally important to Kuleshov's development." Conversely, research can be used to support and validate a point or a part of the overall argument: "Both Patrice Petro and Judith Mayne have produced complex feminist readings of silent-era German films that support my interpretation of *Mädchen in Uniform* (1931)." Yet another possibility is to use research sources to back up the validity of facts or critical frameworks necessary for introducing an argument: "In *The Zero Hour: Glasnost and Soviet Cinema in Transition*, Andrew Horton and Michael Brashinsky convincingly show that Russian cinema after 1985 returned to the center of the world stage, an argument that will provide the background for my claims about the importance of *Little Vera* (1989) in Europe and America."

Direct Quotations and Paraphrasing

Once research material has been gathered, selected, and integrated into an essay, all of the sources used must be properly documented. There are two kinds of research material that require documentation: (1) direct quotation from a secondary source, and (2) paraphrasing, in which the writer puts the idea or observation from another source into his or her own words. When information is considered common knowledge and is well known to most people, there is no need to document where you found it. If, however, there is any doubt about whether the observation is common knowledge, always document the source so as to avoid any suspicion of plagiarism. For example, a critic's remark that Ousmane Sembène is one of Africa's premier filmmakers and that his films work in a realist tradition would be considered common knowledge by many seasoned filmgoers. But a writer new to Sembène's work may feel more comfortable documenting the source of that information and, like all writers, should *never* risk the charge of plagiarism. Quotations of dialogue from a film usually do not require documentation.

Documentation Format

There are various documentation formats for listing authors, titles, and publication data. Here we will describe the format advocated by the Modern Language Association (MLA) and widely used in the humanities. (See the *MLA Handbook for Writers of*

▶ **VIEWING CUE**

How will you collect the research you need to formulate and present your argument? What sources will you use? Keep a detailed list of each for later documentation. ⏸

▶ **VIEWING CUE**

As you prepare to integrate research into your essay, think about a particular quote or critical position you will argue against. What factual or historical material will support your argument? Note passages you can use to bolster a central part of your essay. ⏸

Research Papers, 7th ed. [2009].) The primary components of the MLA format are in-text citations and the Works Cited list. An in-text citation is required wherever the writer refers to, or quotes from, a research source within the essay's text. The in-text citation includes the author's name and the page number, enclosed in parentheses. Note that "p." and "pp." are not used.

> Filmmakers such as Stan Brakhage and Jonas Mekas "appropriated home-movie style as a formal manifestation of a spontaneous, untampered form of filmmaking" (Zimmerman 146).

When the author's name appears in the discussion that introduces the quotation, only the page number or numbers are given.

> As Patricia Zimmerman has noted, filmmakers such as Stan Brakhage and Jonas Mekas "appropriated home-movie style as a formal manifestation of a spontaneous, untampered form of filmmaking" (146).

The same citation formats are used whether the material is quoted directly or paraphrased.

> Much of the American avant-garde movement experimented not so much with the techniques of modern art but with the spontaneous actions associated with home movies (Zimmerman 146).

When you use two or more sources by the same author in your essay, you must distinguish among them by including an abbreviated version of the title. The title can be part of the introductory text, as in "Zimmerman writes in *Reel Families . . .*" or in the parenthetical citation: "(Zimmerman, *Reel Families* 146)." Each source cited in the text must also appear in the Works Cited section with full bibliographic detail.

Another type of annotation is the content note or *explanatory note*, which may or may not include secondary sources. These notes offer background information on the topic being discussed or on related issues, suggest related readings, or offer an aside. They should be placed on a separate page after the text (but before the Works Cited list) or as footnotes at the bottom of the page. Thus a writer discussing horror films and Brian De Palma's *Carrie* (1976) might include this text and content note:

> Although *Carrie* focuses on female anxiety and violence, it is difficult to pinpoint a specific audience for this film.[1]

> [1]Especially since *Psycho*, horror films seem fixated on violence against women, but there is good reason to consider how both female and male audiences identify with these films. An important discussion of this issue is Carol Clover's *Men, Women, and Chain Saws* (3-21).

Full documentation for every source cited in your essay should be included in the **Works Cited** section, positioned on a separate page immediately after the last page of the essay text. Sources that have been consulted, but not cited in the text or notes of the essay, can be included in an optional **Works Consulted** section, which follows on a separate page after the Works Cited list. (Note that for reasons of space, we do *not* show the Works Cited and Works Consulted sections as separate pages in the essay beginning on p. 461.) Punctuation of the different entries must be absolutely correct. Titles should be typed either in italics or underlined, according to your instructor's preference. Finally, the end of each entry should indicate the medium of the publication as either "Print," "Web," or others (such as "DVD" or "Performance").

Examples of some of the most common types of Works Cited entries follow.

Book by One Author

Zimmerman, Patricia. *Reel Families*: *A Social History of Amateur Film*. Bloomington: Indiana UP, 1995. Print.

Book by More Than One Author

Bordwell, David, Janet Staiger, and Kristin Thompson. *The Classical Hollywood Cinema: Film Style and Mode of Production to 1960*. New York: Columbia UP, 1985. Print.

Edited Book

Cook, Pam, and Mieke Bernink, eds. *The Cinema Book*. 2nd ed. London: British Film Institute, 1999. Print.

Article in an Anthology of Film Criticism

Gaines, Jane. "Dream/Factory." *Reinventing Film Studies*. Ed. Christine Gledhill and Linda Williams. London: Arnold, 2000. 100–13. Print.

Journal Article

Spivak, Gayatri. "In Praise of *Sammy and Rosie Get Laid*." *Critical Quarterly* 31.2 (1989): 80–88. Print.

Articles in Daily or Weekly Periodical

Corliss, Richard. "Suddenly Shakespeare." *Time* 4 Nov. 1996: 88–90. Print.

Interview (Printed)

Seberg, Jean. Interview by Mark Rappaport. "I, Jean Seberg." *Film Quarterly* 55.1 (2001): 2–13. Print.

Article in an Online Journal (including Access Date)

Include the URL (in angle brackets) after the access date only if your instructor requires it or readers would need it to find the Web site.

Firshing, Robert. "Italian Horror in the Seventies." *Images Journal* 8 Nov. 2001. Web. 23 July 2011.

Information from an Online Site (including Access Date)

Magnolia: The Official Movie Page. 1999. New Line Productions. 14 Nov. 2003. Web. 12 May 2011.

A Videocassette or DVD

Always identify whether you are referencing a videocassette or a DVD. Include the director, main performers, and original release date of the film, followed by the video/DVD distributor and year.

Fearless. Dir. Peter Weir. Perf. Jeff Bridges, Isabella Rossellini, Rosie Perez. 1993. Warner Home Video, 1999. DVD.

Always remember to keep in mind that plagiarism—using sources without giving the proper credit to them—is one of the most serious offenses in writing and research. For more information on attribution formats for other types of sources, consult the *MLA Handbook for Writers of Research Papers*, 7th ed. (2009).

FILM IN FOCUS

157010

From Research to Writing about *The Cabinet of Dr. Caligari* (1920)

Responding to the strange look and feel of this silent film from Germany and looking for some basic information, a student writer might start his research by examining the introductory material in David Cook's *History of Narrative Film* (2003). In the index, he checks various headings, such as "German cinema" and "Weimar cinema," as well as the title of the film and the name of its director, Robert Wiene. Next, he searches the Internet by entering the title of the film in a search engine, which results in dozens of different Web sites. Although much of the Internet information is too general, he keeps a list of his Web sources and their bibliographic details, noting one particular site that provides early reviews of the film. Even this preliminary research starts to shape his thinking about a topic involving the period known as the Weimar era.

Following this preliminary work, the writer then checks the databases at his college library for more substantial critical books and essays on the Weimar period in German history. This initial search leads him to dozens of books and critical articles, but he decides to concentrate on books that deal with films made during the Weimar period; he discovers numerous scholarly studies devoted to this particular film culture and even whole books devoted to *The Cabinet of Dr. Caligari*. He reads and takes notes on appropriate sections of well-known books, such as Siegfried Kracauer's *From Caligari to Hitler* (1947) and Lotte Eisner's *The Haunted Screen* (1973). He also consults two fairly recent scholarly books, Mike Budd's edited collection *"The Cabinet of Dr. Caligari": Texts, Contexts, Histories* (1990) and Thomas Elsaesser's *Weimar Cinema and After* (2000).

Armed with information about how the Weimar era became the prelude to fascism and the rise of Hitler, the writer realizes he needs to refine his topic so that he has a more focused thesis. He reviews the film on DVD and realizes that the violence and horror seem connected to the social context of a prefascist Germany. As his thesis about social violence begins to take shape, he returns to the library, where he finds a good recent study of film violence, Stephen Prince's edited collection, *Screening Violence* (2000).

With each step, the writer makes notes, double-checks quotations for accuracy, and makes certain to record accurate bibliographic information on all the sources he consults. As he formulates his thesis statement and constructs an outline, he tries to indicate where the different parts of his research would be most effective in directing and supporting his argument. His final essay, reproduced here, clearly demonstrates the important contribution that careful research makes to writing about film.

Steven Thompson

Professor Corrigan

Film Criticism 101

10 Dec. 2010

History, Violence, and *The Cabinet of Dr. Caligari*

In his detailed study of *The Cabinet of Dr. Caligari* (1920), Mike Budd identifies the complex cultural history of the film's arrival in the United States, an arrival that intentionally obscured the origins of one of Germany's most famous movies. When the film premiered in New York on April 3, 1921,

Background research clearly sets up the writer's argument.

it followed a well-crafted promotion and distribution campaign that stressed *Dr. Caligari*'s novelty, global appeal, and generic formulas. One 1921 poster identifies the film as "a mystery story that holds the public in suspense every minute," while another describes it as "thrilling, fantastic, bizarre, gripping." However accurate these descriptions may be, these promotions, as Budd notes, intentionally present the film "out of context, [with] its origins both cultural and national deliberately obscured" (56–58). That obfuscation has continued to dog *The Cabinet of Dr. Caligari* in the many decades since its initial release, so that American and other viewers have remained less attuned to the specific historical and social realities dramatized in the film than to the psychological mysteries played out in its thrills, fantasies, and horror. Exploring the social drama of *Dr. Caligari* reconnects the film more concretely to its original German context and makes clear that this film is about national unrest and violence, both of which are far more historically tangible than the usually acknowledged fantasy of the film's madmen and monsters.

The film's story tells of the hypnotist Dr. Caligari who comes to a town with a carnival [**Figure CDC.1**]. In his sideshow act, Caligari presents Cesare, a somnambulist who can supposedly see the future. At the same time, a series of murders occurs in the town. Francis, a student who discovers that Caligari and Cesare are behind the killings, pursues Caligari to an insane asylum. The final twist occurs when the narrative shifts its perspective and we discover the truth: Francis has been the narrator of the tale, he is in fact the mad patient in the asylum, and Caligari is the kind director of the hospital allowing Francis to tell his delusional tale.[1]

While watching this film, many (if not most) viewers understandably fixate on the exaggerated sets and backdrop paintings. These factors, together with the twisted narrative that turns the story into the vision of a madman, place this film squarely in the cultural and aesthetic tradition of expressionism, a movement in which unconscious or unseen forces create a world distorted by personal fears, desires, and anxieties. According to this position, Cesare acts

The thesis statement announces the argument.

This summary paragraph assumes readers know the film, but refreshes their memory of its story and plot.

A content note provides additional information about a point raised in the text.

CDC.1 *The Cabinet of Dr. Caligari* (1920). The malevolent or benevolent Caligari.

This image shows a main character, followed by a caption that identifies a key question in the film and the student's argument about that character.

out the evil unconscious of Caligari, while the violence and chaos associated with that unconscious spread through the entire community.

Many critics have, in fact, made intelligent connections between the psychological underpinnings of expressionism and the German society that, bereft of so many fathers after the devastation of World War I, gravitated toward malevolent authority figures. Most famously, Siegfried Kracauer's *From Caligari to Hitler* offers the most direct statement of Dr. Caligari as the unconscious of a social history predicting the imminent arrival of fascism **[Figure CDC.2]**. He writes that Caligari becomes "a premonition of Hitler" (72):

> Whether intentionally or not, *Caligari* exposes the soul wavering between tyranny and chaos, and facing a desperate situation: any escape from tyranny seems to throw it into a state of utter confusion. Quite logically, the film spreads an all-pervading atmosphere of horror. Like the Nazi world, that of *Caligari* overflows with sinister portents, acts of terror and outbursts of panic. (74)

Although *Dr. Caligari* certainly responds to readings like this, which see the film as part of an expressionist aesthetic or a projection of the unconscious of the German masses around 1920, the more concrete social realities informing the film frequently get overlooked. In *The Weimar Republic Sourcebook*, Anton Kaes, Martin Jay, and Edward Dimendberg have assembled a compendium of documents on this period in German history, and many of the topics for this cultural history of Germany from 1918 to 1930 could act as a social blueprint for the thematic history that permeates *Dr. Caligari*. Three topics stand out as especially pertinent: the traumatic legacy of war (creating a fatherless generation), economic upheaval and social instabilities (that rattled almost every social institution at the time), and the rise of fascism (through repressive authority figures). With traces of each of these three motifs throughout the film, *Dr. Caligari* becomes, from one angle, a study of social violence within the interpersonal relationships and the cultural institutions of Weimar Germany.

At the heart of *Dr. Caligari* is a social melodrama concentrated on conscious sexual activities that quickly turn violent. According to Thomas Elsaesser, "It is essentially the tale of a suitor who is ignored or turned down" (184). The threesome at the center of the story—Francis, Alan, and Jane— suggests both male bonds and a heterosexual romance that moves toward the conventional outcome of marriage. However, like Jane's anxious worry over "her father's long absence," each member of this standard social group seems physically and emotionally handicapped by a missing parental or patriarchal figure. Essential to the plot is the rivalry that creates a tension among the three characters, with Alan and Francis competing for the affections of Jane. That seemingly normal and playful tension, however, turns dark when Cesare becomes a stand-in for the simmering violence implicit in this group, murdering Francis's rival Alan and seducing and abducting Jane. In the midst of these events, the dazed Jane can only mutter that "we queens may never choose as our hearts dictate," and Francis goes mad **[Figure CDC.3]**. If heterosexual melodramas take many forms through history and in different cultures, here a common love triangle suddenly and inexplicitly erupts with unusual violence, suggesting that

This overview of a major scholarly position establishes the writer's authority and prepares readers for what will distinguish his argument.

A succinct quotation sums up a complex critical viewpoint. Because it is more than four lines in length, the quotation is presented without quotation marks in the block (indented) format.

Against the backdrop of these other critical positions, the writer reasserts and develops his thesis.

The writer refines and focuses his thesis as three motifs in the film.

A strong topic sentence presents the first motif, supported by a secondary source.

An exact quotation from the film's dialogue provides supporting evidence for the writer's claim.

CDC.2   *The Cabinet of Dr. Caligari* (1920). A premonition of Hitler?

CDC.3   *The Cabinet of Dr. Caligari* (1920). Horror, or a romance gone awry?

the problem may be less about Caligari and Cesare than about the enormous social stress and strain within this fundamental social grouping.

    The violent stress and strain of this heterosexual drama spreads and appears through every social institution in *Dr. Caligari*. If the home is where the melodrama explodes, the film identifies this violence with three other social spaces: the city government, the carnival, and the mental hospital. With the first, an officious town clerk is murdered on a whim for enforcing restrictions that annoy Dr. Caligari. With the second, entertainment turns ominously threatening when a sideshow amusement tells Alan, "You die at dawn." With the third, a traditional institution for healing becomes a prison to subjugate or control human beings who have lost all ability to interact socially. In each case—and most notably in the hospital where the narrative pretends to return to a normal world—the visual disturbances of the graphically twisted walls and out-of-kilter windows become a measure of not merely an unbalanced expressionistic mind but, more importantly, of the social violence that surrounds all individuals as part of the institutions in which they must live.

    If violence has always been an ingredient and attraction of films, the brand of social violence in *Dr. Caligari* is clearly linked to a specific time and place, a Weimar Germany from which the Nazi regime would soon spring. In "Graphic Violence in the Cinema" from *Screening Violence*, Stephen Prince correctly argues that "screen violence is deeply embedded in the history and functioning of cinema" and the "appeal of violence in the cinema—for filmmakers and viewers—is tied to the medium's inherently visceral properties" (2). Although Prince claims that "screen violence in earlier periods was generally more genteel and indirect" (2), there is nothing genteel about the social violence of *Dr. Caligari*, even if it lacks the physical excess of contemporary movies. With the crucial insights of historical hindsight, this violence should not be relegated merely to the unconscious and the psychological distortions of dark fantasies, but should be recognized as the shadow of a historical and social reality. In its original historical context, the melodramatic violence in the relationship of Alan, Francis, and Jane

A smooth transition is made from the previous paragraph to the second motif about "social institutions," analyzed here as three different "social spaces."

Visual details strengthen the argument.

The third motif builds on a more general secondary source on "screen violence."

maps a frustrating and often desperate problem with heterosexual romance in a fatherless Germany, while the troubled, anxious, and repressive interactions at town halls, carnivals, and hospitals refer to a real political and structural crisis in the social arenas of post-World War I Germany. If the social violence of *Dr. Caligari* seems tame (to modern eyes accustomed to Technicolor bloodbaths), there is no doubt that such violence reverberates with more extensive, if less intensive, implications for the state of German society in 1920.

Many viewers without a precise sense of German history and *Caligari*'s original cultural context can still appreciate its dark tale, striking visual effects, and unsettling frame tale. The psychological dimension that permeates this murder mystery is, moreover, an undeniable and critical component to its disturbing plot and expressionistic mise-en-scène. Yet, in the wake of World War I, the nightmarish violence of the film resonates with particular historical and social meaning that cannot be explained as fantasy. *The Cabinet of Dr. Caligari* will always be a specific cultural space whose violence remains historically tangible.

> The assertive conclusion restates the central thesis.

Note

1. In *A History of Narrative Film*, David Cook notes that it was the great German director Fritz Lang who urged this frame tale: "Lang correctly thought that the reality frame would heighten the expressionistic elements of the mise-en-scène" (110).

[According to MLA, begin new page here]

Works Cited

> The Works Cited list starts on a new page at the end of the research essay.

Budd, Mike, ed. *"The Cabinet of Dr. Caligari": Texts, Contexts, Histories*. New Brunswick: Rutgers UP, 1990. Print.

Cook, David A. *A History of Narrative Film*. 4th ed. New York: Norton, 2003. Print.

Elsaesser, Thomas. "Social Mobility and the Fantastic: German Silent Cinema." Budd 171-90.

Kaes, Anton, Martin Jay, and Edward Dimendberg. *The Weimar Republic Sourcebook*. Berkeley: U of California P, 1994. Print.

Kracauer, Siegfried. *From Caligari to Hitler: A Psychological Study of the German Film*. Princeton: Princeton UP, 1947. Print.

Prince, Stephen. "Graphic Violence in the Cinema: Origins, Aesthetic Design, and Social Effects." *Screening Violence*. Ed. Stephen Prince. New Brunswick: Rutgers UP, 2000. 1-46. Print.

[According to MLA, begin new page here.]

Works Consulted

> The Works Consulted list, when included, starts on a new page following Works Cited.

Carroll, Noël. "The Cabinet of Dr. Kracauer." *Millennium Film Journal* 1.2 (1978): 77-85. Print.

Eisner, Lotte. *The Haunted Screen: Expressionism in the German Cinema and the Influence of Max Reinhardt*. Berkeley: U of California P, 1973. Print.

Elsaesser, Thomas. *Weimar Cinema and After: Germany's Historical Imaginary*. London: Routledge, 2000. Print.

CONCEPTS AT WORK

In this chapter, we've examined both the aims and mechanics of good writing about film. Some of the important preliminary steps in this kind of writing include identifying an audience, balancing subjective and objective perspectives, taking notes, and sketching an outline that develops a particular argument and interpretation. The actual writing requires a clear and detailed thesis, strong topic sentences, and concrete evidence from the film, and is always followed by a series of revisions of first drafts that work to clarify the argument, its ideas, and its presentation. Careful proofreading then follows final revision, double-checking mechanics such as spelling and punctuation. Students should beware of indiscriminately using images from a film if they are simply ornamental; if used, images should provide precise and detailed evidence for a part of your argument and be connected to that argument with a short caption that reinforces that connection. Finally, we have discussed both why research can be crucial to a strong critical paper and how that research can be pursued and integrated into the writing.

Activities

- Practice taking detailed and productive notes on a film. Select one key scene in a film you viewed recently to annotate as precisely as possible. Describe the position of the characters, camera, and frame. Note any sounds, including dialogue. Support your description with a rough sketch.
- Many filmmakers, such as François Truffaut and Peter Bogdanovich, also work as fine film critics and scholars, and much of the work of making a film—research, planning, organizing, and revising—can resemble the work of writing a critical essay. In fact, film and video can work like a critical essay—as a commentary on, or interpretation of, another film. Try making a short video or film that comments on or interprets a film. Does this method offer new critical or analytical possibilities that writing does not? Does it lack some of the powers of traditional critical writing?

Glossary

above-the-line expenses: A film's initial costs of contracting the major personnel, such as **directors** and stars, as well as administrative and organizational expenses in setting up a film **production.**

abstract films: Formal experiments that are also nonrepresentational. These films use color, shape, and line to create patterns and rhythms that are abstracted from real actions and objects.

academy ratio: An **aspect ratio** of screen width to height of 1.37:1, the standard adopted by the Motion Picture Academy of Arts and Sciences in 1931 and used by most films until the introduction of **widescreen ratios** in the 1950s; similar to the standard television ratio of 1.33:1 or 4:3.

activist video: A confrontational political **documentary** using low-cost video equipment.

actor: An individual who embodies and performs a film character through gestures and movements.

actualities: Early **nonfiction films** introduced in the 1890s depicting real people and events through continuous footage; a famous example is Louis and Auguste Lumière's *Workers Leaving the Lumière Factory* (1985).

adaptation: The process of turning a novel, short story, play, or other artistic work into a film.

agents: Individuals who represent **actors**, **directors**, writers, and other major personnel employed by a film **production** by contacting and negotiating with writers, **casting directors**, and **producers.**

alternative film narrative: Film **narratives** that deviate from or challenge the linearity of **classical film narrative**, often undermining the centrality of the main character, the continuity of the plot, or the **verisimilitude** of the **narration.**

analytical editing: **Continuity editing** that establishes spatial and temporal clarity by breaking down a **scene**, often using progressively tighter **framings** that maintain consistent spatial relations.

analytical essay: The most common kind of writing done by film students and scholars, distinguished by its intended audience and the level of its critical language.

anamorphic lens: A **camera lens** that compresses the horizontal axis of an image or a projector lens that "unsqueezes" such an image to produce a widescreen image.

ancillary market: A venue other than theatrical release in which a film can make money, such as foreign sales, airlines, pay television, cable, or home video.

animated musical: A subgenre of the **musical** that uses cartoon figures and stories to present songs and music.

animation: A process that traditionally refers to moving images drawn or painted on individual **cels** or to manipulated three-dimensional objects, which are then photographed onto single frames of film. Animation now encompasses digital imaging techniques.

antagonists: Characters who oppose the **protagonists** as negative forces.

anthology films: See compilation films.

A picture: A feature film with a considerable budget and prestigious source material or stars or other personnel that has been historically promoted as a main attraction receiving top billing in a double feature; see **B picture.**

apparatus theory: A critical school that explores the cinema as an ideological phenomenon based on a physical set of technologies, including the camera and the arrangement of projector and screen, that reinforces the values of individualism and the transcendence of the material basis of the cinematic illusion.

apparent motion: The psychological process that explains our perception of movement when watching films, in which the brain is actively responding to the visual stimuli of a rapid sequence of still images exactly as it would in actual motion perception.

archetype: An original model or type, such as Satan as an archetype of evil.

art director: The individual responsible for supervising the conception and construction of the physical environment in which the **actors** appear, including sets, locations, **props**, and costumes; see **production designer** and **set designer.**

art film: A type of film produced for aesthetic rather than primarily for commercial or entertainment purposes, whose intellectual or formal challenges are often attributed to the vision of an **auteur.**

aspect ratio: The width-to-height ratio of the film frame as it appears on a movie screen or television monitor.

asynchronous sound: Sound that does not have a visible onscreen source; also referred to as **offscreen sound.**

auteur: The French term for "author"; the individual credited with the creative vision defining a film; implies a **director** whose unique style is apparent across his or her body of work; see **auteur theory.**

auteur theory: An approach to cinema first proposed in the French film journal *Cahiers du cinéma* that emphasized the role of the **director** as the expressive force behind a film and saw a director's body of work as united by common themes or formal strategies; also referred to as *auteurism*.

automated dialogue replacement (ADR): A process during which **actors** watch the film footage and re-record their lines to be dubbed into the **soundtrack**; also known as **looping**.

avant-garde cinema: Aesthetically challenging, noncommercial films that self-consciously reflect on how human senses and consciousness work or explore and experiment with film forms and techniques. Avant-garde cinema thrived in Europe in the 1920s and in the United States after World War II.

axis of action: An imaginary line bisecting a **scene** corresponding to the 180-degree **rule** in continuity **editing**.

backlighting: A **highlighting** technique that illuminates the person or object from behind, tending to silhouette the subject; sometimes called **edgelighting**.

below-the-line expenses: The technical and material costs—costumes, sets, transportation, and so on—involved in the actual making of a film.

blaxploitation: A **genre** of low-budget films made in the early 1970s targeting urban, African American audiences with films about streetwise African American **protagonists**. Several black **directors** made a creative mark in a genre that was primarily intended to make money for its **producers**.

block booking: A practice in which movie theaters had to exhibit whatever a studio/distributor packaged with its more popular and desirable movies; declared an unfair business practice in 1948.

blockbuster: A big-budget film, intended for **wide release**, whose large investment in stars, **special effects**, and advertising attracts large audiences and economic profits.

blocking: The arrangement and movement of **actors** in relation to each other within the **mise-en-scène**.

boom: A long pole used to hold a microphone above the **actors** to capture sound while remaining outside the frame, handled by a *boom operator.*

B picture: A low-budget, nonprestigious movie that usually played on the bottom half of a double bill. B pictures were often produced by the smaller studios referred to as Hollywood's Poverty Row; see A **picture**.

camera lens: A piece of curved glass that focuses light rays in order to form an image on film.

camera movement: See mobile frame.

camera operator: A member of the film crew in charge of physically manipulating the camera, overseen by the **cinematographer**.

canted frame: Framing that is not level, creating an unbalanced appearance.

casting director: The individual responsible for identifying and selecting which **actors** would work best in particular roles.

cels: A transparent sheet of celluloid on which individual images are drawn or painted in traditional **animation**. These drawings are then photographed onto single frames of film.

character actors: Recognizable **actors** associated with particular **character types**, often humorous or sinister, and often cast in minor parts.

character analysis: A formal topic, concentrating its argument on a single character or on the interactions between more than one character.

character coherence: A quality created within a fiction of **characters** displaying behavior, emotions, and thoughts that appear consistent and coherent.

character depth: A quality created within a fiction of **characters** displaying psychological and social features that distinguish them as rounded and complex in a way that approximates realistic human personalities.

character development: The patterns through which **characters** in a particular film move from one mental, physical, or social state to another.

characters: Individuals who motivate the events and perform the actions of the **story**.

character types: Conventional **characters** (e.g., hardboiled detective or femme fatale) typically portrayed by **actors** cast because of their physical features, their acting style, or the history of other roles they have played; see **stereotype**.

chiaroscuro lighting: A term that describes dramatic, high-contrast **lighting** that emphasizes shadows and the contrast between light and dark; frequently used in **German expressionist cinema** and **film noir**.

chronology: The order according to which **shots** or **scenes** convey the temporal sequence of the **story**'s events.

chronophotography: A sequence of still photographs such as those depicting human or animal motion produced by Eadweard Muybridge and Étienne-Jules Marey; the immediate precursor of the cinema.

cinematographer: The member of the film crew who selects the cameras, **film stock**, **lighting**, and lenses to be used as well as the camera setup or position; also known as the *director of photography* or *D.P.*

cinematography: Motion-picture photography, literally "writing in movement."

cinéma vérité: A French term literally meaning "cinema truth"; a style of **documentary** filmmaking first practiced in the late 1950s and early 1960s that used unobtrusive, lightweight cameras and sound equipment to capture a real-life situation; the parallel U.S. movement is called **direct cinema**.

cinephilia: A love of cinema.

clapboard: A device marked with the **scene** and **take** number that is filmed at the beginning of each take; the sound of its being snapped is recorded in order to synchronize **sound recordings** and camera images.

classical film narrative: A style of narrative filmmaking centered on one or more central **characters** who propel the **plot** with a cause-and-effect logic wherein an action generates a reaction. Normally plots are developed with **linear chronologies** directed at definite goals, and the film employs an omniscient or a restricted **third-person narration** that suggests some degree of **verisimilitude**.

classical film theory: Writings on the fundamental questions of cinema produced in roughly the first half of the twentieth century. Important classical film theorists include Sergei Eisenstein, Rudolf Arnheim, André Bazin, and Siegfried Kracauer.

classical Hollywood narrative: The dominant form of **classical film narrative** associated with the Hollywood **studio system** from the end of the 1910s to the end of the 1950s.

claymation: A process that uses stop-motion photography with clay figures to create the illusion of movement.

click track: Holes punched in the film corresponding to the beat of a metronome that can help **actors**, musicians, and the composer keep the rhythm of the action.

close-up: Framing that shows details of a person or an object, such as a character's face.

code: A term used in linguistics and **semiotics** meaning a system of **signs** from which a *message* is generated. In a communication act, a code must be shared by the sender and the receiver for the message to be understood. For example, traffic signals use a color code. Film analysts isolate the codes of **camera movement, framing, lighting**, acting, etc., that determine the specific form of a particular **shot, scene**, film, or **genre**.

color balance: Putting emphasis on a particular part of the color spectrum to create realistic or unrealistic palettes.

color filter: A device fitted to the **camera lens** to change the **tones** of the filmed image.

comedy: A film genre that celebrates the harmony and resiliency of social life, typically with a **narrative** that ends happily, and often emphasizes episodes or "gags" over plot continuity.

comparative analysis: An analysis evaluating features or elements of two or more different films, or perhaps a film and its literary source.

compilation films: Films comprised of various segments by different filmmakers; also known as *anthology films*.

computer-generated imagery (CGI): Still or animated images created through digital computer technology. First introduced in the 1970s, CGI was used to create feature-length films by the mid-1990s and is widely used for **visual effects**.

continuity editing: The institutionalized system of Hollywood **editing** that uses **cuts** and other transitions to establish **verisimilitude**, to construct a coherent time and space, and to tell stories clearly and efficiently. Continuity editing follows the basic principle that each **shot** or **scene** has a continuous relationship to the next; sometimes called *invisible editing*.

continuity script: A screenplay that presents in detail the action, **scenes**, dialogue, transitions, and often camera setups in the order planned for the final film.

continuity style: The systematic approach to filmmaking associated with classical Hollywood cinema, utilizing a broad array of technical choices from **continuity editing** to scoring that support the principle of effacing technique in order to emphasize human agency and **narrative** clarity.

costume designers: Individuals who plan and prepare how **actors** will be dressed for parts.

counterpoint: Using sound to indicate a different meaning or association than the image.

crane shot: A shot taken from a camera mounted on a crane that can vary distance, height, and angle.

credits: A list at the end of a film of all the personnel involved in a film **production**, including cast, crew, and executives.

crime film: A film genre that typically features **characters** who live on the edge of a mysterious or violent society (both criminals and individuals dedicated to crime detection); **plots** that involve criminal acts and increasing mystery, with often ambiguous resolutions; and urban settings.

critical objectivity: Writing with a detached response that offers judgments based on facts and **evidence** with which others would, or could, agree.

crosscutting: An **editing** technique that cuts back and forth between actions in separate spaces, often implying simultaneity; also called **parallel editing**.

crossover: An independent film (typically with a modest budget) that gains success with a broader audience.

cue: A visual or aural signal that indicates the beginning of an action, line of dialogue, or piece of music.

cultural analysis: A formal topic that investigates the relationship of a film to its place in history, society, or culture.

cultural studies: A set of approaches drawn from the humanities and social sciences that considers cultural text and phenomena in conjunction with processes of **production** and consumption.

cut: In the **editing** process, the join or splice between two pieces of film; in the finished film, an editing transition between two separate **shots** or **scenes** achieved without **optical effects**. Also used to describe a version of the edited film, as in **rough cut, final cut**, or director's cut.

cutaway: A **shot** that interrupts a continuous action, "cutting away" to another image or action, often to abridge time.

dailies: The footage shot on a single day of filming.

deadline structure: A **narrative** structure that accelerates the action and **plot** toward a central event or action that must be accomplished by a certain time.

deep focus: A focus in which multiple planes in the **shot** are all in focus simultaneously; usually achieved with a **wide-angle lens.**

depth of field: The range or distance before and behind the main **focus** of a **shot** within which objects remain relatively sharp and clear.

dialectical montage: A concept developed in the theories and films of Soviet silent film **director** Sergei Eisenstein that refers to the cutting together of conflicting or unrelated images to generate an idea or emotion in the viewer.

diegesis: A term that refers to the world of the film's **story** (its **characters**, places, and events), including not only what is shown but also what is implied to have taken place. It comes from the Greek word meaning "**narration.**"

diegetic sound: Sound that has its source in the **narrative** world of the film, whose **characters** are presumed to be able to hear it.

digital cinematography: Shooting with a camera that records and stores visual information electronically as digital code.

digital sound: Recording and reproducing sound through technologies that encode and decode it as digital information.

direct cinema: A documentary style originating in the United States in the 1960s that aims to observe an unfolding situation as unobtrusively as possible; related to **cinéma vérité.**

directional lighting: Lighting that may appear to emanate from a natural source and defines and shapes the object, area, or person being illuminated.

director: The chief creative presence or the primary manager in film **production**, responsible for overseeing virtually all the work of making a movie.

direct sound: Sound captured directly from its source.

disjunctive editing: A variety of alternative **editing** practices that call attention to the **cut** through spatial tension, temporal jumps, or rhythmic or graphic pattern so as to affect viscerally, disorient, or intellectually engage the viewer; also called *visible editing.*

dissolve: An **optical effect** that briefly superimposes one **shot** over the next. One image fades out as another image fades in and takes its place; sometimes called a *lap dissolve* because two images overlap in the printing process.

distanciation: Derived from the work and theories of Bertolt Brecht, an artistic practice intended to create an intellectual distance between the viewer and the **performance** or artwork in order to reflect on the work's **production** or various ideas and issues raised by it.

distribution: The means through which movies are delivered to theaters, video stores, television and Internet networks, and other venues that make them available to consumers, or to educational and cultural institutions. The entity that performs this function is a *distributor.*

documentary: A nonfiction **film** that presents real objects, people, and events.

dolly shot: A shot in which the camera is moved on a wheeled dolly that follows a determined course.

duration: Denotes the temporal relation of **shots** and **scenes** to the amount of time that passes in the **story.**

edgelighting: See backlighting.

editing: The process of selecting and joining film footage and **shots.** The individual responsible for this process is the *editor.*

ellipsis: An abridgment in time in the **narrative** implied by editing.

epic western: A subgenre of the **western** that concentrates on action and movement, with a hero whose quests and battlers serve to define the nation and its origins. This genre has its roots in literature and epic paintings, and appears early and often in film history.

establishing shot: Generally, an initial **long shot** that establishes the location and **setting** and that orients the viewer in space to a clear view of the action.

ethnographic film: Documentary films that record the practices, rituals, and people of a culture.

evidence: Concrete details that convince readers of the validity of a writer's interpretation.

exclusive release: A movie that premieres in restricted locations initially.

executive producer: A producer who finances or facilitates a film deal and who usually has little creative or technical involvement.

exhibition: The part of the film industry that shows films to a paying public, usually in movie theaters.

existential western: A more introspective **subgenre** of the **western** that features a hero plagued with self-doubt and troubled by his changing social status. These films tend to feature a more populated and civilized frontier.

expanded cinema: A term coined in 1970 by Gene Young-blood that describes how video and computer technology can allow moving-image media to extend consciousness; also designates a number of installation or **performance**-based **experimental film** practices.

experimental films: Films that explore film form and subject matters in new and unconventional ways, ranging from abstract image and sound patterns to dreamlike worlds.

exploitation film: A cheaply made **genre** film that exploits a sensational or topical subject for profit.

extras: Actors without speaking parts who appear in the background and in crowd **scenes.**

extratextual: Characterizes aspects of the film experience available to the scholar that exist outside of the film itself, including **production**, **distribution**, **exhibition**, and reception.

extreme close-up (ECU): A framing that is comparatively tighter than a **close-up**, singling out, for instance, a person's eyes, or the petal of a flower.

extreme long shot: A framing from a comparatively greater distance than a **long shot**, in which the surrounding space dominates human figures, such as in distant vistas of cities or landscapes.

eyeline match: A principle in **continuity editing** that calls for following a **shot** of a **character** looking offscreen with a shot of a subject whose screen position matches the gaze of the character in the first shot.

fade-in: An **optical effect** in which a black screen gradually brightens to a full picture; often used after a **fade-out** to create a transition between **scenes**.

fade-out: An **optical effect** in which an image gradually darkens to black, often ending a **scene** or a film; see **fade-in**.

family melodrama: A **subgenre** of the **melodrama** that focuses on the psychological and gendered forces restricting individuals within the family.

fanfic (fan fiction): Fan-written stories that continue or reimagine the **plot** and **characters** of a film.

fast motion: A cinematic special effect that makes the action move at unrealistic speeds, achieved by filming the action faster than normal and then projecting it at standard speeds; see **slow motion**.

feature film: Running typically 90 to 120 minutes in length, a **narrative** film that is the primary attraction for audiences.

fill lighting: A **lighting** technique using secondary fill lights to balance the **key lighting** by removing shadows or to emphasize other spaces and objects in the **scene**.

film gauge: The width of the **film stock**—e.g., 8mm, 16mm, 35mm, and 70mm.

film noir: A term introduced by French critics (meaning literally "black film") to describe Hollywood films of the 1940s set in the criminal underworld, which were considerably darker in mood and **mise-en-scène** than those that had come before. Typically shot in black and white in nighttime urban **settings**, they featured morally ambiguous **protagonists**, corrupt institutions, dangerous women, and convoluted **plots**, and they used stylized **lighting** and **cinematography**.

film review: A short essay that describes the **plot** of a movie, provides useful background information (about the **actors** and the **director**, for example), and pronounces a clear evaluation of the film to guide its readers.

film shoot: The weeks or months of actual shooting, on **set** or on location.

film speed: The rate at which moving images are recorded and later projected, standardized for 35mm sound film at twenty-four frames per second (fps); also, a measure of **film stock**'s sensitivity to light.

film stock: Unexposed film consisting of a flexible backing or base and a light-sensitive emulsion.

filters: Transparent sheets of glass or gels placed in front of the lens to create various effects.

final cut: The final edited version of a film.

first-person narration: Narration that is identified with a single individual, typically (though not always) a **character** in the film.

flare: A spot or flash of white light created by directing strong light directly at the lens.

flashback: A **sequence** that follows images set in the present with images set in the past; it may be introduced with a **dissolve** conveying a character's subjective memory or with a **voiceover** in which a character narrates the past.

flashforward: A **sequence** that connects an image set in the present with one or more future images and that leaps ahead of the normal cause-and-effect order.

focal length: The distance from the center of the lens to the point where light rays meet in sharp **focus**.

focus: The point or area in the image that is most precisely outlined and defined by the lens of the camera; the point at which light rays refracted through the lens converge.

foley artist: A member of the sound crew who generates live synchronized sound effects such as footsteps, the rustle of clothing, or a key turning in a lock, while watching the projected film. Named after their inventor, Jack Foley, foley tracks are eventually mixed with other audio tracks.

following shots: A pan, tilt, or **tracking shot** that follows a moving individual or object.

formalist: A scholar who believes a work's form or structure is primary, and posits that objective meaning is to be found in the work itself and not in an outside source, such as the author's biography.

framing: The portion of the filmed subject that appears within the borders of the frame; it correlates with camera distance—e.g., **long shot** or **medium close-up**.

French impressionist cinema: The first of a series of radical experiments with film form between 1920 and 1939. This movement aimed to destabilize familiar or objective ways of seeing, and to revitalize the dynamics of human perception.

French New Wave: A film movement that came to prominence in the late 1950s and 1960s in France in opposition to the conventional **studio system**; designates films by a group of young writer-directors involved as critics with the journal *Cahiers du cinéma*. The films were often made with low budgets and young **actors**, shot on location, used unconventional sound and **editing** patterns, and addressed the struggle for personal expression.

frontal lighting: Techniques used to illuminate the subject from the front. Related terms are **sidelighting**, **underlighting**, and **top lighting**.

fullscreen: Format in which the image fills the entire screen. Widescreen films are sometimes converted to this using a "pan-and-scan" process.

gangster films: Films about the criminal underworld, typically (but not necessarily) set in the United States during Prohibition in the 1930s.

genre: A category or classification of a group of movies in which the individual films share similar subject matter and similar ways of organizing the subject through **narrative** and stylistic patterns.

German expressionist cinema: Film movement drawing on painting and theatrical developments that emerged in Germany between 1918 and 1929; expressionism depicted the dark fringes of human experience through the use of dramatic **lighting** and **set** and costume design to represent irrational forces.

graphic editing: A style of **editing** creating formal patterns of shapes, masses, colors, lines, and **lighting** patterns through links between **shots**.

graphic match: An edit in which a dominant shape or line in one **shot** provides a visual transition to a similar shape or line in the next shot.

green screen technology: A technique for creating **visual effects** in which **actors** are filmed in front of a green screen and later superimposed onto a computer-generated or filmed background.

grip: A crew member who installs **lighting** and dollies.

handheld camera: A lightweight camera (such as the 16mm Arriflex) that can be carried by the operator rather than mounted on a tripod. Such cameras, widely used during World War II, allowed **cinematography** to become more mobile and fostered the advent of on-location shooting.

handheld shot: A film image produced by an individual carrying the camera, creating an unsteady **shot** that may suggest the **point of view** of an individual moving through space.

hard-boiled detective film: A subgenre of the **crime film** featuring a flawed or morally ambiguous detective **protagonist** battling a criminal element to solve a mystery or resolve a crime.

hard lighting: A high-contrast **lighting** style that creates hard edges, distinctive shadows, and a harsh effect, especially when filming people.

***heimat* films:** Set in idyllic countryside locales of Germany and Austria, these films depict a world of traditional folk values in which love and family triumph over virtually any social evil.

high angle: A **shot** directed at a downward angle on individuals or a **scene**.

high concept: A short phrase that attempts to sell a movie by identifying its main **marketing** features, such as its stars, **genre**, or some other easily identifiable connection.

highlighting: Using **lighting** to brighten or emphasize specific **characters** or objects.

historiography: The writing of history; the study of the methods and principles through which the past becomes organized according to certain perspectives and priorities.

Hong Kong New Wave: A movement in Chinese cinema led by producer-director Tsui Hark, which introduced sophisticated style, lucrative **production** methods, and a canny use of Western elements to the **genre**.

horror film: A film **genre** with origins in gothic literature that seeks to frighten the viewer though supernatural or predator **characters**; **narratives** built on suspense, dread, and surprise; and visual compositions that anticipate and manipulate shocking sights.

hybrid genres: Mixed forms produced by the interaction of different **genres**, such as **musical horror films**.

iconography: Images or image patterns with specific connotations or meanings.

ideology: A systematic set of beliefs, not necessarily conscious or acknowledged.

IMAX: A large-format film system that is projected horizontally rather than vertically to produce an image approximately ten times larger than the standard 35mm frame.

independent films: Films that are produced without initial studio financing, typically with much lower budgets; they include feature-length **narratives, documentaries**, and shorts.

Indian cinema: Approached as a national popular cinema, this is the most prolific film industry in the world. Indian cinema is notable for *Bollywood* films, as they are often referred to, as a dominant cultural form, and critically prized films with a presence on the world stage, such as those of Satyajit Ray.

insert: A brief shot, often a **close-up**, filmed separately from a **scene** and inserted during **editing**, that points out details significant to the action.

integrated musical: A subgenre of the **musical** that integrates musical numbers into the plot.

intercutting: Interposing **shots** of two or more actions, locations, or contents.

internal diegetic sound: See semidiegetic sound.

intertextuality: A critical approach that holds that a text depends on other, related texts for its full meaning.

intertitle: Printed text inserted between film images, typically used in silent films to indicate dialogue and exposition and in contemporary films to indicate time and place or other transitions.

invisible editing: See continuity editing.

iris: A shot in which the corners of the frame are masked in a black, usually circular, form. An *iris-out* is a transition that gradually obscures the image by moving in; an *iris-in* expands to reveal the entire image.

Italian neorealism: A film movement that began in Italy during World War II and lasted until approximately 1952 depicting everyday social realities using location shooting and amateur **actors**, in opposition to glossy studio formulas.

***jidai-geki* films:** Period films or costume dramas set before 1868, when feudal Japan entered the modern Meiji period.

jump cut: An edit that interrupts a particular action and intentionally or unintentionally creates discontinuities in the spatial or temporal development of **shots**.

key lighting: The main source of non-natural **lighting** in a scene. *High-key light* is even (the ratio between key and fill light is high); *low-key light* shows strong contrast (the ratio between key and fill light is low).

leading actors: The two or three **actors**, often stars, who represent the central **characters** in a **narrative**.

lighting: Sources of illumination—both natural light and electrical lamps—used to present, shade, and accentuate figures, objects, spaces, or **mise-en-scène**. Lighting is primarily the responsibility of the *director of photography* and the *lighting crew*; see **key lighting**, **fill lighting**, and **highlighting**.

limited release: The practice of initially distributing a film only to major cities and expanding **distribution** according to its success or failure.

linear chronology: Plot events and actions that proceed one after another as a forward movement in time.

line producer: The individual in charge of the daily business of tracking costs and maintaining the **production** schedule of a film.

location scouting: Determining and securing suitable places besides studio **sets** to use for shooting particular movie **scenes**.

long shot: A framing that places considerable distance between the camera and the **scene** or person so that the object or person is recognizable but defined by the large space and background; see **establishing shot**.

long take: A shot of relatively long **duration**.

looping: An image or sound recorded on a loop of film to be replayed and layered.

low angle: A shot from a position lower than its subject.

machinima: A new media form that modifies video-game engines to create computer **animation**.

magic lantern: A device developed in the seventeenth century for projecting an image from a slide; a precursor of motion pictures.

marketing: The process of identifying an audience and bringing a product such as a movie to its attention through various strategies so that they will consume (watch or purchase) it.

masks: Attachments to the camera or devices added optically that cut off portions of the frame so that part of the image is black.

match on action: A cut between two **shots** featuring a similar visual action, such as when a shot in which a **character** opening a door cuts to a shot depicting the continuation of that action, or when a shot of a train moving left to right cuts to a character running in the same direction.

matte shot: A **shot** that joins two pieces of film, one with the central action or object and the other with additional background, figures, or action (sometimes painted or digitally produced) that would be difficult to create physically for the shot.

media convergence: The process by which formerly distinct media, such as cinema, television, the Internet, and video games, and viewing platforms such as television, computers, and cell phones become interdependent.

medium close-up: A framing that shows a comparatively larger area than a **close-up**, such as a person shown from the shoulders up; typically used during conversation **sequences**.

medium long shot: A framing that increases the distance between the camera and the subject compared with a **medium shot**; it shows most of an individual's body.

medium shot: A middle-ground **framing** in which we see the body of a person from approximately the waist up.

melodrama: Theatrical, literary, and cinematic **narrative** mode often centered on individual crises within the confines of family or other social institutions, frequently characterized by clearly identifiable moral types, coincidences and reversals of fortune, and the use of music (*melos*) to underscore the action.

metteur-en-scène: French term for "director" (particularly a theater director); in **auteur theory**, this term refers to a director who conveys technical competence without possessing a strong streak of individual vision, in contrast to an **auteur**.

mickey-mousing: Overillustrating the action through the musical score, drawn from the conventions of composing for cartoons. An example of mickey-mousing is accompanying a character walking on tiptoe with music played by plucked strings.

miniature model: A small-scale model constructed for use during the filming process to stage **special effects sequences** and complex backgrounds.

mise-en-scène: A French theatrical term meaning literally "put on stage"; used in film studies to refer to all the elements of a movie **scene** that are organized, often by the **director**, to be filmed and that are later visible onscreen. They include the scenic elements of a movie, such as **actors**, **lighting**, **sets**, costumes, make-up, and other features of the image that exist independently of the camera and the processes of filming and **editing**. A *naturalistic mise-en-scène* appears realistic and recognizable to viewers, while a *theatrical mise-en-scène* emphasizes the artificial or constructed nature of its world.

mix: The combination by the sound mixer of separate **soundtracks** into a single master track that will be transferred onto the film print together with the image track to which it is synchronized.

mobile frame: A property of a **shot** in which the camera itself moves or the borders of the image are altered by a change in the **focal length** of the **camera lens.**

mockumentary: A film that uses a **documentary** style and structure to present and stage fictional (sometimes ludicrous) subjects.

modernism: An artistic movement in painting, music, design, architecture, and literature of the 1920s that rendered a fragmented vision of human subjectivity through strategies such as the foregrounding of style, experiments with space and time, and open-ended **narratives.**

modernity: A term designating the period of history stretching from the end of the medieval era to the present, as well as the period's attitude of confidence in progress and science centered on the human capacity to shape history.

montage: The French word for "editing." It can be used to signify any joining of images, but it has come to indicate a style that emphasizes the breaks and contrasts between images joined by a **cut**, following Soviet silent-era filmmakers' use of the term; also designates rapid **sequences** in Hollywood films used for descriptive purposes or to show the rapid passage of time. *Intellectual montage* was defined by Sergei Eisenstein as an intentional juxtaposition of two images in order to generate ideas. See **dialectical montage** and **disjunctive editing.**

motion capture technology: A special effects technology used to incorporate an **actor's** physical features into a computer-generated character.

movement editing: An **editing** technique through which the direction and **pace** of actions, gestures, and other movements are linked with corresponding or contrasting movements in one or more other **shots.**

movie palaces: Lavish movie theaters built between the 1920s and 1940s with ornate architecture and sumptuous seating for thousands.

multiple narrations: Found in films that use several different **narrative** perspectives for a single **story** or for different stories in a movie that loosely fits these perspectives together.

multiplex: A movie theater complex with many screens. Most are found in suburbs or small towns, and many are connected to malls.

musical: A genre popular since the introduction of **synchronous sound** that typically features **characters** who act out and express their emotions through song and dance; **plots** that are interrupted or moved forward by musical numbers; and spectacular **sets** and **settings.**

music supervisor: The individual who selects and secures the rights for songs to be used in films.

narration: The telling of a **story** or description of a situation; the emotional, physical, or intellectual perspective through which the **characters**, events, and action of the **plot** are conveyed. In film, narration is most explicit when provided as asynchronous verbal commentary on the action or images, but it can also designate the storytelling function of the camera, the **editing**, and verbal and other **soundtracks.**

narrative: A story told by a **narrator** or conveyed by a narrational **point of view**; see **plot.**

narrative analysis: A formal topic that concentrates on the **story** and its construction.

narrative frame: A context or person positioned outside the principal **narrative** of a film, such as bracketing **scenes** in which a **character** in the **story's** present begins to relate events of the past and later concludes her or his tale.

narrative frequency: How often certain **plot** elements are repeated.

narratology: The study of **narrative** forms, encompassing stories of all kinds, including films. From Russian narratology are derived the terms *fabula* (story), all the events included in a tale or imagined by the reader or viewer in the order in which they are assumed to have occurred, and *syuzhet* (**plot**), the ordering of narrative events in the particular narrative.

narrator: A **character** or other person whose voice and perspective describe the action of a film, either in **voiceover** or through strict limitation of what is shown by a particular point of view.

natural lighting: Light derived from a natural source in a **scene** or **setting**, such as the illumination of the daylight sun or firelight.

negative cutter: The individual who conforms the negative of the film to the **final cut.** Release prints are then struck from the negative.

New German cinema: A film movement launched in West Germany in 1962, when a group of young filmmakers declared a new agenda for German film in a film festival document called the Oberhausen Manifesto. These films were known for their confrontation with Germany's Nazi and postwar past and their emphasis on the distinctive, often maverick, visions of **directors** whose creativity earned the movement the designation *Autorenfilm* within Germany.

new media: A term used in both information science and communications as well as the arts to refer to an array of technologies, including the Internet, digital technologies, video-game consoles, cell phones, and wireless devices, and the applications and imaginative creations they support.

niche market: A term referring to a segment of the audience with specialized tastes, which Hollywood increasingly has come to recognize as lucrative and to target with films and **marketing.**

nickelodeons: Early movie theaters, typically converted storefront or arcade spaces, where short films were shown continuously for a five-cent admission price to audiences passing in and out. They were prominent until the rise of the **feature film** in the 1910s demanded more comfortable settings.

nitrate: The highly flammable chemical base of 35mm **film stock** used until 1951.

nondiegetic insert: An **insert** that depicts an action, object, or title originating outside of the space and time of the **narrative** world.

nondiegetic sound: Sound that does not have an identifiable source in the **characters'** world and that consequently the characters cannot hear; see **diegetic sound** and **semidiegetic sound**.

nonfiction films: Films presenting (presumed) factual descriptions of actual events, persons, or places, rather than their fictional, or invented, re-creation.

non-narrative films: Films organized in a variety of ways besides storytelling; they employ organizational forms such as associations, lists, repetitions, or contrasts.

objective point of view: A point of view that does not associate the perspective of the camera with that of a specific character.

offscreen sound: A term used to distinguish **diegetic sounds** related to the action but whose source is not visible on the screen.

offscreen space: The implied space outside the boundaries of the film frame.

omniscient narration: Narration that presents all elements of the **plot**, exceeding the perspective of any one **character**; see also **third-person narration**.

180-degree rule: A central convention of **continuity editing** that restricts possible camera setups to the 180-degree area on one side of an imaginary line (the **axis of action**) drawn between the **characters** or figures of a **scene**. If the camera were to cross the line to film from within the 180-degree field on the other side, onscreen figure positions would be reversed.

onscreen sound: Sound with a visible onscreen source, such as when dialogue appears to come directly from the speaker's moving lips.

onscreen space: Space visible within the frame of the image.

optical effect: Special effects produced with the use of an optical printer, including visual transitions between **shots** such as **dissolves**, **fade-outs**, and **wipes**, or **process shots** that combine figures and backgrounds through the use of **matte shots**.

optical printer: The photographic equipment used by technicians to create **optical effects** in films by duplicating the already exposed image onto new **film stock** and altering the **lighting** or adding additional components.

optical sound recording: A sound recording process that converts sound waves into electrical impulses that then control how a light beam is projected onto film. The process enables a **soundtrack** to be recorded alongside the image for simultaneous projection.

orphan films: Films that have been abandoned by their owners or copyright holders, or have otherwise been neglected. This category can include everything from amateur films, training films, and **documentaries** to censored materials, commercials, and newsreels.

orthochromatic: A property of black-and-white **film stock** used in the 1920s, sensitive to greens and blues but registering red light as black.

overhead shot: A **shot** that depicts the action from above, generally looking directly down on the subject; the camera may be mounted on a crane.

overlapping dialogue: Mixing two or more **characters'** speech to imitate the rhythm of speech; the term may also refer to dialogue that overlaps two **scenes** to effect a transition between them.

overlapping editing: An edited **sequence** that presents two **shots** of the same action; because this technique violates continuity, it is rarely used.

pace: The tempo at which the film seems to move. It is determined by the **duration** of individual **shots** and the style of **editing**, as well as by other elements of **cinematography** and **mise-en-scène** and the overall rhythm and flow of the film's action.

package-unit approach: An approach to film **production** established in the mid-1950s whereby the agent, **producer**, and **casting director** assembled a script, stars, and other major personnel as a key first step in a major production.

pan: A left or right rotation of the camera, whose tripod or mount remains in a fixed position that produces a horizontal movement onscreen.

pan-and-scan process: The process used to transfer a **widescreen**-format film to the standard television **aspect ratio**. A computer-controlled scanner determines the most important action in the image, and then crops peripheral action and space or presents the original frame as two separate images.

panchromatic: A property of a black-and-white **film stock** introduced in the 1920s that responds to a full spectrum of colors, rendering them as shades of gray, for a more nuanced and realistic image.

parallel editing: An editing technique that alternates between two or more strands of action in separate locations, often presented as occurring simultaneously; see **crosscutting**.

parallelism: An instance in which the **soundtrack** reinforces the image, such as synchronized dialogue or sound effects or a **voiceover** that is consistent with what is displayed onscreen; see **counterpoint**.

performance: An **actor's** use of language, physical expression, and gesture to bring a **character** to life and to communicate important dimensions of that character to the audience.

periodization: A method of organizing film history by groups of years defined by historical events and/or during which movies share thematic and stylistic concerns.

personal or **subjective documentaries:** Documentary formats that emphasize the personal perspective or involvement of the filmmaker, often making the films resemble autobiographies or diaries.

perspective: The manner in which the distance and spatial relationships among objects are represented on a two-dimensional surface. In painting, parallel and converging lines were used to give the illusion of distance and depth; in film, perspective is manipulated by changes in the **focal length** of **camera lenses.**

physical horror film: A subgenre of the **horror film** that features graphic violence.

physical melodrama: A subgenre of the **melodrama** that focuses on the physical plight and material conditions that repress or control the **protagonist's** desires and emotions.

piracy: The unauthorized duplication and circulation of copyrighted material.

pixilation: A type of **animation** that employs **stop-motion photography** (or instead simply cuts out images from a continuous piece of filmed action) to transform the movement of human figures into rapid jerky gestures.

platforming: The **distribution** strategy of releasing a film in gradually widening markets and theaters so that it slowly builds its reputation and momentum through reviews and word of mouth.

plot: The **narrative** ordering of the events of the **story** as they appear in the actual work, selected and arranged according to particular temporal, spatial, generic, causal, or other patterns; in **narratology,** also known by the Russian word *syuzhet.*

point of view: The position from which a person, an event, or an object is seen or filmed; in **narrative** form, the perspective through which events are narrated.

point-of-view (POV) shot: A subjective **shot** that reproduces a **character's** optical **point of view,** often preceded and/or followed by shots of the character looking.

political western: A more contemporary and critical **subgenre** of the **western,** this subgenre tends to foreground the ideology and the politics that have always informed the western.

postclassical narrative: A term used to characterize cinema after the decline of the **studio system** around 1960.

postmodernism: An artistic style in architecture, art, literature, music, and film that incorporates fragments of or references to other styles; or the cultural period in which political, cultural, and economic shifts engendered challenges to the tenets of **modernism,** including its belief in the possibility of critiquing the world through art, the division of high and low culture, and the genius and independent identity of the artist.

postproduction: The period in the filmmaking process that occurs after **principal photography** has been completed and usually consisting of **editing,** sound, and **special effects** work.

postproduction sound: Sound recorded and added to a film in the **postproduction** phase.

poststructuralism: An intellectual development that came after **structuralism** and in some sense supplanted it, calling into question the rational methodology and fixed definitions that structuralists bring to their various objects of study.

postsynchronous sound: Sound recorded after the actual filming and then synchronized with onscreen sources.

premiere: A red carpet event celebrating the opening night of a film.

preproduction: The phase when a film project is in development, involving preparing the script, financing the project, casting, hiring crew, and securing locations.

primary research sources: These sources have a direct and close relationship with the original film, such as a DVD. Some of these materials are readily available in libraries, including the many classic scripts now published as books; others, such as 16mm films, can be far more difficult to locate, except in film archives.

principal photography: The majority of footage filmed for a project; takes place during **production** phase.

process shot: A special effect that combines two or more images as a single **shot,** such as filming an **actor** in front of a projected background.

producer: The person or persons responsible for steering and monitoring each step of a film project, especially the financial aspects, from development to **postproduction** and a **distribution** deal.

production: The industrial stages that contribute to the making of a finished movie, from the financing and scripting of a film to its final edit; more specifically, the actual shooting of a film after **preproduction** and before **postproduction.**

production designer: The person in charge of the film's overall look.

production sound mixer: The sound engineer on the production **set**; also called a *sound recordist.*

production values: An evaluative term about the quality of the film images and sounds that reflects the investment expenses.

promotion: The aspect of the movie industry through which audiences are exposed to and encouraged to see a particular film; promotion includes advertisements, **trailers,** publicity appearances, and product **tie-ins.**

prop: An object that functions as a part of the **set** or as a tool used by the **actors.**

propaganda films: Political documentaries that visibly support, and intend to sway viewers toward, a particular social or political issue or group.

prosthetics: Artificial facial features or body parts used to alter actors' appearances.

protagonists: Individuals identified as the positive forces in a film; see antagonists.

psychoanalysis: The therapeutic method innovated by Sigmund Freud based on his attribution of unconscious motives to human actions, desires, and symptoms; theoretical tenets developed by literary and film critics to facilitate the cultural study of texts and the interaction between viewers and texts.

psychological horror film: A subgenre of the horror film that locates the dangers and distortions that threaten normal life within the mind.

race movies: Early-twentieth-century films that featured all–African American casts and circulated to African American audiences in the North and South.

rack focus (or pulled focus): A dramatic change in focus from one object to another.

reaction shot: A shot that depicts a character's response to something shown in a previous shot.

realism: An artwork's truthful picture of a society, person, or some other dimension of everyday life; an artistic movement that aims to achieve verisimilitude.

reception: The process through which individual viewers or groups make sense of a film.

reception theory: A theoretical approach to the ways different kinds of audiences regard different kinds of films.

reenactment: Re-creating presumably real events within the context of a documentary.

reestablishing shot: A shot during an edited sequence that returns to an establishing shot to restore a seemingly "objective" view to the spectator.

reflected sound: Recorded sound that is captured as it bounces from the walls and sets. It is usually used to give a sense of space; opposed to direct sound.

reflexive narration: A mode of narration that calls attention to the narrative point of view of the story in order to complicate or subvert its own narrative authority as an objective perspective on the world.

reflexivity: Referencing the film's own process of storytelling or cinematic technique.

reframing: The process of moving the frame from one position to another within a single continuous shot.

restricted narration: A narrative in which our knowledge is limited to that of a particular character.

retrospective plot: A plot that tells of past events from the perspective of the present or future.

rhythmic editing: The organization of editing according to different paces or tempos determined by how quickly cuts are made.

road movie: A film genre that depicts characters on a journey, usually following a linear chronology.

romantic comedy: A subgenre of comedy in which humor takes second place to the happy ending, typically focusing on the emotional attraction of a couple in a lighthearted way.

room tone: The aural properties of a location that are recorded and then mixed in with dialogue and other tracks to achieve a more realistic sound.

rotoscoping: A technique using recorded real figures and action as a basis for painting individual animation frames digitally.

rough cut: The initial edited version of a movie in which an editor approximates the finished film.

safety film: Acetate-based film stock that replaced the highly flammable nitrate film base in 1952.

saturation booking: The distribution strategy of releasing a film simultaneously in as many locations as possible, widely implemented with the advent of the blockbuster in the 1970s. Also called *saturated release.*

scale: Determined by the distance of the camera from its subject.

scene: One or more shots that depict a continuous space and time.

scenics: Early nonfiction films that offered exotic or remarkable images of nature or foreign lands.

screenplay: The text from which a movie is made, including dialogue and information about action, settings, etc., as well as shots and transitions; developed from a treatment. Also known as a *script.*

screenwriter: A writer of a film's screenplay; the screenwriter may begin with a treatment and develop the plot structure and dialogue over the span of several versions; also called a *scriptwriter.*

screwball comedy: A comic subgenre of the 1930s and 1940s known for fast talking and unpredictable action.

script doctor: An uncredited individual called in to do rewrites on a screenplay.

segmentation: The process of dividing a film into large narrative units for the purposes of analysis.

selects: The director's chosen takes to use in editing a scene.

semidiegetic sound: Sound that is neither strictly diegetic nor nondiegetic, such as certain voiceovers that can be construed as the thoughts of a character and thus as arising from the story world; also known as *internal diegetic sound.*

semiotics: The study of signs and signification; posits that meaning is constructed and communicated through the selection, ordering, and interpretation of signs and sign systems, including words, gestures, images, symbols, or virtually anything that can be meaningfully codified. Also called *semiology*.

sequence: Any number of **shots** or **scenes** that are unified as a coherent action or an identifiable motif, regardless of changes in space and time.

sequence shot: A **shot** in which an entire **scene** is played out in one continuous **take**.

set: Strictly speaking, a constructed **setting**, often on a studio **soundstage**, but both the setting and the set can combine natural and constructed elements.

set designer: The individual responsible for supervising the conception and construction of movie **sets**.

set lighting: The distribution of an evenly diffused illumination through a **scene** as a kind of **lighting** base.

setting: A fictional or real place where the action and events of the film occur.

shallow focus: A **shot** in which only a narrow range of the field is in focus.

shock cut: A **cut** that juxtaposes two images whose dramatic difference aims to create a jarring visual effect.

shooting ratio: The relationship between the overall amount or length of film shot and the amount used in the finished project.

shot: A continuous **point of view** (or continuously exposed piece of film) that may move forward or backward, up or down, but not change, break, or cut to another point of view or image.

shot/reverse shot: An **editing** pattern that begins with a **shot** of one **character** taken from an angle at one end of the **axis of action**, follows with a shot of the second character from the "reverse" angle at the other end of the line, and continues back and forth through the **sequence**; often used in conversations; also called *shot/countershot*.

Showscan: A projection system, developed by Douglas Trumbull and marketed in 1983, that projects at sixty frames per second (rather than twenty-four frames) and creates remarkably dense and detailed images.

sidelighting: Used to illuminate the subject from the side.

sign: Term used in **semiotics** for something that signifies something else, whether the connection is causal, conventional, or based on resemblance. As defined by Ferdinand de Saussure, a sign is composed of a *signifier*, the spoken or written word, picture, or gesture, and a *signified*, the mental concept it evokes.

slapstick comedy: Films known for physical humor and stunts; some of the first films were slapstick comedies.

slasher films: A subgenre of contemporary **horror films** depicting serial killers, often considered to have originated with *Psycho* (1960).

slow motion: A cinematic special effect that makes the action move at unrealistic speeds, achieved by filming the action slower than normal and then projecting it at standard speeds; see **fast motion**.

social documentaries: **Documentaries** that examine and present both familiar and unfamiliar peoples and cultures in a social context, with an emphasis on authenticity and discovery in their representations.

social melodrama: A subgenre of the **melodrama** that extends its reach to include larger historical, community, and economic issues.

soft lighting: Diffused, low-contrast **lighting** that reduces or eliminates hard edges and shadows and can be more flattering when filming people.

sound bridge: The term for sound carried over a picture transition, or a sound belonging to the coming **scene** playing before the image changes.

sound continuity: The range of scoring, **sound recording**, mixing, and playback processes that strive for the unification of film meaning and experience by subordinating sound to the aims of the **narrative**.

sound designer: The individual responsible for planning and directing the overall sound of a film through to the final **mix**.

sound editing: Combining music, dialogue, and effects tracks to interact with the image track in order to create rhythmic relationships, establish connections between sound and onscreen source, and smooth or mark transitions. Performed by a *sound editor*.

sound mixing: An important stage in the **postproduction** of a film that takes place after the image track, including the **credits**, is complete; the process by which all the elements of the **soundtrack**, including music, effects, and dialogue, are combined and adjusted; also called *re-recording*.

sound perspective: The apparent location and distance of a sound source.

sound recording: The recording of dialogue and other sound that takes place simultaneously with the filming of a **scene**.

sound reproduction: Sound playback during a film's **exhibition**.

soundstage: A large soundproofed building designed to construct and move **sets** and **props** and effectively capture sound and dialogue during filming.

soundtrack: Audio recorded to synchronize with a moving image, including dialogue, music, and sound effects, as well as the physical portion of the film used for recorded sound.

source music: Diegetic music; music whose source is visible onscreen.

special effects: A variety of illusions created during the filmmaking process through mechanical means, such as the building of models, or on-set explosions, or with the camera, such as slow motion, color filters, process shots, and matte shots. Sometimes used interchangeably with visual effects, which more often denotes digital effects added in postproduction.

spectatorship: The process of film viewing; the conscious and unconscious interaction of viewers and films as a topic of interest to film theorists.

spotting: The process of determining where music and effects will be added to a film.

star system: Employing one or more well-known actors (*stars*) whose appearance in movies builds on audience expectations and promotes the movie. In a studio system or a national film industry, the star system will often have a specific economic organization of contracts, publicity, and vehicles.

Steadicam: A camera stabilization system introduced in 1976 that allows a camera operator to film a continuous and steady shot without losing the freedom of movement afforded by the handheld camera.

stereotype: A character type that simplifies and standardizes perceptions that one group holds about another, often less numerous, powerful, or privileged group.

stinger: Sound that forces the audience to notice the significance of something onscreen, such as the ominous chord struck when the villain's presence is made known.

stop-motion photography: A process that records inanimate objects or actual human figures in separate frames and then synthesizes them on film to create the illusion of motion and action.

story: The subject matter or raw material of a narrative, or our reconstruction of the events of a narrative based on what is explicitly shown and ordered in the plot.

structural film: An experimental film movement that emerged in North America in the 1960s with filmmakers like Hollis Frampton and Michael Snow in which films followed a predetermined structure; developed into *structural/materialist* film in the United Kingdom in the 1970s.

structuralism: Derived from linguistics and anthropology, an approach to literary and filmic narratives that looks for common structures rather than originality.

studio system: The industrial practices of the large production (and, until 1948, distribution) companies responsible for the kinds and quality of movies made in Hollywood or other film industries. During the Hollywood *studio era* extending from the late 1920s to the 1950s, the five major studios were MGM, Paramount, RKO, Twentieth Century Fox, and Warner Bros.

stylistic analysis: Offers a wide variety of topics that engage the formal arrangements of image and sound, such as shot composition, editing, and the use of sound.

subgenre: A specialized genre that defines a specific, more limited version of a more general genre, often by refining it with an adjective, such as the spaghetti western or slapstick comedy.

subjective point of view: A point of view that re-creates the perspective of a character.

supernatural horror film: A subgenre of the horror film that features a spiritual evil that disrupts the human realm.

supporting actors: Actors who play secondary characters in a film, serving as foils or companions to the central characters.

surrealist cinema: One of the most influential of the avant-garde movements, surrealist films confronted middle-class assumptions about normality using the powers of film to manipulate time, space, and material objects according to a dreamlike logic.

suture: A term that refers to our sense of being inserted in a specific place in the film, from which to look at its fictional world through editing and point of view.

synchronous sound: Sound that is recorded during a scene or that is synchronized with the filmed images; as used by scholar Siegfried Kracauer, a term that describes sound that has a visible onscreen source, such as moving lips; also referred to as onscreen sound.

syntagma: A term derived from linguistics for sequential units of meaning and used by Christian Metz to refer to the smallest combinable narrative units of film—sequences, scenes, and autonomous shots.

take: A single filmed version of a shot during production or a single shot onscreen.

talking heads: An on-camera interview that typically shows the speaker from the shoulders up, hence "talking head."

Technicolor: Color processing that uses three strips of film to transfer colors directly onto a single image; developed between 1926 and 1932.

telephoto lens: A lens with a focal length of at least 75mm, capable of magnifying and flattening distant objects; see also zoom lens.

theatrical musical: A subgenre of the musical that is set in a theatrical milieu.

theatrical trailer: A promotional preview of an upcoming release presented before the main feature or as a television commercial.

thesis statement: A short statement (often a single sentence) that succinctly describes and anticipates each stage of an essay's argument. A *working thesis* is a rough version of a thesis used to draft an essay.

Third Cinema: A term coined in the late 1960s in Latin America to echo the phrase and concept "Third World," Third Cinema opposed commercial and auteurist cinemas with a political, populist aesthetic and united films from a number of countries and contexts.

third-person narration: A narration that assumes an objective and detached stance vis-à-vis the **plot** and **characters**, describing events from outside the **story**.

30-degree rule: A **cinematography** and **editing** rule that specifies that a **shot** should only be followed by another shot taken from a position greater than 30 degrees from that of the first.

3-D modeling: A computer imaging technique that uses software to create visual representations from three-dimensional models.

three-point lighting: A lighting technique common in Hollywood that combines **key lighting**, **fill lighting**, and **backlighting** to blend the distribution of light in a **scene**.

tie-ins: Ancillary products that advertise and promote a movie, such as T-shirts, CD **soundtracks**, toys, and other gimmicks made available at stores and restaurants.

tilt shot: An upward or downward rotation of the camera, whose tripod or mount remains in a fixed position, producing a vertical movement onscreen.

titles: Generally the opening **sequence** of a film, including the film's title and the names of the main **actors**, **director**, **producers**, **screenwriter**, and **cinematographer**.

tone: The shading, intensification, or saturation of colors (such as metallic blues, soft greens, or deep reds) in order to sharpen, mute, or balance them for certain effects.

topicals: Early films that captured or sometimes re-created historical or newsworthy events.

topic sentence: Usually the first sentence of a paragraph that announces the central idea around which all other sentences within the paragraph cohere.

top lighting: Used to illuminate the subject from above.

tracking shot: A **shot** that changes the position of the **point of view** by moving forward, backward, or around the subject, usually on tracks that have been constructed in advance (see **dolly shot**); also called a *traveling shot*.

trailer: A form of promotional advertising that previews edited images and **scenes** from a film in theaters before the main **feature film** or on a television commercial or Web site.

treatment: A succinct description of the content of a film written before the **screenplay** or *script*.

two-shot: A shot depicting two **characters**.

underground film: Nonmainstream film, associated particularly with the **experimental film** culture of 1960s and 1970s New York and San Francisco, characterized by the intersection of **performance** and sexual subcultures.

underlighting: Used to illuminate the subject from below.

underscoring: A film's background music; contrasts with **source music**.

unit production manager: A member of a film's production team responsible for reporting and managing the details of receipts and purchases.

unreliable narration: A type of **narration** that raises questions about the truth of the **story** being told; also called *manipulative narration*.

verisimilitude: The quality of fictional representation that allows readers or viewers to accept a constructed world, its events, its **characters**, and their actions as plausible; literally "having the appearance of truth."

vertical integration: The industrial organization of the major studios in the 1930s and 1940s, in which film **distribution** was controlled through production companies' ownership of theater chains.

video: Electronic medium that captures, records, stores, displays, and transmits moving images.

video on demand (VOD): The distribution of films through cable or online services that allow consumers to purchase and view movies on computers and home video screens.

viral marketing: A phenomenon in which consumers pass along a **marketing** message through word of mouth, electronic messaging, or other means.

visible editing: See disjunctive editing.

visual effects: Special effects created in **postproduction** though digital imaging.

voice-off: A voice that originates from a speaker who can be inferred to be present in the **scene** but who is not visible onscreen.

voiceover: A voice whose source is neither visible in the frame nor implied to be offscreen; it typically narrates the film's images, such as in a **flashback** or the commentary in a **documentary** film.

walla: A nonsense word spoken by extras in a film to approximate the sound of a crowd during sound dubbing.

western: A film **genre** set in the American West, typically featuring rugged, independent male **characters** on a quest or dramatizing frontier life.

wide-angle lens: A lens with a short **focal length** (typically less than 35mm) that allows **cinematographers** to explore a **depth of field** that can simultaneously show foreground and background objects or events in focus.

wide release: The premiere of a movie at many locations simultaneously, sometimes on as many as 1,500 to 2,000 screens nationally.

widescreen processes: Any of a number of systems introduced in the 1950s that widened the **aspect ratio** and the dimensions of the movie screen.

widescreen ratio: The wider, rectangular **aspect ratio** of typically 1.85:1 or 2.35:1; see **academy ratio**.

window: The period of time when a film is in theaters before it is shown on television or the Internet or distributed on DVD.

wipe: A transition used to join two **shots** by moving a vertical, horizontal, or sometimes diagonal line across one image to replace it with a second image that follows the line across the frame.

women's picture: A category of films produced in the 1930s–1950s, featuring female stars in romances or **melodramas** and marketed primarily to women.

Works Cited: List of sources cited in an essay, positioned on a separate page immediately after the last page of the essay text.

Works Consulted: Optional list of sources that have been consulted but not cited in the text or notes of an essay; appears on a separate page after the **Works Cited** list.

zoom-in: The act of changing the lens's **focal length** to narrow the field of view of a distant object, magnifying and **reframing** it, often in **close-up**, while the camera remains stationary; see **zoom-out**.

zoom lens: A lens with variable **focal length**.

zoom-out: Reversing the action of a **zoom-in**, so that objects that appear close initially are distanced and **reframed** as small figures.

The Next Level: Additional Sources

Introduction

Mayne, Judith. *Cinema and Spectatorship*. New York: Routledge, 1993. This excellent book summarizes and rethinks models of identification at the movies to develop more varied and dynamic descriptions that account for different audience responses.

Plantinga, Carl. *Moving Viewers: American Film and the Spectator's Experience*. Berkeley: Univ. of California Press, 2009. A wide-ranging study of the viewing experience focused on mainstream Hollywood film; it examines film viewing from different angles, including cognitive, philosophical, and social perspectives.

Williams, Linda, ed. *Viewing Positions: Ways of Seeing Film*. New Brunswick, NJ: Rutgers Univ. Press, 1995. This varied collection of essays on spectatorship at the movies presents critical discussions addressing a range of viewing experiences, from early cinema to postmodern malls.

Chapter 1

Acland, Charles R. *Screen Traffic: Movies, Multiplexes, and Global Culture*. Durham, NC: Duke Univ. Press, 2003. Examining the changes in the movie business since the mid-1980s, this book explores the new global reach of the cinema today and the changing production, distribution, and exhibition structures of business enmeshed in the economics of megaplexes, pay-per-view distribution, and accelerating viewing patterns.

Gomery, Douglas. *Shared Pleasures: A History of Movie Presentation in the United States*. Madison: Univ. of Wisconsin Press, 1992. A well-researched and discriminating history of the many changes in film exhibition from 1895 to 1990, this study provides a wealth of detail about the evolution of distribution of U.S. movies.

Lukk, Tiiu. *Movie Marketing: Opening the Picture and Giving It Legs*. Los Angeles: Silman-St. James, 1997. Less a scholarly work than a series of case studies, this book concentrates on a variety of contemporary movies—from *Four Weddings and a Funeral* to *Mrs. Doubtfire*—and describes a range of different marketing and promotion strategies.

Stokes, Melvyn, and Richard Maltby. *American Movie Audiences: From the Turn of the Century to the Early Sound Era*. London: BFI, 1999. This excellent collection of essays maps the remarkable diversity of moviegoing patterns in the first part of the twentieth century. Arguing the diverse social compositions of early film audiences, the book presents convincing evidence of those audiences often resisting the homogenization and standardization being promoted by a corporate Hollywood.

Vachon, Christine, with Austin Bunn. *A Killer Life: How an Independent Producer Survives Deals and Disasters in Hollywood and Beyond*. New York: Simon & Schuster, 2006. A lively account of the production process by a founder of the New York–based independent film company Killer Films, which produced such innovative films as *Boys Don't Cry* and *I'm Not There*.

Chapter 2

Affron, Charles and Mirella. *Sets in Motion: Art Direction and Film Narrative*. New Brunswick, NJ: Rutgers Univ. Press, 1995. Concentrating on the work of set designers, this study examines a number of films to demonstrate how sets do far more than embellish a film, often becoming the center of its meaning.

Brewster, Ben, and Lea Jacobs. *Theatre to Cinema: Stage Pictorialism and the Early Feature Film*. Oxford: Oxford Univ. Press, 1997. The book is a careful, scholarly investigation of the transition from stage to screen in early film history.

Dyer, Richard. *Stars*. Rev. ed. London: BFI, 1998. A landmark study of the many ways that stars organize and focus a reading of film, this work explores both their onscreen presence and their offscreen activities.

Gaines, Jane M., and Charlotte Herzog, eds. *Fabrications: Costume and the Female Body*. London: Routledge, 1990. This collection of essays addresses the role of costume and costume design in defining film narrative, shaping female star images, and appealing to women audiences.

Gibbs, John. *Mise-en-Scène: Film Style and Interpretation*. New York: Columbia Univ. Press, 2002. Devoted exclusively to the importance of mise-en-scène, this book is a historical survey of this critical dimension of film and a detailed examination of its aesthetic powers.

Naremore, James. *Acting in the Cinema*. Berkeley: Univ. of California Press, 1988. A lucid introduction and survey of forms and styles of film acting that also ventures into theoretical and ideological issues underpinning different acting strategies.

Neumann, Dietrich. *Film Architecture: Set Designs from* Metropolis *to* Blade Runner. Munich: Prestel Art Press, 1999. This book that accompanied an art exhibition is a lavishly illustrated study of modernist architecture and urbanism's influence on set design.

Williams, Christopher. *Realism and the Cinema*. London: Routledge, 1980. A wide-ranging examination of the arguments about film realism, this book also looks at different filmic practices of realism and the ideological stakes implicit in those movies.

Chapter 3

Belton, John. *Widescreen Cinema*. Cambridge, MA: Harvard Univ. Press, 1992. This book examines the technical, economic, social, and aesthetic forces that have been a part of widescreen cinema since 1896, shaping and reshaping the film image to respond to different cultures and audiences.

Berger, John. *Ways of Seeing.* Harmondsworth: Penguin, 1972. Small and well illustrated, Berger's book offers a remarkably broad perspective on how images of all kinds—from paintings to television advertisements—are informed by powerful historical and cultural values.

Manovich, Lev. *The Language of New Media.* Cambridge, MA: MIT Press, 2001. This book presents an influential theory of the philosophy, technology, and impact of digital cinema.

Pierson, Michele. *Special Effects: Still in Search of Wonder.* New York: Columbia Univ. Press, 2002. Pierson's work is an important contribution to theorizing this persistent and ever more dominant dimension of the moving image.

Schaefer, Dennis, and Larry Salvato. *Masters of Light: Conversations with Contemporary Cinematographers.* Berkeley: Univ. of California Press, 1984. Fascinating discussions with acclaimed directors of photography give insight into their art and craft.

Smoodin, Eric. *Animation Culture: Hollywood Cartoons from the Sound Era.* New Brunswick, NJ: Rutgers Univ. Press, 1993. This book offers an examination of not only the technical strategies in film animation (from 1930 to 1960), but also the complex political and ideological agendas that often drove those strategies.

Winston, Brian. *Technologies of Seeing.* London: BFI, 1997. A critical review of the development of the technological image—from 16mm film to HDTV to holography—this study emphasizes the logic behind these changes and how they engage other historical and social shifts.

Chapter 4

Bazin, André. *What Is Cinema?* Edited and translated by Hugh Gray. 2 vols. Berkeley: Univ. of California Press, 2005. Originally published in 1967. This translation of Bazin's own selection of critical essays on the language of cinema, published posthumously, includes his classic theorizations of montage and the long take. This new edition includes forewords by Bazin scholar Dudley Andrew.

Bordwell, David. *The Way Hollywood Tells It: Story and Style in Modern Movies.* Berkeley: Univ. of California Press, 2006. An examination of Hollywood films since the 1960s, this study looks at the changes in narrative style to argue, among other issues, that continuity editing has evolved dimensions of what the author calls "intensified continuity."

Burch, Noel. *Theory of Film Practice.* Translated by Helen Lane. Princeton: Princeton Univ. Press, 1981. In this influential study originally published in 1973, a contemporary French theorist and filmmaker considers the construction of space and time in Hollywood and avant-garde films.

Dancyger, Ken. *The Technique of Film and Video Editing: Theory and Practice.* 4th ed. Boston: Focal Press, 1997. Aimed at directors and focusing on the history, theory, and practice of film editing, this highly readable book is designed as an update to Karel Reisz's 1953 classic, *The Technique of Film Editing,* and its 1968 revision by Gavin Miller.

Eisenstein, Sergei. *The Eisenstein Reader.* Edited by Richard Taylor. London: BFI, 1998. A collection of shorter writings by the Soviet filmmaker that illuminate his film practice and his theories of montage, this work covers his entire career from 1923 to 1947.

Figgis, Mike. *Digital Filmmaking.* London: Faber & Faber, 2007. This book is a guide to the dramatic changes and opportunities ushered in by the digital revolution and non-linear editing, written by a filmmaker who took early and creative advantage of that revolution.

Metz, Christian. *Language and Cinema.* The Hague: Mouton de Gruyter, 1974. Outlining the field of film semiotics in this dense but influential work, Metz presents his framework for analyzing the syntagmatic components of the narrative film (the *grand syntagmatique*). He sees editing as being crucial to supporting the comparison of film with language via the definition of a grammar of film.

Oldham, Gabriella. *First Cut: Conversations with Film Editors.* Berkeley: Univ. of California Press, 1992. Editors share secrets of their craft.

Chapter 5

Altman, Richard, ed. *Sound Theory, Sound Practice.* New York: Routledge, 1992. This anthology addresses the under-theorizing of film sound and includes perspectives on the history of film sound and on non-narrative film sound.

Chion, Michel. *Audio-Vision: Sound on Screen.* Edited and translated by Claudia Gorbman. Foreword by Walter Murch. New York: Columbia Univ. Press, 1990. This translated work by a leading theorist of film sound stresses the inseparability of sound and image and introduces original terminology to explore the experience more precisely.

Dickinson, Kay, ed. *Movie Music: The Film Reader.* London: Routledge, 2003. This collection of essays includes a classic statement by Theodor Adorno and Hans Eisler as well as discussions of animation, the record industry, and formal analysis of music.

Donnelly, Kevin. *The Spectre of Sound: Music in Film and Television.* London: BFI, 2005. This study examines the use of music in both films and television to elicit emotional reactions; it explores the use of pop music, horror music, orchestral music, and other types of film music.

Eisenstein, Sergei, Vsevolod Pudovkin, and Grifore Alexandrov. "Statement on Sound." In *The Eisenstein Reader,* edited by Richard Taylor, pp. 80–81. London: BFI, 1998. Originally published in 1928, this manifesto by Soviet montage theorists anticipates the creative uses of sound in film.

Gorbman, Claudia. *Unheard Melodies: Narrative Film Music.* Bloomington: Indiana Univ. Press, 1987. A thorough examination of how music works in narrative cinema. Drawing on narratology and semiology, this book introduces important theories of film music with extensive examples.

Kozloff, Sarah. *Overhearing Film Dialogue.* Berkeley: Univ. of California Press, 2000. A rare comprehensive study of film dialogue, this book examines the critical neglect of dialogue in American movies. The second part of the book analyzes the distinct use of dialogue in four genres: westerns, screwball comedies, gangster films, and melodramas.

Lastra, James. *Sound Technology and the American Cinema.* New York: Columbia Univ. Press, 2000. Linking practices and rhetoric of film sound in the 1920s and 1930s with nineteenth-century technologies, Lastra demonstrates persistent ways of speaking about the aural dimension and tracks social and sensorial changes wrought by modernity.

O'Brien, Charles. *Cinema's Conversion to Sound: Technology and Film Style in France and the U.S.* Bloomington: Indiana Univ. Press, 2005. This work is an innovative crosscultural analysis of how two different film cultures—those of France and the United States—assimilated the sound revolution in often notably different ways. Unlike traditional studies of sound technology, the book argues less for the common stylistic strategies associated with Hollywood and instead emphasizes the significant role that cultural differences can play in the production of cinematic sound.

Weis, Elisabeth, and John Belton, eds. *Film Sound: Theory and Practice.* New York: Columbia Univ. Press, 1985. A comprehensive anthology covering history, technology, aesthetics, and classical and contemporary sound theory, this work includes a section on practice that comprises essays on the work of directors who have used sound innovatively, from the early sound period to modern Hollywood cinema.

Chapter 6

Altman, Rick. *A Theory of Narrative.* New York: Columbia Univ. Press, 2008. This ambitious study of narrative ranges from the Bible through twentieth-century cinema, debating both theoretical issues about narrative and practical considerations.

Branigan, Edward. *Narrative Comprehension and Film.* New York: Routledge, 1992. Branigan offers an analytical account of the structures of narrative cinema and of how audiences learn to identify and process them.

Elsaesser, Thomas, and Adam Barker, eds. *Early Cinema: Space/Frame/Narrative.* London: BFI, 1990. Representing leading British, American, and European scholars, this collection of essays explores the first twenty years of the cinema, including the exciting multitude of filmic practices and experiments that fashioned early narrative cinema.

Fell, John L. *Film and the Narrative Tradition.* Norman: Univ. of Oklahoma Press, 1974. This collection of essays traces the many different historical and cultural backgrounds of narrative cinema.

Gaines, Jane. *Classical Hollywood Narrative: The Paradigm Wars.* Durham, NC: Duke Univ. Press, 1982. A reinvestigation of the classical Hollywood paradigm, this collection of essays by leading film scholars describes how that paradigm has been challenged by television, new gender relations, and other cultural changes.

Turim, Maureen. *Flashbacks in Film: Memory and History.* New York: Routledge, 1989. This book is a complex theoretical investigation of how flashbacks have structured narratives from silent films to the present.

Chapter 7

Barnouw, Erik. *Documentary: A History of Non-Fiction Film.* 2nd rev. ed. New York: Oxford Univ. Press, 1993. This survey of major twentieth-century documentary films distinguishes kinds of nonfiction films by the rhetorical stances they initiate (such as those of "the explorer," "the prosecutor," and "the guerrilla").

Barsam, Richard M., ed. *Nonfiction Film Theory and Criticism.* New York: Dutton, 1976. One of the first and still most important collections on the aims and distinctions of nonfiction filmmaking, this book features essays by John Grierson, Joris Ivens, and others.

Bruzzi, Stella. *New Documentary: A Critical Introduction.* 2nd ed. London: Routledge, 2006. This book is a serious, polemical, and succinct introduction to practical and theoretical issues regarding documentaries, such as the changing roles of gender, spectatorship, and authorship.

Grant, Keith Barry, and Jeannette Sloniowski. *Documenting the Documentary: Close Readings of Documentary Film and Video.* Detroit: Wayne State Univ. Press, 1998. A collection of individual essays on specific documentary films, ranging from *Nanook of the North* to *Tongues Untied.*

Nichols, Bill. *Blurred Boundaries: Questions of Meaning in Contemporary Culture.* Bloomington: Indiana Univ. Press, 1994. This demanding and insightful investigation explores the "blurred" middle ground between fiction and nonfiction films; its historical scope moves from Sergei Eisenstein's *Strike*, to the infamous Rodney King videotape, to the work of a host of exceptional contemporary filmmakers.

Renov, Michael. *The Subject of Documentary.* Minneapolis: Univ. of Minnesota Press, 2004. Renov's collection of critical essays explores the various fashionings of self through different documentary traditions: from newsreels and autobiographies to domestic ethnographies and new interactive technologies.

Rosenthal, Alan, and John Corner, eds. *New Challenges for Documentary.* 2nd ed. Manchester, England: Manchester Univ. Press, 2005. Thirty-five essays by different authors address six sets of topics: documentary as genre, documentary producers and directors, ethics and aesthetics, documentary and television, representations of history, and docudramas.

Chapter 8

Benjamin, Walter. "The Work of Art in the Age of Mechanical Reproduction." In *Illuminations*, edited by Hannah Arendt. New York: Schocken, 1969. This seminal essay written in Weimar-era Germany discusses how film and photography have transformed the work of art and contemporary ways of seeing.

Gunning, Tom. "The Cinema of Attraction: Early Film, Its Spectator and the Avant-Garde," *Wide Angle* 8.3–4 (1986): 63–70. Important theorization of early cinema's solicitation of the spectator and the implications of such a mode for non-narrative traditions, including the avant-garde.

Hall, Doug, and Sally Jo Fifer, eds. *Illuminating Video: An Essential Guide to Video Art.* New York: Aperture, in association with the Bay Area Video Coalition, 1990. This is an authoritative study of video as an art medium before the advent of digital video.

James, David E. *Allegories of Cinema: American Film in the 1960s.* Princeton: Princeton Univ. Press, 1989. This study contextualizes underground and avant-garde cinema on the political and social movements of the period.

Le Grice, Malcolm. *Abstract Film and Beyond.* Cambridge: MIT Press, 1977. An important experimental filmmaker himself, Le Grice begins by comparing these films to avant-garde paintings and then maps their development from the futurist movement through various post–World War II movements in the United States.

MacDonald, Scott. *A Critical Cinema: Interviews with Independent Filmmakers.* 5 vols. Berkeley: Univ. of California Press, 1988–2006. In this vital series, one of the foremost scholars and advocates of experimental cinema interviews hundreds of filmmakers spanning several generations of the U.S. avant-garde.

Manovich, Lev. *The Language of New Media.* Cambridge: MIT Press, 2001. Provocative and influential theorization of new media and their relation to old media.

Petrolle, Jean, and Virginia Wright Wexman, eds. *Women and Experimental Filmmaking.* Urbana: Univ. of Illinois Press, 2005. An anthology of new writings on filmmakers who are sometimes overshadowed in canonical accounts.

Rees, A. L. *A History of Experimental Film and Video.* London: BFI, 1999. Addressing subjects ranging from Jean Cocteau to Stan Brakhage and contemporary avant-garde video, this is a meticulous, smart, and readable account of twentieth-century experimental film and video.

Renov, Michael, and Erika Suderburg, eds. *Resolutions: Contemporary Video Practices.* Minneapolis: Univ. of Minnesota Press, 1996. A comprehensive anthology of theoretical and historical essays on activist and art video.

Rieser, Martin, and Andrea Zapp. *New Screen Media: Cinema/Art/Narrative.* London: BFI, 2002. Features writings by a wide range of critics, theorists, and artists about the impact of new media forms on narrative and aesthetics.

Sitney, P. Adams. *Visionary Film: The American Avant-Garde, 1943–2000.* 3rd ed. Oxford: Oxford Univ. Press, 2002. This classic text establishing the terminology with which the American avant-garde film and its key filmmakers were discussed for decades. Originally published in 1974, it now includes a new chapter surveying recent developments.

Wees, William C. *Light Moving in Time: Studies in the Visual Aesthetics of Avant-Garde Film.* Berkeley: Univ. of California Press, 1992. Provides accounts of the aesthetics of many of the principal filmmakers of the North American avant-garde.

Chapter 9

Altman, Rick. *Film/Genre.* London: BFI, 1999. A balanced survey of genre theories since Aristotle, this study addresses the importance of film genres both for the industry and for movie audiences, examining the historical variations of genres and their relationship to social life.

Browne, Nick, ed. *Refiguring American Film Genres.* Berkeley: Univ. of California Press, 1999. This collection features articles by many top scholars on film genre and gathers pieces on particular films and genres (including the war film and the jury film) that develop new theoretical stands on film genre.

Clover, Carol. *Men, Women, and Chain-Saws: Gender in the Modern Horror Film.* Princeton: Princeton Univ. Press, 1992. Clover's bold study of the slasher film argues that the "Final Girl" who survives the carnage is a figure of cross-gender identification for male fans.

Gledhill, Christine, ed. *Home Is Where the Heart Is: Studies in Melodrama and the Woman's Film.* London: BFI, 1987. This collection contains essays by some of the field's finest feminist theorists on silent melodrama, women's films of the 1930s and 1940s, and the family melodramas of the 1950s.

Grant, Barry, ed. *Film Genre Reader III.* Austin: Univ. of Texas Press, 2003. An indispensable anthology of essays on film genre, this volume covers a range of theoretical issues and analyzes numerous film genres. Contributors represent a range of traditional and contemporary critical methods.

Kitses, Jim. *Horizons West: Directing the Western from John Ford to Clint Eastwood.* London: BFI, 2004. This new edition of a classic genre study first published in 1969 establishes the western at the center of American film genres and elegantly combines auteurist and genre criticism.

Neale, Steve. *Genre.* London: BFI, 1980. Neale's brief but intellectually provocative account of film genre emphasizes the institutional and textual contract between the movie industry and the audiences that genre films crystallize and require in order to create systems of meaning.

Shatz, Thomas. *Hollywood Genres: Formulas, Filmmaking, and the Studio System.* New York: Random House, 1981. A lucid and carefully organized introduction to how film genre operates as an organizing principle for movies, this work gives special attention to westerns, gangster and hard-boiled detective films, screwball comedies, musicals, and family melodramas.

Chapter 10

Allen, Robert C., and Douglas Gomery. *Film History: Theory and Practice.* New York: Knopf, 1985. A successful combination of theoretical savvy and pragmatics, this study is a rare look at the different ways film histories can be constructed and used to illuminate individual films.

Beauchamp, Cari. *Frances Marion and the Powerful Women of Early Hollywood.* Berkeley: Univ. of California Press, 1997. A lively and readable history of the women screenwriters, producers, and stars active in the early years of Hollywood's influence.

Bordwell, David, Janet Staiger, and Kristin Thompson. *The Classical Hollywood Cinema: Film Style and Mode to 1960.* New York: Columbia Univ. Press, 1985. An extensively researched and detailed exploration of U.S. film history based on industrial standards that, according to the authors, have altered little in sixty years.

Bruno, Giuliana. *Streetwalking on a Ruined Map: Cultural Theory and the City Films of Elvira Notari.* Princeton: Princeton Univ. Press, 1993. Focusing on the fascinating career of a woman producer of early films in Italy, Bruno makes an argument about gender, cities, and the new experiences of space and time offered by the film medium and the institution of cinema in the context of modernity.

Cook, David A. *A History of Narrative Film.* 4th ed. New York: Norton, 2004. Large and exact, this excellent history of world cinema moves from the original to recent movie cultures. A superb source of information and dates that is punctuated by analysis of film masterpieces.

Cripps, Thomas. *Slow Fade to Black: The Negro in American Film, 1900–1942.* New York: Oxford Univ. Press, 1977. A richly detailed social history of the representation of African Americans in U.S. films until World War II that continues in the author's *Making Movies Black* (1993).

Grant, Catherine, and Annette Kuhn. *Screening World Cinema.* London: Routledge, 2006. This anthology of contemporary essays on transnational cinema explores many of the most current theoretical issues (for instance, the relation of modernity to international cinema) and also discusses some of the most important national cinemas to emerge in recent years (such as the Iranian, Chinese, and Latin American cinemas).

Hansen, Miriam. *Babel and Babylon*. Cambridge: Harvard Univ. Press, 1991. Looking at the specific contexts of U.S. silent film reception as well as at such examples as the popularity of Rudolph Valentino, this book argues that audiences found a new public experience of the modern world at the movies.

Harpole, Charles, general ed. *History of American Cinema*. 10 vols. New York: Scribner's, 1990–2002. With each volume edited by a different scholar, this monumental history provides a decade-by-decade compendium of details and facts that map the industrial, social, and stylistic development of American movies.

Hill, John, and Patricia Church Gibson. *World Cinema: Critical Approaches*. New York: Oxford Univ. Press, 2000. A wide-ranging collection of essays by film scholars from around the world, the book features some general essays on topics such as "Concepts of National Cinema" and "Issues in European Cinema," as well as case studies on individual film cultures, including "East Central European Cinema" and "Taiwanese New Cinema."

Naficy, Hamid. *Accented Cinema: Exilic and Diasporic Filmmaking*. Princeton: Princeton Univ. Press, 2001. An influential study of the migratory aesthetics of contemporary films whose stylistics and perspectives bear the marks of crosscultural dialogues within transnational cinema; it considers filmmakers as diverse as Canadian Atom Egoyan, Iranian Abbas Kiarostami, and American Trinh T. Minh-ha.

Nowell-Smith, Geoffrey, ed. *The Oxford History of World Cinema*. New York: Oxford Univ. Press, 1996. A comprehensive volume featuring contributions from experts on periods, topics, and regions of world cinema.

Sklar, Robert, and Charles Musser, eds. *Resisting Images: Essays on Cinema and History*. Philadelphia: Temple Univ. Press, 1990. A collection of essays by contemporary film scholars and critics that examines the relationship between cinema history and social history through such topics as "Soviet worker clubs of the 1920s" and the "politics of Israeli cinema."

Chapter 11

Andrew, Dudley. *Concepts in Film Theory*. Oxford: Oxford Univ. Press, 1984. A thoughtful introduction to issues taken up in contemporary film theory.

Corrigan, Timothy, and Patricia White, with Meta Mazaj. *Critical Visions in Film Theory: Classic and Contemporary Readings*. Boston: Bedford/St. Martin's, 2011. An extensive collection of the major documents in film theory, featuring introductions to major topics and individual readings, along with reading cues to guide students through the essays.

Elsaesser, Thomas, and Malte Hagener. *Film Theory: An Introduction through Senses*. New York: Routledge, 2010. A guide to the primary schools of film theory based in the spectator's different experience of film as, for instance, "window," "mirror," and "mind."

Hill, John, and Pamela Church Gibson, eds. *The Oxford Guide to Film Studies*. Oxford: Oxford Univ. Press, 1998. Introduction to the field, with strong sections on classical and contemporary film theory as well as film history and culture.

Kaplan, E. Ann. *Feminism and Film*. Oxford: Oxford Univ. Press, 2000. Collection of many significant contributions to feminist film studies, covering authorship, genres, spectatorship, race, sexuality, and more.

Lehman, Peter, ed. *Defining Cinema*. New Brunswick, NJ: Rutgers Univ. Press, 1997. Essays and contemporary commentaries on five major theorists, from Sergei Eisenstein to Christian Metz.

Stam, Robert. *Film Theory: An Introduction*. Malden: Blackwell, 2000. A concise, vivid account covering contemporary classical contributions and including fresh examples from global traditions.

Chapter 12

Corrigan, Timothy. *A Short Guide to Writing about Film*. 8th ed. New York: Pearson/Longman, 2012. A short but complete guide to writing about film, replete with a variety of professional and student essays.

Donald, James, Anne Friedberg, and Laura Marcus, eds. *Close Up, 1927–1933: Cinema and Modernism*. Princeton: Princeton Univ. Press, 1998. Featuring some of the earliest and best writers about film—such as Dorothy Richardson, Harry Potamkin, and H.D., who still have much to tell contemporary writers about style and substance—this volume collects relatively early, passionately serious, and important reviews and essays on the art of film as it moved from the silent to the sound era.

Lant, Antonia, ed. *Red Velvet Seat: Women's Writings on the First Fifty Years of Cinema*. London: Verso, 2006. While filmgoing was one of the most important cultural activities for women throughout the twentieth century, this collection of writings is the first widely inclusive survey of the many ways women wrote about film. The book features not only the writings of actresses, filmmakers, and writers, such as Virginia Woolf and H.D., but also social activists such as Jane Addams and Barbara Deming.

Lopate, Phillip, ed. *American Movie Critics: From the Silents until Now*. New York: Library of America, 2006. A wide-ranging anthology of American film criticism, this recent collection spans the history of cinema, from Vachel Lindsay's prophetic writings in 1915 to Roger Ebert's modern reviews, and it offers an exceptional range of voices and perspectives, from Manny Farber's 1930s writings to poet John Ashbery's contemporary reflections of the cinema.

Rich, B. Ruby. *Chick Flicks: Theories and Memories of the Feminist Film Movement*. Durham, NC: Duke Univ. Press, 1998. Covering a range of topics and films that engage several decades of feminist film criticism, Rich writes as both a journalist and a film scholar, with each essay demonstrating a skillful balance of personal experience and intellectual argument.

Acknowledgments

Photo Credits

p. 3: (left) Courtesy Everett Collection; (right) © Summit Entertainment/Courtesy Everett Collection; p. 4: Courtesy Everett Collection; I.1: Francis Specker/Landov; I.2: Mary Evans Picture Library/The Image Works; I.3: Rue des Archives/The Granger Collection, NY; I.5: Photofest; I.13: The Kobal Collection/Art Resource, NY; I.16: Courtesy Everett Collection; p. 18: © Summit Entertainment/Courtesy Everett Collection; 1.2: Kevin Winter/Getty Images; 1.5: Courtesy Everett Collection; 1.8a: Courtesy Everett Collection; 1.11: Courtesy Everett Collection; 1.14: © Weinstein Company/Courtesy Everett Collection; 1.27: Courtesy of Milestone Film & Video; 1.30: Photofest; 1.33: AP/Wide World Photos; 1.41: © New Line Cinema/Courtesy Everett Collection; 1.46: Bettmann/Corbis; p. 60: The Kobal Collection/Art Resource, NY; p. 61: (left) The Kobal Collection/Art Resource, NY; (center) Yash Raj Films; (right) The Kobal Collection/Art Resource, NY; p. 62: The Kobal Collection/Art Resource, NY; 2.2: TM & Fox Searchlight Pictures. All rights reserved/Courtesy Everett Collection; 2.6: Courtesy Everett Collection; 2.26: Courtesy Everett Collection; p. 94: The Kobal Collection/Art Resource, NY; 3.3: Tiger Darson/Alamy; 3.5: Hulton-Deutsch Collection/Corbis; 3.6: Courtesy, the George Eastman House; 3.15a: *Icon of St. John the Baptist* (tempera on panel) by Andrei Rublev (c. 1370–1430) Andrei Rublev Museum, Moscow, Russia/The Bridgeman Art Library Nationality/copyright status: Russian/out of copyright; 3.16a: Andy Kingsbury/Corbis; 3.42f: Lorey Sebastian/© Paramount Pictures/Courtesy Everett Collection; 3.20: The Kobal Collection/Art Resource, NY; p. 132: Yash Raj Films; 4.1a: Gianni Dagli Orti/Corbis; 4.1b: Erich Lessing/Art Resource, NY; 4.1c: François PERRI/REA/Redux ; 4.2: Etienne Jules Marey/Getty Images; 4.3: © 2011 Artists Rights Society (ARS), New York/VG Bild-Kunst, Bonn; 4.41: MTV/Photofest; p. 176: The Kobal Collection/Art Resource, NY; p. 178: (2nd from left) From the collection of Joseph Yranski; 5.2: Courtesy Edison Historic Site, NPS; 5.3: MPI/Getty Images; 5.4a: From the collection of Joseph Yranski; 5.4b: Marnan Collection/Minneapolis, Minnesota; 5.6: Photofest; 5.16: Samuel Goldwyn/Photofest; 5.25: Think Film/Courtesy Everett Collection; 5.38a: "Shrek" 2001 DreamWorks Animation LLC, used with permission of DreamWorks Animation LLC; 5.38b: "Shrek" 2001 DreamWorks Animation LLC, used with permission of DreamWorks Animation LLC; 5.46: A Women Make Movies Release. Courtesy of Women Make Movies www.wmm.com; p. 212: The Kobal Collection/Art Resource, NY; p. 213: (left) Lions Gate/© Dog Eat Dog Films/Photofest; (center) The Film Company; (right) © Rogue Pictures/Courtesy Everett Collection; p. 214: The Kobal Collection/Art Resource, NY; p. 216: (far right) © The Weinstein Company/Courtesy Everett Collection; 6.1a: Erich Lessing/Art Resource, NY; 6.1b: © National Gallery, London/Art Resource, NY; 6.2a: Spider-Man, © TM

Marvel Entertainment, LLC. Used with permission; 6.10a: Photofest; 6.10b: Photofest; 6.10c: Photofest; 6.10d: Photofest; 6.13c: © The Weinstein Company/Courtesy Everett Collection; p. 254: Lions Gate/© Dog Eat Dog Films/Photofest; 7.1: Courtesy Everett Collection; 7.4: Jacob August Riis/Corbis; 7.5: Archival film and/or video materials from the collections of the Library of Congress; 7.6: Courtesy of Milestone Film And Video; 7.7a: Contemporary Films Ltd./NA/Photofest; 7.11a: AP/Wide World Photos; 7.11b: The Kobal Collection/Art Resource, NY; 7.16: The Kobal Collection/Art Resource, NY; 7.17: Courtesy British Film Institute; 7.24: © Bridgewater Film Company, Inc. permission granted by Zipporah Films, Inc.; 7.32: Courtesy Everett Collections; 7.36: Courtesy of Filmmakers Library; 7.37: Courtesy of DER; 7.40: Courtesy of Women Make Movies; p. 284: The Film Company; p. 287: (far left) Courtesy Everett Collection; (3rd from left) Shirin Neshat, *Untitled* (Rapture Series–Women Pushing Boat), 1999. Gelatin silver print, 44 x 68 1/4 inches. Edition of 5. Copyright Shirin Neshat. Courtesy Gladstone Gallery; 8.2: Courtesy of the Video Data Bank, www.vdb.org; 8.3: Hulton Archive/Getty Images; 8.4: Monet, Claude (1840–1926). *Water Lilies*. 1914–26. Oil on canvas, three panels, each 6' 6 3/4" x 13' 11 1/4" (200 x 424.8 cm), overall 6' 6 3/4" x 41' 10 3/8" (200 x 1276 cm). Mrs. Simon Guggenheim Fund. (666.1959.a-c) The Museum of Modern Art, New York, NY U.S.A. Digital Image © The Museum of Modern Art/Licensed by SCALA/Art Resource, NY; 8.12: Courtesy Everett Collection; 8.18: Courtesy of Michael Snow; 8.21: Hirshhorn Museum and Sculpture Garden, Smithsonian Institution, Holenia Purchase Fun in Memory of Joseph H. Hirshhorn, 1996. Photo by Lee Stalsworth; 8.25: Courtesy Everett Collections; 8.26: Courtesy of Anthology Film Archives, All Rights Reserved; 8.27: Léger, Fernand (1881–1955) © ARS, NY. *Three Women*. 1921–22. Oil on canvas, 6' 1/4" x 8'3" (183.5 x 251.5 cm). Mrs. Simon Guggenheim Fund. The Museum of Modern Art, New York, NY U.S.A. Digital Image © The Museum of Modern Art/Licensed by SCALA/Art Resource, NY; 8.34: Courtesy of Michael Snow; 8.35: Courtesy of Anthology Film Archives, All Rights Reserved; 8.36: Shirin Neshat, *Untitled* (Rapture Series–Women Pushing Boat), 1999. Gelatin silver print 44 x 68 1/4 inches. Edition of 5. Copyright Shirin Neshat, Courtesy Gladstone Gallery; 8.37: Photofest; 8.38: Buena Vista Pictures/Photofest; 8.39: Photofest; 8.45: Erich Lessing/Art Resource, NY; 8.48: Courtesy the artist and Roslyn Oxley 9 Gallery, Sydney; p. 319: © Rogue Pictures/Courtesy Everett Collection; 9.3: Erich Lessing/Art Resource, NY; 9.4: The Art Archive/Art Resource, NY; 9.14: Courtesy of Anthology Film Archives. All Rights Reserved; 9.24: MPI/Getty Images; p. 353: (left) Focus Features/Courtesy Everett Collection; (center) author's collection; (right) Posteritati Movie Posters, NYC, www.posteritati.com; p. 354: Focus Features/Courtesy Everett Collection; 10.37: Ft. Lee Public Library, Silent Film Collection, Ft. Lee, NJ; 10.39: Photofest; 10.43:

AP/Wide World Photos; **10.45**: Courtesy Everett Collection; **10.46**: Photofest; **10.49**: Courtesy Oscar Micheaux Society, Duke University, with thanks to Jane Gaines; **10.50**: Courtesy Oscar Micheaux Society, Duke University, with thanks to Jane Gaines; **10.51**: Courtesy Oscar Micheaux Society, Duke University, with thanks to Jane Gaines; **10.54**: Photofest; **10.58**: Courtesy of DER from The Video in the Villages Series by Vincent Carelli; **10.60**: Courtesy Prelinger Archives; **10.61**: Fox Movietone News Story 4-171: World's Youngest Acrobat (November 8, 1929. Outtakes from the Hearst Metrotone/Fox Movietone Newsreel. Courtesy Moving Image Research Col-

lections, University of South Carolina; **p. 398**: author's collection; **11.3**: Courtesy of Anthology Film Archives, All Rights Reserved; **11.6**: Courtesy Everett Collection; **11.7**: The Kobal Collection/Art Resource, NY; **11.11**: The Granger Collection, NY; **11.12**: © Moviestore collection Ltd/Alamy; **11.13**: Courtesy of Anthology Film Archives, All Rights Reserved; **11.21**: © 2011 C. Herscovici, London / Artists Rights Society (ARS), New York; **11.22**: The Kobal Collection/Art Resource, NY; **11.29**: © Allen Eyestone/Palm Beach Post/Zuma Press; **11.31b**: Jean Baptiste Lacroix/WireImage; **11.32**: Hubert Boesl/dpa/Landov; **p. 434**: Posteritati Movie Posters, NYC, www.posteritati.com.

Index